Mario Reading was brought up in England and the south of France. He speaks four languages. He studied Comparative Literature under Malcolm Bradbury and Angus Wilson at the University of East Anglia, where he specialized in French and German Literature and translation. During a passionately misspent youth he sold rare books, taught riding in Africa, studied dressage in Vienna, played professional polo in India, Spain and Dubai, helped run his Mexican wife's coffee plantation, and survived a terminal diagnosis for cancer. He is the award-winning author of two novels, *The Music-Makers* and *The Honourable Soldier,* for which he won an Arts Council Writing Award, and author of the highly personal *Dictionary of Cinema*, re-issued as *The Movie Companion*, and *Nostradamus, The Complete Prophecies for the Future.*

S0-BND-567

The Watkins dictionary of DREAMS

Mario Reading

THE ULTIMATE RESOURCE
FOR DREAMERS
WITH OVER 3,000 ENTRIES AND
15,000 CROSS-REFERENCES

WATKINS PUBLISHING
LONDON

Distributed in the USA and Canada by
Sterling Publishing Co., Inc.
387 Park Avenue South, New York, NY 10016

This edition first published in the UK and USA 2007 by
Watkins Publishing, Sixth Floor, Castle House,
75–76 Wells Street, London W1T 3QH

Reprinted 2009

3 5 7 9 10 8 6 4 2

Designed by Jerry Goldie

Typeset by Dorchester Typesetting Group

Printed and bound in Great Britain

Library of Congress Cataloging-in-Publication Data Available

ISBN 978-1-84293-171-4

www.watkinspublishing.co.uk

For information about custom editions, special sales, premium and
corporate purchases, please contact Sterling Special Sales
Department at 800-805-5489 or specialsales@sterlingpub.com.

Acknowledgements

I have a number of people to thank for their help and support during the course of this project's quickening and parturition, amongst whom my editor, Michael Mann, for his tolerance of a book which, like the now near-ubiquitous Topsy in Harriet Beecher Stowe's *Uncle Tom's Cabin*, 'just growed'; my agent, Anthea Morton-Saner, for her elegant persistence in cracking champagne bottles on what must have, at times, appeared to be the sister ship of the *Titanic*; my ex-wife and not uncoincidental mother of my son, Anna-Clare Hillier, who kindly donned her psychoanalytic psychotherapist's garb and checked out my introduction for blunders; Dr Gerald Phillipson for steering me towards my entry on Dream-Founded Churches; my copy editor, Fiona Brown, for her ever-tactful prinking and preening; and finally my wife, Claudia, who listened to countless readings of projected entries and even intervened, when terminal cross-referencing was threatening to drive me into the waters of Lethe, and hauled me, wet and dripping, back towards the Elysian Fields.

'Sometimes dreams are wiser than waking.'
Black Elk, holy man (shaman) of the Oglala Lakota Sioux

DREAMS

A maid to dream of verdant Groves,
She'll surely have the man she loves;
But if the Groves are nipt with Frost,
She'll be as sure in Marriage crost.
A Peacock tells t'will be her lot
To have a fine Man but a Cot.
To dream of Lambs or Sheep astray,
Her Sweet-heart soon will run away.
To dream of letters far or near,
She soon will from her Sweet-heart hear.
To dream of bad Fruit, her Sweet-heart
A fair Face has but false at Heart.
To dream her Sweet-hearts at Church zealous
If she has him he will be Jealous.
A Maid to dream of Cats, by Strife,
She'll lead but an unhappy Life.
To dream her Sweet-heart will not treat her,
Tis well, if she have him, he don't beat Her.
To dream her Sweet-heart gives a Kiss,
Instead of Blows, she will have Bliss.
If she dreams of Bees or Honey,
When Wife he'll let her keep her Money
And be the Mistress of his Riches,
Nay if she will, may wear the Breeches;
And some time life is not the worse,
When GREY MARE is the BETTER HORSE,
To keep things right in stormy Weather,
Thong and Buckle, both together.
To dream of Timber she'll be wed
To one who'll be a Log in Bed;
But she'll be Wed who dreams of Flies,
To one that will be Otherwise.

Taken from *The New Book of Knowledge* (1758)

Introduction

There is a strong body of thought amongst the psychoanalytical and psychotherapeutic communities that feels that it is impossible, to any really effective degree, to analyze one's own dreams; that the tacit (and active) presence of a second party is necessary in order to isolate, break down, and free the repressions that exist in one's unconscious mind. There is probably some truth in this. What this book aims to do is to allow the individual access to some of the perhaps collective and unconscious values of the symbols our minds choose when we dream, and to do no more than suggest from whence they might have come. The rest is up to the individual, or to the client/practitioner relationship. As Sigmund Freud suggested in his seminal *The Interpretation of Dreams*, each individual dream, in terms of interpretation, is absolutely specific to the dreamer, and any arbitrary or universal interpretation of archetypes that appear in such a dream, without taking into account the life situation of the dreamer, is futile. This book is an aid to dream work, therefore, and not an answer to it.

Carl Jung – a former pupil who at first collaborated with and then distanced himself from Freud – maintained that ready-made, rule-of-thumb interpretations of dreams are worthless, and I agree with him. That is why I have slanted *The Watkins Dictionary of Dreams* rather towards suggestion than towards certainty. He consistently reminded himself that he could never understand someone else's dream well enough to interpret it correctly, and that it was incumbent upon him, the analyst, to curb the flow of his own associations and reactions so that they might not influence the uncertainties and hesitations of the analysand, as so much depends on the personal differences between the two. Dream analysis, when it is conducted in the presence of another, is a dialectical exchange between two minds, and the domination by one of the other is not appropriate. The individual, in other words, is the only reality. Mutual agreement must be reached before progress can occur, despite the fact that a so-called 'normal' society is one in which people habitually disagree, and in which both introversion and extraversion have their rightful place. To understand another's dream, one's own predilections, projections, and prejudices need to be sacrificed. To understand one's own dreams, the exact opposite needs to take place. No general rules exist, therefore, for the interpretation of dreams.

Before it is possible to correctly interpret the symbols appearing in a dream, it is necessary, first of all, to understand their archetypal significance, and it is for this reason that I have devoted a major part of *The Watkins Dictionary of Dreams* to the philology, history, and origin of symbols. People often know things without knowing them – that is why I so often bring in traditional meanings, alongside potentially more 'accurate' symbolical meanings. In this context, the traditional, half-remembered (or inferred) meaning can often be more important than the more obvious 'core' meaning. A dream is significant as much for what it includes (however seemingly aberrant) as for what it leaves out. In addition, the context within which the images appear is also crucial, and their interpretation, outside that context, is pretty much a hit or miss affair. The symbols, then, must be taken together, and viewed as cumulative, rather than exclusive – as an aid, rather than as an answer.

My advice to interested readers would be to go to the alphabetical section marked D, and to begin their investigation into the workings of the unconscious mind by reading every entry prefixed with **Dream** (barring, needless to say, the slang entries, although these might be said to provide something of a necessary, albeit somewhat jaded, objective correlative). In this way the basic premises of dream interpretation will be understood, and the rest of the book will fall, as it were, into place.

Occasionally, to somewhat leaven the symbolic mix, I have added a carefully selected KEY LINE to stimulate the reader even further towards lateral thought. I have chosen a great deal of poetry for these key lines, because, in my opinion, poetry is the closest (or most kindred) literary form to the dream, in that it draws from the unconscious far more, even, than most novels will draw. The sheer concentration of a great poem echoes the concentration of a dream, and the aftershocks of a poem are again akin to the concentric lapping waves that echo the diminishing remembrance of a dream.

As far as the cross-referencing goes, I had to make a decision early on that it was impossible for every cross-referenced word to match exactly that to which it applied. I am therefore relying on my readers to assume, when they see **cheat** cross-referenced, for instance, and only discover **cheating** when they look it up, that the one inevitably refers to the other. Also, when they happen upon two normally unlikely words linked and cross-referenced together (a good example might be **eunuch priests**), that the cross-referencing then refers to two separate entries under **eunuchs** and **priests**. I've also placed the vast majority of my symbols in the plural, as in **Dreams**, and not **Dream, A**. This means that singular textual cross-references are likely to appear in their plural forms when you look them up – I don't feel that this is too much of a burden (given the no doubt rattlingly high IQ of most of my projected readers), but for the sake of clarity, here are a number of examples: when you see **bed** in bold in the text, look it up under **beds** – when **cat** is tagged as a cross-reference, it will appear under **cats** in the list of symbols. Capisce?

I'm not sure any other book in the history of literature has taken the art of cross-referencing to quite the same degree as I have in this one (there must be a good 15,000 cross-references within 200,000 words of text). As my excuse I have taken the Jungian (even post-structuralist) view that more lies latent in the text than even I, the author, suspect, and that by cross-referencing in this way, I may lead the reader to serendipitous discoveries or unexpected cross-connections and associations that would not otherwise make themselves available. These associations will then become an actual part of the dream work itself, leading to a richer, more unplanned, and therefore potentially more significant interpretation.

A lot of serendipity inevitably goes into the writing of a book like this – during the year or so in which one prepares it, anything and everything one encounters may be perceived to have some relevance to the final article. There have been times, of course, when I have felt like George Eliot's Mr Casaubon in *Middlemarch*, grandiloquently failing to finish his *The Key to all Mythologies* – a victim of the so-called Casaubon Delusion, in which one sets oneself an impossible task and then dementedly persists in its realization despite occasional intimations of normality.

Sir Arthur Conan Doyle (1859–1930), a noted spiritualist, member of the Psychical Research Society, and believer in the power of dreams, puts the following into the mouth of his sinister collector of esoterica, Lionel Dacre, in his story *The Leather Funnel*: 'The charlatan is always the pioneer. From the astrologer came the astronomer, from the alchemist the chemist, from the mesmerist the experimental psychologist. The quack of yesterday is the professor of tomorrow. Even such subtle and elusive things as dreams will in time be reduced to system and order.'

Despite the existence of this present volume, together with all the history of dream research that went before it and by which it is imbrued, one finds oneself rather hoping that he will be proved wrong.

How to Use This Book

The best way to explain how to use *The Watkins Dictonary of Dreams* is to describe one of my own dreams (the only time I do this during the course of the book), and to chance an interpretation of it via a mixture of intuition, reference to the text, and the use of lateral thought – just as I would advocate anyone to approach one of their own dreams if they possess this book, but are without the aid of an enlightened second party. So here goes. I give my diary entry exactly as I wrote it immediately upon waking up from the dream, at 8 am on the morning of 26th April 2006:

'An excellent dream. My party had been travelling some way together, by land and sailing boat at the same time. We arrived (on foot, although we moored the boat) at the most perfect hillside inn, unknown to strangers, set into the hill, overlooking the sea. Only fishermen were there, and the dining area was snug, and closed down from outside light. "We'll eat here." We arranged for the landlord to open the outside doors, for one of our party did not want to eat inside. When the doors were opened, the restaurant was as good as outside, and we were all delighted and agreed to eat there. The light was wonderful and the place perfection, bathed with light, high up above the sea (which felt like the Mediterranean). I wandered back and found a room in which a man had hung all his leather goods for sale around the wall. I was delighted, and wished to buy something. Someone shouted "Our boat has gone." I ran through, and realized that one of the fishermen must have taken it. I ran down to the beach and swam after him. I found him, and the boat, and brought him back to the restaurant. He had white/red hair and a strong accent (Irish?). We sat him down. My friends had been preparing a contract. "We're going to fine you the equivalent of one day's fishing." We had it all written out. (For some reason he had quite a lot of money on him, in cash.) He counted out the money. When all was concluded he hugged me very strongly, moved, and said that I was a gentleman, and a kind man. Then he left. The important thing about the dream was the feeling of walking for a long time and then coming across a place so perfect that we all knew it was the place we wanted to be. It was the most perfect inn – the owner was just right. The interior, though pokey, was full of character, and when we asked for the doors to be opened it became bathed with light, and showed its position above a cove and the sea. I forgot to say that we were in the sea when we realized the boat had gone, swimming with a friendly shark (or killer whale). When I went after the robber, it lashed its tail at me, but in an unthreatening way. I had a sudden feeling that it would one day be threatened by humanity's actions, and I felt sorry for it. This feeling may have transferred itself also to the place, which I felt could not last in its present form – that one day it would change.'

I must reiterate here that this is *exactly* how I wrote down the dream, at most two minutes after I had woken up from it, in one of the notebooks I have been keeping near me at all times for the last 25 or so years (for I am an inveterate diarist). I have not changed a word or edited the text in any way beyond disguising my doctor's name, when it appears in the following entry, behind an initial.

First, therefore, it is important to accept that the dream relates, in its entirety, to me. It is not an ecological dream (the shark/whale), a utopian dream, or a fantasy. It is entirely grounded in what has been happening to me, in how I feel about it, and in my unconscious response to events that I have either undergone, fear that I might undergo, or wish that I might undergo. The 'I' character and his friends are all aspects of me – this is why they weren't defined in the dream, even in a sexual (i.e. gendered) way. My instinct (and that is all that it was) tells me that we four travellers were equally balanced, comprising two male aspects and two female, but my friends/aspects were indistinct (probably because they were an integral part of me). Now here are my immediate diary thoughts, written immediately after – and concurrent with – the writing down of the dream:

'Musing on it retrospectively, I suppose the place was fuelled by my thoughts on Daquise, twinned with a Moroccan shoe shop and parts of Essaouira (the fish grills on the harbour), and also on stasis, and fears of change. The fear of change (although fear is too strong a word – it was almost a sadness) was probably fuelled by Doctor K's explanation of the three possible courses my cancer might take, given my results. He was more optimistic, he said, than he had been. Before (last summer) he had given me a one in two chance of having a treatment failure (the radiotherapy). He had assumed my PSA would have risen to between 1 and 2 by now. In fact it's .42, having been .32 in November. This showed him three scenarios – either that the treatment had still failed, but that we had bought some time (five years, maybe); or that the treatment had succeeded, and that what we were seeing was the radiotherapy still killing off old cancer cells; or, thirdly, that some cells had survived, were trying to rekindle themselves, but they had been damaged to such an extent that they were having difficulty, and thus causing peaks and troughs in the reading. Either way, future readings were crucial – ideally they should remain under 1. We would see, in other words, what we would see. But he felt considerably more optimistic than he had done.'

Again, this is exactly as I wrote it immediately following the depiction of the dream, and I should also add that I was not aware that I was going to use the dream in this book, nor was I intending, at that stage, to use any of my dreams in the book. As I was engaged in writing the entry, the image of the restaurant above the harbour, and the throwing open of the shutters to admit the day and the view, began to make sense. I was experiencing what amounted to a rebirth. This was reinforced by the restaurant image, for on the previous day, an hour before my visit to the Royal Marsden for my regular cancer check – I should perhaps mention here that I had had a terminal cancer in 1992, from which I had recovered, followed by another, entirely separate cancer, in 2001, from which I was still residually suffering following surgery in 2002 and salvage radiotherapy in 2004 – I visited a favourite old Polish restaurant in South Kensington, Daquise, which had previously been destroyed by fire.

To my astonishment, the phoenix had risen from the ashes in exactly the same form as it had entered them – the restaurant, in other words, had been reborn in exactly the same state as it had been in before the fire, even down to the set menu and the prices. This had seemed close to miraculous at the time, and had doubtless struck a chord that was waiting to be struck, namely that what had happened to the restaurant might conceivably happen to me, even for a second time. My unconscious mind, therefore, elated at the possibility of yet another reprieve, had latched on to this phoenix image (the surviving of the fire) and used it in the dream – my unconscious mind which was, to all intents and purposes, far more optimistic than I had allowed myself to be in real life. For in an attempt at emotional protection (something serially ill people unfortunately learn to do over a period of many years) I had quite consciously repressed the good news of Dr K's tentative optimism, and played it down, both in my head and in front of my wife, because I did not want us to be let down again.

My unconscious mind had instantly rebelled at this and constructed an optimistic dream scenario which more clearly reflected the reality of what I had heard – namely that the restaurant (me) had apparently survived all onslaughts, and though it would one day change (just as the shark/whale would one day be threatened by humanity's actions), for the present it was perfect. The potential robbery of the boat and its return, and the gratitude of the robber (my doctor?), and the contract (equivalent to the chart Dr K had shown me detailing my PSA count over a period of four years since the operation), all reinforced the 'good news' aspect of the dream. Even the shark/killer whale (equivalent to the cancer?) had behaved out of character, and although it had brushed me with its tail, still, apparently, it presented – whilst remaining intrinsically threatening – no immediate threat.

I should perhaps add here that the previous day had been a particularly significant one in other ways than the Royal Marsden visit – I had also visited the bedside of a sick old friend (a father figure, almost) who had nearly died, and was now recovering, and following my Royal Marsden visit I had been to see my new agent – feared endings, then, and possible new beginnings.

Now to the symbols. Having had such a dream, and having entered upon a tentative preparatory interpretation, I would then advise the dreamer to turn to this book and look up a number of the symbols. In the case of my dream I would look up the following: **Robbing, Birth, Rebirth, Restaurants, Harbours, Sharks, Whales, Fire, Water, Seas, Shoes, Leather, Boats**, and **Light**.

To further facilitate the process, therefore, I append the entries, in the order I have instinctively given them, to follow:

Robbing The act of robbing in a **dream** suggests that the **dreamer** feels that they have, at some crucial point in their lives, been robbed of something that was rightfully theirs. This may refer to **energy**, rights, respect, health, or even material things, depending on the imagery that surrounds the robbery, and on the residual images that remain after the robbery has been perpetrated – paradoxically, this rule will tend to apply even if it is the dreamer themselves who appears to be the **guilty party**. A fundamental case of 'robbery', of course, is that of the **mother** by the **father** (or vice versa), or alternatively of the mother from the father by the **son** – leading to what **Freud** termed the **Oedipus Complex**.

Birth Birth in **dreams** may often, paradoxically, represent **death**. This is yet another example of dream **ellipsis**, and may also apply to **life** and death, rejoicing and **mourning**, luck and the **loss** of luck, and so forth. Birth and death are inextricably **linked** in the **unconscious**, primitive mind, to the extent that birth can sometimes appear in dreams as a **compensation** for either a literal or a symbolical death. It is a not entirely unconnected fact that unhappily **married couples** will often resort to a 'birth' to try and save the 'death' of their **marriage**. See **Pre-Birth Dreams & Rebirth**

Rebirth A primeval concept relating to the solstices and to the hope that **winter** will once again turn into **summer**, or that **illness** will one day transform itself back into health. This **archetypal** notion threads through virtually all **world religions** and dogmas, but it is notable for its absence in almost all secular faiths. Balder, Osiris, Tammuz, and Orpheus, for instance, were all **killed**, and subsequently restored to **life**, at the order of the **Gods**. See **Resurrection**

Restaurants Restaurants are amenable and open to everybody just so long as that person has both the **money** and the nous to dress appropriately. Because restaurants are primarily **public** forums, there is an element of **ritual** about their use, implying that the subject is not necessarily being themselves in the restaurant environment – they are showcasing, in other words, and playing to the gallery, possibly as a result of a craving for **companionship** or for the anonymity of public places. As a result restaurants have an element of neediness about them, and of latent **fear**. Will we behave correctly? Will we order or do the **right** thing?

Harbours Harbours and **towns** can represent the **anima** when they occur in **dreams**. They are maternal **symbols**, implying both emotional succour and the affective equivalent of rest and recreation, before the inevitable return to the fray.

Sharks Sharks are **danger** signals, usually relating to emotional issues (in that they are **water**-borne). The indiscriminate aspect of the shark is also important, in that it tends to **eat** up whatever comes into its **path**. If a shark makes off with a particular limb in its **mouth**, then that limb, and what it represents, is of specific importance (both semantically and metaphorically). A shark coming up from **below** the **dreamer**, for instance, and **tearing** off the dreamer's **leg**, might imply a desire for freedom of **movement**, but the inability to put that desire into practice – the shark then becomes a convenient excuse for not indulging in forward or upwards movement (see **Above**). Sharks may also symbolize mortal **disease**, or threats of mortal disease. See **Amputation, Floating & Swimming**

Whales Whales are significant **symbols**, and have been so since **pre-biblical times**. The whale may **represent** the emergent **soul** (as in Jonah), or the **lower** passions externalized (as in the **Buddha**'s Nirvanic cutting of his bonds with the **world** and its '**monsters** of desire'). This apparent paradox – this at once concreteness and luminosity – is at the **heart** of the whale's fascination, and stems from its function as one of the few beasts (**vehicles**) that can span the very bounds of the **oceans** (*ergo* the emotions).

KEY LINE: 'When I'm playful, I use the meridians of longitude and parallels of latitude for a seine, and drag the Atlantic ocean for whales. I scratch my head with the lightning and purr myself to sleep with the thunder.' (From Mark Twain's *Life on the Mississippi* 1883)

Fire Fire is often a concretized symbol of the **abstract** concept of **love**. Fire can also relate to sexuality – the making or creation of a fire can symbolize the sexual act. There is, in addition, a strong **link** between fire and **water**, between **sex** and conception, and this may find itself reflected in fire-dousing **symbols**. Fire, in that aspect, is **phallic** and masculine, whereas water is **uterine** and feminine. This becomes even more apparent when the properties of the two elements are investigated, fire being characterized by its devouring, licking, **burning** aspects, and water being characterized by its dousing, slaking, extinguishing aspects. Both elements, while seemingly antithetical, are equally precious, and both may, of course, be used as **cleansing** or purificatory agents. Finally, fire may equate to **blushing** and to loss of control in puberty.

Water Water implies the possibility of unknown powers or emotions, and deep water represents the **unconscious**, or the **psyche**. Hesitating before entering the water can imply doubt as to one's inner depths, and where the discovery of them may **lead**. Water, particularly when it is circumscribed, can also **represent** the **uterus**, while uncircumscribed water may represent urine. In **Freudian** terms, water almost always means **birth**, especially when dreamt of by a woman – and when a young **child** is associated with the **dream**, and perhaps **blood** as well, this becomes even more apparent, and may point towards **fears** of a **miscarriage**. See **Aquarius, Fire, Kelp & Secretions**

Seas The sea, according to **Jung**, is a **symbol** of the **collective unconscious**, due to the unfathomable depths it hides. The regenerative aspect of the sea is also important, in that the sea is to a large extent **self-fuelling** and **self**-fulfilling. In symbolical terms the sea represents the aspect of the astral plane that deals with our desires and, according to Plutarch, our passions (in the guise of Typhon, or Set). Diving into the sea in a **dream** might then suggest giving in to – or allowing ourselves to be subsumed by – our emotions. See **Oceans**

Shoes Shoes have many **superstitions** attached to them. One such was that to place them beside the **bed** in the form a T would bring **dreams** of a future mate. In dreams, shoes tend to symbolize the desire to advance spiritually, whilst the discarding of shoes usually implies the shucking off of **lower** things, for shoes *per se* can suggest an excessive attachment to the material **world**. An ill-fitting shoe might **lead** one to suppose that the **dreamer** feels uncomfortable in taking on another person's mantle ('standing in another's shoes') – **black** shoes, in this context, might suggest that there has been a **death**, possibly triggering the identity crisis.

Leather Leather and human **skin** are all but synonymous in **dreams**, and the piercing of leather in any form probably **reflects** a fear by the **dreamer** of being pierced – i.e. of being shown to be mortal – in their turn. To 'leather' was to beat with a **belt**, and although **beatings** of any form are frowned upon nowadays in most civilized societies, collective physical memories persist, fuelled by images from **films** such as Lindsay Anderson's 1968 movie *If...*, **television** (ITV's 2005 dramatization of Robert Hughes's *Tom Brown's Schooldays* being a case in point), and the **internet**. **Anxieties** (or **repressed** desires) about a restoration of 'leathering' probably relate to hidden **fears** of a loss of civilized amenities and a return to anarchy – a situation in which the strongest (the best leathered) will always prevail. See **Spanking**

Boats   In purely **Freudian** terms, boats, being receptive, are frequently synonymous with the **vagina**. Sikhism, however, equates a boat with the True **Guru**, further reinforcing the boat's equation with the **soul**, floating on the **river** of **life**. A boat was also used to **ferry** the dead to Hades, and the image is repeated in the Arthurian Legends, when the mortally **wounded** King Arthur is ferried away from Lyonesse in the company of the Lady of the **Lake's** handmaidens. This powerful image takes us back to the age-old reference to the boat as a vessel of apotheosis, **mirrored** in the frequent depiction on **coins** of sovereigns and **kings** afloat. See **Hell** & **Ships** KEY LINE: 'So said he, and the barge with oar and sail/Moved from the brink, like some full-breasted swan/That, fluting a wild carol ere her death,/Ruffles her cold plume, and takes the flood...' (From Alfred, Lord Tennyson's *The Passing of Arthur – Idylls of the King* 1859–85)

Light   Light equates with **life** and the putting out of the light equates with **death**. Shedding light on something may be to give it life, or, otherwise, to focus on it in a particular and concentrated way. To light up from within presupposes a spiritual **transformation**, or a desire, at least, for **change** and **truth**. **Holiness** was traditionally called the '**candle** of the Lord', and the appearance of **daylight** after a long period of **darkness** heralded **rebirth** and the possibilities of **resurrection** – indeed the Realm of Light is another name for the **Buddhic** plane, in which wisdom becomes consciousness.

Readers, no doubt, will have their own views on what symbols I should have looked up, but that is as it should be. One's own instincts must be followed in the interpretation of any dream. But readers will agree, I hope, that by using the approach advocated in the book, and by an at once generalized and specific reading of the symbols contained within the dream, I have come to a useful and enlightening understanding of the actions of my own unconscious mind, and, what's more, in onionskin process, have succeeded in revealing myself, just a little more, to myself.

For David Whately

A

Abambou/Obambou An **evil** spirit, conjured up in **dreams** by members of the West African Camma tribe. A **fire** always **burns** in Abambou's **house**, and if he emerges during the **night**, **sickness** and **death** will follow.

Abandonment Our first experience of abandonment usually comes when we realize that we are no longer the primary focus of our **mother**'s attention – at the **birth** of a sibling, perhaps, or when we experience a **primal scene** involving our **parents**. Later, there is the **fear** of being excluded from something significant and in which we may **wish** to participate – of not belonging, in other words. Such **anxieties** commonly recur, often in the strangest possible forms, in our **dreams**, and are part of their fundamentally protective **nature**.
KEY LINE: 'He heeded not; but, with his twofold charge/Still in his grasp, before me, full in view,/Went hurrying o'er the illimitable waste,/With the fleet waters of a drowning world/In chase of him;' (From William Wordsworth's *The Prelude*, Book V, 1850)

Aberfan Disaster On 21st October 1966, in the small village of Aberfan in southern Wales, a landslip of mining waste tumbled down a hillside and onto the local village **school**, **killing** 144 **people**, 116 of whom were **children**. In the two **weeks** before the **disaster**, more than 200 **people** were found to have had **dreams** or **precognitions** about the tragedy, including nine-year-old Eryl Mai Jones, one of the **victims**, who had told her **mother**, on the 20th October, of a dream she had had the **night** before: 'I dreamed I went to school and there was no school there. Something **black** had come down all over it.'

Aberration In psychological terms an aberration is a morbid departure from the norm, or from normal functioning.

Abon Hassan The Great Caliph of the **East**, Haroun al Rashid (765–809), decided to play a **trick** on a **rich** merchant of his acquaintance. He ordered his courtiers to transfer Abon Hassan, whilst still **sleeping**, from his **bed** on the outskirts of **town**, into Haroun's own bed at the **palace**. When he **woke** up, Hassan was to be treated in every way as the Caliph, until he eventually began to doubt his own identity (From *The Sleeper Awakened*, a tale of the *Arabian Nights*). **William Shakespeare** uses a comparable device in *The Taming of the Shrew*, and Robert Burton (in his *Anatomy of Melancholy* ii, 2, 4) tells of Phillipe the Good, Duke of Burgundy, playing a similar **waking dream** trick on the occasion of his **marriage** to Isabel, daughter of the **King** of Portugal.

Abortions When a woman **dreams** of an abortion, it may represent a hidden **fear** of **pregnancy** or of the responsibilities and perceived loss of

independence that a pregnancy can bring. It can also carry with it connotations of outside forces – a *deus ex machina*, perhaps – magically
resolving issues that are not, in reality, so easy to resolve. Should a man
dream of an abortion, there are usually overtones of powerlessness, or of
losing control over something that he considers fundamentally his own,
to others (perhaps to women).

Above The state of being above something in a dream may reflect the
dreamer's desire for a resolution of an uncomfortable moral dilemma.
This displacement from **below** to above is usually a **transformative** one
– a movement from the carnal towards the spiritual, if you like, or from
the sensual to the intellectual. The reverse, needless to say, is also true,
and may point to **castration complexes** or the existence of **psychoses** or
other pathological **neurotic** complications, such as **obsessive compulsive
disorders** (a shift from the important 'above' to the trivial 'below' which
is carried over into real life). **Adler** felt that the 'upper' in **dreams** represented the dreamer's ambitions, while **Freud** took the view that the
'below' and the 'behind' represented the **unconscious**, while the above
symbolized the dreamer's moral conscience or **superego**.

Abraham The **biblical** patriarch Abraham was pronounced the first-ever
dream interpreter by Philo Judeas in his *Book of Giants and of Civil Life*
(25 BC). This is a somewhat debatable point.

Abreaction A **Freudian** term indicating a removal of emotional blocks
through the re-experiencing of their causation in a therapeutic setting.

Absence Absence, or the sense of loss absence brings, is one of the cornerstones of existential **anxiety**. The feeling that we are alone, and have
no one to look after or to comfort us, is one of the fundamental motivators of religious thought, and an invaluable spur to the imagination.
Writers, **artists**, and **poets** thrive on the **fear** of absence, and the act of
drawing, or of **writing** something, or even of creating something in the
sand, is one of mankind's few (albeit, temporary) answers to the problem
of existential loneliness. See **Aloneness** & **Amputation**

Absinthe The original absinthe was made with extracted wormwood, and
turned habitual drinkers blind. It is psychoactive, and causes unnatural
dreams and **hallucinations** when overindulged in. It was reputedly
brought over to Europe from Algiers by addicted French **soldiers**, some
time during the 19th century. See **Artificial Dreams, Blindness &
Hallucinatory Dreams**

Abstinence A concentration on the higher rather than the lower human
aspects. Abstinence in **dreams** may be a manifestation of spiritual
desires, or the **wish** to overcome one's animal **nature** – for **animals**,
needless to say, do not abstain from anything which may lead to the satisfaction of their **urges**. See **Id**

KEY LINE: 'Abstinence is whereby a man refraineth from anything which he may lawfully take.' (From Sir Thomas Elyot's *The Governour* 1531)

Abstract Thoughts Abstract thoughts or theoretical principles in **dreams** usually find themselves personalized or concretized in some way, often by the substitution of a person or an object representing the thought for the actual thought itself. An example might be comedy, depicted in the form of a **clown**, or freedom, depicted in the form of a **cowboy** riding the range. **Freud**, however, did acknowledge the difficulty of translating abstract thought into effective **dream work**. See **Comical Dreams**, **Figurative Expressions** & **Personalization**

Abudah Abudah, in *Tales of the Genii*, was a merchant of old Baghdad, who used to be tormented, every **night**, by **nightmares** of a terrible old hag. He finally discovered that the only possible way to rid himself of these unceasing visions was to 'fear **God**, and keep his commandments'. See **Descartes**

Abysses In purely symbolical terms, abysses are bottomless, because we can, by definition, only know the extent of them if we are already **falling** to our **deaths**. To that extent they are perfect images for the **dream** to grasp when it wishes to leaven, or diffuse, our everyday **anxieties**. Crossing an **abyss** (by a shaky rope **ladder**, perhaps) shows our desire to regain control – very possibly over our own mortality. See **Emptiness** & **Voids**

Accidents Dreaming of accidents reinforces our **fear** of the unexpected disrupting the comforting flow of our everyday lives (*inter os atque offam multa intervenire posse* – 'between the mouth and the morsel many things may happen' (Cato the Elder, a.k.a. Cato the Censor 234–149 BC)). There may also be a fantasy element involved, because it is normal to fantasize over how we would behave in an **emergency**, and creating a controllable crisis in our **dreams** provides a particularly safe **harbour** for such thoughts.

Aces The Ace in a deck of **cards** is both the **lowest** card and the highest. It incorporates both power and powerlessness. The Ace of **Spades** is traditionally the **death** card, and the Ace of **Clubs** may equate, in symbolical terms at least, with the threefold nature of **God**, given the trefoil design, which also suggests the **cross**. Diamonds, it hardly needs to be added, imply both **wealth** and symmetry (see **Gems**), and **Hearts**, **love**.

Aches The presence of an ache or a **pain** in a **dream** may point to an underlying mental or spiritual disharmony.

Active Analysis Analysis by direct **guidance**, rather than by enlightened inference.

Actors Actors may represent flippant or non-serious aspects of the dreamer's personality which the **dreamer** may, or may not, wish to discard (particularly if the actor is associated with a transient object). **Jung** recounts just such a **dream**, in which the 'actor' throws his **hat** against a wall. In this particular context, the 'hat' took on the guise of a **mandala**, which represented the aspect of the dreamer that was a **stranger** to himself, and which was ultimately embodied by the 'actor' persona.

Adders In superstitious terms, to see an adder and to let it live was meant to bring bad luck. Such deep-seated **superstitions** have simply added to the generally ill-omened **nature** of **snakes** when they appear in **dreams**.

Addiction Fears about – and the **neurotic** acceptance of – addiction ('I shall do as I see fit, and to hell with the consequences'), can both foment **anxiety**, and are therefore likely to infest our **dreams**, especially when others, in everyday life, are putting pressure on us to behave in a more responsible manner. Addiction equates with a perceived loss of self-control, and usually refers, in a dream context, to underlying **death** fears and intimations of mortality.

Adler, Alfred (1870–1937) An eminent Austrian psychologist and founder of a neo-**Freudian** school of psychology, Adler believed that inferiority, rather than the **sex** drive, was the fundamental motivator of human development – to this end he coined the term 'inferiority complex'. Adler believed that the **breaking** down of **inferiority complexes** and their compensatory defence mechanisms was the main purpose of **psychoanalysis**. In addition he believed that mental equilibrium depended on the individual's correct adjustment in three crucial spheres relating to the outside **world**, namely 'work', 'sex' and 'community'. He believed that **dreams** represented an arranging, by the **dreamer**, of their life plans, and were therefore useful only insofar as they formed part of an 'unmasking' process. That their function, in other words, was either anticipatory or prescient – nothing more. See **Neurosis & Will to Power**

Adoption Adoption, in purely symbolical terms, relates to the assimilation of the lower nature into the higher, creating unity. It therefore has a redemptive quality which, in a dream context, may be healing. See **Adultery**

Adultery Adultery, in direct opposition to **adoption** in symbolical terms, represents the forsaking of the higher part of **nature**, for the lower.

Advice Advice, in dreams, is frequently given to us by the **Wise Old Man** or the **Great Mother**, **symbols** mankind has created for itself to negate its natural powerlessness in the face of **nature**. The **question** to be asked is why our **dreams** have felt the need to conjure up these images in the first place – the underlying message may be that our **unconscious** is telling us that we *ought* to heed outside **advice** (or enlightened inner awareness), and not force our way towards often specious answers to otherwise insoluble questions.

Aeroplanes Aeroplanes are predominantly masculine symbols, for they are undoubtedly **phallic**, and are frequently associated, particularly in the **male** mind, with images of domination and control. This may be seen not only in terms of **flying**, but also of entering or **crashing** down, which may equate to a catastrophic loss of control (or a libido crisis). Such a crashing down frequently occurs in a back **garden**, potentially implying a **fear** of, or a suppressed attraction to, **homosexuality** – an alternative and less sexualized reading, however, might suggest revocations of a loss of the innocence or of the security formerly afforded by the parental home (or by parental unity), either as a result of **divorce**, or of the **death** of one or both **parents**. In addition, aeroplanes can be both aspirational and **terminal**, and the experience of travelling in one may, in purely symbolical terms, be closely akin to the **pre-birth** or intra-uterine experience. In the **female** mind they can be both threat and promise – literally speaking they are **dangerous**, but if you decide to take them (or allow them to take you – see **Captains**) you may **travel**, and enjoy the experience.

Aesculapius Aesculapius was the Greek **God** of **Medicine**, who was eventually killed by Zeus with a thunderbolt because he threatened the natural order of the **world** by bringing **people** back from the **dead**. The sick would practice 'incubation' at his **temple**, which involved going to **sleep** and **dreaming** of the God, who would, if they were lucky, descend and diagnose their **illness**, recommending a cure which his **priests** would then **carry** out.

Affirmation A **move** from affirmation to **negation** in a **dream** usually implies its direct **opposite**. The **dreamer**'s will is in fact cutting in and manipulating the dream to protect the dreamer from persons or objects that may be uncongenial in real life.

Agoraphobic Dreams These **dreams** usually contain **inhibitions** of one sort or another, and may stem from the **dreamer**'s fear of enacting otherwise safely hidden impulses. **Adler** believed, in addition, that the concealed purpose of agoraphobia (the morbid **fear** of open **spaces**) was as a **mask** behind which the sufferer might attempt to impose their will on their environment.

AIDS AIDS (or any sexually communicable **disease**, for that matter) is a convenient **symbol** for the dream world to latch on to in order to castigate, or morally contain, an otherwise rampaging **id**.

Airplanes See **Aeroplanes**

Airports Airports are **harbours** for **aeroplanes** to come into. To that extent they are predominantly **female** symbols, usually implying a safe and secure landing place after a **dangerous** (i.e. **male**) interim.

Alarms Alarms are convenient **fear-** or **anxiety**-inducing **symbols**, and have **archetypal** connotations in that they would have been one of our first civilized, communal acts, and a fundamental trigger for human intelligence. They are at the same time unsettling and comforting – unsettling, because one is not at first aware of the severity of the **danger** being trumpeted, and comforting, because one is, by definition, still alive to hear them.

Alchemy The word alchemy derives from the Arabic, *al kímía*, meaning 'the **secret** art'. In its scientific form it equates most closely with modern **chemistry**, but in its philosophical form it endeavoured to solve the three great **secrets** of **science**, namely the discovery of the universal solvent, the transmutation of base **metals** into **gold**, and the secret of the elixir of life – all these aims found themselves drawn together within the concept of the **Philosopher's Stone**, or 'universal panacea'. To the alchemist, each **planet** corresponded to a **metal**: Apollo, or the **sun**, equated to gold; Diana, or the **moon**, equated to **silver**; **Mercury** to quicksilver; **Venus** to **copper**; Mars to **iron**; Jupiter to tin; and Saturn to **lead**. In purely symbolical terms, alchemy represents the transmutation of the **lower** into the higher. **Jung**, in particular, associated alchemical insight and **symbols** with **dreams**, believing that the concept of the alchemical *illuminatio* or *solificatio* (enlightenment or elucidation) potentially corresponded to the **males'** acceptance of the **anima**, and to the **females'** acceptance of the **animus**. See **Above & Below**

Alcohol Alcoholic **dreams** (i.e. dreams under the influence of alcohol) tend towards the freeing of normally repressed **instincts**, and, in extreme cases of alcoholic poisoning (in which **hallucinatory dreams** are common), they may even contain **voices** or other such **projections**. Dreaming of alcohol *per se* is more likely to contain elements of **wish fulfilment** than to imply anything more than a temporary change in perception or **consciousness**. See **Artificial Dreams**

Aliens When a woman **dreams** of aliens she may simply be allowing her entirely rational but possibly repressed fear of **rape** (particularly in strange, unknown places – whilst **travelling**, perhaps?) to take its rightful place in her **unconscious** – rightful, because it is not possible to function in a larger society if one is perpetually in fear of something happening which could catastrophically overturn one's normal life pattern. In this case the dream acts as a safety **valve**, allowing the violation **fears** to be expressed (or theatrically re-enacted), but in an innocuous and physically unthreatening form – for so-called rational people do not really believe in aliens, or if they do, they do so theoretically, without ever expecting to encounter one. *Ergo* rapists.

Allan Apples The old Cornish name for Hallowtide (Halloween) was Allantide. At this **season**, each member of the **family** was given a very large **apple**, called an Allan Apple. If an unmarried maiden slept with such an apple tucked beneath her **pillow**, she would **dream** of her future **husband** (or so the legend had it). This tradition continued to the very turn of the 20th century, when it fell into decline. See **Ash Leaves & Dumb Cake**

Alleys Alleys are predominantly anal or uterine **symbols** – one can be trapped in alleys despite wishing to **exit**. For breech-born **children**, dreaming of alleys may reflect back on the trauma of their **birth** (the instinctive desire to emerge, but the inability to do so without help). The **claustrophobic** element is present, too, in the symbol of an area that finds itself, as it were, situated between two stools. See **Anal Erotism, Anal Retention & Uterus**

Alligators Archetypally speaking, alligators, like caimans, gavials, and **crocodiles**, are amongst the most mysterious of **animals** in that they dwell both **above** and **below** the water, and are thought to carry their prey to strange abodes. Dreamed of by a **female**, they probably have **phallic** connotations, and may disguise a **fear** of, or **anxiety** about **sex**. Dreamed of by a **male**, they may imply **emasculation** fears, or **castration complexes**.
KEY LINE: 'Each crocodile was girt with massive gold/And polished stones that with their wearers grew:/But one there was who waxed beyond the rest,/Wore kinglier girdle and a kingly crown …' (From Christina Rossetti's *My Dream* 1855)

Alnaschar Dream Any dream in which **chickens** are **counted** before they are hatched. The eponymous Alnaschar invested everything he had in a **basket** of glassware, and then constructed a **waking dream** in which he sold the **glass** at a profit, these transactions **spiralling** ever upwards until, a **rich** man, he finally came to **marry** the Vizier's **daughter**. The only **problem** being that he went on to dream that he was **angry** with his imaginary **wife**, **kicked** out at her, and **broke** the very glassware that would have started him on his **road** to riches in the first place.

Aloneness There are subtle differences between being alone, being solitary, and being **abandoned**. The dream image may, in many cases, appear to be the same, but the emotion contained within the image is categorically different. Aloneness is primarily an existential state – we are born together, but die alone. Aloneness, or the **fear** of being alone, is therefore one of the main motivators of human existence. Being solitary can be a **rich** and productive state (though technically, or at the very least seemingly, aberrant) – however, the products of such a solitary state are usually best consumed communally, or at the very least *à deux,* for few human beings can remain solitary for long periods without the onset of **neurosis**. See **Solitude**

Alpleich Also known as the *Elfenreigen*, this is the (possibly apocryphal) **spirit music** that can sometimes be heard, more often than not in a **dream state**, just before **death** occurs. The word comes from the German, and means, literally, **mountain body**.

Altars Altars symbolize religious consciousness. They may also have **sacrificial** overtones, and are not immune to desecration or misuse, as in the **Black** Mass.

Amazement Amazement, in a **dream**, may equate with the process of metaphorical **awakening**, or revelation.

Ambivalence See **Bipolarity**

Ambulances Ambulances are **anxiety**-carriers in **dreams**, and are chosen by the **unconscious** to provoke terror or uncertainty as a means of alleviating it in real life. The adjunct of the **siren**, or **alarm**, may represent a clarion call for the **dreamer** to pay attention to something of importance that the unconscious wishes to communicate.

America America, according to **Jung**, is the **symbol** of untrammelled, practical thinking, in which the intellect is seen as the employee rather than as the *chef d'usine*.

Amina Amina is the **orphan heroine** of Vincenzo Bellini's opera *La Sonnambula* (*The Sleepwalker*), who sleepwalks her way straight into the **bed** of Count Rodolpho on the very eve of her **marriage** to Elvino, a **rich** farmer. Disgusted, Elvino renounces the girl, despite the count's pleas that Amina is innocent, and was in a **dream state** when she came to him. When Amina sleepwalks once again, however, and this time publicly – along the edge of the **roof** under her **adoptive father's** **mill wheel**, and then, in **peril** for her life, across a dangerous **bridge** – Elvino realizes his mistake and marries the vindicated **girl** forthwith. **Freud**, however, would immediately have pooh-poohed any idea that Amina was innocent, and would have described her **sleepwalking** into Count Rodolpho's bed as the **unconscious** enactment of hidden, underlying impulses – in the society in which she lived, who could blame the girl for secretly preferring the bed of a noble count to the cot of a farmer, however rich he may be?

Amplification A **Jungian** term describing the directed clarification and amplification of a **dream** image through enlightened symbolical parallels (folklore, mythology, religion, etc.).

Amputation Amputation, in a dream, often reflects a **castration complex**. The lack of an organ may represent the withdrawal of that organ's emotional base or charge. In this context the identity of the lost organ is important, and may represent an element of the **dreamer** that they **fear** is calcified, or otherwise non-functioning. Such 'losses' often have a semantic base, as in a 'loss of face', or a 'loss of manhood' or 'femininity', represented by an organ that has those specific semantic connotations (**heart, shoulders, hips, breasts**, etc.). Traditionally, amputees have feared being buried in their incomplete form, as this would disadvantage them through all Eternity – as a consequence, severed limbs were often kept for later **burial** alongside their original host (Sir Arthur Conan Doyle's short story *The Brown Hand* is a marvellous case in point). See **Menopause & Voids**

KEY LINE: 'Accordingly, I went over to the fire-place in the usual English way, proposing to wait there. And there, after the same fashion, I lounged with my arm upon the mantel-piece; but only for a few moments. For feeling that my fingers had rested on something strangely cold, I looked, and saw that they lay upon a dead hand: a woman's hand newly cut from the wrist.' (From Frederick Greenwood's *Imagination in Dreams* 1894)

Amulets An amulet represents our desire to change the course of our fate, or to stave off **evil**. As such, its presence in a **dream** is often part of a **wish-fulfilment** scenario, and may equate with the ancient Roman practice of dressing in **rags** when appearing as the defendant in a court case in order to excite pity in the **hearts** of the spectators. See **Strangling**

Amusement Parks Amusement parks are a **symbol** of childhood being carried over into adulthood. They are nominally for **children**, but adults, too, can enjoy them, on the understanding that they are only there because accompanying children need protecting from the mysterious and possibly destructive forces of unfettered joy. Our **dreams**, too, make use of such images in a number of ways – either by using the fact that one has to **pay** to derive **pleasure** from them, or on the principle that **danger** may be lurking behind their otherwise jolly **façade**, or finally by virtue of the fact that our enjoyment is being provided by **people** whom we perceive (even inadvertently) to be beneath us and who may, in consequence, conceivably try to gain their **revenge** on us by **cheating** us. Thus their use in such seminal and psychologically acute **films** (*ergo* dream fantasies) as Alfred Hitchcock's *Strangers on a Train* (1951), or Carol Reed's *The Third Man* (1949), often, paradoxically, as scenes of horror. See **Childhood Dreams & Dreamland**

Anaesthesia Dreams under anaesthesia often incorporate motion of some sort, to counterbalance or compensate for the **dreamer**'s feeling of **imprisonment** and subjugation. Dreams with a religious motif may also occur in this context. The images chosen in the dream may conceivably reflect (in purely symbolical terms, of course) the medical machinery inevitably surrounding the dreamer, be they in a dentists' surgery, surgical unit, or operating theatre. Even the name of the place in which the surgery is being enacted may find itself echoed within the dream, as in **dreams** of a real **theatre**, in which **actors**, rather than **doctors** or

dentists, appear. Such dreams may also reflect the **toxic** element of the dreaming process, which was not, in this case, caused by fatigue, but by artifice. Occasionally, too, they may reflect back to a **pre-birth** condition, triggered by the **death fear** we all have when undergoing anaesthesia, i.e. are we going to **wake** up again? (For a filmic example of this, try Powell & Pressburger's *A Matter of Life and Death* (1946)). Such an exalted degree of **anxiety** is not usually present when we go into a natural, rather than an artificial **sleep**, however. See **Artificial Dreams**

Anagogic Tendencies Anagogic tendencies in **dreams** are those tendencies which point up the **dreamer**'s desire for everything spiritual, high-minded and ideal. See **Catagogic Tendencies**

Anal Erotism An early stage in infantile sexuality in which **libido** development is centred on the anal area. The stuff of many **dreams**, in other words. See **Anal Retention**

Anal Retention A catch-all quasi-**Freudian** concept relating to the **anal erotism** phase of infancy (from around 18 months to three years of age) in which the principal gratification of the libidinal drive is considered to stem from the retention and expulsion of faeces (see **Excrement**). This is then extrapolated forward to adulthood, and behavioural characteristics which involve excessive cleanliness (in mimesis of a bid to please, and not alienate, the **mother**), often twinned with certain **fetishistic** forms of sexuality. See **Cleansing** & **Torpedoes**

Ancestors To the Taoists of ancient China, dreaming of ancestors meant that good fortune would follow the **dreamer**.

Anchors Anchors tie us down to things, but they also protect us in case of **storms** and uncertain **seas**. They serve to attach us to the **land**, when we are nominally on an element (the sea) over which we have but little control. They can be a drag (quite literally), but they are also beautiful objects which we should not like to **lose**. All this to say that when anchors occur in our **dreams**, they may indicate a desire for stability in stormy **waters**, or, obversely, a desire to cast aside what is holding us down and set ourselves free.

Angels Angels represent a ministering influence – they also carry messages. Dreaming of angels may point to an **unconscious** desire on the part of the **dreamer** to evolve from their present position. See **Messengers**
KEY LINE: 'An angel stood and met my gaze,/Through the low doorway of my tent;/The tent is struck, the vision stays; – /I only know she came and went.' (From J. R. Lowell's *She Came And Went*)

Anger The appearance of anger in a **dream** is usually a direct response to a real attitude. Only occasionally does it betoken its exact **opposite** (see

Transformation), and then only through lack of a real means of expression in a real environment.

Anima According to **Jung**, the anima is the **female** element in the **male unconscious** (the animated psychic atmosphere) with which a man needs to come to terms if he is to live a balanced psychic life. Insecure males often keep their animas concealed, both from themselves and others. Throughout history, **hermaphroditic** images have hinted at mankind's psychic **bisexuality**, and in certain Eskimo and **Indian** tribes **shamans** and **medicine** men would even dress up as women, the better to be able to connect with the **ghost**-world (the unconscious). In the male, the anima is usually most influenced by the **mother** – if in a positive, constructive way, all very well. If in a negative way – the *femme fatale*; the **poison** damsel; destructive illusion; the nursing of fantasies; anima **projections** onto inanimate objects such as **cars**, etc. – **depression** and irritation can occur. If the male is finally able to exorcise or address these negative maternal residues, however, his positive masculinity may be enhanced. See **Animus**

Animals When an animal pursues someone in a **dream**, it can reflect the splitting off of an instinct from formal consciousness. The animal part of the **dreamer** is striving to be readmitted, or reintegrated, into the dreamer's consciousness, but the dreamer fears the return of the suppressed **instinct** and sets up barriers to its entry. Certain animals may also reflect a desire on the part of the dreamer to **discipline** themselves, or to control their lower **nature**. See **Cats**, **Dogs**, **Snakes**, etc.

Animism The **archetypal** belief that all things, both animate and inanimate, have a **soul**. Animism is important in a **dream** context because its influence may be present outside the span of the **dreamer's** intellectual volition.

Animus According to **Jung**, the animus is the collective **male** element in the **female unconscious**. Each human organism has two sets of chromosomes (one relating to each **parent**) and a balance must exist between the two for a healthy psychic life. If the animus gets out of hand, obstinacy, **frigidity**, or inaccessibility may occur in the woman. The animus is fundamentally influenced by the female's **father** – if the father acts as a benevolent **bridge** to the adult, relational **world**, all very well. If the father inhibits the **daughter's** psychic **journey**, however, her relationship with her animus may well be **wounded**, and lead to a series of destructive relationships in adult life, or to other **secret**, injurious attitudes. Should the adult woman be able to come to terms with these negative aspects of her paternal inheritance, her femininity and creative potential may nonetheless be unleashed. See **Anima** & **Beauty and the Beast**

Anise The Elder Pliny (23–79 AD), **author** of the 37-volume *Historia Naturalis*, maintained that the anise **seed** prevented disagreeable **dreams** if sprinkled on the **pillow** before **sleeping**.

Anorexia Anorexia, or the morbid loss of appetite, most frequently appears in **dreams** in terms of extreme **thinness** or emaciation. It is most probably a **symbol**, like the seven thin kine in the **Bible** (see **Pharaoh's Dream**), that something is not quite **right** with the **dreamer**.

Antelopes It is almost impossible to think of an antelope without also entertaining thoughts of its **skin**. Traditionally, the skin of the **black** antelope was seen as reflecting the manifesting surface of the **soul** in its involuted form. To this extent at least it may symbolize evolution, or a desire to evolve.

Antiques See **Old Things**

Antithesis The **teasing** out of a **neurosis** through its antithesis (or direct **opposite**). Such apparently contra-indicative currents frequently run through **dreams**, and need to be identified. An example might be of an innately conservative person consistently dreaming of anarchic events. This does not necessarily mean that the anarchist hidden within the reactionary wishes, pupa-like, to emerge, but rather points up tensions and prejudices within the **dreamer** that need to be resolved in their everyday life.

Antennae Antennae are most obviously **phallic**, but they are also indicative of the capacity, or the necessity, to hear something – they prick up at **danger**, or feel their way towards a **secret**. The **animal** to which the antennae are attached, be they **ants**, **butterflies**, or **beetles**, is also important. See **Deafness**

Ants Ants symbolize frugality and prevision. In Christian art they symbolize prudence, for they, like humans, behave in an **archetypal** way in the formation of organized societies. In ancient Cornwall they were known as Meryons, and considered to be **fairies** in the final stage of earthly existence. Dreaming of them may imply a **fear** of something disintegrating, or even a fear of the power of **nature** over the individual. In Morocco they were traditionally fed to lethargic people in order to gee them up, and to prevent them from wasting their lives in the pursuit of **daydreams**. See **Dali**

Anus, The Dreaming of anuses usually implies a **regression** (or an unconsciously desired regression) back to the **anal erotic** state of early **childhood**. Anuses have both **sexual** and olfactory overtones, and it is important to note that even so-called 'normal' human beings usually have a marked love/hate relationship with the waste, sounds, **smells** and sensations that the anus produces. In addition, anuses are shaped like **rings**, and the movement of the **hand** or the **finger** towards a **ring** has strong symbolical connotations in virtually every society. See **Odours**

Anxiety Dreams Anxiety, in a dream context, is often related more to apprehension than to actual **fear**. These types of **dream** can throw a valuable **light** on a **dreamer**'s emotional **regression**, for they are at the service of the **ego,** and do not relate to 'real threats'. **Freud** saw them as being defined by the 'contradictory meaning of primal words' – this means that they frequently express desires that have been **repressed** by the conscious mind, and which can manifest themselves in stark oppositions or juxtaposed opposites, i.e. bad/good, **right**/wrong, **light/dark**, **fear**/comfort, **guilt**/freedom. They may also contain elements of hypocrisy stemming directly from the dreamer's own persona, which need to be teased out before the full meaning of the dream can become apparent. What appears to be happening in the dream, in other words, may simply represent a carefully hidden (even from the dreamer) **wish-fulfilment** scenario. See **Pepys** & **Warnings**

Apes Apes traditionally symbolize uncleanliness and **dirt**, and also the automatic, or subjective mind. In Christian art they represent malice, lust, and cunning. If a woman **dreams** of an ape, it may represent her **fear** of, or fascination for, the **male**. The **Beauty and the Beast** myth is a longstanding one (**Freudian slip**?), and comprises within it both the **hero** and the **heroine archetype**. See **Monkeys**
KEY LINE: 'When I awoke again, I was a baby-ape in Bornean forests, perched among fragrant trailers and fantastic orchis flowers … But I grew and grew; and then the weight of my destiny fell upon me.' (From Charles Kingsley's *Alton Locke* 1850)

Apnoea A sudden temporary incapacity to **breathe** caused by a relaxation of the **throat** muscles while **sleeping.**

Apollonian The Apollonian principle, according to the **philosopher** Friedrich Nietzsche (1844–1900), is reflected in balance, calm, and intellectual order. This is in direct **opposition** to the more creative, anarchic, **Dionysian** chaos. The name Apollonian stems from the **cult** of the **Sun God,** Apollo.

Applause Dreaming of applause inevitably contains within it elements of a **wish-fulfilment** scenario. We all like praise, and when we do not receive enough of it in our everyday lives, our **dreams** are there to **compensate** us so that we may **sleep** on without disturbance.

Apples Apples, while symbolizing, in one sense, the **fruit** of the **spirit,** are often synonymous with **female breasts** when they appear in **dreams**. The apple's association with the Fall from the **Garden** of Eden appears all-encompassing, but it is arguable (if one consults the Authorized

Version of the **Bible**), that another fruit may have been involved, and that
the apple is therefore innocent of taint. See **Allan Apples**
KEY LINE: 'Apples are thought to quench the flame of Venus, according
to that old English saying, He that will not a wife wed, Must eat a cold
apple when he Goeth to bed, though some turn it to a contrary purpose.'
(From Thomas Cogan's *Haven of Health* 1588)

Appointments Appointments and **anxiety** are inevitably connected. In
dreaming of appointments kept, missed, or near-missed (see **Missing**),
our **dreams** may be reminding us that something is niggling us – something that needs to be attended to. The dream architecture surrounding the
appointment then needs to be investigated, and its symbolical value
assessed.

Aprons Aprons are most likely to represent womanhood, or femaleness,
to the **dreamer**. They may also reflect domesticity and order. When associated with **blood** (implying **butchery**), they can reflect a **breaking** up, or
breaking down, of an established order.

Aquarius In Buddhistic terms, Aquarius, the water carrier (see
Carrying), is the vehicle of the spirit and the container of **truth**, in the
form of **water** taken from the **fountain** of Divine Reality. While this may
seem a little far-fetched when related to **dreams**, it certainly works on an
archetypal level, even when taken outside a religious context – the symbol of the offering of water (*ergo* life) is an ancient one, and almost
invariably benevolent. See **Zodiac**

Archaic Remnants According to **Freud**, dream images that involve
primitive aspects of **myth** and **ritual** are simply psychic survivals or
hang-overs from our ancestors – a position **Jung** profoundly disagreed
with. He believed that these images were still functioning in the form of
archetypes, creating a **bridge** between the modern **world's** conscious
expression of its thoughts, and a more primitive means of articulation.

Arches In purely symbolical terms, an arched **gateway** hints at the existence of mental qualities which may (or indeed may not, if a worst case
scenario is adhered to) open the way to an increase of knowledge. They
represent **entrances** to **secret**, hidden places, and possibly even the abode
of the **self**.

Archetypes Archetypes are elements that occur in a **dream** which are not
individual, and do not derive from the **dreamer's** personal experience.
Such archetypes, which equate in some measure only to **Freud's** concept
of **archaic remnants**, are, according to **Jung**, expressions of an inherited,
aboriginal, or innate old **psyche**, which predates the so-called 'rational'
mindset of the 'civilized' man – they are, as he put it, 'organs of the **soul**'.
These archetypes appear in the form of **primordial images**, and are, at
one and the same time, both images and emotions. Without this crucial

tie-up, they would lack the numinosity, the psychic energy, necessary to make them significant and subject to dynamic consequences. Archetypes differ from **instincts**, however, in that instincts are physiological urges, susceptible to perception by the senses, whereas archetypes may also manifest themselves through fantasies and symbolic images, and have no known origin. In addition, they appear to be subject to a form of spontaneous morphology, and can reproduce themselves anywhere, at any **time**, in any part of the **world**. Archetypes frequently work in anticipatory ways, preparing the ground for oncoming crises, and they only really come to life when it is possible to discover in what exact way they are significant to the individual dreaming of them. They are the cornerstones of creativity to the extent that they can be accessed – or are amenable to accession – by the putative creator. A list of archetypes might include the kindly **mother** or the kindly **father**, the destructive mother or the **ogre** (encapsulating **male** negativity), the **siren** (encapsulating the **female** temptress), the **tramp**, the sorcerer, the Amazon (see **Shears**), the **witch**, the villain, the youth, and the competitor. See also **Anima, Animus, Hero, Heroine, Priests/Priestesses, Princes/Princesses, Wise Man & Great Mother**

Arenas Arenas are places of confrontation, and can be either benevolent, when they function as areas of intellectual confrontation or debate, or malevolent, when they function as areas of morbid competition and threat. Arenas also act as a focus for our attention, and their appearance in **dreams** may act as a **warning** that we are not concentrating our energies sufficiently on a desired object or outcome. They are also private places (in the sense of private conflict) into which the public is only invited on sufferance, and when dreamt of by an **introvert**, can come perilously close to **nightmare**.

Arguments Arguments, in **dreams**, are usually between the **self** and oneself (i.e. the **ego**). They are not **extroverted**, in other words, but **introverted**, and usually imply an inner **conflict** that needs to be resolved.

Armies Armies often have positive ramifications in **dreams**, symbolic of the disciplining of mental qualities, or of the organizing of certain capacities necessary to the fruitful enjoyment of one's life. Imaginary armies may also be used in the treatment of **cancer** and other invasive **diseases**. If, however, the **dreamer** finds themselves **attacked** by an army, a different interpretation must be sought, and the sources of the dreamer's **anxiety** (which may find themselves inadvertently expressed in the **make-up** of the attacking army) identified.

Armour We protect ourselves with armour, but such protection is often specious, as with the child who hides itself under the bedcovers in the mistaken belief that no one can see it because it cannot see them. Armour, too, is rigid and inflexible, and its protective capacities may only serve to alienate us, rather than to hide us, from the real **world** (think of the survivalist cults in certain parts of the USA). In a more positive light, dreaming of armour may imply a desire to be chivalrous, or to be of help to others.

Arms Arms and **weapons** frequently represent outgoing, ejective forces relating to the mental plane, which is also, needless to say, the plane of **conflict**. On a more mundane level, they may appear to be a means of putting **wish-fulfilment** fantasies into practice, or, in **Adlerian** terms at least, to imply the existence of an **inferiority complex**.

Arrival The act of arrival in a **dream** may often be equated with the attainment, or the desire to achieve, an **orgasm**. Arriving can also, on occasion, mean **death**. See **Lateness**

Arrows Arrows are likely to have **phallic** connotations when they appear in **dreams**. In symbolical terms, however, they may express a higher, divine will, as exemplified by the cherub bowmen so beloved of the **gods**. They may also, paradoxically perhaps, indicate a desire to communicate. See **Targets**

Artemidorus of Daldis Artemidorus, who lived in the second half of the second century AD, and was one of the first recorded workers with **dreams**, recounts the following **prognosticatory** dream. A patient of his dreamed that he watched his **father** die in a house **fire**. A short time later, the patient himself succumbed to a *phlegmone* (or fiery fever), while his father went on to live out his normal span. The **house**, in this instance, was the patient's own 'house' (i.e. his **body**), and the fire that raged within it was the **fever** that would later **kill** him. Traditionally of course, when a father dies, even symbolically, the son frequently sees in the **death** a foreknowledge and forewarning (an *adumbratio*) of his own mortality – in certain ancient societies this was considered such a *sine qua non* that it was even customary for the son to inhale his dying father's last **breath** in order to take over his father's **soul**. Apart from one or two **gems** such as this, Artemidorus's *Interpretation of Dreams* (*Oneirocriticon*) is a pretty dotty concoction, *viz.* his equating of the **hands** of a man who dreams that he is **masturbating** as symbolic of his **servants** (either **male** or **female**). Artemidorus goes on to say that if the dreaming man is without servants, he may expect a loss (*ergo* 'the emission'), but if the servant dreams of masturbating the **master**, he will be **whipped** (i.e. extended) by the said master, thus fulfilling the dream's prophecy. There's an awful lot on **incest**, too, which would, on the surface, appear to connect Artemidorus with **Freud** in a roundabout way, except that Artemidorus is rather pro incest, to the extent that he advises poor men to have **sex** with their **rich daughters** (only in dreams, needless to say) as they will benefit both materially and by way of enjoyment should they choose this course of action. **Mothers**, too, are fair oneiric game, except that Artemidorus does not advise variations of sexual position in this particular case, as it would be insulting – as indeed, would *fellatio* be (one man, Artemidorus assures us, even lost his **penis** after such a dream). One final Artemidorean note: if a man dreams he is having **sexual intercourse** with himself, he will lose everything, because, and I quote, 'sexual intercourse with oneself would involve great agony'. Readers may be pleased to note, however, that, on the whole, Artemidorus rather disapproves of necrophilia. See **Ezekiel**

Arthritis Arthritis, or the deformation of **limbs** (thus negating their functional ability), frequently involves a **resistance** of some form or other in **dream** terms. If one is deformed, or in **pain**, one cannot, by definition, act in certain ways – one is scuppered, as it were, by *force majeure*, taking away some of the pressures of personal responsibility. In everyday life, **illness** can be used as an excuse not to act, while also (it goes without saying), providing perfectly justifiable reasons for creative inertia.

Artificial Dreams Dreams induced by the use of herbs, **drugs**, **alcohol**, **anaesthetics**, painkillers or soporifics. Such **dreams**, unless they are spiritually prepared for as part of a noumenal experience, do not stand or bear interpretation. However, **dreamers** often claim that a **dream** they have had and whose significance they may not wish to address occurred as the result of artifice on their part, and is therefore not significant – this is, of course, delusional, and rarely stands up to detailed analysis.

Artists Amongst the many artists who acknowledge being directly influenced or driven to create by their **dreams**, we find **William Blake, Francisco de Goya**, Edward Burne-Jones, Frida Kahlo, Peter Birkhauser, Pierre Puvis de Chavannes, Odilon Redon, Max Beckmann and Jim Dine.

Ascension Ascension, in both religious and noumenal terms, usually implies a **movement** onto a higher plane of being – a union between the terrestrial plane and the spiritual one, in other words. People 'ascend' in **trances**, and the **sun**, too, ascends into the **sky** – we understand, of course, that the sun's apparent descent is not in fact a descent at all, but merely the movement of 'our' **planet** around its orbit. See **Ladders** & **Sublimation**

Asceticism Asceticism represents the **bridge** being two states of being, the corporeal and the spiritual – its active principle being that of self-denial. See **Abstinence**

Ash Leaves In a Yorkshire variation on the Cornish **Allan Apples** legend, an unmarried young girl might secretly gather an **ash** leaf, place it underneath her **pillow**, and intone the following: 'Even-ash, even-ash, I pluck thee,/This night my own true love to see,/Neither in his rick nor in his rare,/But in the clothes he does everyday wear.' Her future **husband** would then appear to her in a **dream**. See **Dumb Cake**

Ashes Ashes from a **fire** were considered to have **magical** properties, because they contained a residue of both the fire they were part of, and the substance that had been burned. In the same way ashes in **dreams** may be residues, or **memorials**, left over from **past** events. They also symbolize the transitory quality of the **nature**-world. See **Burning &** **Sackcloth**

Asps In Christian art the asp symbolizes **Christ**, or the Christian faith. See **Serpents & Snakes**

Assemblies Assemblies, or **meetings** of **people**, often equate with a **drawing** together, or a desire to have things out. A result is being called for, but the **dreamer** may feel either incapable of achieving such a result themselves, or anxious that the desired result may be dispersed or even lost amongst the multitude – that the impetus of the original thought is being fragmented, in other words. See **Losing**

Asses Asses traditionally symbolize stupidity and stubbornness. In **Christian** art they were generally taken to symbolize sobriety, or the Jewish Nation. The phrase 'the burial of an ass' indicated no burial at all (Jeremiah xxii, 19). **Jesus'** calling for the ass and its colt, in Matthew xxi, 2, represented his method of **drawing** our attention to old doctrine, in the form of the ass, and new **truth**, in the form of the colt, to which it was perceived to have given **birth**.
KEY LINE: 'Until the Donkey tried to clear/The Fence, he thought himself a Deer.' (From Arthur Gutterman's *A Poet's Proverbs*)

Association The voluntary expression of an idea or a word that may (or may not) relate to a dreamed experience – its very non-relation, in a **dream** context, may also be of significance. See **Free Association**

Assurbanipal, King (668–626 BC) See **Assyrian Dream Book**

Assyrian Dream Book The Assyrians of ancient Mesopotamia believed that every object and every occurrence had predictive significance. Contrived **sacrifices** (involving the dissection of the internal organs of slaughtered **animals**), the particular glow of a precious **stone**, the **spirals** evolving from **smoke**, the **shape** of a **fruit**, the sounds emanating from natural **springs**, the creaking of **trees**, the **whistling** of **wind** through **rock** striations, the accidental transposition of a **word** – all had tales to tell. Most important of all omens, however, were the dreams of **kings**, **priests** (magi), and **heroes**. King Assurbanipal's *Dream Book* (discovered on a series of **clay tablets** at Nineveh, and dating from circa 660 BC) describes a series of formal **dreams** which the king contrived during times of **peril**, after **nights** spent within the inner sanctums of particular **gods** and **goddesses**. One of these dreams, experienced under the aegis of the goddess Ishtar, allowed Assurbanipal to **lead** his **army** safely across the torrential **river** Idid'e, protected by the goddess. It was alleged that the dreams of kings were often dreamed simultaneously by many sleepers, thus reinforcing their message. If the dreams were negative or portentous, their **poison** could be diluted by recounting them to a lump of **clay**, which might then be dissolved in **water**.

Astrology The belief that events on **earth** are subject to planetary, or astronomical influence. Astronomical symbols frequently appear in **dreams**, and must be looked at **archetypally**, in the first instance, before wider contexts are sought. See **Zodiac**

Astronauts Astronauts may imply freedom (the desire to reach out), hermeticism (the artificial sealing in of experience), or the existence of **secrets** beyond the normal human sphere and only amenable to a select few. The astronaut's suit is also important in this context, as there may be an **unconscious** desire present in the **dreamer** to protect themselves, in some artificial way, from the outside or 'real' **world**.

Athletes Athleticism, or the turning of the **dreamer** into an athlete, is usually (except where the dreamer is, indeed, an athlete) indicative of a **wish-fulfilment** scenario – the desire to transcend one's present physical incarnation without the need for the amount of real effort necessarily involved in such an enterprise. Most of us fantasize about being better than ourselves, and the 'athletic **cult**' now prevalent in so many nations whose citizens are technically **obese**, is merely a non-dreaming, real-life manifestation of what is normally a dream scenario.

Atomic Bombs Difficult as it may be to accept, dreaming of atomic **bombs** tends to be primarily **sexually** driven, in that the mushroom **cloud**, the sense of release, the 'little **death**' (in that someone who sees an atomic **bomb** go off, is, by definition, either not within the actual blast area, or already dead), all point towards **ejaculation** rather than enlightened pragmatism or outraged political or environmental virtue. An atomic bomb may also imply the **end** of things (again, the sexual connotation), or the **destruction** of something that has formerly been cherished.

Atonement Atonement is the **wish** to provide reparation, leading to a resumption of upward growth. It implies work still to be done – unfinished business, if you like. Its aim is reconciliation, and in dream terms it may imply a desire to reconcile with oneself, as well as a desire to reconcile with those one believes one has wronged. There exists, of course, a false atonement syndrome, which is **masochistically** charged and **neurotic** in **nature**, and this needs to be watched out for, as it may stem from inappropriate feelings of **guilt**, often fomented in **childhood** when self-censorship is virtually non-existent.

Attacks The **key** to interpreting such an attack is whether the **dreamer** is the aggressor or the aggressed – the **murderer** or the murderee (see Chapter Two of D. H. Lawrence's *Women in Love*: 'It takes two people to make a murder: a murderer and a murderee. And a murderee is a man who is murderable. And a man who is murderable is a man who in a profound if hidden lust desires to be murdered.') If the dreamer is the symbolic murderer, or attacker, they are probably attempting to defend the indefensible (a low self-image or an **inferiority complex**, perhaps). If they are the symbolical murderee, then they need to ascertain why the **death** (or **failure**) desire is so present in them, and attempt to rectify this facet of their personality.

Attics Attics are **above**, and we already know how significant this factor can be in a **dream**. They are also places where old things are hidden (or even forgotten about). When moves are being made or changes are occurring, these old things can come back to haunt us, requiring, at the very least, our attention and address. See **Hiding**

Auctions The presupposition in an auction is that everything can be either bought or sold. This is palpably untrue in real life (you can't go around **buying** or **selling** intelligence or real affection), and therefore, in a **dream** context, auctions are merely fantasy representations of desired (or **feared**) outcomes.

Audiences Audiences and the possibility of **applause** may seem synonymous in everyday life, but there is also such a thing as a silent, disapproving audience, or even a barracking one. Some **people** do not believe that anything exists if it is not observed (the 'seeing is believing' school of perceptual causalists), and such people may unconsciously provide audiences for themselves through the medium of **dreams**. The **question** then arises as to what hitherto unresolved area in their lives needs the presence of an audience for its **affirmation**, and what manner of audience this consists of? Is the audience made up entirely of themselves?

Augury Augury is the art of divination, which consists in predicting what is going to happen in the future. The augurs of ancient Rome were soothsayers belonging to a priestly **college** who interpreted the words of the **gods** as they were passed down to human beings, either through the movement of **birds** (ornithomancy or *avis-spicere*) or through the taking of other auspices such as **thunder** and **lightning**, the movement of **animals**, the manner of feeding of **chickens**, or the content of **dreams**. *Haruspices* (a caste which originated in the *Etruscan Disciplina* and were later hijacked by the Romans), foretold the future through the observation of the entrails of **sacrificial** victims, as described in Cicero's *De Divinatione*.

Auras See **Haloes**

Authority Figures See **Officers, Teachers**, etc.

Authors Dreaming of being an author is the ultimate in wishful thinking and is closely akin to **masochism**. One must assume that the **dream** is protecting such a **dreamer** from the terrible reality that the realization of their desires would bring down on them. **Poverty**, loneliness, opprobrium, **failure** and disdain all await the putative author, and the authorial **wish**-fulfilment fantasy may shelter them, in some part, from such an objectionable, but almost certainly inevitable, reality. CYAAFAD, or the 'Call Yourself An Author For A Day' club, was founded way back in 1982 for just such eventualities, and allows would-be authors to enjoy the spurious prestige of authorship without actually having to write anything at all. **Books** are mocked up, with the **fake** author's name on the cover, and he or she can then **wander** around waving the book in front of their friends' **noses** and enjoying the little cries of envy and respect this will no doubt elicit. Murphy's Law dictates, of course, that this **waking dream** will last no more than a day, for, sooner or later, one of the author's so-called friends will no doubt check the book's existence on Amazon. The pretend author will then experience some of the horrors and indignities all real authors know so well, often in the form of **recurring dreams** or **nightmares**.

Autism Autism has recently been defined (by T. Peeters & C. Gillberg) as hyper-realism, or the almost complete inability to interpret **symbols** or symbolic language, a condition leading to a failure to relate in any significant way to the outside **world**. It is now associated with a specific brain dysfunction, which may or may not incorporate an element of inner brain damage. Curiously, however, more able autistic **people** (i.e. those with no learning disability) still retain the capacity to dream (insofar as we can tell) while often having difficulty, because of the tendency to literality endemic in their condition, in distinguishing between **daydreams**, night-time dreams, and mundane reality – in this sense alone they are similar to the Chaco Indians of Argentina (see **Dreams**) who have reached a roughly similar state via an entirely different route.

Auto-Eroticism A term coined by Henry Havelock Ellis (1859–1939) to imply a non-participatory **sexual** act, i.e. without the need for a second party. See **Masturbation**

Avalanches Dreaming of avalanches often disguises an unconscious **fear** of sudden **disasters** disrupting an established life pattern. There is also a connection, of course, with the **orgasm**, which is often called the 'little **death**', and which, in **females** at least (or so the author has been reliably informed), often resembles the gradually building downhill **rush** of an unstable snowfield. See **Landslides**

Avenging Avenging and self-vindication are often linked, and can imply a desire towards an unachievable and unrealistic perfection. Outraged virtue seldom appears in **dreams**, possibly because the **unconscious**

mind does not necessarily mimic diurnal variations of morality. 'Vengeance is mine; I will repay, saith the Lord.' (Romans xii, 19)

Awakening During the (one hopes) gradual process of awakening from our **dreams**, the **ego** slowly reconstructs itself and **dream-censorship** levels are gradually restored. A process of coordination is entered into with the emergent **world**, just as physical necessities (a full bladder, noise consciousness, a rise in ambient temperature, **hunger** pangs, **light** stimulation) reassert themselves. By the time we are fully awake, the ego has readapted itself to **reality**, having been temporarily protected and nurtured by the dreaming state during **sleep**.

Awards See **Prizes** & **Trophies**

Axes Axes, to the Taoists of Ancient China, symbolized **authority** and the possibility of **punishment**. Dreaming of a ceremonial axe implied the **death** of sensuality. In Christian iconography axes represent the Divine Truth, and the possibility of culling spiritual dead **fruit** (Matthew iii, 10). To that extent their appearance in **dreams** may have a cathartic value, or, if seen in purely **Adlerian** terms, act as part of a **wish-fulfilment** fantasy disguising feelings of **inferiority**.

B

Babies Most women will automatically assume that dreaming about babies is quite simply a literal reflection of an inner biological drive. To some extent, this is no doubt true. However, the question the **dreamer** needs to ask themselves is: 'What do babies represent for me?' Such a **question**, if answered honestly, is likely to throw a very different light indeed on the content of the dream. Should a **male** dream of babies, a similar question needs to be asked, always bearing in mind that a man is – how shall we put it? – one step in detachment away from the **female** position on the subject. See **Children**

KEY LINE: 'Dream that my little baby came to life again; that it had only been cold, and that we rubbed it before the fire, and it lived. Awake and find no baby. I think about the little thing all day. Not in good spirits.' (From Mary Wollstonecraft's *Journal*, 19th March 1815)

Bacchus See **Dionysian**

Backwards Movement Backwards movement in a **dream** can indicate a desire to return to the **past**. Backwards movement through **rooms** is often related to the **dreamer** reviewing past aspects of their life – that there are things, perhaps, still lurking in there that need straightening out (or even spring **cleaning**). One is being prevented from going forward, as it were, by a backwards, or recalcitrant, current. See **Retreating**

Badges 'Badges? We ain't got no badges. We don't need no badges. I don't have to show you any stinking badges!' (Mexican bandit Alfonso Bedoya's Gold Hat to Humphrey Bogart's Fred C. Dobbs in John Huston's 1948 film of *The Treasure of the Sierra Madre*). Bedoya was right, of course. Badges mean nothing, and are in fact simply another disguise – a method of seeming to belong to a **group** without having to answer all the necessary questions. Bedoya *knew* he belonged, and he also knew what he was after (plunder, **raping** and fun). As such, he is the perfect filmic equivalent of the **id**, which needs the **fake** authority badges give to others in order to be controlled. The badge, in the context of this argument, is the **superego** – the individual-in-society's method for limiting the anarchy of the id and bringing it to heel. In Bedoya's case it didn't really work, and Dobbs (a far more dangerous psychopath altogether), is forced to **kill** him, in a surfeit of intoxicating hypocrisy. See **Masks**

Baggage Baggage, when taken semantically, implies the **carrying** of some sort of **burden** without which we would be freer. However, there may also be a comfort element to baggage, implying something we do not wish to disburden ourselves of, but wish to continue carrying, just in case it may someday be of use to us.

Bags Bags are **female** symbols and customarily equate with the **vagina**. Movements within bags frequently represent coitus fantasies. Things running out of bags may reflect a **fear** of **sex** or of sexually motivated fantasies, or even a fear of their **repression**. Normally pleasant daytime fantasies can become unpleasant ones when they occur in **dreams**, and may find themselves expressed by unpleasant things, such as **surprise**, shock, or fear of the unknown, e.g. **rats** emerging from the bag.

Balconies Balconies are often synonymous with the **female breast** when they occur in **dreams**, especially if one equates the architecture of **houses** with the human **body**. They are also upper things, towards which one may aspire (see **Above & Below**). People tend to throw things (or themselves) off balconies, too – *ergo* Rapunzel and her hair, Juliet and her **virginity** ('And none but fools do wear it. Cast it off.'), or the Lady of Shalott's embroidery web ('Out flew the web and floated wide; the mirror crack'd from side to side').

Baldness Baldness contains mixed messages for both men and women. To a genetically bald man it will probably be taken as a sign of virility, to compensate him for the **trick nature** (and the paternal relatives of his **mother**) has played on him, and this comes under the **wish-fulfilment** fantasy umbrella. To a man suffering from male pattern baldness, it might be seen as a premature sign of ageing, with all the concomitant **baggage** which that entails in terms of **anxiety**. The collective **symbol**, and no doubt tacitly understood as such by both **male** and **female** dreamers, would seem to be one of spirituality, taken from the habit of partial or complete tonsure by **monks** and Buddhist **nuns** (and the cutting and covering of the **hair** by Christian nuns, which equates, of course, with virtual baldness).

Ballerinas A ballerina implies both flexibility and fun (we enjoy **dancing**), but there is also a voyeuristic, **erotic** element for both sexes in the display of a female **dancer**. The ballerina symbolizes both the 'perfect' and the 'desired' qualities of the **female** – 'perfect' in that she is usually young, fruitful, and physically available (she is exhibiting herself, after all), and 'desired' insofar as both **males** and females want her (the males to possess her, the females to be her).

Balloons Balloons take off and **fly** away, and thus their appearance in a **dream** may expose a desire for freedom on the part of the **dreamer**, or for loosing the shackles which they perceive as binding. Balloons are also **fragile**, in the sense that they will eventually pop or **shrink** away to nothing, and it is this temporary element of the balloon which is probably the most significant. **Colour**, too, is important, with a **black** balloon possibly signifying **death**, and a **red** balloon, life, or **love**. For a **female** dreamer the balloon may have further significance, in that **pregnancy** manifests itself by the ballooning of the **stomach** (which will eventually shrink down after **birth**) – and the loss of **virginity**, too, may find itself expressed in the symbol of the balloon, whose fracturing may infer the **loss** of girlhood's freedoms and the eventual taking on of maternal responsibility.

Balls Balls, as well as being **round**, with **mandala**-like properties, can also have semantic overtones in a **dream** context, in the sense of 'juggling too many balls', 'missing a catch', or 'going to a masked ball'. They can equate with both fun and threat (if a ball hits you, it hurts). They are the symbolical **shape** of **bombs** (even though real bombs tend not to be spherical), and as such may be used for either defensive or aggressive purposes. They are the shape of the **sun** and the **moon**, and to that extent at least, they may express the noumenal.

Bamboo Dreaming of bamboo will have very different connotations for an Asian or a European. In Asia, bamboo is all things to all **people**, in that it is pliant, craftable, edible, and aesthetically pleasing. It is also, dare one say it, **phallic**. In symbolical terms, it yields under pressure, and can survive the worst **storm**, and even aid in the rebuilding after the storm is over. To an Asiatic or a Caribbean, the sound of **wind** through a bamboo grove is the sound of life.

Bananas Bananas can often be **symbols** of the **phallus** in **dreams**, equating with fertility and masculinity. The context in which the banana appears is important, too, with its presence in the **hand** or **mouth** having strong **sexual** connotations for both men and women.

Banks Banks are meant to be safe places, independent of ourselves, which we can trust. They are symbolical areas in which valuable things are **stored**, such as memory (see **Screen Memory**), **wealth**, intelligence and energy. We draw from the bank when we need access to these things, but we are aware that their existence is finite, just as our own is. Banks can also be plundered, and **secrets** which we may wish to be kept hidden from others may be garnered from them without our permission. In this sense only, banks, in modern times, have begun to be symbolically equated in the **unconscious** mind with **computers**, and both, to a certain extent, with the human **body**. The storming of a bank or the pillaging of a computer is therefore the symbolical equivalent of **rape**.

Banquets Banquets may stand for a period of growth consolidation – the gathering in of experience, possibly related to the **soul**. See **Growing**

Bantam Cocks A bantam **cock** traditionally symbolizes pluckiness, or priggishness. It may also carry with it revocations of self-importance or vainglory.

Baptisms Baptisms are **symbols** of moral purification. In **dream** terms they may signify an aspiration towards higher things, particularly vis à vis the growth of the **soul**. See **Morality**

Barbers There is no escaping the concept of Sweeney Todd, the **demon** barber of Fleet Street, when we talk of barbers. He is the bogeyman who will serve you up in a **meat** pie if you misbehave. He is the stuff of **nightmares**, and attacks **people** when they are at their most vulnerable and relaxed. And if he doesn't **kill** you, he will force you into unwitting **cannibalism**. The cutting off of **hair** can also act as an adjunct to the **castration complex**, which is usually evident in **male** dreaming patterns whenever someone threatens someone else with a **knife** or bladed instrument. The bleeding **body** is then disposed of through a trapdoor (see **Below**), reinforcing the **sexual** content of the **dream**. The barber's **chair**, when dreamt of by a **female**, inevitably holds echoes of the gynaecological chair and the **dentists**' chair, both environments in which women feel particularly vulnerable, and which equate, in certain areas, to the submissive, forcibly sub-dominant position taken by the woman when engaged in the more conventional forms of **sexual** congress.

Barley See **Rice & Wheat**

Bars Bars, as in **iron** bars, imply **frustration** and rigidity of thought and action. Drinking bars are largely artificial environments where we go to enjoy ourselves, but they, too, encompass **inhibition**, in that we need **money**, or the generosity of **friends**, in order to benefit from them – and, in addition, there is a **time** limit to that enjoyment and, most probably, a physical price to pay as well. Archetypally, then, bars bear more than a little resemblance to **prostitutes**, and this **archetypal** similarity (**paying** for **pleasure**) should be taken into account when any readings involving bars are made.

Baseball Bats Baseball **bats** can frequently substitute for the **penis** when they appear in **dreams**. They may also act as an empowering or assertive extension of the **hand**.

Basements Basements in **houses** often represent the **dreamer**'s **unconscious**. The basement in Alfred Hitchcock's *Psycho* (1960) was the one **arena** in which Anthony Perkins' Norman Bates could conjoin with his **mother** to become one single, notional entity. See **Split Personalities**

Basic Rule A fundamental **psychoanalytical** technique in which the analysand expounds, without mental intercession, all that comes into their **head** at a certain moment. See **Free Association**

Baskets Baskets are largely feminine symbols, being yielding, enclosing, and sharing. They are also porous, and while not entirely opaque, are nevertheless amenable to mystery. It is not entirely uncoincidental that **Pandora's Box** is often depicted as a **horn**-shaped basket – Pandora, the first woman on **earth**, was given every possible gift by the **gods**, except perverse **Hermes**, who taught her not only **charm**, but also guile and the arts of manipulation to boot. Curiosity eventually persuaded Pandora to open the **box** Zeus had given her, causing every **evil** under the **sun** to **fly** out, save only Hope, to which she managed to bar the **exit** at the last possible moment.

Bathing Bathing equates with **cleansing** in **dream** terminology. The **question** this begs is, what aspect of ourselves do we feel needs such a cleansing? The dream, if carefully deconstructed, should **point** this up.

Baths Baths are frequently synonymous with **urination**, or urine, in **dream language**. They may also carry revocations of purification and of **sexual** availability. See **Secretions**

Bats A bat (the mammalian version) symbolizes **blindness**. It was regarded by the Caribs as a good **angel** which protected their **houses** at **night** while the inmates were asleep, and it was considered sacrilegious to **kill** one. Bats may also represent the **unconscious** mind of the **dreamer**, in particular when the dreamer doubts the strength of their own **repressive** capacity. Bats are connected with **vampirism**, too, and a woman dreaming of bats may unconsciously and illicitly (see **Taboo**) **harbour** a fantasy desire to be taken sexually against her will.

Batteries Batteries are **driving** forces. They may represent the **lungs**, which drive the **heart** (see **Ignition**), or they may represent the heart itself, and a **fear** of winding down, and of the inevitable depredations of old age. Batteries are only really good when **new**. Even rechargeable batteries deteriorate at every new charging, just as the heart takes us on a pretty steady downward **spiral** towards **death**.

Battles Battles often signify mental **conflicts** on the part of the **dreamer**, or the opposition of two apparently incompatible ideas (the mind and the emotions, for instance). The battling individuals or **armies** represent the two sides of the **dreamer**'s unacknowledged, contrasting impulses.

Bay Leaves If placed underneath the **pillow** at **night**, bay **leaves** were said to promote cheerful, happy **dreams**.

Bays Bays are nurturing **symbols**, in that they imply safety from **stormy seas** or the return from a long **journey**. They are crescent-shaped and **female** in **archetype**, and there is a strong **sexual** and **wish-fulfilment** element involved in any **dreams** in which **ships** (especially, **God** forbid, **steamers**) enter receptive, storm-free bays. See **Steam**

Beaches Beaches are boundary areas and points of rest. We **travel** to them and from them, but rarely live on them. To that extent they occupy a largely fantasy role in our **unconscious** minds, usually related to relaxation and comfort. Even the most common words associated with beaches (beachcomber, beach-bum, beach-bunny) continue this fantasy theme – let's face it, even Robinson Crusoe decided that he was far too vulnerable living on the beach, and pulled back a little inland.

Beacons Beacons draw our attention to things – they also shed **light** on the area surrounding them. They symbolize communication, too, and the need to concentrate our **minds**, both mentally and spiritually. They encapsulate light, and draw us towards themselves. And in **archetypal** terms, they objectify the beginnings of a communal civilization.

Beads Beads, as objects, have had special significance throughout human civilization. They are **ornaments** and religious **symbols**; they simplify **counting**; and they can be a means of payment (see **Paying**). They have been used for trade, too, and in Anglo Saxon English the word 'bead' meant to **pray** (a beadsman was responsible for rosary prayers in almshouses). To this extent, the appearance of beads in a **dream** may equate with counting one's blessings, or the possession of – or desire to possess – something of value.

Beans Beans are associated with **death** and **ghosts**, and were thought, by many, to contain the **souls** of the dead. Could this be why the Pythagoreans (see **Plato**) banned their consumption before **sleeping**? They were certainly passed around and **eaten** at Roman **funerals**. The aroma of bean **flowers** is said to induce bad **dreams**, **nightmarish** visions, and even lunacy, and to some (Empedocles, for instance) they were a **symbol** of false philosophy. To Aristotle, the word bean equated with venery, and this idea is echoed in old-fashioned **slang**, in which beans (from the French *biens* – goods) meant property or **money** (in this case, a guinea).

Beards Beards are customarily of a roughly similar **shape** to a woman's pudenda. Although this comparison may seem a little far-fetched, it is certainly not so within the architecture of a dream, for the **unconscious** often snatches at the first thing it can find to reinforce the points it wants to make. Take the word 'snatch', for instance, which I have just used. It is a **slang** euphemism for the **female vagina**, and I used it quite without thinking – what had actually happened, of course, was that my unconscious mind had instantly made the link between the word 'snatch' and the word 'pudenda', and had imposed the word on me without any by your leave. Exactly the same thing happens in the course of **dreams**. My unconscious, not to put too fine a point on it, had 'bearded' me.
KEY LINE: 'If you think that to grow a beard is to acquire wisdom, a goat is at once a complete Plato.' (From Lucian's *Greek Anthology*, Book xi, epigram 430)

Bears Traditionally a bear symbolizes ill-temper, or uncouthness, and illusions which stifle creativity. They can also symbolize dominating **parents**, given the **double** meaning in the word 'bear', as in 'bearing' a child. Emanuel Swedenborg (see **Plato**), in his *The Apocalypse Revealed*

(1761), has this to say: 'Bears signify fallacies – the literal sense of the Word, read indeed, but not understood.'

Beating To beat something is often to **cleanse** it – the two acts are symbolically intertwined. **Teachers** used to beat their pupils to cleanse them of sin (or so it was purported), and Latin poetry was metaphorically beaten into the **heads** of recalcitrant **scholars** until they could quote it by rote. To beat someone or something in a dream is to show that we have power over them or it, a power that we may wish to possess in real life, but most probably do not have. The prevalence of spanking in **pornographic** literature is a further case in point, for we know that pornography is, beyond everything, a waking form of the **wish-fulfilment** ethos so prevalent in **dreams**.

Beauty and the Beast A female **rite-of-passage** myth which reflects the two different **archetypes** of **male** and **female** – the forceful, dominant, but still susceptible male archetype, and the slowly awakening, nominally passive, female archetype, needing to be released from the bond with her **father** before she can accept a relationship with another male. The message of the **myth** is that, for both elements to enter into the necessary **sacred marriage**, each must complement and influence the other, and be acknowledged as significant in their own **right**. See **Apes**

Beavers Beaver is a common euphemism for the **female vagina**, and the appearance of one in a **male**'s **dream** is most likely to **point** in this direction. Beavers also construct **dams**, enjoy **play**, and relish the **hunting** and catching of **fish**. To that extent they epitomize a largely benevolent and idealized **nature**, which may find itself echoed in the **dreamer**'s desire for comfort and control of their environment.

Beds In popular legend, the position of a bed was considered crucial to the peace of mind of its occupants. **East** and **west** were the preferable pointings, as **north** and **south** were considered to promote **nightmares** – other authorities, it has to be said, maintained the direct opposite. In purely symbolical terms, a bed was often taken to signify doctrine, for 'as the body rests in its bed, so does the mind rest in its doctrine.' (Swedenborg: *The Apocalyptic Revealed* 1761)

Bed Wetting See **Wetting the Bed**

Bees A bee symbolizes industry. It was also the Emperor Napoleon's emblem. There is a traditional connection between the bee and the **soul** – the prophet Muhammad admitted bees to **paradise** for this very reason, and it was long considered sacrilegious to **kill** one. To the Romans, however, a flight of bees was a bad omen, whereas to the Greeks it could be a good one (even an emblem of purity, according to Isaac Myer's *Qabbalah*), for a flight of bees allegedly descended on **Plato**'s mouth while he was still in his cradle, according him the gift of oratory and

enlightened thought, and the priestesses of Demeter (Mother **Earth**) were colloquially known of as 'bees'. Bees behave in an **archetypal** way when they engage in their tail-wagging **dance**, and are usually unthreatening in a **dream** context – one ancient saw, however, has it that bees may emerge and then return into the **mouths** of sleepers while they are dreaming, but if they are killed in the interim, the sleeper will die.
KEY LINE:'My dreams are flowers to which you are a bee,/As all night long I listen, and my brain/Receives your song, then loses it again/In moonlight on the lawn.' (From Harold Munro's *The Nightingale Near the House* 1919)

Beethoven, Ludwig van (1770–1827) The great German composer was frequently beset by **dreams** of **music**, particularly after his descent into **deafness** circa 1818. In 1821, during a **journey** to Vienna, he found himself dreaming of the Middle **East**, and the sequence of a particular musical canon entered his **head**: 'But scarcely did I awake when away flew the canon, and I could not recall any part of it.' Frustrated, Beethoven retraced his journey, and this **time** he had a **waking dream** of the same piece of music, which he held fast 'as Menelaus did **Proteus**', and was then able to **write** it down, 'only permitting it to be changed into three parts.'

Beetles Beetles symbolize **blindness** and bad luck. Tradition has it that if a **black** beetle runs across someone's **shoe**, or across their recumbent **body**, a **death** will occur in the household. See **Scarabs**

Befana Befana is the good **fairy** of Italian **children** – she appears on Twelfth **Night**, while they are sleeping, and brings them **gifts**. Her **name** is a corruption of Epiphania. See also **Bertha, Dame Abonde** & **Santa Claus.**

Beginnings Continually starting something without being able to bring it to fruition is a common dream image, and equates with **running** on the **spot**. It is a common manifestation in **anxiety dreams**, and usually **points** to the existence of unacknowledged **frustrations** in everyday life.
KEY LINE: 'All glory comes from daring to begin.' (From Eugene F. Ware's *John Brown*)

Beheading Possibly a **symbol** of the **split** between the lower and the higher mind – the **cutting** off of opinion, in other words.

Behind Persons lurking behind the **dreamer**, with indistinguishable **faces**, can often represent the dreamer's **unconscious**. See **Above** & **Below**

Belated Obedience An **unconscious**, affirmative response to a consciously repressed or rejected command. Such a scenario may be replicated in a **dream** environment, in which the **dreamer** finds themselves performing an action that they would not consider performing outside the context of the dream.

Belladonna Meaning 'beautiful woman' in Spanish, belladonna, or deadly nightshade (the name alone is enough to indicate its **poisonous** qualities), was much used by Mediterranean **females** for dilating the pupils of the **eye** as a prelude to seduction. Taken in the form of *solanum*, however, it induces **sleep** and vivid, fantastical **dreams**. See **Artificial Dreams**
KEY LINE: '... merry craziness, dreams of undressing and of walking through the streets undressed. Walks around the churchyard gathering herbs, and in his dream converses with his late sister in the churchyard.' (From the notes of Dr Herring & Dr Jahr, of the Liga Medicorum Homeopathica Internationalis)

Bells The sound of bells was long considered to ward off **illness** or the **plague**, and even to help in the delivery of **babies**. Bells in **dreams** may be either protective (in the sense of **warning**), or predictive (in the sense of being ominous). The texture of bells is also most important, and the fact that they are man-made may be significant if the dream otherwise unfolds within a natural setting. To **sailors**, bells were frequently equated with the **souls** of the **ships** they inhabited, whilst in ancient Chinese culture they were considered to predict good luck.
KEY LINE: 'She felt that in another instant the whole world would fall from her – her heart was full of agony. And as the last breath was passing her lips, she heard a very faint, sweet sound, like the tinkling of a silver bell.' (From Arthur Machen's *The Great Return* 1915)

Below People situated below the **dreamer**, whose features are difficult to make out, frequently represent the **unconscious**. A move from below to **above** may represent the dreamer's aspirations to move from carnality towards spirituality, with the opposite also holding true. **Freud** believed that, on a **sexual** level, the below symbolized the genital area.

Belts A belt holds things up or gathers them together. It can also be used for striking, and for giving **pain**. The appearance of a belt in a **dream** may suggest that the **dreamer** feels in need of support, or even sponsorship – that they are not yet prepared to go it **alone**. Alternatively, the belt may appear as some kind of threat – 'belt up' is common **slang** usage, as is 'put a belt on it'. The putting on of a belt can also be a manifestation of power or even an accolade – an **officer**'s Sam Browne belt, for instance, a boxer's Lonsdale Belt, or a belt of office. See **Girdles**

Bertha Frau Bertha, a snow **white** lady who brings presents to sleeping **children**, is the personalized German form of the **Christmas** Epiphany. It is alleged that she creeps into children's nurseries and rocks them to **sleep** when they are abandoned by their **nurses** or their **mothers**. Bertha is the stuff of **nightmares**, however, to naughty children, for she has an iron nose and extremely large feet, which crash and beat at the ground on her approach. See also Befana, Dame Abonde & Santa Claus

Berryman, John (1914–72) Berryman wrote his long poem, *77 Dream Songs*, in 1964, and won the 1965 Pulitzer Prize for poetry on the basis of it. Haunted by dreams of his father's suicide, which occurred when Berryman was just 11 years old, Berryman was to commit suicide himself, 47 years later, by jumping into the Mississippi River from the railings of Washington Bridge, Minneapolis.

Betting See Wagers

Bible, The Once again, the context of a Bible dream is all important, as is the significance that the Bible has for the dreamer – a Muslim or a Jew will of necessity view the Bible in a markedly different way than will a Christian. The actual book itself symbolizes morality, and the wish to attain some form of spiritual wholeness, but it may also be viewed as a warning that these things are not occurring, and that the dreamer needs to pay attention to the message their unconscious mind is transmitting to them.

Bicycles Riding a bicycle may sometimes be a symbol for masturbation, in dream terms. Bicycles are also synonymous with freedom. Through the use of a bicycle we can become more than we are in reality – we can move faster and even shirk responsibility (it is hard to think on a bicycle). Bicycles are also symbols of duality, in both the form of the wheels (mandala-like), and the presupposition that a bicycle, by definition, needs a rider to complete itself.

Bigness Things often appear larger than they are in real life when we dream of them. This probably harks back to infancy, when everything seemed big from our diminutive perspective. Big things may simply be significant things, and small things insignificant in dream terms, although large things may also be threatening, and seek to impose themselves on us, just as our parents and our teachers did when we were children. Curiously, when ether was in regular use as an anaesthetic, dreams which occurred under its influence were often characterized by looming, enlarged figures and objects. This is also true of morphine-induced dreams, of which the author, needless to say, only has experience in a medical setting. See Smallness

Binoculars Binoculars bring important things closer, and allow us to see things we would not otherwise be able to make out with the naked eye. They are an aid (a crutch, if you like), and the need for their use during a dream is probably suggestive of our need to look more closely at something that is niggling at us – something that we may not wish to confront close to.

Bipolar Disorder See **Manic Depression**

Bipolarity The coexistence of two directly contrasting affects in the **mind** of one individual. Examples might include pleasure/**pain**, **love**/hate, greed/asceticism or confidence/suspicion ambivalences.

Birds Roman augurs studied the flight and activities of birds (ornithomancy) as a formal prelude to interpreting **dreams** and **visions**. **Owls**, **crows** and **ravens** were considered unlucky birds ('birds of ill-omen'), while **swallows** and **storks** were lucky – a stork apparently flew around **Jesus Christ** on the **cross**, crying '*Styrka, Styrka*,' according to one Swedish **myth**. To the Taoists, dreaming of birds could imply freedom of **spirit**, but also, on occasion, unpleasant events. Birds act in an **archetypal** way when they build **nests**, just as humans do. They are also **symbols** of aspirations (particularly if one equates the air to the mind, as the ancients did) and also, in **Jungian** terms, of the flight of thoughts.

Birth Birth in **dreams** may often, paradoxically, represent **death**. This is yet another example of dream **ellipsis**, and may also apply to **life** and death, rejoicing and **mourning**, luck and the **loss** of luck, and so forth. Birth and death are inextricably **linked** in the **unconscious**, primitive mind, to the extent that birth can sometimes appear in dreams as a **compensation** for either a literal or a symbolical death. It is a not entirely unconnected fact that unhappily **married couples** will often resort to a 'birth' to try and save the 'death' of their **marriage**. See **Pre-Birth Dreams** & **Rebirth**

Birthdays Birthdays are synonymous with **ego** movements, in the same way that human **birth** may symbolize the **entrance**, or creation, of the ego, in the form of an out-breathing (when viewed in purely astral terms).

Bisexuality Dreaming is by its very **nature** an unconventional act. The content of our **dreams** frequently expresses unconventional, not to say threatening, desires. The act of dreaming about these desires may protect us from the castigation we would normally expect to receive were we to enact them in a conventional social sphere. It is at least arguable that we are all essentially **bisexual**, and that society, in order to protect itself, forces us into monosexual relationships. **Plato** famously declared that **love** consists of two halves that were once whole searching for and finding each other again.

Bishops Bishops symbolize spiritual principles – free, in theory at least, from contamination. They oversee, direct, and discipline the Higher **Self**, and equate, **archetypally**, with **teachers**.

Biting If a woman **dreams** of biting it may indicate a resentful, **sadistic**, or **castrating** attitude vis à vis men, particularly if the bitten object is

phallic. If the bitten object is **breast**-like, or has **vaginal** connotations, and the **dreamer** is **male**, a similar unsexing attitude may be present.

Black   The **colour** of **death**, of **night**, and of **mourning** (a Roman custom, borrowed from the Egyptians), black can also indicate constancy, wisdom and prudence. In certain eastern nations it was the colour of **slavery**, servitude, and low **birth**. Black was also the colour of the **devil** and those who communed with him – practitioners of the Black Arts, in other words.

Black Magicians   Black **magicians** may be taken to symbolize the unbalanced **ego,** and the destructive power of uncontrolled knowledge. See **Magicians, Wizards & Witches**

Blacksmiths   Blacksmiths are usually positive **dream symbols**, incorporating qualities of discipline and the creative direction of energy.

Blake, William (1757–1827)   An English **poet, painter** and engraver, Blake's masterwork is the series of engravings he did for the *Illustrations of the Book of Job* (published in 1825). Amongst these is *Job's Evil Dream*, in which Satan visits Job in a dream, and tempts and torments him. The engraving shows Job encircled by horrendous **visions**, in the clutch of **demons**, and unable to move. Blake's **drawing** entitled *O, How I Dreamt of Things Impossible*, shows a **horse** breaking free from the ground and carrying two **dreamers** with it on its flight through the heavens. In 1793 Blake wrote a poem called *The Angel*: 'I dreamt a dream! what can it mean?/And that I was a maiden queen,/Guarded by an angel mild:/Witless woe was ne'er beguil'd!'

Blindfolds   Blindfolds have a number of different connotations, many of them anarchic. They may, for instance, manifest a desire to be led without the need for taking personal or moral responsibility for one's actions (thus their frequent use in **pornographic** iconography). They may also suggest that the **dreamer** feels themselves to be in a state of suspension, or tense **waiting**, particularly when a **kidnap** motif is either apparent or suggested.

Blindness   It may seem like a contradiction in terms to dream that one is blind, as a dream is, by its very definition, a form of 'seeing', but blindness nevertheless has strong symbolical value in a dream context. It can, for instance, imply ignorance of some sort, or a **rite-of-passage**, as in St Paul's symbolical blindness on the **road** to Damascus – or simply that we are not seeing something that is right before our **eyes**. **Dreams** by congenitally blind **people** very often use 'touch' symbols, indicating denseness, heaviness, warmth, roundness, softness, hardness, abrasiveness, etc., and frequently contain significant auditory elements, too, as well as **anxiety** elements such as **fire** or claustrophobia fears. Dreams by people who have become blind later in life may contain strong **wish-fulfilment**

aspects including **colour**, **light**, seascapes, skyscapes and **horizons**. There is a general acceptance within the psychoanalytic community that **children** who become blind before the age of five do not 'see' in their dreams, whereas those who become blind after that age do. The American writer Helen Keller (1880–1968), who was both blind and **deaf** from the age of 19 months, dedicated a chapter of *The World I Live In* (1908) to the dream world, which she found morally inconsistent: 'Oh, dreams, what opprobrium I heap upon you – you, the most pointless things imaginable. Yet remove the dream world and the loss is inconceivable.'

Blizzards A dream blizzard reflects directly on the state of mind of the **dreamer**, implying flux, threat and uncertainty. We wish to shelter from blizzards, and, at least in **archetypal** terms, they threaten to undermine all the civilized values that we hold dear. Blizzards are neither moral nor immoral, selective nor unselective, random nor unforeseeable. Only a confident person, correctly attired (in an ethically or morally sound **coat**) is able to confront one with impunity.

KEY LINE: 'For some time the trees and flowers grew on, despite the intense cold. Birds flew into the houses for safety, and those which winter had overtaken lay on the snow with wings spread in vain flight.' (From Helen Keller's *The World I Live In* 1908)

Blood Blood has numerous meanings in dream symbolism. These can include **family** ties, fears of **menstruation** or **abortion**, **anger** or quarrels (bad blood), and the desire to do **violence**. Some primitive peoples believed that blood was the seat of the **soul**, and that losing blood was synonymous with spiritual impoverishment. **Witches**, too, it was felt, could be weakened by the taking of their blood, particularly from above the **nose** and **mouth**, which was called 'scoring above the breath'. In religious terms, blood is equated with Divine Truth, both spiritual and natural. See **Secretions**

Blossoms The existence of blossoms implies a fundamental process of **rebirth**. To the Japanese the arrival of the cherry blossom (*sakura*) is the happiest time of the year, its message leavened, however, by the bittersweet undertone of the **fragility**, temporariness – and temporality – of all things.

Blue Blue is the symbolic **colour** of Divine eternity and human immortality, and often denotes the function of thinking (the higher mental plane). When worn by an **angel** it indicates faith and fidelity. The **Virgin Mary** wears blue in much Christian iconography, to signify her modest nature. The **alchemist** and **chemist** – Paracelsus (1493–1541) maintained that the colour blue was injurious to the health and spirits, and could induce melancholy. See **Stockings**

Blushing Ereuthophobia is a morbid **fear** of blushing. Sufferers from this condition (which usually, but not always, strikes women) tend to dream of actions or events occurring to the **face**, such as injury by **fire**, boiling **water**, **volcanoes**, the spray from **syringes**, or the explosion of liquid from pressurized containers. There, is, inevitably, a sexual element contained within such **dreams** (a displacement of sexual excitement from the genitals to the face), which may reflect back on the perceived hormonal element to blushing (while conveniently ignoring the psychological).

Boars In Norse mythology, boars were sacred to the God Wotan. Freyr, the deity of the **sun**, of peace, and of plenty, and the rider of the boar Gullinbursti, was said to have been killed by one, necessitating an annual **sacrifice** in his honour forever after – a sacrifice which traditionally took place at the.**winter** solstice (Yuletide), and was the precursor to our **Christmas**. Boars also symbolized **rebirth**, in that the boar Saehrimnir was **eaten** every evening by Aesir, in Valhalla, only to find himself restored to perfect health the very next **morning**. The **Gautama Buddha** died from a meal of dried boar's flesh – in this context, the boar referred to was the boar avatar of Vishnu, and the dried flesh of the boar implied an excess of esoteric knowledge made palatable to the uninitiated. Plutarch tells us, in his *Symposiacs*, that Adonis, too, was killed by a boar, and this is backed up by Nonnus, in his *Dionysiacs*, who equates the boar with Ares (Mars). All this to say that boar mythology and symbolism is a complex issue, ranging through many cultures, and that the appearance of one in our **dreams** is almost certain to reflect back to well beyond our own knowledge and towards a **collective unconscious**, as well as, in more literal terms, symbolizing wildness, wilderness, and the free and constructive use of **nature**.
KEY LINE: ''And up and doun as he the forest soughte,/He mette he saugh a bor with tuskes grete,/That slept ayeyn the bryghte sonnes hete./And by this bor, fast in his armes folde,/ Lay, kissyng ay, his lady bright, Criseyde.' (From Geoffrey Chaucer's *Troilus and Crisyede*, Book v, 1380)

Boats In purely **Freudian** terms, boats, being receptive, are frequently synonymous with the **vagina**. Sikhism, however, equates a boat with the True **Guru**, further reinforcing the boat's equation with the **soul**, floating on the **river** of life. A boat was also used to **ferry** the dead to Hades, and the image is repeated in the Arthurian Legends, when the mortally **wounded** King Arthur is ferried away from Lyonesse in the company of the Lady of the **Lake's** handmaidens. This powerful image takes us back to the age-old reference to the boat as a vessel of apotheosis, **mirrored** in the frequent depiction on **coins** of sovereigns and **kings** afloat. See **Hell & Ships**
KEY LINE: 'So said he, and the barge with oar and sail/Moved from the brink, like some full-breasted swan/That, fluting a wild carol ere her death,/Ruffles her cold plume, and takes the flood …' (From Alfred, Lord Tennyson's *The Passing of Arthur – Idylls of the King* 1859–85)

Bodies Bodies, in dreams, may be equated with **houses**. Also, taken literally, they may imply the heavenly bodies of the **sun**, the **moon** and the **stars**, or the alchemical bodies, in the form of physical transmutations between **planets** and **metals**. See **Alchemy**

Bodily Fluids Primitive man believed that all things which stemmed from the body – **hair**, **nails**, excrement, urine, **saliva**, **semen**, **mucus**, etc. – were creative and dynamic elements that could be used in sympathetic **magic**. See **Secretions**

Body Image Body image is the relationship between the **ego** and the body. It is not uncommon, for instance, for amputees to dream that they still have the **arm**, or the **leg**, or the **hand**, that has been taken from them. In certain cases, the phantom limb appears shorter in the amputee's **dream** than it was in real life, implying a **regression** to **childhood** and to the powerful **foundations** laid down at that time – foundations which form many of the bases for our dream **worlds**. See **Amputation, Bodies & Compensatory Dreams**

Boils Boils were frequently seen as **plagues** from either **Heaven** – *ergo* the story of the **magicians**, the Egyptians, and Moses, in Exodus ix, 8–11 – or from **Hell**, as in Job's affliction from Satan, described in Job ii, 7. Taken metaphorically they may imply a deep-seated failure or shortcoming simmering away within the individual which will eventually emerge for all to see. Their appearance in **dreams** probably echoes this **fear**, rather than any more purely metaphysical apprehension.

Bombs Bombs are synonymous with the noise that they make – in fact the word itself stems from the Greek, *bombos*, and the Latin, *bombus*, meaning a 'deep noise'. As noises are only intermittently heard in **dreams**, the appearance of a bomb is probably trying to tell us something – namely to go about **waking** up. To this extent bombs customarily stop things, or put an end to them, and this is reflected in their **dream symbolism**. Paradoxically, many physicists believe that the universe began with a 'big bang' – but if **time** runs **backwards** beyond the event **horizon** of a **black hole**, as others amongst their **number** believe, it will no doubt *end* with a big bang too. Consider yourselves forewarned.

Bones The appearance of bones in **dreams** may point to **past** experiences that appear to have been **buried**, but whose influence is still felt by the **dreamer**. Pointed bones are usually **phallic** symbols. In medieval times, bones were considered to be the seat of psychic powers, and in Christian iconography they represented virtue and inner firmness – 'The Lord keepeth all his bones; not one of them is broken.' (Psalms xxxiv, 20)

Bonfires Bonfires are **warnings**, as well as being places by which one may warm oneself. They may also have **sacrificial** connotations in a **dream** context, and can point to either **rebirth**, as in the phoenix emerging from the replenishing flames, or extinguishment, as in the ritual burning of **witches**, heretics and inconvenient artefacts such as **books**.

Books Books may appear, at first glance, to represent knowledge, but they can also represent hidden things (virtues, possibly, or **secrets**) that need looking up and rediscovering. Books are rarely read in **dreams**, usually existing merely as concepts or suggestions about the nature of their true function. They are therefore very convenient as **symbols**, and efforts should be made when interpreting the dream to discover first to what extent, if any, the **dreamer** values them – a dyslexic person, for instance, may fear them; for an analphabetic they may represent **chains**, or even, paradoxically, freedom. See **Pages**
KEY LINE: 'In Books lie the *soul* of the whole Past Time; the articulate audible voice of the Past, when the body and material substance of it has altogether vanished like a dream.' (From Thomas Carlyle's *On Heroes and Hero-Worship: The Hero as Man of Letters* 1841)

Borders Borders and boundary lines traditionally represent inhibitions and moral restrictions in **dreams**. In real life borders are put in place to stop people crossing them, and their appearance in dreams represents a similar function – they are there, in other words, to prevent people carrying out actions that they might otherwise regret.

Borrowing The act of borrowing from others in **dreams** often reflects a desire to take on some aspect of that person that the **dreamer** either envies or admires.

Bosses For a customarily dominant person the appearance of a boss in a **dream** may represent an irritant, or even a sign of **failure** – if your **unconscious** calls for a boss, it must surely fear a descent into **chaos**. For a customarily sub-dominant person (a prevalent, but largely unacknowledged majority of the population), the appearance of a boss may represent comfort cravings, or the return to an infantile desire for a firm **hand** at the tiller – a hand against whom you may also rail, as a child will rail against its **parents**, but whose authority you nevertheless still acknowledge.

Boswell, Connie Connie Boswell (1907–76) is in here because of a smashing song in waltz time she recorded back in September 1932, called 'I'll Never Have to Dream Again' (Newman, Jones). There must be 10,000 songs with 'dream' in the title, so this will have to stand in for all of them. Connie developed polio as a small child, and was paralyzed from the waist down, but this didn't stop her from perfecting a spectacular bluesy contralto, with a redolent southern twang to it. Listen to the second chorus – just after the horn interlude – of 'I'll Never Have to Dream Again' and, well, dream.

Bottles Bottles tend to be **male** symbols in **dreams**, just as **bowls** tend to be **female**. However, it is arguable that a bottle can also have **bisexual** symbolism, being both a receptacle and its antonym.

Bowing See **Kneeling**

Bowling If a man dreams of bowling, it is usually synonymous with **sexual intercourse**. If a woman dreams of bowling the effect is likely to be reversed, possibly suggesting a desire to instigate penetration, or, in the case of a lesbian, to indulge in penetrative sex in the guise, as it were, of a man.

Bowls Bowls tend to be **female** symbols in **dreams**, just as **bottles** are ususally **male** symbols. Bowls are nurturing, containing and circular, with the implication that, because they represent vulnerable and fragile parts of the **psyche**, they need cherishing.

Bows The firing of an **arrow** at a **target** is a strongly **male** sexual symbol, and carries within it both the hunter's desire to **kill** his prey, and the male's desire to mate with a **female**. The bow itself is, paradoxically perhaps, a feminine **symbol**, both in its **shape**, and in its manipulation and cherishing in the hands of a male. In Victorian times, archery was taken up by women, largely, one suspects, because of the attractive way the stretching and setting of a bow showed off the female form, but also, perhaps, as an **unconscious** arrogation of a traditional male pursuit.

Boxes Boxes frequently represent the **vagina**, or hidden, illicit things. They can also symbolize coffins, and the fear of **death**. See **Jewellery Boxes**

Boys Boys are often **symbols** of the primitive mind, synonymous with early stages of mental development. Physically, they are precocious, and to that extent they exemplify the physical put before the mental, with all that may entail. They are also prone to anarchy, or rioting, if not disciplined, and their appearance in **dreams** may signify such a **wish** on the part of the **dreamer** – the wish to give in to a younger, freer self, with a consequent implied refutation of personal responsibility.

Branches Branches symbolize the spreading of things, the stretching out towards things, and even, in some cases, the search for **roots** (for the growing of branches necessitates strong foundations, or the tree will overbalance). **Trees** send out branches to gather **rain**, and such branches probably represent human **arms** when they appear in **dreams**. Symbolically, branches conjure up inevitable revocations of Yggdrasil, the great **ash** tree of life (from the *Prose Edda*), and also of the tree near Bhudd Gaya underneath which the **Gautama Buddha** sat. See **Christmas Trees, Oak Trees, Poplar Trees, Redwood Trees & Yew Trees**

Bread Bread is one of the fundamentals of human life. The breaking of bread is symbolic of the partaking of **food**, but it also contains the spiritual connotations of the body of **Christ**. Dreaming of bread can also imply creativity – the making of something out of nothing. The throwing away of bread was at one time considered to be close to sacrilegious. KEY LINE: 'When you came, you were like red wine and honey,/And the taste of you burnt my mouth with its sweetness./Now you are like morning bread,/Smooth and pleasant./I hardly taste you at all, for I know your savor;/But I am completely nourished.' (From Amy Lowell's *A Decade* 1919)

Breaking Breaking and ending are near synonymous in **dreams**, and both imply a process of inevitable, even if occasionally uncongenial, change. The breaking of **bread** is of fundamental symbolical value, and carries with it revocations of both friendship and the possibility of deceit. The breaking of a stick forms a significant part of the **wedding ceremony** of a number of Native American tribes, just as the breaking of a **wine glass** fulfils a similar function within the Jewish tradition. The breaking of certain childish objects may refer back to the 'breaking' that occurs when a child puts aside infantile innocence and infantile things (his **parents**, for instance) in favour of a non-guilt-assigning maturity.

Breastfeeding All mammals breastfeed their young, and infant and **animal** suckling is therefore a constantly recurring image which the **unconscious** mind will inevitably latch on to in order the better to express itself. We begin and end life with an **oral fixation** (and many individuals continue their fixation in-between times). To that extent the role of **breasts**, and the **milk** that they express, is a fundamental one, and more often than not reflects a desire on the part of the **dreamer** to return to the certainties and simplicities of **childhood**.

Breasts Breasts are primarily symbols of affection and charity. It is easy to be swayed by their **sexual** connotations, but it should be remembered that, to at least half the population, this is not considered their primary function. One '**gives**' a breast – one doesn't take it. That said, their appearance and symbolism in **dreams** is complex, and care needs to be taken in interpretation, incorporating a refusal to be swayed by the obvious. Breasts may represent comfort, nurture, sustenance – they may also be threatening, arousing, inconvenient and even unwanted, as with the Abyssinian Gallas people, who amputated the *mammae* of boys soon after **birth**, fearing that a warrior who possessed them could not possibly fight bravely. Breasts may be stifling, or they may symbolize an earlier lost innocence or simplicity – even their **shape** may find itself reflected in disparate objects and **symbols** appearing in the dream, and when this occurs, the object chosen is also likely to be of some significance to the **dreamer**. See **Breastfeeding**

KEY LINE: 'I had a dream of nourishment/Against a breast/My infant face was presst/Ah me the *suffisance* I drew therefrom ...' (From Stevie Smith's *A Dream of Nourishment* 1966)

Breaths Breathing is synonymous with life. A dying person breathes their last breath, and an infant child takes its first one after emerging from its **mother**. In the interim we judge health and contentment by the capacity to breathe – rattling, jagged breaths imply **illness**; short, rapid breaths infer **excitement** or threat; long, languorous breaths suggest ecstasy, contentment, or **sexual** satiation. The same rules apply to **dreams**. Even the fact of their existence in a dream refers back to the **dreamer**, and to the state their **unconscious** has mapped out for them. At the end of the day, breathing is a simple reinforcement of the fact that we exist, or that we are alive.

Breton, André (1896–1966) A prominent **leader** of the **Surrealist** movement, Breton tried to describe what surrealism meant in an essay written in 1922, and published in 1924 as *Les Pas Perdus* (*The Lost Steps*): 'We use it to illustrate a certain psychic automatism which comes very close to dream, a state that is extremely hard to circumscribe today.' In 1935 he produced a cardboard collage called *Dream Object*, in which everyday items appear and disappear through **holes** in the construction. 'I believe that the apparent antagonism between dream and reality will be resolved in a kind of absolute reality – in surreality.' The single-minded Breton was much influenced by his study of the works of **Freud**, but Breton's obsession with the **unconscious** to the exclusion of all else (save 'chance') finally led to Surrealism's marginalization as merely another influential historical phenomenon.
KEY LINE: 'Man is above all the plaything of his memory.' (Breton)

Bricks Bricks are symbolical of the lower plane – they are conduits through which things may be made that transcend their fundamental constituents. To that extent they are developmental objects (exemplified, if you like, by their use in **childhood** as creative objects).

Bridegrooms It could be said that dreaming of a bridegroom (from the Old Dutch *gom*, meaning a young man) is an example of a **wish-fulfilment** fantasy. Western society as a whole may appear to have turned its back on **marriage** *per se* in favour of looser relationships, but the **archetype** still persists, and for many people marriage remains the ultimate emotional challenge, despite what they may find themselves under pressure to mouth, in public, to the contrary. **Dreams** will tend to reflect this underlying **truth**, and not the partial truth society imposes on such young people, particularly women, which is more likely to emerge in terms of **anxiety**.

Brides The bridal **wreath** refers specifically back to the *corona nuptialis* worn by the Greeks and Romans in order to indicate triumph, and, for most of its history, bride-hood was indeed an indication of success in a girl's **rite-of-passage**. Thus, for a **female** to dream of a bride may infer a societal **wish-fulfilment** fantasy, while for a **male** to dream of a bride may suggest the desire to benefit from unfettered or exclusive access to one **girl's** sexual favours.

Bridges Bridges are traditionally associated with the **passage** of **souls**, and therefore with **death**. In Norse mythology the dead crossed Bifröst, the rainbow bridge between Midgard and Asgard, and in Celtic mythology the Irish Bridge of the Cliff could only be crossed by the brave – **cowards** would find the bridge tilting beneath them, and **fall** off. Muslims, too, have the bridge of Al-Sirat, as sharp and **thin** as the blade of a scimitar, while in Yorkshire folklore (as John Aubrey tells us in his *Remaines*) the Brig o'Dread had to be passed before Whinney Moor could safely be crossed by the **souls** of the dead. Such stories are enfolded unconsciously within **dream symbology**, and must be taken account of as part of the context of any dream which includes them.

Bridles Bridling something equates with control, and traditionally to 'bite on the bridle' was synonymous with suffering intense hardship, as indeed did scolds and harridans, who were sometimes forced to suffer such indignities as bridling, by their peer group, until well into the 19th century. To a Frenchman, on the other hand, bridling up, or *se rengorger*, implied the tossing back of the **head** in pride, just as a lively **horse** will toss its head when severely bridled back. In **dreams**, however, the **symbol** of the bridle is most likely to apply to something the **dreamer** wants to free or unburden themselves from, and to that extent its appearance can act as a welcome catalyst for conscious divestment. See **Reins**

Briefcases We hide vital things in briefcases, and there is also an aura of self-importance about someone who carries one, as if they wish to be judged by how they look, rather than by what they are. The significance of this carries over into **dreams**, and the question to be asked is probably 'what does the briefcase conceal?'

Brightness Brightness equates with clarity of **vision** and with **holiness**. If something is bright, it will catch our notice and force us to pay attention to it. A similar thing is probably occurring in **dreams**, when we favour bright objects. For some reason the **unconscious** wishes to draw our attention to such an object – even to trigger a response from us.

British Premonitions Bureau Set up in January 1967 in the aftermath of the **Aberfan disaster** by London psychiatrist J. C. Barker, the bureau set out to harness, and use, the power of **premonition**. A year later, in 1968, the Central Premonitions Agency was established in New York. Both associations met with little success in averting future **disasters**.

Broken Things Should a woman dream of broken things, this often equates with the loss of her **virginity**, or with the act of defloration. A concomitant male image might suggest a fear of the effect one's masculinity may have on a fragile (possibly female) object.

Brontë, Charlotte (1816–55) The English novelist Charlotte Brontë, when asked by her friend Mrs Gaskell if she had ever taken **opium**, said no, but admitted that, in common with many others of her ilk, she would think in a concentrated fashion about her work just before she laid her **head** on the **pillow**, and then 'sleep on it'. In this way 'she wakened up in the **morning** with all clear before her, and then could describe it, word for word, as if it had happened.' See **Authors, Novels, Writers & Writing**

Brooks When young **children** dream of a tinkling brook it very often alludes to **urination**, or a desire to pee without having to get out of **bed**. To an adult, brooks can have **magical** overtones, but also overtones of 'egress and regress', as was amply demonstrated by Ford's annexation of the name, Master Brook, when he encountered Sir John Falstaff, in Shakespeare's the *Merry Wives of Windsor* Act ii, scene 1 in an effort to tease out the truth or not behind Falstaff's carnal relations with his wife. See **Adultery, Streams & Wetting The Bed**

Brooms Brooms are natural **phallic** symbols, to the extent that in medieval folklore, if a girl stepped inadvertently over a broom, it was deemed that she would become a **mother** before she became a **wife**. Brooms also **sweep** things away, and when they occur in **dreams**, both of these attributes (the phallic and the fresh) may find themselves intertwined.

Brothels Brothels can represent ambivalence about **sexuality**, and also **fear** of the unknown, or of femininity. To some extent they are **taboo**, and may represent aspects of the **mother** complex, in that any connection between client and **prostitute** is, by definition, lacking in emotional depth, and as such may, at first glance, appear unthreatening to the mother/**son** relationship – whilst, in reality, deriving from it.

Brotherhood Brother Jonathan became the John Bull of the United States during the War of Independence – the man you would consult when the chips were down. Brotherhood naturally implies such trust, and with it, comradeship. However, we are also well aware, from even a cursory reading of the **Bible**, in, say, the case of Cain and Abel, that brotherhood is not always all that it is cracked up to be. Much care, therefore, needs to be taken in the disentangling of the meaning from the **taboos** surrounding it. See **Brothers & Sisterhood**

Brothers There are many verbal and symbolical associations for brothers in **dreams**, amongst which those of **clergyman** and **monk** are only the most obvious – this is due to their semantic links to confraternity, and also to the **taboos** associated with them, which equate to the **incest** taboos relating to **brotherhood** and **sisterhood**. A brother may also suggest something that is a part of you and yet still different (and possibly threatening in its difference) – something which you must come to terms with.

Brown Going into a 'brown study' can imply reverie, or drifting into a **dream state**. *Sombre* and *brun* in France (from where the expression originally came) can mean either sadness, melancholy, gloominess, or dullness. Brown, however, is also the colour of the **earth**, and of natural things, and a 'Brownie', in Scotland, was the nickname for the brawny and familiar **farm spirit** who emerged at **night**, while the **family** were sleeping, and did the household chores (he was called Robin Goodfellow in England). The Brownie was rewarded with offerings laid out on a familiar **stone**, named the 'Browny's Stone'. The writer Robert Louis Stevenson believed that Brownies came to him in dreams and helped him compose his work – in particular *Dr Jekyll and Mr Hyde*. Brown, needless to say, is also the **colour** of **defecation**.

Browne, Sir Thomas (1605–52) Sir Thomas Browne, one of the great masters of English prose, wrote the following in his magisterial 1650 essay *On Dreams*: 'If some have swounded [archaic word for swoon] they may also have died in dreams, since **death** is but a confirmed swounding. Whether **Plato** died in a dream, as some deliver, he must rise again to inform us. That some have never dreamed is as improbable as that some have never laughed.'

Brushes Brushes are often penile symbols in the context of **dreams**, but may also imply new **beginnings**, as in the expressions to 'brush up' or 'make a clean sweep'. See **Brooms**

Brutality The expression of brutality in a dream, in any guise, frequently implies **frustration** and a desire for **artificial** (or even miraculous) empowerment. Brutality is a simple answer to a complex question and is thus in the service of the **id**, rather than of the **superego**.

Bryony The Elder Pliny (23–79 AD), writing in his *Historia Naturalis*, alleged that the berry plant, bryony, was a soporific, triggering intense **dreams**, and even, on occasion, **sleepwalking** in the susceptible. See **Artificial Dreams**

Bubbles Bubbles are both attractive and ultimately **empty**. The bursting of a bubble implies the sudden ending of something that was, in itself, artificial or contrived.

Buckles 'Buckling under', 'buckling in' or 'buckling to' all have largely negative connotations, and a buckler was, itself, a **shield**, carrying with it the implication that one needed to defend oneself from something or respond in some way to a challenge. Traditionally, buckles on **shoes** were strictly for show purposes, and served no other useful purpose.

Buddha See **Gautama Buddha**

Buds Buds symbolize new life, twinned with the prospect of reincarnation. They may also find themselves symbolically equated with the clitoris, as in the famous passage in Orson Welles's *Citizen Kane* (1941) in which Kane mouths the words 'rosebud, rosebud,' as he dies, which many believed was the nickname William Randolph Hearst (on whom Kane was allegedly based) gave to his mistress Marion Davies' clitoris. See **Blossoms**

Bugs Bugs are signs of deterioration and anarchy – to a woman, bugs may imply an unclean **house**, or an unclean child. Bug comes from the Welsh *bwg*, or hobgoblin, while a bugbear was a **scarecrow**, with all the sinister connotations that such a figure may sometimes imply.

Buildings Buildings very often reflect the physical **body** of the **dreamer**, or some aspect of that body that wishes to draw attention to itself. A toppling building may have **sexual** overtones, while movement up into a building may imply the desire to better things, and a movement down may infer a **fear** of **failure**, or even humiliation. See **Above & Below**

Bulldogs A bulldog traditionally symbolizes pertinacity and relentlessness. There may also be salivatory revocations (see **Secretions**), in the sense of feeling one is the object of an unattractive person's lust, or alternatively fearing that one's own feelings of lust or desire for someone else are unwelcome – or a cause of disgust – to their object.

Bulls A bull symbolizes strength and straightforwardness and the ability to 'take the bull by the **horns'** and get on with things. Bulls are also **symbols** of the Divine matrix (in the Zoroastrian system), into which all living creatures were deposited. A bull may therefore represent a concatenation (i.e. more than the sum of its parts), and to that extent it is one of the most symbolic of all **animals**. To a woman **dreamer**, a bull may at first seem threatening, but it may also represent something (some aspect of herself, perhaps) that may be amenable to taming, or even seduction. When a torero kills the bull, he becomes a part of it through the very act of plunging his **sword** into its vitals – this may be a displeasing thought to some, but there is no avoiding the possibly cathartic effect of the ritualistic **killing** of something that appears, at first glance, to be stronger than oneself (*ergo* the Mithraic *taurobolium*, in which Mithras sacrifices a bull, following which a **dog** and a **snake** leap into the **wound**, symbolizing the dualism of good and **evil** brought together in creation).

Bullying Bullying **dreams** are, by definition, **anxiety dreams**, but in Shakespearean times the word bully could also be used as an endearment

– in fact a bully-boy was a jolly companion, rather than a thug, and stemmed from the Old German word *buhle*, a **lover**, or *buhler*, a gallant. That said, the word is normally used pejoratively, and the appearance of a bully in a dream will probably represent deep-seated **fears** of being forced to behave or act in a way the **dreamer** does not wish to.

Bunsby Jack Bunsby, a character from Charles Dickens' *Dombey and Son* (1846–48), gave to the world the words 'to bunsby', which means living in 'an invisible dreamland somewhere beyond the outer limits of invisible space.'

Bunyan, John (1628–88) Bunyan was the lowly born and puritanical English **author** of the *Pilgrim's Progress* (1678–84), the **dream** journey of a **pilgrim** in search of salvation. Christian, the **hero**, makes a circular **journey** through the antechambers of his own **soul**, meeting, on the way, a series of **archetypes** which show him, in allegorical form, the way to **heaven**. See **Dante**

Buñuel, Luis (1900–83) The Spanish filmmaker Luis Buñuel claimed that his groundbreaking **surrealist** film *Un Chien Andalou* (1928) represented 'an encounter between my dreams and (Salvador) **Dali's**'. He further asserted that if he had only 20 **years** left to live, he would accept two hours a day of activity 'and I'll take the other 22 in dreams.' Two of his later **films** were marked, in particular, by his use of **dreams**: *El Angel Exterminador* (1962), in which *haut bourgeois* dinner **guests** find themselves sealed, first inside their host's **house**, then inside a **church**, and *Belle de Jour* (1967), in which a bored surgeon's wife, prone to **masochistic** fantasies, goes to work each afternoon in a **brothel**. Both were considered, even by Buñuel himself, to defy rational explanation.

Burdens Burdens on the chest, when they appear in a woman's **dreams**, are frequently synonymous with the **sexual** act. Other forms of burden, particularly on the **stomach**, may be synonymous with **pregnancy**. Should a man dream of burdens, particularly on the back, this may suggest unwanted responsibilities, or even, in some cases, a fear of **homosexuality** (possibly equated with the losing or arrogation of power).

Burglars When a woman **dreams** of a burglar, it is likely that she unconsciously desires a change of **sexual** partner. The **criminal** element reflects her **guilt** and **anxiety** at entertaining such thoughts, twinned with the frisson a flirtation with **danger** and the unknown can bring. Male burglar images tend to be nominally more positive while being ethically more negative, in that they can reflect underlying **rape** desires, or a wish to get something for nothing (i.e. without the necessity of paying for it or taking responsibility for its emotional ramifications).

Burials Should the **dreamer** see themselves buried or in their coffins in a dream (as happened to the main protagonist in the famous dream sequence from Ingmar Bergman's 1957 film *Wild Strawberries*), it may mean that they have buried, lost, or estranged themselves from some aspect of their personal consciousness that may again – if capable of resurrection – be of value to them. Burial places are traditionally viewed as of **evil** omen, in that they were seen as infected by **death** and by the dead, and this belief still lurks at the basis of most systems of cremation and open-air (sky) burial. See **Depersonalization**

Burning Burning may be purifying or it may be destructive. One may burn with lust, with **fever**, or with a passion to learn. One may burn the past (see **Ashes**) or the **past** may burn its way into our **psyches** like a brand. The **Bible**, too, speaks of 'burning fiery furnaces' and 'burning bushes', equating the possibility of torment with that of revelation. Dreamers rarely feel **pain** in **dreams**, and this oneiric protection accords considerable value to burning in a dream context, as it is immediately apparent that it means more than simply the sum of its collateral function in **waking** life (i.e. that it also causes pain). We burn votive **candles** when we offer up **prayers**, and the ancients **sacrificed** burnt offerings (*olah*/ascension; *kalil*/consumption) to the Lord in an effort to obtain Grace. In certain countries (including our own) **bodies** are burnt after **death** for later reconstitution back into the **natural** world, and **books** are regularly burnt by insecure governments or religious factions as manifestations of thought control. All these possibilities must be taken into account when interpreting 'burning' dreams, together with the physical and emotional condition of the **dreamer** (are they in a feverish state? does burning have a particular significance for them?). Finally, burning may also be a symbol of man's civilizing nature, as the **smoke** from a distant **fire** may be the first visible **sign** that we are not **alone** in this **world**.

Buses Buses, and **time**, and **anxiety**, are often interlinked. A bus presupposes a desire to go somewhere, and this is true also of **dreams**, in which being bussed to one's destination can imply a process of movement independent of one's own volition. Bussing, too, is another word for **kissing**, and there may very well be a **sexual** connotation to the dream, in that buses are environments in which we are forced to confront, and occasionally even touch, **strangers**. See **Bus Stops**

Bus Stops Bus stops are in many ways similar to **subways** in that they can represent, especially in symbolical terms, an environment in which unexpected **sexual** encounters may potentially take place. They are locations, therefore, in which **strangers** are forced together, through need, and possibly against their will, only to find themselves placed into positions where they have to look at each other (or otherwise be made aware of each other) almost regardless of inclination. Such a magnificently convenient image frequently finds itself transmuted into **anxiety dreams** or **wish-fulfilment** fantasies. It may seem a little invidious to mention (but I shall do so nonetheless), that the word 'bus stop' also provides a convenient semantic **imago** (i.e. bust top) which may find itself reflected, unknowingly, in any potentially idealized dream image. See **Buses**

Butchers There is something a little unsavoury about butchers (just as with undertakers), in that we need them, but we don't necessarily entirely approve of what they do for us. This apparently hypocritical quasi-paradox may find itself reflected in butcher **symbols** in **dreams**, for such a symbol is rarely benevolent, and can even, on occasion, seem threatening – the butcher's **apron**, for instance, covered in **blood**, has strong revocations of the surgeon's gown, and also, of course, of the Freemason's ceremonial garb, suggesting secret **rituals** or processes which may potentially involve us but of which we may be more than a little ignorant. The image may therefore hark back to a **primal scene** or other **childhood** occurrence in which we infer more than we can possibly know about a suspicious event (*ergo* the **killing** of **animals** or the sexuality of our **parents**).

Butter Butter implies **richness** and natural softness, but may also take the meaning of **self**-satisfaction, as in 'she looked as if butter would not **melt** in her **mouth**'. In many religions butter also has a strong spiritual significance, and is frequently used as part of a **burnt** offering (usually in terms of, or symbolic of, nourishment). It can also act as a symbol of 'civilization', for the making of butter requires stasis and order, rather than movement and disorder.

Butterflies Traditionally, a butterfly symbolizes sporting capacity or living for **pleasure** (See **Pleasure Principle**). To the Mexican Aztecs it was the emblem of **fire** and of the purified **soul**. The Chinese Taoist Chuang Tzu once dreamed that he was a butterfly. It seemed to him, in his dream, that he had always been a butterfly, flitting from flower to **flower**, and living in a state of perfect existential happiness. When he awoke, he realized, with some distress, that, far from being a butterfly, he was merely Chuang Tzu – but then the happy thought occurred to him that perhaps he was the butterfly after all, dreaming that he was Chuang Tzu. The butterfly (*leyp-lya*) was considered by the Taoists to be the cause of **dreams**, but, when it left the **body** of the **dreamer**, it could not stray from already known **paths** for **fear** of permanent disassociation, possibly leading to the dreamer's **death**. In Burma, the *win-laik-pya*, or soul butterfly, would leave the body of a sleeper, and go to meet other soul-butterflies, of men and of **animals**, before returning to the sleeper just before the moment of **waking** – it was therefore considered particularly ill-advised to wake a person suddenly, as the *win-laik-pya* might then not have the chance to return to its host in time.

Buying 'Buying' is the opposite of 'making' – it is the easy option, in other words. We may 'buy' our freedom, or 'buy' our way out of **danger**. The act of buying has taken on more positive revocations in the new post-

1960s consumer age, but the **unconscious** may still see it as a short cut rather than as an acceptable basis for an ethical way of life.

Byron, Lord (1788–1824) The English poet Byron wrote his *The Dream* in 1816, in an effort to reflect, and if possible, coalesce, the significance of **dreams** and dreaming to the Romantic imagination:

> 'And dreams in their development have breath,
> And tears, and tortures, and the touch of joy;
> They leave a weight upon our waking thoughts,
> They take a weight from off our waking toils,
> They do divide our being; they become
> A portion of ourselves as of our time,
> And look like heralds of eternity;'

C

Cabbages Cabbages frequently represent the **vagina** in **dreams** – the fact that they are shaped like a baby's **head**, and are of roughly the same size, merely reinforces the vaginal connotations. Coelius, Suidas, Rabelais, Ovid, Pausanias and Rhodiginus all wrote that cabbages were first formed when a few drops of Jupiter's sweat (See **Secretions**) fell upon the **earth**, and they are, in addition, renowned for their capacity to instil **thirst** in the eater, as well as flatulence (oneirically speaking a somewhat diffuse threat, perhaps). For this reason, dreaming of cabbages may also be associated with **stomach** problems, which, in the case of a woman, may also include **pregnancy** or even the **fear** of **abortion** (chopped cabbage).
KEY LINE: '... physicians will tell us that some food makes turbulent, some gives quiet dreams. Cato who doated on cabbage might find the crude effects thereof in his sleep; wherein the Egyptians might find some advantage by their superstitious abstinence from onions.' (From Sir Thomas Browne's *On Dreams* 1650)

Cabins Cabins can equate with shrines, in symbolical terms, for they offer comfort and **shelter** (physical safety allows us the chance to think, and to construct communities). They can also seal us off from the natural **world** in a quasi-hermetical way, and **blind** us to what is happening outside.

Cables Cables are almost inevitably **umbilical** when they appear in **dreams**, in that they are designed to attach one thing to another. In **archetypal** terms, this inevitably refers back to the **mother**/child connection, and a breached cable usually implies a cessation, or threatened cessation, of the mother/**child** relationship.

Cacti The cactus, as well as carrying implications of **water** retention and hallucinogenic properties (See **Hallucinations** & **Hallucinatory Dreams**), also supports the idea of defence from unwanted intrusion/ **invasions**. To that extent cacti may imply **frigidity**, or, in the case of a **female dreamer**, unwanted **male** attention, given their aggressive **phallic** shape allied to distinctly anti-pleasurable spines. See **Mescal**, **Mescaline** & **Peyote**

Cader Idris Another name for King Arthur's Seat. If a man were to spend a **night** in King Arthur's Seat, or so the legend has it, the **dreams** he would have would turn him into either a **poet** or a madman. Cader Idris (to which the same legend applies) is also the name of a **mountain** ridge in southwestern Wales, which may or may not be the original location of the kingly settle.

Cafés Cafés are pleasurable and safe environments in which we may interrelate with apparent impunity while still according ourselves the frisson of speculative **sexual** encounters. They are also **meeting** places – places of rendezvous. Dreaming of cafés may imply that the **dreamer** feels that they are waiting for something or somebody, but that there is an element of expectant **pleasure** rather than of **anxiety** in the prospect.

Cages Cages are sometimes representative of the **vagina**, but they are also places of imprisonment, in which the **prisoner** may be put on unwanted display. There may also be a **masochistic** or **sadistic** element involved when they appear in **dreams.**

Cakes Cakes are nutritious, portable, and also, according to the Egyptian *Book of the Dead*, **symbols** of the perfected **soul**. To that extent they draw together both domestic virtue (the ability to make cakes) and spiritual nourishment (the ability to derive significance from them).

Calculators Calculators may symbolize the power of the **machine** over the mind. They may also indicate a desire to be **right**, or, alternatively, a **fear** of trusting one's own instincts over those of an unemotional, and possibly unconnected or disinterested, third party.

Caldéron de la Barca y Henao, Pedro (1600–81) The last great figure of the Golden Age of Spanish literature, Caldéron was a **poet** and dramatist whose greatest work, *La Vida es Sueño* (*Life is a Dream*), written in 1635, relates, in symbolical and philosophical terms, the **nightmare** of a young man in **love**. See **Davoine & Johannot**

Calendars Calendars symbolize the passing of **time**, but not necessarily in a negative, doom-laden way. Their appearance in a **dream** may represent the **unconscious** mind's attempt to remind the **dreamer** of something important they have forgotten, or that they feel obliged, but reluctant, to do.

Calpurnia According to the Roman biographer Suetonius, Calpurnia, Julius Caesar's wife, dreamed of his **death** just a few hours before it happened, on 15th (ides of) March, 44 BC. However, she failed to convince her **husband** to cancel his doomed visit to the Senate, and he was duly **murdered** by a cabal of former **friends** and associates. In Plutarch's version of the event, Caesar **awoke** and actually saw Calpurnia having the **dream** beside him. Livy (reflecting his essential **nature**) saw the whole thing more symbolically, describing Calpurnia's dream as that of a gable-ornament, reflecting Caesar's glory, being pulled down. Caesar was obviously moved by his **wife's** quite uncharacteristic feyness, for he double-checked with his own seers, but even when they confirmed the portents, he refused to follow Calpurnia's advice for **fear**, one supposes, of being perceived as weak (he turned his back on his **anima**, in other words).

Calves A calf traditionally symbolizes lumpishness, cumbrousness, or **cowardice**. They are also **sacrificial** objects, and synonymous with plenty and with future possibilities.

Camels A camel, in Christian iconography, symbolizes submission, or **obedience** to higher **guidance**. Camels are also stubborn creatures (see **Asses**) and represent individuality and even eccentricity in the face of coercion. When a Muslim **dreams** of camels, there may also be revocations of the Prophet Mohammed's camel, Al Kaswa, which accomplished the **journey** from Jerusalem to Mecca in four enormous bounds. In addition, the **toe** of the camel may also carry **sexual** connotations, in that they are traditionally perceived as resembling a certain particular configuration of the depilated **female vagina**.

Cameras Cameras potentially provide us with **pictures** of ourselves the way others may see us. Many primitive tribes feared **cameras** for this very reason, suspecting that a photographer might be intent on stealing part of their essential natures, thereby placing them in the power of others. More recently, cameras may be taken to illustrate or signify the power the State has over our lives, *ergo* 'Big Brother' – the Orwellian rather than the Reithian, needless to say. Cameras, and the images taken from them, show only the exterior of a person and not the interior (i.e. what a person does, and not what they think), however their products, especially in the digital age, are amenable to **fakery** and misconstruction, and they may also, on occasion, shed an uncomfortable **light** on misperceived **truths**. See **Double** & **Photographs**

Camouflage The desire to **hide** ourselves, or aspects of ourselves, from the view of others. The wearing of camouflage may also have more sinister connotations, in detaching the wearer from the rules, or oversight, of normal society. Dreaming of camouflage may also imply a desire to cover up something that the **dreamer** has done, or **fears** that they might do.

Camphor See **Incense**

Camps Camps imply not only a mingling together, but also the possibilities of either protection or **imprisonment**. Constructing an entrenched camp about oneself in a **dream** suggests the need for comfort, or even, dare one say it, a desire to return to the **womb**, for an entrenched camp would appear, at first glance, to be self-sufficient. There is one bugbear, however. Entrenched camps are difficult to **escape** from, particularly if one is surrounded by one's **enemies**.

Canals Canals are inherently mysterious things. They are that ultimate paradox – seemingly natural, although of necessity man-made, objects. In **dream** terms they suggest conduits or **passages**, and to that extent they may take on some of the symbolical function of the **heart** and of its arteries. **Locks** are then seen to represent clots or blockages, which may be amenable to wishful opening (See **Wish-Fulfilment**), allowing free passage once again. To this extent the country containing the canals represents the **body**, and the canals its circulatory system, transporting **food** and **fuel** and **pleasure** around and within.

Cancellation Cancellation, or the cancelling of things, may, when dreamt of by a woman, suggest the loss of her **virginity** or the fear of defloration. In another context, it may be a convenient euphemism for **frustration**, or for the pique one feels when one's best-laid plans are upset or interfered with by outside forces.

Cancer Symbolical of the fourth period of life, the crab (or in Indian astrology, the **tortoise**), was, according to **Plato**, the **mouth** through which the **soul** descends (it ascended through **Capricorn**). Like the crab, which feeds on flotsam and jetsam, the **disease** of cancer is perceived to feed off the human **body**, and eventually to destroy it. Dreaming of cancer may therefore imply the existence of unacknowledged **guilt**, or a fundamental lack of **self**-worth – even the doubting of established orders or frameworks. To that extent it may have positive connotations, too, pointing to aspects of the **psyche** that need urgent attention.

Candles When a woman **dreams** of candles they can represent the erect **penis** – in addition, when lit, they **burn**, and may, in this guise, indicate the repression of **sexual** desires. Traditionally, lit candles were left next to the dead to protect them from **evil** spirits, and to that extent their appearance in a dream may be the **unconscious** mind's way of drawing attention to something, just as Jessica, in Shakespeare's *Merchant of Venice* Act ii, Scene 6, says to Lorenzo, 'What, must I hold a candle to my shame?' Within Christian iconography, candles represent the **light** of **truth**.

Candlesticks Candlesticks can symbolize the **superego** when they appear in **dreams**, for they are an age-old **symbol** of wisdom, in the sense that they stand **tall**, throw **light**, and benevolently overlook us. Upset, they can threaten the status quo (in the form of the **scorching**, let's say, of our *amour propre*/**ego**). See **Wise Old Man**

Candy See **Sweets**

Canes Apart from their obvious **phallic** and sadomasochistic overtones, canes also have the capacity to bend under pressure, and even to protect, in the sense of building a **shelter** with them when under threat. A cane is also a traditional **symbol** of regal or magisterial authority, and therefore of the **superego**, as exemplified in the Roman *fasces*, which consisted of a bundle of canes tied together with scarlet thongs and carried by a *lictor* – the canes symbolized the power to punish, and, when an **axe** was added to the bunch, also the power of life and **death**. See **Masochism** & **Sadism**

Cannibalism Cannibalism, in **dreams**, as well as being a reversion to the atavistic, or **id**, may also imply an incorporative process (often of a hate object) – otherwise known as the 'transmissibility of properties'. Examples of similar symbolic incorporations often occur in real life, too, as exemplified by such crimes as those of Issei Sagawa, in Paris, in 1981, who **killed**, **raped**, and then partially ate a **female** student. He was pronounced insane by the French authorities, and then freed, three years later, from the asylum to which he had been transferred. See **Eating** & **Manic Depression**

Canoes Canoes are at one and the same time both **phallic** (they are driven **male** images, covered in **skin**, which **plough** through **water**) and transitional, in that they allow fast and non-invasive movement across otherwise impossible environments. When a **female** dreams of a canoe it may imply a desire to be 'as the male' – i.e. free from female appurtenances such as menses and the ability to bear **children**. See **Menstruation**

Canyons Canyons are largely female **symbols** into which one **falls**, or in whose **shadow** one resides. There are hidden and unexplored depths to them, and if a man is apprehensive or suspicious of them in his **dreams**, it may indicate a **fear** of women or a desire to avoid (or refuse to acknowledge) the feminine aspects of his own **nature** (his **anima**). If he welcomes them, on the other hand, and acknowledges that the **river** that formed them may contain nourishment, he is probably at ease with this aspect of his nature. Should a woman dream of canyons, it may indicate a coming-to-terms with, or acceptance of, her own **female** condition.

Capricorn The **Zodiacal** Capricorn, or **goat** (in Indian **astrology**, the **elephant**), equates with the tenth period of the cycle of life, and was considered by **Plato** to represent the **gate**, or **mouth**, through which the **soul** ascends to a higher plane.

Caps Caps have obvious prophylactic connotations, with the Dutch cap, the **condom**, and the **female** condom **falling** within their symbolical framework. In theory, they protect – either from inclement **weather**, inclement **sex**, or inclement identification. There is also the more obvious 'setting one's cap at someone', which, in its original form, applied exclusively to **female** mating behaviour, in the sense that a girl would put on her best bonnet in an effort to capture one particular man's attention.

Capsizing Capsizing is an obvious oneiric euphemism for **failure** – **sexual**, emotional, or what have you. There may also be a **wish-fulfilment** aspect to a dream which contains, or repeats, a capsizing motive, as there is often an element in our **psyches** which seeks to fail, or which, perversely, feels **guilt** for its success.

Captains There is an aspect to nearly everyone which responds to firm leadership, and the symbol of the Captain is a powerful one, therefore, and perilously close to an **archetype**. The bad Captain or the **female** Captain seem almost a contradiction in terms when seen purely in this archetypal light, and **dreams**, despite the nominal prevalence of political correctness in our everyday lives, usually revert to pre-PC prototypes such as this at the very first opportunity. See **Leaders**

Captive Woman See **Captivity**

Captivity The captive woman is an age-old **symbol** and occurs in most mythologies. Its origins may lie in the **stealing** of other tribe's women by our Neanderthal **male** ancestors (intent on **sexual** gratification and/or reproduction) but it has more recently come to symbolize, particularly in the guise of the Andromeda legend, forward movement, and the activity of desires. In **Jungian** terms the freeing of the captive woman reflects the acknowledgment and possible liberation of the male's inner **anima**, while the stealing of other people's women is by and large contra-indicated, as potentially leading to a determinedly non-Jungian animus. Captivity *per se* usually indicates a **fear** of the enslavement of our mental qualities, as well as a reaction against possible physical domination by faceless individuals or institutions. See **Slaves & Slavery**

Cards Cards imply randomness twinned with hierarchy – an odd concatenation when one comes to think of it. Given the amount of superstitions associated with them, it is hardly surprising that they represent such a mass of disparate symbolic pointers when they occur in **dreams**. To a **gambler** they will mean one thing, and to a puritan another. Whatever one's religious or moral persuasion, they inevitably suggest an easy way out, or, at the very least, a pleasurable answer to a difficult question – i.e. what to do with one's life. See **Aces**

Car Parks See **Parking Lots**

Carpenters Carpentry is traditionally a **symbol** of divine artifice – **Jesus Christ**, it goes without saying, trained as a carpenter in his **father**'s workshop, and later majored in divine carpentry. In purely dream terms carpentry may suggest the need to mend something, or to engage in a slow process of construction.

Carpets Carpets cover things. It's as simple as that. To that extent they equate with **clothes** – as window-dressing perhaps, or as a means of impressing or cutting a dash. To a Mohammedan, however, they have a further significance, in that they are often used as **prayer** mats, or as carriers of the words of the **Koran**.

Carroll, Lewis (1832–98) In his second Alice book, *Through the Looking Glass*, Carroll confronts his **heroine** with Tweedledum and Tweedledee –

all three contemplate the sleeping Red King: 'He's dreaming now,' said Tweedledee: 'and what do you think he's dreaming about?' Alice said, 'Nobody can guess that.' 'Why, about *you*!' Tweedledum explained, clapping his hands triumphantly. 'And if he left off dreaming about you, where do you suppose you'd be?' 'Where I am now, of course,' said Alice. 'Not you!' Tweedledee retorted contemptuously. 'You'd be nowhere. Why, you're only a sort of thing in his dream!'

Carrots More **phallic** connotations, I'm afraid, with a hefty dose of seduction thrown in (as in the carrot and the donkey). The **cutting** up of carrots in a woman's dream may have little to do with cookery, but considerably more with a desire to diminish **male** power, or to puncture male bombast. A male dreaming the same thing may **harbour** a fear that a woman's domestic skills will harness or **bridle** his essential virility – the only way to soften a carrot, after all, is to cook it. See **Asses** & **Cooking**

Carrying Carrying inevitably leads us towards **pregnancy** and motherhood, particularly when dreamt of by a woman. Whether the carrying is of something that is burdensome or **light** depends entirely on the context of the **dream**, and on the woman's **unconscious** feelings about the benefits, or potential bondage, of maternity. See **Mothers**

Cars Cars frequently symbolize **sexual** urges in **dreams**. A car is also an easy answer to a complicated **question**, i.e. how does one get about quickly – the 'easy' part is the getting about, the 'complicated' part is to know what to do when one gets there. Joking aside, cars are an interesting example of something that may have either a **male** or a **female** connotation, depending on the context of the dreaming. In **Freudian** terms, a car is usually a male **symbol**, and any **damage** to a car represents the **castration** idea. Cars, however, are also objects one enters, and into which one puts things. They are vanity objects, which one cleans and beautifies (see **Cleansing**), possibly with status in mind. They are desired by other **people**, and they give power (even if only temporary) to their possessor. A car can be stolen, or entered illegally by others (**raped**). Cars are felt to **reflect** their owners – one can even, narcissistically, see one's own image in a car, either in the (vanity) **mirror**, or in the polished paintwork, just as an elderly man, for instance, may wish to see himself reflected in a much younger woman, or the concomitant, but rather rarer and traditionally more **taboo** image, of an elderly female with a younger male in tow. This predominantly female aspect of the car (ownership, vanity) may be subject to the whims of the male owner without any input from the 'vehicle' itself. It is therefore a perfect fantasy object for the male, in terms of ownership, power and control, and for the female, in terms of power and control over a male simulacrum. Finally, cars can represent a sort of freedom – the possession of a car puts the owner less in the power of others in terms of transport, choice, and the liberty to say no (and leave). This sense of freedom, though, is arbitrary, and partially dependent on luck (i.e. not having an accident – *ergo* 'defloration'), and upon the consonance of others. Thus, their **richness** in terms of dream imagery. See **Driverlessness & Lorries**

Caskets Precious things are usually concealed in caskets – think, for example, of Alexander the Great's copy of Homer, with Aristotle's corrections, which became known as the 'Casket Homer', and which Alexander carried with him wherever he went – and also, of course, the dead. There is as much reason to **fear** the opening of a casket, therefore, as there is to rejoice, and particular care must be taken to identify the actual **feeling** or atmosphere behind the appearance of such a vessel in a **dream**, for its presence may be reminding us of something we had thought was locked away.

Castles 'Castles in the air', 'sandcastles', 'castles in Spain' – yes, castles are often fantasy objects, which we create to comfort ourselves when reality is uncongenial. They may also be places of terror, like Castle Terabil (in the Arthurian Legends), with moats and keeps and **torture** chambers. A castle, too, may stand in for the **body** of the **dreamer**, with **entrances** and **exits** equating with the usual areas, and armouries, treasuries, alcoves and parapets standing in for the rest. See **Buildings & Houses**

Castration Complex Primitive peoples who believed in the power of the **phallus** and of the act of coition to form a connection with the divine, naturally feared castration (or emasculation) as a diminution of that power. Active and passive castration complexes are therefore evident in the unconscious of most **males**, and are likely to occur in **dreams** of one form or another at some point in the **dreamer's** life. Castration fears are often the product of **guilt**, and may be connected atavistically with an inability to procreate, equating, in the **unconscious** mind, with an unwanted disconnection from the divine. A **biblical** example of the castration complex occurs in the story of Samson and Delilah (Judges 13–16), in which Samson has his **hair** cut off (thus losing his masculine power) and is also blinded (see **Blindness**). A psychological study conducted by the US Office Of Strategic Services (a precursor of the CIA) in 1943, found, amongst other things, that Adolf Hitler had an active and crippling castration complex. See **Barbers, Circumcision Complex, Eyes, Hymen Complex & Razors**

Catagogic Tendencies Catagogic tendencies in **dreams** point up everything in the **dreamer's** mind that is destructive, anarchic, or selfish. The transformation of the antisocial into the heroic, in other words. One example might be the glorification of suicide bombing. See **Anagogic Tendencies**

Caterpillars The most important faculty of caterpillars (at least in dream terms) is that they incorporate within themselves the capacity for fundamental change. They perform a similar function, needless to say, in

dreams, in which they appear as much to subvert expectations as to reinforce them.

Catacombs Catacombs even rhyme with '**wombs**', with the added implication that they are empty, dead, or barren. For a woman to **dream** of them may imply, quite strongly, that she **fears** such barrenness, or suspects it in herself. If, in addition, she pictures herself inside the catacombs, perhaps looking for an **escape** route, the **reading** is even further strengthened.

Catharsis The dramatic discharge, through conscious enactment, of an **unconscious** emotional block. Such an eventual discharge may be facilitated through an enlightened interpretation of **dreams**. See **Theatres** & **Theatrical Performances**
KEY LINE: 'He had long been a lover of dreams, even bad dreams, because thanks to them, thanks to the contradiction they present to the reality which we have before us in our waking state, they give us, at the moment of waking if not before, the profound sensation of having slept.' (From Marcel Proust's *La Prisonnière* 1923)

Cathedrals Cathedrals, like **churches**, presuppose aspirations towards a higher plane. They rise upwards, connecting human beings with ethereal things, rather than with the mundane. And yes, unfortunately, they do have **phallic** connotations, too.

Cats A cat traditionally symbolizes deceit. In German mythology it was **sacred** to Freya, goddess of **love**, fertility and beauty. Cats can also represent the **unconscious** mind of the **dreamer**, particularly when the dreamer doubts the strength of their own **taboo** control. In old English folklore, if a **sick** person dreamed of a cat, he would die – the same thing would happen if the invalid saw two cats **fighting**. They were also renowned as the 'familiars' of **witches**, given that Satan particularly liked to make his appearance in the guise of a **black** cat. Cats can also engender extreme antipathies, as with Henry III of France, who fainted away whenever he saw one, and Napoleon, who loathed the very thought of them. In addition, they can carry within their **name** strong revocations of whipping, as in the cat-o'-nine-tails. See **Devil** & **Whips**
KEY LINE: 'Confound the cats! All cats – alway –/Cats of all colours, black, white, grey;/By night a nuisance, and by day –/Confound the cats!' (From Orlando Dobbin's *A Dithyramb on Cats*)

Cattle See **Oxen**

Caves Our ancestors saw **mountain** caves as the **homes** of **demons** ('Now was Loki (the trickster) taken without any chance of respite. The Aesir (sky gods) conducted him into a cave.' *Prose Edda*). To a modern person, caves are more likely to represent the unknown or the

unconscious. In purely symbolical terms, the cave represents the **vagina** and the process of **birth** – from **darkness** into **light**, in other words.

Cavities When a tooth has been extracted in a **dream**, the ensuing cavity is usually **vaginal**, or **anal**, in connotation, with the implication that it is a **space** needing to be filled. See **Tooth Dreams**

Cayce, Edgar (1877–1945) The Kentucky-born Cayce was known as the 'sleeping prophet', thanks to his capacity for healing and prophesying whilst asleep. A deeply committed Christian who read through the **Bible** every **year** of his life, Cayce refused to charge, or benefit in any way, from his **gifts** (he even doubted his own prophetic abilities, believing that the 'true' future depended on free will). Despite these misgivings, Cayce devoted his life to helping others, believing that he was merely part of a communally-charged, Universal, or Akashic, Knowledge (communicated by a sort of spontaneous, but still fallible, reincarnative morphology), and to which we all have a certain degree of access if only we care to look for it. **Dreams**, to Cayce, stand at the **crossroads** of the individual personality we briefly inhabit, and the collective cosmic **soul** of which we all form a permanent part. The **records** of his Life-**Readings** are still held at ARE (The Association of Research and Enlightenment), at Virginia Beach, Virginia, USA. See **Healers**
KEY LINE: 'Dreams are today's answers to tomorrow's questions.' (Edgar Cayce)

Ceilings In purely symbolical terms ceilings are **symbols** of the higher mental plane, and may be taken as representing the firmament (or our aspirations towards it). We tend to look upwards, and not downwards, when we die, and when we go outside at **night** our **eyes** are inevitably (atavistically?) drawn towards the **heavens**. See **Above & Below**

Celebrations The definition of celebration really depends on whether the **dreamer** feels part of the celebrations they are dreaming about, or excluded. Either way, celebrations imply some form of special, or out of the ordinary, event, to which the **unconscious** mind obviously attaches particular significance.

Celebrities In the so-called modern **world** (all worlds, of course, were modern in their **time**) the culture of celebrity will tend to have a different significance for the young than for the old – or even for the middle-aged. For the one it may have largely positive connotations, for the other it may have neutral, or even negative connotations, and imply unwanted attention or even intrusion by outside forces into internal (*ergo* emotionally charged) affairs.

Celibacy The concept of celibacy is now such a rarefied one – even though, paradoxically, the same proportion of **people** may be celibate now as in Victorian times – that **dreams** about the state itself are of extreme significance. They mean, of course, what they don't seem to mean, and need to be disentangled from the **fears** of societal opprobrium, mistrust, or even disdain that now surrounds the 'c' word. **Archetypally**, celibacy implies a desire for higher things (beyond the physical, in other words) and aspirations to become wiser, or deeper, than one was initially.

Cemeteries The significance of a cemetery in a **dream** would seem, at first glance, to be obvious, but nothing is ever as simple as it seems in the dream world. The **key** word is 'buried', and the appearance of a cemetery attests more to that fact than to any precognitive anticipation of **death**. Something lies buried in the dreamer's **unconscious** – something that wishes to draw attention to itself. The fact that that something may or may not have morbid overtones is not **self**-evident either, and the grave-yard emphasis may simple lie in the peace and detachment from so-called normal life that one customarily derives from such a place. See **Burials**

Centaurs Centaurs (half man, half **horse**) represent wildness and anarchy. They live by their instincts (see **Dionysian**), and are synonymous with an uncontrolled **id**. Centaurs, should they appear in **dreams**, represent man ruled by his **animal nature** – the desire to live without the need to subject oneself to society's rules.

Central Idea A dream's central idea, teased out after effective **dream work**, usually reflects the central problem of the dreamer's **neurosis** (if they have one) – the unfulfilled wish, if you like, that hampers normal behaviour.

Centres Centres usually connote **mandalas**, and to that extent they tend to be aspirational, and to appear in the form of **bulls-eyes**, for instance, or **clocks** (both, in their different respects, **targeting** something). They may be rotational, or perpetually in movement, and it is at least arguable that their symbolic centre is inhabited by **God**.

Ceremonies Ceremonies tend towards the transmutative – they ritualize the progression from a lower plane to a higher one. They are also an acknowledgement from the outside of what is happening on the inside. To that extent they act in exactly the opposite way to **dreams**, and should be viewed, in consequence, as largely external symbolizations of inter-nally salient features. See **Rituals**

Cesspools Cesspools and the word 'excess', for instance, may find themselves linked in the strange symbolical **language** from which **dreams** are often made. Such odd **marriages** are common in dream architecture, and frequently make up considerably more than the sum of their apparently disparate parts. Another semantic link (to take but one example) might be with the word 'cease', as in 'cease pool', implying a place where things end up. See **Neologisms**

Chagall, Marc (1887–1985) The Russian-born Chagall was always heavily influenced by **dream** imagery in his **paintings**. His 1930–9 *Le Temps n'a Point de Rive* (*Time Has no Riverbanks*), as well as being a pun on *rive* (bank) and *rêve* (dream), contains within it many common dream **symbols**, including a **flying fish** with **wings**, a **ticking clock** (also flying), a **hand** dropping a **violin** into a **river**, and a **sexual** assignation (or possibly even a **rape**), involving two insubstantial figures in the foreground.

Chains Chains bind, and the obvious questions to ask are, 'What are they binding? And why?' If the **dreamer** finds themselves bound up and unable to move, they are likely to be both anxious and frustrated, and this is going to be reflected in the architecture of the dream – the **unconscious**, in other words, will select clues that point to the underlying **neurosis** or **central idea** behind the dream's formation.

Chains of Dreams See **Dream Series**

Chairs Chairs have particularly strong symbolic value. People have their favourite chairs; **heads** of **family** sit in chairs at the head of the **table**; **crowned** heads sit on **thrones**; and **murderers** are attached to **electric** chairs. **Pregnant** women were often confined to groaning chairs (see **Groaning Cake**), or placed in them after a successful parturition to receive the congratulations of well-wishers, and chair-days was an ancient term for old age. As a result, their specific appearance in a **dream** (as opposed to a 'by default' appearance, as in a **hotel** lobby) is usually of significance, and may point to status **worries**, or to other hierarchical anxieties. Their resemblance to a **skeleton** (i.e. ribbed) may also need to be taken into account.

Chalk One either plans or demonstrates things with chalk, and the inference taken from such signifiers may be either good or bad – merit marks might be perceived as good, for instance, and **plague** marks bad. Chalk may also imply an otherness, as in the expression 'chalk and **cheese**', suggesting two very different and nominally incompatible things. To dream of chalk, then, carries with it the inevitable implication of the message that the chalk will make.

Champagne The assumption must be that champagne equates with the need for a **celebration** or is a **symbol** for exuberance, but **bottles**, and particularly champagne bottles – with their froth potentially equating with **semen**, and their firing of corks potentially equating with **orgasm** – are also **phallic** objects.

Chandeliers Chandeliers reflect both **light** and glory, and in that sense they are status objects, as well as being **symbols** of civilization.

Changing Personae Should one person 'morph' into another during dreaming, the first person is usually a **symbol** or a carrier of qualities that the second person also possesses. Such morphing is often an indication that a change of **dream symbolism** is on the **cards**.

Channels Channels, **passages** and **corridors** all imply communication. They are conduits from one stage, or state of being, to another (just as in **birth**). They allow both forward and **backwards movement**, and the harder the passage, the more important the eventual **goal** probably is. To be stuck in a passage is inevitably transient – some movement has to occur (a decision has to be made) or one is forced into a position of emotional stasis, equating, in some measure, with **death**. See **Pre-Birth Dreams**

Chaos Chaos equates with formlessness. Primal matter is perceived as chaotic – pure being, without an infusion of **spirit** or humanity to leaven its pre-neanic state. The Orphic Mysteries declared that Chaos first existed 'eternal, vast, uncreate; it was neither darkness nor light, moist nor dry, hot nor cold, but all things intermingled' (From the as yet unattributed *The Clementine Recognitions* – translated circa 400 AD).

Chariots Chariots have traditionally been taken as metaphorical vehicles of consciousness, and to that extent they were often used by the **Gods** during spiritual or otherwise significant **journeys**. In dream terms they have a similarly strong symbolical value, and the choice of them, as an image, is of immense importance. In addition to their role in transporting **consciousness**, they are also, in **archetypal** terms, vehicles of perfection, and to that extent they may imply a desire to strive on the part of the **dreamer**, which may, when seen in terms of aspirations towards maturity, equate with a desire to make the **soul** before **death**.

Charles IX (1550–74) Charles IX of France was tormented by **nightmares** and **waking dreams** of **blood** and dead **victims** after his dominant **mother**, Catherine de Médicis, persuaded him to trigger the 1572 St Bartholomew's Day Massacre of Huguenot Protestants. He lived for only another two **years**, and died at the age of 24. There is speculation that his death was a result of **poisoning** – possibly at the orders of his mother.

Charms Charms equate with wishful thinking, in that it makes no rational sense to take a lucky charm with one for protection, but many of us feel better if we persist in such behaviour despite the **absence** of any compensating logic. It's the equivalent of trusting to fate, in other words, and the implication must be, when charms appear in **dreams**, that we do not wish to take personal responsibility for some of our actions. For real-life examples we need look no further than the woman who carries a **rabbit's** foot but persists in **smoking**, or the man who drives at breakneck **speed** while trusting to a St Christopher or a St Anthony. A charm, it should be

added, can also be a song or an incantation, and to that extent may at one time have had the same virtues as an **amulet** or **talisman**.
KEY LINE: 'I know of a charm by way of a prayer that will preserve a man from the violence of guns and all manner of fire-weapons and engines, but it will do me no good because I do not believe it.' (From Rabelais's *Works*. Book i, Chapter 42)

Charts Charts help us to find our way, and this will tend to be their significance in **dreams** as well. The **questions** that need to be asked are 'In what way are we lost?' And why?' The dream is indicating something to us, and we need to pay attention.

Chasing Chasing, like **flying** and **running** on the spot, is one of the commonest of all **dream** images. When one does not catch the chased object, but persistently misses it, **anxiety** is probably the most prominent motivation of the dream, twinned with **frustration** at some aspect of one's life or behaviour. A 'chase', in terms of woodland, is a private domain held outside the royal prerogative (such as Cranborne Chase), and it would not be uncommon for a **dreamer** to mix the two images up inside a dream in a form of semantic stew.

Chasms Chasms instil **fear** – they open up suddenly beneath our **feet** and threaten us. Symbolically they, too, can equate with the **vagina**, but this time making of it a fearsome object rather than one in which a heterosexual **male**, for instance, might earnestly desire to re-immerse himself. It's possible, of course, that repeated **dreams** of chasms or crevasses merely refer back to unfortunate **birth** or **pre-birth** experiences, but they may, in addition, indicate **death fears** (which are often linked to birth images, anyway), as a result of an **unconscious ellipsis**.

Cheating Cheating may seem, at first glance, to be an easy way out, and our **unconscious** minds are not above seeking such convenient **escape** hatches when they are confronted by uncomfortable **truths**. Who or what are we cheating in the dream? And what is the narrative our unconscious mind has constructed to justify the cheating?
KEY LINE: 'Like strawberry wives, that laid two or three great strawberries at the mouth of their pot, and all the rest were little ones.' (From Francis Bacon's *Apothegms* Number 54)

Checkers See **Draughts**

Cheese Cheese, for Wallace and Gromit, may conceivably represent all that is good in the **world**, but for a non-Plasticine human being there might be other associations – smiling or **happiness**, say (via 'saying cheese' or the 'Cheshire Cat'), or possibly even suggestions of frugality (**cutting** small pieces off a **wedge** of cheese, *ergo* cheeseparing). Traditionally, to **dream** of cheese was considered ill-omened, and suggestive of great disappointment and sorrow.

KEY LINE: 'Many's the long night I've dreamed of cheese – toasted, mostly.'(Marooned pirate Ben Gunn speaking in Robert Louis Stevenson's *Treasure Island* 1883)

Chefs The appearance of a chef in a **dream** may well fall under a **wish-fulfilment** fantasy codification, in that we would all like to be one, or, failing that, to have one at our beck and call. Joking apart, there is also a **phallic**, sensual element about the image of a chef, exemplified by his upstanding **hat**, and by his dominant position in the **kitchen** (where goodies and other desirable articles are traditionally stored).

Chemistry The appearance of chemistry in a **dream** is often a **symbol** of **death** or of **poison**, but the particular associations that the **dreamer** may have with chemistry need to be taken into account carefully before a correct analysis can be made. There is, too, an inevitable connection with **alchemy**, and with the **transformative** or transmutative process.

Chess Chess implies an extended process of rational thought, and also the capacity to respond in a constructive way to vicissitude. In the checkmate, though, we also have a **symbol** for endless **frustration** and **anxiety**, twinned with a dominant and sub-dominant endplay with potentially **sexual** undertones.

Chewing Chewing, infantile **oral fixations**, and oral **sex** are pretty much linked in the **unconscious,** so that the one predisposes towards a proportion, at least, of the other. Chewing, of course, also draws attention to the **mouth**, which most human beings acknowledge as either a direct erogenous zone, or, at the very least, a **seat** of considerable sexual interest. To that extent **eating** and sex are conjoined in the unconscious, and the chewing or mastication of **food** is merely a **symbol** of a justifiable (and usually **guilt**-free) form of sensual gratification.

Chickens The Taoists believed that dreaming of a chicken in a **tree** foretold **money**. The fear of **counting** one's chickens before they are hatched (see **Alnaschar Dream**) may find itself represented by the appearance of a certain **number** of chickens in a dream, with strict significance being given to the actual number present (*ante victoriam canere triumphum*, as the Romans said – don't crow before the triumph). The word 'chicken', as well as being intrinsically funny (try saying it out loud and not smiling), also has connotations of **cowardice** and funk, and this must also be considered when analyzing the fowl's significance.

Chiefs A chief is often interchangeable with **God** in a **dream**. The image may also contain links to the **father** and the **teacher archetype**.

Childhood Dreams Children instinctively possess a very un-adult sense of completeness which is inevitably **lost** following the emergence of **ego**-consciousness around the time of pubescence. This sense of complete-

ness is reflected in **dreams** which often manifest, in symbolic form, the future basic structure of the **psyche,** together with the more traditional pairing of unfulfilled **wishes** and **anxiety dreams** (a child's first dreams usually occur between the ages of two and five **years** old, following the beginnings of ego integration). Such dreams, as well as reflecting the child's psychic make-up, can also provide a framework – an anticipation, if you like – for the later development of the individual. Adults may occasionally reconnect with this sense of completeness (if only briefly) in what psychologist Abraham Maslow (1908–70) called the capacity for 'peak experience'. This describes a sudden moment of intense **lucidity** which equates, in some measure, with G. K. Chesterton's concept of 'absurd good news'. See **Children**
KEY LINE: 'I durst not, even in the day-light, once enter the chamber where I slept, without my face turned to the window, aversely from the bed where my witch-ridden pillow was. Parents do not know what they do when they leave tender babes alone to go to sleep in the dark ...'
(Charles Lamb's *Witches, and Other Night Fears* 1823)

Children A child may symbolize **Christ** in a dream, or a new state of being. Children may also find themselves represented by **lice** or **vermin** when they occur in an adult's **dreams**, but the author abjures all responsibility for this **reading**, which stems from psychoanalytic therapist Sandor Lorand. A childish consciousness, according to **Jung**, is always tied to the **father** and **mother**, and a return to childhood is always a return to the **parents**. See **Satellites**
KEY LINE: 'Diogenes struck the father when the son swore.' (From Robert Burton's *Anatomy of Melancholy* 1621)

Chimneys Complex things, chimneys. They are at one and the same time **vaginal**, they move up through **houses** (the **body**), they need regular **phallic** sweeping – a service which was historically done, in **reverse**, as it were, by small **children** – and they both radiate **heat** and let in the **cold**. If that's not enough in the way of symbolical paradoxes, their externals are phallic while their internal architecture is **female**, giving rise to **hermaphroditic** or **bisexual** connotations.

Chocolate Since its belated discovery in Mexico in 1519 (it had been in use since at least 600 BC), chocolate has been a desirable commodity, largely associated with comfort and **ritual**. After Fry & Sons (of Bristol) produced the first **eating** chocolate in 1847, chocolate would have rapidly become part of dream architecture, particularly because of its convenience in the alleviation and servicing of **oral fixations**, and its resemblance (dare one say it) to faeces. See **Cocoa** & **Excrement**

Choirs Dreaming of John Cleese's 'the choir invisibule' – whether or not accompanied by a dead **parrot** – probably implies a **fear** of, or at the very least a fascination with, **death**. There can be something ethereally nonhuman about the collective sound of a massed choir, particularly when it is singing Bach or Mozart. It takes us momentarily beyond ourselves, and causes us to aspire to higher things. The choirs' purpose in a **dream** is probably a similar one, and consists largely in calling us, or drawing our attention to, something that is, in itself, of more importance than our mundane cares. One cannot easily both **kill** and **sing** at the same **time**.

Choking Dreaming of choking may stem from a perfectly literal rendition of an actual state, for very often when we snore, a sudden blockage or interruption to our **breathing** will have occurred, forcing us, if only briefly, awake. Dreaming of choking may also be referring us back to a **pre-birth** state, or even to the sense experiences that may have occurred during a difficult breech **birth**.

Choughs The **soul** of King Arthur allegedly migrated into a chough, and the birds are still protected in Cornwall for that reason. **Archetypally**, alongside **crows** and **ravens**, choughs may form part of our **collective unconscious**.

Christ Christ, as an **archetype**, appears to relate to the pre-Christian **hero** and **rescuer myth**, in which the hero, attempting to subdue a **monster**, appears to be devoured, and yet returns later, miraculously unharmed. In purely symbolical terms, the Christ figure relates to the Higher **Self**, and, in Christian terms, to the idea of personal Godhood. See **Cannibalism**, **Figurative Expressions** & **Jesus Christ**

Christmas The concept of Christmas, alongside its more obvious Christian associations, often indicates an **unconscious** desire for comfort – even a **regression** back to **childhood** certainties. It may also have more negative connotations, depending on personal circumstances, symbolizing all that the **dreamer** is missing and may feel that they deserve (or not, as the case may be).

Christmas Trees Christmas trees are particularly rich tree **symbols**, relating to both Christian and pagan **rituals**. They may often imply hidden **treasures**, either spiritual or mammonish, depending on context. Seen without the protective **veil** of **myth**, they are uprooted entities, transient and finite – the opposite of **trees**, in other words – and of only cursory, consumerist value.

Churches Churches are often replacements for the **superego** in **dreams**. They imply established forms of thought, and the organization of human aspiration. The **destruction** of churches is often the first step towards **repression**, and a ruined church frequently symbolizes the loss of civilized moral values – anarchy, in other words. See **Dream-Founded Churches** & **Mosques**

Churchill, Sir Winston (1874–1965) After he lost power in the popular vote of 1945, the ex-Prime Minister of Britain, Winston Churchill, busied himself with a **number** of **writing** projects. One of these was his posthumously published **book**, *The Dream* (actually written in 1947), in which he imagined that his beloved **father**, Lord Randolph Churchill, reappeared in the flesh whilst his now 73-year-old **son** was copying a tattered old **painting** of the eminent **politician** sent to him from the Belfast Conservative **Club**. Churchill proceeds to give his appalled father a rundown of the horrors that have occurred in the half-century since his **death**, including the loss of India to Empire, and the Nazi concentration **camps**. A particularly clever conceit lies in the fact that Randolph is entirely unaware (and remains so) of his son's glittering career, and assumes that he is still the rather unfocused duffer who left Harrow without much in the way of scholastic achievement to his name.

Cicadas Cicadas symbolize poetry. They also have revocations of **summer** and leisure, and even joy for the sake of joy. In addition, they are also convenient **symbols** for the brevity of perceived **happiness**, and for the transience of human aspirations. See **Poems** & **Poets**

Cigarettes Cigarettes, as well as being obvious **phallic symbols**, may also imply (particularly in recent times) a refusal to conform to the dictates of the State, or to a so-called higher authority. One could also, if one were feeling a little perverse, view them as arcane manifestations of the **death**-wish. Most ex-smokers admit to **anxiety dreams** in which they find themselves still **smoking**, and still at risk of all the things they thought they had succeeded in avoiding. See **Cigars**

Cigars Cigars, as well as **cigarettes**, are strong **phallic symbols** – for a long time the **smoking** of them was considered the sole realm of men (a symbol of maleness, even). They are still strong images of confidence and leisure (it is virtually impossible to smoke a cigar quickly), and imply assertiveness and confidence rather than timidity. Women who dream of them are often admirers and likers of men – save when the cigar is seen as threatening or distasteful in the **dream**, when the exact opposite is the case. **Males** who dream of them may feel in need of asserting themselves, and unable to do so without the use of a prop. To that extent a cigar, like **clothes**, may represent a desire to disguise one's true **self**, particularly when taken in the male context.

Circles Circles are ancient **symbols** of unity, and also the symbol of the **Self**. In addition, the circle represents the totality and wholeness of the **psyche**, and may also indicate a **secret**, protective, or potentially spellbinding purpose. Circles also equate to the haloes of **Christ** and of the Christian **Saints** in religious iconography. Circular 'sun wheels' appear in many Neolithic **cave paintings** and **rock** engravings, predating any conceivable notion of the functioning **wheel**. Circles may sometimes have **anal** connotations, too. See **Mandala**
KEY LINE: 'The eye is the first circle; the horizon which it forms is the second; and throughout nature this primary figure is repeated without

end. It is the highest emblem in the cipher of the world.' (From Emerson's *Essays: First Series* 1841)

Circumcision Complex A **fear**, frequently reflected in **dreams**, of either the presence, or lack of it, of circumcision. Physical symbols like the eyelid, the fingernail, or the **toe** often stand in for the prepuce, the labia, or the clitoris in such cases. Circumcision, in its purely symbolical form, may indicate a wish to control, or cut off, desire, either by the **dreamer**, or an outside party. See **Castration Complex** & **Hymen Complex**

Circuses There is an element of controlled **chaos** about a circus, as well as a sense of indefinable threat – they are not just benevolent places, in other words, or **theatres** of enjoyment. Roman circuses, for instance, were all very well and good if one was not required to form a part of the entertainment. In addition to pleasure, therefore, they can also suggest venality and brutalization. See **Clowns**

Cities A city on a **mountain**, even in its most **skeletal** aspects, can represent cultural aspirations, or, alternatively, the 'region of the **soul**' in which the **Self** lives. **People** and things congregate around cities, and they are also places of temptation – 'Then the devil taketh him up into the holy city; and setteth him on a pinnacle of the temple.' (Mat. iv. 5). When populous cities appear in **dreams** they can indicate a desire for communion, or, in the case of a **deserted** city, our **fears** of **abandonment** – 'Once I passed through a populous city … yet now of all that city I remember only a woman …' (Walt Whitman 1819–92). In his original draft for this poem, Whitman had made his 'woman' a man, even further fuelling the oneiric sense of alienation which the poem (and composer Frederick Delius's musical setting of it) so beautifully encapsulates.
KEY LINE: 'In my sleep I saw a gothic city rising from a sea whose waves were stilled as in a stained-glass window.' (From Marcel Proust's *Le Côté de Guermantes* 1920)

Clams The appearance of clams in **dreams** frequently relates to the **shape** of, and the expectations aroused by, the female **vagina** (at least in the case of men). The contents of a clam may well equate with the **carrying** of a child, in **female** dream symbology, or with the capacity to say no in terms of the dispensing of **sexual** favours. A woman who fears that she is **frigid** may well 'clam up' when confronted by an over-assertive **male** sexual partner.

Claustrophobic Dreams These often equate to **pre-birth dreams** (intrauterine fantasies), and may reflect underlying **anxieties** or as yet undiagnosed respiratory complaints. See **Birth**

Claws Claws may be threatening, with their **danger** of scarification – one is 'armed' with a claw, after all – but they may also imply human interaction, as the verb to claw was for a long time synonymous with scratching, both aggressively, and in the form of 'you scratch my back and I'll scratch yours'. T. S. Eliot's **lines** 'I should have been a pair of ragged claws/Scuttling across the floors of silent seas' (From his 1917 poem *The Love Song of J. Alfred Prufrock*, lines 73/4), are the epitome of the **wish-fulfilment** fantasy, implying that there is perhaps something 'other' to which we might, not unreasonably, aspire.

Clay We are all made of symbolic clay, with the implication that we originate from the **earth** and shall one day return there. Certain Native American tribes, such as the Algonquins, believed that Kitche Manitou (the 'Great Spirit') formed Man out of clay and then baked him in a kiln. The first batch he overcooked, creating the **black** man. The second batch he undercooked, creating the **white** man. But the final batch he cooked perfectly, in the form of the **red** man. Thus Romans ix, 21: 'Hath not the potter power over the clay, of the same lump to make one vessel unto honour, and another unto dishonour?' The very formlessness of clay, which is capable of almost infinite transformation, can therefore act not only as a **symbol** of the power of the Godhead, but also as a convenient metaphor for our earthly aspirations.

Cleaning See **Cleansing**

Cleansing Cleaning and purging are often interrelated in dream terms, and both can have strong symbolical value. A **biblical** example might be **Jesus'** cleansing of the **temple** (John ii, 13–16) – he was purging the '**soul**' of the Church, of course, and not simply the money-changers and the dove-sellers who were abusing its premises. Similarly, in **dreams**, the act of cleansing suggests that there is something in the dreamer's **unconscious** that *needs* cleaning out.

Clergymen Clergymen are very often **linked** to the **dreamer**'s **brother**, and are (or at least should be) subject to similar **taboos**.

Cliffs The fear of **falling** over a cliff, equating with the **fear** of vertiginous heights, is a frequent **dream symbol**. We all fear **failure**, just as our **unconscious** minds fear **risk** (even though our well-trained conscious minds pooh-pooh the fact that we may be apprehensive). Going higher in a dream may symbolize the strength of our aspirations, while the **fear** of a sudden fall shows us what lurks underneath. See **Climbing**

Climbing The act of climbing can indicate the **ego** of the **dreamer** ascending towards an increased state of consciousness. Climbing can also be a **symbol** of ambition and of idealistic cravings. At certain times, too, the act of climbing can have **sexual** connotations relating back to infancy, and to the child climbing up on the **mother** or **father** and pressing against them, seeking comfort.

Cloaks Cloaks are usually **symbols** of mental coverings, or protective carapaces of the **psyche**. They may also be symbols of desired status, as in **teacher**'s gowns, or the flowing robes of dons and professors. See also **Clothes, Coats & Diplomas**

Clocks Clocks imply the passing of **time**. Stopped clocks may suggest **death**. Clocks that do not keep the correct time may represent the vanity of human wishes. Clocks in **dreams** are usually **anxiety** pointers, but they may also have religious connotations, in that their original clepe stemmed from the word for **church bells**, namely *cloca* in medieval Latin, *cloche* in French, and *glocke* in German. They may also, on occasion, symbolize the **heart**.

Closets Closets may represent the dreamer's **unconscious** mind. A partially open closet **door** might therefore suggest an encounter that the **dreamer** half dreads and half looks forward to – a situation that may go either way, in other words, with as yet undetermined ramifications.

Clothes Taking off clothes in a **dream** may, when viewed purely in **transference** terms, reflect a desire by the **dreamer** for frankness, or for being truthful about themselves. Clothes, of course, are a disguise (see **Masks**) and a signifier, as well as an **ornament**, and they may serve multiple capacities, of which protection from the elements may be one of the least important. In purely symbolical terms clothing can signify limitations of thought in relation to the **ego** – prejudices, conventional opinions, ingrained habits, etc., which may need to be shucked off if the dreamer is to move forwards. See also **Cloaks, Coats, Diplomas, Nakedness & Wardrobes**

Clouds The Taoists of Ancient China predated modern trends by viewing **white** clouds as lucky, and **dark** clouds as foretelling misfortune. In Buddhism, white clouds are the sheath of the Atman. Metaphorically speaking, clouds are **symbols** of **truth** and divinity, and their appearance in **dreams** is often linked to the **dreamer's** aspirations, and may, as a result, be taken to encapsulate ideals rather than strict realities.
KEY LINE: 'So clouds replenish'd from some bog below,/Mount in dark volumes, and descend in snow.' (From Alexander Pope's *The Dunciad*, Book ii, l. 363 1743)

Clover In old English folklore to **dream** of clover was particularly beneficial, especially for betrothed **couples**, who would have a happy and well-founded **marriage** as a result of the dream. Clover was perceived to have **magical** qualities, too, and even to promote or facilitate **visions** of **fairies**.

Clowns Clowns may appear at first glance to be moderators, but they may also constitute threatening presences. Clowns, too – and almost by definition – appear to be one thing while actually being something other. It may not be inapposite to mention here that clowns and comedians are frequently seen to suffer from **manic depression** in their everyday lives, and there is no doubt that those who **play** them or inhabit their personas carry a certain continual **weight** of expectation, which may, at times, be uncongenial and hard to fulfil. See **Circuses** & **Comical Dreams**

Clubs Clubs (the sort one strikes with) are not always blunt instruments, and the **unconscious** may very well be responding to them in their purely **archetypal** form, as **symbols** of the higher emotion overcoming lower emotions such as **jealousy**, selfishness, and inappropriate desires. Clubs in which **people** gather rarely appear in that particular form in **dreams**, simply because a group of individuals meeting together usually indicates differing aspects of the **dreamer**, rather than the gathering of unrelated **strangers** or acquaintances that such a dream image may at first seem to imply.

Coal Coal is full of paradoxes, for it carries within it both implications of **heat**, as in the **burning** of coal, and **cold**, as in the **water**-fuelled creation of coal from fossilized **tree** and **plant** residues. Coal also darkens and blackens, and may be used for **camouflage** purposes. This blackness throws up yet another **opposition** – that of **black** and **white** – to set beside hot and cold, **darkness** and **light**. Coal is natural and yet unnatural; amenable to **flame**, and yet hard to **handle**; buried deep underground, while originally stemming from light-loving, light-embracing origins. To that extent it represents the symbolical pattern of human life – from the **void**, to the neanic, and then back, once again, to the void.

Coats Coats may represent the contrived identity or persona that the **dreamer** presents to the outside **world** – the protective cover or **mask**, in other words, protecting what is on the inside from prying **eyes**. Coats, as in 'mantles', are also something that may be passed on, either through **inheritance**, or as an adjunct to **king**-making. **Freud** considered them **phallic**, while **Stekel** characterized their occurrence in a dream as being a **symbol** of love. See also **Cloaks, Clothes** & **Diplomas**

Cobwebs Cobwebs are inextricably linked to **myth**, as in the thread that Ariadne gave Theseus to guide him back out of the **labyrinth** after he had **killed** the Minotaur. Cobwebs can also imply traps, as in the **spider** waiting for the **fly**. A more positive connotation might be when a person finds themselves surrounded or overtaken by cobwebs, for cobwebs can also offer healing properties alongside their other more cliché-ridden, sinister-seeming implications.

Cocaine Cocaine is a highly addictive **drug** traditionally distilled from the **leaves** of the Andean coca shrub. In dream terms, cocaine tends towards **regression**, or regressive **dreams**, in which previously repressed or inhibited instincts are brought to the fore and are made to seem reasonable. Consistent overuse (which is more or less endemic, due to the addictive qualities of the drug) may eventually lead to **neurosis**.

Cocks A cock (the avian kind – see **penis** for the other) traditionally symbolizes vigilance and overbearing insolence, for it is easy, of course, for the cock to **crow** on his own dunghill ('*gallus in suo sterquilinio plurimum potest*') or for a man to 'cry cock' even though he has nothing whatsoever to boast about. To a Muslim, however, the cock may have a different significance, for Mohammed allegedly discovered a cock in the first **heaven** of such a size that its coxcomb touched the second heaven, and its call could rouse everything on earth except Man. It is said that when this cock ceases to crow, the day of **judgement** will be upon us. In Christian iconography the third crow of the cock symbolizes St Peter's denial of **Christ**. See **Roosters**

Cocoa Dreaming of cocoa may relate to **anal** erotic fixations (the comfort element, twinned with the **colour** and the suggestion of **oral** ingestion), connected to an underlying infantile **neurosis**. **Freud** made this link in a famous **case** study, and suggested, in addition, that it might be allied to **childhood** concepts of procreation involving either anal **birth**, or birth from the **mouth** as a result of **eating** (as sometimes occurs in **fairy tales**). See **Chocolate**

Cocteau, Jean (1889–1963) The French **writer**, **poet** and **surrealist** Jean Cocteau believed explicitly in the power of **dreams**, not least in their use to a poet. Such a person, he maintained, 'is at the disposal of the **night**. His role is humble. He must clean **house** and await its due visitation.'

Coffee Coffee (from the Turkish *Kauhi or Kahveh*) has become one of the **earth**'s great comfort **foods**, even though it offers but little formal nourishment. To that extent, the drinking of it equates with non-procreative **sex** and comfort **eating**, in that we do it by choice and not through necessity. This comfort element was taken to its illogical, ritualistic conclusion by the Ardennes French, who customarily drank no fewer than ten **cups** of coffee after dinner, with each cup being afforded a different **name**. Not a formula for untroubled **sleep**, one might suppose.

Coffins Coffins and sarcophagi tend to reflect the **ego** of the **dreamer**, in the sense that one's view of oneself (or one's view of how others should see one) may ultimately be reflected in the pomp and expense involved in a **funeral** (*ergo* the glorification of the defunct, or the glorification of defunct values). To that extent, coffins are **symbols** of the **past**, and of buried **history**. See **Burials**

Cognitive Theory Cognitive theory holds that **dreams** are simply a reflection of our waking concerns, and as such are only one of a number of means we can use to understand, perceive, or interact with our everyday environment. Cognitive **psychologists** look for obvious themes and

patterns within dreams, and believe that these are amenable to codification. Suitably dissected dreams, in other words, can allow us to make sense of the **world**.

Coins Coins symbolize both the provision of and the payment for services. They can also represent value, in that to this day in certain cultures a particularly beautiful or desirable **wife** might wear coins about her person in the form of **necklaces** and headgear to demonstrate the value her **husband**, or her **family**, places upon her. A coin (an *obol*) was also traditionally given to Charon before the conveyance of any dead person across the **River** Styx – this coin was placed in the dead person's **mouth**, from where the aged Charon would pluck it before agreeing to undertake the **ferry**-crossing to Hades.

Cold Cold and **heat** may be viewed as fundamentally **oppositional** qualities, covering similar ground to **love** and hate, good and **evil**, movement and inertia, matter and **spirit** – the appearance of one, in other words, presupposes the existence of the other.
KEY LINE: 'Here sadness rules; and here thy drooping head/Instead of down shall have a frozen bed:/Love rocks thy panting cradle; and to bring/Thy thoughts asleep, melancholy shall sing.' (Thomas Lovell Beddoes 1803–49)

Cole, Thomas (1801–48) A monumental painting, 54 × 84 inches (137 × 213.5 cm), Cole's *The Architect's Dream* (1840) shows an architect dreaming on a Doric plinth, the entire known panoply of **world** architecture disappearing into infinity behind him. An early member of the American Hudson River School, Cole painted *Dream* for architect Ithiel Town, who belatedly decided he didn't want it.
KEY LINE: 'In the early stage of my malady, the splendours of my dreams were indeed architectural: and I beheld such pomp of cities and palaces …' (From Thomas de Quincey's *Confessions of an English Opium Eater* 1822)

Coleridge, Samuel Taylor (1772–1834). The English Romantic **poet** Samuel Taylor Coleridge claims, in *Kubla Khan: or, a Vision in a Dream* (1798), that his great poem, *Kubla Khan*, was the result of a **hallucinatory dream**, triggered by a dose of **opium** he had taken as the result of an indisposition. When he awoke the next **morning**, the entire poem was clear in his **head**, but he was disastrously disturbed in full creative flow by 'a person on business from Porlock', and he only ever managed to get down the tiniest part of his **vision**.
KEY LINE: 'My dreams become the substances of my life.' (From a letter from Coleridge to William Wordsworth dated 1803)

Collapsing Edifices **collapsing** and things **falling** are very often taken as **symbols** of pre- or post-sexual penile diminution in the **male** – brewer's droop, in other words. All joking apart, the **fear** of collapse is a fundamental human frailty, and is inherent in every human undertaking. Physical collapse is often symbolized by falling **buildings** and falling **houses**, while mental collapse may find itself objectified by **storms** or other natural **disasters** which threaten the stability we all crave.

Collective Unconscious The portion of the **psyche** which contains and transmits our common psychological inheritance. The collective unconscious contains **symbols** that are not individual, but collective in **nature**, emanating from primeval **dreams** and creative fantasies whose origins are buried in the mysteries of the **past**. It is therefore prelogical and inferential, rather than logical and rational. See **Telepathic Dreams**

Colleges London's infamous Newgate **prison** was known as the 'college' during the 18th and 19th centuries, and to 'take one's final degree' was a euphemism for being **hanged**. Colleges have positive connotations, too, although one's **instinct** is that they are very often an adjunct of **anxiety** when they appear in **dreams**. Colleges may also indicate a desire for personal growth, or an aspiration upwards – sometimes, even, ambitions unfulfilled.

Colonna, Francisco Colonna, a 15th-century Franciscan **monk**, wrote a fantasy called *The Dream of Poliphilo*, which was illustrated with numerous woodcuts, one of which featured a **dragon** (Satan, of course), conjured up in a **dream**, pursuing the hapless Poliphilo through a **monastery** towards a looming, darkened archway. A close investigation of the woodcut reveals that the terrified Poliphilo's bladder has let him down, for a puddle of urine lies on the ground beneath his fleeing figure. See **Secretions**

Colours As well as the collective symbolic significance of certain colours, their individual associations to the dreamer also need to be addressed if any sense is to be made from them. Some **dreamers** consistently see bright or cheerful colours in their **dreams**, while others see only drab colours, or dream in **black** and **white**. Drab colours tend to reflect **depression** and gloom, while bright colours represent elation, or the manic stage of a depressive cycle. (Go to individual colours for a more detailed analysis) See **Manic Depression**

Traditional colour symbolism gives us the following:

Black: Ignorance and Witlessness
Blue: Intellect and Understanding
Green: Astral Growth and Spiritual Development
Purple: Wisdom and Acumen
Rose Red: Love and Tenderness
Red: Power and Ambition (allied to Mars)
Scarlet: Life Energy and Fundamental Vitality
Yellow: Kingship and Authority

White: Purity and Perfection

Columns Columns, as well as being nominally **phallic**, also point us towards higher things. Statues of famous or beloved **people** are placed above us in this way in public settings, and the Stylites lived on columns (or pillars) in order to be nearer to **heaven**. Even the **Tower** of Babel was, in its perverse way, an aspirational **symbol**.

Combs Traditionally, a many-toothed comb was a **symbol** of knowledge and of evolutionary change. The act of combing, in a **dream**, as well as having the usual **narcissistic** overtones, may also imply a **cleansing** process, or the desire to be clean. Also, more literally, the disentangling of something or somebody, particularly when performed by a woman.

Comets Comets encapsulate elementally disruptive forces, and are thus primary instillers of **anxiety**. 'What if a comet were to strike the **earth**? Would we go the same way as the **dinosaurs**?' They also appear when least expected and from a largely unknown direction, and we are reliant on others for news of their coming. Traditionally, too, comets were seen as ill-omened, foretelling great and possibly undesirable change.

Comical Dreams Comical dreams may (paradoxically) reflect important issues in the dreamer's mind that they wish to belittle or downplay in some way. As a result of this, comical dreams are rarely, if ever, intrinsically funny, and may often be manifestations of a desire to avoid or modulate justifiable guilt feelings that still haunt the dreamer's **unconscious** as a result of repressed or forgotten occurrences.

Coming Coming to a place, in **dream** terms, may often be equated with the achievement of an **orgasm**. There may also be a sense of completion, perhaps in terms of a duty performed. See **Arrival**

Commanders A commander is often a dream euphemism for **God**. See **Leaders**

Communes Communes reflect a desire for fellowship and support, but there are also likely to be **sexual** connotations which may hint at certain underlying polygamous tendencies inherent (if, for the most part, unacknowledged) in many otherwise monogamous **people**.

Companions An alternative **symbol** for the **shadow** or **double**. The appearance of companions in a **dream** may also **reflect** other aspects of ourselves that we may feel **separated** from, but which are still close enough to attract our notice.

Compasses Compasses are designed to show us the way, but when we dream of them they may have the exact opposite meaning – i.e. that we are **lost**, and need, rather than already have, guidance.

Compensatory Dreams Jung believed that, on occasion, our **dreams** could act as compensations for conscious attitudes – of superiority, perhaps, or lack of proper respect. 'Only the wounded physician heals,' was one of his favourite sayings. See **Body Image**

Complexes When repressed, emotionally-charged ideas appear, disguised, in conscious forms, to dominate normal thoughts and behaviours. **Jung** believed that the active interpretation of **dreams** could act as an objective correlative to such ideas, and, in certain cases, dilute or negate them.

Compulsion An overriding urge (verging on morbidity) to act in opposition to our conscious desires.

Computers Computers may be equated with the **body**, and the **secrets** they hold with the secrets we all wish to **seal** up or **lock** away behind unbreakable code-words or other forms of encryption. They are equally as subject as the human body to viruses, old age and antiquation, and equally as vulnerable to **attacks** by others. The main difference is that they are not fundamentally self-fuelling, as the human body is, and they are therefore not able to function without a certain measure of human intervention, so, in that sense, they are more akin to precocious infants than to fully-grown adults. See **Banks**

Concentration The act of concentration may sometimes reflect a desire to **urinate** or **defecate**. A lack of concentration may reflect a fear of incontinence.

Condensation A **Freudian** term relating to the variety of ideas that may be contained within a single dream image, depending on its associations. These, he felt, might serve as disguises between moral and instinctive conflicts, and need, in consequence, to be unpicked. **Dreams** are therefore the products of multiplied condensations, and may have several explanations – some essential, and some contributory. When objects or ideas metamorphose during the course of a dream, it is called 'incomplete condensation'. See also **Displacement**, **Dream Work**, **Representability** & **Secondary Revision**
KEY LINE: 'The key to dream interpretation is the recognition of resemblances.' (Aristotle 384–22 BC)

Condoms Condoms may reflect a desire to protect ourselves – to **coat** ourselves in a protective **layer**, while at the same time persisting with the enjoyment of our pleasures – 'to have our **cake** and **eat** it' as the saying goes.

Conductors A **symbol** of the 'father'. Taken further, a conductor may symbolize someone who takes over responsibility for others, and to that extent they equate, to some extent, with **captains, chiefs** and **commanders** when they appear in **dreams**.

Confessions In some ways **dreams** themselves are confessional, in that our **unconscious** is revealing to us certain things, certain aspects of ourselves, of which we may otherwise be unaware. Specific confessions, though, would appear to imply the existence of subordinated, possibly even inappropriate, **guilt**, and the original source of this guilt needs to be addressed.

Confirmatory Dreams Dreams dreamt only after discussion with a second party – **dreams** that, in **Freud**'s phrase, 'lag after analysis'.

Conflict Immediate or of-the-moment conflicts of the sort that are frequently thrown up in **dreams** are often predicated on infantile experiences. These infantile experiences are then re-enacted in a **neurotic** way in a desire to re-experience the comfort of **childhood** innocence and ignorance – they are, in effect, pre-programmed reproductions of childhood situations. Conflict may also represent the conscious mind's endeavour to **defeat**, deflate, or otherwise suppress the **unconscious**.

Conscience An aspect of the **superego** that modifies instinctual expression in favour of so-called reasoned behaviour.

Consciousness According to **Jung**, consciousness does not create itself, but wells from unknown depths. 'It is like a child that is born daily out of the **primordial womb** of the **unconscious**.' See **Pre-Conscious State** & **Unconscious**

Conservation of Energy An **archetypal** image, common to all cultures, and duly found in ancient rites, **initiations**, **alchemical** formulae, **baptisms** and **rites-of-passage**. For a sublime example (of an admittedly extreme case) of the conservation of 'precious bodily fluids' syndrome, an early viewing of Stanley Kubrick's 1963 movie *Dr Strangelove; or, How I Learned to Stop Worrying and Love the Bomb* – the early scenes with Peter Sellers's Group Captain Lionel Mandrake, and Sterling Hayden's General Jack D. Ripper – is heartily recommended.

Consolation Dreams See **Post-Operative Dreams**

Constantine The Great (274–337) In 312 AD, on the eve of his great battle against his rival, Maxentius, the Sun **God**-worshipping Constantine had an unexpected **dream**. **Jesus** appeared to him, and asked him to place the *chi-rho* (a **symbol** of **Christ**, equivalent to the X and the P of ancient Greece) onto the **shields** of his followers. The next day, Constantine saw a great **cross** superimposed on the **sun**, with the words *in hoc signo vinces* ('with this sign you will prevail') written upon it. He went on to win the Battle of Milvian **Bridge**, and immediately issued the Edict of

Milan (313 AD), according freedom of belief to Christians throughout the Roman Empire. The Emperor was himself baptized into the Christian Faith shortly before his **death** on 22nd May 337, becoming a **key** figure in the foundation of medieval Christian Europe.

Constipation Dreaming of constipation would seem to imply that something important which needs to come out, isn't. This may, on the surface, seem amusing, but the image may be disguising an important logjam in the dreamer's life – a logjam which desperately needs to be released, and of whose origin and existence the **dreamer** may be rationally unaware.

Construction Construction implies a desire to improve oneself, or to strive towards higher things. It may also suggest a need to reshape, or reform the **body**. This would be particularly telling, for instance, in the case of an obese person who consistently **dreams** of building a **house** to their own specifications. This would then be the **unconscious**'s way of lessening that person's **anxiety** about their condition, thus allowing them to **sleep**.

Contact 'Contact' images, such as those represented by using the **telephone**, sharing a meal, **travelling** together, rescuing another person, or **dancing**, often represent the **sexual** act.

Contests Contests (see **Contact**) may have **sexual** overtones, as the pitting of one person against another implies a degree of intimacy. The actual sexual act itself is in some **archetypal** way akin to a **race**, in which, from the very beginning, each party to the proceedings is striving towards a specific and desirable end, dictated by their biological 'a-gender'.

Contraceptives See **Condoms**

Convents Depending on one's point of view, convents can be either positive places, in which **prayer** and meditation occur, and which are of general benefit to mankind, or threatening places, in which inhibitions are rife, and hypocrisy all-consuming. Either way, they seem to be places in which **shelter** is sought, and this is probably the most important element of their symbolic value in a **dream**.

Conversation **Freud** maintained that fragments of conversation recalled from **dreams** are actually fragments of real conversations that have taken place some time previously in the course of the **dreamer**'s life. Many **psychoanalysts** dispute this finding, but few dispute that such word condensations, mutilated words, and **neologism** coinings are fundamental components of **dream work**, and have important significance in **dream interpretation**. An example of word mutilation might be 'Dresther', implying both 'dread' and a person's name. Or even 'beautilation', implying both mutilation and the possibility of beautifying oneself as a result – let's say via piercing, **tattooing**, or infibulation.

Convicts Convicts are usually threatening (think of Abel Magwitch, in Charles Dickens' 1860/1 novel *Great Expectations*), and imply the existence of **superego** forces in control of the **id**. When we **dream** of a convict, or convicts, some hidden aspect of ourselves would seem to identify with the felon, and feel empathetically threatened by society at large (even, curiously, when we think the convict may be **guilty**). In the case of a **female** dreaming of a convict, there may, in addition, be a possible **sexual** leitmotif threading its way through the dream (see **Burglars**), as well as aspects of a saviour **neurosis** (the desire to change somebody for their own good and for the self-esteem of the **saviour**, rather than for the good of society in general).

Cooking Cooking and **alchemy** are closely connected in **dreams**, for both are transmutative. Disparate elements are gathered together to make for a satisfying whole, and the end result is definitely more than the sum of its parts. The semantic aspect of the word 'cook' may also be significant, as in 'cooking the **books**', or 'your **goose** is cooked'. See **Cooks**

Cooks According to Athenaeus in his second-century-BC *Deipnosophistai* (or *The Learned Banquet*), cooks were the first **kings** of the **earth**. There is something almost regal about a **male** cook in his **kitchen**, **phallic hat** aslant and arms akimbo, **cock** of his roost. This alpha role carries over into the dream-world, and often counts as part of an anagogic **wish-fulfilment fantasy**, predicated on a desire to be well viewed by one's fellow human beings – to provide **food** is, after all, one of the fundamental roles of the **head** of the **family** (something to which nearly all men secretly aspire). Cooks can also be threatening, and this, too, has its role to play in the cook's phallic presence, rather as a **lion**, confident in his strength, will amiably cuff his cubs or his lionesses into place before rolling lazily back to **sleep**. It's the **symbol** of the benevolent dictator, who provides his **people** with everything they need just so long as they ritually recognize his supreme dominance – gainsay him, and his **claws** will emerge. See **Cooking**

Copper Copper was once the alchemical **totem** for **Venus**, **goddess** of **love** and courtship – and think, too, of the protective uses still adhering to copper bracelets in terms of arthritis – but it is also an ancient euphemism for **money**, and the two may find themselves linked or admixed when they appear in a **dream**, even though the **dreamer** may **count** themselves formally ignorant of the **alchemical** connection. Even now, in both the US and Britain, a 'copper' is also a **policeman**.

Coral Coral was felt to have many beneficent and protective qualities. A coral **necklace** worn to **bed** was thought to prevent **nightmares**, and coral **beads** were felt to be particularly beneficial to **children**, protecting against 'fits, sorcery, **charms** and **poison**'.

Cords Dreaming of cords straightaway brings to mind **umbilical cords**, and the connection to the **mother**, but there is also a connection to the **serpent** (the **symbol** of seductiveness), and to the possible mistaking of the cord as real substance (truth), in favour of the cord as mere symbol (appearance). If this sounds too esoteric, it should be remembered that **dreams** very often work upon a quasi-metaphysical level, and that inferences may be both literal and figurative.

Corks Corks are ejected from **bottles** and bob up in **water** (both symbolical equivalents of the **birth** process), but they also stopper potentially threatening things (as in Aladdin's **lamp**) and prevent them from **escaping**. There is a **sexual** element, too, involved in thrusting a cork back into a bottle, an element that is carried through to the popping of a **champagne** cork.

Corn Corn equates with nourishment, for in western society it forms the foundation of **bread**. Symbolically, it represents the higher mental qualities, in that it has been sown into the **earth**, from whence it thrusts its way inexorably upwards towards the **light**.

Corners Corners prevent **escape**. They suggest, too, that things are not always **straight** and easy. To 'corner' someone or something means to dominate them, and nobody likes to be driven or sent into a corner. Corner-**stones**, however, were felt to be positive things (uniting two disparate elements into one), and **Christ** was known, in consequence, as the corner-**stone** which united the Jews and the Gentiles, a concept originally generated in Job xxxviii, 6–7: 'Whereupon are the foundations thereof fastened? Or who laid the corner stone thereof; When the morning **stars** sang together, and all the sons of God shouted for joy?' In the **world** of coursing (possibly society's most ancient **sport**), the ability of the **hare** (puss) to corner faster than the courser provided the edge that allowed it to escape 98 times out of a 100. All these disparate elements adhere, in some form or another, to the **symbol** of the corner, when it appears in **dreams**.

Corpses Corpses, in a **dream**, imply the existence of something dead, or of something that the **dreamer** *wishes* were dead. In purely symbolic terms, corpses suggest the personality in its lowest possible aspect, bereft of Divinity and the Divine **spark**. Corpses have traditionally been considered impure, particularly by the Hindus and the Zoroastrians, and there is a strong element in Buddhist thought that holds this earthly coil to be purely transient. St Luke, too, takes this view, in ix, 24: 'For whosoever will save his life shall lose it: but whosoever will lose his life for my sake, the same shall save it.' The image of a corpse being eaten by **birds** is a very common one (quite literally so, to the Parsees), with the birds symbolizing the elementals of the lower plane in their task of freeing the spiritual **ego** (or **soul**) for its flight away from earthly corruption.

Corridors Corridors are ineradicably **uterine**, and carry within themselves inevitable revocations of the **birth passage**. They can also be transitional areas, or nomanslands, between one physical or mental state and another. To that extent they are **limbo**-like, when they appear in **dreams**, and suggest, almost by default, the necessity for movement if stasis is to be prevented.

Cosmetics Cosmetics equate with, while at the same time being antonymic to, **camouflage**. They are designed to highlight aspects of an individual that would otherwise go unnoticed, but, when well applied, they can also be used to direct attention away from certain areas that the individual might feel ill-served by. Cosmetics, for instance, are used to make the dead palatable to the living, and they may also be used on **buildings**, as in, for instance, Matthew xxiii, 27's 'whited sepulchres, which indeed appear beautiful outward, but are within full of dead men's bones, and of all uncleanness.'

Cosmic Man Cosmic Man (the First Man, or the Super-**Soul**) equates with the basic principle of the **world**, embodied in the Judaic Adam, the Hindu Purusha, the Chinese P'an Ku, and the Persian Gayomart. His principle is fourness, fourfoldness, or the **quaternity** – for example, **East**, **West**, **North** and **South**; **Red**, **Black**, **White** and **Yellow**; or the **Beginning**, the Middle and the End brought together into the unity of One. His **female** counterpart is the **Great Mother**.

Cotton The appearance of cotton in a **dream** most probably refers to 'cottoning on' to something or someone, particularly if the cotton finds itself attached to an individual person or object. There may also be a suggestion of Ariadne's thread (see **Cobwebs**), or even to the **umbilicus** (see **Cords**).

Couches Couches to some extent equate with **beds**, with the usual **sexual** byplay. In the animal kingdom, the **male** couches before **killing**, while the **female** also mirror couches before mating. In embroidery a couch implies filigree (the threading of something through something else), and a **knight** will couch his **phallic** lance before an **attack** that may, conceivably, puncture his opponent. For the male to couch is therefore seen as dominant, while for the female to couch is seen as passive or submissive. Such established **archetypes** may seem under threat, but the **unconscious** is generally impervious to political and social diktat, and one of the main functions of **dream work** is to ignore temporary moral fashion (except in terms of its symbolic influence, needless to say) in favour of a longer and more psychologically enduring archetypal significance.

Counting Counting can equate with anticipation, in **dreams** – the anticipation of an **inheritance**, for instance, or of a **death**, or perhaps the morbid counting of remaining **family** members. Counting frequently presents itself illogically, as in the counting of apparently random objects which at first seem to have no special significance to the **dreamer**. Their very randomness is significant, however, and their meaning needs to be teased out so that the often inappropriate **anxieties** underlying them may be neutralized.

Countryside The countryside may represent a blissful place to **escape**, full of desirable activities, or it may represent a fearful, threatening environment, full of unwelcoming yokels – which of these two aspects the **dream** chooses is entirely dependent on the **dreamer**'s point of view. The whole thing becomes a great deal more interesting, of course, if the dream subverts convention or otherwise **plays** against type by choosing an aspect that appears to go against the **grain** of the dreamer's convictions. See **Interchangeability** & **Interpretation by Opposites**

Couples Dreaming of couples may seem to **fall** most easily under the **wish-fulfilment** scenario (i.e. the **dreamer** desires to form part of a couple, and their **dream** is a rendition of that desire), but the appearance of a couple may also, on occasion, represent an undesired situation – even a symbolical harking back to the perceived exclusion of the **child** by the **parents**, possibly as a result of the witnessing of a **primal scene**. Couples, by their very nature, exclude more than they include.

Courtyards Courtyards are usually open **spaces** surrounded by the '**body**' of the house, and their presence in **dreams** may reflect this corporeal aspect quite literally, in that the courtyard may represent the **stomach** or even the back. The 'imprisoning' aspect of a courtyard also needs to be taken into account – one is inevitably overlooked, while there is, quite possibly, no view out. To that extent there may also be a **uterine** or **pre-birth** connection to such a dream.

Cowards The appearance of a coward in a **dream** almost inevitably represents some self-referential aspect of the **dreamer**, or some action that the dreamer has either undertaken (or failed to undertake) and that they are ashamed of. There may also be a voyeuristic element to such a dream, in that the 'coward' element refers to the perceived public view of the dreamer rather than to the reality – a situation analogous to that of John Clements' Harry Faversham, in Zoltan Korda's film of *The Four Feathers* (1939).

Cowboys Cowboys are **wish-fulfilments** personified, in that they never really existed except in the imagination of the **writers**, directors and professional **yarn**-tellers of old Hollywood. They are an entirely imagined species, in other words, conjured up through **archetypal** need. It is only in recent **years** that some effort has been put into defusing the **myth** of the cowboy, and injecting a little reality into the **picture**. **Self**-respecting **dreamers**, though, will have none of this, and the cowboy resolutely remains one of the most comforting of **id** placebos – a sort of pacifier of the plains.

Cows See **Oxen**

Crabs Crabs move sideways, which means that they often represent **inhibitions** in **dreams**, or a desire to return to the **past**. There is also the **cancer** connection (i.e. the fear of **illness**), and the inevitable association with crabbiness. The **Great Mother** is sometimes represented by a crab.

Cracks Cracks can be either vulval (for obvious reasons), or they can imply **flaws** or fragilities. Cracks, by their very definition, inevitably spread, and to that extent they can constitute a warning to **dreamers** of some inherent **weakness** in an otherwise sound structure. See **Vaginas**

Cradles To **dream** of cradles may imply, quite literally, a desire to have a **baby** or to become a **parent**, but there may also be a **wish** present to be 'cradled', or otherwise nurtured, oneself. Whether the cradle is full or **empty** is also significant, particularly in the case of a woman's dream, when an empty cradle might imply a **fear** of **miscarriage**, or the dread of sterility. Should the baby in the cradle be **alien** to the woman in some way – *pace* Roman Polanski's *Rosemary's Baby* (1968) – there may be an implication that she is not entirely **happy** with her **husband**, or with the putative '**father**' of her **child**.

Crashes Crashes, derailments, and sudden crises are the very stuff of **dreams**, and often predate or pre-indicate coming, or feared, conditions. The smashing together of two objects can also exemplify the **sexual** act – even the **fear** of **virginity** (in a **male**) or the fear of losing one's virginity (in a **female**).

Craters In Buddhist thought craters are **symbols** of the World-**soul** (the Hindu Atman), and to that extent are symbolic of the Higher **Self**. In a secular sense, craters inevitably refer back to blemishes on the **skin** of something (the **moon**, the **face**, an **orange**, the otherwise smooth surface of a **planet**), and may therefore suggest a **fear** of imperfection.

Crayons Crayons carry within themselves the concept of a message, or alternatively of drawn **symbols** or communications. They are also, quite inevitably, **phallic**.

Craziness Craziness (or lunacy, or mental decadence, or senile dementia, or schizoid disintegration) is something many otherwise sane people **fear**, in that succumbing to it appears, even more than physical **illness**, to threaten our fundamental personalities. There is a real argument that our personality is the only thing that we 'possess' – that we can, with some justification, call our own – and it is therefore hardly surprising that we feel vulnerable when confronted by the possibility of **losing** it. One has only to think of a mind the calibre of **writer** and moral **philosopher** Iris Murdoch, and its sad descent into the moraine of Alzheimer's Disease, to understand how the **unconscious** mind may quake at the prospect of no longer running its own **shop**.

Cream   Cream may, at first glance, most obviously equate with **semen**, or even with vaginal fluid (see **Secretions**), but it may just as well refer to other desired objects, such as the cream on top of the **milk**, or the cream of the **crop**. Semantic considerations may also enter the equation, such as the close connection between the words 'cream' and 'scream' (with all their inherent **sado-masochistic** overtones).

Creative Dreams Psychologists tend to view **artists**, composers and **writers** as conducting a never-ending **battle** with their encroaching **neuroses** through the liberating medium of creative **repetition**. As each such attempt is inevitably doomed to **failure**, it is only through the actual process of confessional reiteration that the artist can find peace. It is precisely because of the repetitive **nature** of the artist's struggle, of course, that their **dreams** are of such significance to them, frequently completing, or suggesting the means to complete a troublesome work. Examples abound of creative artists (and novelists in particular, it seems), taking their **problems** to **bed** with them and **waking** up in the **morning** with the problems solved. The **unconscious** mind is particularly conducive to connections, and E. M. Forster's dictum of 'only connect ...' beautifully sums up the lurking dynamic behind most artistic aspiration. See **Berryman**, **Bunyan**, **Chagall**, **Coleridge**, **Daydreams**, **Dr Jekyll and Mr Hyde**, **Goethe**, **Greene**, **Shelley**, **Tartini**
KEY LINE: 'I opened mine with terror. The idea so possessed my mind, that a thrill of fear ran through me, and I wished to exchange the ghastly image of my fancy for the realities around ...' (From Mary Shelley's *Introduction to Frankenstein* 1831)

Credit Cards   One supposes that dreaming of credit **cards** might suggest a **wish-fulfilment** fantasy (or even the fear of **debt**), but the shape of the credit card is also important, as these rectangular obloids have increasingly taken over the role of **money** in modern society, with all the comfort aspects and **anxiety** entrainments that money once stood for. See **Coins**

Creeks   Creeks may equate with **urination**, with **wounds**, or with the tributaries of the **heart**. When associated with sound in a **dream**, there may possibly be a semantic or linguistic link with the word 'creaks'.

Crests   Crests, coxcombs and plumes (see **Plumage**) of all sorts tend to be **male symbols**, both in the human and in the **animal world**. There is a strong vanity aspect to their meaning, as even when the crest is a sign of nobility, it still carries within itself the fleeting implication of vainglory or self-satisfaction. The term 'crest of the **wave**' suggests not only **victory**, but also the **pit** that potentially lies in wait underneath – the existence of **death** within life, so to **speak**. For many centuries it was the male's role to ignore the fear of death in favour of glory, and to that extent any recent pejorative aspects of the word 'crest' should be leavened with our human need for glory, and for the altruistic recognition of glory in others.

Cricket To many, cricket equates with fair play and gentlemanly virtues – something bad, or the manifestation of shabby behaviour, 'just isn't cricket'. There is a manuscript in the Bodleian **Library**, dated 1344, showing **monks playing** with a *cric* (a **crutch** or **staff**) and a **ball**, and this monkish element has carried through to the present **day**, in that cricket, although occasionally played by **females**, is quintessentially a **male** game. Even the **symbol** of the ball and the **bat** (not to mention the **stumps**) is a virile one, and there is an inevitable element of **emasculation** in getting somebody out (putting them 'out of the **game**'). The collective element of the fielding side equates neatly with the **hunting** parties of our **ancestors**, with the batsmen representing the prey, and the bowler the huntsman, or carrier of the **bow**. The fact that **tides** can turn in cricket, just as out hunting, is satisfying archetypally, and the respect traditionally shown one's opponent, both during and after the game, was probably initiated by the respect traditionally shown towards one's **animal** prey by enlightened hunters (e.g. prehistoric **cave painters**, who most likely attributed **magical** qualities to such images). All such **archetypal** aspects may find themselves reflected in the use **dreams** make of **symbols** such as cricket, and, in addition, there is the figurative aspect of 'squaring the **circle**' to take into account – if the movement of the bowler and the batsmen and the fielders is viewed in the graphic abstract, a satisfyingly circular, **mandala**-like configuration may be descried.

Criminals Sancto de Sanctis maintained (allegedly as the result of much study) that the **dreams** of criminals were unusually peaceful, and sometimes even verging on the beautiful, whilst the dreams of innocent **people** were horrifying in the extreme. See **Burglars**, **Criminal Thoughts** & **Gangsters**

Criminal Thoughts Criminal thoughts are usually next to unrecognizable in the **dream** context, as the **unconscious mind** will tend to protect the **dreamer** from the possible dreamed consequences of their criminal actions. See **Burglars**, **Chemistry**, **Criminals** & **Gangsters**
KEY LINE: 'Wherever a man commits a crime, God finds a witness ... Every secret crime has its reporter.' (From Ralph Waldo Emerson's *Uncollected Lectures* 1932)

Cripples Dreaming of a cripple, or of someone who is disabled in some way, usually refers to something that is holding the **dreamer** back from doing what they wish to do. The **symbol** of the cripple, or of the amputee (see **Amputation**), is a powerful one, and harks back to underlying **fears** of being unwanted (i.e. of no use to wider society), or of being castrated (see **Castration Complex**). We all have fantasies of perfection, and our

dreams are there to puncture them, protecting the **id** from the consequences of its own inconsequent desires.

Critics Critics are both hearkened to and feared – courted and hated. These two aspects are probably what the **dreamer** picks up on most when dreaming of a critic, **judge** or arbiter, for the three are interrelated. The critic in a **dream** is usually the dreamer themselves, and what they draw attention to will be of undoubted significance even when seen elliptically (See **Ellipsis**).
KEY LINE: 'He that fears his blotches may offend,/Speaks gently of the pimples of his friend.'(From Horace's *Satires* Book i, satire 3, line 73)

Crocodiles A crocodile traditionally symbolizes hypocrisy, possibly on account of the smile that appears to be on its **face** even when it is **eating** you. See **Alligators**

Crooked Lines Crooked lines equate with havering and obfuscation. Their appearance in **dreams** (often using the **symbol** of a meandering **river** or a circuitous **road**) suggests that we may not wish to confront the results of our own actions.

Crooks See **Criminals**

Crops Crops imply fruitfulness – the concrete results of labours past. Blighted crops suggest that we have not prepared correctly, or that we have **hurried**, and therefore spoiled, some important element in our lives. Crops suggest both the **past**, the present and the future (almost by default) and to that extent they are a universal **symbol** of the different cycles of our lives, and how one inextricably interrelates with the other.

Cross, The A deeply symbolic, pre-Christian concept that equates, in many ways, with the **tree** and the **lingam** in its focus on creativity and growth. In Christian iconography, the cross also symbolizes **death** and **resurrection**. The four points of the cross may also **lead** us towards the idea of **quaternity**, or 'fourness', a concept that played a great role in numerous ancient **religions** and philosophies (including the Hermetic philosophy of the Middle Ages) before being superseded by the Christian concept of the **Trinity**. The cross can also stand in for the **superego** in a **dream** context.

Crossings Crossings are usually moments of **danger** – we are in a transitional phase, and consequently vulnerable to unexpected setbacks.

Crossroads Crossroads imply moments of decision or of crisis. We are faced with a series of possible choices, and must decide how to act, or stasis will set in. All those who were excluded from Holy Rites (up until the time of George IV of England, circa 1820) were traditionally buried at a crossroads (saving **suicides**, who were buried on verges or on highways with a stake driven through the **heart**) – to that extent at least cross-roads were quasi-holy places, symbolic of the **cross**, and of pre-Christian **quaternity**.

Crowds Crowds may, paradoxically, indicate a desire for secrecy on the part of the **dreamer** – we can, of course, lose ourselves in crowds. They may also suggest a **fear** of individuation and a desire to belong. See **Interpretation by Opposites**

Crowns As well as suggesting the possible existence of a *folie de grandeur* on the part of the **dreamer**, the wearing of a crown may also imply a desire to be chosen or singled out from the **crowd**. Symbolically, crowns equate with the realization of the supremacy of the state of the **soul**, and the possibility of Divine Rule. **Jesus'** crowning with **thorns** was a symbolical attempt to devalue the Higher by a false veneration of the Lower, roughly equivalent to what the French call a *nostalgie de la boue*, and to what we English term 'enlightened social engineering'.

Crows A crow symbolizes longevity. They are also **death birds**, renowned for following **armies** and predating off the detritus of **war**. KEY LINE: 'With rakish eye and plenished crop,/Oblivious of the farmer's gun,/Upon the naked ash-tree top/The crow sits basking in the sun.' (From William Canton's *To the Cuckoo* 1845)

Crucifixion Crucifixion equates with martyrdom and **sacrifice** in **dream** terms, whether we are thinking about the crucifixion of **Jesus**, Spartacus, Andrey Tarkovsky's filmic *Andrei Rublev*, or the two thieves. Crucifixion itself was designed by the Romans to be both public and undignified – a Roman citizen could not be crucified, as the **punishment** was reserved for **slaves** and **criminals**. In Christian symbology crucifixion represents the final anguish of the incarnate **soul** on its **journey** towards perfection. See **Cross & Martyrs**

Cruising Cruising may have positive overtones for certain of the homo-sexually inclined (despite the threat of **AIDS**), but it has distinctly pejo-rative overtones for some non-**homosexuals**, who consider it a threat, either to society at large, or to their own stated view of their own sexual identity. The fear of overt sexuality is deeply ingrained in many **people**, and the rise and rise of (a largely solipsistic) **pornography** is merely a symptom of that discomfort. Even the more traditional view of cruising – as of going nowhere fast, whilst still enjoying the ride – sits uneasily with the work ethic and religiously-inspired **guilt** that many feel when confronted by their own baser instincts.

Crutches Crutches suggest that we need help – that we are **fragile** in some way, and incapable of standing on our own two **feet** without out-side support. The **symbol** of the throwing away of crutches (both **biblically** and in evangelical/faith-healing **circles**) is a powerful one, suggesting that we are taking control of our own lives by the simple expedient of arrogating that control to a Divine Being. The crutch in this case equates with the **cross** (the words come from the same Latin root – *crux*), and the symbolical throwing away means not that we are rejecting the symbol, but rather that we are replacing the **artificial** with the real, in the sense of the noumenal.

Crying   Crying and beseeching are very often twinned. Should a **dreamer** hear cries, it suggests that they are being besought to do something – to respond in some way to the stimulus of the sound, rather as a **mother** will rush to her **baby** when a certain non-reflexive **wail** is given out. Should the dreamer be keening or weeping, it is likely that they are **mourning** some aspect of themselves that they feel they have lost.

Crystals   Crystals are perceived to have healing qualities, but they can also be opaque, although paradoxically suggestive of the passage of **light** – they transmit rather than comprehend, in other words. This suggestion of light carries through into folklore and **fairy tales**, but it also has its foundations in the real **world**, as manifested in the Crystal **Hills** on the Caspian coast, near Badku, where there exists a **mountain** so rich with crystals and **sea glass** that it glitters like a mother-lode of **diamonds**. In the symbolism of the Scriptures, crystals refer to **truth** received through the **mind** and later transmuted into the personality, while Ptolemy believed that a crystalline sphere existed between the Primum Mobile and the fixed **stars** of the firmament – it is at least arguable that what he was describing was a **dream** (or transubstantial) **world**, a suggestion partially mirrored in Milton's *Paradise Lost*. See **Healers**

Cuckoos   A cuckoo symbolizes **infidelity**, or cuckoldry. The cuckoo's habit of infiltrating its **eggs** into other **birds**' **nests** affords it more or less free **rein** in our **dreams**, potentially representing **jealousy**, envy, possessiveness, and the dread of betrayal. For a **male** to dream of a cuckoo may imply that he doubts that the child that carries his name is his – for a **female**, that she **fears** dispossession by another, perhaps younger, woman.

Cuddling   To **dream** of cuddling is usually a straightforward reference back to the more tactile era of our infancy and youth, when physical closeness was not restricted by societal **taboos**. However tactile we may think we are, we were probably more so when we were young.

Cul-de-Sacs   Cul-de-sacs are **anxiety** triggers, affording little prospect of **escape** from an acutely uncomfortable situation. The **dream** may find us leaping seven storeys to **escape** from a blind **alley**, or have us skittering up the obstructive **wall** like a **lizard** – but if its subtext is that we are in a quandary of our own making, it is unlikely that the architecture of the dream will allow us to escape so easily. An alternative reading would have the cul-de-sac representing inertia, and a loss of the will to move forward. Also, possibly, the **vagina**, with the woman's **legs** in a position that denotes both **birth** and **sexual** compliance.

Cults The presence of cults suggests both a desire to belong and a **fear** of belonging. It's pointless to pretend that the Branch Davidian massacre, near Waco, Texas, in 1993, and the mass **suicide** of 974 members of the People's Temple Christian Church, under its leader, Jim Jones, in Guyana in 1978, haven't entered the **unconscious** mind of most well-informed **people**. This has led to a generalized suspicion of cults and of breakaway religions, with the inevitable subtext that only rather unintelligent and easily-led people are likely to **join** them. At the time of the Cathars, cults were perceived as a brave alternative to state- or **church**-led tyranny. Now they are perceived as the final recourse for the non-belonging and the disenfranchized.

Cupboards Cupboards frequently represent the **dreamer**'s **unconscious** mind ('**skeletons** in a cupboard'), whilst also, on occasion, suggesting the corporal. Much depends on whether they are **empty** or full, rather as an optimist views a **cup** as half full, while a pessimist sees it as half empty. In addition, cupboards and their contents are an investment for the future, and may therefore equate with the Five Wise Virgins in the **Bible**, who wisely took along extra **oil** for their **lamps**, and were thus not excluded from the **wedding**.

Cupids Cupids facilitate the life of the affect, as well as the progress of the **soul** towards perfection, in the form of virtuous **love**. They are both playful and mischievous, and a **dreamer** may conjure them up as an aid to emotional satisfaction. In addition, there may be a voyeuristic subtext to the **dream**, and the physical correlation between Cupid (Eros) and a **baby**, or infant – or, in Apuleius's magnificent *Cupid and Psyche* episode in the *Golden Ass* (Books iv–vi), a beautiful young man, beloved of the **Gods** – has a strong **archetypal** resonance, particularly for women.

Cups Cups and chalices have extremely strong symbolic value in the **Bible**, the *Corpus Hermeticum*, the *Iliad*, the Grail Legend and the Buddhist *Tripitaka* (to name only a few). They are **symbols** of the purified psychic **body** transcending the human vehicle, and, as such, they usually suggest the garnering or offering of wisdom when they appear in **dreams**. The involuted cup resembles the **breast**, and to that extent the cup equates with the feminine and the **Apollonian**.

Cursing Cursing implies a negation of the Divine Will by human ambition. Traditionally, it was often accompanied by the tolling of the **bell**, the closing of the **Bible**, and the quenching of the **candles** (cursing by bell, book, and candle). Superstitiously, too, it was felt that 'curses, like **chickens**, come home to roost', and to that extent alone the arrogation of the Divine Will was a dangerous course to take. In Old English, the word *curst* equated with **anger**, and cursing as a **dream symbol** often has this connotation, rather than the more formal one of execration. See **Hexes** KEY LINE: 'And oftentimes such cursing wrongfully returneth again to him that curseth, as a bird that returneth again to his own nest.' (Geoffrey Chaucer's *The Parson's Tale*, Section 41)

Curtains Curtains **hide** or **veil** things from outside view. Throwing curtains wide open lets in **light**, and implies a desire not to conceal oneself, or aspects of one's personality, from others. 'Ringing down the curtain' was a **theatrical** term implying the bringing to an end of some outstanding matter. See **Drapes**

Cutting Cutting or slicing into things may imply a desire to truncate or hasten on an ending to something, before its naturally appointed **time**. It may also imply the cutting of ties with the **past**, or the weakening of established bonds (*ergo* the **umbilical cord**).

Cymbals Cymbals proclaim things. They are designed to capture our attention. In addition, one cymbal cannot function without the other – a single cymbal being less than useless, for obvious reasons. The euphonic similarity between '**symbols**' and 'cymbals' is also relevant, and to this extent a pair of cymbals is probably symbolic of a **couple**, or pair of **people**, working together to produce a harmonic whole.

D

Daggers See **Knives**

Dali, Salvador (1904–89) Dali's 1932 painting, *Le Rêve* (*The Dream*) conjures up a **landscape** in which **ants** take the place of a human **mouth**, and strange figures appear to bemoan their fate behind a windswept **marble statue** of a **sleeping** woman. Accused of being a genuine paranoiac after the invention of his 'paranoiac-critical method' in 1930, Dali countered with: "The only difference between me and a madman is that I am not mad."

Damage Damage happening in a **dream** – to a **car** for instance – often refers back to the **dreamer**'s body, and to damage sustained (or suspected) there. The position of the damage is therefore important – is it on the **left** side, or on the **right**? At the front of the car, or at the back? Are the headlights (the **eyes**) damaged? Or maybe the rear **window** (which might relate to the back of the **neck**)? Once this concept is grasped, and the awakened **mind** finds itself able to think laterally, many fascinating **body** correspondences will reveal themselves.

Dame Abonde The French equivalent of **Santa Claus**, Abonde is the good **fairy** who descends at **night**, while **children** are asleep and **dreaming**, to fill their **pillow**-cases with **toys**. Unlike Santa Claus, she chooses New Year's Day as her moment to make little **children's dreams** come true. See also **Befana** & **Bertha**.

Dams Dams symbolically control pent-up emotions (see **Water**), and are also susceptible to corruption and to **sabotage**. When a child **dreams** of dams, it most probably conceals a desire to **urinate**, and the dam is conjured up as a temporary stopgap which may (or, unfortunately, may not) allow the child to continue sleeping without disturbance (see **Wetting the Bed**).

Dancing An integral part of initiations and **rites of passage**, dancing holds **magical** overtones to this day – one can 'lose oneself' in a dance (think of Hans Holbein's *Dance of Death* woodcuts of 1538, and the many *Danses Macabres* that appear both on medieval **churches** and in incunabula). Dancing is also a **symbol** of unity (think of King David's Sacred Dances, and those of the Whirling Dervishes). Dancing, in **dream** terms, is often synonymous with the **sexual** act.

Danger Danger, in its generalized form, is an obvious extension of the **anxiety dream**, conjuring up **symbols** which may or may not shed **light** on the cause of the underlying apprehension. If light is not being shed, it is because the element of danger is being used by the **unconscious** as a deception, or ruse, in order to draw the **dreamer**'s attention away from the real (and therefore sleep-threatening) cause of their anxiety. See **Peril** KEY LINE: '*Pericula qui audit, ante vincit quam accipit* – He who dares dangers overcomes them before he incurs them.' (From Publilius Syrus' *Sententiae* Number 538)

Dante Alighieri (1265–1321) The greatest Italian **poet**, Dante was also a moral **philosopher**, a historian and a political theorist. His masterwork is the *Divine Comedy* (*La Divina Commedia*), completed just before his **death**, which describes a spiritual dream **journey** through **hell**, purgatory, and **heaven**. '*Nel mezzo del cammin di nostra vita mi ritrovai per una selva oscura che la diritta via era smarrita.*'('In the midst of life's journey I found myself in a dark **wood** where the **straight** way was lost'). Following Dante's death, the last 13 cantos of the *Paradiso* were deemed to be **lost**, or never completed, but eight months after his **burial**, Dante appeared in a **dream** to his **son** Jacopo, and told him that they were hidden behind a **wall** in his old bedchamber. Accompanied by Piero Giardino, one of Dante's disciples, Jacopo roused the new owner of the **house** and they duly discovered the now disintegrating cantos hidden in a hitherto unnoticed **window** sconce. See **Bunyan**

Darkness Darkness is both symbolic of ignorance and suggestive of Divinity, in the guise of the Unknowable – this apparent paradox goes some way towards explaining why we are at the same time both attracted and repelled by it. We literally, in the form of our **birth** experience, come from darkness into **light** ('He sent from above, He took me, He drew me out of many waters') and then, at the end of our lives, return to darkness (except in the case of the purified **mind**, which is capable of recognizing darkness as light). The Egyptians viewed darkness as the mystery of all mysteries, while Psalm xviii gives us, as well as verse 16 above, verse 11: 'He made darkness His secret place; His pavilion round about Him *were* dark waters *and* thick clouds of the skies.'

Darts Cupid's darts instilled **love** in whoever was pierced by them, and to that extent they are quite obviously **phallic**, in that physical love is the almost inevitable by-product of profane or earthly passion (*pace* the post-castration correspondence between religious **philosopher** Peter Abelard, and Héloïse, later prioress of Argenteuil **convent**). Darts may also equate with **injections**, and this is reflected in the curious story of 'the darts of Abaris'. Abaris was given a golden **arrow** by his mentor, **Apollo**, to ride with through the air – the dart also made Abaris **invisible**, gave him oracular powers, and cured **illness**. Abaris, in a rather remarkable fit of generosity, reputedly gave the dart to Pythagoras, and one wonders whether this quasi-mythical brainstorm wasn't at the root of much later medical theory. To be pierced by a dart in a **dream** – to be 'cured' or 'injected' or 'killed', in other words – is a pretty straightforward **wish-fulfilment** fantasy, depending entirely on the **dreamer**'s orientation and **sexual** worldview for its accurate interpretation.

Dates Dates (temporal) are significant in that they imply deadlines – times by which things must be done. Dates (fructal) are emblems of fertility, and the date-palm itself was seen as a **symbol** of **self**-sufficiency and **shelter** by much of the near Eastern ancient **world**. The mingling of the two symbiotically (something that frequently occurs in **dreams**) might throw up erotic overtones of desired and sweet-seeming assignations. See **Fruit**

Datura A toxic herb much used by the ancient **Druids** for inducing **dreams** and **visions**. See **Artificial Dreams**

Daughters The use of words such as 'my daughter' in a dream can often have **vaginal** connotations. Daughters themselves, particularly when dreamt of by a woman, are more likely to apply to her (the **dreamer**) as daughter, rather than to her daughter as daughter (if you take my meaning). This is because **dreams** are usually **self**-referential, rather than scrupulously objective.
KEY LINE: '*Der Mutter schenk'ich, Die Tochter denk'ich* – I give presents to the mother, but think of the daughter.' (From **Goethe**'s *Sprüche In Reimen*, Part iii 1827)

Davoine *Nightmare* (1859) is Davoine's only known lithograph, and is a homage to **Johannot**'s illustrations for Alfred de Musset's 1843 *Voyage où il Vous Plaira* (*Journey Where You Will*), incorporating all of the **monsters** that Johannot portrays as part of the narrator's **dream**. The French word *cauchemar* (**nightmare**) appears in the middle of the lithograph, composed of nine tormented figures hanging from a wall.

Dawn Dawn is usually a **time** of hope (except, of course, if one is condemned to **death** by hanging or firing squad), and new dawnings tend to presuppose the capacity for revival or resurrection. They are, in fact, nothing of the sort, being merely a continuance of the old in revivified guise, and **dreams** may reflect this latent fact, but often in subtle ways.

Daydreams The act of dreaming whilst still awake, both in terms of **wish-fulfilment** fantasies and in terms of a **regression** to often infantile modes of thought (and the **unconscious** replication of infantile experiences). Viewed in this way, daydreaming is most akin to **music**, in that it frequently represents itself as a series of symphonic vibrations, or feelings, rather than as words. It is, to that extent at least, pre-literary. The women and **children** of the Aranda Aborigines of Australia played a game, called *altjira*, a word that also means a dream. The game was in the form of a daydream, in which an individual would strike out at apparently random **leaves** or sticks, giving them the names of **people**, and noticing which way they fell. Then a narrative would be made, incorporating the imagined people and their actions into concrete realities. It was only when more than one person became involved in the game that it took on a more traditional, less imaginative, form. *Altjira* aside,

excessive, unstructured daydreaming may point to inner complexes, and needs to be addressed. **Freud**, in particular, considered extreme daydreaming a precursor to **hysteria**. Daydreaming can, in effect, be a substitute for action, as James Thurber's **Walter Mitty** belatedly discovered. See **Creative Dreams**
KEY LINE: 'Seven or eight hours is a competent time for a melancholy man to rest, as Crato thinks; but as some do, to lie in bed and not sleep, a day, or half a day together, to give assent to pleasing conceits and vain imaginations, is many ways pernicious.' (Robert Burton 1577–1640)

Daylight Daylight may appear to be the opposite of **darkness**, but in fact the two are very much conjoined, in that the one (at least in our experience) presupposes the other. Daylight in **dreams** probably equates with perception, as in something 'throwing daylight' on something else.

Day's Residues The second **layer** of **Freudian** dream analysis, which consists of the identification of those areas in the **dream** which may be associated with the previous day's experiences – the day's unfinished business, in other words. See also **Manifest Content, Latent Content & Dream Work**

Deafness The **dreams** of deaf **people** often contain compensatory factors for the **dreamer**'s deafness – they may, for instance, concentrate on or show **symbols** from the side of the **body** which still hears the best. There may, too, be strong areas of **wish-fulfilment** about such dreams, and the deafness of the dreamer needs to be taken into account when making any interpretation. When deafness itself appears in a dream, it can be an indication that the dreamer is not listening to something that they need to hear. See **Antennae, Muteness & Silence**
KEY LINE: 'In my dream I was deaf./He touched my ear in friendship/ but when he felt my deafness,/the ball of wax blocking my hearing,/he turned sadly away/leaving me alone in the dark foreign room.' (From Penelope Shuttle's *The Dream* 1980)

Death It was a commonly held belief amongst the ancients that the approach of **death** casts an anticipatory shadow (an *adumbratio*), which infuses both the **life** and the **dreams** of the person involved – that sudden death, if you like, may be unconsciously prepared for. Death in dreams may often, paradoxically, represent life, just as, in ancient days, a dreamed **funeral** was often considered to be the sign of a **wedding** to come, with each separate aspect – life and death, *Eros* and *Thanatos* – representing the other. Thus luck may represent loss of luck, or **birth** may represent death, etc. (see **Ellipsis**). Specific dead **people** reappearing in dreams, particularly if they are trying to damage the **dreamer**, usually signify the **fear** of death itself, or, in the case of benevolent appearances, that the dead person is still alive in the dreamer's mind. **Children**, in particular, see death more in terms of absence than of physical deterioration, and this can sometimes be reflected in the quality of their dreams.

Death, in astral terms, can imply a cessation of direction from the higher plane (an in-breathing). See **Death Clause** & **Dying**
KEY LINE: 'As I walk'd a stilly wood,/Sudden, Death before me stood:/In a hollow lush and damp,/He seem'd a dismal, mirky stamp …' (From Gerard Manley Hopkins's *Spring and Death* 1865)

Death Clause Involuntary (and thus usually **repressed**) thoughts or **dreams** which involve either the subject's **death**, or that of another person. The Aru Islanders of Eastern Indonesia took this possibility to its logical conclusion by refusing to **sleep** in a dead person's house on the first **night** after their death for fear of being made **sick** through meeting the **soul** of the defunct in their dreams.
KEY LINE: 'To dream your are dead announces freedom from anxiety.' (Astrampsychus's *Oneirocriticon* of 350 AD)

Death Wish See **Death, Death Clause** & **Dying**

Debts Monetary debts can equate with metaphorical debts when they occur in **dreams**, as in the debt one owes to one's **parents** appearing as a literal payment made to an individual or a **couple**. There may, too, be a reference to the 'debt of **nature**' (which traditionally means **death**), implying that life is but a loan and not a **gift**, and needs to be repaid. See **Mortgages**

Decay The **fear** of decay is in us all. Art, **film** and literature have done much to fill in the blanks for those **people** who, at another **time**, would have had neither the imagination nor the bad luck to experience real decay for themselves. **Dreams** will frequently take this subliminal **anxiety** (the anxiety of ageing, if you like) and transpose it to a more amenable, less threatening, context. **Nightmares**, on the other hand, are apt to turn a perfectly reasonable fear into a raging, incipient **neurosis** that may even go on to affect how we run our lives. See **Death Clause**

Deer Both traditionally and allegorically, deer, and, in particular, the **hunting** of deer, have inescapable **sexual** overtones relating to the pursuit and subjugation of the objects of our sexual desire. **Springing** deer have their place in Hindu religious iconography, representing both aspirations towards the **truth**, and the **rain-cloud** bringing familiars of the Maruts (who were the **servants** of Indra).

Defeat Dreams may prepare us for the defeats inherent in real life by creating, through theatrical mimesis, something akin to Greek cathartic drama. If we continually fail to do something in a **dream**, the effect is leavened by the context of the **failure** – we are not, in other words, undone (which is the original French meaning of the word 'defeat'). As François I wrote to his mother after the Battle of Pavia in 1525: '*Tout est perdu, Madame, fors l'honneur.*' (All is lost, Madame, save **honour**). To dream of defeat is to fail without the loss of honour – it is to fail, if you will, by proxy.

Defecation Defecation is frequently a symbolic parallel for other activities that the **dreamer** may consider unclean, such as fetishistic **sex**, buggery, or **menstruation**.

Deformation See **Deformity**

Deformity As we know from **fairy tales**, deformities can often conceal great beauty, a beauty that is only revealed by the appearance of the **right** man or right woman. Deformity in a **dream**, therefore, is a trigger for change, and for movement towards a superior form of consciousness that does not view the deformity literally, but can see through its apparent ugliness to the beauty potentially imprisoned within. See **Beauty and the Beast**

Delay **Dreams**, protective of the **id**, driven by the **ego**, and sheltered by the **superego**, love to delay **wish-fulfilment** in favour of **anxiety**. They act as the courtesans of our **pleasures**, teasing us through **ellipsis** and obfuscation, tempting us with codes and hijacked images, reused, like random **car** parts, to create new wholes. The id is out for instant gratification, and the ego, possessive of its freedoms and its pleasures, **fears** the power of the id and its capacity for mischief. Try to imagine the id as Mr Hyde, eager for the fray, and the ego as Dr Jekyll, vainly trying to stop himself from **drinking** the potion (see **Dr Jekyll and Mr Hyde**). The superego then becomes society-at-large, intent on **suppressing** anything that threatens the status quo – anything that tempts its citizens to question its laws and the **fabric** of its moral carapace.

Delvaux, Paul (1897–1994) Renowned for his **surreal** dream images, Delvaux painted *Venus Asleep* in 1944, during a series of **flying bomb** raids over Brussels. **Venus** lies **naked** on a **velvet couch**, dreaming. Watching over her are a **skeleton** and a dressmaker's dummy. Disporting themselves amongst the classical architecture of the surrounding piazza are various naked ladies, either in flight, or worshipping the **moon**. What this all means is anybody's business.

Demolition Destroying things can be **cathartic**, and destroying them in **dreams** has the added attraction that we secretly know that they are not really being destroyed at all – that they will **magically** restore themselves upon our awakening, just like those reversed cine **films** showing crumbling **chimneys** inexplicably re-erecting themselves like gas-filled sausage **skins**. So yes, we are into **wish-fulfilment** again, and the eternal cycle of **phallic** and **sexual** reawakening – but there is some element in us that understands the mechanics of motion **pictures** and therefore knows that the **buildings** really *are* destroyed, and that we are letting ourselves down in some way by choosing to believe the special effects spin, rather than simply the substance. Such a thing can happen in **dreams**, too, which is why we sometimes wake up with the uneasy feeling that what we have just dreamt not only *resembles* **reality**, but *is* reality, in some unfathomable way. That simply by imagining it, we have experienced, at the very least, a mimetic **truth**.

Demons Demons are **nature spirits**, designed to undermine human will and human aspirations on behalf of the **Devil** – if one falls, all fall (see **Falling**). In **dreams**, then, demons represent **temptation**: 'Then the demons shouted out of the darkness thus: "You are man, worship the demon! So that your demon of malice may repose."' (The Zoroastrian *Bundahis* Chapter xv, 18). See also **Fuseli, Goya, Incubi, Raimondi & Succubi**
KEY LINE: 'I sometimes dream of devils. It's night, I'm in my room, and suddenly there are devils everywhere. In all corners and under the table, and they open doors, and behind the doors there are crowds of them, and they all want to come in and seize me.' (From Fyodor Dostoevsky's *The Brothers Karamazov* 1880)

Dentists Dentists hold a strange place in our **unconscious** minds. They do something to us that we don't like, but which we nevertheless feel we need – i.e. look after our **teeth**. We put ourselves entirely under their control (we take, in other words, the sexually subordinate position, upon which we are entered by the dentist's **drill**, and filled with his amalgam). As the dentist may very well be **female**, and as the patient may very well be **male**, this largely symbolic state of events naturally gives rise to a certain amount of mental confusion (even, dare one say it, **resistance**). It is for this reason that dentists (and **doctors**) appear so regularly in both heterosexual and homoerotic **pornographic** literature and iconography – imagining they are them (and in control, for a change) compensates the sexually insecure for the humiliations they are forced to, or in some cases are willing to, endure in the service of good health. This state of affairs naturally finds itself reflected in **dreams**, with the **dreamer** (depending on taste, context, and subliminal proclivity) recreating the dentist/patient relationship, with themselves, of course, in the starring role. See **Extractions**
KEY LINE: 'I imagined that I was with a dentist who was about to extract a tooth from a patient. Before applying the forceps he remarked to me (at the same time setting fire to a perfumed cloth at the end of something like a broomstick, in order to dissipate the unpleasant odour) that it was the largest tooth he had ever seen.' (From Havelock Ellis's *The World of Dreams* 1911)

Dents Dents, to the Taoist, suggested misfortune to come. To the conventional **dreamer**, dents evoke fallibility, vulnerability, and the bitter realization that all will not remain as it was. They may also suggest **rape**, brutalization, or **damage** to a beloved object (frequently oneself).

Depersonalization Depersonalization occurs when the **dreamer** feels as if they are outside their own **body** or in some way disconnected from their real selves. This can reflect emotional detachment from a tricky situation, or a **repression** of unwelcome experiences or impulses. Out-of-body experiences often have similar **root** causes, and may be part of the bodies' defence mechanism in times of extreme stress or **danger**. **Hysteria** can act in a similar way, even to the extent of causing psychogenic or psychosomatic symptoms like **deafness**, **blindness**, or **paralysis**. **People** in the grip of depersonalization may occasionally **fear** that they are going **insane**, and this fear may find itself reflected in the **fabric** of their **dreams**. See **Derealization**

Depravity Dreamed depravity is the **ego**'s way of protecting itself from the results of its own desired actions.

Deprecation When a **dreamer** deprecates a **dream** that they have had, this often disguises the importance of the dream, or of a detail in the dream, which the dreamer is unconsciously (or consciously) attempting to **suppress**.

Depression Depression, in a dream, very often finds itself objectified by extreme sadness or by a continual, morbid, disappointment. The **dreams** of depressives are often larded with themes of **self-punishment** and a near-**masochistic** satisfaction at being let down. This 'being let down' syndrome may even manifest itself in an overtly literal manner within the symbology of the dream, as in 'going down in a lift', 'crashing in a plane', 'suffering from a **disease**', or '**falling** down a chute'. To this extent the dream is failing the depressive, acting merely as a reinforcement of, rather than as a safeguard for, the state of their mental health. If this continues to be the case, medical care should be sought, as it is, quite literally, unsustainable to feel continually undermined in both **waking** life and in **sleep**. See **Cannibalism**, **Devouring**, **Lowness** & **Manic Depression**

Derealization A morbid **fear** that reality is in fact unreal.

Descartes, René (1596–1650) Much of French **philosopher** and mathematician René Descartes' work was based upon a sequence of vivid **dreams** he had when he was 23 years old, in Ulm, on 10th November 1619 – fearing for his life, he decided to 'look to philosophy for an explanation'. Like **Abudah**, in *Tales of the Genii*, Descartes decided that **God** was his only refuge, and that **Truth** would then descend on him through the **writing** of books in which he would endeavour to prove 'the unity of all the human sciences'.
KEY LINE: 'I am accustomed to sleep and then in my dreams to imagine the same things that lunatics imagine when awake.' (Descartes 1641)

Deserts Deserts may be places of isolation and want, but they may also be places of **retreat** and fruitful contemplation. As well as symbolizing **primordial chaos** and formlessness beyond the reach of reason, they may also suggest reincarnation and the fulfilling power of asceticism. In **dream** terms they may evoke **abandonment** or **frigidity** (in the sense of dryness), twinned with the **fear** of an infinity of choice.

KEY LINE: 'The sea-like, pathless, limitless waste of the desert.' (From Longfellow's *Evangeline*, 1847, Part ii, section 4, line 140)

Designs Enlightened design, and not dry intellectual concept, is at the **root** of all creativity. When the Islamic carpet **masters** of the 15th and 16th centuries used non-figurative designs for the greater glory of Allah, they were joining **nature** and artifice together in a harmonic whole (the Ardabil carpet at the Victoria and Albert Museum in London is one such example). Paul Cézanne (1839–1906) achieved a similar effect in his **paintings** of still lives and of the Mont St Victoire, distilling the essence of nature's own designs onto canvas. Dreaming of abstract designs might therefore imply that we are responding to their inferences – desiring them, even, to stave off **chaos** – and to that extent these are benevolent, creative, reflective, **dreams**, rather than ambitious, conceptual, over-intellectualized **wish-fulfilments**.

Desks Desks take us straight back to **school**, with all the **anxieties** inherent in a return to institutional life after the apparent freedoms of adulthood. Desks equate with **authority**, even outside the schoolroom – they can act as both **bridge** and **dam**, although the dam effect is definitely the most frequent. Desks are easily sexualized, given all the dominant/subdominant corollaries that attach to them, in particular because many of our adult **sexual** predilections are cemented during the formative **years** we spend at school.

Dessert Dessert can be a **symbol** for what the **dreamer** feels that they are owed. Symbolically speaking, it represents a happy end – when in reality we all know that it is **death** that awaits everybody, and not a pavlova. In dream terms, pudding can be a compensation for perceived slights and injustices, as well as a metaphor for sweetness and plenty. See **Sweets**

Destruction When a woman **dreams** of destruction, or of things being destroyed, this can refer back to the loss of her **virginity**, or to the fear of defloration. More generalized destruction may refer to things that are not being valued – the **dreamer** is symbolically destroying them in order to draw attention to them. Such an apparently paradoxical use of dreams is very common, with the dream acting rather as a child will act when it breaks its favourite **toy** in an effort to gain its **mother**'s or **father**'s attention. The child would appear at first glance to be acting against its own interests, but the reality is that it is acting in favour of its interests, but taking a long-term view – namely that it will benefit considerably more in the future than the simple loss of its toy in the present would at first presuppose.

Detectives   A simple trawl through the average **television** guide should be enough to convince even the most sceptical of **souls** of the now almost **archetypal** significance of detectives in the modern mind-set – it is hardly surprising, then, that they crop up, with increasing frequency, in **dreams**. It is normal to desire solutions, and when we can't discover them for ourselves, it is customary to call in someone who can. When the **unconscious** mind is presented with an apparently insoluble conundrum, who does it turn to, therefore? Well, Sherlock Holmes and Inspector Morse, of course. Both **male** patterns of authority, perhaps, but eccentric and outsider enough not to be threatening to **females** (quite the contrary, in fact) – they have authority because they are intelligent, in other words, and not because they have happened upon power through the medium of ambition. They are, dare one say it (and *pace* natural selection), potentially good mating material.

Deus ex Machina   A convenient dream trope (stemming from the Greek theatrical device of allowing a **God** to descend, via a mechanical pulley, to intervene in the affairs of men), designed to disengage the **dreamer** from mental activities that might otherwise threaten the **sleeping** state.

Devil, The   We need the Devil, just as any **self**-respecting **fairy tale** needs a bogeyman (or bogeywoman), and just as any thriller needs a baddie. Sometimes known as the **Evil** One, the devil is often pictured as an **animal** – a **goat**, a **camel**, a black **cat**, a **dragon**, a **fox**, a swine, or even, for **Dante**, a **dog**. His dam was supposed to be Lilith, who was so malevolent that Adam could not bear to live with her, giving rise to the expression 'the Devil and his dam', implying the devil and something worse. 'Dream of the devil and he's sure to come' was a variation on 'talk of the devil', and probably stemmed from medieval **fears** of witchcraft and **night** possession. See **Witches**
KEY LINE: 'Antonia shrieked. The Monster clasped her in his arms, and springing with her upon the Altar, tortured her with his odious caresses.' (From Matthew Lewis's *The Monk* 1796)

Devouring   Devouring or being devoured possibly refers back to the **cannibal** dreams of **shamans**, and to the Greek mythological stories of Orpheus and Pentheus. Very young **children** are often **orally-fixated**, in that everything is trial ingested before being either approved or rejected for future use – **manic depressives** frequently have cannibalistic **dreams**, in which hate objects are devoured and, as it were, incorporated into the cycle of self-**punishment** engendered by the condition, a cycle which could be construed as a partial return to infantilism.

Dialling   Dialling equates with communication, in that it represents an almost **magical** conjuring up of a desired connection. There are negative overtones, of course, as in the dialling of the emergency services, or of being called by someone one does not wish to communicate with, but by and large the **unconscious** probably views dialling as a desirable activity – a tuning in, if you like (or even, in certain circumstances, a tuning out). Curiously enough, the **telephone**, with its adjunctive **line**, also carries with it revocations of the **umbilicus**.

Diamonds See **Gems**

Diapers See **Nappies**

Diaries Diaries are **records** of what we think we have done. Any claims to objectivity are entirely spurious, and they are therefore biased narrations of ourselves as we would like others to see us. Even a warts-and-all story is never all that it seems, being necessarily one-sided. Dreaming of diaries may imply that we secretly desire that our lives should be recorded – this reflects the natural human fear of oblivion. If one believes, of course, as the Theosophists do, in the Akashic Records, or as **Jung** did, in the **collective unconscious**, or as Christians, Mohammedans, Hindus, Jains and Buddhists do, in reincarnation or **resurrection**, or as the Pythagorean Greeks and ancient Egyptians did, in **transmigration**, or simply as the Hebrews did, in Jehovah, such **fears** are palpably unnecessary. Or are they?

Diarrhoea It's bad enough having diarrhoea, let alone dreaming of it – the symbolism is, however, far too convenient for the **unconscious** to pass up. The simplest explanation for such a **dream** is that there is something **dirty** lurking inside us (see **Excrement & Secretions**) which we wish to hide away, unacknowledged or unwitnessed, or to flush away, abrogating all responsibility for it.

Dice Dice equate with fate – one can load them, **trick** them, swear by them, or contrive to ignore them, but their symbolism is simply too convenient. 'As false as dicers' oaths', says Hamlet, after slaying Polonius (Act iii, scene 4), implying that one cannot believe the oath of any man who claims that he will forego his **compulsions**. While seemingly objectifying fate, dice also have a curious facility that allows us to feel that we might, just might, be able to **cheat** it.

Dictionaries Ever since Galfridus Grammaticus' 1440 *Promptorium Parvulorum Sive Clericorum* (*pace* Dr Johnson and the Assyrians, who also produced roughly similar tomes), we have looked to dictionaries for the **judgement** of Solomon on how we can and cannot use our **language**. The **truth** is that each and every dictionary is as partial and as biased as we are ourselves, and they should really be called 'dictatories'. Such semantic mix-ups are the very stuff **dreams** are made of, and we are therefore forced to construe the appearance of dictionaries in a dream as yet another form of **wish-fulfilment**, along 'look here, I'm right' **lines**.

Diets Diets are entirely **anxiety**-driven – one doesn't, by definition, diet because one is feeling good about oneself. Their appearance in **dreams** is usually indicative of an underlying malaise or discomfiture, and possibly even a lurking **depression**, given the near-endless possibilities for **self-punishment** a diet can hold.

Digging Digging, in a **dream**, equates with unearthing – and for there to be an unearthing, there must be something lurking below **ground** to be unearthed. For that to be the case, somebody, somewhere, must know about it, or sense that it is there. Who better than the **dreamer**? In purely symbolical terms, digging indicates a desire for self-consciousness through the medium of our **earth**-natures, suggesting that the objects dug up (however unsettling) will all have significance for us, and be helpful on our spiritual **journey**.

Dinosaurs The word dinosaur has pejorative overtones now, as of large, clumsy creatures, out of time and out of place, which are doomed to eventual extinction. Most rational **people** realize that this is an absurd simplification, and that dinosaurs were as significant, in their way, as we will no doubt prove to be – i.e. not at all. All this notwithstanding, they are a convenient oneiric trope for antediluvian, out-of-date, and occasionally threatening aspects of the **past** that may (or may not) come back to haunt us.

Dionysian The Graeco-Roman religion of Dionysus – a.k.a. Bacchus, the **god** of **wine** and vegetation – gave us the term Dionysian (via the German philosopher Friedrich Nietzsche), implying intuitive and spontaneously creative, rather than exclusively rational behaviour. A somewhat benevolent god (except to those who refused to indulge in his **orgies** celebrating the oneness of man with **nature**), Dionysus formed the **bridge** between man's creative instincts (the **Phallus**) and the mysteries of **Mother Nature** (the **Earth** Mother, or **Great Mother**). The catalyst to an understanding of these mysteries was wine, which lowered man's consciousness to a sufficient extent to allow him to see things as they really were, rather than as he would have them be – to connect the spiritual with the physical, in other words, in order to make a single unity. As a **symbol** of this unity, the culmination of all Dionysiac orgies was the **sacred marriage** of Dionysus to Ariadne (granddaughter of the **Sun** God, Helios). The raising of the Chalice during Christian Mass is quite possibly a carry-over from this earlier Dionysiac **ritual**. See **Apollonian**, **Centaurs**

Dionysus See **Dionysian**

Diplomas Diplomas may be nominally satisfying, but they are, in the author's opinion, ultimately meaningless, in that the ability to pass **exams** or hang in during lengthy and largely uninformative seminars does not necessarily equate with intelligence or intellectual ability. It may even be a sign of intelligence to *avoid* certain diplomas, in recognition of their significance as the fodder of the mediocre, and to strike out on one's own. To that extent they equate with **clothes** and **masks** in **archetypal** dream terms (and as agents of self-satisfaction), being of use only to **hide** or disguise what lurks underneath. See **Cloaks & Coats**

Dirt The **fear** of dirt returns us to the infantile stage of **oral fixations** and **anal eroticism** – how can we ever hope to please mummy and daddy if we are dirty, or if we don't tidy our **room**? Dirt also has a correlation with **death**, in that it implies a loss of control on the part of the begrimed, with all the usual threatening revocations of 'nature red in tooth and claw', etc. Traditionally, we 'dig the dirt' on others, or **buy** something 'dirt cheap' – if we are humiliated, we 'eat dirt'. When we die we inevitably return to dirt, whether we are cremated, **buried**, **fired** out of a cannon, or dunked at **sea** – sooner or later we'll all settle back into the primal ooze from whence we came. Our **dreams** (in the temporary form of our **unconscious** mind) already know this.
KEY LINE: 'And if the corpse of any one I love, or if my own corpse, be duly/render'd to powder and pour'd into the sea, I shall be satisfied,/Or if it be distributed to the winds I shall be satisfied.' (From Walt Whitman's *Of Him I Love Day and Night* 1860)

Disablement See **Amputation**, **Blindness**, **Cripples**, **Deafness** & **Deformity**

Disasters We dream of disasters to make ourselves anxious, but also to protect us from real-life disasters through what one might term 'dream preparation'. There may also be an element of 'there but for the Grace of God …' about the dream, as well as a possibly underlying feeling that we deserve to undergo a disaster on account of our behaviour (the Sodom and Gomorrah syndrome). **Manic depressives** frequently dream of disasters occurring to themselves or their loved ones as an extension of **self-punishment**, but there may also be a **cathartic** effect inherent in disaster **dreams**, when we **wake** up and find out that the disaster has not really happened.

Discipline Discipline and nominal control go hand in hand in the relatively limited dream lexis, at least in the simplistic terms that **dreams** often view or contrive to present such things. The notional **argument** is likely to go something like this:

Superego: 'I don't like the way you are living your life.'
Ego: 'I feel I deserve to enjoy myself.'
Superego: 'Aren't you ashamed?'
Ego: 'Well I am, a bit. What do you suggest?'
Superego: 'You need to pull yourself together. Set some ground rules. Get some control over yourself.'
Id: 'Pay no attention to what Superego says.'

Ego: 'But I know Superego is right. I feel so guilty every time I let myself go.'
Id: 'But it's fun, isn't it?'
Superego: 'Fun must be paid for.'
Id: 'Why?'
Superego: 'Because that's just the way things are. The alternative is chaos.'
Id: 'Chaos sounds fun.'
Ego: 'No, it doesn't.'

Discs See **Disks**

Disease Disease as **punishment**, disease as discomfiter, and disease as the procurer of **anxiety** – all of these are aspects of the disharmony that disease, together with its **symbols**, can bring. To some extent disease fractures our link with the normal **world** and makes us something other – a number in a **hospital**, say; or the quality of our disease anticipating, in **people**'s **minds**, the nature of our character, perhaps; or even the disease as excuse for not participating in communal activity. Each of these aspects may be carried through into **dreams**, but it is the **guilt** aspect that appears to predominate, and the appearance of a specific disease in dreams is often an aspect of the **self**-punishment drive. See **Depression**

Dishes Dishes, if you like, seem made to be broken (see **Breaking**). One **eats** off them, true, but the richer they are, and the harder they are to replace, the higher the **anxiety** inherent in their use. John the Baptist's **head** was brought to Herod Antipas on a dish, after Herod promised Salome (of the Dance of the Seven Veils fame) anything she reasonably desired, so long as it didn't amount to more than half his kingdom. The **symbol** of the dish is a strong one, therefore, and represents both the receptacle of the spirit and a means of offertory. Traditionally, a dish was offered to a **guest** with both **hands**, as a sign of peace (no hands were in consequence left free for grasping the sword).

Disks The most obvious thing about a disk is its circular **shape** (see **Circles**), and this is what the **dream** is most likely to latch on to. The image of the **sun** in disk form, with its revocations of life and fecundity, was fundamental to ancient Egyptian thought, and this concept of the sun as nourisher of **souls** has carried through to the present day, at least in **archetypal** terms. Nowadays, too, we see disks as storehouses of knowledge, or as safety devices (backups) in the event of **disasters** – it would be inconceivable if the dream were to ignore this aspect of diskery, just as it would be were the dream to ignore the disk as the **body** of **Christ** (as represented in the communion wafer), or the disk as **pill** or placebo.

Disorientation Disorientation is defined as a loss of certainty in one's environment or identity, which can occasionally occur in the aftermath of **nightmares** or **anxiety dreams**.

Displacement A **Freudian** concept that describes the ability of the **mind** to move from one uncomfortable image to another, more comfortable one, which may, nevertheless, still reflect the initial dilemma of the dreamer in some transmogrified form. Displacement could be construed, therefore, as the mind's way of disguising the true import of a **dream**. See also **Condensation, Dream Work, Representability & Secondary Revision**

Dissociation The splitting off of one aspect of the personality from the other. See **Dr Jekyll and Mr Hyde**

Distortion See **Displacement**

Ditches Ditches can represent both diversions from the mainstream (as in tributaries), or divisions between different states of being. It is important to ascertain whether the **dreamer** is in fact inside the ditch (in the sense of being locked into old habits and established **patterns**), or outside the ditch (which consequently remains an unknown quantity), and fearing to **fall** in.

Divorce Divorce is a splitting asunder (either apparent or delusional), and to that extent it represents, at least in terms of the Divine Law, a separation of **love** from wisdom, goodness from **truth**, and emotion from reason. This is the problem that Catholics face when it comes to the formal splitting of the 'one flesh' of **husband** and **wife**: 'What therefore God hath joined together, let no man put asunder' (Matthew xix, 4–6). To that extent the concept of divorce and the belief in **God** would appear to be contra-indicative, and although this may seem foolish in the **light** of our modern laws, the **archetypal** belief in the sanctity of **marriage** is a strong one (incorporating, as it does, the giving and receiving of oaths), and even though the rational mind may make light of such things, the **unconscious** mind may not.

Dizziness Dizziness is often a precursor of **disease**, or else a **symbol** that something is 'not quite **right**'. If we see someone reeling, it acts like a mute call for help, and it is a rare human being who would not go to that person's aid. Dizziness, though, may also equate with self-abuse (through either **drink** or **drugs**), and then the situation rapidly changes, and the temptation is to despise, avoid, or feel sorry for the person suffering the apparently self-inflicted disorientation. If we reel or lurch in **dreams**, it usually implies that we aren't comfortable or contented as we are – it may also act as a **warning** that we need to get out of our present position (or state) as soon as possible.

Docks Docks may equate either with the return from a **journey**, or the necessity of a servicing (medical, mental, or otherwise). And yes, there may be a **vaginal** element to the docking procedure, in that ships are

phallic – despite their nominally **female** personification – for men both enter them and use them for entering.

Dr Jekyll and Mr Hyde Robert Louis Stevenson had been struggling for two sleepless **days** and **nights** to find a plot for his new **novel**. On the third night he fell into an uneasy doze and had the following **dream**: 'I dreamed the scene at the window and a scene afterward split into two, in which Hyde, pursued for some crime, took the powder and underwent the change in the presence of his pursuers.' He wrote the first draft – which his wife Fanny Osbourne called a 'shilling shocker' – in just three days. It was published in 1886, and has never been out of print since. In purely **Jungian** terms, what happened to Dr Jekyll in the **book** was called **dissociation**, or a splitting of the **psyche**, leading to inevitable **neurosis**. See **Double** & **Shadow**

Doctors Gertrude Lawrence (renowned for her risqué and marginally off-key vocal renditions) sang a marvellous Cole Porter song about doctors, called 'The Physician' (1933), from *Nymph Errant*: 'Once I loved such a shattering physician,/Quite the best looking doctor in the state,/He looked after my physical condition,/And his bedside manner was great.' Doctors, as **authority figures**, may represent the **superego** in **dreams**, but their appearance may also imply that something fundamental, although not at first visible, may be wrong. To 'doctor', too, carries with it numerous more pejorative connotations, as in 'doctoring' a drink, 'doctoring' dice, or 'doctoring' the accounts. Doctors, such as Dr Diafoirus in Molière's 1673 *Malade Imaginaire*, were also renowned for being set in their ways, or, like Dr Rezio, in Cervantes' *Don Quixote* (1605), for forbidding the partaking of anything enjoyable – alternatively, they were viewed as sinister, as in the sublime 'I do not like thee, Dr Fell,/The reason why I cannot tell;/But this I know, I know full well,/I do not like thee, Dr Fell.'

Does Does are symbolic of shy, maidenly, elusive femininity.

Dogs A dog symbolizes not only fidelity, but also promiscuity, lack of discrimination, and dirty habits – on the plus side, of course, a dog may also represent freedom, in the sense, perhaps, of running free. The **black** dog was a **fiend**, native to country places, and, thanks to Winston Churchill, he is now synonymous with **depression**. Dogs were long considered to have the power of seeing **ghosts**, **fairies**, and the **Angel** of **Death**, and their appearance in **dreams** may be either protective, threatening, or iconic, depending on the context.
KEY LINE: 'I dreamed that my wife's dog – a dog who, in real life, was constantly getting into trouble – had killed a child in the neighbouring town.' (From Havelock Ellis's *The World of Dreams* 1911)

Dolls Dolls may be both sinister and comforting – what joins the two is imagination. Dolls may also represent our **double**, or doppelgänger, and what happens to the doll may act as a **warning**, or even a euphemism, for something that is occurring, or may be about to occur, to the **dreamer**. If the doll is being tormented or abused, for instance, particularly in the case of a **child**'s **dream**, extreme care needs to be taken in the interpretation of the dream, because the child may well be extrapolating onto the doll things that are occurring in real life, and which the child may, as yet, be incapable of understanding. The doll may then be acting as a suppressant – or *in loco adolescens* – so that reality is distanced through the use of a simulacrum.

Dolphins Dolphins are **archetypal symbols** of wisdom and, in medieval art, of social **love**. They personify the natural life, free of appurtenances, and to that extent they deliver us back (by inference) towards the pre-civilized nomadism of our distant **ancestors**. They also suggest extreme (i.e. beyond human) possibilities of communication, and to that extent the dolphin, in its **fish**-like and un**stained** aspect, may, to some degree at least, represent **God**.
KEY LINE: '… parting day/Dies like the dolphin, whom each pang imbues/With a new colour as it gasps away,/The last still loveliest.'
(From Byron's *Childe Harold*, canto iv, stanza 29, 1817)

Donkeys See Asses

Doors Doors symbolize hope as well as **sexual** anticipation. A front door usually symbolizes the **vagina** and a back door, the **anus**. Dead **bodies** were only ever carried out through the front door of a **house**, or, failing that, by the front **window** – and always **feet** first. **Jung**, in *Civilization and Transition*, described the dream itself as 'a little hidden door in the innermost and most secret recesses of the psyche …'
KEY LINE: 'Dreams are the subtle Dower,/That make us rich an Hour/Then fling us poor/Out of the purple door.' (Emily Dickinson, Number 1376, 1870)

Dormitories Dormitories will tend to have particular connotations for privately educated **children** who have boarded at **school**, just as they will for those who have been in the **army**. For such **people** dormitories represent communally shared areas, possibly with same-**sex** connotations, twinned with the institutionalizing aspects and conservative **nature** of pre-established patterns. This may seem quite a heavy burden of symbolism for one seemingly mundane image, but **sleeping** and sexuality are inextricably linked, and to that extent a dormitory has revocations beyond the apparent simplicity of its nominal significance.

Double, The Ancient **cave paintings** of **animals** often contain real **spear** marks, made by the troglodytes themselves, who appeared to believe that by symbolically **killing** a double of their prey, a **magical** identification could be triggered between the image and the living creature. Certain tribal **peoples** (in parts of Mexico, for instance) still refuse to be **photographed** for this reason, and also insist that previously **amputated**

limbs be conserved for as long as is needed so that they can be buried with their original owner, thus retaining the primal unity of the **body**. Our psychic 'doubles' can also equate, although in some measure only, to the **Jungian** and Rankian (see **Rank, Otto**) concept of the **shadow,** or doppelgänger. See **Doubling**

KEY LINE: 'I dreamed that I was arranging my toilet before this glass – just as I had done that evening – when on a sudden the face of the portrait I have mentioned was presented on its surface, confronting me like a real countenance, and advancing towards me with a look of fury ...' (From Sheridan le Fanu's *Wylder's Hand* 1864)

Doubling If a patient, client, or analysand has a split personality, or a tendency towards **bisexuality**, they may engage in doubling within the **dream** context – that is, they may conjure up a **twin**, or **double** of themselves, who acts in their capacity (*in loco somnis*), protecting them from the consequences of their desired but **repressed** actions. These doubles are usually, but not always, of the same **sex** as the **dreamer** themselves. See **Condensation & Representability**

KEY LINE: 'I remember of dreaming on one occasion that I possessed ubiquity, 20 resemblances of myself appearing in as many different places, in the same room; and each being so thoroughly possessed by my own mind, that I could not ascertain which of them was myself, and which my double.' (From Robert Macnish's *The Philosophy of Sleep* 1830)

Doubting Dreams See Obsessive Compulsive Disorder

Doves Doves appear to symbolize innocence and harmlessness, but there is a hybrid edge to their symbology which carries with it revocations, too, of hardness and usury – of a **fist** of **steel** inside the **velvet glove**. That is why **Jesus** 'overthrew the **tables** of the moneychangers and the **seats** of them that sold doves' during his purging of the temple of **God** (Matthew xxi, 12). They are there, if you like, to persuade and to lull (gull?).

KEY LINE: 'The sight of doves is the introduction of injury.' (From Astrampsychus's *Oneirocriticon* 350 AD)

Downward Movement See Below

Dragonflies Dragonflies may symbolize freedom, but they also carry suggestions of the brevity of human **wishes** and the possible foolishness of long-term aspirations. They appear to live entirely for the moment, and their appearance in **dreams** may conceivably reflect our natural desire to make the most of every **day** without needing or caring to fret about the future.

Dragons In Christian iconography, the dragon symbolizes Satan. To Taoists, on the other hand, dragons indicate **money** and **fame**. Future status was dependent on the number of **toes** the dragon appeared to have, with the Royal Dragon possessing five. **Winged** dragons, it appears, symbolized the transcendent powers of both the **snake** and the **bird**, while a thousand-mile-long dragon, known as the 'Enlightener of Darkness', could produce **daylight** or **darkness** merely by **opening** and closing his **eyes**. The psychologist, A. von Winterstein, somewhat belatedly interpreting one of **Swedenborg's** dreams for his 1936 book on the philosopher, demonstrated a splendid example of **fixed symbolism** when he insisted that Swedenborg's image of the dragon (over which he flew, in the dream) represented 'the deceitful **mother** as castrator'. See **Spiders**

Drains   Drains are, quite literally, fundamental, and symbolize both the repository of **dirt** and the human waste system, as it functions within the **body**. To some extent, also, the image of a drain may act as a release valve for the bad things we no longer wish to keep – we simply flush them down the drain. The problem then arises – where do they go? Does the smell linger? Have we eradicated them for good, or do they lurk in our recesses and in the folds of our (metaphorical) bowels?

Dramatis Personae   The identity or significance of the **people** who appear in a dream is of the utmost importance in **dream analysis**. Transfigurations often occur, hiding the origin of the 'person **symbol**' two or more stages back in the dream. A system of reverse exposure then needs to be put into place, teasing out the meanings of each stage of the **chain**, the one leading inexorably to the other, as in a **detective** story. Each individual person represents the **dreamer** themselves (to some extent or other), with **dreams** being, in that sense at least, absolutely egoistical.

Drapes   Drapes conceal things. Their appearance in a **dream** may suggest the desire to hide something, or the sensation by the **dreamer** that something is being kept hidden from them. Polonius was killed by Hamlet while he was lurking behind some drapes in the **queen**'s bedroom – Hamlet believed (because he wanted to believe) that Polonius was the **king**, and that by stabbing through the queen's arras (a **phallic** movement, if ever there was one), he was symbolically avenging his **father**'s cuckolding and **death**. See **Curtains**

Draughts   A classic use of wordplay and a fine example of **dream** semantics. Draughts may mean either 'the game of draughts', 'the taking of drink', or 'wind finding its way in through nominally sealed spaces'. Each may find itself interchangeable within the architecture of the dream, so that we discover, for instance, a game of chequers being played in a howling **wind** with each player throwing back pints of beer – at first sight, there appears to be no logic or connectivity to the image, but the word 'draughts' alone provides the clue to the apparently random **train** of events. Once this **key** is discovered, the dream may be open to a more rational interpretation.

Drawers Drawers often represent the **vagina** when they appear in **dreams**. They are also store-places for things that we may wish to keep, but not, necessarily, to confront. See **Cupboards**

Drawing Drawing is a non-verbal form of communication. To that extent it is unique, in that it relies on nothing more than luck, conservation factors, and the capacity for lateral thought (in the eventual viewer) in order to carry its message across millennia. In **dream symbolism**, drawing is a useful trope for non-verbalized emotion.

Dream Analysis Dream analysis is a key psychotherapeutic tool. No one school of psychological thought, however, possesses all the answers, and care must be taken to distance oneself from mental rigidity when engaging in **dream analysis**. The emotions displayed in our **dreams** provide us with the **key** to their interpretation. These are most readily expressed in the dream's **latent content**. Dreams, however, are usually far less emotional than the events or **anxieties** which trigger them, and it is here that an element of **repression**, or of **unconscious dream censorship**, most readily comes into **play**. The dreams of intellectuals and neurotics (often one and the same) are consequently the hardest to interpret. Dream images **mirror**, to a larger extent than we might at first care to acknowledge, our individual thought processes. See **Neurosis**

Dreamboat The 1940s word for a particularly beautiful or sexually attractive man or woman.

Dreambox Early 20th-century US black **slang** for an intelligent or thoughtful person's **head**.

Dream Censorship As we dream, the normal processes of critical analysis that we exercise in everyday **waking** life are increasingly put on hold. Our capacity to be surprised is the first thing to decline, and things that might shock or disconcert us in the normal course of events no longer do so. It is for this reason that such images as appearing in a **hotel** lobby in the nude (see **Nakedness**), or defying the laws of gravity by **flying** over **trees**, can so easily occur – we no longer benefit from the full force of the **superego** to correct them. Dream censorship, which largely takes place in our preconsciousness, is therefore specifically designed to **head** off immoral or antisocial thoughts – it is a form of mental scotoma, in other words.

Dream Content The content of a dream, at least in its external form, simply reflects the mentality, or the intelligence quotient, or the semantic capacity, of the **dreamer**. The basic substance of a dream, therefore, is pretty much universal – it is simply the design of the **wallpaper** that varies. **Symbols**, in other words, replace emotions. New inventions or fads may invade our **dreams**, but they afford us no more than a series of different **colours** – and possibly a differently contoured palette or two –

with which to **paint** the same old **picture**. The **nature** of the dreams we dream is fundamentally unchanged. Only the essential nub matters.

Dream Dust 1960s **slang** for any narcotic drug in powder form.

Dreamer 1980s **slang** for morphine. See **Morphine Dreams**

Dreamer, The When the dreamer appears in their own dream, it is usually only the conscious **ego** that is represented. Other figures and personages in the dream stand for the largely unknown, **unconscious** qualities of the dreamer. To this extent **dreams** are naturally anthropomorphic, and one is reminded of Johann Wolfgang von **Goethe**'s famous epigram, 'Man never knows how anthropomorphic he is.'

Dreamers 1930s **black** US **slang** for blankets, carrying the implication that one **sleeps** between them.

Dream-Founded Churches The following **churches** were all founded as a direct result of the **dreams** or **visions** of their founders:

1. The Christian Fellowship Church is the largest independent church in Melanesia. It was founded in 1959, in New Georgia on the Solomon Islands, by healer/prophet Silas 'Holy Mama' Eto (1905–84), following a series of dreams spurred on by his admiration for John Wesley, and which featured pioneer New Zealand missionary J. F. Gouldie. Fundamentally Pentecostal in tone, the Church is centred on a Holy Village in which spiritual and dream healing takes place.

2. Alice Lenshina's Church (a.k.a. the New Lumpa Church) came into existence following founder and prophetess Alice 'Lenshina' Mulenga Mubisha's (1924–78) series of dreams and mystic visions in the early 1950s, in which she found herself carried up to heaven and charged with the task of destroying witchcraft and sorcery in Zambia. A Bemba tribeswoman, born in a Church of Scotland mission in northern Zambia, Lenshina (meaning **Queen**) and her acolytes clashed with government forces in 1964, leading to the **death** of over 600 people, and the banning of her church.

3. The Nazarite Church, founded in 1910 following Zulu religious leader Isaiah Shembe's (1867–1935) vision of a revelation and covenant on the 'cosmic **mountain**' of Nhlangakazi, was based on the Hebrew **cult** of the same name (see Numbers vi, 2–13) in which members consecrated themselves to **God** by pledging never to cut their **hair**, drink **wine**, or touch a **corpse**. Leadership disputes arose between Shembe's **sons** following his **death**, but the Church still remains, with its centre at Ekuphakameni, near Durban, and boasts up to 80,000 acolytes, at least according to the last available figures (1970).

4. The Maori Ratana movement (largest of the Maori movements, with 25,000 members in the mid 1980s, and a good deal of political clout) was founded following the 1918 dream of Tahupotiki Wiremu Ratana (1873–1939). This **healer** of the 1918 influenza epidemic saw himself appointed as the Mangai, or mouthpiece of God, in his native New Zealand, with **angels** as his mediators and intermediaries, channelling, through them, God's opposition to the traditional Maori belief in *tapu* (the **taboo**, or mana of spiritual powers).

5. The Handsome (Hansom) Lake Religion, founded by Seneca prophet (and alcoholic) Handsome Lake (1735–1815), following a series of dreams and mystic visions in 1799, in which he was given specific instructions for the Iroquois tribe, leading to the foundation of the Longhouse religion. An early example of syncretism, the religion incorporated Quaker beliefs and Puritan ethics, together with more traditional tribal beliefs and **rituals**. The Handsome Lake Religion is still active in Upper New York, Ontario and Quebec.

6. Various Melanesian Cargo Cults, including the very first Fijian Tuka Movement Cult of 1855. Later cults, particularly during and after the Second World War, believed that the **soldiers** and **sailors** who received regular 'gifts from the skies' (cargo drops) must have had special relationships with their **ancestors**, and that these could be recreated by the cargo cultists themselves through the expedient use of simulacra, leading to a revival of the Golden Age.

7. The Native American Church, which was formally incorporated in 1918, but with links back to 1880 and Comanche chief Quanah Parker's (1850–1911) dream vision of a wolf and an eagle, and which includes peyotism (the veneration of the **peyote** cactus) amongst its religious practices.

Dream Girl 1920s US **slang** for the perfect woman.

Dream Gum Early 20th-century US **slang** for **opium**.

Dream Guy 1920s US **slang** for the perfect man.

Dream-Hole A **hole** built into the **wall** of a **tower** or **castle** to let in **light**.

Dream Interpretation Whether the dream interpreter is a psychotherapist, an enlightened observer, a **friend**, or, of course, the **dreamer** themselves (auto-analysis), they need to be well informed, well read, and capable of a degree of lateral thought. **Fairy tales**, religious texts, literature, **films**, **television**, folklore, popular culture, **archetypes**, mythology (see **Myths**), and every sort and form of **symbol** need to be taken into account, predicated, needless to say, on the cultural references available to the dreamer, and on the context in which they dream. It should perhaps

be mentioned here that not all **dreams** are capable of interpretation, and that in such cases a simple cross-section of the dream should be taken for later, retrospective relation against other dreams. See **Dream Series**
KEY LINE: 'My conclusion is that obscure messages by means of dreams are utterly inconsistent with the dignity of the gods.' (From Cicero's *De Divinatione*, Book II, 70 BC)

Dream Journeys Gypsies of Russian or Tartar extraction traditionally believe that 'dream **journeys**' are triggered by **ancestors** who wish to encourage the **dreamer** to make the **right**, rather than the wrong, decision.

Dreamland Early 20th-century **slang** for unconsciousness. Also Margate's famous seaside amusement park, opened in the 1920s, and home to the Grade II listed Scenic Railway **rollercoaster**, the oldest functioning rollercoaster in Britain. Dreamland featured in Margate-born conceptual artist Tracey Emin's debut feature **film**, *Top Spot*.

Dream Language Dream language is the psychic energy contained within the hidden symbolism in our **dreams**. This psychic energy, when we listen to it, may force us to change our behaviour. If messages from the **unconscious** such as these are not heeded, a psychic imbalance, leading to **neurotic** dissociation, may occur.

Dream Off 1930s US **slang** for nodding off on the **job**.

Dream of the Rood *Dream of the Rood* is one of the earliest Anglo-Saxon poems, and is significant for its close, almost symbiotic identification between **Christ** (as redeemer), the **Cross** (as salvator), and the **Dreamer** (as witness). It is probably the earliest English dream vision in written form, and a telling example of 'affective piety', in which the notion of the attainment of the Kingdom of **Heaven**, despite having been born into sin, is shown as possible.
KEY LINE: 'Listen! The choicest of visions I wish to tell,/which came as a dream in middle-night,/after voice-bearers lay at rest./It seemed that I saw a most wondrous tree/born aloft, wound round by light/brightest of beams.' (From *Dream of the Rood*, early 8th century AD, from the Vercelli Book)

Dream On 1980s **slang** designed to deflate unrealistic expectations.

Dream Puss 1940s US college **slang** for an idealized young woman.

Dreams Dreaming is mental activity that differs, in essence, from **waking** thought. Dreams are perceptual rather than conceptual, for while we dream, the **ego** is temporarily put on hold – in fact it is almost as if it no longer existed. Dreams incorporate events of which we have not consciously taken note, and they remain, in consequence, below the level of our conscious minds in the form of symbolic, or metaphorical, images. As a result, dreams appear to be the most universally accessible source for the investigation of mankind's symbolizing faculty, and are amenable to **free association**. Images produced in dreams may seem far more powerful than they do in everyday life, because of the restraints and limitations we put on things when thinking consciously about them. They are, however, a normal and natural phenomenon, and even the Talmud states that 'the dream is its own interpretation' – it is what it is, in other words, and its meaning differs in no essential way from its contents. In addition, dreams can allow us to move towards what **Jung** called 'the realization of the **shadow**' – the confrontation of those aspects of ourselves that we would normally consign to the **unconscious** as too difficult or uncomfortable to address (equivalent to Hercules' cleaning of the Augean **Stable**). The Chaco **Indians** of Argentina go even further, by acknowledging no difference between dreams and reality. If a man **steals** something in someone else's dream, he will be punished, even if he finds himself many miles away from the scene of the 'purported' crime. The Maoris of New Zealand, on the other hand, found themselves faced with the apparently insurmountable problem that, if the **soul** can leave the **body** in a dream, or inhabit **animal doubles** (the bush soul, psychic identity, or mystical participation), something else must, by process of elimination, be left to run the body in the meantime. They therefore invented a number of different principles, adjunctive to the soul, which took on the role in its absence. Certain tribes in East Africa still believe that ordinary **people**'s dreams have no meaning, and that only the dreams of **chiefs** or of **medicine** men are significant. Once colonized, the chiefs and elders of such tribes decided that their dreams no longer had any substance, and that the capacity for significant dreaming had been arrogated by the **head** of the colonizing power. The Taoists of ancient China believed that dreams split into three different forms; those dreamed early in the **sleep** process, those dreamed around midnight, and those dreamed early in the **morning** – these were construed as the 'false', the 'mixed' and the 'true'. The ancient Romans had a traditional saying that is also apposite to this discussion: 'Life is a short dream.' Jung expanded on this Roman concept by stating that 'one does not dream: one is dreamed.' We 'undergo' our dreams, in other words, and function as its 'objects'. See **Dream Series**, **Punishment Dreams**, **Recurring Dreams**, **Recollective Dreams**, **Recovery Dreams**, **Waking Dreams**, **Why we Dream** & **Wish-Fulfilment**

KEY LINE: 'But whether dreames delude, or true it were,/Was never hart so ravisht with delight,/Ne living man like wordes did ever heare,/As she to me delivered all that night;' (From Edmund Spenser's *The Faerie Queene*, Book I, Canto IX, 1589)

Dreams, Self-Analysis of Freud believed that the chronological method of analysis (i.e. the bringing up of associations in the order in which they first appeared in the dream) was the best method to use if analysing one's own **dreams** without the presence of a second party.

Dream Series Chains of dreams (or particular dream series) usually point to some central idea seeking to force its way from deep within the **dreamer's unconscious** mind towards the conscious state. Such chains of **dreams** can sometimes appear to proceed logically, enacting apparently rational sequences of events, or even, at times, to continue on from one previous dream topic to another seemingly related one – they present themselves in instalments, in other words. According to **Jung**, these dreams invariably have a common significance – they radiate from around a central idea like a **wheel** in relation to its hub. By correctly identifying the central idea or motif lying behind the dream series, Jung felt that previous mistakes in interpretation might be amenable to rectification. It should also be mentioned that a 'same **night**' series of dreams (often as the result of broken **sleep** or a number of random awakenings) usually points to a related emotional backdrop or theme, with each dream connecting to the other, at least in terms of emotional genesis. To sum up: series of dreams may be taken both chronologically (in the sense of dream plots) and psychologically (in the sense of a gradual build-up of **latent content**). The second, psychological route, is by far the most significant in terms of underlying issues.

Dream State The condition, or process, or function, of dreaming. KEY LINE: 'To nothing more aptly can I compare the working of our brains after we have unyoked and gone to bed than to the glimmering and dazzling of man's eyes when he comes newly out of the bright sun into the dark shadow.' (From Thomas Nashe's *The Terrors of the Night* 1594)

Dream Stick 1920s US **slang** for a pipe of **opium**. Later, circa the 1940s, the expression began to be used for a **marijuana cigarette** (a reefer).

Dream Street US journalist and short story writer Damon Runyon (1884–1946) gave this name to the heartbeat of US Vaudeville, which he narrowed down to the stage door of B. F. Keith's Palace Theater, on New York City's 47th Street, between Sixth and Seventh Avenues.

Dream Symbols Dream symbols are message carriers from the instinctive to the rational parts of the human **mind**. Virtually unclassifiable, no dream symbol can be separated from the individual who dreams it, and a generalized, pedagogic, or pedantic interpretation can only ever be inconclusive. The symbol-producing function of **dreams** is therefore a means to an end – that of restoring the fundamentally primitive and irrational mind of man through a state of advanced, or differentiated consciousness, leading to a condition of critical self-reflection following **individuation**. To summarize, then: deciphering **symbols** alone is not enough – first, the dynamics of the dream have to be addressed.

Dreams Within Dreams Dreams within **dreams** often disguise protective measures on the part of the **dreamer**, in which uncomfortable or challenging events are made 'unreal', and therefore unthreatening.

Dreamtime The ritualization of the **nature** of **dreams** by the Australian Aborigines. A celebration of the sacred, Dreamtime exists outside time proper (A. P. Elkin called it 'the eternal now') allowing for the transmogrification of men into **animals** (and **ancestors**, and **heroes**) and vice versa. It is, in effect, the undermining of an existing order, allowing an already established society the possibility of infinite change. Identities can be amended, to be replaced by trial identities, allowing the **dreamer** to try on different guises and selves. Ayer's Rock (a.k.a. *Uluru*), situated **southwest** of Alice Springs, is sacred to the Aborigine, being the place where collective dreams are **ritualistically** enacted in real **time**, leading to the creation of potentially **cathartic** mythologies. See **Myths**
KEY LINE: 'Those who lose dreaming are lost.' (Aboriginal proverb)

Dream Work The gradual elucidation (or retranslation, if you like), either by **self**-analysis or through the analyst/analysand relationship, of the various unconscious meanings and **anxieties** concealed within our **dreams**. This amounts to the fourth stage in Freudian **dream analysis**, being the transformation of the **latent content** into the **manifest content**, and is a function of the dream itself. The analyst's job is to reverse the procedure, and to show how it occurred in the first place. In **Freudian** analysis, for instance, this is done by means of a four-stage process. The first stage is called 'distortion and **displacement**'; the second stage is called 'symbolization' or '**representability**'; the third is '**condensation**'; and the fourth is 'secondary elaboration' or '**secondary revision**'. Each of these four stages is dependent on the single fact that dreams are prelogical, and depend on delusion for their primary rationale – they mimic, as it were, primitive modes of thought. Each individual dreamer dreams the dreams that suit them. See **Day's Residues** & **Central Idea**

Dreamy 1940s US **slang** for **sexual** or idealized perfection.

Drilling The obvious sexual connotation exists here, alongside a rather more subtle one, which accords more with the suggestion of a 'search' than of a 'forcible seduction'. We can drill for oil or water, or we can drill for decay (as in teeth) – the choice of image rests with the dreamer's **unconscious** mind.

Drinking In symbolical terms, drinking sustains the **spirit** – to drink in company is to proffer **friendship**, to drink **alone** is a sign of alienation. It was the ancient Greeks who devised the idea of drinking to someone's health, and it was the Romans (inevitably) who took the custom over and honed it to its present ritualistic **heights** (see **Rituals**). There are, of course, the obvious revocations with drinking from the **breast**, together with the **oral fixations** that we all retain to some degree or other from our infancy, but, by and large, the act of drinking in a dream most probably refers back to a simple desire to be nourished in some way.

Driverlessness The **dreamer** sitting helplessly in the back of a driverless vehicle is a frequent dream motif. How better to instil **anxiety** in oneself than to conjure up a situation in which all control of one's life is arrogated to an arbitrary fate? But **dreams** are protective, too, and it is a rare dream in which an **accident** will actually occur as a result of driverlessness. A continuous recurrence of the image is a far more likely outcome, as one part of the dreamer struggles to impose order, while the other part seems almost to enjoy the near-**death** frisson, and even attempts to lengthen it until dramatic stasis (and a possible reawakening) is achieved.

Driveways Driveways equate with **docks**, in that they tend to be female **symbols**, a reading strengthened by the domestic environment in which they are found. A man places his **car** (his status symbol) in full view in his driveway, in an effort both to claim the space for himself (marking his territory), and to proclaim the degree of his worldly success to his neighbours. The car in the driveway has similar revocations for the **female**, or it may reflect her ability to capture and keep a valuable mate (and a **father** for her **children**). The car, to that extent, is the **penis**, and the driveway the **vagina**, with the **house** acting both as joint corporeal symbol (the two **bodies** as indissoluble one), and symbol of the swollen maternal belly.

Driving To drive is to take control, which is why it is usually (but not always) **males** who drive when in the car alone with a **female**. Driving appears to be a natural adjunct to masculinity, which is why cars represent such iconic male **talismans** in a **world** in which physical strength and bravery are no longer requisites for civilized living, and also why they are so frequently the sites of marital and relational strife – for how dare the wife or the **children** argue with someone who controls the **road**? Driving, then, in **dreams**, is the perfect **symbol** for a **wish-fulfilment** restoration of a lost control – the returning to a perceived **archetypal** norm. The question to ask oneself is: what aspects of my life, my persona, and my conduct am I dissatisfied with, if I need to be conjuring up images of comfort/domination in my dreams?

Dropping Dropping things, particularly such valuable things as **coins**, can represent the **loss** of something the **dreamer** feels is important, like **babies**, or even **semen** – to that extent 'dropping' may have **masturbatory** connotations.

Drowning For many centuries it was considered unlucky to save a person from drowning, as the **sea**, deprived of its **victim**, would then search for another through the 'four russet divisions of the universe' – most probably, indeed, the **rescuer**. In any other context, drowning probably equates with losing effective control over one's emotions. See **Submerging**, **Underwater** & **Water**

KEY LINE: 'This August I began to dream of drowning. The dying/went on and on in water as white and clear/as the gin I drink each day at half past five.' (From Anne Sexton's *Imitations of Drowning* 1966)

Drowsiness The stage between waking and **sleeping** in which the **dreamer** finds it increasingly difficult to maintain contact with their own **self** or **ego**, which slowly **sinks** to the level of the **id**. This is sometimes experienced as equivalent to – if rather less permanent than – a form of **dying**.

Drugs Drugs inhibit normal dream modes because they affect thinking. Under the influence of drugs, the **unconscious** is adulterated, and no longer free-ranging. While **dreams** experienced under these circumstances may be exciting, horrifying, or even enlightening, they are not significant in terms of the **psyche**, except insofar as the actual taking of drugs may reflect on the psychic condition of the person indulging in them – it could even be said that the dreams of such a person (a drug taker) are already in the process of secondary or tertiary elaboration, and that they are therefore no longer in an associative state. See **Hashish** & **Psychedelic Drugs**

Druids To dream of druids is often to dream of a perfect order that does not need to be questioned – their laws, and rules, and even the basis of their religion are so far in the **past** that we can only *feel* that we know them. They are therefore convenient ciphers (just as the pre-Christian Goths were for the Nazis) from whom we can take with impunity to **fuel** present ambitions.

Drums Drums draw attention to things, and even transmit messages. They may also be threatening, and suggest hidden or even nefarious **rituals** (just think of the mass of British Empire stories in which surrounded **whites fear** the sudden discontinuance of native **drums**). Drumming is also a dream euphemism for **masturbation**, sexual tension, or the **sexual** act (possibly suggesting the real meaning of the British Empire stories), while it can also have **menstrual** or even circulatory connotations – when the drumming stops, in other words, we're dead.

Drunkenness Drunkenness is a **victory** for the **id**. A drunk arrogates for themselves the **right** to behave in a way that is inconsistent with normal (i.e. non-threatening) societal interaction. A drunk effectively **loses** all **self**-awareness, and to that extent may feel themselves equated, if ever so briefly, with **God**. Thus was born the great temperance movement of the latter half of the 19th century – the phrase 'that man is drunk as blazes' refers, of course, to the **devil**. To that extent drunkenness in **dreams** represents the **dreamer**'s attempt to fight free of societal restraint, and carve out their own (albeit anarchic) new series of laws. Archetypally, then, drunkenness is akin to reverting to our **animal** state, and for a long time the **seven** degrees of drunkenness were viewed as follows: 1. **Ape** drunk. 2. **Lion** drunk. 3. Swine drunk. 4. **Sheep** drunk. 5. Martin drunk. 6. **Goat** drunk. 7. **Fox** drunk. 'Why martin?', I hear my readers ask, 'Why compare a drunk to a **bird**?' Martin was the traditional name for a jackass, as well as being the patron **saint** and protector of drunkards, thanks to his festival falling on 11th November, the day of the feast of Bacchus (see **Dionysian**).

Ducks A duck symbolizes deceit. The French even call a hoax, or practical joke, a *canard* (duck). In **dream** terms a **lame** (or limping) duck (in the sense of someone inadequate) would be significant, as is the link between a duck and **drowning** (a ducking) or the ducking of one's head. The duck of Ilmater (the Finnish **water mother**) provided the primal **eggs** that created the **sun**, the **sea** and the **sky**, and to that extent at least the duck egg may represent **primordial** matter in the **collective unconscious**.

Dumb Cake In old English folklore, unmarried girls would bake themselves a dumb **cake** (flour, **water**, **eggs** and **salt**) and then **eat** it, having walked **backwards**, without **speaking**, towards their bedrooms, with all their clothes unpinned as a precaution against any apparition trying to grab them on their way upstairs. Once safely in **bed**, they would intone: 'Sweet St Agnes, work thy fast./If ever I be to marry man,/Or even man to marry me,/I hope him this night to see.' They would then **dream** of their **husbands**-to-be. Another variation on the same theme saw the dumb cake left out on the **hearth**, at **night**, on Christmas Eve, St Mark's Eve, Halloween, or on the Eve of St Agnes (20th January), with the girl's initials pricked into it and the front **door** left open. During the night, her intended young man's **double** would come inside the **house** and prick his initials next to hers on the cake. If the door happened to be shut against him, there would be a tragedy in the offing. See **Allan Apples** & **Ash Leaves**

Dunces The word 'dunce' came from the followers of Duns Scotus, who resented both theological and social change (a position of ignorance also mocked in Alexander Pope's satire, *The Dunciad*). The dunce's **cap**, of course, was conical, and akin to the cuckold's (or Actaeon's) **horns**, and to that extent it implied a slow, dim-witted person, too bound up in the trifling to see what is happening under his own **nose**. In a **dream**, the dunce figure almost certainly applies to the **dreamer**, and to that extent it may suggest the dreamer's view of themselves, or of certain of their actions.

Dürer, Albrecht (1471–1528) Dürer's magnificent engraving *The Dream of the Doctor* (1496) shows an elderly **doctor**, asleep by his **stove**, and beset by a whispering **demon**. The doctor is obviously dreaming of a nubile young woman, for she stands at his side, a cloth neatly protecting her pudenda, and points disparagingly at the old man's stove, with the obvious implication that there are other ways to warm oneself up than simply by **burning wood**. A **Cupid** lurks close by, trying on a pair of stilts – for the woman, in a marvellous surge of the artist's wit, happens to be nearly half as **tall** again as the fantasizing doctor. See **wish-fulfilment**

Dusk Dusk is generally seen as a time of **death** or **dying**, in that the **falling** off of the day is synonymous with diminishing energies and the **retreat** of the **sun** in its role as the **cradle** of life. Traditionally, too, dusk implied the beginning of the end of the working day, and in a **dream** it may also be taken to imply the ending of something – be it a relationship, a **friendship**, a particular experience, or even a business association.

Dwarves **Dreams** of dwarves can indicate a **regression** back to **child-hood** fantasies, when **fairy tales** and stories provided glimpses of an as yet unexplained adult **world**. They can also represent the **dreamer**'s **unconscious**, and may even occur as **phallic symbols** in certain contexts. See **Smallness**

Dying Dying, in **dreams**, may often equate with the desire for, or the achievement of, an **orgasm**. Dying is also frequently a disguise for other things, and does not actually represent the dreamer's **death**, or even a desire on the part of the **dreamer** to die. Its use in dreams may, in fact, be more along the lines of a convenient **symbol** for the dreamer to 'resist', thus reinforcing and protecting the dreamer's **ego**. The 'dying' aspect of the dream may also originate from a recent traumatic experience that the dreamer has had, or has heard about, and by which they were emotionally or psychically affected. Another convenient aspect of 'dying' in a dream may be the old but persistent walnut that 'death solves all problems' – the reality, needless to say, is usually somewhat different.

Dylan, Bob Bob Dylan's '115th Dream', from his 1965 album *Bringin' It All Back Home*, describes a number of **dream** sequences relating to the foundation and condition of America, based on an amusing semantic conceit inspired by the now perhaps somewhat clichéd concept of 'the American dream'.

Dynamite Dynamite appears to wipe things away – in the occasionally simplistic world of the **dreamer**, it may be called upon to provide an instant answer to a complex question. Don't understand it? Don't like it? Well then, blow it up. Somewhat akin to terrorism, then, in its specious logic. And terrorism, of course, is the temporary – or, in the case of the **suicide** bomber, permanent – triumph of the **id**. See **Terrorists**

E

Eagles An eagle symbolizes majesty, inspiration, height, and, in heraldic terms, fortitude, for a **white** eagle, the Bird of Estë, was the cognizance of the **house** in Tasso's *Jerusalem Delivered*. According to **Ezekiel**, the eagle also represents John the Evangelist, who, like the **bird**, was able to gaze upon the 'sun of glory'. The dream eagle, then, is a positive image, imbued with ancient meaning, not least in its reincarnative qualities, for, like the phoenix, the eagle was considered capable of **flying** into the 'fiery regions', every ten **years** or so, from whence it fell into the **sea**, translating its old **feathers** into fresh ones.

Earrings Earrings have been with us since around 3000 BC, and they have very different significances for men and women. For a woman, earrings are often a **symbol** of her value to her **husband**, her **lover**, or herself, and to that extent, when they appear in **dreams**, they may reflect the self-image of the **dreamer**. For a man they frequently reflect status and symbolical possession – a good example appeared in Tracy Chevalier's novel *Girl With a Pearl Earring* (1999), in which painter Johannes Vermeer falls foul of his neglected **wife** by pinning one of her precious **pearl** earrings onto his 16-year-old **maid**, Griet, whom he has chosen to be the subject of one of his **paintings**. The moment that Vermeer pierces the girl's **skin** with the shaft of the earring is a symbolical **sexual** act of the highest order, and the putting on of an earring in a dream context often has similar sexual revocations.

Ears Ears indicate both receptivity and alertness. They are private places for public words, and to this extent their appearance in **dreams** may imply the need to pay attention or to 'bow down the ear'. A torn (see **Tearing**) or amputated (see **Amputation**) ear may suggest that something is 'ear-marked' for our attention – in Elizabethan times, ears were cropped for **punishment**, and in **schools**, until only recently, a child might be taken by the ear to see the headmaster, or given a 'flea in the ear' by a **policeman**. Such quasi-**archetypal** traditions often continue in the dream **world** long after they have been vanquished in the real one.

Earth Earth is often an **archetypal symbol** for the **mother** in **dreams**, as in Mother Earth and the Earth Goddess. It is also **primordial**, and carries with it implications both of **death** (in terms of **burial**) and life (in terms of sustenance). It may also act as a disguise, covering up or concealing things that we do not wish to be seen. See **Great Mother** & **Planets**

Earth Goddess See **Great Mother**

Earthquakes When a woman **dreams** of an earthquake it is frequently synonymous with the **sexual** act, while for a **male** it is more likely to indicate a feeling of powerlessness or a lack of restraint – there are also implications of upheaval and permanent change, and of disruptive forces outside the control of the **dreamer**. Some Hindus believe that the **earth** rests on the **head** of a great **elephant**, and that when this elephant seeks to refresh itself, an earthquake results. The ancient Greeks, on the other hand, felt that earthquakes were caused by **giants** whom Jupiter had buried beneath certain **mountains**, while early Buddhists saw the earth as resting on the back of a **frog** (or even a **tortoise**).

Ear Wax Clearing out ear wax is a deeply satisfying act, rather like watching **people** swiftly exiting in front of one from inside a packed **aeroplane**. The implication of ear wax in a dream is of something being dammed up or stoppered, and needing urgently to be cleared so that normal service, as it were, may be resumed. (See **Ears & Wax**)

East, The **Christ** was perceived to rise in the east, as with the **morning** dayspring, and any hopes of **resurrection** are also easterly, *ergo* the Creed and the **burial** of **people** with their **feet** towards the **rising**, rather than the setting, **sun**. Dreaming of the east may imply a desire for enlightenment, or it may simply suggest the need for physical **light**, or even light to be shed upon something that mystifies us. See **North**, **South** **& West**

Easter Eggs Easter **eggs** symbolize creation, or the resurgence of **spring**. It was the Zoroastrian Persians who originated the idea, basing their **gifts** on the concept of the mundane egg, with which Ormuzd (good) and Ahriman (**evil**) were forced to contend before perfect consummation could be achieved. The practice of giving an egg became so widespread (Jews, Egyptian and Hindus all practised it), that it has become an **archetypal symbol**, bearing little or no relation to any specific religion. Occurring as part of a **dream**, a **coloured** egg may predispose towards thoughts of **rebirth**, or simply of **birth** itself.

Eaten, Being **Children** sometimes have **dreams** of being eaten. This usually reflects a fear of the outside **world** and what it may contain. **Eating** and emotion have strong correlations, while also symbolizing the acquisition of knowledge – dreaming of being eaten, therefore, may **harbour** symbolical **fears** of having one's essence taken away, or of having it subsumed by others. The image of having one's **head** eaten is a simple semantic juxtaposition of the term 'eating one's head off', implying excess and the triumph of one's **animal nature**, while the eating of a **heart** has a similar link to 'eating one's heart out'.

Eating Sharing a meal with another person frequently implies the act of coition in a **dream**. In infantile terms, of course, it suggests a desire to incorporate, or assimilate. Both bulimia (binge eating) and anorexia (morbid loss of appetite) may have their sources in this infantile desire to assimilate (or explore with one's **mouth**), followed by expulsion of that which is deemed unpleasant or undesirable. Eating also has links with temptation and **taboo** (the **apple** of knowledge, for instance, or the **golden** apples of the Hesperides, which Ge (or Gaea) gave to Hera at her **marriage** to Zeus). It is also a **symbol** of life triumphing in the **face** of **death**, particularly, of course, when the **food** is flesh.

Echoes Echoes are at once mystical, and a necessary confirmation of our existence. We are all drawn to shouting inside **caves**, comforting ourselves when the echo of our shout returns to us. To that extent echoes are like reappearances after a **journey**, or the redefining of ourselves against an **unknown**, but still familiar, quotient. The nymph Echo pined away for unrequited **love** of Narcissus, and there is an element in every echo of a gradual diminishment towards **death**. See **Wells**

Eclipses Eclipses symbolize the power of **nature** and the natural **world** to change the expected **pattern** of our lives. However scientifically we approach an eclipse, few **people** remain un-awed or unmoved by the prospect of permanent **darkness** (ergo **blindness**). The Greeks and Romans both viewed eclipses as **evil** omens, and many primitive peoples believed that the **sun** or **moon** was actually being **eaten** by some unnamed **monster** during astronomical transits – to counteract the threat they would beat **drums** and howl until the 'monster' was driven away. The **symbol** of the eclipse may also be taken literally, when it occurs in a dream, as in the **dreamer** being 'eclipsed' by someone or something.

Eddas, The The prose *Edda* (Snorri's) and the poetical *Edda* (Saemund's) represent the **flower** of Scandinavian/Icelandic **mythology**, delineating both the creation of the **world** by the **Gods**, and the triumphs and exploits of the great **heroes** who succeeded and served them. Dreaming of the *Eddas* may therefore represent a desire both to understand and to mesh with the **past**, morphologically recombining with our **ancestors** to form more than the sum of our present parts.

Education Education. Education. Education. For those who don't have it, it seems the answer to everything, and for those who do it can be a source of **guilt**, joy, bafflement, or regret. Our **dreams** very often take us back to places we have known in the **past**, and **schools**, together with their sense-remembered atmospheres, are favoured locations for the posing of **questions** that we didn't necessarily know we needed to ask. Taken literally, education is about control. Taken metaphorically, education is about freedom – the freedom to choose. The **path** the **unconscious** is directing us towards is entirely dependent on the context and tone of the remembered dream – trepidation equates with control; equanimity with freedom.

Eggs The Cosmic Egg traditionally implied totality. In the Taoist philosophy, the Cosmic Egg was believed to have **split** apart at the very moment of creation, to form the Earth and the Sky. Traditionally, eggs are a **symbol** of **resurrection** and the continuity of life. It was considered unlucky to **dream** of them, however, and more especially of spoiled eggs – such a dream foretold a **death** in the **family**.

KEY LINE: 'To hold eggs, or to eat eggs, symbolizes vexation.' (From Astrampsychus's *Oneirocriticon* 350 AD)

Ego, The The ego's main **goals**, according to **Freud**, are the pursuit of **pleasure** and the avoidance of displeasure. As well as ruling voluntary motion through perception and muscular action, the ego also anticipates displeasure through the medium of **anxiety** – a state of **mind** invariably reflected in our ego-deprived **dreams**. See **Id, Self & Superego**

Egyptian Dream Papyrus Possibly the oldest known written account of the meanings of **dreams** occurs in *Papyrus Chester-Beatty III*, dating from the Egyptian Middle Kingdom period (2000–1785 BC), in which dream **symbols** are related to a set formula of interpretation. Examples include that of a man dreaming that his **bed** was on **fire**, implying that his **wife** would be **raped**, or a man dreaming of a dead **ox**, which allegedly suggested the **death** of his enemies. **Snakes**, on the other hand, symbolized abundance of provision, which neatly returns us to the **phallic** – dare one even say seminal? – **reading** favoured by **Freud**.

Egyptian Dream Stele A pink granite stele, resting between the feet of the Great Sphinx of Giza, tells how the Pharaoh Thothmes IV (1425–08 BC) fell asleep, while **hunting**, beneath the image of Harmakhis (the sun god, Re). The young prince dreamed that the **god** came to him and offered him the Kingdom of Egypt, and a full and worthy reign, if only he would look after and preserve the now almost sand-buried Sphinx. This Thothmes did, conveniently proving, at one and the same **time**, his respect for the **past**, and the divine providence (preordination) of his reign to his people.

Ejaculation Even though we may occasionally be tempted to deny or subsume our **sexual** feelings – particularly, of course, if they are inappropriate – our **unconscious** mind will rarely allow us to get away with such a degree of hypocrisy. Dreamed ejaculations, however disguised they may be (**fountains, volcanoes, geysers**, exploding pustules, **rocket** launches, and billowing funnels are merely the most commonplace images) nearly always refer back to the **dreamer**'s earliest conditioned responses to the sexual act.

Elastic Elastic symbolically holds us back, preventing us from achieving those things which we may feel we wish to achieve. Our elasticated **dream** would appear to be telling us that something is wrong with the course we intend to take, and that, in addition, we may be spreading ourselves too thinly. Even more literally, if we force the issue, either through vanity or vainglory, the elastic may break and snap back in our **faces**.

Electra Complex The female version of the **Oedipus Complex**, in which the **female** gains power through the manipulation of men (in particular those of her immediate **family**). In Sophocles' tragedy, Electra gains revenge on her **mother** and stepfather by persuading her **brother**, Orestes, to avenge their beloved **father** Agamemnon's **death**.

Electricity Electricity is a largely invisible power, carrying within itself revocations of both the bringing of **light**, and of potential harm (negative and positive energy). Such a seeming paradox lies at the **centre** of most **dream symbols** and images. If the electrical wiring lies within a **house**, then the wires probably represent the veins and arteries that carry our life-force around the **body**. If the electricity is coursing along outside **wires**, then communication, or a desire to communicate, may be the intended message.

Elephants An elephant symbolizes sagacity and ponderousness. In India, the elephant symbolizes royalty. The elephant-**God** Ganesha is supposed to have dictated the entire *Mahabharata* after tearing out his tusk to use as a **pen**. Dreaming of an elephant with a raised trunk means the overcoming of **obstacles**, but may also have **phallic** connotations. See **White Elephant**

Eleusinian Mysteries A Greek fertility **ritual** that linked the **worship** of Demeter (**Goddess** of **corn** and the **harvest**), Persephone (Goddess of the **earth** and agriculture), and Dionysus (**God** of **wine** and vegetation). A union, if you like, of the **Apollonian** with the **Dionysian**. It constituted, also, a preparation for **death** and reincarnation through submission.

Elevators Elevators may move us from **below** to **above**, suggesting that we are on a good and positive **path** (perhaps towards **heaven**), but they may also take us down, in the direction of the **genital** area, or below that, even, to the area of **darkness** (equating with **hell**). The downward path is not all bad, though, as it may equate with **flying**, if it takes place in an open, airy environment, and offers us a wide, rather than a truncated, prospect.

Ellipsis The **missing** out or obliteration of **key** elements in a **dream** through the **unconscious** wish of the **dreamer**.

Eloping Eloping is fundamentally making off with something to which we have no societal (as opposed to moral) **right**. To that extent it is an adjunct of the **id** – a thumbing of the **nose**, if you like, at the establishment. The downside is that, once eloped (metaphorically, not literally, of course), one no longer benefits from the rights accorded by society to those who agree to live by its rules. This presents the dreaming person with a curious **ego** dilemma, which may be reflected in the difficulty the **dreamer** often has in getting away or freeing themselves from apparently rejected (but still vaguely desired) societal ties. The **superego**, in other words, is doing its job, by saving the dreamer from the results of possibly ill-considered actions.

Elves Elves traditionally represent the **golden**-haired and sweetly **singing spirits** of the **mountains**, **woods**, and **streams**, and to that extent their appearance in **dreams** is utopian, even crinkum-crankum, in its allusion. Elves are fun. They also play pranks. They are childlike, too, in their simplicity, and it is for this reason that their appearance in dreams carries with it a strong desire for a return to the comforts of **childhood**.

Emails See **Mail**

Emasculation An emasculated man, in a **dream**, means a woman. **Fear** of emasculation in the man may mean a fear of the **anima**.

Embryos Embryos are things which swell inside other things (from the Greek word *embruon*), and they are, for that reason, **pregnant** with possibility. However, they are also unformed, vulnerable and incomplete, and may also be suggestive of partialness and possible truncation. See **Pre-Birth Dreams**

Emeralds See **Gems**

Emergencies Emergencies equate with **anxieties**, and also with a **fear** of the unexpected. They are the **unconscious** mind's way of suggesting that something may be wrong, and may possibly need to be rectified. See **Warnings**

Emission Dreams Symbolic **ejaculation** (the explosion of **bombs**, the switching on of a **fountain**, **fireworks**) frequently takes the place of pictorialized ejaculation in the context of a **dream**. This is a case of **layer symbolism**, in which the **sex** act and the subsequent ejaculation are present, but symbolically disguised. See **Wet Dreams**

Employment Employment frequently equates with self-worth. This may be a false equation, in that self-worth should come from some fundamental wellspring inside the individual, and not simply from how society sees that individual in terms of use. To that extent, being 'gainfully employed' in a **dream** may be a **red** herring, throwing attention away from something that is really troubling the **dreamer**, towards something with which they are, on the surface at least, content.

Emptiness Uncertain people fear emptiness. Grounded **people**, and people with faith, often crave it. Saints and Lamas achieve it. Emptiness implies acceptance, which is a difficult **trick** for someone actively engaged with **life** to carry off. Emptiness in a **dream** may suggest **death** or aridity. It may also suggest the draining of emotions, or the desire to free oneself from the clutter of material possessions. See **Voids**

Enchantress, The The Enchantress is a **Jungian archetype**, common to both **male** and **female dreamers**. She carries within her both the power to seduce and the power to destroy. She is in some ways similar to a **Siren**, or to Adam's first wife Lilith, in terms of **sexual** predation and destructive capacity, and she symbolically represents a number of the more negative aspects of femininity. If a woman **dreams** of her, it suggests that she may need to review her self-destructive urges – if a man dreams of her, it may suggest a hidden desire to be re-consumed by the feminine, this time carnally, of course, rather than obstetrically. Her antithesis is the **Madonna**, or **Good Mother**.

Enclosures Enclosures tend to have links with the **womb**, but also, possibly, with the **stomach**. When we **dream** of enclosures we tend to view them as comforting and safeguarding **spaces**, except when they impinge upon our freedom of movement – then they become threatening, and their interpretation darkens.

Ending See **Breaking**

Enemas Logically, an enema would appear to imply a desire to be **cleansed** or purified of something that is **poisoning** us. The **sexual** connotations, though, are impossible to ignore, and these would tend to equate enemas with **vaginal** or **anal** intercourse, with the added complication of sterility. In anal terms, such a thing goes without saying, but in vaginal terms the enema **symbol** may suggest that the **dreamer** considers the sexual act to be fruitless, or ultimately without point.

Enemies Dreaming of enemies is an effective way to channel our **anxieties** and to protect ourselves from the realities adherent to them. Our dreamed enemy is frequently only a threatening aspect of ourselves that we need to understand and **interpret** if we are to disarm it. If an object becomes our enemy, then the object needs interpreting too – the morbid **ticking** of a **clock**, for instance, might imply a **fear** of **death**, or of **time**'s predations.

Energy Energy is largely an aspect of **wish-fulfilment** when it appears in **dreams**, for we all seek to benefit from energy, either spiritual, elemental, physical or mental. Energy also equates with youth, with creativity, and with the **sexual** urge, while lethargy suggests illness, age and a lack of dynamic thinking – our **unconscious** mind both understands and seeks to compensate for any shortcomings we may have in this department, and this will be **reflected** in our dreams.

Engagements Engagements fuel **anxiety**. They also bind us, even against our wills, to ourselves and others. To that extent they are a valuable **tool** of the **ego** in its **battle** to prevent us from letting ourselves down. They are inextricably bound up with our expectations, too, in that we often **weight** our engagements with a spurious significance even when we know that, as a result, we may be **riding** for a **fall**. In our **dreams** we often have 'engagements' with aspects of our own personalities, and whether we let ourselves down or come up trumps becomes of acute significance – for a person who doesn't match up to their own ambitions may ultimately prove to be a loser in the **game** of life.

Engines Engines frequently represent the life force, or **heart**. If they go wrong, we may need to call upon an outsider to put us back on the **right track** again. To this extent they reinforce our communality, and our almost morphological connection one to another.

Engineers Engineers may often be a **symbol** of the **father** in our **dreams**. They can also represent **God**.

Engram The lasting traces left by a psychic, paranormal, or **dream** experience on the neural tissue, offering one possible explanation for the 'persistence of memory'.

Entrances Entrances tend to be feminine **symbols**, in that it is the **female** who allows her mate access to her **vagina**, her **baby** to her **womb**, or her **child** to her **breast**. Men tend to force their way through entrances for this very reason (think of **policemen**, **footballers**, or even **storm** troopers), often forgetting, in the process, that if one destroys the entrance, the reception **room** inside will no longer remain secured. History, when one comes to think of it, is largely a mass of **raped** entrances.

Entrapment Entrapment is yet another **anxiety** trigger (see **Engagements**) – there we are, blithely going about our own business, when someone or something (life perhaps?) sets a trap for us. Such traps allow us to arrogate the responsibility for our own **failures** onto others – well, he always had it in for me, so what could I do? There are times, though, when we may wish to be voluntarily entrapped (into **marriage**, for instance, or even a moral covenant) and thereby prevented from doing something that we may later regret.

Envelopes Envelopes hide **secrets**, but secrets that are easy rather than hard of access. They may contain goodies, too, or a cheque – perhaps, unfortunately, a bill, or the reminder of some obligation we may not wish to confront. They can be left unopened, even thrown into a **corner**, but their contents lurk, working away at our **unconscious**, and frequently reappearing in **dreams** under different guises. Envelopes, particularly when dreamt of by a woman, may also suggest **pregnancy**, or at least the possibility of a pregnancy.

Envy See **Jealousy**

Epilepsy Epilepsy suggests a total loss of control. Images of epileptic seizures, of **people** swallowing their own **tongues**, or of having to be restrained, or gagged, have strong revocations within **dreams**. It must be emphasized here that dream images are rarely what is now termed 'polit-ically correct' – the **unconscious** mind is often unregenerate and fre-quently innately conservative to boot, and is rarely amenable to either logic, rational moral constraints, intellectual expostulation, or outraged virtue. It tends to go straight for the jugular, and will snatch any images that are suitably strong, and use them without compunction, and for its own ends. See **Amputation**, **Cannibalism**, **Cripples**, etc.

Epona Epona was the Celtic **horse** goddess, and one of the **Goddesses** of Creativity, as well as being associated with the fertilizing aspect of **water** on **earth**. She was often personified as a **white** mare, with a foal at **foot**, and, together with Oghma (Ogmios), the **God** of Eloquence, was the only Celtic deity to be hijacked by the Romans as one of their own, official, deities. See **Mares** & **Stallions**
KEY LINE: 'The sight of white horses is a vision of angels.' (From Astrampsychus's *Oneirocriticon* 350 AD)

Eroticism We love eroticism and we fear it – it can be either a **pleasure** or a threat, and frequently both at the same **time**. Most of us are rather more cautious than we care to let on as to how we filter and channel our erotic thoughts. The **dream world** reflects this, dragging lost images of our **childhood** out of the woodwork, or showing us, in lateral terms of course, the possible results of our actions were we to give way to our lower (or base) emotions, at the instigation of the grandiloquent **id**.

Eruptions Eruptions are usually synonymous with **ejaculations**, **orgasms**, and other such **earth**-shattering events. They both undermine and reinforce reality – the one, humanly conceived, the other, an adjunct of **nature**.

Escalators See **Elevators**

Escapes Escapes carry within them the inevitable implication that there is something that needs to be escaped from. That 'something' may be either an aspect of ourselves that we wish to deny, a responsibility that we may wish to disinherit, or a moral constraint that we may wish to outpace. In order to escape, we frequently turn ourselves into something that has a positive significance for us (a **horse**, for instance, or the fleetest of run-ners). The fact that our **unconscious** mind rarely lets us get away with such a flagrant obfuscation (and frequently **leaves** us bouncing up and down like a jack-in-a-box on the very same **spot**) may imply that what we wish to escape needs facing, and if possible, **lancing**.

Estate Agents Estate agents try to **sell** you things you think you want, but secretly suspect that you may not need. None of us actually needs to own a **house**, but we choose to do so because it gives us a (possibly false) sense of security. Estate agents are therefore the perfect embodiment of the **wish-fulfilment** fantasy, in that they rely on us to **trick** ourselves into an expedient (to them) conformity.

Eternal Principles An **archetypal** concept relating to such universal **symbols** as the **mandala**, the **circle**, and the **cross**.

Ether Dreams See **Bigness**

Eunuchs Eunuchs are likely to relate to **castration complexes** when dreamt of by men, and to a non-threatening (i.e. Utopian) version of masculinity when dreamt of by women. One could also infer a possible confusion about **sexual** identity, or even a desire to suppress one's sexuality, should it prove inconvenient or over-demanding.

Evenings A **time** when consciousness opens and becomes more receptive to the **unconscious**. A time, also, when both men and women become more responsive to the **anima** and **animus** respectively.

Evil The concept of pure evil has been pretty comprehensively arrogated by most of the great **religions** (largely as a convenient recruitment aid), but its existence probably predates a communally held faith, reflecting, instead, individually perceived **dangers** of the unknown. **Paranoia** (a convenient justification for **neurosis**, if ever there was one) has long been understood to reflect back onto the individual, rather than out towards society-at-large – to this extent dreamed evil implies the only partially formed **soul**, and infers ignorance, rather than active malevolence. See **Devil**
KEY LINE: 'Evil is not true being, but the negation or privation of it.'
(From Andrew Jukes's *The Names of God*)

Examinations Examinations are another frequent dream motif, much like **falling** and **flying**, and are very often dreamed about *after* the event. To that extent they are often comforting, as the **dreamer** knows that they have already fulfilled what was expected of them and are merely going over old **ground**, as it were, and reinforcing lessons already learned. Such **dreams** may often occur just before important milestones in the dreamer's life, or when decisions need to be made that the dreamer may be putting off – the **examination**, in the dream, stands in for one of life's 'tests'. To that extent they may be morale boosters, and act cathartically *before* the feared event.

Examples in Dreams A **dreamer** who is convinced of something in everyday life, will often reinforce this belief in their **dreams** by the use of specific, or literal, **examples**. For instance, a man who believes that **money** is inherently **evil** may dream of thieves **stealing** money from the poor. Or a woman who feels that her **marriage** is stifling may picture a married **couple** sweating over a hot **stove**, making inedible **bread**.

Excavations The presence of excavations in a **dream** (architectural, occurring in ancient **cities**, etc.) often implies that there is something the **dreamer** would like revealed, or even that such a revelation may be on the **cards**. Excavations may also symbolize the process of **psychoanalysis** itself.

Exchange Exchanges of one sort or another frequently occur in **dreams** – the **pouring** of **water** from one basin into a second, for instance, or the transformation of a **river** into the **sea**. These exchanges symbolize transformations (either intended, serendipitous, or unintended), and often refer to the movement from the traditional (the **father**, or collective consciousness) to the intuitive (the **mother**, or **collective unconscious**). It is a freeing, if you like, from the infantile attitude of obedience, to one of intuitive equality – the taking on, in many cases, of either the **anima** or the **animus**, depending on the **sex** of the recipient.

Excitement The steady accrual of excitement in a **dream** (**climbing** a **staircase** or a **mountain**; taking off in **aeroplane**) is usually a **symbol** of **sexual intercourse**.

Exclusion Human beings, as largely social **animals**, **fear** exclusion more than almost anything else. Few of us feel able or willing to survive **alone**, and companionship appears to be essential to us, not only in terms of mental **health**, but also for our physical well-being. To **dream** of exclusion, therefore, is to foment **anxiety** on oneself, and it may be necessary to ask from *what* one is excluded, before a suitable interpretation can be made.

Excrement The desire to **eat** our own excrement is an atavistic one, and not simply limited to coprophiliacs. It frequently occurs in **dreams**, and can indicate a desired, albeit incipiently **neurotic**, **regression** to **childhood**. There may also be an element within the **dreamer**'s character or persona which they may secretly wish to expel – a sort of reverse assimilation, so to speak. See **Cannibalism & Secretions**

Executions Executions may suggest the imposition of permanent solutions on otherwise insoluble **problems**. They are short **cuts** (often quite literally) and may seem to offer an end to all **argument**. As they provide such a radical answer, one must assume a concomitant size and significance for the **questions** they are addressing.

Exercise To an obese person, dreaming of exercise may represent the blunted edge of a **wish-fulfilment** fantasy – dream of it, and you don't have to do it. To a fit person, exercise may provide a positive reinforcement for a seemingly enlightened life choice. For any **dreamer**, consistently dreaming of exercise, or the functions of exercise, may suggest the need to metaphorically stretch some part of themselves that is not, at present, being stretched.

Ex-Husbands When women dream of their ex-**husbands**, the ex-husband can often represent some aspect of themselves that they are dissatisfied with, or wish to reject. When **marriages** fall apart, partners frequently become (albeit briefly, one hopes) **mirror** images of each other, reflecting largely negative aspects. In a good marriage, of course, both partners tend to mirror positive aspects of one another.

Exile We **fear** exile, just as we fear **exclusion**, although exile, thanks to worldwide communications, no longer carries within itself the myriad connotations that it did in the **past**. In symbolical terms, though, exile is as powerful as ever, and may represent the failure to better oneself, or to attempt to make one's **soul**. It may, in addition, imply dismemberment, or the separation of one part of the **psyche** from the other (see **Amputation**). Most importantly, of course, it may imply the voluntary **separation** of oneself from **God**. See **Quarantine**

Exits Exits often symbolize the **anus** in **dreams**.

Experiments The **alchemists** experimented in an apparently vain, although laterally productive, effort to discover how to transmute base **metals** into **gold**, how to prepare the elixir of life, and how to create the universal solvent. Faced with this precedent, fantasies have been produced throughout the ages (think of Frankenstein, the Golem, or the Evil Maria in Fritz Lang's 1926 **film**, *Metropolis*) in which easy answers were serendipitously found to the most demanding of **questions** (and often with the most appalling results). The rapaciously questing **id** searches for such easy answers, and the concept of the experiment is an easy one to harness for such purposes.

Expertise Ersatz expertise in anything equates with **wish-fulfilment**, particularly when it appears in **dreams**. When we find ourselves playing the **piano** like Sviatoslav Richter, or **dancing** like Astaire and Rogers, we can be pretty sure that the image is obscuring a less congenial **reality**. We are compensating for our lack of expertise, in other words, by a sudden, magnificent outpouring of undeserved skill. **Children** lie when confronted by their shortcomings – **dreamers** fabulate.

Explosions Explosions tend to have **sexual** connotations in **dreams**, particularly when dreamt of by men, for whom **guns** and firearms of all sorts tend to stand in for the **penis**, and the power they would like to see derogated to it. See **Nuclear Explosions**

Extractions Extractions lead us back to **dentists**, and to all the **sexual baggage** those who **monkey** about with our **mouths** carry with them. Extractions leave **holes** which need to be filled, and **nature**, as we know, abhors a **vacuum**.

Extraversion See **Extrovert**

Extrovert A person whose attentions are turned more towards the outside **world** than towards themselves. A **Jungian** term, whose antonym is **introvert**.

Ex-Wives See **Ex-Husbands**, and transpose the **sex** of the dreaming party.

Eyes Eyes have paradoxical uses in **dreams**. They can be, at the same time, both receptive and aggressive – at the service, in other words, of both the **male** and the **female**. The eye can be both **phallic** and uterine, flirtatious and assertive, and to this extent the eye is a concatenation of the two sexes, and of strong symbolical value. Eyes may also be neutral, or ever-watchful, as in the eyes of the **Gautama Buddha** – or they can be intrusive and threatening, as in the **Evil** Eye. A single eye often has **anal** connotations. Loss of sight, or **blindness**, can symbolize loss of **sexual** power (**castration complex**) in the **male**, or the loss of fertility, or a **hymen complex**, in the **female**. In addition, it was traditionally believed that if a **corpse**'s eyes were still open after **death**, they were looking for someone to accompany them to the **grave** (thus the covering of the eyes with **coins**, or pennies).
KEY LINE: 'A most frightful dream of a woman whose features were blended with darkness catching hold of my right eye and attempting to pull it out – I caught hold of her arm fast – a horrid feel …' (From Samuel Taylor Coleridge's *Notebooks* of 28th November 1800)

Ezekiel The **biblical** Book of Ezekiel **dates** from the first half of the 6th century BC. In Chapter 37, i–xiv, Ezekiel describes his dream **vision** in the **Valley** of the Dry Bones, in which 'there was a noise, and behold a shaking, and the bones came together, bone to his bone.' The **bones** then grafted sinews, and became covered by **skin**, and the four **winds** entered them and they became a mass of **people**, far exceeding a great **army**. **God** then explained to Ezekiel that what he was looking at was not a human, fleshly '**house**', but the House of Israel. See **Artemidorus of Daldis**

F

Fabric In symbolical terms fabric represents the vibrating structure and mechanisms of the universe, while in metaphysical terms it stands for the frame and stuff that lies behind otherwise seemingly abstract philosophical **argument**. We frequently **judge** a person by the fabric of their **clothes** – cheap rayon, nylon or artificial fibres denoting someone of a lower class, while **wool**, cashmere, mohair, **silk** and the finest lawn **cotton** would appear to be tokens of someone of worth and taste. Our **dreams** often see behind our hidden aspirations, however, whether they represent *folie de grandeur* (**above**) or *nostalgie de la boue* (**below**). Dreams of tears in fabric may represent a young girl's trepidation before the loss of her **virginity** (something whole becoming partial), or even a concealed **rape** fantasy (fabric as spurious protection), while a **male** dreaming of such tears, particularly when threatened, is probably receiving his first intimations of mortality – the torn uniform of the dead **soldier**, or the shattered valance of the **knight** spring to **mind**.

Façades Clothes are façades, veiling the inner person from outward scrutiny. **Dreams** are adept at constructing façades of all kinds, snatching at **symbols** and images in order to protect our **sleeping** selves from the full horrors of reality. Our **bodies** become **houses**, our minds **vaults**, our **enemies snakes**, and our **friends mirror** images, or **doubles** of ourselves. We construct architectural façades in our dreams, even complete **towns**, to represent challenges we feel we are being asked to confront. When stripped of our façades (see **Nakedness**) we try and **run**, often without avail, for the tempering power of the **superego** still dominates our dreaming minds. **Freud** felt very strongly that the dream itself was a façade, behind which it's meaning lay hidden – a meaning quasi maliciously withheld from consciousness. **Jung** vigorously disagreed with this view, however, feeling that dreams were parts of **nature** and therefore not, by definition, designed to deceive – that they involve no arbitrariness and no legerdemain.

Facelifts A facelift may express itself literally in a **dream**, as in a face lifting off its skeletal structure, or the word may simply split, giving two separate symbols of a **face** and a **lift**. The implication of a facelift is that we can, through outside forces, transcend our present reality. This is not true, of course – we only appear to transcend present reality. In **truth** we have simply created another **façade**, or wall, to protect us from the threatening world outside our **stained glass windows**.

Faces Faces in **dreams** are often reflections of the **dreamer** themselves – differing faces for differing moods or aspects of the dreamer's personality. There is also the face we put on for the outside **world** – the 'brave face', or the 'put upon face'. Perfidy was traditionally seen as double-faced, and the Janus image in dreams, of a person with two faces, front and back, may reflect this. They say that you get the face that you deserve at 40, but there is a tendency, in the modern mind, to prefer **façade** over reality, and this will be reflected in the **fabric** of our dreams. What we deserve, and what we feel that we deserve, are two very different things altogether.

Faeces See **Excrement** & **Secretions**

Failure We often dream of failure to protect ourselves from its influence (see **Examinations**). It's as if the **dream** acted in a similar way to the three small bows superstitious **people** give when confronted by a **black cat** or a single **magpie**, or to the statement, 'Let's not paint the devil on the wall, shall we?', when someone too categorically states the optimistic obvious.

Fairgrounds Fairgrounds are places where the unexpected may happen, and they play a similar role in **dream** symbolism, too. They are designed to entertain and give us **pleasure**, but at the same **time** we **fear** being taken advantage of by **people** with more **street** wisdom or savvy than ourselves. To that extent fairgrounds equate, symbolically at least, with visiting a **prostitute**, which is why show-people have traditionally been disapproved of, and equated with **gypsies**, tinkers and **circus** entertainers, in the communal mind. We want them, we are entertained by them, but we fear them a little also – we fear their 'lack of restraint'. By going to the fairground and paying our entrance fee we give them temporary **rights** over us – think of Charon requiring his penny before **ferrying** the dead across the **River** Styx. We pay in a similar way for the privilege of **travelling** through the Chamber of Horrors, on the understanding, of course, that we will be allowed out again at the opposite end. See **Dreamland**

Fairies Fairies were significantly more likely to appear in the **dreams** of Victorians than they are in the dreams of today's **dreamers**. That said, however, fairies are considerably more important to **children** than they are to adults, and this can carry over into adult dreams, in which previously innocent infantile fixations may take on new and sometimes unnerving aspects. There are both good and bad fairies, and we may conjure up the one for **wish-fulfilment**, and the other as an **anxiety** adjunct, often linked to **demons** such as **incubi** and **succubi**.

Fairy Tales Fairy tales are largely comforting, but, like **fairgrounds**, they can **harbour** uneasy truths as well. These, as Bruno Bettelheim tells us in his 1976 book, *The Uses of Enchantment*, are of great importance to the maturing individual, who desperately needs to learn about reality, although preferably through mimesis rather than personal experience. The images from such cathartic fairy tales may carry over into adulthood, however, transmogrifying themselves, when they appear in **dreams**, into images of **repression**, **frustration** and **anxiety**. Thus we may get Humpty

Dumpty standing in for a fear of obesity, the **ogre** representing an abusive **male**, or the **witch** in **Snow White** representing a threatening or undermining **female**.

Fakery Fakery and **dreams** go hand in **hand**, as no one really likes to confront unpleasant **truths**, and the construction of dreams frequently **mirrors** and relates to the consequent **repression** of our natural **urges** and **instincts**. The **joke** is often on us, however, as our **superego** is adept at both **building** up and **tearing** down fake edifices, despite all our efforts to impose our wills upon the more awkward of our dreams. See **Clothes, Cloaks, Dream Censorship, Masks & Façades**

Falling Falling or **tumbling**, in a dream, may constitute a **warning** that the **dreamer**, in their everyday life, is acting in too grandiose or highhanded a fashion, disproportionate to their real capacities – living above themselves, in other words. Such **dreams** can provide a valuable forewarning of **dangers** to come, and may disguise a **secret** longing to become unstuck. Falling can also symbolize 'loss', as in a loss of equilibrium, a loss of self-control, or a loss of moral judgement. Even the gradual drifting away into **sleep** is a sort of falling, incorporating, as it inevitably does, the 'loss' of our comforting **ego** consciousness. Falling, in semantic terms, may indicate a descent from a state of grace or a loss of virtue, and because of this, when women dream of 'falling', it can sometimes imply **sexual** intercourse, with all the ambivalent feelings that such an act can sometimes contain. Dreams of others falling, but not ourselves, may occasionally occur as a result of subliminal or **unconscious death** wishes on the part of the dreamer. Falling out of **bed** may represent a literal fulfilling of an unconscious desire not to succeed in what one is doing – i.e. sleep – because the very act of sleeping might be depriving us of the capacity to do something which our **id** instinct might prefer. Finally, certain dreamers are convinced that falling implies a re-entering of the physical **body** by the etheric **double** after involution.

Falsification of Memory The changing or manipulation of a memory so that it is no longer 'true'.

Fame We are told that the youth of today values fame and celebrity (see **Celebrities**) above everything else. If this is so, then fame will have a significant value in terms of a young person's **dreams** – either as an **anxiety** pointer ('I shall never be famous') or as a **wish-fulfilment** fantasy ('If I do such and such a thing, I shall be famous') or as a **displacement** activity ('If I make myself desirable enough, perhaps a famous person will notice me, and sprinkle some of their stardust in my direction'). It's a cop out, of course, replacing notoriety with achievement, and to this extent it represents the easy answer callow **people** crave to what are usually complicated questions – i.e. how are we to live our lives, and what significance do they, or should they, have?

Family See individual elements of the family, i.e. **father**, **mother**, **son**, **daughter**, etc.

Family Romance The (usually) erroneous belief that one has secretly been born into a higher social bracket (the Royal Family being a firm favourite) than the real **world** is capable of acknowledging. Such delusions often find themselves reflected in grandiloquent **dreams**, or similar *folies de grandeurs*. See **Celebrities** & **Fame**

Fans The purpose of fans would appear to be the forcible movement of **air** in order to procure a draught – but in the flamenco tradition, for example, they are also **tools** of seduction, which both conceal and draw attention to desirable features. This capacity to 'draw attention' may well be the **key** to fan symbolism within **dreams**, in that fans may also, when closed, be used as pointers towards things, or even, when clacked smartly shut, as attention gatherers in terms of noise, or as instruments of upbraiding. Dreaming of fans (in the sense, say, of football supporters) might suggest either a desire to belong (possibly tribally), or a desire to be seen as behaviourally supportive, thereby gaining parental or peer recognition for one's conformity.
KEY LINE: 'Wer't not better/Your head were broken with the handle of a fan?' (From Beaumont and Fletcher's *Wit at Several Weapons* 1855)

Farms Farms equate with **food** and sustenance (the word stems from the Anglo-Saxon *fearme*, food), but, in modern terms, they may also imply isolation – this is, of course, something of a paradox, for in ancient times they might, with some justification, have been seen as representing community. This fact throws up, yet again, the importance of the individual significance **symbols** have for each separate **dreamer** – there are **archetypes**, yes, but significances are often interchangeable, much along the lines of philosopher Ludwig Wittgenstein's theory of the existence, in each individual, of both a 'public' and a 'private' **language**. There simply *are* no rules, and inferences must be made according to the most flexible of guidelines.

Fasting In symbolical terms fasting implies abstention from the external in favour of the internal. In some ways this capacity for abstention is the fundamental thing that separates us from other **animals**, and is a strong pointer towards the existence of the **id**, the **ego**, and the **superego**, which, between them, would appear to call such a capacity into being. It is also an argument for the existence of **God** (as if such an argument were needed!), in that the human being, outside the presence of God, would feel no need of betterment, but would remain animal-content.

Fat See **Fatness**

Fathers The father often appears as an authority figure in dreams (a **king**, an emperor, a **conductor**, a **pilot**, a **wise old man**, a **teacher**, a **captain**, etc.) and can be equated with the **sun**, in **mythological** terms, and with **God**, in religious terms, and with the collective consciousness in noumenal terms. Such **symbols** are the 'masks' or 'imagos' by which the **dreamer** protects themselves from a too overt undermining of a societally instilled respect for the paternal figure. The father can also represent the **superego**. In **Jungian** terms, the father is often seen to represent the embodiment of the 'traditional **spirit**', but this may be subject to change given the recent (but possibly short-lived in **archetypal** terms) breakdown of **family** values in the Western **world**. In English, of course, the words 'Dad' and 'dead' are very close to each other euphonically, and, given that the father is usually the first to die in a close-knit family (being customarily older than the **mother**, and, being **male**, more short-lived), there may also be a semantic element to the appearance of the father in a dream context. See **Mothers**

Fatigue Fatigue **dreams** may have correlatives with **frustration dreams** and **inhibitions**, and often point to a depletion of the dreamer's **superego** resources. The **dreamer**, in other words, may feel that they no longer have the self-control or the physical stamina necessary to live in harmony with the outside **world**. They can also serve as reminders that we need to 'pull ourselves together' if we are not to let ourselves down. **Running** on the spot dreams can have a similar **root** cause, suggesting that the dreamer is torn between two modes of action and feels that they no longer have the necessary energy to make a morally informed decision.

Fatness The pejorative overtones of fatness are relatively recent in origin, and often reflect more on the condition and **unconscious** predilections of the speaker than on any fundamental problem inherent in fatness itself. In many ways fat is a good thing – it may protect us from the **cold**, dissuade others from being aggressive towards us, or serve as a **sacrificial** object implying the offering of affection. The rejection or repudiation of fatness can only occur in a society which is itself 'fat' with privilege and the capacity for idleness. This, in itself, implies that 'fat' feeds off 'fat', and may go some way towards explaining our society's, and, not uncoincidentally, the dream **world**'s, fragmentation in the **face** of the fat issue. Like William Shakespeare's Julius Caesar, our **dreams** often prefer 'men about [us] that are fat.' See **Thinness** & **Upholstery**
KEY LINE: 'And I will satiate the soul of the priests with fatness, and my people shall be satisfied with my goodness, saith the Lord.' (Jeremiah xxxi, 14)

Faucets **Children** often dream of faucets when they wish to urinate. The dream may even go so far as to show a faucet being tightened and then (oh no) loosened again, often leading to a bedtime gusher, and to all the **guilt** feelings bed-wetting (see **Wetting the Bed**) traditionally triggers. Faucets and taps equate to 'civilized' control of the environment, while bed-wetting frequently stems from the **fear** that an apparently civilized edifice (the parental relationship, for instance) may be in imminent danger of collapsing.

Faxes Faxes are a relatively modern form of message-bearing and communication, so if they appear in **dreams**, this would reasonably seem to be their significance. The speed of a fax would also be significant, implying that the message was an urgent one, possibly associated with work.

Fear Symbolically, fear implies a lack of intellectual willpower, in that most things of which we are fearful may be rationally downplayed until they are no longer quite so threatening. Our **dreams**, however, will often filter through and replay such **suppressed** fears, in an effort, one supposes, to prevent psychic damage. It is for this reason that fear of the unknown, twinned with a fear of often inappropriate objects, plays such a large part in our dream architecture. In the ancient French romance *Croquemitaine*, Fortress Fear is a fantastical **castle** near Saragossa conjured up in dreams by those who give in to their fear – if the fear can be overcome, the castle immediately disappears into thin air.

Feasting See **Banquets**

Feathers Feathers have revocations both of lightness and of **cowardice** – of the ephemeral and of the lower personality. Being **light**, feathers are temporal, and do not carry a great deal of **weight** – they are easily discarded, in other words, even by the **birds** who need them to **fly**. **Death**, too, is often signified by the **falling** of a feather, particularly, of course, when birds are **killed** for our **food**, or when, in parts of ancient Asia and North America, the native **peoples** would add a new feather to their bonnet for each **enemy** slain, thus triggering the expression 'another feather in your cap' (the same is still done in modern sporting **circles** when a woodcock is **shot**). This **rich** vein of suggestibility makes of feathers powerful dream image material.

Feeling The feeling one has when first awaking from a **dream** is a powerful clue to its **manifest content**. This, together with the unvarnished sequence of remembered dream events needs to be **written** down as soon as is feasible, so that as little as possible of the dream is **lost**.

Feet Feet are our connection with the **ground**. Traditionally, if our feet are placed firmly, it means that we are well-seated as personalities, and able to absorb setbacks better than if we are flibbertigibbets, with our **heads** (and feet) in the air. The **washing** of feet by another has a strong symbolical significance in many Middle Eastern countries (viz. **Jesus'** washing of Peter's feet at the Last Supper).

Fellow Traveller An alternative symbol for the **double**, or the **shadow**. There is also a suggestion of betrayal about the phrase, as in the Senator

Joseph McCarthy's (1908–57) **witch**-hunt era phrase 'fellow travellers' meaning communist adherents.

Female, The The **Great Mother**, or Mother **Earth**, was one of the two **archetypal** principles at the foundation of both Eastern and Western functional **mythologies** – what the German poet **Goethe** called the 'Eternal Feminine'. The feminine principle is traditionally both passive and receptive, important adjuncts of the so-called 'higher emotions'. Despite its recent denigration (at least in concept) as a result of the **rush** towards the imposition of an often spurious, and even capricious, ersatz 'equality', the feminine principle, in its pure form, is an essential part of the **male/female** duality, as objectified in **spirit**/matter, **mind**/emotion, **love**/wisdom, life/form, force/matter, intellect/intuition, etc. Only by a complete understanding of the opposing principle (rather than by its plundering) can an accommodation be reached with either the **anima** or the **animus**, depending on the **sex** of the **dreamer**. See **Male**, **Oppositions**, **Widow & Widower**

Femininity See **Female**

Fences **Dreamers** often place fences in front of themselves either to trigger the facing of uncomfortable issues, or to prevent actions that might be thought premature by the **unconscious** mind. Fences require both strategies (to devise how to overcome them) and patience (particularly if they are large and obstructive). The size of the fence is of crucial importance here, as is its makeup. Fences in **dreams** can represent perceived social barriers, and also relational boundaries – even, on occasion, **taboos**.

Ferries Ferries are conveniences, as without them we would have to **swim**. This might seem **self**-evident at first glance, but nothing, of course, is self-evident in **dreams**. 'The **night**', as the old saying goes, 'has its own laws.' When we conjure up ferries, therefore, it indicates a wish to move forwards, or across barriers – even, possibly, to die (think of Charon ferrying **souls** across the **River** Styx). The **death** may be a metaphysical or spiritual one, though, and not necessarily that of the **body**. See **Boats**

Fertilizer The use of a fertilizer implies that something is drying up or needs nourishing. Fertilized ground (both spiritual and geophysical) announces itself ready for seeding, which brings us to the **Freudian** view of fertilizer, as implying, perhaps, a desire to bear **children** – to *be* fertilized, in other words.

Festivals Festivals are **ritualistic**, occurring outside desire and generally on pre-announced occasions. This may be why they are so often dreaded, as one may simply 'not be in the mood' on the day in question. Festivals exert a sort of *force majeure* upon us, bending us to their service, rather than the opposite way around. It is therefore not surprising that festivals, when they occur in **dreams**, may often be pretty lowering or lacklustre affairs, smacking more of duty than of joy. On the occasions that they do take off, it is usually when they are not intellectually prearranged – other **people**'s festivals are more fun, in other words.

Fetishes Fetishes are abnormalities (or the products of abnormal thinking) which rule our object-choices. In the case of **males** (in whom fetishes predominate), **Freud** considered that most fetishes were substitutes for the mother's **phallus** 'which the little boy once believed in and does not wish to forego' – for the obvious reason that if the **mother** can be castrated, so can the little boy. An extreme example of this might be the fetishising of the deformed **female** foot in ancient Chinese custom – first the foot was deformed and then it was revered, a chain of events that Freud compared to the Chinese thanking the woman for the courtesy of having voluntarily submitted to castration in the first place. See **Castration Complex & Primal Scene**

Fevers Fevers break. They also generate breaks between the pre-fever state and the post-fever state. **People** change as a result of fevers, either by having an increased awareness of their own mortality, or through the selfless help they are able to give to others. Fevers, then, can both nourish and diminish – they can suggest a generalized disharmony, or they can trigger an often unexpected altruism. See **Thermometers**

Fields In purely physical terms, fields provide nourishment (either to us or to our **animals**), while also giving us aesthetic pleasure. In the Bhagavad-Gita, the *Kshetra*, or field, is the environment in which the **soul** evolves – the *Kshetra* allows movement from the lower to the upper, just as a connection with **nature**, during the Romantic Era, was felt to bring enlightened adherents nearer to the ineffable.

Fiends Fiends are elemental, auto-intelligent **spirits**, who may or may not be connected to the **Devil**. We can conjure up fiends for ourselves (through self-abuse or **neurotic** gratification), or have them conjured up for us (through **manic depression** or malicious **poisoning**). In **dreams** they may well serve as a reminder of where we may be headed if we do not succeed in changing the patterns of our behaviour.
KEY LINE:'And he likes to relate his success on the Halls,/When the Gallery once gave him seven cat-calls/But his grandest creation, as he loves to tell,/Was Firefrorefiddle, the Fiend of the Fell.' (From T. S. Eliot's *Gus, The Theatre Cat*)

Fighting Fighting in **dreams** often has a **sexual** meaning. It can, for instance, imply a fight against an 'undesirable' sexual tendency such as **homosexuality**, lesbianism, or even heterosexuality, depending on context and proclivity. Or it may signify the sexual act itself, particularly in the case of younger **dreamers** – for the young **child**, when inadvertently witnessing such an act (see **Primal Scene**) between their **parents**, may reasonably assume (through the ignorance we often impose upon youth) that their parents are fighting or roughhousing. Fighting, just as with **battles** and **wrestling**, may also point towards other, non-sexual, mental conflicts.

Figs Figs are symbols of the **vagina** – Adam and Eve covered their pudenda with fig **leaves**, indicating both fruitfulness and modesty, and possibly giving rise to the expression 'full fig' for being fully dressed (*pace* the Italian word *fiocchi*, meaning 'in gala costume', and which probably stemmed from a similar source). When we see a fig we immediately imagine it open, i.e. the significance is more on the inside than on the outside. In addition, figs contain **seeds** (ergo **eggs**), and symbolize, in many cultures, the **Tree** of Life.
KEY LINE: 'The proper way to eat a fig, in society,/Is to split it in four, holding it by the stump,/And open it, so that it is a glittering, rosy, moist, honied, heavy-petalled four-petalled flower.' (From D. H. Lawrence's *Figs*)

Figurative Expressions Figurative expressions that occur in **dreams** are invariably depicted literally, as in, for instance, a grey **cat**, for 'all cats are **grey** in the **dark**', or the appearance of a number of **cooks**, for 'too many cooks spoil the broth'. See **Abstract Thought** & **Personification**

Filmic Dreams See Films

Films The arrival of moving **pictures** arguably gave a marginally different structure to our **dreams**. The **unconscious** mind steals with impunity from any available source, and, thanks to television, the DVD player, and the **internet**, our intake of contrived images and stories is now at an all-time high. It would be inconceivable were this not to affect the quality and arrangement of our dreams, particularly in terms of **doubles**, and **shadows**, and **wish-fulfilment** fantasies. Amongst films which are based directly on dreams experienced by their directors are Ingmar Bergman's *Hour of the Wolf*, Robert Altman's *Three Women*, and Akira Kurosawa's *Dreams*.

Finding It is more usual to search in a dream than to find. This is because **dreams** are very often triggered, not by joy or by **happiness**, but by **frustration**, **anxiety** and the **repression** of **guilt** feelings. **Searching**, then, reflects what we may sense is wrong in the way that we live our lives, while finding may suggest that we are doing something **right**, and deserve good fortune, or even success in our **journey** of self-realization. If what we find is unpleasant, however, measures may need to be taken to **root** out the cause of the psychological misfire the dream is pointing up.

Fingers While fingers which appear in **dreams** may sometimes possess **phallic** connotations (one can be 'finger and glove' with someone when one is intimate), in symbolical terms they may also be manifestations of what has been demonstrated to have been done. Going further along these lines, they are also **symbols** of **truth** and of the **love** of goodness, as suggested by the Christian Blessing and also by the sign of the fingers of Horus often found on **amulets** within Egyptian tombs. In dreams, fingers frequently **point** the way towards things, but they can also be used to stop forward movement, and, in extreme cases, movements to the rear.

Finishing Finishing something may possibly have **death** connotations (death is, after all, a completion), but it can also suggest misplaced or inappropriate satisfaction with what one has achieved. Young ladies used to be 'finished', when everybody knew that they hadn't, in reality, even 'started' – and **furniture**, too, was given a 'finish'. Semantic complications abound for 'finish', amongst which 'Finnish' and '**fish**' stand out, giving us, for instance, a **dog** sled **race** in the **snow** (in Finland), whereupon we make through the finishing line and dig into the ice for fish to prevent ourselves from **starving** (dying/finishing). This may seem far-fetched, but it is actually a very good example of how the dream **world** manipulates and moulds meanings to suit itself.

Fire Fire is often a concretized symbol of the **abstract** concept of **love**. Fire can also relate to sexuality – the making or creation of a fire can symbolize the sexual act. There is, in addition, a strong **link** between fire and **water**, between **sex** and conception, and this may find itself reflected in fire-dousing **symbols**. Fire, in that aspect, is **phallic** and masculine, whereas water is **uterine** and feminine. This becomes even more apparent when the properties of the two elements are investigated, fire being characterized by its devouring, licking, **burning** aspects, and water being characterized by its dousing, slaking, extinguishing aspects. Both elements, while seemingly antithetical, are equally precious, and both may, of course, be used as **cleansing** or purificatory agents. Finally, fire may equate to **blushing** and to loss of control in puberty.

Firecrackers See **Fireworks**

Firemen Firemen frequently represent **wish-fulfilment** fantasies in **dreams**, with either the **dreamer** desiring to be saved by a man (for it *is* usually a man) they do not wish to have to **judge**, or else desiring to be that man, saving others. The iconic status of the fireman was further enhanced during and after the Twin Towers **Disaster** in the US in 2001, in which firemen were seen, for a short time at least, as the purificatory elements that represented all the **archetypal** characteristics that the US was deemed to have **lost** during the post-Kennedy era – the self-sufficient working man taking responsibility for his **family**, the sense of community, the capacity for **self-sacrifice** in favour of the general good, etc.

All these factors underline and are incorporated within the fireman's dream identity.

Fireplaces See **Hearths**

Fireworks The desire to let off firecrackers or fireworks is often symptomatic of a desire for **sex**. **Rockets** may occasionally equate with **ejaculation**, just as they may suggest a desire to be noticed or even helped (one may, after all, be sending off a signal or distress rocket). It is a striking fact that it is nearly always men and boys who are fascinated by fireworks, and this strengthens the assertive sexual element of the firework image – every exploded firework presupposes a 'successful **launch**' (unless, of course, they blow your **fingers** off).

Fish To the ancient Chinese the words for fish and abundance were similar in intonation, making them entirely transposable in **dream** interpretation. Fish were, in addition, believed to have knowledge and wisdom, and were often used in folk remedies. In Christian iconography a fish often represents **Jesus Christ**, or the Higher **Self**, and it is surprising how often fishermen who practise catch-and-release will admit that they feel that a recently released **salmon** (for instance) **carries** away with it something of themselves. However, it was the **Devil**, paradoxically, and not Jesus Christ, who was known as the great 'fisher of **souls**'. This **richness** of image imbrues each and every fish appearing in a dream, and makes interpretation particularly difficult unless individual contexts are taken into account. To **weight** the **scales** even further in the fish's direction, it should be added that the **collective unconscious** may well have its own take on the possibility of our having begun our morphological development as protozoan fish. See **Fishing**
KEY LINE: 'Rapidly changing in shape and size from pretty one-pound trout to great-eyed, loose-mouthed cod-like monsters, they presently fill the whole bed of the stream – fill it pile-high in a horrible sweltering heap; which becomes more horrible still in another moment, when the ghastly creatures die and fall to pieces.' (From Frederick Greenwood's *Imagination in Dreams* 1894)

Fishing If a man **dreams** of fishing, it is usually a euphemism for the **sexual** act. The act of fishing may also imply a search for something **hidden** just beneath the surface – even for sustenance, whether mental or spiritual. See **Fish**

Fishing Rods Fishing rods are usually penile symbols in **dreams**. They may also equate with divining **rods**, however, implying a search for something precious (and possibly even something feminine, like **water**).

Fists Fists are assertive, masculine **symbols**, used to imply or to force dominance over others. If a woman **dreams** that she is threatened by a fist, there is undoubtedly a **phallic** element to the **fear**, and possibly even a fear of conception, in that a fist may equate with the imposition of a **birth** or a **baby**, necessitating possibly unwanted life changes. **Fisting** (the voluntary insertion or 'forcing' of a fist into the **vagina** or **anus** for sexual pleasure) is in widespread use in lesbian, **homosexual** and heterosexual **pornographic** iconography, and one can only infer a subtextual echo of sterility from its recently more prevalent status. This will no doubt find itself reflected, even if unknowingly, in dreams.

Fixed Symbolism The temptation, given in to by some **psychoanalysts**, to affix set meanings to certain **symbols**. There is a **danger**, when this mode of thought is too slavishly followed, that symbols which already have a 'full value' will not be heeded, leading to **false**, and possibly even distorting, interpretations. See **Spiders**

Flagpoles Flagpoles often represent the **penis** in **dreams**. There is, in addition, a triumphalist element to a flagpole, which may equate it with the self-proclaimed crowing of a **cock** – it is a visible expression of the abstract notion of **possession**, in other words. See **Flags**

Flags Flags and banners tend towards reactionary meanings – they usually represent reversions back to old norms, rather than movements towards the **new**. Crusades require flags to hold them together, and to this extent flags are binding agents for otherwise disparate **groups**. They can, on occasion, also suggest a desire to **celebrate**, when they appear in **dreams**, or a desire to signal some fundamental change in status (such as **pregnancy**, **marriage**, or **recovery** from **illness**). See **Flagpoles**

Flailing We flail when we are uncertain, but also when we wish to separate the lower qualities from the higher qualities (the **wheat** from the chaff). There is also an element of **masochism** involved in flailing, as one may, quite easily, strike oneself in the process. Flailing, **whipping**, **beating** and flagellation are virtually synonymous with each other, while flailing may also imply the desire to impose one's will on others, without, perhaps, any justification for so doing.

Flames To the Taoists, flames indicated **danger**, **anger**, or **speed**. Flames may be purificatory (see **Fire**), and also **sexual** in content, as in, 'I was consumed with passion'. In Christian iconography they often represented spiritual **truth**, as in Daniel iii, 15's 'burning fiery furnace', to which Shadrach, Meshach and Abednego were condemned by Nebuchadnezzar for refusing to worship graven images.

Flashlights See **Torches**

Flaubert, Gustave (1821–80) Flaubert, in his *The Dictionary of Accepted Ideas* supplement to his posthumous last novel, *Bouvard et Pécuchet* (1881), has the following to say about **dreams**. 'Dreams: (Vague) The sum of great ideas one does not understand.'

Flaws Flaws or **cracks** in existing structures are pointers to underlying **problems** that may need immediate rectification, before tragedy (the destruction of the structure) occurs.

Flaying Stripping something of its flesh may have both positive and negative revocations. A **snake** sloughing its own flesh is in the actual process of regeneration, and the expression 'I feel like a new person' implies a similar development. But 'I'm not comfortable in my **skin**' suggests the need for spiritual renewal – the rejection of something precious (the skin) in favour of something inchoate and noumenal. To 'flay a **fox**' is an age-old expression for **vomiting**. See **Shamans**

Fleas Fleas are outside irritants. Symbolically they can equate to **gossip**, malicious intent, **illness** caused by environmental factors, or parasites feeding on us or on those we cherish.
KEY LINE: 'Hobbes clearly proves that every creature/Lives in a state of war by nature;/So naturalists observe a flea/Has smaller fleas that on him prey,/And these have smaller still to bite 'em,/And so proceed ad infinitum.' (From Jonathan Swift's *On Poetry: A Rhapsody* 1733)

Fleeces Fleeces may protect us from the **cold** (and to that extent they are precious), but they may also disguise us, or suggest that we are something other than what we seem to be (think of Ulysses and his men hiding in the fleeces of Polyphemus' **sheep** on the Island of the Cyclops, and the '**Golden** Fleece' of Jason and the Argonauts fame, which was probably perceived to have **magical** properties for similar reasons). To 'fleece' someone is to forcibly take something of value from them (their fleece), and a '**wolf** in sheep's **clothing**' is someone who hides their true, aggressive **nature**, under a non-aggressive exterior.

Flies A fly symbolizes feebleness and insignificance. The ancient Greeks used to sacrifice an **ox**, once a **year**, at the **temple** of Actium, to the **God** of Flies, as did the Syrians, and it is probably for this reason that the fly can sometimes be taken to symbolize the **Devil**, or Beelzebub, **Prince** of the Flies. The Koran states that all flies shall perish except one – the **bee-fly**.

Floating To float, in a **dream**, implies that we may be in a state of stasis or inertia, and that a decision must, at some time, be made, in terms of forwards, backwards, upwards, or downwards movement. **Freud**, however, associated floating with **sexuality**, particularly in terms of allowing our emotional **natures** to dictate to our rational natures. Floaters, or pieces of detached retina, get in the way of clear sight, and this, too, may find itself reflected in dream imagery. See **Above & Below**

Flogging Flogging may equate with **beating, flailing, selling**, and **hitting** in **dream** terms, and will almost certainly have sexual as well as aggressive or punitive connotations. The fundamental link between **sex** and

violence, and sex and dominance, is well documented, and even the age-old schoolboy use of the word 'to flog', implying **masturbation**, is a case in point. Boys were 'flogged' and thus dominated in terms of **punishment**, and would 'flog' their own **penises** in a desire to dominate in their turn – a sexualized action they might later project onto **females**. Religious flagellation and self-flagellation, however, probably stems from the concept that we are symbolically healed by the stripes given to **Jesus** on the way to the **Crucifixion**.

Floods Floods may represent **urination**. They can also be concretized **symbols** of an abstraction, such as **love**. Noah's Flood represented a down-pouring of **Truth** onto an as yet unevolved **world** in the form of spiritual dissolution. Many **Eastern** religions suggested that the Great Flood consisted of boiling hot **water**. See **Flames**

Flowers In old English folklore, to **dream** of **white** flowers was a **death** omen. This belief probably stemmed from the association of white flowers with the dead, and also to the belief that if a plant with **coloured** petals showed a freak white petal, a death would occur in the **family** to which the flowers belonged. Flowers in a dream may also equate with the concept of a reward, either self-proclaimed ('You love me, so you ought to give me flowers to prove it'), or unwitting ('I love you, therefore I feel a desire to demonstrate my love for you by giving you flowers'). See **Mark Twain** & **Picking Flowers**

Flowing The motion of flowing in a dream can often have its source in thoughts of **menstruation**, and sometimes even of **orgasm**. Flowing, too, may imply the eventual reaching of a **goal** (even **death**, or the 'little death' of **sexual** ecstasy), and to that extent it will probably associate itself with **rivers**, **oceans**, or even an **avalanche**, when it appears in **dreams**.

Flutes Flutes are suggestive of the **penis** when they appear in **dreams**, particularly when associated directly with the **mouth**. Even in Mozart's *The Magic Flute*, the flute was accorded **magical** properties (*ergo* the propagating of **children**) which, unless purified by **love** and the powers of **light**, simply reflected **darkness** and the **vices** of lust and unfocused carnal desire. The flute, in other words, may be used to make beautiful **music**, but only in the hands of an adept.

Flying One of the commonest **symbols** to occur in **dreams**, the act of flying usually signifies a desire for independence – for breaking free from something that would normally tie us down. **Freud** believed that such fantasies of flying were the product of a natural regression to our **childhood**, in which we felt freer, and more capable of unencumbered movement than we do as adults. In addition, the process of looking down from a **height** can appear to offer us a perspective on our destiny, as well as affording us the prospect of an easy **escape** from a difficult situation. The act of flying may also serve as a compensation for deficiencies in the character of the **dreamer**, as well as **warning** them of **dangers** already present in the course which they are taking in their everyday life. If action is not taken to remedy the situation, real **accidents** may occur. Flying, when dreamed of by a **male**, can also suggest an erect **penis**, or a penis in the process of erection, and when dreamed of by a woman may suggest coitus fantasies. Other **psychoanalysts** (**Stekel**, for instance) saw flying as a symbol of **death**, or, in the case of **Adler**, as a desire to dominate. See **Levitation**, **Swinging** & **Wings**

KEY LINE: 'Thus, the dreamer sometimes thinks he is flying in unknown regions, sometimes skimming only a few inches above the ground, and wondering he never did it before.'(From Leigh Hunt's *Of Dreams* 1820)

Foetuses See **Embryos**

Fog Fog both occludes and obfuscates, and may imply an inability to make up one's **mind**. One may approach **danger** in a fog and not even be aware of it. One may also **lose** one's way. In addition, our **voices** are dampened in the fog, and may not easily be heard – the very same thing applies to others calling us, of course, and asking us for help. See **Mist** & **Smog**

Following To be followed, in a **dream**, often represents anxiety over something that has occurred in the **past** – this is particularly true if we are unable to make out exactly what it is that is following us. If it is we who are following someone or something, it may indicate that we need **guidance** or help of some sort – we may even feel the need to act as a disciple or as a **servant** to some greater **goal** than that afforded by expedient self-interest. See **Anxiety Dreams**

Food Food is an expansive **symbol**, covering both the mental, the physical and the spiritual. If we are actively **hungry** in a **dream**, it implies a perceived lack of something fundamental to our well-being, whereas if we dream of surfeit, we may be experiencing an underlying guilt at some real or imagined inequity. Food may also equate with **truth** (if we do not eat, we die), and can present itself as a **bridge** between **reality** and illusion (think of the **biblical** concept of *manna*). See **Cannibalism**

KEY LINE: 'It is certain enough ... that dreams in general proceed from indigestion; ... The inspirations of veal, in particular, are accounted extremely Delphic; Italian pickles partake of the same spirit of Dante; and a butter-boat shall contain as many ghosts as Charon's.' (From Leigh Hunt's *Of Dreams* 1820)

Fools To dream of fools is often to imagine oneself a fool ('every man hath a fool in his sleeve'). Fools do not acknowledge or learn by their errors, and it is possible that our **dream** is telling us that we have committed an error ('been a fool') and that we are, in consequence, not using our intelligence to its full capacity ('living in a fool's paradise').

Football   The significance of football lies in its import to the **dreamer**. To a non-sporting person, football might have revocations of time-wasting and triviality, whilst to a sporting person it might represent strategy, teamwork and community. To dream of individual footballers (George Best, before his death, was a firm favourite) is a pretty clear **wish-fulfilment** fantasy – the emphasis being on what he achieved during, rather than after, his career.

Footprints   Footprints are manifestations of existence. We have only to think of Robinson Crusoe and his discovery of Man Friday's footprint in the sand to remind ourselves of their significance in human terms – pictures of the first footprint on the moon's surface hold an equally iconic status. In a stranger's footprints we recognize someone akin to ourselves, and to that extent they imply the continuing succession of physical forms. See **Handprints**

Forests   Symbols of meditation and of the primeval **forest** from which we all stem, forests also **hide** things. Individual **trees** are generally seen as benevolent, but masses of trees together may **harbour** bizarre **numina**, **monsters** and **wolves**. **People** often enter forests with a feeling of dread, and forests in **fairy tales** are almost always **secret** places, in which unforeseen things may occur, or in which wild **animals** may lurk. Forests are **symbols** of the **unconscious**, therefore, and may suggest the multitude of different **paths** that potentially lie ahead of us. A single mistake, in a deep forest, is hard to rectify – as if to illustrate this, Dante began his *Divine Comedy* with the words '*Nel mezzo del cammin di nostra vita mi ritrovai per una selva oscura che la diritta via era smarrita.*' ('In the midst of life's journey I found myself in a dark forest where the straight path was lost.')
KEY LINE: 'Yet I never dreamed of cities; nor did a house ever occur in any of my dreams. Nor, for that matter, did any human being ever break through the wall of my sleep. I, who had seen trees only in parks and illustrated books, wandered in my sleep through interminable forests.' (From Jack London's *Before Adam* 1908)

Forges   Forges are **alchemical symbols**, and suggest the making of something from something else (the concatenation of two or more elements). One can forge a **friendship**, or forge an alliance between two disparate **parties**, and the element of **fire** that a forge presupposes is potentially purificatory.

Forks   Forks may denote choices, as in a road that forks two ways, or they may suggest **lightning** and sudden changes occurring as a result of outside forces. Traditional **dream interpretation** (possibly influenced by thoughts of the **Devil**) sees a fork as representing **enemies** working against the **dreamer**, or unhappiness in the domestic sphere and separation from loved ones. If the fork is driving us on, it may suggest that, emotionally at least, we are between a **rock** and a hard place, and that we need to make a decision before too much **time** elapses. 'Forks' was also another word for the gallows, and originates from the Latin word *furca*, meaning a prisoner's **yoke**.

Formulae The presence of formulae in a **dream** may suggest difficult answers to difficult questions. Codes may also be implied, together with **secrets** that may only be teased out through the acquiring of esoteric knowledge.

Fortresses The conjuring up of a fortress in a **dream** may suggest that the **dreamer** is fundamentally insecure, and stands in need of a haven or **sanctuary** or some other form of outside help (for one cannot, of course, build a fortress on one's own).
KEY LINE: 'And he [David] said, the Lord is my rock and my fortress, and my deliverer;' (2 Samuel xxii, 2)

Foundations For anyone who has studied the **Bible**, firm foundations brings St Matthew's 'the **house** built on **sand**' parable immediately to **mind** (Matthew vii, 24-27), in which the **wise** man builds his house upon a **rock**, while the foolish man builds his house upon sand. Foundations can also apply to the **past**, or to our antecedents – and even to the Law, both moral and civil.

Fountains These may often be seen as a representation of the **uterus**, i.e. the 'font of life' or the 'life principle'. They can also symbolize the **female breast**, and even, to a young **child**, the act of **urination** (see **Wetting the Bed**). The 'Fountain of **Death**', in Torquato Tasso's 1581 poem, *Jerusalem Delivered*, excites thirst in whoever sees it, but then goes on to **kill** with **laughter** anyone who tastes its **water**, while the Fountain of Youth (situated somewhere in the Bahamas, apparently) was guaranteed to prolong active life beyond rational **borders**. Fountains, then, suggest activity, both spiritual and physical, and will tend to have a similar significance when they appear in **dreams**. See **Representability**

Fourness The number four equates with wholeness and completeness, and represents a healing and unifying force when it occurs in **dreams**. Individual aspects of the four, when undifferentiated, can imply both evolution and the possibilities of progression in psychic terms. See **Quaternity**

Foxes A fox symbolizes cunning or artifice. In Christian iconography, the presence of a fox's image implies **fraud**. Tycho Brahé, the 16th-century Danish astronomer, would faint if he caught sight of a fox, while Elizabethans would **fight** with one (a broadsword), and if they were **killed**, the decaying matter of their **bodies** might find itself surrounded by fox-**fire** (phosphorescence). All this *à propos* of nothing in particular.

Fragility To **dream** of fragility is to connect with our ethereal **nature** – it may also suggest a sense of the inchoateness of much human endeavour, despite what we are told to the contrary.

Fraud Fraud may suggest either outraged virtue or submerged **guilt**, depending on its context within the dream. There may also be an element of **living** under false pretences, for most of us put on a front of some sort in our everyday existences in order to ease life's little **burdens** – **dreams**, unfortunately, are remarkably adept at pointing up these minor peccadilloes, and making us feel guilty about them.

Free Association A technique, developed by **Freud**, for reducing **dreams** to certain basic **patterns**, free association formed a significant part in the development of **psychoanalysis**, allowing the **unconscious problems** of patients to be explored. **Jung** later veered away from 'free association', (acknowledging that it was the most fickle aspect of **dream interpretation**, particularly in the **light** of partial mass knowledge of psychotherapeutic techniques) in favour of concentrating more on the actual form and content of a dream – the so-called 'active **dream analysis**'.

Freeways Freeways suggest access to an easy **passage** – to something that will facilitate and speed up our enjoyment or our capacity to interrelate. Freeways, however, offer little **time** for concentrated thought, as one is forced into a state of preternatural concentration if one is not to collide with other acolytes of instant gratification.

Freezing See **Cold, Ice, Igloos** & **Snow**

Freight Cars Freight cars carry **burdens**, and it is this which is likely to be the most significant factor in their interpretation – the **train** engine, in this context, may be the **dreamer**, and the freight cars the **dreamer**'s past. Uphill, the **engine** may struggle – downhill, there is the **danger** of the **past** catching up with, and possibly even overtaking, you.

Freud, Sigmund (1856–1939) The founder of **psychoanalysis** and the practice of **psychotherapy**, Freud published his groundbreaking *The Interpretation of Dreams* in 1900. Freud noticed links between **dreams** and **free associations**, and deduced from this the existence of an inner censor that protected the patient from the **anxiety** inherent in a rational, that is to say, conscious, analysis of their dream images. By leading the patient towards an understanding of the sources of their **anxieties** and the **conflicts repressed** in their **unconscious** minds by means of **transference** and **dream work**, Freud believed that **light** could be thrown on the patient's emotional state, and that their unconscious **wishes** might thus be revealed. See also **Archaic Remnants, Condensation, Displacement, Day's Residues, Dream Language, Dream Work, Latent Content, Manifest Content, Representability** & **Secondary Revision**

Freudian Slip The sudden occurrence, in an otherwise innocent **conversation** or series of thoughts, of an **unconsciously** uttered word or phrase that throws unexpected **light** on an underlying **problem** or **neurosis**, and which is, therefore, of psychological significance.

Friends Friends, and in particular old friends, may symbolize the **super-ego** in a **dream** context. They may also indicate aspects of the **dreamer** themselves which the dreamer has unconsciously projected onto 'significant others'. In addition, they may suggest a need for support, comfort, or the reinforcing of already established prejudices and convictions. See **Friendship** & **Pets**

Friendship A dream of friendship can imply the successful subsumation of the **ego**. A literary case in point might include the friendship between **Goethe** and Schiller, or that between Montaigne and De la Boëtie. Dream friendships tend to imply the yearning to be selflessly benevolent, but they can also, on occasion, reflect selfish desires, too, as in the **wish** for a *deus ex machina* (a perfect, or expedient friend) to sort out all our **problems**. See **Friends**

Frigidity Women who suffer from frigidity frequently dream of interruptions, disturbances, or other third-party interventions during the run up to a potential **sexual** encounter. Such interruptions can reflect the **dreamer**'s **unconscious** frustration at their condition, which is often **masked** in real life by an apparent acceptance of the frigid state as unchangeable, or indeed unmanageable. Frigidity, too, can find itself equated with **death** in **dreams**, just as **male impotence** can. See also **Frustration Dreams** & **Inhibitions**

Fringes Being on the fringes of things can imply shyness, diffidence, **inhibition**, and possibly even active prejudice. Many overtly confident **people** secretly feel marginalized, and use assertion or self-emphasis to **mask** their real feelings – feelings which frequently emerge in **dreams** under other guises. Ancient Jewish tradition saw the priestly wearing of fringes as symbolically sacred, and the **touching** of the priestly fringe as auspicious.

Frogs A frog symbolizes inspiration, as does a **toad**. In traditional (i.e. pre-**Freudian**) dream interpretation, to **dream** of **eating** frogs suggested but a small gain from social connections. Post-Freudian **dream interpretation** might concentrate on the **colour** of frogs (predominantly **green**, needless to say) possibly equating with **jealousy**, a reading further enhanced by the prevalence of frog spawn implying a too liberal spreading of one's own **seed**, or that of one's partner, perhaps? Properly speaking only Parisians, and not Frenchman *per se*, are termed as frogs, due to Paris' ancient heraldic device figuring three frogs or three toads (and possibly stemming from Paris' ancient origins in the swampland known as Lutetia).

Fruit Fruit often equates with **creativity**, or with the enjoyment of some-thing we feel that we have earned. **Rotting** fruit may suggest that we have not achieved what we set out to achieve, or that something we hold dear is in the process of decay. See **Apples**, **Oranges**, etc.

Frustration Dreams Frustration dreams, such as late arrival (See **Lateness**), or **running** on the spot without getting anywhere, frequently point up contrasting desires in the **dreamer** which are crying out for **neu-rotic** fulfilment. In this context the dreamer both **wishes** to enjoy the desired experience, while at the same time hoping that they will have suf-ficient self-control *not* to enjoy it. This neurotic dilemma then finds itself reflected in the activity of the **unconscious** mind. See **Inhibitions**
KEY LINE: 'Last night I dreamt I went to Manderley again. It seemed to me I stood by the iron gate leading to the drive, and for a while I could not enter for the way was barred to me.'(From Daphne Du Maurier's *Rebecca* 1938)

Fuel Fuel is a fundamental human need, and its appearance under any guise in a **dream** probably suggests **anxiety** about its lack, rather than relief over a surfeit. Fuel being thrown onto a **fire** may reflect a desire to purge oneself of the **past**, or it may simply be the dream's way of saying that the **dreamer** is adding to an already existing **problem** (i.e. 'adding **fuel** to fire'), and that some measure of control needs to be exerted.

Fugue A hysterical symptom in which an individual inhabits a **dream**-like state during normal life with no residual memory of what has occurred.

Functional Analysis The teasing out not only of the **symbols** used in our **dreams**, but also of their origins. In this way we can identify not only our **repressed** impulses, but also the forces repressing those impulses.

Functional Economy The architecture of **dreams** relates to functional economy in that the simplest conceivable solution is usually the one **unconsciously** chosen by the **dreamer** to address the most complicated of underlying **problems**.

Funerals To dream of one's own funeral or **burial** suggests that the **dreamer** feels that they have **lost**, or are about to lose, something of value to them. Funerals are about **mourning** for the **past**, but they can also indicate a buried desire for sympathy, or they may even suggest, par-ticularly in the case of a **parent's** funeral, the dreamer's desire for inde-pendence. Roman funerals always took place in the **dark**, by torchlight, for **fear** that the sight of the dead might violate the sacerdotal capacities of **priests**, or the jurisdictive impartiality of **magistrates**.

Fungi See **Funguses**

Funguses Funguses and fungi equate with growths, and they may suggest a **fear** of **cancer**, of ganglions, or of **tumours**, when they appear in **dreams**. In addition, they may suggest, when in the form of mushrooms, something which eats, or is **eaten**, further reinforcing their invasive properties.

Fur Fur may be both **sexual** (as in pubic **hair**, or the difference between **male** and **female** hair types), protective, or even, in the case of a convinced **vegetarian**, pejorative, in that someone covered in fur may seem primitive or threatening to such a person. Traditionally, fur denoted power and **riches**, and it still retains these connotations in the colder, more easterly parts of Europe.

Furnaces Furnaces often have **anal** connotations. They may also carry purgative qualities, and, at least for non-Muslims, overtones of **death**, as in cremation. For Jews (and enlightened non-Jews) furnaces and **ovens** will have **anxiety** and threat implications stemming back to the Second World War, and their function as mechanisms in Adolf Hitler's Final Solution. To that extent they may also figure as misused or misconstrued artefacts, just as **lorries**, trucks and **trains** may be seen to function as both conveyances of the living, and unwanted harbingers of death. See **Fire & Flames**

Furniture Furniture, in the sense that it **peoples** or provides the framework within a house, can equate with the **skeleton** when it appears in **dreams**. The **breaking** of furniture can suggest the destruction of, or damage to, the **body**. Furniture may also represent established mores or the **repression** of initiative, particularly when it is **dark** and indicative of **burdens** passed from generation to generation. Furniture can also equate with outward show, in that, like **clothes**, how we furnish our **houses** suggests how we wish to be seen to the outside **world**. Sloppy **clothes** or slapdash furniture may suggest a lack of interest in outward show, or it may suggest **illness**, and inner turmoil.

Fuseli, Henry (1741–1825) An aristocrat from Zurich, Fuseli specialized in depicting **dreams** and **nightmares** in his **paintings**. His *The Nightmare* (1781) depicts a **sleeping** woman on a **couch**, with a malevolent **incubus** seated on her **stomach**, and a bulging-**eyed horse** emerging from the **drapery** nearby. See also **Raimondi** & **Succubi**

Fuses Fuses can relate to the **heart**, in dream terms, in the sense that when they blow, the **lights** go out. This may seem, on the surface a least, rather a simplistic equation, but **dreams** frequently choose the easiest route between two idioms.

Futility There is a particular category of **dreams** that appears to represent 'futile' actions. These dreams tend to show situations where, despite every effort, the **dreamer** finds themselves stymied. Such dreams may use **symbols** such as U-Turns, no-through **roads**, barred entries, objects that prohibit ingress, etc., to achieve their purpose. As well as being **frustrating** in themselves and manifesting the **dreamer**'s 'doubt', their continuation or repetition may also be a sign of a **latent** or **manifest manic-depressive** cycle. See **Repetitive Motifs**

G

Galaxies Galaxies suggest mysteries, in that, despite scientific advances, they are still fundamentally unknowable, and therefore open to all manner of speculative charges. Galaxies may also suggest **belts**, **girdles**, or even **wombs**, hemming us in and protecting us, in certain measure, from what lies beyond. Pythagoras believed that the **soul**, in spherical form, descended from the boundary where the Zodiac and Galaxies **meet**, elongating itself into a conical form during its downward **journey**.

Gamblers We are all gamblers to some extent, and gambling, in its turn, seems to relate, in some **measure** at least, to progress, in that we need gamblers to risk themselves in order for discoveries, outside the bounds of the normal, to be made. This said, gamblers also threaten stability, in that they personify chance and the random throw of often fateful **dice**. We are drawn to gamblers, but do not **wish** to be led by them – we are attracted by the ability to achieve sudden **wealth**, while being wary of the emotional costs involved in not taking seriously the conduct and significance of our everyday **struggles**. See **Games, Poker, Roulette** & **Wagers**

Gambling See **Gamblers, Games, Poker, Roulette** & **Wagers**

Games Games and playing are important **dream** images – both are necessities, but both can threaten stability and imply immaturity when taken to extremes. They can be compensations for feelings of **frustration** and pointlessness, but they can also become ends in themselves when allowed to dominate everyday consciousness. Games can also equate with simplicity (in that they **waste** time, and are not 'serious'), while at the same time leavening seriousness, and diluting solemnity. See **Gamblers, Roulette** etc.

Gangs Gangs are usually threatening when they appear in **dreams**, in that they often equate with **packs** (as in **wolves**), predation, and **bullying**. **Weak-**willed **people** are often attracted to gangs, in that they can feel that membership accords them an identity that they do not benefit from – or have the strength to carve out for themselves – in normal life. One can hide in a gang, due to its collective, amorphous quality, just as one can hide in a **crowd** made up of a similar race to oneself – for **races**, of course, just as **religions**, are merely another form of gang.

Gangsters Gangsters suggest easy ways out – just as does the harbouring of **criminal thoughts**. **Dream censorship**, however, is likely to come into **play** when such images rear their **heads**, stepping in to protect the **dreamer** from the consequences of any potentially immoral thoughts or actions.

Garages Garages tend to be **female** symbols, into which **male** symbols (i.e. **cars** and other such paraphernalia) are frequently placed. They are security **symbols** as well, in that we **seal** off a garage against outside interest or interference. It is the source, too, of one means of **escape** from the **house** (*ergo* the **body**), and a suitable symbol for the evacuation of **waste** and of other unwanted artefacts – for we can keep the things we need (but which we nevertheless consider a little **dirty**), isolated from the house, but still within reach in a connecting garage.

Garbage Garbage equates with **waste** and with the detritus of discarded ideas and concepts. The act of cleaning something out (see **Cleansing**) suggests the possibility, at least, of a new start, or of a start from a different location. The first thing we do when we wish to begin anew is to clean out our surroundings, and impose our will upon them. The retention of garbage suggests an inability to address the future.

Gardens Gardens, in **dreams**, are frequently seen **archetypally**, as **symbols** of the Garden of Eden or an Edenic period – **childhood**, for instance – that occurred before the 'fall' into puberty. The oft-occurring dream symbol of an **aeroplane** crashing into one's back garden (particularly if dreamt of by an adolescent), might then be seen as a fear of **sexual** maturity (or of a repressed **homosexuality**) and the loss of innocence and security that inevitably accompanies it – a tragedy, in fact, coming out of a clear **blue sky**. It may even, *in extremis*, suggest the loss, or the **fear** of loss, of one's **parents**. See **Losing**

Garlands Garlands are usually given to victors, or to **people** who are being admired beyond the norm. They are also used to celebrate **weddings**, both temporal and spiritual. They may also be seen as compensations for perceived losses, or as **symbols** of the aesthetic triumphing over the expedient. See **Celebrations & Victory**

Garlic Traditionally, garlic was used to ward of the **evil** eye, and its appearance in **dreams** is still likely to **mirror** that largely protective function. Such superstitions stemmed from garlic's alleged **alchemical** capacity for destroying the magnetic power of the loadstone. Sir Thomas Browne pooh-poohed this idea by placing garlic in his book of *Vulgar Errors*, with the implication that those who felt that a clove of garlic might secure them from the attentions of a **vampire** were labouring under a potentially lethal delusion. Nowadays, garlic is more likely to be seen as preventing a **heart** attack, or even flatulence, and one can only imagine Sir Thomas Browne's view on that eventuality.

Garters In English folklore, a girl might pin her garters to the **wall** above her **bed**, arrange her **shoes** in the form of the **letter** T, and after reciting a certain rhyme, get into bed without saying another word. She would then **dream** of her future **husband**.

Gas Gas is **claustrophobic**, and therefore a convenient addition to any **anxiety dream** list. Dreaming of gas may be triggered by something as simple as lying next to someone who has inadvertently broken **wind**, or it may have deeper overtones, including a **fear** of suffocation that may have been engendered in the **womb** (possibly as a result of a breech **birth**), or else through botched or mal-perceived anaesthesia. See **Artificial Dreams**

Gates Arched gateways are thresholds – they both **separate** and unite. They may even contain **dangers**. Gateways may also suggest either new **beginnings**, or in the case of barred gateways, cyclical endings. In religious terms they may be taken as **symbols** of the higher, causal being, and its capacity for receptivity on the spiritual plane. See **Doors**
KEY LINE: 'Two gates for ghostly dreams there are: one gateway of honest horn, and one of ivory. Issuing by the ivory gates are dreams of glimmering illusion, fantasies, but those that come through solid polished horn may be borne out, if mortals only know them.' (From Homer's *The Odyssey*, Book xix, ninth Century BC)

Gauges Gauges are designed to reflect **levels**, and their appearance in **dreams**, together with their semantic meaning (i.e. to 'gauge someone's worth'), may possibly reflect back to perceived levels of psychic **energy**.

Gauguin, Paul (1848–1903) The French post impressionist painter, Paul Gauguin, painted his *Manao Tupapau, the Spirit of the Dead Watching* (1892), in an effort to create something that was the direct embodiment of a **dream**. It shows a **naked** Kanaka woman, lying on her **stomach**, and frozen with **fear** as the result of a visitation by the *tupapau*, or **spirit** of the dead, who sits behind her, by the **bed**, silently watching her. See **Wrestling**

Gautama Buddha (563–483 BC) The avatar, Gautama Buddha, found the concept of the transiency of duration overwhelming. He joined forces with five ascetics (the five senses), and disparate other **masters**, in a bid to understand unity. This attempt failed. At the age of 35 he then sat under a **tree**, in Bhudd Gaya, and vowed not to move until he had reached enlightenment. Despite a succession of **dreams** in which Mara (the lord of illusion, and master of **death**, **evil**, and desire) assaulted him, he maintained his position – and his concentration on the Four Noble **Truths**, and the Noble Eightfold **Path** – until he became wholly awakened, and reached Nirvana (the Great Enlightenment).

Gavels Gavels imply **judgement**, and the power of one person, or state, over another. They may also relate to **auctions**, and to that extent they are **anxiety** pointers – we may desperately want something, but sense that there is a time limit to our desires or ambitions beyond which the auctioneer's symbolical **hammer** will **fall**.

Gear Sticks Gear sticks are quintessential **phallic symbols**, a reading strengthened by the plethora of no-doubt apocryphal stories concerning their use and misuse in compromising situations. The **unconscious** mind has a tendency to latch on to such apocryphal images, transforming them according to its **lights**, and re-jigging their meaning to suit itself. A gear stick might become entirely independent from the **car**, for instance, or come off in the **dreamer**'s **hand** – even force its way down through the floor, leaving the car driverless (see **Driverlessness**). This may imply that in the dreamer's **eyes** the **male** driving force is ineffectual, or else, in the case of a **female** dreamer, threatening in some way.

Geese A goose traditionally symbolizes conceit and folly. Geese behave in an **archetypal** way when they migrate in formation, and this may be reflected in **dreams** of **pointing**, or of mass migration towards a considered end. Geese may also represent freedom to the **dreamer**, since they share the capacity of all **birds** simply to get up and go. A dream of a 'cooked goose' has obvious semantic revocations, and may reflect on the dreamer's potentially morbid conception of their own perceived **failures**.

Gems Gemstones and birthstones were considered to have **mystical** qualities, and this may be **unconsciously** reflected in the context in which they occur in **dreams**, together with the month to which they symbolically belong:

January: Garnet: **Truth** and constancy.
February: Amethyst: Sincerity and sobriety.
March: Bloodstone: Courage and presence of mind.
April: Diamond: Innocence and **light**.
May: Emerald: Success in **love**.
June: 1. Agate: Health and long life; 2. Pearl: Purity and tears.
July: 1. Carnelian: Contentment and **friendship**; 2. Ruby: Courage and chastity.
August: Sardonyx: Marital **happiness**.
September: 1. Sapphire: Magic; 2. Chrysolite: Protection from melancholy.
October: Opal: Hope and luck for those born in October: misfortune for others.
November: Topaz: Fidelity and the antidote to **poison**.
December: Turquoise: Prosperity and protection.

Genealogy They say that **sex**, genealogy, and **Nostradamus** are the three main sources of hits on the **internet**, and it is therefore not uncoincidental that they are, to a certain extent at least, related. Sex without physical input, and **family** without emotional effort – it hardly reflects well on our affective ambitions. Dreaming of genealogy, then, may carry with it implications of present emptiness, for we would hardly feel the need to search for a possible spurious, and certainly unverifiable **past** (or, in the case of Nostradamus, a future), did we not feel even marginally dispossessed in the present.

Generals Generals usually relate to the **father** figure when they appear in **dreams**. One may also infer a desire for **guidance**, perhaps, or even for a *deus ex machina* to appear from out of the woodwork and save the day.

Generators The **heart** is a generator, especially if the **body** is perceived as a **house**, with all the necessary **baggage** in terms of radiators, piping, and electrical wiring representing the circulatory and nervous systems. Should the generator be **damaged**, or run out of **fuel**, a crisis will occur, and the fundamentals of the house may need urgent **repair**.

Genitals We **judge** a person by their genitals (or by our perception of what their genitals are likely to consist of, thanks to certain external signifiers); just as a dog will judge other **dogs**, deciding whether to be dominant, sub-dominant, placatory, or aggressive; its entire response dependent on perceived threat or **self**-interest and the pheromones it picks up during its initial exploratory sniff. It's hardly conceivable that human genitals, when they appear in **dreams**, don't perform a similar function. Even suggestions of genitalia, as in dresses, trousers, kilts, etc., influence the way we respond to each other in everyday life. Most women will admit that men respond to them very differently depending on whether they wear trousers or a dress (and in particular when a woman wears something that emphasizes the child-bearing nature of her **hips**), while women (often despite their better **natures**) instinctively respond to **uniforms**, sporting **clothes**, and other virile signifiers, in what may fairly be termed an **archetypal** way. Dreams, quite naturally, reflect this.

German Language The German **language** has two expressions for the dreaming state: *Ich traume*, meaning 'I am dreaming', and *es traümt mir*, meaning 'it is dreaming me', or, less literally, 'the **dream** comes to me'.

Germs Germs are threats, and in **dream** terms they may represent any form and sort of threat, not merely of **illness**, but also of a personal, spiritual, or social **nature**. Germs are also **small**, and this may be reflected in the trivial aspect of the threat – in its needling quality, for instance.

Gestalt *Gestalt* means 'configuration'. The word lies behind a psychological and psychotherapeutic approach to **dream analysis** that bears largely on 'perception'. Contexts are crucial, and **dreams** need not so much to be interpreted as rekindled and re-enacted in the present, achieving something akin to insight. One desired end might resemble the holistic bringing together of the three levels of 'awareness', namely the **world**, the dream-world, and the **self**, in an act of spontaneous integrity.

Geysers Geysers are ejaculatory, and to that extent they most probably represent **orgasm**, the emission of spermatozoa/**semen**, or even, on occasion, **menstruation**, when they appear in a **dream**. They may also represent an emotional outburst or some other such occurrence, particularly when they occur in the presence of identifiable beings. See **Ejaculation**

Ghettos Ghettos equate with **exile**, and possibly even with low **self-esteem**. Nobody chooses to live in a ghetto (unless they can benefit in some way from its particular aspects), and the formulation of a ghetto area in a **dream** may conceivably apply to some lack or misuse of creative potential which the **dreamer** secretly perceives in themselves.

Ghosts As far as the Taoists were concerned, arguing with ghosts in a **dream** was a good thing, indicating a long and auspicious life for the **dreamer**. In traditional western **dream interpretation**, however, ghosts were said to represent one's **parents**, or even one's **enemies**. In modern dream interpretation ghosts are far more likely to refer to aspects of the **past** which still haunt the **dreamer** – they may also suggest hidden aspects of the **self** which are either misunderstood or which threaten to undermine the dreamer when they least expect it.

Giants Images of giants can often be sparked by an infantile **regression** in the **dreamer** during which they metaphorically revert to a **dwarf** state, and in which their **parents**, just as in the **fairy tales** they were most probably told at the time, appear as mysterious giants. It should be remembered that the dwarf, in a fairy tale, very often gets the upper hand, and that an element of **wish-fulfilment** is therefore present in such **dreams**. See **Largeness & Smallness**

Gifts Being given a **horse** in a dream, for instance, and not being allowed to check its **teeth** for age, might be suggested by the old saw of 'not looking a gift horse in the mouth' – **dreams** frequently take such verbal elaborations and present them literally. Gifts may otherwise betoken abilities or capacities, and the **giving** away of such a gift may exemplify a desire to procreate, or to pass on one's 'gifts' to others. The word 'gift' in German means **poison**, and this suggestion, if it is known to the **dreamer**, may also underlie the image, as in, for instance, the gift of a 'poisoned chalice'.

Giraffes Giraffes are both gentle and incredibly powerful, and this apparent paradox makes them very useful **dream** material indeed. Metaphorically, they may represent upward movement (see **Above**) towards growth, added to which their **necks** are undoubtedly suggestive of the male **penis**, particularly when associated with the giraffes' mating **ritual**, which involves two **animals** interlinking necks in a highly suggestive **dance**.

Girdles Girdles, just as **belts**, probably imply a need for support. In the case of girdles this would seem to be **invisible**, even unacknowledged support – the sort of support given by an unselfish **friend**, perhaps, or by a **parent** who holds your best interests at **heart**. Girdles are also circular (see **Circles**), and even **mandala**-like, and carry with them spiritual revocations and suggestions of **rebirth** and the Divine Order (the belt of Orion), and it is possibly for this reason that they were traditionally worn by as yet unmarried **girls** – St Colman's girdle, for instance, would meet only around the chaste.

Girls If a male **dreams** of young **girls**, the dream may not necessarily have sexual connotations, but may imply a search for the feminine (see **Femininity**), or **anima**, through the medium of the dream. There is also a deep-seated, almost **archetypal** male need to **father daughters**. This desire to share the attributes of the opposite **sex** has its parallel in the often overwhelming **female** desire to give **birth** to a **son**, so that the **mother** may better connect with her latent **male** energy, or **animus**. See **Finding**

Giving To dream of giving is often to **dream** of **wishing** to receive, because the act of giving in a dream presupposes its opposing **mirror** function. Giving can also suggest connectedness, or the acknowledgement of some form of otherwise hidden relationship. See **Gifts**

Glaciers Glaciers can suggest hidden depths beneath possibly frigid coverings. They can also suggest **emptiness** and **death** (the inability to live). To strike a glacier, possibly with one's **ship**, implies a **fear** of the unknown, twinned with the desire to avoid unnecessary confrontation, the implication being that your **enemy** is **cold** and quite possibly immovable.

Glass Glass is aesthetically pleasing, useful, a **symbol** of **truth** on the higher mental plane, and also exceedingly **fragile**. It would seem, then, that glass has predominantly **female** characteristics, and this is likely to be reflected in its **dream** relevance (as it were). If one also adds the significance of glass to a woman in the protection of her **home** and the reflection and reinforcement of her **sexual** attraction, it is obvious that glass imagery has powerful connotations, particularly for women **dreamers**. See **Mirrors**

Glasses Glasses and magnifiers are used for aiding and abetting **vision** – for throwing (metaphorically at least) more **light** on things. Should a person wear glasses in a **dream** where they do not normally wear glasses, it might suggest that the **unconscious** mind is endeavouring to draw the **dreamer's** attention to certain particular aspects of the dream imagery. In this case, where the glasses are put becomes important, as does the direction or tenor of the placing – glasses placed on a **book**, for instance, or on a document, may imply the need to concentrate on non-verbal, even coded, communications. See **Spectacles**

Gliders Gliders have links with **flying**, in **dreams**, with all that that entails in terms of a desire for freedom from temporal, or indeed earthly, ties. A glider may also take us closer to **God**, or to the condition of **birds**. Flight by glider is a strictly temporary affair, though, and dependent on air currents – which may equate, in dream terms, with finding oneself unduly influenced by the whims of others (or oneself), if one is to take this metaphor to its logical conclusion.

Globes Globes are breast-like, and they also suggest the **earth**. One looks into a globe (or **crystal ball**) in order to discern the future, and **breasts**, too, in their palliative function, also evoke the future rather than the **past**. Globes may also be suggestive of **light**, the amplification of **vision**, and even rewards.

Gloves Gloves are predominantly feminine artefacts, into which **fingers** and **hands** are slipped for either comfort, protection, or for purely aesthetic reasons. The 'marrying' of a glove and a hand has undoubted **sexual** connotations, therefore, but may also imply something underhand (glove **money**, or a bribe), hidden, or sly (going hand in glove with someone). Gloves can also be descriptive of status, and may, in addition, be used as a **symbol** of rebuke, or in order to trigger a duel, or **argument**.

Glue Glue attaching us to some object or person may imply the existence of unbreakable ties, or, depending on context, a desire to break free twinned with an inability (especially if the subject is struggling) to do so – that something, in other words, is holding us back from fulfilling our desires. For both **males** and **females**, glue may also carry with it revocations of **semen**/seminal fluid, in the sense that impregnation of another (a spermatozoa attaching itself to an **egg**, for instance) may glue us to that person and to any progeny eventually stemming from the union. See **Bodily Fluids, Gum** & **Secretions**

Gnawing Gnawing, **chewing** and mouthing often refer back to **childhood oral fixations**, but they may also be taken more literally, as in 'something gnawing at us' in order to indicate worry. Alternatively, the architecture of the **dream** may be reflecting a real-life (although **unconscious**) **grinding** of **teeth**.

Goals In the case of goals, a figurative goalmouth (on a **football** field, say), may just as well be taken metaphorically – as in a stated goal, e.g. the winning of the **game** – as literally. If we miss the goalmouth, the implication may be that we feel that we have let ourselves down, or have not achieved what we set out to achieve in our lives. If we are taking a penalty shot from a very long way out, we may very well have set ourselves too high, or even impossible to achieve, standards.

Goats A goat traditionally symbolizes lasciviousness and lust, possibly twinned with an element of **mute** obstinacy. Goats are indiscriminate eaters, and are also highly individualistic, and to that extent they are the very opposites of **sheep**, whom they nominally resemble – this might

imply a stubborn desire, in the **dreamer**, to follow their own **path**, rather than to remain part of the herd. Goats sometimes carry with them revocations of the **devil**, too, and of the lower qualities of **nature**.
KEY LINE: 'And before him shall be gathered all nations: and he shall separate them one from another, as a shepherd divideth his sheep from the goats: and he shall set the sheep on his right hand, but the goats on the left.' (Matthew xxv, 32, 33)

God To dream of God is to be blessed. It's really as simple as that. 'For God speaketh once, yea twice, yet man perceiveth it not. In a dream, in a vision of the night, when deep sleep falleth upon men, in slumberings upon the bed, then He openeth the ears of men and sealeth their instructions.' (Spoken by Elihu, the son of Barachel, to Job)

God-Image The image of **God** (the *imago Dei*) which is imprinted, according to **church** teachings, on every human **soul**. It is also a **symbol** of the **self**, and of **psychic** wholeness.

Gods & Goddesses The great God El, in the cuneiform texts of Ugarit (the Ras Shamra tablets) is attested as learning of important events through **dreams**. This predates the settlement of Canaan by the Israelite tribes, who also viewed **oneiromancy** as a useful **tool** through which God might communicate to the individual, and via the individual, to the tribe. This idea is again carried over in Greek and Roman society, where Gods and Goddesses regularly appeared in **people**'s dreams, either **warning**, ordering, deceiving, or in some cases, even, seducing – this process was called 'seeing a dream', and many cases occur in Homer's *Iliad* (circa 9th century BC). One could argue, therefore, that the conjuring up of numerous Gods, rather than simply one **God**, merely reflected a desire on the part of acolytes to exemplify masculine and feminine principles in an easily digested, extramundane form.

Goethe, Johann Wolfgang von (1749–1832) The great German writer Goethe, author of *Faust* (1808/32) and *The Sorrows of Young Werther* (1774), admitted that he wrote many of his **poems** in a **dream state**. 'In such a somnambulistic condition, it has frequently happened that I have found a sheet of **paper** lying before me all aslant, and I have not discovered it till all has been written, or I have found no room to write any more.'
KEY LINE: On dreams: 'These whimsical pictures, inasmuch as they originate from us, may well have an analogy with our life and fate.' And also: 'I believe men only dream that they may not cease to see. I have fallen asleep in tears, but in my dreams the loveliest figures came to give me comfort and happiness and I awoke the next morning fresh and cheerful.' (From a letter by Goethe to Erckmann).

Goggles Goggles protect the **eyes**, but they may also, to some extent, prevent the eyes from seeing – they truncate as well as safeguard **vision**, in other words. This dual purpose is highly suggestive, and may indicate paradoxical feelings on the part of the **dreamer**, relating either to individuals or to life tendencies.

Gold The **colour** of the **sun**, creativity, and the **harvest**. The Emperor Charlemagne's **spirit** is said to cross the Rhine on a Golden **Bridge** at Bingen during **seasons** of plenty, before blessing the **vineyards** and the cornfields. The colour gold is also indicative of Divine Wisdom, of philosophy, and of the capacity for intellectual rigour.

Golden Age Dreaming of a Golden Age implies discontent with the present state of affairs – this may seem an obvious reading, but Utopianism, sentimentality and nostalgia are so omnipresent in modern society, that clear 'golden' thought is no longer held at the premium it benefited from during the Age of Enlightenment (the end of the 17th to the end of 18th century). The dreamed-of Golden Age, therefore, most probably refers back to an individually idealized **childhood**, rather than to the collectively significant era it might seem to imply. The **father** of Rabelais's Gargantua was Grangousier, **King** of Utopia, who was happy to spend his life scratching on the **hearth** with a **burnt stick**, while watching his chestnuts slowly roasting. See **Gold**

Golf Clubs Golf **clubs** frequently substitute for the **penis** when they occur in **dreams**. They are also convenient **wish-fulfilment** fantasy objects, particularly for competitively inclined **males** and **females**, who may be tempted to seek social acceptance through sporting success, rather than through a more genuine (i.e. less instantly gratifying) process of peer respect. The image of striking a **ball** which then **travels** a very long way indeed, may well suggest a fantasy desire for empowerment, or the presence of a marginally inappropriate vainglory (for nothing travels that fast or that far), whereas a ball that persistently comes back at the striker will tend to fall under the heading of a **frustration dream**.

Gongs Gongs may indicate a desire for public acclamation on the part of the **dreamer**, with the **metal disk** (with its attention-garnering sound) standing in for the **medal** whose name it semantically reflects. It may also act in the capacity of a wake-up call, or even a call-to-**arms** (in a metaphorical sense, of course).

Good Mother, The The good **mother** is a necessary **archetype**, probably inspired by the **guilt children** unconsciously feel at the **sacrifices** and **pain** their mother must endure (in a less than perfect society) in order to bring them, **kicking** and squealing, into the **world**. There is a strict **taboo** in most societies in ascribing selfish motives to maternal impulses – this is as much to protect the **feelings** and **self**-worth of the progeny, of course, as it is to protect the mother's good **name**. As we need our mothers to nurture us (or we die), so we also need our mothers to be selfless (i.e. to put our interests before their own) – thus the archetype of the good mother. Necessity breeds convention.

Gossip Gossip, in a **dream**, equates with self-doubt on the part of the **dreamer**. Traditionally speaking, a gossip was also a sponsor or mentor (the word stems from the Anglo Saxon *gesib*, for kinsman), and there may be a sub-text, here, in that a shy person may feel the need for a spokesman, while at the same time fearing the speaking out of others (or what they might inadvertently reveal). Dreams feed on such **unconscious**, but nevertheless reality-driven, paradoxes. See **Speech**

Government Government, in a **dream** context, may refer more to parental regulation than to societal steering. **Self**-government, or even the lack of it, may relate to the **dreamer**'s inability to **discipline** themselves over vices or habits that, under stricter parental 'government', might not have found their inception.

Goya, Francisco (1746–1828) Goya's 1799 *El Sueño de la Razon Produce Monstros* (*The Sleep of Reason Produces Monsters*) was number 43 of his *Caprichos* series of engravings, and shows a **sleeping** young man, at his **desk**, beset all around by monstrous **owls**, **cats**, **bats** and ghouls. Goya has this to say about the piece: 'Imagination, deserted by reason, foments impossible **monsters**. United with reason, she is the **mother** of all the arts, and the source of all their wonders.'

Grades Grades, and the necessity of being graded, **play** on our **anxieties**. Any imposed **exercise** or **examination** attempts to conceal this effect beneath a carapace of 'if you act or conform in such and such a way, such and such a good thing will no doubt happen to you.' The **unconscious** is notoriously wary of such potentially specious justifications (or imposed **rites-of-passage**).

Grail See **Holy Grail**

Grain 'Going against the grain' implies a desire to be non-conformist in some way, and this, in turn, requires courage. Grain is, in addition, at the foundation of something greater than itself – e.g. **bread**. If one adds the concept of each human being constituting a grain of **sand**, it becomes apparent that a desire for non-conformity – an unwillingness to participate in the communal making and **breaking** of bread, in other words – is a classic **anxiety** indicator. Dreaming of grain is therefore comforting to the conformist (implying **harvests**, abundance, and justified plenty), and threatening to the non-conformist (suggesting the potential for a loss of individuality amongst the mass).

Grandfathers Dreaming of grandfathers may suggest a desire for longevity, twinned with a concomitant **fear** of **death**, for **males** traditionally live for shorter spans than **females**. A grandfather, being non-threatening, may represent the **animus** for a female **dreamer**, or a mentor figure for a male dreamer.

Grandmothers Dreaming of grandmothers may suggest the cyclical **nature** of human life, and our desire for spiritual continuance in the face of certain **death**. To a **male** dreamer, the unthreatening figure of the grandmother may simplify the acknowledgment of the **anima**, and to a **female dreamer** the grandmother figure may represent an exemplar, or approachable paradigm.

Grapes Grapes are virtually synonymous with the production of **wine**, which is, in itself, synonymous with leisure and sustenance. The '**fruit**' aspect of grapes is also important, as a **fat** bunch of grapes traditionally represents plenty, while **thin**, desiccated grapes represent want and a poor **harvest**. Should the grapes be inedible, 'sour grapes' may be suspected, whereas shiny black wild grapes (or **wolf**-grapes, as the Arabs call them) come from the plant Deadly Nightshade (***belladonna***), and may mortally intermix with domestic grapes, giving rise to Othello-like revocations to **dreamers** in the know.

Grass Grass and **death** go hand in **hand**. This may seem a strange thing to say, but our **unconscious** minds are sure to acknowledge both that grass traditionally covers **graves**, and that grass dies as **winter** comes. Conversely, and rather more cheeringly, grass also suggests the possibilities of **rebirth** and regeneration.
KEY LINE: 'A child said *What is the grass*? fetching it to me with full hands;/How could I answer the child? I do not know what it is any more than he./I guess it must be the flag of my disposition, out of hopeful green stuff woven./Or I guess it is the handkerchief of the Lord, a scented gift and remembrancer designedly dropt .../And now it seems to me the beautiful uncut hair of graves.' (From Walt Whitman's *Song of Myself*, Section 6 1855)

Grasshoppers A grasshopper symbolizes old **age**, and it is also the traditional sign of the **grocer**. The Anglo-Saxons believed that it was made up of the parts of **seven animals**, consisting of 'the **head** of a **horse**, the **neck** of an **ox**, the **wings** of a **dragon**, the **feet** of a **camel**, the **tail** of a **serpent**, the **horns** of a **stag**, and the **body** of a **scorpion**.' To many, the grasshopper symbolizes **summer**, and the **devil**-may-care attitude of the truly capricious. The Chinese, on the other hand, believed that the grasshopper represented spiritual enlightenment, and it is conceivable that the very simplicity of the grasshopper's life and needs will carry this reading across into the **dream world**.

Graves For many centuries it was believed that if an old grave were accidentally disturbed, the culprit would suffer from bad **dreams** until he had restored the **bones** to their rightful place. Graves represent hidden (see **Hiding**) things, too, together with the mysteries of dissolution. To '**dig**

one's own grave' has obvious **dream** revocations, as has the word 'gravely', as in 'gravely **ill**'. The linking of a relative, for instance, with a grave, might demonstrate that the **dreamer** fears for their own mortality, and finds belief in an afterlife somewhat questionable. See **Inscriptions, Shrouds & Tombstones**

Grease Grease is both a simplifier and a contaminant. If things are not running quite as they should, **palms** might need to be greased, or we may need to **climb** up the greasy **pole** in order the better to view our situation – continually **sliding** down the pole before we can reach the top might demonstrate either a lack of real desire on the part of the **dreamer**, or a hidden **fear** of impotence or **failure** (*ergo* the **masturbatory** context).

Great Mother The Great **Mother** is the **archetypal** image of pure matter, allowing the emotional meaning of Mother **Earth** to be expressed in symbolical terms, understandable to the human **mind**. In her role as the container of all life, the *Magna Mater* can appear in **dreams** in a number of roles tailored to the individual **dreamer**, **Pandora** and Eve being only amongst the most obvious. See **Anima, Animus, Baskets, Female, Good Mother & Wise Man**

Green The **colour** of **vegetation**, **nature** and the astral plane. In ancient folklore green symbolized hope (see **Pandora's Box**) and the possibilities of growth. The colour green is also traditionally associated with **jealousy**, as in **Shakespeare**'s 'green-eyed **monster**' (*Othello*), and also immaturity, as in '"He is so jolly green," said Charley,' from Charles Dickens' *Oliver Twist*. See **Grass & Growing**

Greene, Graham (1904–91) The English **writer** Graham Greene was obsessed by **dreams**, and admitted that they formed the basis of two of his **novels**, *It's a Battlefield* (1934) and *The Honorary Consul* (1973). He further believed that when he identified too much with one of his characters, he would actually start dreaming *their* dreams instead of his own. This, he maintained, happened in the case of Querry, in *A Burnt-Out Case* (1961) – he later transposed the dream, as it was, to the novel. Greene further claimed that, as a seven-year-old boy, he had dreamed of a maritime **disaster** on the **night** of the **sinking** of the Titanic (14th April 1912).

Grey Grey is the colour of twilight, old **age**, and neutrality. The folk **myth** of the *Grey Washer by the Ford* tells of an Irish wraith who appears to be **washing** clothes by a **river**. When her **victim** approaches, she holds up the **clothes**, which prove to be a **shadow** of the doomed man, complete with the **wounds** from which he will soon suffer.

Grief Grief and **mourning** are synonymous, and grief in **dreams** carries with it the inevitable implication that we are still in mourning for something that we feel we have **lost**. Grief may also imply **failure**, as in 'they came to grief'. When these two meanings find themselves twinned, a powerful regret for the **past**, or for past occurrences, may be suggested. KEY LINE: 'Grief is as intense in dreams as in reality, but we can bear horrors in sleep which would certainly deprive us of our waking senses, if not of life.' (From Robert Southey's *Diaries* 5th October 1823)

Grinding Teeth Teeth grinding during **sleep** may disguise repressed **anger**, **jealousy**, or hatred. There may also be a pure **anxiety** element to the grinding, suggestive of remorse, **depression** ('grinding down'), or misplaced **labour**.

Groaning Cake It was traditional in many parts of England to prepare a groaning **cake** against the **birth** of a **child** (the **mother**'s confinement was known as a 'groaning'). The **father** would then symbolically **cut** the cake and **hand** it to everyone in the household – if he cut his **finger**, however, the baby would **die**. Unmarried girls would eat only part of their share and then place the remainder underneath their **pillows** in the hope that their future **husbands** would then appear to them in a **dream**.

Groceries Groceries imply things put away for the future, or against a **rainy** day. As the principle meaning of such an image would seem to involve **nurturing**, it is likely that the **dreamer** may feel subtly undervalued, or in need of care and attention.

Grocery Stores Grocery stores are comfort providers. We can visit them at will and, as long as we have **money**, we are able to purchase anything that we wish without any further effort on our part. No **growing**, tilling, manufacturing or **labour** of any sort is required, beyond carrying the articles back **home**. Grocery stores, therefore, equate with instant gratification, and with the accoutrements of peace. See **Shops** & **Storing**

Grooming Grooming, both of the **self** and of others, is an **archetypal animal** characteristic, and offers many unseen benefits, not least amongst which is the process of self-acknowledgment. We groom our own idealized **reflections**, and those we choose to groom, or lavish our attentions on – most frequently our mates, or our **children**, or grateful, **paying** clients – tend to reinforce that process. Grooming in a **dream**, then, is a reinforcement of the **ego**.

Groups Groups traditionally provide **shelter** and protection, but they may also be threatening, particularly when we do not belong to them. Disparate groupings within the **dream** context often refer back to the **dreamer's** own **self**, and to aspects of that self that may seem in **danger** of rioting or of being **lost**. Groups may also refer to **family** pairings and to underlying **fears** that all is not well within one's intimate social group (a group which also acts as a **reflection** of the **ego**, or, in the worst case scenario, of the **id**). See **Gangs**

Growing Growing infinitely **big** is a recurrent motif in **children**'s **dreams**. It can be both a compensation for not being adult, and a tacit declaration by the child that they **wish** to have more power over their own lives – a power arrogated, without permission, by their **parents**. Growing, in an adult's dream, may represent a desire for spiritual growth, or for growth within a specific, possibly even diminished, area of the **dreamer's** personality. See **Shrinking**

Guardians See **Guards**

Guarding Dreamers frequently find themselves guarding areas of their personae from outside onslaught in a **dream**. This can carry over into **daydreams**, too, with fantasies occurring synonymously with **ritual** practices, like going to the **lavatory**, locking the back **door**, or **switching** off the **lights**. There is sometimes a very narrow **path** between enlightened **guarding** of important aspects of the **self**, and **paranoia** – care must therefore be taken if guarding themes become too recurrent or over-**ritualized**.

Guards The use of outside guards or guardians to protect threatened aspects of the **dreamer** may well relate to hidden **fears** of **illness**, or to the desires we all share for a *deus ex machina* (a **doctor**, a **priest**, a mentor, a **teacher**, a **healer**, or a miracle cure, for instance) to make all well again in our inevitably fractured **worlds**.

Guests Guests may be welcome or unwelcome. Unwelcome guests include **illnesses**, **emergencies**, invasive bacteria and inconvenient moral imperatives that engender **guilt**. Welcome guests may include employers, benefactors and **people** who appreciate us beyond the apparent span of our abilities. **Friends** are usually welcome guests in **dreams**, as the **unconscious** quickly identifies and recognizes mutual realms of **self**-interest within such relationships, and often seeks to use them to relieve **anxiety**. See **Employment** & **Invasions**

Guidance Guidance, or the appearance of a guide in a **dream**, may often represent the intervention of the **superego**. The search for a guide may also reflect a desire for proximity to **God**, or to the Higher **Self** – the desire for self-betterment, in other words. See **Finding** & **Ushering**

Guillotines See **Maury**

Guilt There is a fundamental difference between the **guilt** reactions of a normal person, which largely stem from conscience, and **neurotic** feelings of guilt, which are associated with the **unconscious** and which demand **self-punishment**. In dream terms, fancied or projected guilt is punished by the **superego** exactly as if it were real guilt. See the 'Chaco Indians' section under **dreams** for an interesting reversal of this concept.

Guinea Pigs A guinea **pig** was traditionally someone who fell between two stools, like a midshipman, an honorary but inactive director of a company, or a **clergyman** without cure. The modern definition still contains an element of this, with the addition of **risk**, in that the guinea pig is always the first in line to try something different. This aspect is obviously of use in **dreams** in which the dynamic is all about the expansion of experience, rather than the contraction of opportunity.

Guitars A guitar is shaped like a woman. Picasso knew this, as did **Goya** and Watteau. Our **unconscious** knows it too, and guitars are frequently feminized in **dreams** for this reason. If the sound of the guitar is discordant, it may mean problems with an affective relationship, or with women *per se*. If the guitar is in tune and euphonic, it implies a strong sense of harmony, and may even be suggestive of the **golden** mean, and unity with the **anima**.

Gulls A gull traditionally symbolizes gullibility. A seagull soaring, though, might indicate a desire for freedom, or for the power to rise above mundane **problems**. Traditionally, too, **dreaming** of dead gulls was taken to imply a separation from **friends**. See **Birds** & **Flying**

Gum Gum is both sticky, tasty and useful. It has an attractive smell, and the name, gum Arabic, has exotic revocations of idealized foreign **lands**. In a **dream**, we may wish to adhere to something or someone in particular, and gum may be used as a vehicle for this thought. Or we may wish to prevent ourselves from doing something – like regurgitating **pills** – and either gum or **glue** our **mouths** shut to achieve this end. See **Odours**

Gums Gums equate with old **age** and decrepitude, in that, if we lose our **teeth**, we lose an active part of ourselves for good, and have to replace that active part with **artifice**. Gums may also imply a desire to say something, without the ability to do so clearly. See **Tooth Dreams**

Guns A gun is a common **symbol** for the **penis** – it is fundamentally oblong in **shape**, may be used aggressively or competitively, and is capable of emission. Thus, its symbolical nature in **dreams**. For a **female dreamer**, being shot might imply the **sexual** act, while running from a gun, or a person carrying one, might imply a **fear** of her own sexuality, or, at a somewhat further pinch, **lesbianism**. For a **male** dreamer the gun can often be a simple penis substitute (**shoot** someone and you don't have to think), or fear of a gun might imply a fear of **homosexuality**, or same-sex attraction. See **Shooting**

Gurus Gurus equate with mentors, **teachers**, guides and **shamans** in suggesting the existence of the spiritual, as opposed to the mundane, or purely physical, **mind**. If the **dreamer** is searching for a guru, this might imply a simple desire for **guidance**, or it might suggest a deeper problem stemming from a lack of **self**-actualization – the unresolved **heart**, if you like. The guru, of course, also stands in for **God**, or **Jung's** concept of the **Wise Old Man**.

Guts Guts, when seen in terms of bravery, might infer a desire to **face** up to something particularly painful, or particularly difficult, in the **dreamer's** life. When seen in terms of innards, there are probably revocations of **hanging**, **drawing** and quartering (a notably powerful pictorial image, in that the killing, the torturing and, yes, the symbolical unbirthing of another human being, is usually **taboo**). There may also be revocations of **cannibalism** and the undergoing of the nominally (and literally) discombobulating **rite-of-passage** normally leading towards the acquisition of **shamanic** powers. See **Fourness**

Gymnasia Gymnasia are places where the **body** or the **spirit** may be trained to surpass their perceived boundaries. There are revocations, too, of **self-discipline**, and even betterment. Given the Greek origin of the word, an element of debate may also enter into the reading, as well as the symbolic concept of **nakedness**.

Gypsies Dreaming of gypsies can indicate a conjoining of the concepts of freedom and trickery – of both living by one's wits, and irregularity. To that extent the **symbol** mixes both **nature** and contrivance, the conscious and the **unconscious**, depending on the context within which the gypsy motif appears. See **Tricks**

H

Haemorrhoids Dreaming of haemorrhoids draws attention to the **anal** area, which was, no doubt, a source of erotic satisfaction during the anal fixation stage of early infancy. The suggestion of **pain** associated with a comfort zone is now most probably **guilt** associated.

Haggard, Sir Henry Rider (1856–1925) The English **author** of those splendid books, *King Solomon's Mines* (1885) and *Allan Quatermain* (1887), experienced an extraordinary premonitory **dream** concerning his **daughter**'s dog, Bob. In his dream Haggard saw the **dog** lying motionless near some **water**, and as he watched, his own personality seemed to rise from the **body** of the dog so that the dog seemed as if it was trying to speak to him. Without words, the dog then communicated that it was **dying**. Haggard's **wife** awoke him at that exact moment to ask why he was making 'such horrible and weird noises'. Later that morning, at breakfast, he told the dream to his wife and assembled **friends**. Only afterwards did he find that the dog was **missing**. Everyone went out to search for it. Its body was eventually found, bumping against a weir, a mile from where a **train** had knocked it off a railway **bridge** on the previous **night**, a good three hours before the time of Haggard's dream. See **Finding**

Hail Hail, and other inclement **weather** forms, frequently stands in for the **superego**, in that they can get in the way of, or censor, the **dreamer**'s desired actions. An example might be that of a hailstorm suddenly occurring when the dreamer **wishes** to **fire** a **gun** at someone – or should the dreamer wish to **fly** up to the top of a **building**, say.

Hair Hair has **erotic** connotations, and it is also a **sex** fixer, in that it is one of the easiest and most demonstrable ways of visually differentiating between men and women. In symbolical terms, hair is also a **symbol** of faith and intuition, while the hair tuft between the **eyes** of the **Buddha** is an emblem of spiritual **truth** in the making of the **soul**. The **shaving** of hair is frequently seen as a symbol of contrition, of visible asceticism, or as a **punishment** for inappropriate actions against the wider community (a desexualizing, in other words), while the leaving on of a tuft of hair was designed to simplify an aided ascent (see **Ascension**) to **heaven**, in the case of certain Muslim sects, or a **scalping** by a triumphant **enemy**, in the case of a number of North American **Indian** tribes.

Halloween Halloween is one of a flurry of non-Christian or pre-Christian **festivals** that have been hijacked by the conspicuous consumption lobby (*ergo*, the **id**) for instant gratification purposes. In **dream** terms, Halloween is significant because it gives us permission to wear **masks** and playact in an otherwise mask-free and predominantly seriously minded environment. We can role-play, in other words, and revert to infantile forms of behaviour without the usual concomitant **guilt**.

Hallucinations Hallucinations are sensory perceptions of non-existent occurrences and objects.

Hallucinatory Dreams Hallucinatory **dreams** mimic real life, but are not of it.

Hallways In Freudian terms, hallways are often equated with the **uterus**. **People** meet in hallways, and **Freud** took the concept of **meeting** to its furthest possible stretch when he suggested that the **child**, when adult, might fantasize about meeting its **father** while it was on its way out of the uterus, and while he, the father, was on his way in (as it were). To that extent the uterus acts as a metaphorical two way street on which an unborn child may bond with both its **mother** and its father at one and the same time, in a beyond verbal manner.
KEY LINE: 'I dreamt I dwelt in marble halls,/And each damp thing that creeps and crawls/Went wobble-wobble on the walls.' (From Lewis Carroll's *The Palace of Humbug* 1855 – originally written as a skit on Alfred Bunn's *The Bohemian Girl* 1843)

Haloes Haloes may suggest **saints**, and they may suggest auras. Some **people** are able to make out auras or personal **colours** in everyday life, and it is suggested by others that meditation may add energy to already existing auras. A **dream** is more likely to use a halo or aura to draw attention to something or somebody, or to suggest goodness or benevolence at a time when verbal communication is impossible – in a crisis, say, or at a time of **illness** or extreme decrepitude. See **Holiness**

Hammers Hammers are **tools** for change, whether it be constructive change or the destructive variety. This paradox makes them convenient **dream** vehicles, and, like **guns**, their use depends entirely on the mental and educative state of the user (or abuser). They may also stand in as **symbols** of virility and masculine power, particularly when in, say, the hands of a **blacksmith**. See **Sickles**

Hams Hanging hams suggest provision for the future, or even **fear** about future want. The pig is often associated with the human being, too, and one recalls from schooldays the old (but apparently true) chestnut about **cannibals** referring to missionaries as 'long pig'. Ham may also symbolize good things preserved from the **past**.

Hamsters Hamsters can be **symbols** of the captive **heart**. Like songbirds, they cater to the human desire to control things, rather than to accord them freedom.

Handcuffs If a **dreamer** finds themselves in handcuffs, it seems that they are being constrained from free expression by outside forces. Should they be handcuffing others, a similar but diametrically opposed **reading** may be assumed – in both cases, over-possessiveness may also be implied. A third reading would see the presence of handcuffs as a **self**-control measure against unnatural or inconvenient desires (the **id**).

Handicaps Handicaps are often about perceived **self**-image, in that, in **dream** terms at least, a handicap of whatever sort may be a convenient excuse for not acting when we know that we need to act.

Handles Handles may be **phallic symbols**, and they may have **female** connotations (in the sense of protruding **hips**, bottoms, **breasts**, etc.) depending on **shape** and size. We can also attempt to get a 'handle' on a galling situation, or give someone a 'handle', in the sense of a **name**, or nickname.

Handprints See **Footprints**

Hands Hands symbolize the public expression of private **feeling**. In that sense they are both receivers and givers of **energy**, for the laying on of hands may imply healing, but it may also imply a **curse** – an ambivalence (see **Bipolarity**) that may find itself reflected in the context in which the hands appear. Hands are also the most obvious way that we may reach out for **God**, or for salvation, while the movement of our hands may also be **self**-directed, as in the assumption or repudiation of **guilt**.

Hanging The hanged or hanging man is a **key symbol** of the tarot, and may be taken to mean a human being caught between two **worlds** – the spiritual and the mundane. Hanging may, in addition, suggest both a **pregnant** pause (we are 'left hanging') and a terminal state (**death**). If we hang we are also vulnerable – to the attack of carrion **crows**, say, or to **people** pelting us with rotten **fruit**. We may wish, of course, to make ourselves vulnerable as a proof of our **love**, and this is a very positive manifestation, throwing the onus upon the loved object, and not on the hanging person themselves.

Happiness Dreaming of happiness may conceivably be an enlightened forerunner to what occurs at **death**. Those **people** who have seen, or been in the presence of, **God**, often speak of a sense of perfect happiness, twinned with total capitulation to a greater will than that which is implied by the simply human. To that extent happiness is a symbol of fusion with the Godhead, and with the capacity to thank and to accept, rather than to require and to ask.
KEY LINE: 'Suddenly, I see myself on a road that skirts the top of a cliff and I know that the dream is beginning and with it, a feeling of happiness such that human speech cannot give the faintest idea of it.'
(From Julian Green's *Diaries* 12th December 1934)

Harbours Harbours and **towns** can represent the **anima** when they occur in **dreams**. They are maternal **symbols**, implying both emotional succour and the affective equivalent of rest and recreation, before the inevitable return to the fray.

Hardware Computer imagery has an ever increasing place in the **dream** world, simply as a result of its convenience as a signifier. Hardware in its traditional sense implies the capacity to find the right **tools** for the job, together with the capacity to mend problem areas of the **psyche** or of the **body**, and get them working again. See **Internet**

Harems The fantasy of possessing a harem is one that occurs to most men at some **time** in their lives, and is merely an acknowledgement of the existence of the **id**, and its capacity for wishful thinking. Harems represent a complete abrogation of **male** responsibility and a refusal to acknowledge the **anima**, while for a woman they may suggest a desire for subsumation inside the purely feminine, with a concordant suppression of the **animus**.

Hares A hare symbolizes timidity. **Meeting** them was also considered to be unlucky, except in certain parts of England, where the exact opposite was true. **White** hares were considered to **harbour** the **souls** of young maidens who had died of grief after being **abandoned** by their **lovers**. To **dream** of a hare was considered to be a sign that the **dreamer** had **enemies**, or that a **death** was about to occur in the **family**.
KEY LINE: 'The sight of a hare portends an unlucky journey.' (From Astrampsychus' *Oneirocriticon* 350 AD)

Harlot Fantasies Harlot fantasies in women are frequently symbolized by the presence of **money** or **coins** in a **dream**, and in particular to the '**spending**' of money, which is at one and the same time both exciting and **guilt** inducing. **Freud** believed that the so-called 'harlot complex' could sometimes stem from deep-rooted **incestuous** fantasies twinned with possibly unresolved **homosexual** complexes. See **Shops**

Harps Harps, while only nominally represented in John Cleese's 'the choir invisibule' (from Monty Python's perennial *Dead Parrot* sketch), may also suggest harmony and the Aeolian (the ability to give oneself up to whatever may come, without the added need for human intercession). This aspect of the harp's symbology may represent a desire for spiritual awakening, or it may simply suggest a desire to return to natural, rather than **artificial**, ways.

Harvesting Harvesting presupposes the earlier spreading of **seed** – an investment, in other words, that is finally **paying** off. There may also be revocations of fertility (or the desire for fertility), together with a wish to continue on in some form after **death** (regeneration).

Hashish Hashish, like most **drugs**, exemplifies the **wish-fulfilment** fantasy taken to its logical conclusion – i.e. we want what we want now, and to **hell** with the long-term consequences. This is a fundamental human (and **animal**, and **id**) characteristic, and only the desire for spirituality of some sort or another offers us any hope of transcending it. Hashish in **dreams** probably represents this form of easy option – the 'why not?' convention that has been used as one of the main justifications for **self-abuse** since **time** began.

Hats Hats are often **penile** symbols, but they may also symbolize the head. They are also **symbols** of power. A hat may seem to represent who we really are, because we have, on the surface at least, chosen it – but in reality, it has probably chosen us. The doffing of a **cap** (the uncovering of our **heads**) has strong **phallic** connotations, particularly when it is done by a **male** in the presence of a woman.

Hawks A hawk traditionally symbolizes rapacity and penetration. It may also suggest the capacity or desire to see ahead for long distances, or with conspicuous (and perhaps rare) clarity. To the ancient Egyptians, the hawk, or sparrowhawk, was the emblem of the **Sun God**, Rā, and the image of the human turning into a hawk implied a subsumation into the deity.
KEY LINE: 'The hawk is called in the Egyptian language *baieth*, from *bai* soul, and *eth* heart, which organ they consider the seat or enclosure of the soul.' (From Horapollo's *Hieroglyphica*, circa 5th century BC)

Hawthorn In Lincolnshire folklore, a girl of marriageable age would partially **break** a hawthorn **branch** in **flower**, and leave it in position all **night**. If it had not blown down by the next **morning**, she would soon **dream** of her future **husband**.

Hay Hay, and the scent of hay (see **Odours**), implies both **pleasure**, **nourishment** and forward provision. Hay also represents **summer**, carried through and memorialized in **winter**. To that extent it may be dreamed of by elderly **dreamers** to indicate an idealized aspect of a **lost** youth.

Hayter, Alethea (1911–2006) The author of *Opium and the Romantic Imagination* (1968), Alethea Hayter was a convinced exponent of **creative dreams**, with particular reference to the works of **Coleridge**. She concentrated, inevitably, on the effects of **opium**, while disdaining to try it herself: 'No curiosity or wish for new experience could nerve me to enter such a world of wretchedness.' She did maintain, however, that opium could never give the power of vivid dreaming to those who had not got it already.
FOOTNOTE: 'I think my only immortality will be in other people's footnotes …' (Alethea Hayter)

Hazards To **dream** of hazards suggests that the course the **dreamer** has started upon may be **dangerous**, unwise, or overly challenging.

Head, The The head was for a long time considered the symbolical seat of the higher mental powers. Should the head be **cut** off it may suggest, as in the case of the Egyptian **God** Horus (God of **sky**, and **light**, and goodness) who cut off the head of Set (**chief** of the powers of **evil**), that the head is also the seat of the intellectual qualities of evil. To that extent the head can be symptomatic of thought without **feeling**, while a bowed head, in a dream, may imply supplication or remorse. See **Hair** & **Scalping**

Healers To dream of healers implies that there is something in the **dreamer** that needs to be healed. **Jesus**, of course, was a healer, and his raising of the dead implied the possibility of a reawakening of the dormant **soul**. Healing by the 'casting out of **devils**' suggests the need to puncture or undermine our existing illusions, while the spontaneous healing of the **body** implies a desire for purification and clarity.

Hearses Hearses are **symbols** of physical **death**. They are both demonstrations of continuity – in the sense that they are status symbols referring, not to the dead, but to the living – and symbols of brevity and the mortal sway.

Heart, The The heart is traditionally the seat of the **soul** and of essential energy. If one **dreams** of a tired heart, it may mean that one no longer wishes to engage with the **world**, and that one is now predisposed towards an accommodation with dissolution. The natural vibrations of the heart (those vibrations which prove that we are still living) symbolically concord with the vibrations of beyond physical desire. It was for this reason that the Aztecs (amongst others) tore the still pulsing heart out of the **bodies** of **sacrificial victims**, feeling that only in this way (in the giving of what was most valuable) could the **Gods** be placated.

Hearths The hearth and the fireplace were for untold centuries the nerve centre of the **home**, taking an almost maternal place in the scheme of things. If one wanted comfort, sustenance, nurturing, or **light**, one turned towards the hearth. A fragrant, well-filled hearth reflected on the quality of the **people** who provided it, just as a thin, unkempt fireplace showed a lack of **self**-worth that would no doubt find itself reflected in the physical condition of **family** members. This **archetype** carries over, even today, within the **bones** of **dreams**, for we are nothing if not the products of a morphologically remembered **past**.

Heat Heat, in a **dream**, often suggests heightened emotions or a warning against going in a particular direction, or touching a particular thing. Heat may also be nurturing and energizing, and, in its rawest form, purificatory. See **Cold, Scorching** & **Thermoses**

Heaters Heaters may equate with the **heart** on their most obvious level, but they may also suggest a desire on the part of the **dreamer** for **nurturing** and tender loving care. To that extent they may symbolize the maternal (we are heated and kept warm in the **womb**), or even the lifeforce (we grow **colder** before **death**, as the **body**'s essential maintenance structure gradually shuts down). When we thaw out before a heater we gradually become more open, and more receptive, to outside forces and influences.

Heaven It is said that we carry heaven and **hell** within us, and the semantic similarity of 'heaven' to 'haven' may also be significant. Heaven and **earth** represent **spirit** and matter, and also, respectively, the **Yang** and the **Yin** – on these two principles depends the whole of existence and the duality of **primordial** manifestation, at least according to the Chinese. See **Paradise**

Heaviness If the **dreamer** feels heavy or unable to move with any great alacrity, something is, quite literally, weighing them down. Whether this is an eternal **burden** (disability or terminal **illness**, perhaps), or merely a burden that may one day be discarded, like obesity, thereby freeing the dreamer to concentrate upon other things, depends entirely on the context of the **dream**. Heaviness may also imply physical or mental abuse of some sort, or even the abuse of **drugs** or of soporifics. See **Fatness**

Hedgehogs Traditionally, the hedgehog represented bad manners and malevolence, aspects which don't sit well with our modern fluffy bunny approach to certain unthreatening, undomesticated **animals.** The hedgehog's prickles are an undoubted hindrance to true cuddly pet status, however, and may be seen to imply an **iron glove** in a **velvet fist**. The hedgehog is also ineradicably associated with **gypsies**, both because they **eat** him, and because he shares certain of their independent characteristics.

Hedges Overly well-tended hedges may suggest a certain predisposition towards **anal** retention, if one takes the **Freudian** view. Hedges also delineate boundaries, and they can be status **symbols**, also, as well as potentially 'hedging in' the **dreamer** by protecting them from outside interference and influences.

Heels High heels carry within themselves a delicious paradox, for they are both **phallic**, and at the same time suggestive of the **womb** – by tightening and **drawing** attention to a woman's **legs**, of course, they tend to **carry male** attention to other aspects of the **female** anatomy than merely the **arch** of the **foot**. Achilles, too, was beset by heel paradoxes, in that he was both invulnerable, thanks to his **mother** dipping him in the **River** Styx, and vulnerable, because she grasped him by the heel, which did not, in consequence, get wet. Achilles was a 'bit of a heel', too, given the way he treated Hector (whom he attached to his **chariot** by straps through the heel), and he also endeavoured, again through his **mother**, to show the Trojan **war** a 'clean pair of heels' by pretending to be a girl.

Heights The fear of heights is a magnificent **anxiety** image, as it besets about 90 per cent of the human population, always excepting the Mohawk **Indians** from the Kahnawake Reservation near Montreal, who specialize in working up the tallest skyscrapers. Heights are also redolent of spiritual aspiration and of the unknown – we can aspire to them, but we can't easily understand them.

Helicopters Helicopters might suggest the brief upward movement of rotor-shaped **seeds** (for we know they will both eventually come down), but they may also be assertive and intrusive, and to that extent they are probably masculine pointers, particularly when dreamt of by women who are not entirely comfortable with their **sexuality**, or with being an object/subject of interest to men.

Hell Hell is where we go when the **ego** can no longer be controlled. The four lower planes of **nature**, namely the physical, the astral, the etheric, and the lower mental, all presuppose towards the need for some sort of enlightened teaching environment before they can be jettisoned in favour of **heaven**. Hell would seem to be that place (at least according to scriptural authority), but human beings will persist in allocating **fire** and brimstone to the **spot**, and therefore it is these aspects that most often appear in **dreams**. See **Tar**

Helmets Helmets are not only **masks**, but also symbolical devices which protect the unformed mind from the rapaciousness of physical desire. Other aspects of the helmet image can include an inability to suspend our capacity for fantasy, and also an inordinate desire to protect oneself from the potential vicissitudes of the natural **world**.

Hemlock Hemlock, the plant used in the philosopher Socrates' (470–399 BC) enforced **suicide**, triggers **nightmares** and horrendous **dream visions** when taken in smaller doses. It is, needless to say, highly toxic. See **Artificial Dreams**

Henbane The herb henbane contains scopolamine (the **truth** drug), and was much used at one time to induce **visions**. It is now recognized as highly toxic. See **Artificial Dreams**

Hens A hen traditionally symbolizes maternal care. The concept of the '**mother** hen' has certain pejorative overtones, and so, for instance, were a woman to **dream** of a hen clucking around large numbers of chicks, it might imply that she was being over-maternal and pernickety vis-à-vis her **children**, her **family**, or her employees. See **Chickens**

Herds Herds suggest plenty, and also multiple aspects of the same thing. There is also an element of something being more than simply the 'sum of its parts'. Should a herd be rioting or stampeding, the **dreamer** may feel that different aspects of their own personality or life are spiralling out of control.

Hermaphrodites Dreaming of hermaphrodites may imply insecurity regarding the **dreamer**'s sexual orientation. Often, in a **dream**, the hermaphrodite figure will not be explicitly hermaphroditic, but only so via inference.

Hermes Hermes, alongside **Hypnos**, and his **son**, **Morpheus**, was believed to possess **magical** powers over **sleep** and **dreams** (which the Greeks considered states akin to **death**). The son of Zeus, **King** of the **Gods**, and Maia, **daughter** of Atlas the Titan, Hermes' primary job was as a **messenger** to the Greek Gods. He was renowned for his **tricks** and practical jokes, and was occasionally called Acacetus ('one who does nothing badly') in honour of his **gift** of the gab and his powers of nocturnal persuasion. His actual appearance in **dreams** can represent the **unconscious** mind of the **dreamer** (the nether **world**).

Hermits Hermits represent voluntary isolation, but their meaning in **dreams** may have an involuntary aspect about it – they may, for instance, symbolize old **age**, or the gradual disintegration of the **ego**. **Jung**'s concept of the **Wise Old Man** may manifest itself in the guise of a hermit, just as the hermit may represent a guardian, **teacher**, or mentor who acts as a **bridge** between the real **world** and that of the **collective unconscious**.

Hero, The The most common of all **myths**, the 'hero' is an **archetypal** mythos, stemming from **time** immemorial, and almost always referring to a powerful man (a **God**-man, if you like), who acts as a **cathartic** liberator while under the protective tutelage of **Gods**, guardians, or mentors. This liberation from **evil** usually occurs after an initial **rite-of-passage** demonstrating the hero's strength (the young Arthur drawing the **sword** from the **stone**; the **baby** Hercules **wrestling** two **snakes**), and is achieved by the almost superhuman vanquishing of **serpents**, **monsters**, **dragons**, **demons**, warlocks or **witches** (not always, however – in some hero myths, such as Jonah and the **Whale**, and Jason and the **Serpent**, the hero actually gives in to the monster and is finally regurgitated). In addition, such liberation frequently involves the specific freeing of a **virgin** (an unfallen woman) from the artificial shackles that bind her; a freeing which equates to the freeing of the **anima** inside the **male** hero figure. The **celebrations** that follow usually include **dances**, **music**, or other **rituals** such as **sacrifice**, which involve the participants in a numinous, almost **cannibalistic**, identification with the, usually doomed, hero. St George is the most obvious western personification of such a man, and the **roots** of the myth can be traced back to, and even beyond, the

Osiris/Horus myth of ancient Egypt. Dreaming of such hero figures can often represent a necessary reinforcement of the **ego**, preparing the **dreamer** for the real-life struggles that await them beyond the **dream state**. Care should be taken, however, when interpreting such **dreams**, to take into account the specific stage of the hero cycle that forms the substance of the dream, as this will equate with, and possibly throw **light** upon, the level of the dreamer's ego-consciousness. See **Heroine, Oedipus Complex & Rescue**

Heroine, The Just as with the 'hero', the origins of the heroine **myth** are lost amongst the **seas** of **time**. The heroine is usually of greater moral stature than normal women, and more perfect in her being. She is generally a **virgin** – with the implication that her femininity is intact and unprejudiced – and often young. She leads through example, and is a galvanizer of men, who follow her out of admiration, recognizing and acknowledging in her the feminine aspects of their own **psyche** that they customarily conceal. She is often called upon to **sacrifice** herself at the end of her quest, and her most perfect recent personification is probably contained within the myth (I use the word advisedly) of Joan of Arc.

Herpes Fear of **disease** – and in particular diseases contracted through **sexual** transmission – is the very stuff of **anxiety dreams**. The dream action is akin to someone **lecturing** a smoker on the biological impact of **smoking** on the **body**, thinking in this way to frighten them out of the habit. Very often all that happens is that the smoker becomes so anxious that they increase the number of **cigarettes** they smoke in counteraction.

Hexes Hexes and **cursing** are reliant on **superstition** for their real effect. Very often the hexed person comes to feel that they secretly deserve the hex, if not necessarily for the original reasons given. This **guilt** aspect is likely to manifest itself in **dreams**, and often equates with a *mea culpa* on account of some perceived fault of omission (rather than of commission) the **dreamer** finds in themselves.

Hiding Hiding away from something in **dreams** takes us directly back to **childhood**, and to the half-**games** we played with our **parents** and other **children**. Half-games, because the child takes them very much more seriously than the adult will, never being entirely sure that the game isn't suddenly going to open out into a truly frightening scenario in which the child finds itself pursued by some unnameable **monster**. This sense of doubt carries over subliminally into adulthood, and often infuses our dreams, translating itself into comfort hiding and into escapist fantasies equivalent to the child's hiding of its **head** beneath the **pillow**.

Hierosgamos The concatenation (or spiritual/**alchemical marriage**) of two otherwise disparate parts – **Christ** and the **Church**, for instance, as *sponsus*/**bridegroom** and *sponsa*/**bride**, or, to give another example, the **sun** and the **moon**.

Highways See **Freeways**

Hiking **People** are always hiking to somewhere (although very often only back to their original starting point), and the process, therefore, defines itself more by the act than by the intention. This urge for action (any action!), even if it's largely ineffectual, overcomes us when we find ourselves in emotional stasis, and uncertain of our **path**. In **dream** terms, therefore, hiking probably constitutes a desire for **energy** renewal, or for new **beginnings**. When we **walk**, we don't necessarily have to think.

Hills Hills are both challenges and promises of different vistas. When we see a hill, it is human **nature** to aspire towards it, and this probably **reflects** back upon our nomadic **past**. For there are opportunities inherent in hills for new **beginnings**, new **visions**, and renewed spiritual growth – traditionally, also, **prayers** were offered up from high places, and **temples** built.

Hinges The existence of hinges implies the possibility, at least, of an **opening**. Hinges may also suggest truncated choices, as in everything 'hinging' on some particular action or decision. A hinge also conjures up the **picture** of something that may **fall** back on you, if you do not plan carefully enough.

Hippopotami Hippopotami are notable for their **weight**, and for the **leathery**, viscous texture of their hide. They are also aggressive, and capable of sudden, unexpected appearances, often from beneath where one is sitting (the filmic **canoe** syndrome). To this extent there may be a **sexual** element to their appearance in a **dream**, as in a **fear** of pregnancy (increased weight), or penetration (increased assertion).

Hips The shape of a woman's hips suggests childbirth. Should the **shape** be exaggerated in a **dream**, it may suggest a **fear** of the biological implications of femininity, or even a fear of the process of parturition itself – for when things get bigger, they threaten us, thanks to **childhood regression**. The hips are also intimately bound up with a **female**'s directional ability, leading to links between the hips (childbearing) and the hips (suggestive of will). See **Bigness** & **Shoulders**

Historical Dreams Dreams set in the **past** are usually attempting to redefine the present. We tend to **measure** ourselves against the past, while at the same **time** repudiating it as outmoded or archaic. Deep inside ourselves we know that such an attitude is absurd, as every era has its own integrity, and integrity is absolute and should not (in an ideal **world**) be dependent on fashion or culture for its belated **interpretation**. Such **dreams** may be impelling us to relearn old lessons, therefore, and possibly even to revisit the past and reassess bygone actions.

Hitchhikers The hitchhiker is an alternative **dream symbol** for the **shadow** or **double**. Hitchhikers may also suggest **illnesses**, or viruses, or even, possibly, the unknown. They may also, paradoxically, imply a desire to reach out and connect with the outside world.

Hitting Hitting is a form of communication. For very young children, and even for autistic adults (see **Autism**), it may be the only way they can conceive of to gain the attention of a carer or **parent**. Hitting, in a **dream** context, can also stand in for criticism, or at the very least a desire to lash out in order to prevent or pre-empt it. There may be positive overtones too, as in hitting one's **target**, or making a hit.

Hives The construction of a beehive suggests forethought and enlightened preparation. It also suggests a capacity for communal living and compromise. Hidden sweetness may be an important element, too, as may be a sting in the **tail**, and a desire to protect one's interests or community. See **Bees** & **Honey**

Hobbies Hobbies suggest **self**-fulfilment – they are things we do to please ourselves, and not others. To share one's hobby with someone else is often to bore them, so there are pejorative elements to intense self-absorption as well. Hobbies also suggest peace, continuity, and the opportunity for leisure – those who live at a subsistence level simply do not have time for them, so there may be an element of hidden **guilt** to their appearance in **dreams**. See **Pleasure Principle**

Hoeing Hoeing suggests forced regeneration – the hoer is imposing themselves on an otherwise natural environment in order to dominate it, and force it to **fruit**. The hoe may also act as a **penis** substitute, therefore, and the **cutting** action may suggest **abortion**, or even sterility. There are positive elements to hoeing, of course, but the action of the hoe is what the **dream** is most likely to **pick up**, and that tends towards the intrusive. See **Sterilization**

Hogs In Christian iconography a hog implies impurity, and there are similar revocations in Homer, particularly in *The Odyssey*, when Circe transforms Odysseus's men into the swine they so clearly resembled. Hogs may also equate with **money** (a hog was any **silver coin**) in the sense, too, that a **farmer's** worth traditionally depended on the number of hogs he was able to fatten, or a vintner's on the number of hogsheads he was able to supply. In addition, living 'high on the hog' or to 'go the whole hog' suggests plenty at a time of scarcity. See also **Pig**
KEY LINE: 'I dreamed that I had entered the body of a hog, that I could not easily get out again, and that I was wallowing in the filthiest slime. Was it a kind of reward?' (From the Count of Lautréamont's *Maldoror* 1868)

Holes It's pointless, really, to draw attention to the **sexual** aspect of holes or apertures, as this is **self**-evident. Holes are also things we **fall** into, or into which we **dig** ourselves, and either of these enactments may present themselves in **dreams**. Holes may also equate with **graves**, or **wounds**, and suggest the fundamental fallibility of the human **body**. A hole healing itself up, or being **healed** or stitched, may suggest a desire for forgiveness, or the desire to forgive.

Holidays Holidays are **wish-fulfilment** fantasies, in that, despite taking ourselves *with* ourselves on holiday (in the sense of not being able to escape our own natures), we persist in **feeling** that they are the easy answer to otherwise insoluble **questions**. There is, therefore, a 'resting on one's laurels' aspect to holidays in **dreams**, just as there is a **self**-adulatory aspect, in that we may feel we deserve a holiday for being 'pleasing' – i.e. in recreating the **archetypal** infantile action of 'pleasing our **parents**'. Such a **regression** to **childhood** frequently occurs in dreams, and is one of the most common manifestations of the uncontrolled **id**.

Holiness The desire to be holy lurks within us all, and usually refers back to pre-established **childhood patterns**, for if we are good **children**, our **parents** will **love** us, but if we are bad children, we shall be **punished**. True holiness, of course, is without ulterior motive, and complete in itself, but dream holiness is usually a means to an end, and rarely, if ever, manifests itself selflessly. See **Haloes**

Holly Holly, with its **red** berries, is a **symbol** of enduring life, and is traditionally viewed as lucky for this reason. In the **northern** part of England, a man or woman who wished to know in advance whom they were to **marry** would go out at midnight on a Friday **night** to gather nine she-holly (the non-prickly variety) **leaves**, which they would then tie with **nine knots** in a three **cornered** handkerchief. This would be laid under the **pillow** before going to **bed**. They would then **dream** of their future mate.

Holy Grail, The The Holy Grail is one of the fundamental icons of Christian symbology, and purports to be the vessel into which the **blood** of **Christ** on the **Cross** was poured. He who seeks the Grail must ask the right **question**, and that question is not what the Grail is, or what it can do, but how it can be served. To that extent it is often seen as a peculiarly **male rite-of-passage** myth, just as the Eros and Psyche **myth** relates to women.

Home To the Anglo Saxons, our 'long home' was the **grave**. In symbolical terms, home is the ultimate container of the **soul**, and may be seen, by some, to represent **God** Himself. Home, in the domestic sense, carries with it many different connotations, depending on its significance for the **dreamer**. Its **archetypal** meaning might be 'a community within a community', while its emotional meaning might be 'the place in which I dwell and am accepted'. See **Houses**

Homelessness Homelessness is the ultimate stigma, in that it implies that neither we, nor anybody else, thinks enough of us, or desires us enough, to accommodate us. Symbolically, this equates with an almost total lack of identity, and for this reason images of homelessness are likely to be found most often in the **dreams** of **manic depressives** and sufferers from similar mental disorders.

Homosexuality Homosexual desires appear, in some form or another, in everybody's dreams. To a certain extent they may represent the fascination that we have with our own **bodies**, and the projection of that fascination onto others, similar to ourselves. Heterosexual **dreams** by homosexuals (either men or women) frequently disguise antagonistic feelings towards the opposite **sex**, which may be at the base of the homosexual **urge**, while remaining unacknowledged in everyday life. Such dreams can reflect an underlying **fear** of rejection (by a **mother** or **father**, for instance), twinned with a desire not to invest emotional currency in a relationship the **dreamer** suspects (either through experience or anxious supposition) may be doomed to **failure**.

Honey Honey suggests **nature**'s abundance, and also the worthy products of effort. Dreaming of honey may suggest that the **dreamer** craves **pleasure**, or possibly even regeneration, given the apparent curative qualities of propolis and royal jelly. Traditionally, honey benefited from predominantly positive qualities, although the Puritans insisted that 'it is better to be preserved in vinegar than to **rot** in honey'. A moot point, perhaps. See **Hives & Bees**
KEY LINE: 'The pedigree of honey/Does not concern the bee;/A clover, any time, to him/Is aristocracy.' (From Emily Dickinson's *Poems*, Part ii, No. 56)

Honour To dream of honour may suggest the lack of it in certain of one's dealings with the **world**. It may also suggest a desire to arrogate the honour that should be accorded others, to oneself. To **dream** of others acting honourably may imply the desire for a mentor or guide – perhaps even a return to the moral teachings of our **parents** or **teachers**, from which we have long since strayed. See **Guidance**

Hoods Hoods, or hoodies, are disguises behind which we may **hide** our shortcomings, for, as the old **saw** has it, *cucullus non facit monachum* – it's not the hood that makes the **monk**. There may also be a revelatory element about a hood, both **sexual**, in terms of the uncircumcised **penis** and the clitoris, and non-sexual, in terms of ecclesiastical or scholastic **honour** systems – the longer the hood, the higher the degree, was the traditional take by both Oxford and Cambridge.

Hooks Hooks may stand in place of things (**amputated hands**, for instance), or they may fix things in their place. We may be threatened by hooks, and they may be used to **draw** us towards something we do not wish to approach. **Fingers** or **toes** may stand in for them, and we may use them to explore areas that would otherwise be closed to us (the **underwater** or undersea, for example). Interesting to speculate as to why, when we explore something, we use an aggressive, possibly **phallic** object, to precede us.

Hop Pillows Pillows filled with hops are alleged to cure **insomnia**. Hops were also used in medieval times for their sedative effect, acting directly on the central nervous system.

Horizons To **dream** of horizons is to dream of possibilities, either in a positive sense (the view of the horizon may stimulate one towards exploration), or in a negative sense (the view of the horizon may convince one of the futility of exploration). The choice and context lies with the **dreamer**, and is probably dependent on whether one views a **cup** as half **empty**, or half full.

Horns In Greek mythology, the horn gate was one of the two dream **gates** – the other was made of **ivory**. The horn gate **dreams** were likely to come true, while those that issued from the ivory gate were deceptive in some way – this idea stemmed from puns on the Greek words for horn and ivory, namely *krano* and *elephas*, which suggested verbs meaning 'to bring to an issue' and 'to cheat', respectively. Dreaming of horns may also be suggestive of cuckoldry (in that a cuckold was traditionally presented with a **pair** of metaphorical horns by his nemesis), or a desire to call someone, or bring something to their attention. Unsurprisingly perhaps, the erect **penis** may also be represented by a horn, leading to that perennially popular expression (*pace* Derek and Clive), 'he's got the horn'. Morgan la Faye (a definite bad **egg**, that one), devised a cup called the Horn of Fidelity, out of which no woman could cleanly **drink** who was not faithful to her **husband** – out of 100 women at King Marke's court, only four managed to sip from it without splattering themselves. See **Baskets** & **Uniforms**

Horoscopes Horoscopes are suggestive of the future, and also, to a certain extent (and only by inference), of **predestination**. The desire to know the future (or a **fear** of or for the future) is common to virtually all **dreams**, and the casting of horoscopes can be a convenient alleviatory trope.

Horses Horses symbolize **speed** and grace. In their **winged** state they can imply transcendence (often in **alchemical** terms), and in their wild state they suggest the instinctive drives of the **unconscious**. In their literal sense they can also symbolize **nightmares**, as in **Fuseli**'s painting of *The Nightmare* (1781). In ancient times, a **white** horse was also a **symbol** of life. To the Taoists of ancient China, horses symbolized the **heavens**, fertility, speed and perseverance. In Norse mythology, horses were **sacred** to the **God** Wotan. Horses are the 'great **companions**', in that, with the adjunct of a horse, a person is considerably more than the sum of their two disparate parts. See **Epona**, **Mares**, **Stables** & **Stallions**

Horseshoes Horseshoes traditionally symbolize luck and protection against **witches** (at least when standing upright), but they can also imply resolution, proficiency and initiative. To **dream** of a horseshoe may imply **drawing** something out (even a **poison**).

Hoses The **penis** has hose-like qualities, particularly in the hands of a younger man (older men tend to suffer from jet diminution, thanks to an inevitable hardening of the prostate). The **heart** (and its vessels and arteries) may also find itself pictured as a hose, while a **burning** passion (or any other such flammable entity) may call upon a **dream** hose to put it out. Hoses can also symbolize a **cleansing** process, which may, in the case of a channelling movement (even the splitting off of a number of hoses), verge on the purificatory.

Hospitals Hospitals are there to cure us, but they may also be places in which we die (see **Dying**). This apparent paradox gives hospitals their uncomfortable, almost faceless, quality, in that they are all things to all **people** – at one and the same time the hope of salvation and the **symbol** of transience. Hospitals are also places in which we lose our individuality (even more than in **schools**), and as such they represent, in **archetypal** terms, individual loss in the face of collective nonchalance.

Hostages We are all 'hostages to fortune', in that we often depend on chance rather than on will to get by. And so to see ourselves being held hostage in a **dream** is no great shakes, for everyone feels, from time to time, that a part of them is being imprisoned. To *take* a hostage in a dream, however, may point up a flawed desire by the **dreamer** to attempt to impose their will on a seemingly un-malleable **world**. This is a dangerous **path** to tread (that of forcing issues), and the dream may very well be protecting the dreamer from the consequences of their own actions.

Hotels Hotels appear frequently in **dreams**, and are often linked to **anxieties** over status. They are public places in which we are on show, and in which our actions have immediate ramifications. Like **houses**, too, they can represent the **dreamer**, both bodily and in their mental construct. For French speakers, an *autel* (pronounced hotel with a silent 'h') may also stand in for, or transmogrify into, an **altar**, before which the dreamer finds themselves **sacrificed** in some way – either socially, publicly, or metaphorically. Hotels are also splendid environments for **feeling** out of place in, and shy or overly self-conscious dreamers may find themselves **walking** around **naked** in hotel lobbies, if they are not very careful.

Hourglasses Hourglasses show **time** trickling by. We are all naturally aware of this state of affairs, but our rational minds set it aside in order the better to live our lives while we may, and in as fruitful manner as possible, in the face of inevitably lowering **skies**. For our **unconscious** minds, though, ignorance is the very opposite of bliss, and some accommodation to incipient mortality needs to be made. The **symbol** of the hourglass, with its fragility, its apparent capacity for renewal, and its eventual and inevitable truncation, perfectly equates with the **passage** of our lives.

Houses Houses are living things. The Hebrews equated the house with the human **body**, with the turrets as **ears**, the **windows** as **eyes**, the **library** as the **heart**, the **furnace** as the **stomach**, and the cellar as the fundament. Houses in **dreams** can have similar meanings, whilst also carrying with them revocations of the **past**, in the sense of our ancestry (our **biblical** house). Such a **reading** suggests that the **room** in which the **dreamer** finds themselves is of itself significant, particularly if events are happening in it. In addition, the existence of houses, and their capacity for renewal, may suggest the *gilgoolem* (the Kabbalistic concept of the natural revolution of pre-existing **souls**). See **Ancestors, Artemidorus of Daldis, Ezekiel, Kabbalah, Hotels & Sheds**

Hubris Hubris describes pride, over-confidence, or arrogance taken to excess, and inevitably leading to humbling by the **Gods**. Hubris and **heroic dreams** are a necessary part, though, of the process of **male** maturation (see **Rites-of-Passage**), for without them the young male cannot move from adolescence to maturity.

Hugging Hugging may be the newest and most modish form of social embrace, but it can also be a sign of possession, a hierarchic signifier, and a euphemism for the **sexual** act. A hug may be both healing (hugging **trees** springs to mind) or lethal (one would not wish to be hugged by a grizzly **bear**). The hug may also be hypocritical, as in the hug by a **leader** that marks out a man for later assassination.
KEY LINE: '... if you know that I do fawn on men, and hug them hard, and after scandal them; or if you know that I profess myself, in banqueting, to all the rout, then hold me dangerous.' (Cassius to Brutus, in Shakespeare's *Julius Caesar*, Act i scene 2)

Humour Humorous **dreams** are surprisingly rare (probably because the **unconscious** mind has a tendency to take itself rather too seriously). Traditionally, the **body** was made up of four **humours**: phlegm, **blood**, black bile and choler. A good balance of these led to health and **happiness**, and this carries over into the apparent healing properties of being 'good humoured'. Humour in dreams, therefore, when it is directed outwards, bodes well – but when it is directed inwards, towards the **dreamer**, it may suggest unease with an existing situation. See **Fourness**

Hunger We are usually hungry *for* something, in **dreams**, and this carries over into the identity of the desired object. Hunger suggests dissatisfaction, or a lack of some specific article or artefact whose presence we feel would complete us (e.g. through **cannibalistic** assimilation).

Hunters See **Hunting**

Hunting Hunting is a fundamental human drive which has been rationalized and sentimentalized virtually out of existence in recent **years**. For a woman to dream of being hunted (or to associate herself with the quarry of a hunter) undoubtedly has **sexual** revocations, and the opposite, of course, is also true, namely when the **dreamer** see themselves as hunter, and fulfilling their instinctive urge to **chase** something or somebody down (possibly a mate – possibly supper). Peaceful societies debase and talk down the hunting **instinct** because they feel threatened by it – hunting, after all, is about the freedom to do what one wants to do, when one wants to do it. To that extent, of course, it equates to anarchy.

Hurdles We place hurdles in our way to slow ourselves down, just as we place hurdles in a **field** to protect our flocks from predators. To **dream** of hurdles is the **superego**'s way of placing **inhibitions** in the way of the unregenerate **id**, and to that extent they are probably a wise leavening of an otherwise unruly (because over-yeasted) **cake**.

Hurricanes Hurricanes constitute sudden upsets of an existing, and often comforting, old order. They are symbolical of a total, if brief, loss of control, and to that extent hurricanes may also suggest the sudden intensity of a total submission to **God**'s will. A hurricane seen **tearing** down a **house** (or even **carrying** it away) may evoke either **illness** or the **fear** of **death**.

Hurrying Hurrying is a familiar **dream** motif indicative of **anxiety**, whether it be hurrying through **crowds**, or **running** hard and getting nowhere. Hurrying also presupposes importance, in that the object towards which one is hurrying cannot, or may not, be kept **waiting**. We often hurry for no good reason.

Hurting The part of the **body** that is hurting us in the **dream** will have particular significance in our everyday lives. If it is an **arm**, for instance, it may suggest that we have trouble reaching out – if it is a **leg**, that we may be struggling to make our way towards, or away from something. If we are hurting others in our dream, we may, paradoxically, be hurting aspects of ourselves, and if we are hurting ourselves, then we may, again paradoxically, be failing in our gratitude to others. See **Failure**

Husbands For a woman to dream in an uneasy way about her husband may be suggestive of **anxieties** about her **animus**, or the quality of her **self**-image *vis à vis* men, as seen through the reflective **eyes** of her father (for **fathers** and **husbands** are sometimes interchangeable in women's **dreams**, just as **wives** and **mothers** may be interchangeable in men's). Comforting dreams about a husband may suggest a healthy **animus**, particularly if the woman *becomes* the husband in some form or other – such startling transmogrifications are perfectly normal in the dream **world**, and reflect different, but often complementary, aspects of the self.

Hyenas Hyenas **hunt** in **packs**, and may therefore symbolize **crowds**, or mobs, or **audiences**, when they appear in **dreams**. There is a **tearing** and gnashing (see **Gnawing**) aspect to their presence, too, which may suggest **illness**, or the **fear** of sudden, unexpected changes. Their is also the laughing, mocking aspect of the hyena, which may suggest an over-emphasis on dignity, by the **dreamer**, and a concomitant fear of public ridicule. See **Laughter**

Hymen Complex A **fear** of the loss of the hymen, or of **virginity**, frequently occurs in **dreams**. Many **symbols**, such as **corks**, filters, **sieves** or **spider webs** may stand in for the hymen in such cases. See **Castration Complex** & **Circumcision Complex**

Hypericum See **Saint John's Wort**

Hypersomnia A condition of extreme sleepiness, verging on morbidity.

Hypnagogic State The particular stage, equating to drowsiness, which occurs between **waking** and **sleeping**. See **Hypnopompic State**

Hypnagogic Thought Sudden flashes of thought or insight that occur just before **sleep** cuts in. See **Hypnopompic Thought**

Hypnopompic State The semi-conscious state that occurs between **sleeping** and **waking**. See **Hypnagogic State**

Hypnopompic Thought Sudden flashes of thought or insight that occur just before **waking**. See **Hypnagogic Thought**

Hypnos The word for 'sleep', in ancient Greek, is *hupnos*, and Hypnos was its **God**. His **son**, **Morpheus**, had the delectable task of adding filigree to mortal **dreams**.

Hypnosis A state roughly equivalent to **sleep** induced by psychological, rather than by natural, means.

Hypnotherapy The treatment of certain psychological conditions by the use of **hypnotism**.

Hyponoic State A particular state of decreased consciousness.

Hyssop A perennial herb, native to Europe, hyssop has been used since **biblical** times as a mild sedative. It was also used to induce and to manipulate **dreams**. See **Artificial Dreams**

Hysterectomies Dreaming of a hysterectomy may represent a **fear** of **pregnancy**, or even a fear of permanent change caused by **sexual** activity. The loss of some fundamental aspect of oneself (the ability to give **birth**, for instance) may reflect fears of the break-up of an established interpersonal relationship (equivalent, in symbolical terms, to that between a woman and her **uterus**). Hysterectomies may also imply outside interference in an extremely intimate matter – possibly even the imposition, intrusion, or arrogation by a **male**, of some thing, some aspect, or some adjunct of the **dreamer**, that she considers ought to be exclusively feminine.

Hysteria The visible projection of **neurotic guilt**, often characterized by functional disturbances such as **nausea**, loss of motor control, or hypochondria.

I

Ice To dream of ice is to **dream** of the imposition of frigidity, inertia, or of the **truth** unmanifest. To this extent ice equates with the emotions, and implies a deadening of the senses, or possibly even a blockage that is impossible to **break** through. Should the ice succeed in being broken, however, or in being **melted** (*scindere glaciem*), the resultant **flood** may have just as deleterious an effect. See **Snow**

Icebergs Icebergs are renowned for being three parts **invisible**, and to **dream** of an iceberg, therefore, may reflect hidden depths or **dangers** lurking just below the surface of an otherwise calm **sea**.

Ice Cream Ice cream, like **chocolate**, is comfort **food**, but it can also be **guilt**-inducing. The semantic comparison between **ice**, with its revocations of **frigidity**, and **cream**, with its revocations of **richness** and plenty, may also be significant.

I Ching, The The *I Ching*, or Book of Changes (*Yijing*), dates from between 2400 and 1150 BC, and represents a considerable **body** of ancient wisdom (the source of both Taoism and Confucianism) which is still entirely amenable to us in the present day. The *I Ching* responds more to chance than to causality, and its philosophy represents a move towards oneness and unity, rather than towards a more fragmentary duality. Complimentary **symbols** like the **Yin-Yang** guide us towards courses of action that may lead to integration, rather than to the disintegration fostered on us by many of the appurtenances of modern life. These **signs** are relevant only at specifically given moments, and only after a specific **question** is asked. They are not universal, and they are not a panacea, but rely more on **synchronicity**, and inner **unconscious** knowledge, for their effect.

Icons Icons are now associated more readily with celebrity than with **questions** of faith and mimesis. To destroy an icon (i.e. to act iconoclastically), implies a reversal of existing mores in favour of the unknown – it is far easier to destroy than to rebuild, however, as the eighth-century iconoclasts, under Emperor Leo III, only belatedly discovered. See **Destruction**

Id, The That part of us, according to **Freud**, which controls or **harbours** all our primeval energies and **instincts**. The id is out for total gratification, and needs modifying by our **superego** if we are to function within an ordered society. The anxieties caused by this necessary **repression** often emerge in **dreams**. See **Ego**

Identification The taking on of other **people**'s attributes while dreaming, as a result of envy, admiration, or ambition on the part of the **dreamer**.

An example might be the dreamer finding themselves **stammering**, because someone they admire, or whose success they might secretly wish to emulate, has a slight stutter. The Andalucian Spanish have affected a lisp (the *ceceo*), allegedly in mimicry of a **speech** impediment suffered by **King** Ferdinand V (1452–1516) – many grammarians and **language** experts, however, do not subscribe to this view.

Idiocy To dream of idiocy is to dream of the **fear** of idiocy. We all sometimes doubt our own intelligence, especially when faced with someone more intellectually rigorous than ourselves. Originally, to the ancient Greeks, an idiot (*idiotes*) meant a private person (i.e. one without any public responsibility), and therefore incompetent. Nowadays, an idiot is merely someone we look down upon, or who uncomfortably resembles us, to the extent that we need to deflate him in order to thwart public recognition of his similarities to us. **Dreams** can act in a similar deflationary way – a case, perhaps, of 'not painting the **devil** (or in this case the idiot) on the wall'.

Idols The **destruction** of idols or effigies represents the symbolic **killing** of the person, or entity, concerned. What better way do non-intellectuals have than to destroy the likeness of one who threatens them? We see this in voodoo, and we see it in the depictions of ghouls and **demons** in 14th-century religious **paintings**. We also see it in **dreams**, when the **dreamer** symbolically destroys some aspect of themselves (or another) they find threatening. See **Icons**

Igloos Igloos are a protection against **death**. Ordinary **houses** simply don't fulfil this function. If the **house** didn't exist, we could probably find somewhere else to shelter, and even if we failed, a **night** out in the **cold** wouldn't **kill** us – no igloo, however, and you freeze to **death**. To that extent, of course, igloos are also **womb**-like, and representative of the feminine, nurturing principle, while also containing within themselves revocations of **frigidity**, and of the **mother** possibly turning against her **children**, or thrusting them away from her.

Ignition Ignition probably equates with the **heart** (if looked at laterally, as we need to do in **dreams**). This symbolic suggestibility is further strengthened when we think of the electronic **paddles** that are often used by **hospitals** in attempts to restart, or reignite, a frozen heart. Ignition may also be a manifestation of the **beginning** of something – the firing up, in other words, of something **new**. See **Batteries**

Illness Dreams of illness are common **anxiety** pointers, and are often designed to draw the **dreamer**'s attention towards feelings of general uneasiness, rather than to any specific malady. If the **sickness** *is* specified – flu, for example – it helps to identify the **symptoms** of the illness (**breathing** difficulties, fever, aching **bones**), and then to take these symptoms out of the context of the illness, and into the context of normal life. We must then ask ourselves a series of **questions** – what, for instance, could cause breathing difficulties? Anxiety? **Pre-birth regressions**? **Fear** of **drowning**? An over-possessive partner? In all these cases the dreamed of 'flu' may have very different revocations than its everyday counterpart.

Imago Psychoanalytic term for the forming of the idealized parental image during infancy. This image is often repressed by the adult as forming no more than the remnants of an infantile affect.

Imitations 'Imitation is the sincerest form of flattery' goes the saying, and this is to a certain extent true in **dreams** as well. To imitate is to project, and we often aspire towards what we imitate, whilst **fearing** what we mimic. To that extent it is probably true to say that the **dreamer** craves the attributes of the imitated person or article, rather than the person or article itself. A good example might be were the dreamer to find themselves limping for no apparent reason – this might reflect a desire to be seen as **heroic**, or to have **sacrificed** something, in a public arena, that might reflect well on the dreamer. To grandstand, in other words. See **Identification**

Immaculate Conception The dogma of the Immaculate Conception came rather late to the Roman Catholic Church (8th December 1854, actually, in terms of an article of faith), and therefore probably reflects a roughly similar degree of wishful or expedient thinking in that **arena** to that which it does in **dreams** – namely that it may be possible to sin without actually sinning, and that there really are exceptions that prove the rule. The purely symbolic meaning of the Immaculate Conception reflects the **touching** of, or by, **God**, as the act of conceiving is both a **coming** and a going, and not simply the one-sided relationship it might presuppose.

Immersion Immersion may represent **death**, as in **drowning**, or spiritual **rebirth**, as in **baptism**. It may represent the process of confinement, as in **immersion** inside the uterine sac (see **Uterus**), or it may represent the process of entombment, as in immersion inside the **earth**. **Water** often equates with emotion, in dream terms, and total immersion may imply an overwhelming, and even, on occasion, **suffocating**, emotional charge.

Immobility We are forced into immobility when our **unconscious** mind **fears** the results of our intended actions and wishes to protect us from them. This equates in some way to real life freezing in the face of **danger** – both human beings and **animals** indulge in such freezing behaviour, often to their detriment. There is an aspect to freezing (or remaining immobile) which hopes not to be noticed, just as a pheasant will freeze at the **feet** of a **hunter**, or as an ostrich will stick its **head** into the **sand**. A person might also remain immobile on a **cold** day to conserve **heat**, or to maximize the effects of the **sun** – paradoxically, of course, this action has the effect of making us more cold, for any movement is generally better than a complete lack of it as far as the circulation goes. While movement *in extremis* may at first seem to go against the **grain**, it is a fact that the British SAS and the US Green Berets were specifically trained not to freeze up during ambushes, but to reply to such unexpected attacks with even more ferocity than the **enemy**. The same may also apply to perceived dangers in **dreams**, suggesting that oneiric immobility might in fact be a **warning** signal, telling us to get on the move.

Immoral Dreams Freud addressed the question of the presence of immoral **dreams** in the dream list of a fundamentally moral person in three ways. First, he acknowledged that some apparently immoral dreams were not, in fact, immoral at all, and did not, in consequence, trigger the **dreamer**'s **self**-censoring faculties. Secondly, when a moral person dreams immoral dreams they will frequently awaken in a sweat, their self-censoring faculties having temporarily failed them and neglected their task. And thirdly, that there are occasions when the sheer exuberance of the **sexual** or perverse content of the dreams carries the dreamer along with it, thus negating, for the time being, the usual self-censorship steam valve – the **manifest** content of the dream, in other words, is being viewed with the same tolerance that the dreamer may accord, in real life, to a sudden outburst of **anger**, or to a fleeting sado-masochistic fantasy. Should the moral person, then, take responsibility for the content of their dreams? Yes, says **Freud**. There is no **escaping** the link between the **ego** and the **id** except if we believe (and here comes a rare Freudian joke) that our dreams are 'inspired by alien spirits'. See **Anxiety Dreams, Masochism, Punishment Dreams** & **Sadism**

Impotence Male impotence, occurring in the context of a **dream**, can disguise, or be a defence mechanism against, an **unconscious** antagonism to women. It can also be reflected in images of **death** or **frustration**, and may, in addition, hide a **castration complex**. See also **Frigidity, Frustration Dreams** & **Inhibitions**

Imprisonment The vast majority of imprisonments are **self**-inflicted – either through self-abuse, lack of discretion, mistakes of judgement, or ineptitude. We can be imprisoned by our mindsets, or by our dependence on others to the detriment of our own free will. The **bars** can be of **gold**, or of **iron** – they can be physical, or metaphorical. In such cases our **dreams** are simply **reflections** of existing states – pointers, if you like, to the need for fundamental change. See **Captivity**

Imps Imps can symbolize the **dreamer**'s **unconscious** mind. They can also suggest fate and its sometimes irritating machinations – for the original Anglo Saxon meaning of the verb to imp was to **needle**, as personified by such figures as the 'thrummy cap', who lurked in the basements of Northumberland castles in the guise of an **old man**, and caused havoc. See **Fuseli** & **Incubi**

Impulse An act or thought driven psychologically, rather than rationally.

Incense Incense generally accompanies **ritual** – it is a link between the outer and the inner, epitomized by its symbolical ingestion. It may also indicate or draw attention to the **past**, as well as being a modifier of the present. Examples of narcotizing incense include camphor, which, according to Jahr's *Manual*, 'can conjure strange figures before the **eyes** which do not disappear on **waking**'. Herrick's *Herbal* goes even further, warning of 'anxious, fearful **dreams; suffocation**, oppression'. The East Indians believed that the location of camphor could only be dreamed, and not deduced in a rational way – **speech** must first be **abandoned**, with, later, the freshly cut **crystals** being secured in a thick cloth so that 'they may not **escape**'.

Incest Incest is usually defined as sexual relations between closely related individuals whose **marriage** would be considered unlawful or whose relationship **taboo**. Incest or incest fixations can often project themselves onto innocent partners in **dreams**. In such cases the thought or representative image of the **mother**, the **father**, the **brother**, the **sister**, the **uncle** or the aunt may interpose itself between the **dreamer** and the object of their desire, stopping coition in its tracks – the sexual partner is thereby unconsciously identified with the incest object, thus scuppering the sought-for union. Incest in a dream may also symbolize the dreamer's attempt to better connect with their own essential selves. See **Incest Barrier**

Incest Barrier Cultural, moral, psychological, psychosocial, or societal restrictions prohibiting sexual activity between closely related individuals. See **Dream Censorship** & **Incest**

Income Income equates with comfort. Enough, and one is happy. Too little, and one is miserable. Or so, at least, runs the saw. In terms of energy, incoming power implies openness and receptivity, while outgoing energy implies jadedness and malcontent.

Incubation See **Aesculapius**

Incubi Incubi were medieval folkloric **demons** (the name *incubus* means '**nightmare**' in Latin) reputed to appear when women were sleeping in order to have **sexual** intercourse with them. The resultant **child** would be either a **witch**, a demon, or deformed in some way. The Yoruba tribe of Nigeria held a similar belief, in which **erotic dreams** were attributed to Elgebra, a **God** capable of taking on either **male** or **female** form and mating with men and women in their **sleep**. See also **Fuseli, Raimondi, Succubi** & **Witches**

Indians Indians may represent foreignness to the **dreamer** (if they don't happen to be Indian, of course), or even, possibly, a foreign or unknown aspect of themselves. The Indians who are now known as Native Americans occupy an interesting, quasi-**archetypal** niche in the **unconscious** minds of many non-Indians – a niche informed by a mixture of inappropriate **guilt** (in the sense that one shouldn't hold oneself responsible for the sins of one's own, or indeed anybody else's, forebears), and environmental idealism. Both these aspects are likely to emerge in **dreams**. See **Red Indians**

Indigestion Indigestion implies that one has been forced, or that one has chosen, to stomach something that sticks in the metaphorical craw. Indigestion may also constitute a block of some sort, in the sense that something is not quite right. See **Stomach Ache**

Individual Psychology A **school** of psychological theory founded by **Alfred Adler** in which the sense of **inferiority**, together with its compensatory mechanisms, was perceived as the primary motivating force for human behaviour (rather than the near invidious **sexual** drive).

Individual Symbols Most dreamers use their own individual **symbols** whilst dreaming – a **doctor**, for instance, may lard his **dreams** with medical jargon, or cause them to take place in a **hospital**, while a **teacher** might do the same thing in the **school** environment she finds most familiar. These environments are only a matter of external form, however, reflecting the **time** and place within which the **dreamer** lives, and they need to be interpreted more deeply within the context of the specific dream. An example of this might be a **vegetarian** Hindu dreaming of **eating meat**, which for him would be a **taboo** experience, while for a carnivorous European it would have no real significance whatsoever. Such individual **symbols** tend to appear and reappear during the course of a long sequence of dreams, making their meaning easier to pin down.

Individuation The transcendence, through the **psyche**, to a complete union of the conscious and the **unconscious**. **Jung** discovered that **dreams** followed certain **patterns**, and these patterns he called the process of individuation. Only by recognizing these patterns over a long period of **time** can individuation be completed. This process of individuation often begins with a '**wounding**', a '**call**', or an 'obstruction' by an external force, which acts as a catalyst to the inner **self**, triggering the process of **change**. Such a process of change often needs the presence of an 'inner **friend**' or '**talisman**', rather than merely a *deus ex machina*, to resolve itself.

Infantile Trauma Damage to the **psyche** that occurs in infancy, and whose origins may occasionally be elucidated through the correct interpretation of our **dreams**.

Infantilism Psychosexual activity or behaviour relating back to the infantile stage of **sexual** development. Examples might include excessive use of **oral** or **anal** stimulation, or even the use of **childhood** adjuncts (**nappies**, dummies, teats, etc.) for sexual or psychological inspiration.

Infection When a woman **dreams** of infection, the **symbol** may in fact be disguising a **fear** of **pregnancy** or of the implications that pregnancy may carry for her. Infection may also correspond to negative energy, or to the pressures of external forces on internal integrity, whether spiritual, physical, or moral.

Inferiority Complexes Psychologist **Alfred Adler** coined the term to describe **ego** problems usually acquired in early **childhood**, normally relating to an overdeveloped sense of personal inferiority. See **Individual Psychology**

Infidelity Infidelity, and the sense of wider betrayal, tend to go **hand** in hand. As **dreams** generally refer back to the dreamer's **self**, this can sometimes imply that the **dreamer** has let themselves down, or betrayed themselves in some way. Projections out onto others are also common, and frequently depend on our perceptions of how others should – rather than do – see us. Other **people**, in other words, are required to fulfil our (the dreamer's) moral and behavioural criteria. They are forced, in effect, to *be* us.

KEY LINE: 'In her dreams, when she had no control over her thoughts, her position appeared to her in all its shocking nakedness. One dream she had almost every night. She dreamt that both at once were her husbands, and lavished their caresses on her.' (From Leo Tolstoy's *Anna Karenina* 1876)

Inflation The extension of the personality through an over-identification with other more dominant personalities or **archetypes,** possibly leading to vainglory or to **repressed** or compensatory feelings of **inferiority**.

Ingres, Jean-Auguste-Dominique (1780–1867) Favoured bedtime **reading** of Madame de Staël, James Macpherson's purported translations of the works of Celtic Bard, Ossian, also found favour with Napoleon, who commissioned *The Dream Of Ossian* (1813) from Ingres, and had it hung in a bedroom in the Palazzo di Monte Cavallo, in Rome, which he never actually went on to use. The **painting** shows Ossian slumped over his Bardic **harp**, romantic marble images of **heroes** and **heroines**, **Gods** and **Goddesses**, disappearing into infinity, and the realms of **sleep**, behind him.

Inheritance Inheritance comprises everything, both good and bad, that is passed down to us from previous generations. This places a particular onus on our **parents**, and on those who would be parents themselves. In symbolical terms, inheritance can be a **weight** of accrued knowledge, or it can represent a communal purpose that in its negative aspect may be akin to vendetta, and in its positive aspect may represent fortune.

Inhibitions Real life inhibitions are often depicted literally in **dreams**, as in an inability to move forward when one yearns to, or **running** and not being able to cover ground, or being prevented, at the last moment, from engaging in a much-desired **sexual** act by the unexpected intervention of a third party. Such dreams are usually caused by the tensions set up by the inhibition of our **id** – one part of us wants to do the inhibited thing, the other part (the **ego**) wishes to 'hold us back' from doing it through **fear** of the possible consequences. An amusing correlative would be in 'Tom & Jerry' cartoons, when a little **red devil** appears on Tom's **left shoulder**, and a little **white angel** appears on his **right** shoulder. Tom's **head** is soon flashing faster and faster, backwards and forwards between the two, until he erupts, on the spot, in an agony (ecstasy?) of indecision. See **Frustration Dreams**

Initiation A process of liberation which begins with the rite of submission, and continues through a period of containment, towards a reconciliation of often disparate elements into one unity. In **archetypal** terms all initiations are the same, whether they be called **Baptisms**, Bar Mitzvahs, Confirmations, Hazings, **Blood Brotherhoods**, or whatever. See **Rites-of-Passage**

Injections Injections are when outside elements are infused or received into a static, pre-existing, or inchoate objective. This may represent itself sexually, as in impregnation via the sperm of another, or it may represent itself metaphorically, as in the seeding of the object by knowledge, religious experience, or the action of the **collective unconscious**. The **syringe** itself is predominantly a **phallic** object, infused with phallic knowledge, and this tends to be its probable reading in a dream context. See **Vaccinations**

Injury The receipt or giving of injury **mirrors** one of the fundamental methods in which we communicate as human beings. To injure someone is to disapprove of them, and to **self**-injure is to disapprove of oneself – both in demonstrable ways. To be injured is to be forced to slow down, or to change the way one functions in some essential manner.

Ink Ink is both the **motor** of a fundamental means of **self**-expression, and also a mechanism whereby one can transmit those private thoughts or messages to others. Ink can also **stain**, and this aspect may still carry with it revocations of otherness, and possibly even of outcast status. Ink can also be used in self-defence, and as a means of self-justification.

Insanity A legal term implying the inability to function within the bounds of normal (that is to say, regulated) society due to a psychiatric disorder or a mental disease. Due to its very **nature**, insanity is unlikely to appear in anything but a symbolical form in the **dreams** of a nominally 'sane' person. In such a context its appearance is more likely to reflect the **fear**, or anxiety, of going insane, rather than the actual state of insanity itself.

Recent research has suggested that a person who is not allowed to dream may, indeed, become insane.

Insects Insects swarming around a **dreamer**'s **head** can symbolize oppression by unpleasing or unwanted thoughts. Insects may also double as **people** who take advantage of temporary **weakness** to drive home their own agendas. See **Bugs**

Inscriptions Inscriptions are one way of communicating with the future. The hieroglyphs on Egyptian tombs and sarcophagi are almost the only way we have to even marginally understand a society whose beginnings are almost as obscure to us as their remaining **memorials**. Inscriptions can also double as legends, and this aspect is important in the context of each individual's **fear** of mortality, and of being forgotten. See **Coffins** & **Tombstones**

Insomnia Difficulty in either getting to, or remaining, asleep. Pierre Janet, an eminent French nerve specialist of the first part of the twentieth century, maintained that insomnia was an hysterical symptom depending on an **unconscious** dread that unpleasant **dreams** would repeat themselves if the state of **sleep** was once more attained. See **Repetitive Motifs**

Instincts Innate, primal **urges** that may temporarily override rational control.

Insulation Insulation **doubles** as protection, but it can also **cut** us off from important events that may have an impact on us. To that extent it may be both a comfort and a discomfort – a comfort physically, a discomfort psychically, or intellectually.

Integration The transposing of apparently unrelated or distinct personality traits into one undivided (hopefully harmonious) whole.

Interchangeability The replacing of the main **dream** focus by other, **camouflaged** focuses. See **Interpretation by Opposites**

Interior Decoration Interior decoration can sometimes equate with the healing process. We are, if you like, healing a **house** and turning it into a **mirror** of ourselves when we decorate it, particularly if we view the house as an extension or stand-in for our own **bodies**. There may also be an element of 'whited sepulchres' about the process, implying that unsightly elements in our makeup may be being disguised rather than eradicated. See **Healers**

Internet, The Dreaming of the internet would suggest that we are searching for connections and easy answers that do not rely on either physical effort or mental **struggle** for their elucidation. In addition, the internet has come, symbolically, to represent truncated possibility, in that it only responds to specifically designed questions and has no obvious dynamic of its own. Internet **nuts** are likely to disagree with this **reading**, however, and their **dreams** will tend to reflect their heightened expectations.

Interpretation by Opposites Frequently, in **dreams**, the seeming meaning of an image may in fact be interpreted by its exact opposite meaning. The **dreamer** sees themselves as part of a **crowd**, for instance, but still they feel **alone** – the crowd image may therefore be a failed **ego** compensation in attempted mitigation of the 'alone' **feeling**. Another **trick** to avoid facing the full ramifications of a **dream** is to constantly replace figures in the dream by other, seemingly different figures, of either **sex**. This equates with the young **child**'s desire to **hide** itself behind obvious objects or pieces of **furniture**, half hoping, half knowing that it will be found out, but still thrilling to the experience. See **Interchangeability**

Interviews Interviews are not only **anxiety** causing, but also conducive to possible change. This apparent paradox underlies their significance in a **dream** context – the **dreamer** is acknowledging the need for change, preparing the ground for that change, but nevertheless dreading its possible effects.

Intestines The intestines have links both to parturition and to eventual disintegration. They are a **symbol** both of the extraordinary complexity of the **body**, and of the brevity of existence its **organs** impose upon us – for our **minds** and our intellectual power may continue more or less indefinitely, but our organs, not. See **Guts**

Intoxication Intoxication, in **dream language**, may be synonymous with **pregnancy**, particularly when dreamt of by a woman. It may also represent a desire not to be held responsible for our actions. There are also revocations of **poisoning** in the word itself, which Pliny tells us stems from the *taxa*, or bay **tree**, which was traditionally used for poisoning **arrows**.

Intrapsychic Occurring within the **psyche**.

Intra-uterine Fantasies See **Birth & Pre-Birth Dreams**

Introjection **Intrapsychic** concentration on one object or person to the exclusion of all others, with the possible adjunct of taking on aspects of that object or person in a morbid over-**identification**. A good example occurs in **Edgar Allan Poe**'s short story *The Lady Ligeia*, in which the narrator, in his introjected fervour, succeeds in conjuring the earlier object of his affections back from the dead through the **medium** of his recently deceased **wife**, Rowena – 'Man doth not yield him to the **angels**, nor unto **death** utterly, save only through the **weakness** of his feeble will.'

Introvert A **Jung**-defined personality type notable for the intense attention it turns upon itself, rather than towards the outside **world**. See **Extrovert**

Invasions Invasions of one sort or another frequently occur in **dreams**. We are all, to a certain extent at least, paranoid, as we need caution in order to survive – if we were not always on the look out for **danger**, we might be taken by **surprise** and overwhelmed. **Illness** is invasive, as is **sexual** attentiveness by others. The **unconscious** mind can contrive invasions, too, either to test us and make sure we are on our mettle, or to force our minds briefly away from even more invasive matters.

Invented Dreams Occasionally, in the course of dream analysis, patients are asked to invent **dreams**. These invented dreams are treated exactly as if they were real dreams. This technique stems from **Freud**'s belief that dreams are never arbitrary and invariably stem from the **dreamer**'s own complexes – to that extent, even such 'invented dreams' can have significance in **psychoanalysis**.

Invisibility The attractions or not of invisibility stem from the **dreamer**'s real life perception of their own essential **nature**. A serially shy person might **dream** that they are invisible because that is what they seem to be in real life – they are unable to impose themselves in any satisfying way onto the consciousness of others. To a serially confident person, invisibility might be yet another means to an already partially attained end – e.g. to impose themselves, *according to their own rules*, onto another person's life.

Iron The Taoists believed that the appearance of inflexible iron in a **dream** betokened the power of **evil**. Iron in a normal dream context is infused with inflexibility and **weight** of purpose.

Ironing The act of ironing can be **cathartic**, in that one is rectifying faults, or ironing out inconsistencies. It may also suggest a desire to receive praise, and to be considered a good and useful person – the '**mother's** little helper' syndrome.

Irrigation Irrigation can give new life to desiccated objects, or it can threaten existing structures with the uncertainty of new movement. Subliminally, irrigation may represent the **body**'s circulatory system, while blocks or **obstacles** in the irrigation **canals** might symbolize clots or threatening coalescences. This can then be extrapolated out of the body towards **friendships**, or social interactions. Well irrigated equals happy relationships – poorly irrigated equals the fractured variety.

Islands We can keep to ourselves on an island, or we can be marooned. Perception is everything in this sort of context, and whether we see the existence of the island as salutary, in a stormy **sea**, or menacing, in terms of potential isolation, depends entirely on the **dreamer**. In symbolical terms, islands can be **people** – the size of the island representing the corresponding size of the person, from **child** to fully grown man or woman.

Itching When we itch we are being irritated by something, and itching in a **dream** will probably have a similar meaning. Our **unconscious** mind may also be trying to remind us of something that we have forgotten, or temporarily mislaid. This may even be some aspect of ourselves (for itching is nothing if not **self**-referential), or it could be an aspect of our **past** lives that has made us ill, or that has attached itself to us in an irritating form.

Ivory Ivory, until relatively recently, has always been inordinately valued. It is natural, and it is beautiful, and the **animal** it comes from, whether it be an **elephant**, a narwhale, or a **walrus**, has strong symbolical revocations for most human beings. Ivory contains within itself both the masculine and feminine essence – the masculine, in that it is **phallic**, and needs to be wrested from elsewhere – and the feminine, in that it is mainly used for decoration, and was for many centuries a desired and highly valued object. However, it should be added that there may also be an element of guilt involved in the ivory **symbol**, in the sense that its beyond-symbolical presence in a dream may require either a death or an extraction. See **Female, Horn & Male**

Ivy Ivy smothers and **kills** things, but it is also beautiful. This apparent paradox underlines the dual aspects of human life. We glory in the beauty of **nature**, but it will eventually kill us, by transitory default. Curiously enough, in terms of traditional symbolism, ivy represents immortality and permanence due to its perpetual **greenness**, while also being dedicated to **Bacchus**, in that it was, notionally at least, a preventative of **drunkenness** (it is arguable that the Greeks meant a different sort of ivy, however, to the one to which we accord the name).

J

Jackdaws A jackdaw traditionally symbolizes vain assumptions and empty conceit – to see one denoted ill **health** and quarrels. Jackdaws make a particularly abrasive noise to announce their presence, and this is probably at the basis of their ill-repute, together with their **egg**-stealing proclivities and their reputation as opportunist thieves. The dreamed-of jackdaw, then, is likely to carry with him the threat of plunder, anarchy and alien practices. See **Burglars**

Jacob's Ladder The **ladder** that the patriarch Jacob (Genesis xxviii, 12) saw in a **vision**, with **God** standing above it. 'And he dreamed, and behold a ladder set up on the earth, and the top of it reached to heaven: and behold the angels of God ascending and descending on it.' The ladder represented the mediator between Man (in the guise of Jacob) and God. See **Wrestling**

Jade One of the **key** elements in Chinese **dream interpretation**, jade (or dreamstone) was considered the **jewel** of **heaven**. It had numerous positive inferences, amongst which could be found good fortune, chastity, humility, sincerity, benevolence and the intellect. Jade was also reputed to have healing properties, and to confer wisdom and sagacity on the wearer.

Jail Jail is a **symbol** of stasis, or even, on occasion, **backwards movement**. A jailing is usually (but not always) predominantly **self**-imposed, in that the jailed person is seen to have taken the wrong **path** at the **crossroads**, and to be bent on self-immolation rather than personal betterment. An unfair jailing in a dream is usually a euphemism for self-justification, along the lines of 'the **world** is against me, I simply don't stand a chance'. It is an argument, in other words, for inaction.

Jailors Jailors may represent society, or **family** members who provoke our wrath, or partners whom we perceive to be **imprisoning** us. The transposition of them into jailors, though, argues for special pleading, and may even suggest that there is an element of **masochism** present in the relationship.

Jainism Mahavira (599–27 BC), the founder of the Jain religion, was born to his **mother**, Trisala, after she had experienced a series of 16 **dreams**, delineated in '*Trisala Dreaming*', a famous miniature from the 15th century Kalpasutras series. In her dreams Trisala saw a **white elephant**, a white **bull**, a white **lion**, either Sri or Lakshmi, Mandara **blossoms**, a **silvery moon**, the **sun**, a leaping **fish**, a **golden** pitcher, a **lake** with floating **lotus flowers**, an **ocean** of **milk**, a **heavenly palace**, a **vase** as high as Meru, bulging with precious **stones**, a **fire** fed by **sacrificial butter**, a **throne** made of **diamonds** and **rubies**, and a heavenly **king** ruling the

earth. These dreams betokened the **birth** of a Tirthankara (a being higher than **God**), already possessing the five kinds of knowledge which he would later **teach** on earth.

Jam Both jam, in the sense of a traffic jam, and jam as confiture, contain aspects of stickiness. Transpose this into a **dream**, and one is presented with both **nourishment** and stasis interacting on a parallel metaphorical plane. The nonsense quote from Lewis Carroll, in the **key** line below, perfectly sums up the apparent paradox.
KEY LINE: 'The rule is, jam to-morrow and jam yesterday – but never jam today.' (From Lewis Carroll's *Through the Looking-Glass*, Chapter 3 1899)

Jars Jars preserve, protect and **exclude**. To this extent they equate most directly with the nuclear **family** unit. It is not surprising, therefore, that in the Arabian **Nights** story of Ali Baba, the 40 **evil** thieves chose jars to hide in – for the jars both split them up, one from the other, while apparently allowing them to retain their communal identities. Aladdin's **lamp** functioned as a jar, too, both protecting and excluding in turn.

Jays A jay symbolizes **empty** chatter, and was also the traditional term used for a wanton or a plunger. Jays resemble **jackdaws** in most of their other **dream** relevant characteristics.

Jealousy Misguided **self**-protection is often at the basis of jealousy, and this carries over into **dreams**. To envy is to hate oneself (by default, as it were), and this self-hate aspect may be the motivating force in dreams that include envy, jealousy and possessiveness in their makeup. **Manic depressives**, too, are likely to include jealousy in their dream litanies.

Jellyfish To be stung (see **Stinging**) by a jellyfish is to be disturbed in what one considers to be the rightful and reasonable enjoyment of one's leisure. To that extent jellyfish may act as moderators of joy in a **dream** context, and threateners of the status quo.

Jesting Jesting can easily turn vicious, and there is often an underlying edge to a jest or jape that suborns and informs the good **humour** which incepted it. Jesting has its salutary aspects, as well, which is why **kings** and **people** in positions of power traditionally employed jesters in order to keep their **feet** more firmly planted on the ground. The jester's role in a **dream** may have a similar deflationary purpose. See **Circuses, Clowns & Comical Dreams**

Jesus Christ The role of Jesus for a Christian reflects the Higher **Self**, and the **movement** away from physicality towards spirituality and the Life of the **Soul**. The figure of Jesus may also appear in the guise of a *deus ex machina*, magically resolving issues which in real life are not nearly so convenient of resolution. For an unbeliever or non-Christian,

the appearance of Jesus may represent otherness, or even, in certain circumstances, the possibility of theocratic fallibility. See **Christ**

Jewels   Jewels are precious things, which are frequently kept hidden (see
Hiding), and only brought out when a particular statement or point needs
to be made – i.e. I am an attractive or valuable person. The giving of jewels is therefore a formal valuing, and the receiving of jewels is a formal,
and frequently public, acceptance of that valuation. See **Jewellery Boxes**

Jewellery Boxes   These are most likely to represent the **vagina**, in that
they are capable of being opened with a **key** (the **penis**), they are
desirable items, they contain things, and they are of value to both their
possessor (the woman), and to their inheritor or usufructuary (the man).
See **Jewels** & **Representability**

Jobs   Dreaming about jobs may often represent a reinforcement of one's
importance or value to oneself and society at large. We are often **judged**
by the job we do (i.e. by what we seem to be), rather than by who or what
we really are – to that extent we can become the sum of our jobs, rather
than the sum of our unexpressed desires. The **dream** world frequently
latches on to this dichotomy, transforming our unexpressed desires into a
raft of convenient **wish-fulfilment** fantasies.

Jogging   When we jog we have the impression of getting somewhere (a
place, a state of fitness, a social position) faster and more effectively than
we might get there were we to **walk**. To that extent jogging is a societal
signifier – if we jog, it presupposes that we are well-fed, healthy, and at
ease with our **bodies**. Break into a **run** (outside a ritual environment) and
both spectators and passers-by become instantly more concerned.

Johannot, Tony (1803–52)   One of the greatest of Romantic illustrators,
Johannot made a series of grotesque illustrations for Alfred de Musset's
1843 *Voyage où il Vous Plaira* (*Journey Where You Will*), an idea originally based on **Caldéron**'s 1635 masterpiece, *La Vida es Sueño* (*Life is a
Dream*), in which the **author** delineates the **dreams** and **nightmares** of a
young man in **love**. See **Davoine**

Joining   Groucho Marx famously disdained the joining of any **club** which
could conceive of having someone like him as a potential member. This
is a surprisingly complicated concept, and **points** up both our desire to
belong, and our desire to signal our (nominal) independence one from the
other. In reality we are all interdependent – the rest is just a matter of
jockeying for pole position. **Dreams** can appear to compensate us for
perceived slights and misconstructions, while in reality pointing up the
very faults and weaknesses that trigger both justified and non-justified
discrimination.

Joints Joints are links between otherwise disparate motivating forces. Separate the **leg** and the **hip**, for instance, and both become useless.

Joseph See **Pharaoh's Dream**

Journals Journals **record** our lives. This is a reflection of an underlying **fear** (common to us all) that we may be inconsequential – not really needed. Popeye had it right when he said 'I yam what I yam' – another part of us, though, persists in declaring that we are what we were. This part often finds itself reflected in **dream** imagery relating to the **past**. There can be a particular if short-lived comfort for mortal beings in the form of constructive nostalgia. See **Diaries**

Journeys Journeys are **key** dream triggers, in that we persist in feeling (nomads that we are) that exploration relies on outward, rather than inner, movement. Our **dreams reflect** this misapprehension, sending us on useless journeys that merely reinforce our inability to benefit from the static (i.e. non-verbal and non-transitory) acquisition of wisdom. To that extent dreamed journeys are displacement activities often suggestive of present discomfort, and possibly even **guilt**.

Judas The Judas figure (i.e. the betrayer) frequently represents the **dreamer** themselves. At some time or other in our lives we all feel that we have betrayed others, and that by so doing we have betrayed ourselves. **Self**-justification, then, is twinned with betrayal, and frequently **projects** outwards, so that we blame the object of our betrayal, rather than acknowledging our own sense of **guilt**. This is fertile dream territory, and convenient **symbols** may find themselves snatched, apparently at random, to facilitate the passing of the buck. Judas is a convenient scapegoat, therefore, as he appears, at first glance, to be the object of an entirely justified and communally inspired hatred, while in reality he merely acts as an expedient **displacement** for our own sense of guilt.

Judgement When we err, we require to be judged. When we feel **guilty**, we hope for judgement, but with mitigation. When we sit in judgement in **dreams**, it is often over ourselves, and this carries through to the context in which the judgement takes place. In an open **field**, for instance, we may be dealing with 'natural' judgement, while in a darkened **room** or a **prison**, unnatural, and possibly even unfair judgement is on the **cards**, for it is the **dreamer** who sets up the context in which the desired judgement must take place. See **Judges**

Judges Judges, as authority figures, often represent **God** in **dreams** – they may also represent **parents**, **teachers** or mentors. Judges often appear 'above' us physically as well as morally, in dreams. This harks back to **childhood patterns** in which **judgement** was invariably handed out from on high.

Jugglers Jugglers represent the either/or aspect of a **dream**. 'If I do it that way, then this will happen, but if I decide in the opposite way, other ramifications might occur.' Jugglers, in order to stay on top of their **game**, must exercise inordinate concentration. Should jugglers drop their implements in a dream, it is possibly because the **dreamer** is trying to do too many things at the same time, and the juggler image then becomes a **warning** about what may lie ahead.

Jumping Jumping is largely a **childhood** habit – when one is **light**, and with a low centre of gravity, jumping is easy and pleasant. Adults rarely, if ever, jump, so the image of jumping becomes a **wish-fulfilment** fantasy when it appears in a **dream**, implying getting out of scrapes, or benefiting from superpowers (a common childhood fantasy). Jumping up and down whilst remaining on the spot implies a temporary suspension of willpower, or an inability to **push** something through to its logical conclusion.

Jung, Carl Gustav (1875–1961) A Swiss psychiatrist and co-founder of the analytical school of psychology, Jung fervently believed in the importance of **dreams**, while acknowledging that they could be interpreted in two markedly different ways – either on the subjective plane (where everything in the dream is representational of the **dreamer** themselves) or on the objective plane (where things and **people** in the dream are considered representational of real objects). He taught that dreams were specific expressions of the **unconscious**, and must be taken as sensible facts about which no previous assumptions should be made. Jung found parallels between ancient **myths** and psychotic fantasies (see **Psychosis**), and believed that human motivation could be explained in terms of a larger, collective, human energy (the psychosynthetic, or integrationist approach). He drew extensively on myths, religions, **fairy tales**, fantasies, and other historical **patterns**, and made a clear distinction between the personal unconscious, and an **archetypal**, **primordial**, **collective unconscious**. In an effort to reconcile the **introvert** and the **extrovert** aspects of personality (the feeling, intuitive side, as against the thinking, rational side), Jung encouraged patients towards **individuation**, or the restitution of the whole, individuated, **self**, within a religiously meaningful life. See also **Anima**, **Animus**, **Archaic Remnants**, **Dream Language**, **Dream Work**, **Free Association**, **Psychoanalysis** & **Psychotherapy**
KEY LINE: 'A dream is a theatre in which the dreamer is himself the scene, the player, the prompter, the producer, the author, the public, and the critic.' (From *General Aspects of Dream Psychology* 1948)

Jungles Jungles are threatening, and tend to suggest **chaos**, and the **fears** many of us have about a descent into anarchy or a loss of civilized factors. As **dreamers**, we frequently conjure up jungles when we are uncertain about the **path** we wish to take, and jungles, if seen as welcoming places, may also suggest the **animal** within us, and the temptation we all suffer from, on occasion, to loose that animal, and to hell with the consequences.

Juniper The juniper is a protective **tree** – it was considered to have hidden the infant **Jesus** during the flight into Egypt. Folkard's *Plant Lore, Legends and Lyrics* has it that to **dream** of a juniper bush, while ill, prevents recovery, but that to dream of its berries is a good luck sign, and heralds the **birth** of a **male child**.

Junk Junk and mental detritus tend to be one and the same in **dreams**. When we surround ourselves with junk, we truncate our view of the wider area encircling us. Junk may also represent the **past**, and outmoded, or no longer relevant ideas.

Juries Juries both reflect us (in societal terms) and threaten us, in the sense that we are most in **danger** from the things with which we are most familiar. A formal jury appearing in a **dream** may very well **mirror** various aspects of ourselves, set in **judgement** over other aspects that may threaten our stability, or our capacity to function effectively in the wider (i.e. non-dream) **world**. See **Judges**

Justice To **dream** of justice is often to feel that we have been treated outrageously, or indeed unjustly. There are also balancing aspects, as in the 'scales of justice', the '**weighing**' up and 'weighting' of evidence, and a desire for a balanced, that is to say fair, **judgement**. The **symbol** of justice may also include revocations of **revenge**, as in the **biblical** 'an **eye** for an eye'. See **Judges**

K

Kabbalah The Kabbalah, from the Hebrew word *cabala*, meaning 'secret knowledge', was the mysterious science (somewhat akin to **alchemy**) that was said to have been handed down to the Jews by divine revelation – it was then passed on orally, from **father** to **son**. Dreaming of the Kabbalah, or of Kabbalistic **symbols**, implies the desire or yearning for secret knowledge, but can also carry with it connotations of an inappropriate craving for power over others or oneself.

Kaleidoscopes A kaleidoscope symbolizes changing – but nevertheless consistent – **patterns**. In the context of a **dream**, this may be taken to apply to behaviour, perception, or even a **regression** to the **childhood** capacity for wonderment, which adults often equate with mystery (and its loss).

Kangaroos Kangaroos are synonymous with motherliness, nurturing and **childhood carrying**. They may also suggest the easy movement of heavy things, and the capacity, metaphorically at least, to leave the ground (i.e. something – an idea, perhaps – taking off).

Karate Paradoxically, perhaps, **dreams** of karate are more likely to be about defence than about **attack**. The **hands**, in dreams, are usually raised to stop blows, rather than to give them, and in this case they may also be repositories of **energy** – even means of communication (a sort of semaphore effect, one supposes). Thus it is the movement of the hands that is important, rather than their physical effect.

Karma To dream of karma is to dream of cause and effect, and the interaction between the higher and the lower planes. Even when we defend ourselves (as we so often do in **dreams**), ramifications can occur. Karma rebalances the **books**, as it were, and acts as the **window** to the **soul**.

Keepsakes Keepsakes attach us to the **past**, changing the **fabric** of our thoughts and our perceptions and imbruing them with an often specious significance. **Parents** can lock their **children** – and **lovers** their partners – into outmoded habits of thought by such means. On a more positive note, **dreams** often **home** in on particular objects as a means of **drawing** attention to them, affording them a sort of *barakah* (an integrity, or Divine Grace).

Kekulé von Stradonitz, Friedrich August (1829–96) While researching the molecular structure of the benzene molecule, Kekulé dreamed of a **mandala**, in the form of a **snake** with its **tail** in its **mouth**. In an apparently spontaneous leap of the imagination, Kekulé interpreted this as implying that the structure of the benzene molecule might consist of a closed carbon **ring**. His hunch proved **right**, and he became an important force in the development of organic chemistry.

Kelp Kelp is entangling (both physically and emotionally), and also suggestive of otherness, in that **sea** kelp travels great distances, carrying with it intimations of things we feel we may not completely understand. People fear being dragged downwards or held back by their emotions, and kelp is strongly suggestive of this, given its presence in **water** (the emotional basin), or washed up on the **shoreline**, like memories.

Kennels Kennels are suggestive of some part of us which yearns, perhaps, to be free, but finds itself imprisoned *as if for its own good*. It is unnatural for anything to be locked up, and yet the 'kennelling' of our emotions is something that we find surprisingly easy to justify. To that extent kennels are aspects of the **superego**.

Kenning See **Swans**

Keyholes Keyholes have strong **sexual** overtones, in that one needs permission (i.e. a key) before they can be triggered, and before the anticipated **pleasures** inside them can be enjoyed. There can be negative aspects to keyholes too, as in 'hidden **secrets**', '**skeletons** in the closet', 'Bluebeard's **wives**', etc. The turning of a **key** can sometimes equate with the **movement** of a **clock**.

Keys Keys can symbolize the desire for **God**, as well as having, in certain particular contexts only, **phallic** connotations. When we search for the key for something, it means that we want to possess it. Keys may also represent easy answers and instant gratification, for if someone gives us a key, we may no longer feel the need to ask questions.

Khaki Khaki may represent obfuscation – a desire to disguise something from someone (perhaps even from ourselves). It may also have military or faecal connotations, as well as suggesting the harbouring of illusions and a desire for anonymity.

Kicking Kicking may be aggressive or passive – it may suggest parturition, and it may suggest a desire to lash out at perceived **enemies**. Kicking out at someone's **stomach** may indicate a **fear** of **pregnancy**, or a fear of the maternal. Dreaming that an **animal** is kicking you may indicate a fear of the outside **world**, or a suspicion of other **people's** motivations.

Kidnap Kidnap in any form constitutes an upsetting of the status quo. It implies that outside forces may be capable of influencing inner drives and established convictions. The **fear** of kidnap may refer to a fear that aspects of the **Self** are in danger, or subject to emotional or other forms of blackmail.

Killing Killing often means simply 'overcoming' in a dream. If a boy, for instance, **dreams** of **killing** his **father**, it does not necessary imply an Oedipal content (see **Oedipus Complex**) to the dream, but is far more likely to imply a desire to better, outdo, or otherwise impress himself onto his father's notice – to supersede the father, if you like. Women frequently dream of men 'killing' them (i.e. attacking them with **knives**, or other sharp objects) and this is usually a simple transposition of often hidden or subordinated **fears** of powerlessness in terms of the conventional **sexual** act and its possible ramifications (e.g. **pregnancy**, or relational or emotional upheaval). See **Murder**

Kings Kings are usually a **symbol** of the **father** in **dreams**. Kinghood implies both the giving and taking of responsibility, and to that extent the concept may be broadened to include the **self**-governing aspects of the human **soul**.

Kissing Kissing is a form of communication, in that the quality of the kiss, its reception, and the inferences taken from it by society at large, can subtly transform its nominally instinctive **nature**. **Judas** betrayed **Jesus Christ** with a kiss, and kisses between otherwise disparate parties may have strong symbolical (even paradoxical) value, in that everyone may know, but still choose to ignore, the fact that the two parties are not fundamentally attracted, but may simply wish to **seal** an agreement by the mimicking of the **rites** of attraction for the benefit of a wider, no doubt **self**-interested, audience. Rabbinical lore held that the righteous met their **death** as the result of a kiss from **God**, an idea echoed in Italian folklore with '*Addormentarsi nel bacio del Signore*' (to fall asleep in the Lord's kiss) – Abraham, Isaac, **Jacob**, Aaron, Moses and Miriam, were all deemed to have perished in this exalted way. Kissing was also deemed potentially spell-breaking in Greek, Latin and Teutonic **mythology** (*le fier baiser* of Arthurian romance, for instance), often in the sense of the cancelling out of a **taboo**, as in Hans Christian Andersen's version of *The Sleeping Beauty*.

Kitchens Kitchens are domestic 'hearts'. They **feed** and **fuel**, just as a real heart does, and they can also stand in as unthreatening meeting places – for we generally associate **food** with **friendship** and mutual need, rather than with hostility and rebarbative interference. Kitchens may also represent the **mother**, for despite the recent emergence of largely **male** super-chefs, the domestic aspect of a kitchen still constitutes an overwhelmingly **female symbol**.

Kites Kites (the non-avian variety) represent truncated freedom, and to that extent they are **superego symbols**. They may appear to be free, bobbing and jerking in the **ether**, but they are still resolutely attached to the ground, in the form of their 'possessor'. Kites, to the Chinese, symbolized the **wind** – but it is a constrained wind, surely, implying human interference twinned with a desire for **self**-domination. However we wish to look at it, an **escaped** kite usually triggers **anxiety**, except in the case of a true free **spirit**, who may consider the symbolical freeing of something we normally have control over – an affective relationship, for instance – as an enlightened moral choice.

Kittens A kitten symbolizes playfulness. It may also represent the **vagina**. Kittens can also suggest the unthreatening aspects of **childhood**, since we know that kittens will eventually grow into larger **cats**, but we nevertheless trust and assume that the influence and power we exercised over them while they were still 'infants' will restrict and inform their use of adult power.

Klinger, Max The German symbolist **painter** Max Klinger (1857–1920) frequently used **dreams** to trigger his art. His series of etchings entitled *Paraphrases about the Finding of a Glove* used a **dream** which depicted the finding of a woman's **glove** at a skating rink as a symbolical leitmotif for a series of often grotesque images commenting on the dynamics of **male/female** relationships. The glove stands in for the woman, as it were, becoming mimetic, and prefiguring, in many ways, the much later **surrealist** movement.

Knapsacks Knapsacks may, at first glance, suggest **self**-sufficiency, but they may also carry with them revocations of **weights** or **burdens** that are not easily discarded. **Children** may be represented by knapsacks, alongside **guilt** or consequences we carry with us from the **past**. An extra dimension is added by the different **pockets** knapsacks may contain, mimicking the splitting up of **people** and relationships into separate, apparently unrelated, containers – the **dreamer** stands in for the knapsack in such cases, affording the common link between the disparate pockets.

Kneeling We kneel to **pray**, and we kneel to express submission. Kneeling was originally known as '**knee** tribute', and is so described in Milton's *Paradise Lost* (verse 782). Symbolically, kneeling reflects moral strength, and the otherwise unconfined **id**'s acceptance of leavening factors on its activities. Kneeling is also what **children** appear to be doing before adults (simply in terms of **height** differentiation), and this regression to **childhood** through metaphor can be a powerful reflexive image in **dreams**.

Knees The basic purpose of a knee is to support and be flexible – it may also be a site of **sexual** interest, and even an erogenous zone (the back of the knee, in particular). This gives it particularly rich revocations in **dream** imagery. When one adds to that the vulnerability of a knee – it is one of the most obvious places in the **body** to receive a crippling **injury**, and has even given us the term 'hamstrung' to depict **frustration** – together with its capacity for causing harm (i.e. kneeing someone), it is little wonder that its effects are more than made up for by the sum of its parts.

Knights Traditionally, knights represented the perfected vessels of moral rectitude, and we are still sufficiently influenced by the Arthurian Legends and the principles of enlightened chivalry for that to remain the **archetypal** case. For a woman to **dream** of knights probably indicates a desire to be saved from interior torment by outside forces (the woman's own, necessarily inchoate, **animus**) – and for men to dream of knights most probably presents itself as a similar **wish-fulfilment** fantasy, but this time with the unrealized **anima** as **victim** and as **target** for salvation (think Rapunzel, Andromeda, and the doomed Lady of Shalott).

Knitting Knitting is, in effect, to make something out of nothing. To that extent it has almost **magical** revocations, and is an almost entirely constructive image. The **unravelling** of **yarn**, on the other **hand**, is usually a negative image, and may indicate the **fear** of a relationship foundering, or **breaking** under strain.

Knives Knives puncture and they cut away – withdrawn, they take life with them. They threaten and they comfort (many **males** feel completed with a knife about their person, and to this extent they are **archetypal symbols** of **self**-sufficiency). Knives are therefore frequent substitutes for **penises** in **dreams**, and also of intellectual endeavour (the **cutting** edge of wit). They may also remind us of mortality, and of our capacity to precipitate unnatural **death** – symbolically, both the Romans and the Japanese used knives (the shorter cutting **sword**) to end their own lives, and those of honourable losers. See **Sheaths**

Knobs Knobs and excrescences tend to be **male** images – for even **muscles** can have 'knob' qualities in **dreams**. It is true, also, that males tend to be obsessed with adjuncts to things, and with additions to existing entities. For a **female**, taking a knob in her **hand** and opening a **door** has strong relational connotations, but also carries with it uncertainty in the face of the **alien**, i.e. male, **world** that she is approaching (with a view to possibly sharing it).

Knocking Knocking is, by definition, tentative, for even if one **hammers** on a **door**, one is still at the mercy of its occupant (as it were). This tentative aspect is carried forward into the knock as attention grabber, and also into the knock as aggressive overture – for, each and every time, the door comes between the knocker and their desired end.

Knots To the Taoists knots represented long life, and the forces of good holding tight against **evil**. Symbolically, knots may represent both nominal strength and, paradoxically, **weakness**, for the knot in a **fishing line**, for instance, constitutes its potentially **weakest** point. One ties the '**marriage** knot', of course, just as one 'unknots' a mystery. The **umbilical** knot needs severing before the human being may begin the process of freeing itself from necessitousness.

Koran, The For a Muslim, the Koran represents the Word of **God**, while for a non-Muslim the Koran might tend to equate, in symbolical terms at least, with the **Bible**. While most Christians, however, freely acknowledge that the Bible was written by others (infused, however, with the Godhead), the strict Muslim believes that the Koran is the direct word (or very essence) of God. This gives its dream value, dependent on context, a non-noumenal aspect which **dreams** of the Bible may possibly (except to extreme fundamentalists) lack.

Kubin, Alfred (1877–1959) At the age of 19 Alfred Kubin attempted **suicide** on his **mother**'s **grave**, and **years** later, on the **death** of his fiancée, he suffered a nervous breakdown. This tormented Austrian **artist** went on to produce an extraordinary series of expressionist works (largely in **pencil**) dealing with **dream symbols**, and with images stemming from the **unconscious**. His *Each Night a Dream Visits Us* (Albertina, Vienna 1903), depicts a **hooded**, **naked** woman, with **knives** instead of **hands** and **feet**, **sailing** over a lowering, rural **landscape**. The knives which replace her hands suggest, not only that she is a potentially lethal entity, but also that she may be attached to a gigantic medieval **punishment wheel**, similar to that depicted in Hieronymus Bosch's *Paradise and Hell* (1510).

L

Labels To **dream** of labels is to wish to give **names** to things – 'to put your damn **mouth** on it', as Ernest Hemingway so tellingly wrote (see **Writing**). Once you've labelled something, of course, you don't need to think about it again, but simply to repeat the label, like a litany. Labelling something is to make the inessential essential, and René **Magritte** showed up the fundamental vapidity of this concept in a series of paintings quietly (and amusingly) suborning mankind's need for nomenclatures and classifications.

Laboratories Laboratories are places in which **scientists cook** up answers to imponderable **questions**, and this **reading** is likely to be reflected in a dream context. Laboratories are also associated with **alchemy**, and, curiously, with order, in that they presuppose existing structures of thought and behaviour, and the leisure within which to explore them.

Labour When something is seen as particularly – or even unnecessarily – laborious within a **dream**, attention should be paid both to the task and to the details surrounding the task, for the **unconscious** mind is putting up a barrier to its completion.

Labyrinths The labyrinth (which correlates to both the **maze** and the spiral) is usually taken to represent either the human **mind** or the entanglement and confusion of matriarchal consciousness. The boy **child**, represented by Theseus in the Ariadne **myth**, can only confront the labyrinth, and save his **anima**, after a **rite-of-passage** initiation into the **collective unconscious**. The **mother**, if you like, needs separating from the anima before the young man will be able to relate naturally to other women. **Freud**, in an interesting example of **fixed symbolism**, equates the labyrinth to an exemplification of **anal birth**, in which the 'twisted ways' represent the **intestines**, and Ariadne's thread, the **umbilical cord**. See **Guts**

Lacan, Jacques (1901–81) See **Scopophilia**

Ladders Ladders represent conduits from one stage or place to another. They can also act as mediators, or symbolical connections. **Burials** in ancient Egypt were often accompanied by ladders, to symbolize the potential ascent of the defunct person through the **seven** spheres of the **planets**. See **Ascension, Jacob's Ladder** & **Sublimation**.

Lagoons Lagoons are peaceful and tranquil places, in that they are separated, as a rule, from the direct influence of the **sea**. When we take the sea as representing the emotions (see **Lakes** & **Water**), lagoons become (usually feminine) comfort **symbols**, into which one can immerse oneself without **fear**. One potentially negative aspect of the lagoon symbol, however, is its possible sterility, in that it may **cut** itself off, if it is not careful, from the source of life – i.e. it may lapse into introspection and introversion. See **Sterilization**

Lakes Lakes conceal things. Articles withdrawn from lakes can be useful to our **psyches**, and can provide a valuable release for **repressed** potential. **King** Arthur's **sword** Excalibur was concealed in a lake, and the Lady of the Lake, who released the sword to him, was his inner **anima**. Arthur only returned the sword to the Lady of the Lake on the point of his **death**, reluctantly freeing his **psyche** from the bonds of the **earth** in the process. Only then, following this act of acceptance and submission, could the Lady of the Lake send her handmaidens to **ferry** the dying king across to the Great Beyond. The lake can also stand for the **vagina** or the **uterus**, as can the **boat**, and the masculine and feminine aspects of Arthur's end-story (the sword, the lake, the boat, the **wound**), imply that both sides of Arthur's psyche are finally joined together in a **sacred marriage**.

Lambs A lamb symbolizes innocence and **sacrifice**. In Christian iconography, it was also the **symbol** for **Christ**, who was known as the Lamb of **God**. This sacrificial aspect would appear to be **archetypal**, in that the lamb may easily be seen to represent a **child**, or the child lurking inside us. Should an **evil** person (a **wolf**) wish to approach without causing **fear**, they traditionally dress in lamb's (or **sheep's**) **clothing**. Lambs are also entirely non-threatening, and **dreams** may suddenly conjure them up to placate otherwise threatened aspects of the **dreamer** – to give the dreamer a breather, in other words.

Lameness Lameness suggests that something is holding the **dreamer** back from a duty or an obligation they may find unconducive. Being lame may also suggest that some aspect of the dreamer feels unbalanced or otherwise out of kilter. Lameness can also point to incompleteness, either metaphorical or literal – something that remains unfinished, for instance.

Lamps Lamps are generally brought in to shed **light**. They may also act as notice gatherers, in that one is drawn towards a light (especially when one is in the **dark** about something). Lamps may also suggest ways of reaching out to **people**, as the sharing of light (i.e. a **fire**) is an **archetypal** form of friendly – *ergo* non-aggressive – expression.

Lancing Lancing is usually **sexual** in connotation, although the lancing of a pustule may represent the sudden freeing up of an otherwise encumbered **channel** (of thought, communication, or even a desired loss of **virginity**). Lancing, as in jousting, tends to be predominantly sexual, too – the **sliding** down of a lady's **colours** onto the lance end of her champion has to constitute one of the most overtly sexual signifiers in medieval iconography.

Land Symbolically **speaking**, land represents manifest change and the power of the lower quaternary (the so-called 'natural man'). Bearing this in mind, land would appear to imply a grounding or a centring when it occurs in a **dream** – a return, if you like, to a state of pre-flux. The very fact that land is 'dry' implies that it is far from the (usually wet) seat of uncontrolled emotions. Land is therefore fundamentally rational, nurturing and retroactive. See **Landscapes**

Landscapes Dream landscapes frequently symbolize the inexpressible. They are a reflection of the **dreamer**'s inner **nature**, and as such they can be seen to represent the dimming of normal consciousness.

Landslides Landslides constitute sudden unwanted descents, usually when we are least expecting them. To that extent they may equate with the **orgasm** (see **Avalanches**) or with the sudden swoop of despair triggered by unexpected vicissitudes.

Langland, William (1332–1400?) Langland is the **author** of a famous medieval **poem** in Old English which recounts the dream **visions** of *Piers Plowman* after he **falls** asleep on the Malvern **Hills**. The poem is satirical in **nature**, and criticizes the corruption of both the secular authorities and the clergy, while praising the virtues of manual **labour**.

Language Language itself is designed for clarification of communication – it is also subtly recognitive of sameness, and predicative of difference. A foreign language, or an obtuse response by the **dreamer** to someone who is speaking to them, may imply inner **frustration** at an inability to grasp important concepts. Glossolalia – i.e. **nonsense** speaking, or the speaking with **tongues** – may well constitute a flashback to former states of being, in which formal language was replaced by sounds, and in which meaning was as much grunt or cough led, as it was lingually engendered.

Largeness See **Bigness & Smallness**

Larks A lark symbolizes cheerfulness and the **defeat** of the ordinary. To **dream** of having – or going for – a lark, suggests a desire to revert back to the simplicities of **childhood**. The presence of a lark in a dream may also imply a **fear** of seeming to be too simple, or of existing only on the surface of things – a fear of vulnerability, too, as a lark (or any other small **bird**) often presupposes the existence of a threatening **cat**. This threatening aspect harks back to infancy, and to the fear that childhood innocence may be at the mercy of adult expedience.

Lasers Lasers suggest the concentration of energy on one particular point. Such a concentration may be triggered by **fear**, jealousy, or indeed any of the major emotions. Seen positively, a laser is an aid to achievement – seen negatively (in terms of a **weapon**, say), it can be destructive of relationships.

Lateness Feeling that one is going to be late for an **appointment**, or that one is **running** late generally, often refers to **repressed** tendencies (or inner retardings) relating to the way of life of the **dreamer**, and may, in consequence, have **neurotic** overtones. Examples of such repressed tendencies might include **incestuous** desires or morally dubious schemes – events, in other words, that one is already 'too late for'. Late arrival **dreams** may also signify nostalgia, or a desire to **regress** to the **past** for comfort purposes – to wind back the **clock**. In addition, fearing lateness can point to age differences between the dreamer and significant others in their lives, be they siblings, **lovers**, or **friends**. In **Freudian** terms such dreams were perceived as relating back to **childhood** fears of arriving too late at the **lavatory**, or of shaming oneself in public. In **female** terms, they were taken to imply a **fear** on the part of the woman that she might 'arrive' too late at her **orgasm**, after her partner in the **sexual** act had already enjoyed his. See **Frustration Dreams**, **Running** & **Time**

Latent Content The third level of **Freudian** analysis of a **dream**, detailing its actual 'purpose' – i.e. making sense of the **unconscious** thoughts contained within the dream, and their associations, and **teasing** out hidden **wishes**, desires, or **anxieties**. See **Manifest Content**, **Day's Residues** & **Dream Work**

Latent Homosexuality Unacknowledged homosexual desires that may appear in our **dreams** in non-specific forms, **shapes** or images, and may sometimes be at the **root** of apparently unrelated **neurotic** tendencies. See **Homosexuality**

Laudanum A hallucinogenic mixture of **opium** and alcohol, much used in Victorian England as a sedative and painkiller. See **Artificial Dreams** & **Hallucinations**

Laughter Much depends on whether the laughter in the **dream** is aimed towards or away from the **dreamer** – whether it derives or derides, in other words. If the dreamer feels themselves to be an object of fun, the energy is negative and draining – if the dreamer laughs in a benevolent way, the energy is positive and healing. Should the dreamer be scorning others with their laughter, followers of psychologist **Alfred Adler** would immediately identify the existence of an **inferiority complex**, or other manifestation of low **self**-esteem.

Launching Launching may be **sexual** in **nature**, or it may refer to the desire to achieve – 'sexual' usually wins, though. The fact that it is pretty much invariably a **female** who smashes the **champagne bottle** onto the stern of a newly constructed **ship** (traditionally also of female nomenclature and classification, needless to say) tells us a great deal about the **male** sexual drive. It would be perfectly normal, according to this scenario, for a woman to view herself as the **sea** (or the **harbour**) into which this pristine liner **plunges** – itself, something of an achievement.

Laundry Laundry equates with cleanliness, and with a desire to purify, to be purified, or to be perceived as pure. Dirty **washing** suggests (metaphorically, of course) that there are things still remaining to be cleaned up. See **Cleansing**

Lava Lava and hidden emotions share consanguinity. **Suppression** of emotion may also be implied, together with the resultant **explosion** when those emotions finally force their way to the surface. The **burning** or caustic aspects of lava are important, too, and suggest that keeping things bottled up for too long may be injurious.

Lavatories Lavatories are places in which unwanted things are flushed away – out of sight and largely out of **mind**, they suddenly become someone else's responsibility. Should the lavatory be blocked, however, it suggests that the discarded items may be coming back to haunt you. Early toilet training has a large part to play in this **reading**, as infants are traditionally praised for conforming to the standards set by their **parents**, rather than by following their own (unclean) **instincts**.

Lawns Immaculately trimmed lawns suggest a latent **fear** of **nature**, which may be extrapolated onto a fear of following one's own **instincts**, and a compensatory over-espousal of the rational. **Anal** retention, obsessive cleanliness, and a refusal to acknowledge **reality** (*ergo* mortality), are also part and parcel of excessive trimming and preening (in any sphere). See **Cleansing**

Lawyers Lawyers manipulate the law to suit themselves and their clients. To that extent they consider themselves above the law, and the law to be an **ass** – except insofar as it benefits them. Such is the near-**archetypal** image of a lawyer (*pace* Charles Dickens' *Bleak House*, and Jarndyce v. Jarndyce) and it still obtains today. Dreaming of lawyers, then, implies dreaming of advantage or of threat, depending on context – seldom, unfortunately, of **justice**.

Laxatives Laxatives are catalysts of forced (as opposed to natural) change. One forces the issue with a laxative, relinquishing free will as one does so – for once the catalyst is swallowed, it runs *you*. To that extent laxatives are enforced purifications, rather as **diets** are enforced **regressions** to an imagined, or fantasized, norm. The use of laxatives in **dreams** may also point up the existence of suppressed **guilt**.

Layer Symbolism Otto Rank described layer symbolism as the symbolical disguise of normal activity so that it occurs euphemistically in a **dream** context – it could be construed, if you like, as a mental striptease conducted by the **unconscious** mind. **Sexual intercourse** is an obvious example of something that is frequently subject to layer symbolism, appearing in the guise of **trains** entering **tunnels**, **firework** displays, speeding **cars**, exploding **bombs**, bursting **fruit**, and **earthquakes**

(amongst myriad others). Hollywood movies of the 1940s and 1950s were renowned for their layer symbolism, a particular favourite being 'pounding surf' to depict the sexual act, as seen in Fred Zinnemann's *From Here to Eternity* (1953), in which Burt Lancaster and Deborah Kerr seethe amongst the wavelets – a favoured alternative involves sudden pans from the **earth** to the **sky**, as used in the Bette Davis/Paul Henreid 'sheltering from the rain' scene in Irvin Rapper's *Now, Voyager* (1942).

Lead Lead **weighs** us down, and is also perceived as poisonous. If we take the analogy further, we find that our **dream** is indicating that worries may be poisoning our existence. Lead is also the medium of **bullets**, which both **poison** and **kill**, metaphorically implying outside interference in our inner lives.

Leaders Leaders may be mentors, and they may be **Gods**. The desire for a leader may reflect an emotional or spiritual need, but it may also reflect what we feel is expected of us – i.e. that we should look to someone else for **guidance**, and not rely on ourselves **alone**. This desire for a guru figure appears to be universal, and marks us out as predominantly communally-minded, socialized beings, rather than the solitary **souls** romantic imagery would make of us.

Leading Dreaming of leading may, paradoxically, suggest that we wish to be led somewhere (see **Layer Symbolism**), but have as yet no notion of who or what we are going to choose to take us there – it's an image that is more significant for what it leaves out, in other words, than for what it contains. Leading may also be taken literally, to imply a desire to dominate, or to assert oneself. Which **road** one goes down depends on the context, and on the **makeup** of those being led.

Leaks Leaks from sealed containers suggest potentially fatal flaws in otherwise sound vessels – for physical law informs us that leaks invariably get worse, not better (unless urgently attended to by an interested party). There may also be a clandestine aspect to a leak, as in a leaked memo, or a leak of information, and revocations of micturition (often in the form of juvenile bed-wetting) are not uncommon either. Finally, leaks may refer to a perceived loss of energy (or its temporary, but inappropriate, use), such as occur in the bleeding of air out of a **balloon,** or during **menstruation**. See **Wetting the Bed**

Leather Leather and human **skin** are all but synonymous in **dreams**, and the piercing of leather in any form probably **reflects** a fear by the **dreamer** of being pierced – i.e. of being shown to be mortal – in their turn. To 'leather' was to beat with a **belt**, and although **beatings** of any form are frowned upon nowadays in most civilized societies, collective physical memories persist, fuelled by images from **films** such as Lindsay Anderson's 1968 movie *If …*, **television** (ITV's 2005 dramatization of Robert Hughes's *Tom Brown's Schooldays* being a case in point), and the

internet. Anxieties (or **repressed** desires) about a restoration of 'leathering' probably relate to hidden **fears** of a loss of civilized amenities and a return to anarchy – a situation in which the strongest (the best leathered) will always prevail. See **Spanking**

Leaves Leaves imply temporality. To that extent they equate with human life – their finiteness is indivisible with their essence, in other words. Botanomancy was the act of divination by **leaves** which were exposed to the **wind**, those remaining constituting the desired message. Leaves (particularly lanceolate, lobed, ovate and serrate) may also have **vaginal** connotations, given their **shape**, their midribs, and their striations.

Leaving Leaving, in **dreams**, can often be equated with **death**. Thus, if the **dreamer** is left by another individual (or leaves them), they may be fearing either that individual's, or their own, imminent death. Images of being left frequently occur in the dreams of **children** and of early adolescents, and usually equate with inchoate intimations of mortality, parentlessness, or the justifiable **fear** that maturity will see the end of a cherished **childhood**.

Lectures Lectures tend to fall into two categories, namely the personal and the impersonal. Impersonal lectures inform, while personal lectures can often provoke **resistance**. As dreamed resistance is generally safe resistance (in that there are no consequences), dreaming of being lectured on a personal or behavioural level tends to represent a **wish-fulfilment** fantasy often manifesting itself in the form of **layer symbolism**.

Leeches Leeches are parasitical, and tend to consume the **dreamer**'s energy. Any **sucking** motion in a **dream** inevitably tends towards the **sexual**, but there may also be hidden revocations of nursing (in the sense of giving **milk**) and of healing, in that leeches are still occasionally used to prevent coagulation, and to drain pooled **blood** from beneath the **skin**.

Left An age-old **symbol** for anything perverse, **taboo** or untoward, the left is traditionally the side of the **criminal** and of the sociopath. More recently, however, as if in compensation for centuries of abuse, the left has gathered to itself revocations of troubled creativity and eccentric genius (largely as a result of one famous left-hander, Leonardo da Vinci). In religious symbolism, the left suggests passivity and the reception of incoming energy. See **Left-Handedness, Right-Handedness & Right**

Left-Handedness In ancient times, the **left** hand, because it was usually the weaker, was associated with feminine traits. In **astrology**, the **moon** was associated with the left **eye**. Left-handed auspices were considered ill-omened, and, even today, the word sinister ('left' in Latin), has negative connotations. In an effort to compensate for the poor deal left-handers have had throughout history, the left is now perceived as the side of intuition, but, despite this, it still retains its psychopathological con-notations. See **Right** & **Right-Handedness**

Legs Legs are traditional **symbols** of duality, just as the legs of a **compass** join two disparate points, the one receptive, the other proactive. Legs also suggest the possibility of motion and of procreation. Standing firm on one's legs equates with positive support – feeling shaky on one's **pins** implies a desire or need to be supported.

Leitmotif Word describing the dominant motive in a **dream**.

Lemons Whole lemons suggest the **sun**, not only in terms of **colour**, but also in terms of the possibilities afforded for growth. The bitter, acidic aspects of cut lemons (their capacity to cause a physical reaction simply by thinking of them), twinned with their semantic connotations ('so and so is a bit of a lemon'), may imply isolation or the **fear** of exile – one tends to move away from a cut lemon in case one is hit in the **eye** by its juice.

Lending Lending suggests an eventual desire for the return of the lent object – it is transitory, in other words, and may be withdrawn at any time. To that extent lending equates with mortality, obligation, and the transient nature of affection.

Lenses Lenses aid perception, but they also suggest **weakness**, in that, if one needs a lens, one is, by definition, incomplete.

Leopards In Christian iconography, a leopard implies sin. Symbolically speaking, a leopard suggests opinionatedness, error, and the triumph of the low. In **dream** terms the **speed** of the leopard and its low-slung phys-icality are probably paramount, twinned with its natural **camouflage** and predatory characteristics. Being **hunted** by a leopard, as well as causing justifiable **anxiety**, may also suggest a lurking **fear** of being **robbed** or set upon by unknown or **alien** forces – to that extent it constitutes the per-fect **paranoiac** image from which one cannot possibly **escape**.

Leprosy Leprosy suggests unjustified torment (see **Torture**) and perma-nent loss. In Christian iconography, the healing of the leper, Naaman, represents the outward manifestation of the inner urge towards purity – the curing of the interior **sickness** of the **soul** externalized, in other words. In **dream** terms, the entirely external aspects of the disease may suggest a **poisoning** of the inner being, suddenly visible to all.

Lesbianism See **Homosexuality**

Letters **Writing** a letter to another person (in terms of **contact**) can imply the **sexual** act. Letters, being non-verbal, may also suggest a desire to be communicated with on an instinctual, rather than a purely rational, level. See **Mail**

Levels Levels are important in **dreams** (see **Above & Below**). As well as suggesting the parts of the **body** pictorially equivalent to the specified level (**head**/high, **feet**/low, for instance), they also imply tendencies, desired directions, and involuntary pressures.

Levitation Levitation implies a desire to **rise** above one's usual station or situation, affording oneself a wider **picture**, and wowing spectators in the process. To that extent at least, levitation may be linked with desired status and cravings for public recognition, as well as with **male** fantasies of **sexual** domination and physical assertion. It would be churlish, however, not to mention the spiritual aspects of levitation, and the very different connotations levitation may have for the resolutely pure in **mind**. See **Flying**

Libidinal Fixation Libidinal fixation is said to occur when the **libido** is fixed onto one source – be that source **parent**, sibling, object, other, or erogenous zone – usually in early **childhood**, or, at the very least, early on in the course of psychic development.

Libido **Jung** used the word libido in a beyond **sexual** sense, to describe the fundamental **driving** force of life. **Freud** defined it as the **energy** of **sexual** desire.

Libraries Libraries are repositories of knowledge, and to that extent they may equate with the human brain when they occur in **dreams**. The **carrying** of **books** suggests the retention of knowledge, and the housing of books in a public library suggests the desire to disseminate that knowledge to a wider public. Libraries may also symbolize the **collective unconscious**, in that virtually all the knowledge transferred to us from the **past** relies on a permanent cycle of enlightened benevolence for its continuance. See **Reading**

Lice Lice, ironically, may sometimes stand in for **children** in **dreams**. In old English folklore a dream of lice was considered a herald of **family** illness to come. Their disappearance from an otherwise infested person was a sign of imminent **death**, rather as **rats** will **abandon** a **sinking ship** well before the actual event. In dream terms, lice may equate with **illness**, and, more specifically, with fears of **cancer**.

Lies Lies in **dreams** tend to appear (perhaps inevitably) as unjustified calumnies against the **dreamer** – we project outwards, in other words, and by default. Rarely, indeed, do we confront our own shortcomings, and the desire for truthfulness in dreams often manifests itself in its opposite, antonymic expression, possibly as a result of our natural human **fear** of unintended consequences.

Lifeguards Lifeguards offer metaphorical safety in potentially troubled emotional **waters**. To that extent they may be conjured up by the **dreamer** as a sort of *deus ex machina*, designed to sort out potentially stifling problems as a medium of last resort.

Life Plan Alfred Adler noted the existence of an **unconscious** or secret life plan in many individuals subject to neurotic behaviour patterns. He believed that, in many cases, this life plan was at the cause of the **neurosis** – even the **driving** force behind it.

Life Rafts Life rafts protect us from the **dangers** lurking underneath them. They are a thin membrane separating us from **nature**, and from hidden emotions that threaten to unsettle us. Although by their very nature **fragile**, life rafts, like **lifeguards**, are mediums of last resort, and to that extent they will probably find themselves garnished with a succession of extra utilities – **food**, **water**, **fishing** gear, **sails**, or even extra durability – in perfect tandem with any increase in our **anxieties**.

Lifts See **Elevators**

Light Light equates with **life** and the putting out of the light equates with **death**. Shedding light on something may be to give it life, or, otherwise, to focus on it in a particular and concentrated way. To light up from within presupposes a spiritual **transformation**, or a desire, at least, for **change** and **truth**. **Holiness** was traditionally called the 'candle of the Lord', and the appearance of **daylight** after a long period of **darkness** heralded **rebirth** and the possibilities of **resurrection** – indeed the Realm of Light is another name for the **Buddhic** plane, in which wisdom becomes consciousness.

Lighthouses Lighthouses act as **warning beacons** – they can also imply security and the benefits of civilization, in that, traditionally, they were manned outposts in places which human beings normally found unconducive. The lighthouse built by Ptolemy Soter at Pharos was one of the **Seven** Wonders of the Ancient **World**, and exemplified, even then, mankind's desire to emulate the **Gods**. Bearing this in mind, lighthouses may also represent – like the **Tower** of Babel – the vanity of human wishes, vulnerable to being swept away by the natural order as a **punishment** for their vainglory. To this extent they can also symbolize the **male** member, and its fundamentally **fragile nature**. See **Searchlights**

Lightning In **archetypal** terms, lightning was the preferred missile of certain **Gods** (such as the Scandinavian deity Thor), whose **voice** was deemed to be heard in the sound of **thunder**, and whose power over the lightning signified his omnipotence. To be struck by lightning was considered auspicious by the ancient Romans – if one survived, one was deemed to have been honoured by the Gods, and if one died, one was considered incorruptible. In **dreams** lightning may represent sudden revelations, or the selection of the **dreamer** for a particular purpose. Lightning may also embody a sudden discharge of tension – even a 'lightening'.

Lilies Lilies are emblems of pureness, innocence and **virginity** – they were even said to have sprung from Eve's **tears** of repentance after the **Fall** from Eden. Traditionally, to dream of lilies brought good luck, although, more recently, they have become associated with **death**, and eventual **rebirth**. They are **flowers** of transition, therefore, and their presence in **dreams** may imply the existence of a **waiting room** (something along the lines, perhaps, of the classic **limbo**).

Limbo Limbo can represent the **fear** of uncertainty, or the lack of resolution in an issue that is hanging over us. It can suggest inertia, too, and a particular form of fatalism that we are all sometimes prone to, and which tells us that there is no earthly point in **struggling** because everything is preordained anyway. Limbo may also represent parturition, and, in particular, the period just before **birth**.

Limbs See **Amputation**

Limousines Limousines are exalted forms of transport, implying importance and unnatural selection. They are status signifiers, and can imply conceit, vainglory, and an over-inflated sense of **self**. The traditional darkening of the **windows** can suggest **blindness**, or a desire not to see, or to have seen, what one really is.

Lincoln, Abraham (1809–65) Shortly before he was assassinated, President Lincoln had the following **dream**, which he recounted to his **wife** and to Ward Hill Lamon, who wrote it down: 'Then I heard subdued sobs, as if a number of **people** were weeping. I thought I left my **bed** and wandered downstairs .... There I met with a sickening surprise. Before me was a catafalque, on which rested a **corpse** wrapped in funeral vestments, guarded by **soldiers**. "Who is dead in the White House?" I demanded of one of the soldiers. "The President," was his answer. "He was killed by an assassin!" Then came a loud burst of **grief** from the **crowd** which awoke me from my dream.' Lincoln was shot at Ford's Theatre, Washington DC, on 14th April 1865 by a Southern actor, John Wilkes Booth. He died the next morning. See **Crying**

Linen Linen requires care, **time** and effort before it can be shown to its best, or natural, advantage. To that extent it is not, perhaps, a **symbol** of modernity, but rather of existing values in a **fast**-changing **world**. In religious symbology (itself borrowed from classical literature), linen represents the Divine Truth, and to **dream** of linen in the context of **death** suggests a desire to **cleanse**, purify and give significance to a condition that at first glance may seem dirty and tarnished.

Lines Lines may, at first glance, suggest a desire to get somewhere – but they can also suggest obfuscation, or long periods of apparent inaction before an end is reached. **Straight** lines may denote boundaries, or forbidden areas (lines one should not **cross**). Curvy lines may relate to havering, or to a perceived inability to keep to one course of action. Upward-moving lines point to possibilities, while downward moving lines suggest consequences.

Lingam The **phallic** symbol of all-embracing creativity representing the **God** Shiva in Hindu mythology. The lingam, set on a base representing the **yoni**, or vulva, forms the basis of Shiva's potency and depth of paradox. The phallic and vulval connotations have very little to do with **sex**, however, and everything to do with transcendent power. It is perhaps worth reiterating that **dreams** involving phallic **symbols** do not always have specifically sexual meanings, and that the lingam was the symbol of both **male** and **female** creativity. See **Penis** & **Vagina**

Liniment Liniment benefits from a placatory (placebo-like) – as well as real – effect. The very act of rubbing (*linire* means to smear) is comforting in itself, and takes us back to **childhood**, and the benevolent caresses of our **parents**. Liniment is usually **sweet**-smelling, and its implications are social and inclusive, rather than solitary and exclusive.

Links Links suggest connections, and the individual contributing to the collective strengthening of the whole. They also suggest that beauty may be practical as well as aesthetically pleasing, and that applied intelligence may solve apparently insoluble **problems**.

Lions A lion traditionally symbolizes both noble courage and God-manifest. According to **Ezekiel**, a lion also represents Mark the Evangelist. To the Taoists, lions stood for strength, energy, and valour in combat. Traditionally, dreaming of a lion could foretell good luck in the choosing of a **marriage** partner. To a contemporary **dreamer**, however, lions may suggest a desire to dominate, or to be perceived as above certain things – lions may also be **symbols** of **self**-sufficiency, and, to a certain extent at least, they can represent both good and **evil**, which affords them the power of paradox.
KEY LINE: 'To see lions announces the contentions of one's enemies.'
(From Astrampsychus' *Oneirocriticon* 350 AD)

Lips Lips suggest the capacity to express what lies within. This – alongside their obvious surface similarity to the **vagina** – is probably the **key** to their status as **sexual** signifier. Lips may also represent **wounds** (just as with the vagina) for they are a direct and visible opening into the vulnerable interior of the **body**, and benefit from no obvious protective carapace. Highly coloured lips, when they appear in **dreams**, indicate sexual excitement and unrepressed desire, as well as the desired vulnerability of the recipient of our attentions.

KEY LINE: 'On a poet's lips I slept/Dreaming like a love-adept/In the sound his breathing kept;' (From *Prometheus Unbound*, 1820, by Percy Bysshe Shelley)

Liquids Liquids suggest flux, and the breaking down of existing orders. We came from the **sea**, and eventually we return to it, simply through the natural collapse (the inherent instability) of our temporary physiological **homes**. Liquids may also suggest the capacity to **flow** through things (**small** spaces for instance), which solidity – or mental rigidity – would inevitably cause to be smashed.

Litter Even litterers often hate litter, and this irritating paradox is at the **heart** of litter's symbolism in **dreams**. We know we should clean up after us, but spring cleaning the **past** requires such a degree of effort and moral consistency that most of us bypass the job, and refuse to acknowledge that the litter we leave behind is ours – first it becomes 'shared', and then, thanks to the **sands** of time, exclusive only to others. Could this be the **driving** force behind the symbolical attachment of tin cans and other detritus to the **cars** of newlyweds? See **Cleansing**

Liver, The The liver, perhaps because of its link with filtration and consumption (particularly of **alcohol**), tends to symbolize the lower human qualities when it appears in **dreams**, including those of **anger** and irritability.

Living Living is the **opposite** of **death**, with the one inevitably presupposing the other. When we dream of living, we are dreaming of being allowed to live, and to that extent, even if we are unaware of it, dreaming of living is akin to **prayer**.

Lizards Lizards appear **primordial**, and suggest great **age** and detached wisdom, as well as, on occasion, indefinable threat. A lizard is pitiless, in that it appears to evince no particular morality. To that extent, lizardry is about as far as one can get (in **archetypal** terms, at least) from enlightened humanity.

Loads Loads are what we perceive of as holding us back from desired outcomes: 'If I didn't need to look after so-and-so, I'd be able to do such-and-such.' **Children** may represent such a load, as may elderly **parents**, sick **relatives**, and needy **friends**. The load in **question**, of course, is frequently a moral one. See **Burdens**

Lobelia Lobelia, part of the bellflower **family**, was much used in quack **medicines**, and was renowned for its hallucinogenic dream-inducing qualities. See **Artificial Dreams**, **Hallucinations** & **Hallucinatory Dreams**

Lobsters Lobsters are strange creatures, in that they are fundamentally defined by their **claws**. To a beast of their own size, or smaller, they *are* their claws, for the remainder of the lobster will never be seen. To this extent lobsters are **mask**-like creatures, and suggest hidden threats, or the desire to force issues without recourse to normal forms of debate.

Locks Locks traditionally symbolize charity, as well as representing illicit, or precluded **sexual** desires. Traditionally, there were no locks on the **doors** to **heaven**, and therefore the imposition of a lock on an object presupposes the existence of a **key**, and is therefore elitist (or exclusive) in meaning. See **Padlocks**

Locusts Locusts destroy whatever they **touch**, and are **biblically** synonymous with **plague** and outside interference. They can suggest **armies**, and other **machines** of **destruction**, as well as intrusion in one's domestic sphere by **alien** parties (the **police**, thieves, meddling neighbours, etc.).

Logs Logs may be **cleansing** and warming, but they can also be threatening and synonymous with natural **destruction**. One can construct a **house** with logs, but that house is also symbolically and literally vulnerable to **fire**. Logs are, in addition, hard to control and hard to the **touch**, and to that extent they may objectify unyieldingness.

Looms Looms produce desirable articles, but they are also mechanical and noisy, and, in consequence, difficult to construe in an entirely positive manner – creative, yes, but also repetitive and soulless.

Lorries Lorries are fundamentally **female** in oneiric significance, which may seem curious, at first glance, but less so if one construes them as **burden** carriers (maternal), and as empty vessels capable of being filled. Lorries are also associated with work and feminine duty, rather than with play and masculine irresponsibility (see **Cars**) and this is another aspect of their maternal symbolism.

Losing If a woman **dreams** of losing things, or of searching for lost things, this may refer back to the loss of her **virginity**, or to the act of defloration. Losing things (**toys**, for instance) can also refer us back to the **past**, and to the perceived loss of **childhood**.

Loss See **Amputation**

Lost, Being Being lost is another carry-over from **childhood anxieties**, and often finds itself transformed into adult **fears** of misguided ambition or unfulfilled potential. **Children** are indoctrinated with what they ought to be when they grow up, and it is inevitable that this unintended brainwashing can often find itself mutating inside the adult mind in terms of a sometimes indefinable sense of loss, or being **lost** – one has bought the

ticket and mounted the **train** (just as one has been told to do), but in the process one has also lost the plot.

Lotteries Lotteries represent the **dreamer**'s desire for a *deus ex machina* to obviate the need for struggle, handing over instead a guaranteed answer to an awkward **question** – namely, what to do with one's life. Lotteries are about the possibilities of apparently endless consumption, with no concomitant need to construct.

Lotuses The symbol of **Gautama Buddha**, implying unity, illumination, and the Divine Intellect. The **prophet** Muhammad says that a lotus **tree** stands in the seventh **heaven**, on the **right hand** of the **throne** of Allah. Lotuses may also be **symbols** of sterile dreaming and the triumph of the **ego**.

Love Love, when it appears in **dreams**, usually reveals itself in another guise entirely, such as a **fire**, **floods**, **money**, or even **pigeons** (**turtle-doves**). Indirect love, or the love of humans for **God**, acts on our capacity for direct, or affective love. See **Lovers**
KEY LINE: 'I think myself into love, and dream myself out of it.' (From William Hazlitt's *On Dreams* 1826)

Lovers A **male** and **female** lover entwined (as in Gustav Klimt's or Auguste Rodin's *The Kiss*) is a classic **symbol** for the mixing of the two **sexes** into one. Such lovers symbolize unity, suggesting the within, without – i.e. the public demonstration of interior expression. See **Love**

Lowness The low (or dwarfed) perspective from which **children** customarily view grown-ups will frequently carry over into adult **dreams**, conveying childish – or occasionally even inappropriate – forms of thought along with it. Lowness may also indicate the way the **dream-er** feels about themselves, or even the way in which the dreamer senses that others may feel about them – if one is low, or positioned at somebody's **feet**, one may easily be crushed. Repeated dreams of lowness may also be triggered by **depression**, or feelings of **inferiority**. See **Above**, **Below**, **Inferiority Complex**, **Manic Depression** & **Repetitive Motifs**

LSD Lysergic Acid Diethylamide is a powerful synthetic psychoactive and hallucinogenic **drug**, related to the rye **grain fungus**, ergot. Even small quantities of the drug may trigger a dream-like state in which the abnormal becomes normal, and in which extreme mood swings predominate. Recent research would appear to indicate that long-term use may lead to **psychosis** and **paranoia**, although numerous **people** – amongst them **psychologist** and drugs guru Timothy Leary, and **writer** Aldous Huxley – have lauded the drug's capacity for consciousness changing and perceptual transcendence. See **Hallucinations** & **Hallucinatory Dreams**

Lucid Dreaming The ability to control and direct one's dreaming (rather than merely to rely on a serendipitous recall) has been an object of keen research for over 100 years, beginning, perhaps, with utopian socialist Frederik Willem van Eeden's *A Study of Dreams* (1913), and leading towards a rather more complicated series of investigations conducted by Stephen LaBerge, at his Lucidity Institute, in Palo Alto, California. See **St Denis**

Luggage See **Baggage**

Lumber Lumber has a **split** meaning – it can represent both a **building material**, fresh and **sweet**-smelling, suggestive of future plans, and it can also represent unwanted articles, kept in a lumber **room**, that can lumber one down and prevent forward movement (thereby causing lumbering). Such semantic tricks frequently occur in **dreams**, and may suggest that the **dreamer** is unsure about the direction they may wish to take. An **example** might run as follows: the dreamer decides to build a **house**, but finds themselves weighed down by the building materials they intend to use. One **reading** might suggest that the building of the house was a vain endeavour, and not founded on good sense, while another reading would have the house as the **body**, and the lumber suggestive of **illness**, or even of past mistakes that the dreamer is still allowing to impinge upon the present.

Lungs, The The lungs are purificatory **organs**, exchanging good **gases** for bad. To this extent they act as the body's ventilators, whilst also representing, in symbolical terms at least, the **life** force. In Chinese **medicine**, the lungs equate with **grief**, sadness, detachment, and the taking of decisions, and their virtues involve the acceptance of the Here and Now, rather than any specious fantasies relating to future prospects – as Chinese medicine incorporates numerous instinctual **archetypes**, it is likely that such meanings will also be present in the **dreams** of non-adepts.

Lu Tung-Pin Lu Tung-Pin, the last of the eight Chinese Taoist Immortals, had many stories told about him, of which the *Dream of the Yellow Sorghum* (*Huang-Liangmeng*) is probably the most famous. When he was a young man, Lu Tung-Pin stopped at an inn, where he was accosted by one of the Immortals in disguise. Later that night he had a **dream**, in which his entire future life was paraded before him. At first, **honours** flooded down on him, and he met with a series of glorious successes, but later, as he grew older, things began to go badly for him, and he met with a **train** of terrible misfortunes, culminating in his brutal **death** at the hands of a brigand. Lu Tung-Pin awoke, horrified, and decided to renounce the world forthwith.

Lynxes A lynx traditionally symbolizes suspicious vigilance. In **dream** terms, therefore, the lynx might suggest objectivity, or the desire for answers.

M

Machines Machines both serve human beings and threaten them. They suggest mechanical rather than emotional responses, and to that extent they are unstoppable, even by logic. Machines can also represent the functioning (or malfunctioning) of the **body**, and even, at times, **frigidity** (rigidity).

Madness To dream of madness is to **dream** of confusion and loss of control. Madness may also represent disintegration (mental, physical, or spiritual), or the presence of unbridled emotion. Traditionally, one can be mad for **love** of someone, with the implication that one is no longer able to behave entirely rationally. Thus madness can equate with anarchy, ecstasy, and even, *pace* certain Native American tribes who treated 'mad' **people** with conspicuously enlightened tolerance, the subsumation of the individual will by that of **God** (being 'touched', in other words).

Madonna, The The image of the Madonna is maternal, virginal and healing. It implies both a loss of **self**, and a nurturing integration into communal thought. The Madonna also symbolizes the feminine principle in harmony with the masculine principle, and to that extent she carries within her both the **anima** and the **animus** – she both serves, in other words, and is served. See **Virgin Mary**

Mafiosi The Mafia, as an institution, exemplifies manipulation – it relies on force and persuasive logic to achieve its ends. Individual Mafiosi represent expediency and moral degeneracy, *ergo* the human **face** of **temptation** by the **Devil**. We all wish to belong – and to benefit by belonging – and the **symbol** of the Mafia (or the Cosa Nostra, the Tongs, or any of a multitude of gangs or **cults**) appears, on the surface, to offer just such a seductive possibility. However, we also fear the Mafia, and to that extent the **dream** may also constitute a **warning**.

Magazines Magazines represent surface consumables – bite-sized chunks of life that flirt with depth without achieving it. They are disposable, briefly seductive, **masturbatory** rather than affective, and cheaply inflammatory, and they engender expectations rather than showing us how to fulfil realizable desires. As a result they are wildly popular, and function as **messengers** of the **id** when they appear in **dreams**, notifying us of suppressed desires without offering us any solutions.

Maggots Maggots symbolize **decay** and the triumph of **nature** over the intellect – they also represent the **death** of the **body**. Maggots, like **lice**, can also indicate a **fear** of **disease** – of being eaten up by something that has access to our insides. Maggots, in certain circumstances, may also suggest a fear of (or disgust for) **sex**, particularly when dreamt of by a woman, as they predominantly threaten orifices and **wounds**. See **Eating**

Magic However rational we may think we are, the concept of magic (of the unnatural dominating the natural), is a regular carryover from **childhood** perceptions. **Artists** like Pablo Picasso believed implicitly that objects could be imbued as much with **evil** as with dynamic potential – that they could be **God**-struck and that they could be **cursed**. Magic and desire are also linked, with both suggesting easy – or even instant – outcomes. See **Black Magicians, Magicians, Witches & Wizards**

Magical Thought The belief that, by adopting a certain posture or mode of thought, one can affect far distant events. Such an idea can find itself reflected, and, indeed, re-enacted, within **dream** imagery, often in terms of **wish-fulfilment** fantasies.

Magicians Magicians are manipulators – masters of appearance and outward show – and they frequently represent desired fantasy outcomes when they appear in **dreams**. The magician's wand has **phallic** overtones, too, and there may well be the added implication that the **dreamer** wishes to indulge themselves in something (possibly **sexual**) that they have not entirely deserved – that they wish, in effect, to be pleasantly surprised. See **Black Magicians, Magic, Magical Thought, Witches & Wizards**

Magistrates Magistrates are responsible for imposing society's rules upon us, even when we disagree with them, or feel that they are unfair. They are authority figures and parental stand-ins (particularly for the **father**), and their presence in a **dream** may reflect on this relationship – even on the continuance (either wanted or unwanted) of the **child/parent** dynamic into adulthood. Magistrates may also act benevolently or in a protective capacity, making sure **weaker** parties, and those who cannot look after themselves, are not discriminated against.

Magnets Magnets, of course, may both attract and repel (depending on how we use them), and to that extent they are often taken to represent the **dreamer**, creating an aura or force **field** which influences anyone who enters its ken. With this in mind, they can become a perfect **wish-fulfilment** fantasy vehicle (rather like **guns**), capable of forcing issues to the benefit of the possessor.

Magnifying Glasses A magnifying **glass** suggests the need for concentrated appraisal, for **paying** attention, or for focusing on a particular object to the exclusion of all else (macropsia). If that object is then brought into keener focus, the implication carried with it is that it must be attended to, or there is no point to the process of magnification. See **Mescaline**

Magpies A magpie symbolizes garrulity, or chattiness. In popular superstition a single magpie could bring sorrow if the person that saw it did not bow his **head** three times. To the ancient Chinese, on the other hand, the magpie was the bird of joy, and a harbinger of glad tidings.

Magritte, René (1898–1967) A leading light of the **Surrealist** movement, Magritte produced his painting entitled *Key of Dreams* in 1930. In it he shows six apparently commonplace objects: an **egg**, a **shoe**, a bowler **hat**, a **candle**, a **glass**, and a **hammer**, and calls them, respectively, the acacia, the **moon**, the **snow**, the **ceiling**, the **storm**, and the **desert** – the implication being that in the world of **dreams**, nothing is what it seems. In his 1927 **painting** of the *Reckless Sleeper*, we see a **bald** man (looking uncomfortably like the title character of F. W. Murnau's 1922 film of *Nosferatu the Vampire*), fast asleep in his own coffin, with the content of his dreams (in the form of the apparently disparate images of a looking glass, a **bird**, a bowler hat, a **bow**, a candle, and an **apple**) **floating** in the **ether** beneath him.

Maids Maids are conveniences – they are there to help us, but they can also function as fantasy objects and vessels for **male sexual** desires. To that extent they exemplify the submissive woman, and it is hardly surprising that, in so-called advanced societies, the tradition of **female** service has gone (perhaps temporarily) into abeyance, making way for other service industries which appear less pointed in their significance. Maidhood hasn't lost its significance for the **unconscious**, though, and remains a convenient oneiric trope for certain representative **archetypes**.

Mail Mail and messages are synonymous in **dream** terms – both are trying to tell us something, and that, urgently. The fact that mail usually consists of **paper** (or, in the case of e-mails, virtual paper) merely reinforces its temporality – mail is a tease, and requires to be opened. See **Letters**

Make-Up Using make-up in a **dream** can often imply a masquerade on the part of the **dreamer** – the **hiding** of something, or some aspect of themselves, that the dreamer does not want revealed.

Male, The The Great **Father** or Father of All (the Creator), was one of the two **archetypal** principles at the foundation of both Eastern and Western functional **mythologies** (the other, needless to say, is the **Great Mother**). The 'male', pure and simple, suggests male characteristics, which may include assertion, aggression, physical strength, and what might be called instinctual rationality. See **Female**, **Widow** & **Widower**

Mana The **spirits**, **demons**, or **Gods** that, in ancient times, formed the wellsprings of our inner motivations. Their existence and significance is entirely antithetical to our modern, flawed concept of 'free will'. An alternative, rather more modern reading might be the containment of 'psychic energy' in a person, an event, a spirit, or an object.

Managers Managers take the place of the **self**-determining will, in that *they* manage us, rather than we, them. Managers may also equate with **teachers**, **gurus**, or spiritual guides.

Mandalas Mandala means 'circle' in Sanskrit, and is often represented by a **snake** or a **serpent** with its **tail** in its **mouth**. It is used as a cosmological diagram and as an aid to meditation in both Hinduism and Buddhism, and may be achieved (at least in the Buddhistic case) by the concentrated use of the imagination via a specific mental image, or *dmigs-pa*, and only by a suitably instructed lama. A similar concept to the mandala was also used by the Navajo and the Naskapi **Indians** to encourage men back towards an inner harmony with themselves and an outer harmony with the cosmos. To that extent they suggest a return towards a previously existing but now forgotten ancient order, which holds out the possibility of renewal and reawakening to its adherents. To **Jung**, they frequently symbolized a movement from the traditional, or patriarchal, towards the intuitive, or feminine (exemplified in the **collective unconscious**, or **anima**). The true mandala is always a mental image, and never concretized. See **Wheels**

Manic Depression Also known as bipolar disorder. Freud noted the frequent occurrence of **cannibalism** in the **dreams** of manic depressives. The **introjected** hate object (often the **dreamer**'s own **superego**) may then be symbolically reincorporated within the dreamer, leading to yet another cycle of **self-punishment**. Recovery from a manic-depressive cycle may be reflected in increasingly 'cheery' dreams, which lack such morbid elements. See **Depression, Futility & Homelessness**

Manifest Content In Freudian terms, this is the first, raw description of a **dream** before any real attempt at interpretation is made. **Freud** called this stage of the dream a rebus (a word or picture puzzle) whose meaning needed to be teased out, revealing the idea behind it. The closer to waking the dream is – the closer to **ego** lucidity, in other words – the less distorted or displaced the content is likely to be. Freud's other euphemism for the manifest content of a dream was as the '*façade*' behind which the real content of the preconscious thoughts and of the **repressed** wishful impulses lay hidden. See also **Day's Residues, Latent Content & Dream Work**

Mansions Mansions are just larger versions of **houses**, and to that extent still probably represent the **body** of the **dreamer**, twinned, perhaps, with the dreamer's hidden aspirations towards greater (or higher) things. Mansions are bulked-up houses, if you like – houses with attitude.

Manure Manure may have its uses, but its fundamental constituent remains, nevertheless, shit. Manure is therefore a **symbol** of fertility bound up with the concept of the midden – just like the human **body**, when one comes to think of it. Fruitful in **decay**; ripe for transmogrification into another state; eager for transmutation.

Maps Maps suggest that there is a **right** and a wrong way – that if we have the capacity for understanding, we may reach our **goal**. Maps need to be clear or they are worse than useless. Our **dream** may be telling us that we need to clarify our position before forward (or auspicious) **movement** can occur.

Marble Marble is at the same time both **frigid** and seductive, and so might suggest something that we desire but nevertheless feel we cannot have. Marble is also suggestive of permanence and longevity – build something of marble and one expects it to last. The song, *I Dreamt I Dwelt in Marble Halls*, by Michael Balfe (1808–70), contains the repeated chorus: 'But I also dreamt, which pleased me most,/That you lov'd me still the same/That you lov'd me, you lov'd me still the same,/That you lov'd me, you lov'd me still the same.' The **wish-fulfilment** aspect of the image was so powerful that James Joyce used it in both *Dubliners* (1914), and *Finnegans Wake* (1939), and it is this repining aspect of exalted nostalgia that is most likely to imbue the marble image.

Marbles Marbles take us back to **childhood**, and to all the secret freedoms lurking behind the nominal restrictions imposed on us during our formative **years**. Marbles resemble **eyes**, too, and this benevolently watchful aspect may contain an **echo** of the forgotten childhood comfort of knowing one was being looked after, or kept an eye upon.

Marching There is a formality to marching – a precision – that is both outward show and inward function. Marching implies order and control, and is thus the very opposite of **chaos**. **Dream** of marching, and one is also dreaming of continuance and **self**-domination.

Mares In symbolical terms, mares correspond to the feminine aspects of the **mind**. They can be **anima** signals when a **male dreams** of them, and expressions of a desire for more freedom in her femininity, when dreamt of by a **female**. See **Epona**, **Horses** & **Stallions**
KEY LINE: 'To see black mares is a thoroughly bad sign.' (From Astrampsychus' *Oneirocriticon* 350 AD)

Marigolds Marigolds have traditionally been associated with the **sun**, with constancy, and with fruitfulness. To **dream** of one was considered to foretell future **wealth**.

Marijuana The drug marijuana consists of the dried **leaves** of the **Indian** hemp plant. **Dreams** experienced under its influence usually involve a slowing down of perceived **time**.

Marines Marines can be either comforting or threatening, depending on context. They may also symbolize disorder within order, in that they are trained to cause **chaos** to an **enemy** while retaining **discipline** themselves. The old **saw** of 'we'd better call in the Marines' can also find itself reflected in a **body** of assertive men suddenly appearing in an **anxiety dream** for 'emergency protective' purposes.

Markets Markets are meeting places as well as being forums for trade, and it is this **meeting** aspect which is often the market's prevalent use in a **dream**. Markets reflect the mundane, too, and the necessity of successful interrelation with others if one is to survive (i.e. **eat**). Markets also attribute value to things, and give us correspondences that we can use outside the market environment. See **Marketplaces**

Marketplaces An **empty** marketplace might imply **abandonment**, or the **fear** of loss. The **absence** of the 'usual **crowd**' may also involve fears of **death**, or of losing one's **friends** and **family**, and those with whom one normally interrelates, to incipient – and inevitable – mortality. See **Markets**

Marriage Traditionally, the linking of two disparate elements – **daylight** and **darkness**, **male** and **female**, strength and passivity – to form one, stronger, whole. Marriage may also be taken to imply the marrying together of ideas, of images, of disparate **peoples**, or of **symbols**, inside a more formalized rearrangement. To that extent marriage may reflect an integration of more than one personality, or the taking on of aspects of another person (the **body** of **Jesus Christ**, for instance) for spiritual gain. See **Sacred Marriage** & **Wedding**

Marshes We lose ourselves in marshes if we are not careful, and become bogged down. Marshes are also wild places, largely unamenable to civilizing influences. Because of this, they often represent the wilder parts of our mind and of our emotions, and even, when the context is **right**, of our imaginative capacities – our capacity to think beyond the civilized, in other words, and in a non-linear fashion. This freedom has a downside, of course, **cutting** us off from the mainstream, with its comforting grassy knolls, and condemning us to a life in what amounts to nomansland – **writers**, composers, **poets**, and **artists** are usually marsh creatures, for this very reason. See **Lost**

Martyrs There is something awkward about a martyr – we tend to respect them but not to like them particularly. To that extent the **self-sacrificial** element of martyrdom may have its pejorative aspects in **dreams**, comprising a certain 'look at me' element often associated with negative energy or extreme solipsism. Martyrdom is as much about influencing others, therefore, as it is about personal abnegation and collective humility.

Masculinity See **Male**

Masks Masks reflect both outwardly and inwardly – the wearing of a mask has implications, in other words, which reflect backwards on the wearer and upon their motives (with the inverse of the mask representing the secret **face** of the wearer, known only to them), as well as frontwards, towards their **audience**. Why are the mask-wearers disguising themselves? Who or what do they wish to emulate? Are they **tricking** us? Do they not wish us to see their real identity? Or is their real identity the mask itself? Masks can suggest a **fear** of **death** (the death mask, or the changes that come over us physically when we die), and they can suggest **disease**, either outward – as in scarification or mutilation – or inward, as in spiritual **decay**. See **Cloaks, Clothes, Coats** & **Diplomas**

Masochism A morbid desire to be ill-treated or humiliated in the cause of **sexual** gratification. The presence of masochism in a **dream** may well point to the latent existence of its antonym (or opposite affect) – **sadism**. The word masochism is derived from the name of the Austrian Count Leopold von Sacher-Masoch (1836–95) who wrote numerous **plays**, **novels** and short stories dealing with the subject.

Massage Massage is both nominally nurturing and potentially unifying (in that it calls for the presence of a second party). The use of both **hands** to massage something suggests **integration**, and the blending of disparate parts into one whole. To that extent, massage is a deeply symbolic bringing together of both the massager and the massaged, and may contain revocations of the intrauterine mother/baby relationship, with the **mother's** natural movement against the **baby** she is carrying equating with the massaging element of the **dream**.

Masters Masters, when they appear in **dreams**, frequently represent **God**, the Holy **Spirit**, or the atma-buddhi, the implication being one of developed individuality within a collective consciousness. On the distaff side of the **coin**, Master Leonard was the familiar and **orgy**-master of the **demons**, and was frequently represented as a **black**-faced man with the **body** of a three-**horned goat**. You have been warned.

Masturbation Masturbatory dreams are very important in the analysis or **self**-analysis of **dreams** because they reflect and can provide a **key** for the specific **love** fantasy of the **dreamer**. The dreamer's conscious **sex** life may appear 'normal' and uneventful, but the conscious or **unconscious** fantasies that the dreamer has while masturbating may reflect their underlying **libido** constellation. Infantile fantasies tend to be largely unconscious, but are often accessible through dreams, while adult fantasies may be subject to considerable distortion and **displacement**, resulting from their **taboo** status.

Matches Matches can both **light** our way and **burn** us. Sudden **ignitions** (as in sulphur or phosphorous catching **flame**) can imply flare-ups of **anger**, or sudden off-the-cuff clarifications – all the more devastating for being unexpected. A match between two players, or involving **teams**, may suggest an inability to make up one's **mind**, or, alternatively, conflicting interests vying for dominance in our everyday lives.

Material Interpretation The interpreting of a **dream** through its 'material' facts. This is an interpretation based on the first – very often **sexual** – **layer** of a dream's **symbols**. **Functional analysis** takes this one step further, by working on the latent ideas hidden behind the material content of the dream.

Mattresses Women, for obvious reasons, often **dream** of being lain upon, or of having things or people **weighing** them down. This can reflect as much on the possibilities for **pregnancy**, as it does on one's natural (i.e. biological as opposed to chosen) **sexual** function. To be treated as a mattress is also significant, in that it implies that one is being taken for granted, or simply as a sexual convenience.

Maury, Louis Alfred (1817–92) Maury was renowned for his investigations into **self**-induced **dreams**, a study which culminated in his book *Sleep and Dreams* (1861). He decided, after an analysis of more than 3,000 different dreams, that external stimuli were the main catalyst that promoted dreaming, and that the dream and the catalyst occurred more or less simultaneously. **Freud** acknowledges his contribution in the *Interpretation of Dreams*, detailing Maury's famous guillotine dream, in which the still adolescent and temporarily ill Frenchman found himself inadvertently starring in a courtroom drama during the revolutionary Reign of Terror. Hauled up in front of a Tribunal consisting of Marat, Fouquier-Tinville and Robespierre, Maury was soon condemned to **death** for a litany of sins. Transported on the tumbril through seething **crowds**, he found himself strapped, **face** downwards, to Madame Guillotine. The trip was sprung, the guillotine fell, and Maury's **head** parted from his **body**, to **fall** with a thump on the ground. **Awakening** with a terrible **anxiety**, Maury discovered that the headboard to his **bed** has fallen down, striking him at the exact same spot on the cervical vertebra where the guillotine would have struck.

Mayors Mayors may be akin to **masters** in their **dream** symbology, taking on mentor-like aspects as guardians or progenitors of spiritually exalted or high moral values. They represent, if you like, formal demonstrations of the collective will.

Maypoles Maypoles are both **phallic** and symbolic of regeneration, and to that extent they usually suggest the possibility or desire for **pregnancy**, when dreamt of by a woman, and of the possibility or desire to incept a **child**, when dreamt of by a man.

Mazes The seven doors to the Egyptian underworld were often depicted as mazes, symbolizing the **unconscious**, together with all of its as yet unknown possibilities. Mazes may also indicate confusion of some sort, or a multiplicity of choices.

Meadows Meadows are fruitful and peaceful places housing a diversity of life-forms, and this aspect may find itself reflected in **pregnancy** or **adoption** undertones when the image occurs in a **dream**. Meadows may also suggest the need for taking a break (a meadow symbolizes the gap between two ranges of **mountains**), or even, when taken **sexually**, the **female** pubis.

Meals See **Food**

Measurement When we measure something we are endeavouring to dominate it (or even to rationalize it). How, for instance, can a simple measurement describe an **ocean**? Or the ineffability of the universe? Measurements may also suggest the extent of our personal expectations, or how we are **judged** by others – how we 'measure up', in other words.

Meat Meat is our essence, both in terms of nutrients (unless we are **vegetarian**) and in terms of physical makeup. Meat is also a reminder of mortality, and even of carnality (carnal, after all, stems from *carnalis*, and means flesh in Latin). Meat **cut** from our **bodies** (*pace* William Shakespeare's *The Merchant of Venice*) can imply the **fear** of a loss of **sexual** potency, and even, in certain circumstances, underlying **castration complexes**.

Mechanics Mechanics are called in to fix things, and this carries with it the implication that something exists in the conscious mind or the physical **body** of the **dreamer** that needs fixing or servicing. We may even need to lie up awhile, and rekindle our forces – to go into dry dock, as it were.

Medals Medals in **dreams** are principally **self**-congratulatory – we pin them on ourselves in the **absence** of an acclamatory public (or in the case of non-demonstrative **parents**, spouses, **children**, etc.). If we accord the medal to others, we are usually reflecting on aspects of ourselves those other **people** represent. Such medals can compensate for the natural withdrawal of unconditional **love** that occurs when we reach adulthood, and no longer benefit from the tolerance traditionally accorded to **youth**.

Medicine Medicine in **dreams** is usually about the perception of healing, or about the desire to be healed (the restoration of balance). Bitter medicine can be a reflection of an unpalatable reality, or it may suggest **guilt** feelings that are hard to **swallow** or keep at **bay**. See **Healers** & **Shamans**

Meditation Meditation carries with it the implication both of a desire for self-knowledge and of a dissatisfaction with the status quo – if everything is perfect, there is no obvious need to meditate. Meditation in **dreams** may also suggest a need for self-**discipline** and **ritual**, and a possible lack of overall structure. Taking **time** out to meditate also presupposes considered, rather than hasty, **judgements**.

Mediums Mediums are, by definition, intuitive, and we call them in when we wish to know something, or to contact someone (or something) we have **lost**. To that extent mediumship is about the **past** and looking **backwards**, and **dreams** containing mediums will have a tendency towards nostalgia, or regret for lost opportunities.

Meetings In life it is remarkably difficult to contrive successful meetings – they are dependent, after all, not only on us, but also on the person whom we wish to meet. **Dreams** obviate this inconvenience, with our **unconscious** mind able to contrive more or less anything it wants, or feels it needs. Meetings in dreams are therefore very often **wish-fulfilment** fantasies – compulsive replays of failed trysts or missed opportunities that the dream allows us to revisit and subtly change. Threatening meetings (or the **fear** of **running** into someone we do not wish to see) may suggest **guilt**, or alternatively aspects of the **past** which still bother us or that we fear are returning to haunt us, possibly along the lines of abuse or **bullying**.

Megalomania Delusions of grandeur. Such delusions can appear in **dreams**, and may point, if they appear frequently, to the existence of an underlying **neurosis** linked to low **self**-worth. See **Inferiority Complexes**

Melons **Freud** believed that dreaming of melons was 'a question of fantasies about women conducive to **masturbation**'. The French philosopher **René Descartes** had just such a melonic **vision** during the course of his now infamous **night** of **dreams** in Ulm, which set him on the fruitful course towards his *cogito ergo sum* ('I think, therefore I am') dictum. If Freud was right, one is tempted to contrive a rather different Cartesian dictum, equally, in its way, as difficult to deny, and merely necessitating the replacement of three-fifths of one crucial word.

Melting Melting is a predominantly affective concept when it appears in **dreams** – it may, in other words, have either **sexual** or emotional implications, and often contains both. The softening of the **male** member after intercourse often heralds the replacement of the physical by the emotional – the aggressive and assertive sexual drive by a nurturing and affectionate post-coital rapprochement. Women, in particular, often find this 'petit tristesse' intensely compelling, as it constitutes one of the rare moments in which **male** partners (particularly when young) are no longer powered exclusively by their testosterone.

Memorials Memorials can symbolize unforgettable recollections or important events that have happened in the **past** and which infuse or inform the present. See **Recollective Dreams**

Menopause The **unconscious** mind is likely to view the menopause as an ending, rather than as the new **beginning** it is now being touted as in magazines, **self**-help publications, and other such popular treatises. To that extent the menopause may equate with **death** in **dreams** (the death of one's fertility) or loss (the loss of one's **sexual** attraction), and may, in addition, suggest desuetude and disintegration. In fact one would be very hard put to contrive a positive slant for the dreamed-of menopause, and for that reason it may well correlate with **amputation**, or with the **castration complex** in men. See **Menstruation**

Menstruation It is arguable that the onset of the **female** menstrual cycle acts as the equivalent, in terms of a **rite-of-passage**, of **male** initiatory rites, both in adolescence and in terms of the **menopause** (when it is seen to be ending). As there is no long-term alternative to menstruation but submission, its occurrence in a dream can indicate missed opportunities, or as yet unfulfilled promise. When **dreams** of menstruation are juxtaposed with specific images of **blood**, for instance, or of other **people**'s **children**, they may be indicating a subliminal desire by the woman to become **pregnant** and give **birth**. Menstruation may also be represented by the act of '**flowing**' in a dream. **Jacob**'s **wife** Rachel, in Genesis xxxi, 35, called menstruation the 'custom of women', and used its **taboo** to deceive her **father**. Certain Australian aboriginal tribes held the firm belief that menstruation stemmed from dreams of a bandicoot scratching the private parts of the **dreamer**.

Mercury Mercury was the **messenger** of the **Gods** (the Roman equivalent to **Hermes**), and his winged **feet** are likely to suggest **flying**, or intense activity – the desire, in other words, to be active and free, and to shake off whatever moral or emotional constraints are holding us down. This constant movement (circulation), may also be mediatory, and Mercury also represents the link between the dead and the living – between **guilt** and resolution. See **Planets**

Mermaids Mermaids and mermen link two apparently disparate elements, namely the **land** and the **sea** – the **dark** and the **light** – the **male** and the **female**. They are **alchemical symbols**, therefore, and representative of unity and **integration**. Men who **dream** of mating with a mermaid are often seeking privileged access to feminine mysteries, and this may also apply to women who dream of being **kidnapped** by mermen, and drawn beneath the sea – such women may feel unfeminine, or not entirely (or sufficiently) connected with their essential selves. See **Anima & Animus**

Mermen See **Mermaids**

Merry-go-Rounds Merry-go-rounds take us continually back to where we started. This may seem amusing at first, but after a while it can become enormously frustrating. One persistently sees only the backs of other **people's heads**, and one is unable, for obvious reasons (the gap between vehicles; the noise) to emotionally or physically communicate effectively with one's fellow **travellers**. Merry-go-rounds threaten not to stop, and, in consequence, they steadily build up tensions and **anxieties** in the **dreamer** which may only be alleviated by **waking** up. There can be a benevolent aspect to them, though, in their symbolic **regression** to **childhood** – although even here, they imply a lack of control over our own destinies. See **Frustration Dreams**

Mescal Native to Mexico, mescal is a colourless **spirit** fermented from the maguey **cactus** (agave). Each **bottle** traditionally contains an agave **worm floating** inside it. Too much mescal can causes **waking dreams**, such as those experienced by the doomed English Consul, Geoffrey Firmin, in Malcolm Lowry's 1947 metafictional masterpiece, *Under the Volcano* (1947). See **Mescaline**

Mescaline Mescaline is an hallucinogenic **drug** (see **Hallucinations & Hallucinatory Dreams**) distilled from the stem nodules of the **peyote**, a variety of **cactus** most commonly found in Mexico and the south western part of the United States. **Dreams** experienced under its influence are similar to those experienced by **schizophrenics**, and include the **speeding** up of **time** and, occasionally, severe disturbances in **ego** perception leading to a conviction that the **dreamer** is an integral or even a functional part of the **landscape** in which they find themselves. Other dream **symptoms** may include **vision** disturbances such as macropsia (seeing the **world** as through a **magnifying glass**) or micropsia (seeing the world as through a **microscope**). See **Mescal**

Mesopotamian Dreams The Babylonians, the Assyrians and the Sumerians all placed great emphasis on **dreams**, viewing them much along ancient **Egyptian** lines, with the addition of that particular **spirit** of moroseness that characterized much Mesopotamian culture of the **time**. The Sumerians named their dreams Ma-Mou, with the implication that they were 'creations of the **night**', triggered by the dream **god** and nocturnal **demon**, An-Za-Qar, and often harbingers of doom. The *Epic of Gilgamesh* (circa 2000 BC) is a case in point, describing Enkidu's dream of a Great Flood, startlingly similar to that described in the **biblical** Noah epic.

Messengers Messengers can imply that we, the **dreamer**, wish to put things **right** – that we wish to communicate with someone (by means of an intermediary, perhaps) who will not otherwise choose to hear us. Alternatively, someone or something may be trying to get through to us in an effort to alter our behaviour or our perceptions – **God**, perhaps, or a **teacher**, or someone whom we have wronged. See **Hermes** & **Mercury**

Metals Metals may be both precious and unyielding. They may constrain us (as in metal fetters), or reflect our value to others or ourselves (as in **jewellery**, rewards and physical ornaments). Metals can objectify emotional hardness, in that only the surface reflects **light**, and they may also symbolize the artificial constraints of our imaginative capacities. The forging of metal by **fire** may also suggest physical or mental **tests** and **rites-of-passage**.

Mice Mice are **female symbols**, often representative of the **vagina**. They can, in addition, suggest small irritations, and traditionally, when a woman dreamed of a mouse, she was well advised to beware of the artfulness and possible treachery of other women close to her. Should a **cat** be chasing the mouse, there may be an element of **sexual** fear, or a **fear** of predation, in the dream. The **soul**, too, was said to take zoomorphic form, often emerging from the **mouth** of a dead person in the guise of a **pigeon**, a mouse, or a **rat** (its constituent degree of sanctity dependent on the **colour** of the **animal**).

KEY LINE: 'The sight of a mouse bespeaks propitious circumstances.' (From Astrampsychus' *Oneirocriticon* 350 AD)

Microcosms To **dream** that we are microcosmic takes us back to medieval beliefs (Paracelsus (1490–1531), in particular) that considered man and the universe as one entity – the **sun** and **moon** stood in for his **eyes**, the **earth** for his **body**, the **sky** for his **wings** and the **ether** for his intellect. The movement of one would presuppose the concordant movement of the other, and so forth, giving us the origins of **astrology**, and possibly even of the **collective unconscious**.

Microphones Microphones receive and transmit what we are saying even when we do not desire them to do so – to that extent they may even equate with **God**, or some other form of moral guide when they appear in **dreams**. They may also imply that we need to speak up, or in other ways make ourselves heard. See **Speech**

Microscopes Microscopes suggest that we need to look again at something, or maybe peruse it in greater detail. They may also be the **unconscious** mind's way of **drawing** our attention to something that we are overlooking because it seems preternaturally **small** or insignificant to us (micropsia), or that is nagging at us and which we are refusing to address. See **Mescaline**

Microsleep Short periods of **sleep** which do not, in themselves, constitute real rest, or real sleep, but which may go some way towards alleviating the sort of mood swings that are prevalent when real **sleep deprivation** exists.

Militarism Militarism or the military may represent, in dream terms, the **fear** of regimentation, or alternately the power and influence other

people have over the **running** of our lives. There may also be an element of unthinking, or even threatening, **obedience** lurking within the concept, which may, paradoxically, tempt us – in the way that all totalitarianism is to a greater or lesser extent tempting to the **superego**. See **Temptation**

Military, The See **Militarism**

Milk Milk is fundamentally nurturing – it is a sustaining **gift** from others, or to others. It represents domesticity, too, as even in nomadic cultures the production of milk necessitates some (albeit brief) cessation of transience. In symbolical terms it represents the lower feeding the higher, and the importance of **nature** as an objective correlative for the **spirit**. See **Secretions**

Mills For many centuries mills were seen in an entirely positive **light**, in that they were places where flour was milled in order to provide us with **bread** – they were, in other words, transformative (see **Transformation**). The industrial revolution changed all that, and layered (see **Layer Symbolism**) the word 'mill' with pejorative overtones it had not previously possessed (or which had lain dormant). Mills translate one thing into another, therefore, either benevolently or malevolently, depending on context – they grind **large** things into **small**, **cutting** them down to size. They **extract** things, too, but they may also be places of concealment and furtive evacuation. See **Millstones**

Millstones Millstones suggest **weight** and **burdens** – a steady **grinding** down of the **large** (the significant) into the **small** (the trivial). Like **mills** (and the action of the **hands** rubbing together), they can also be transformative and transmutative, blending the two into the one. See **Transformation**

Mind, The Freud categorized the mind as a 'modern state', in which the mob (see **Crowds**), eager for enjoyment and destruction, needed to be held down by a prudent superior class (the **superego**). The mind therefore set up and developed organizations to protect it from anarchy, and Freud soon came to realize that dreaming, or dream-distortion, was amongst the most effective of these organizations. Dreaming became, in Freud's words, 'the normal **psychosis** of mankind' – the reliever of unbearable tensions by compromise.

Mines Mines can often represent the **dreamer's unconscious** mind, and to this extent there may a semantic link with the possessive adjective 'mine'. Mines may also suggest hidden resources and concealed emotions, particularly if they find themselves linked with **water**. See **Hiding**

Ministers Traditionally speaking, ministers used to represent the Confucian concept of enlightened **guidance**, but in view of more recent perceptions concerning the downgrading of political **obligations** of duty to ones of narrow electoral expediency, there may be pejorative overtones to ministers, now, as well – in the sense of curtailers of individual freedoms, perhaps, hidden under the guise of social inclusion or dubious (that is to say non-objective) moral imperatives.

Mirrors Mirrors can symbolize the capacity of the **unconscious** to **reflect** the true image of the **dreamer**, an image that may at first shock or dismay the recipient. It may be helpful to remember that in Greek **mythology**, Medusa (the **female**, **snake**-haired Gorgon), could only be viewed in a mirror, or reflected in a **shield**. If her **face** was seen without such protection, the observer would be turned to **stone**. Once killed, though, Medusa's **blood** created the winged **horse**, Pegasus, and poetic inspiration followed.

Miscarriages Many women **dream** of miscarriages, often disguised by other things such as dropped articles, or objects flushed away or swept (see **Sweeping**) down **rivers** into the **sea**. Miscarriages may represent truncated plans, too, as well as ambitions unrealized. The simple derailing of a **train** (a miscarriage, if ever there was one) may form a semantically linked adjunct or correlative to the original emotion, and the concept of **missing** might also find its way into the dream. See **Abortions** & **Waste**

Misers Miserliness of one sort or another afflicts many **people**, and may represent a reasonable response to occasional want, or else a more figured approach, reflecting moral concerns about limited natural resources. Then there is miserliness just for the sake of it, or to afford us power over others. The hoarding of things is also an **anxiety** adjunct, suggesting a **concentration** on the future to the detriment of the present – if we possess something, it carries with it the implication that others cannot possess it at the same **time**.

Missing Missing something or someone is a typical **anxiety** trope, guaranteed to set the **dreamer's** nerves on edge, and to fill them with a sense of incompleteness. We all **fear** or **mourn** missed opportunities, and fantasize (more than we sometimes care to admit) about what-might-have-beens. Missing can also suggest **sexual** malfunction or ineptitude, and may even contain revocations of sterility in a **male**, or, in a **female**, the inability to become **pregnant** when one desires to do so. See **Miscarriages**

Mist Mist obfuscates – it makes it harder to distinguish between **friend** and **enemy**, safety and **danger**. Mist can also trick **people** into imagining they are somewhere they are not, and this element is of particular importance in a **dream** context, because of its possible effect on future behaviour and perception. Mist is also temporary, and presupposes the hope that we shall one day emerge from it, and into the clear **light** of reason and understanding. See **Fog** & **Smog**

Mneme Memories contained in actual **body** cells, according to a theory postulated by German evolutionary biologist Richard Semon (1859–1918).

Moats Moats represent final **obstacles** just before the achievement of a desired **goal** – they are also defences that we put up to stop others from approaching us too closely. The draining of a moat may appear to presuppose a lowering of defences, but it can just as well symbolize the lowering of one's emotional **guard**.

Mobile Phones One really doesn't relish drawing attention to this, but mobile **telephones** are undoubtedly **phallic symbols**, and that is likely to be their major symbolical use in **dream** terms. They are infinitely manipulable, they afford **pleasure** to their possessor, they are intrusive, they demand attention, they are antisocial, and they are about the size and **shape** of the average **penis**, give or take a centimetre or two (and a mild suspension of disbelief). They are, in addition, **fetish** objects, and much care and attention is lavished upon them – their size is significant (in inverse proportion to their power), and they are a means of domination (travel on any train and you'll get my gist), as well as being a sure sign of **sexual** status (ringing, *ergo* erect, implies importance – **silent**, *ergo* flaccid, implies neglect).

Mobs See **Crowds**

Models Models (of the **plastic** and balsawood variety) are virtual recreations of existing dynamic states – they can also act as pointers (see **Pointing**) towards intended outcomes, for we humans are prone to emulate what we covet the most. Fashion models take this concept one step further, acting as pictorialized arbiters of futile aspiration.

Modesty Excessive modesty in a **dream** may disguise invitation, for modesty, like many of its closely allied emotions, is often triggered by **fear**. This is particularly the case when mimicry of **animal** behaviour comes to the fore, as in the approach/retreat syndrome, in which an initial approach is followed by a **retreat** (or a circuit), followed by another, marginally closer approach. The animal or person doing the approaching is thus effectively communicating their desire whilst hedging their bets in case of rejection or aggression on the part of the desired object.

Moles Traditionally, a mole symbolizes **blindness** or obtuseness. Moles seem to be persistent (although how much this is a **projection** of our own discomfort with their presence, is a moot point). They are **velvety** and intrusive, too, and to that extent they may have **phallic** connotations, particularly when dreamt of by a woman – for the act of bursting out into the fresh **air** surrounded by a **shower** of dirt is undoubtedly **ejaculatory** (at least in the pictorial sense).

Monasteries Monasteries appear to be places of **retreat** and tranquillity (at least to non-monks) – to **monks**, of course, they are proactive places, suggestive of confluence with the Godhead. This paradox makes them particularly interesting in **dream** terms, more for what they suggest about the state of **mind** of the **dreamer**, than for any wider symbolical relevance. To dream of a monastery (in the present-day climate of apparently unregenerate non-spirituality) is significant in itself.

Money Money is often a **symbol** of faeces or **excrement** in a **dream**, for the accumulation of money can represent **constipation** (at least in **Freudian** terms). Money is also a concretized symbol for the abstract concept of **love**.

Monkeys A monkey symbolises **tricks** and the automatic **mind**. In dream terms, they may also be taken to represent a perceived loss of freedom, for although monkeys resemble us in many ways and nominally have greater freedom than we do (the capacity to swing from **branches**, for instance), they are also prized as domestic **pets** and as amusing denizens of intrusive **zoos**. Monkeys are also imitators (see **Imitations**) – something we choose to believe is only done by **people** or **animals** of inferior intelligence to ourselves. In **dreams**, of course, we frequently find ourselves imitating monkeys.

Monks A monk can very often represent the dreamer's **brother**, both semantically and symbolically – for similar **taboos** exist in both cases. A monk may also suggest a desire for chastity, or provide a convenient **symbol** with which the **dreamer** can fend off unwanted intrusion, **sexual** or otherwise. See **Monasteries** & **Nuns**

Monsters We conjure up monsters in our **dreams** to dilute their capacity to frighten us in real life, for the true effect of monsters relies largely on first impressions – they shock us, thereby taking away our capacity to think rationally (that's why they're monsters). Their fantasy appearance in dreams rather than in the everyday, therefore, may allow us a crucial few moments to take stock both of them and of ourselves (aspected through the monster), and to formulate a counterattack to the threat that they appear to pose. Monsters, needless to say, can also represent aspects of ourselves that we **fear** to let loose (or wish to **chain** up), like King Kong running amok in New York City's Radio City Music Hall. See **Beauty and the Beast**
KEY LINE: 'I started from my sleep with horror; a cold dew covered my forehead, my teeth chattered, and every limb became convulsed: when, by the dim and yellow light of the moon, as it forced its way through my window shutters, I beheld the wretch – the miserable monster whom I had created.' (From Mary Shelley's *Frankenstein* 1818)

Monuments Monuments frequently symbolize memories when they appear in **dreams**. Monuments may also have **phallic** connotations, but these are not necessarily at the forefront of the **dreamer**'s **mind**. They may also stand in for the **superego**, and a small monument may indicate **Christ**.

Moon, The In many traditional cultures the moon was perceived to have a masculine aspect, with the **sun** taking on the feminine role. Modern western culture sees the moon as predominantly feminine, however, possibly on account of its purported influence on **female** menses and moods. With this in mind, moon **dreams** tend towards the intuitive and the seemingly irrational (**love**, for instance), reflecting the moon's **invisible** influence over so-called rational beings. The moon may also symbolize the **mother**, **wife**, or **daughter**, with the **father**, **husband**, or **brother** role being taken by the sun. The moon may also surprise us by shedding **light** on darkened places, – in imitation of its sudden habit of appearing, particularly when full, from behind **clouds**. See **Menstruation** & **Planets**

Moose Moose are notable for their size (see **Bigness**), and for the **weight** of **horn** that they **carry** around on their **heads**. In dream terms they are likely to symbolize power, therefore, both physical and mental – but as they are constantly being threatened by **cars** and by **guns** and by **people** on motorized sleds, the power they exemplify will tend to derive from **nature**, and not from **mechanical** means.

Morality Dreaming of morality presupposes its **absence** from some aspect of the **dreamer**'s life. The **dream**, in this case, may be acting in a **compensatory** capacity (see **Body Image**), endeavouring to make up for the lack (or the moral lacuna) in the dreamer's everyday routine. Alternatively, the dream may be rectifying a perceived wrong (akin to outraged virtue in the awakened person), and this may be seen as compensatory, too. Finally, the morality image may be acting as a **warning** about the potential social **dangers**, were the dreamer to behave in an uncontrolled and **id**-driven way. See **Immoral Dreams** & **Punishment Dreams**

Morning Morning often represents renewal, and the possibilities of **self**-betterment. It is also the symbol of youth, and of prospects ahead. Morning, too, may imply the lifting of the **fear** of **death** (*ergo* the **night**), or even relief that something unwanted or distressing has – for the time being at least – gone away. Dreaming of morning tends towards the optimistic, therefore, and the upbeat – unless, of course, one is a condemned **prisoner**.

Mortgages Mortgages are **debts**, and they are therefore **anxiety** inducing. They may also stand in for the **fear** of the loss of our **homes** (*ergo* our lives), or for periods when our security is threatened (familial or monetary). Mortgages can also represent pacts we have made, with ourselves or others, and whose details and possible outcome hang heavy upon us.

Mortuaries Mortuaries are temporary places, equivalent, in many ways, to **limbo**. They are neither here nor there, in other words – neither one thing, nor the other. There may also be an aspect of wishful thinking in the mortuary image, as if the **dreamer** were being tempted to say that, well, perhaps **death** *is* preferable to **struggle** after all. The mortuary image may then act as a deterrent, warning the dreamer of whatever such thoughts may eventually lead to.

Morpheus Morpheus was the **son** of **Hypnos**, **God** of **Sleep**. His name, in Greek, means a '**shape**' or a 'form', and the job his **father** gave him was, indeed, to shape our **dreams**.

Morphine Dreams Many **writers** have described their medically-induced morphine **dreams** (most recently playwright Simon Gray, in his *The Smoking Diaries*). This **author**, too, remembers, with unpleasant vividness, the grotesquely enlarged **faces** of those caring for him, and the firm conviction that he was being **tortured** or made to suffer by people (the **night nurses** in particular) who were nominally there to help. The paradox of being **pain**-free, thanks to the morphine, but also beset by imagined discomfort (due to its effects), can therefore be unsettling in the extreme. See **Bigness**

Morse Code S. F. B. Morse claimed to have happened upon the solution to his Morse Code whilst he lay in a state of 'profound abstraction' – or in what is otherwise known as a **waking dream**.

Mosques Mosques will have a different symbolic value for Muslims and non-Muslims. For a Muslim they may represent continuity, identity, and community. For a non-Muslim they may epitomize strangeness, exclusion, and possibly even the exotic. Just as with **churches**, there is likely to be a spiritual element to the **dream** image, as well as a tentative link with the **superego**.

Motels Motels are commonly associated with transience, cheapness, and succour in strange places. We can **count** on a motel, whilst finding it at the same time just a little bit distasteful – rather like an elderly, wise, but notoriously unkempt, uninvited, and *tout-à-fait* drunken friend, who insists on favouring us with his attentions at a status-conscious and rather precious formal reception. In their **sexual** guise, receptive motels (**female symbols**) are entered by **cars** (**male** symbols), and are apt to represent fleeting, or snatched affection.

Mother Earth See **Earth**, **Great Mother**, **Mothers** & **Planets**

Mothers The mother, in **dreams**, is often represented by a **queen**, a **nurse**, a **servant**, the **Virgin Mary**, or some other impersonal symbol such as the **earth** or a **fountain**. These **symbols** protect the **dreamer** from the odium society might conceivably hold them in were they to undermine the maternal force too overtly (the **breaking** down of the mother ideal). The mother is also associated with **Freud**'s notion of the **Oedipus Complex** and **taboos**. In addition, the mother may also represent the **uterus**, the **superego**, or even the Virgin Mary herself. In purely non-noumenal terms she may equate with **Jung**'s notion of the **collective unconscious**. See **Fathers**

Motorcycles A motorcycle balances two mandalas. This may seem a little far fetched, but the **mandala** is a curiously intrusive **symbol**, manifesting itself even when the **dreamer** is ignorant of its significance. A motorcycle may also represent the **eyes**, the **breasts**, or any bodily attribute which contains a parallel, or physical equivalent, to itself. Underway, the two **wheels** of the motorcycle are seen to harmonize, one with the other, and this element (or desire) for harmonic balance often lurks somewhere behind the image.

Motorways See **Freeways**

Mounds Mounds are usually **sexual** in meaning, a **reading** predicated on the shape of the **female breast**, pudendum, buttocks, or the aptly named mound of **Venus**, in the case of **male dreamers**, or the **testicles**, the buttocks, the flaccid **penis**, and the **male** pectoral **muscles**, when dreamt of by women. If one stretches out one's **hands** without aforethought, they generally shape themselves into an inverted mound, as if one were instinctively seeking something conical to grasp. As a result, mounds may also symbolize growth, shaping, or **construction**.

Mountain Passes Mountain passes are often **symbols** of transition from one state (or level of consciousness) to another.

Mountains Climbing mountains represents an upward **journey** by the **dreamer**'s **ego** towards a more elevated state of consciousness. Mountains can also symbolize the **female breast**.

Mourning To **dream** of mourning implies the loss of something or someone close to the **dreamer**'s **heart**. And what is closest to the dreamer's **unconscious** heart? Why, the dreamer, of course. So we are usually mourning some aspect of ourselves during crêpe-laden dreams – our **childhood**, for instance, or the cause of certain unresolved **guilt** feelings that we carry disguised within us.

Moustaches Moustaches are roughly similar to **beards** in their **sexual** significance. They call attention to the **mouth** (an antediluvian stand-in for the **vagina**), and to the **phallic nose**. They are (predominantly) **male** attributes, and their **colour** and texture may delineate the age, or potential sexual potency of the wearer. Moustaches can also be alienating (they may act as a **hedge** in front of the mouth, for instance) and they can have institutional connotations, or even suggest conformity.

Mouth, The Symbolically speaking, the mouth is an expression of the indwelling **self**, of consciousness, and of the given condition. Pictorially, being an external **organ**, it equates with the **vagina** and the **anus** and with **wounds** to the **body**. The open mouth suggests **death** or ecstasy, whilst the closed mouth suggests **anger**, **frigidity**, or displeasure. A disembodied mouth appearing in **dreams** may suggest spiritual communication of one sort or another (perhaps even a message from **God**), while concentration on the mouth of another person tends towards the **masturbatory** or the solipsistic. Silent, although still moving mouths, may suggest difficulties in communication, or the uttering of words one does not want to hear.

Movement Continual movement in **dreams** may indicate disquiet, or other forms of **anxiety** – in certain cases, though, dependent on context (and in the absence of anxiety adjuncts) it may also suggest progression through flux. **Backward movement** may usually be taken to be negative, as is the case with downward movement. Forward or upward movement may have more positive connotations, expressing aspiration or exalted endeavour. See **Above** & **Below**

Movies See **Films**

Mucus Mucus is a by-product of physical change – it is something that usually needs to be expelled by the **body** as fast as possible, or else it will go on to cause chain-reactive physical **damage**. The Hippocratic and Chaucerian concept of **humours** (**blood**, phlegm, **yellow** bile and **black** bile) goes a long way towards explaining mucus' dream symbology, and the **body**'s dependence on environmental and 'natural' factors for its well-being. **Dreams** of mucus would tend to indicate that something is not quite **right** (i.e. disharmonious) with the environment in which the **dreamer** finds themselves. See **Secretions**

Mud Mud equates with primal ooze in **dream** terms – it invests us, and we it. Thanks to its numerous semantic connotations, mud may also be proactive (mud slinging) and reflexive (mud sticks). It may also be constructive, or indicative of hidden **treasures**, prosaically disguised.

Muffs Muffs, thanks to both their **shape** and their semantic connotations, are more often than not synonymous with the **vagina**.

Mules A mule symbolizes obstinacy. A **kicking** mule may indicate **fears** of aggression by **strangers**, or by the **world**-at-large. Traditionally, young women who dreamt of **white** mules were thought to be more than likely to marry **wealthy** foreigners.

Mummies A complex image, this, creating a semantic and pictorial **chain** between Egyptian mummies, **mothers**, swaddling **clothes**, papooses, **life**, **death**, **birth** and disintegration. Symbolically, a mummy suggests both calcification of the personality and purification (putrefaction?), leading to delayed transcendence – the human tampering with **nature**, in other words, ultimately driven by **fear** and not acceptance.

Mumps Dreaming of mumps may suggest blocked energy **channels**, or **fears** of sterility and potential **castration complexes** (in **males**). In **female** terms mumps might suggest **damage** to relationships through faulty communication, twinned with a concomitant **suppression** or **repression** of true **feelings**.

Murder Murder, being an aggressive (and nominally **extrovert**) act, frequently disguises the **killing** off of aspects of oneself in a **dream**. The murderee is all important here, as he or she will indicate what facets of the **dreamer**'s personality are under threat or 'need to go'. **Suppression** of **sexual** feelings, catastrophic **failures** of communication and unfulfilled ambitions, are all potential cause for murderous **feelings** towards oneself or others. To be pursued by a murderer implies a crisis of confidence in oneself, and symbolizes the letting in of outside forces which then threaten to overtake the newly-fledged (and almost invariably **self**-referential) **victim**. See **Murderers**
KEY LINE: 'Filled with disgust and remorse for having destroyed something so great and beautiful, I turned to flee, impelled by the fear that the murder might be discovered. But a tremendous downfall of rain began, and I knew that it would wipe out all memories of the deed.'
(From C. G. Jung's *Memories, Dreams, Reflections* 1963)

Murderers Human beings have a disastrous tendency to **murder** all their darlings (*pace* F. Scott Fitzgerald) in a misguided desire for an unsustainable, and largely unrealizable, perfection. It is as if we can't accept how and what we are, and need to **monkey** with the motherboard in a (usually) futile attempt to improve things. This murderousness tends to develop out of **childhood frustrations** at perceived inadequacies relating to **height**, power, influence, and the **suppressed** envy of others. Psychologist **Alfred Adler** categorized all this inadequately expressed rage as a symptom of the unmasking of the **inferiority complex**.
KEY LINE: 'He was overcome with frenzy and he began hitting the old woman on the head with all his force, but at every blow of the axe the laughter and whispering from the bedroom grew louder and the old woman was simply shaking with mirth.' (From Fyodor Dostoevsky's *Crime and Punishment* 1866)

Muscle Muscle functions underneath the surface of things, acting as an invisible **driving** force. For a **dreamer** to see beneath their own **skin** suggests a desire to scratch below the external strata of perceived motivations and down to the nitty-gritty, as it were.

Museums Museums frequently stand in for memories and recollections when they appear in **dreams**. They are what we inherit from the **past**, and they can either enrich us or **weigh** us down, depending on context and perception. Museums may also symbolize the accretion of unnecessary objects or personal adjuncts which can, if we are not very careful, get in the way of the smooth **running** of our lives. See **Memorials** & **Recollective Dreams**

Mushrooms See **Funguses**

Music The making of music may, at times, be equated with masculinity, or the concept of dominance – such a **reading** might be personified by the image of a **conductor**, say. Music occurring not at the instigation of another person, but as a result of natural rhythmic action and enlightened coordination, is another matter entirely, and suggests creativity and the communality of adaptive acceptance. The Pythagorean notion of the 'music (or harmony) of the spheres' represents a spontaneous, ineffable order, akin to perfection, and is roughly equivalent to the Nirvana concept in Buddhism. See **Pianos**

Musicians The **mother** of the virtuoso violinist, Nicolo Paganini (1782–1840), claimed to have received a **precognition** foretelling her **son**'s particular **gifts**. An **angel** appeared to her in a **dream** and asked her what she most wanted. 'That my son shall become the greatest of violinists,' she answered. When her infant son showed an unfortunate tendency towards the **piano**, Paganini's mother lambasted him with her **vision** until he agreed to returned to the fiddle. See **Tartini**

Muteness Being mute may often equate to **castration** fears in the **male**, being a generally involuntary affliction. There may also be a semantic link between 'muteness' and 'mutilation'.

Myoclonic Jerk A spontaneous muscular contraction that occurs whilst **sleeping** or dreaming. When a myoclonic jerk occurs while dozing, it is often as a result of the **body** beginning to relax, and then catching itself as it falsely perceives itself '**falling**'.

Mysticism Mysticism, in **dreams**, tends to suggest the existence of unknown, or unfathomable, quantities. It may reflect the spiritual ambitions of the **dreamer** (a contradiction in terms, surely), pointing up a desire to force issues, rather than to accept and investigate one's already established condition. See **Mystics**

Mystics Mystics in **dreams** generally equate to spiritual **teachers** or guides who appear to hold **secrets** that we may wish to access – secrets such as the answer to the tantalizing but ultimately frustrating question of the Mystic Knot, which has neither beginning nor end to it, and may or may not hold the **key** to the understanding of the universe. See **Frustration Dreams**

Mythology See **Myths**

Myths Myths are convenient and expedient fictions that nevertheless frequently represent the **truth**. Their importance in **dream** terms lies predominantly in their suggestive quality – why has the dreamer's **unconscious** mind chosen such-and-such a myth as a frame for its metafictions? What does it represent for the **dreamer**? How does it apply to their lives? What does it tell us about their hidden motivations? Replayed in the revealing and lurid **light** of day, what **archetypes** does it throw up, and why? And is it behaviourally consistent with rational morality? And if not, why not?

N

Nails To a Christian, nails inevitably bring to mind the **crucifixion**, and the nails – rumoured to have been forged by a **gypsy** smith, and thus, in many gypsies' eyes, the cause of all the discrimination against them, leading to their curse of perpetual exile – that secured **Christ** to the **cross**. Nails have many other possible revocations, too, including keeping away the **plague** from cottages, and fastening **horseshoes** to **thresholds** in order to ward off the **evil eye**. In certain circumstances they may stand in for the **penis** and its **stabbing** action, and to that extent they can equate to **knives** and other potentially intrusive implements in terms of the first **layer** (the **manifest content**) of **dream** symbology.

Nakedness Nakedness, or being inappropriately clothed in public places, is a **recurring dream** motif. **Freud** maintained that such **dreams** constituted a **regression** to infantile exhibitionism, and that dreams of this sort represented a **wish-fulfilment** fantasy. An alternative theory holds that inapposite nakedness in a dream represents feelings of **inferiority** and the existence of perceived shortcomings in the **dreamer**. Clothing, in this context, is the **mask** behind which the dreamer usually hides. In their dreams, however, this mask is withdrawn, showing the dreamer in their true **nature**, and often in a public **arena** where everybody can see and criticize them, and in which they have no obvious alternative means of protection. See **Clothes** & **Skin**
KEY LINE: 'Some whimsical person died, and it appeared by his will that he had left me an estate of ten thousand pounds a-year, on condition that I should never again wear breeches, pantaloons, trousers, or any other modification of the masculine garb.' (From Robert Southey's *Diaries* 10th May 1832)

Names The names of places, objects and **symbols** in **dreams** often have elucidatory value. The word Brideshead, for instance, might imply a virgin **bride**, a **veil**, or **virginity** (as in maidenhead), as well as indicating a place. The Ancients believed that a **name** actually formed a part of the person who bore it. Common **male** names like John, Dick, Henry and Harry can often carry **phallic** connotations, as can relational euphemisms such as old chap, my **friend**, my **boy**, my **brother**, my chum, etc. **Female** names containing **vaginal** connotations might include Rose, Petal and Carmen (in the sense of the **colour**, carmine), whilst virginal connotations might be carried by Mary, Constance, and, inevitably, Chastity.

Nappies Nappies are both protective and concealing – to that extent they resemble the **biblical** concept of the 'whited' sepulchre'. They allow an infant to mess itself at will, while protecting third parties not from the certainty, but from the suspicion of the certainty. They are the equivalent, therefore, of **sweeping** something under the **table** to be sorted out later.

Narcissism Self-love, as personified by the beautiful Narcissus, who was doomed by the goddess Nemesis to fall helplessly in **love** with his own image in revenge for his slighting of the **nymph** Echo. See **Imago**

Narco-analysis Drug-induced information retrieval of otherwise unretrievable facts from an individual's **unconscious** mind.

Narco-hypnosis The inducing of **hypnosis** by the use of narcotics.

Narcolepsy Falling asleep uncontrollably, and at inappropriate **times** – i.e. during the day (except in the case of Hispanics, Latin Americans and other adherents of the siesta, needless to say). Can also be associated with loss of **muscle** tone due to enforced inertia.

Narcosis A profound state of unconsciousness triggered by the use of narcotics. A **drug**-induced stupor, in other words.

Narco-synthesis The synthesis or concretization of information retrieved by the use of **hypnotic drugs**. See **Narco-hypnosis**

Narrowness Narrowness, **claustrophobia**, and the experience of **childbirth** may all be linked. **Dreams** of narrow **passages** may also represent perceived limitations and the closing down of possible **horizons**. 'Because strait is the gate, and narrow is the way, which leadeth unto life, and few there be that find it.' (Matthew vii, 14)

Nash, Paul (1889–1946) Nash, an official **war artist** for the British in both of the 20th century's World Wars, painted *Landscape From a Dream* between 1936 and 1938. A **hawk** looks at its **double** in a **mirror**, while its mechanical counterpart, a fighter **plane**, **bombs** the **landscape**. In front of it, strange **balls** and circular objects roll around on a canvas laid into the landscape itself, and one of the balls rolls out of the canvas onto what we can only assume is a real **field**, symbolizing war's disconnective power.

Nature Nature, nakedness, and simplicity (even to the extent of **idiocy**) are all connected, both semantically and historically. For centuries, unrestricted nature was viewed as backward and uncivilized – we now pay lip service to the opposite view, while craftily hanging on to all the convenient appurtenances of the mechanized **world**. Nature and simplicity, though, still remain inextricably linked, and are likely to do so in the **dream** world, too.

Nausea Nausea is **nature**'s way of telling us that we have made a mistake, and need to take stock – that we are retaining articles or habits that we don't really need anymore, and that they are making us **ill**. See **Vomiting**

Navel, The The navel represents something that was once crucial to us, but that we no longer have any use for. It is a **memorial** to a past **life**, and symbolic of broken connectivity. On a more positive note, its presence or significance in a **dream** may reinforce the possibilities of connection, given the **right** sort of a context – a tightly sealed navel might suggest security, for instance, whereas a navel through which things **leak** or **escape** would tend to suggest the opposite.

Navy, The The Navy might be taken to represent society and the **super-ego** – an institutionalized **self-discipline** using existing structures, but centred in the emotions (the **water** connection).

Neatness Excessive neatness is now often associated with **anal** retentiveness, and there may be some truth in this. However, neatness is hardly pejorative, and neither does it need to be exclusive. The simple act of getting oneself organized can mitigate **anxiety** issues, and 'neat' **dreams** most probably fulfil such a function.

Nebuchadnezzar King Nebuchadnezzar of Babylon forgot one of his kingly **dreams**. **Frustrated**, he called all his wise men together and insisted that they remember his dream for him and then interpret it, or else he would **kill** them. Faced with this quandary, the wise men cried *caprivi*, and prepared for **death**. The prophet Daniel, though, saw this as an opportunity to demonstrate the power of **God** to the **king**, and God conveniently gave him knowledge of the dream (with His **eye**, one supposes, on the main chance). The dream was of a burnished image with **feet** of clay. Daniel duly interpreted the dream (it somewhat conveniently described the Kingdom of Heaven), and Nebuchadnezzar, not a little taken aback, showered him and his companions with **gifts** and high **offices**. This story was written in the 6th century BC. It certainly couldn't happen now.

Necklaces Necklaces resemble **mandalas**, and, like mandalas, they probably represent **bridges** between our higher and lower **natures**. They may also, on occasion, suggest voluntary possession, as when the acceptance of a necklace symbolizes an acknowledgment of belongingness by the person who receives it to the person who gives it. See **Pendants**

Necks Necks are susceptible areas, and when we trust someone enough to reveal our neck to them and thus make ourselves vulnerable, it usually implies the voluntary undertaking of a **risk** on the understanding that a *quid pro quo* might conceivably come our way – as in the expression 'sticking one's neck out for good reason', or 'you show me yours, I'll show you mine'.

Neckties Neckties are often a **symbol** of the **penis**. They may also suggest **millstones**, or unwanted, even stultifying, responsibilities. A necktie may also be a **badge** of respectability, according a sort of conformist

invisibility to the wearer, **mirrored** in their near iconic status (together with **male sock garters**) in Victorian and Edwardian **pornography**.

Needles Needles are designed to be penetrative, and so there are inevitable oneiric **links** with the **male** member and with **sexual** activity. Moving beyond that, however, needles can represent the outward healing the inward, or the outer **poisoning** the inner (as with **drugs**). Either way, they are external artefacts, pricking us towards change or flux.

Negation Denial. **Freud** maintained that negation is extremely rare in **dreams**, and usually implies its opposite. An example might be a dream in which the **dreamer** states, on **waking**, that 'so and so was not in my dream'. This usually indicates an **unconscious** desire that 'so and so' should not be there, or that the dreamer finds their presence uncongenial or painful in some way and therefore blocks them out of the dream. See **Affirmation**

Neologisms The coining of new words and word orders often occurs in the **condensation** stage of **dream work**. They are a necessary part of the **language** of the **dream**.

Nests Nests, in **dream** imagery, are frequently **symbols** of the **vagina**. They may also prefigure either a desire to **escape** from, or to create, a functional domestic situation.

Nets We generally set out nets to trap (see **Entrapment**) desired objects, or to become trapped, in our turn (sometimes voluntarily) – but nets can, in addition, represent symbolical mechanisms for the acquisition of spiritual, cognitive, and astral (in the sense of exalted) individuality. A **golden** net, for instance, represents the Buddhic image of the idealized universe, to which and in which the infant **Gautama Buddha** was carried by the four wise Brahmins, followed by the four Maharajas (**kings** of the Cosmos).

Nettles Nettles are irritants, holding one back from doing something one wants to do, or preventing one from going where one wants to go. However, they are usually small irritants, and, with willpower and forethought, it is possible to drive one's way through them without undue discomfort. To that extent they may equate with a benevolent **rite-of-passage**, and may even, should one be 'stung into action' by them, present dividends, in the shape of purification or other such salutary mechanisms. See **Stinging**.

Neurasthenia Slightly old-fashioned term implying physical prostration or extreme **fatigue** due to a malfunctioning or disturbance of the nervous system.

Neurosis A common psychiatric disorder which may stem from, or manifest itself in, **depression**, **anxiety**, or hypochondria. The Austrian **psychologist Alfred Adler** maintained that all neurotics strive towards a **secret goal**, and that this goal is a quest for power. Neuroses may appear in **dreams** in the guise of **people**, **animals**, religious or secular iconography, **buildings**, or even mental **symptoms** which disguise the actual workings of the neurosis from the **dreamer**. If this seems a little far-fetched, it should be remembered that **Freud** exemplified the **compulsion** neurosis, for instance, as a 'personal religion'. It is not a great step onwards from this to an understanding of how a sealed-in **church**, to take but one random example, may exemplify a similar neurosis within the context of a dream. The conflict between our **instincts** and our desire for **morality** (the **id** and the **superego**), twinned with its inevitable consequence, **repression**, is at the base of most neuroses. Dreams themselves cannot cause neurosis, but they may anticipate neurotic symptoms. **Wilhelm Stekel** summed up the position with his customary succinctness: 'To be healthy means to overcome the **past**.' See **Neurotic Clauses, Neurotic Arrangement & Obsessions**

Neurotic Arrangement **Adler**'s term for the **unconscious** desire to keep or maintain certain neurotic elements in place, despite an apparent or consciously expressed desire to obviate them. See **Neurosis** & **Neurotic Clauses**

Neurotic Clauses Schemes unconsciously designed by the **dreamer** to counteract discovery of their **neurosis**, or its cause. Such clauses are of fundamental importance in **dream analysis**, and need to be teased out. The most obvious neurotic clauses are probably the '**death clause**' and the 'chastity clause', in which the **fear** of **death**, or the onset of **impotence**, appears to protect the neurotic from the consequences of desired actions, while, in actuality, they merely confirm the presence of the neurosis. See **Neurotic Arrangement**

Newness The sudden appearance of things which are preternaturally new, untouched, or pristine in a **dream,** most probably find their trigger in **fears** about **death**, disintegration, and the loss of physical beauty due to age – real life obsessional shopping may stem from a similar source (the obsessive replacement of the old by the new). Newness may also find itself linked to **virginity**, or to an overly high (even **neurotic**) valuation of it. On a more positive note, new objects may sometimes suggest new approaches, or new ways of looking at existing situations (with the object symbolizing the situation – a **suitcase** representing uprootal, perhaps, or a **book** suggesting the **past**).

Newspapers Newspapers tell us things, and that is their most likely function within a **dream**, too – as **messengers**, or harbingers of ill tidings (headlines, unfortunately, are rarely cheerful). We may even learn of our own **deaths**, or of bad news that we were suppressing and which bursts out of our **unconscious** minds in the form of hack journalism – just as **kings** would often **kill** the messenger who brought them bad news, so **dreamers** can metaphorically throw away the newspaper that brings them news they'd rather not confront.

New Year The New Year inevitably represents the possibility of a symbolical new **beginning**. Its perpetual repetition may indicate that the desire for a new beginning is becoming **neurotic**, as in the repeated but serially failed desire to **diet**, or to give up **smoking cigarettes**. See **Repetitive Motifs**

Niches Niches represent **sanctuaries** – somewhere off the beaten **track** in which we can **hide**. They may also represent **pedestals** upon which we can put things (or ideas) which we wish to cherish. The fact that niches protect us from the back is also relevant, as this may imply a **fear** of intrusion that most probably originates in infancy, when we first descried our vulnerability beyond the orbit of maternal protection (and the niche-like **symbol** of the maternal **stomach**).

Night Night can protect, and it can threaten, depending on one's perception of it. A country dweller (see **Countryside**), for instance, may welcome night as revelatory and softly welcoming – an urban dweller, who rarely encounters true night due to **light** pollution, may view night very differently. Night may also represent **death**, or it may represent the covering up of things that are normally visible – **secrets**, in other words, and things we fear to reveal. Finally, night may represent our inability to make things out, or to see clearly – a form of mental obfuscation which would necessitate firm action (the **striking** of a **match**, for example) to deactivate. See **Darkness**

Nightingales A nightingale traditionally symbolizes forlornness. In Greek **myth**, Philomela was **raped** by Tereus, **King** of Thrace, who then **cut** out her **tongue** to prevent her telling his **wife** (her **sister**) Procnë of what had happened. Philomela then communicated the news to her sister by **tapestry**, upon which Procnë cut up their **son** and served him to Tereus on a platter (see **Plates**). Enraged, Tereus pursued the two women, but the **Gods**, appalled by the **chain** of events, changed all three into **birds** – Tereus into a **hawk** (or hoopoe), Procnë into a **swallow**, and Philomela into a **nightingale** (a rather nice symbolical twist, that one – from **muteness** to euphony in one fell swoop). What all this has to do with **dreams escapes** me, but it's a splendid story.

Nightmares Physically or psychically repressive **dreams**. **Children**'s nightmares are often triggered by outside forces such as respiratory problems, adenoidal complaints, or **stomach** upsets – on occasion, too, they may be triggered by psychic or imaginative over-stimulation. Such nightmares are usually totally forgotten by the **morning**, and it is only when the nightmares consistently reoccur, even after medical treatment, that

something beyond an organic cause should be suspected. An adult nightmare, though, usually has a very different provenance – such nightmares generally correlate with outside, environmental pressures, or with internal **repressions**, often relating to **sexual** or **incestuous** motivations. See **Recurring Dreams** & **Repetitive Motifs**
KEY LINE: 'Restless and not good night, with the most unusual form of unpleasant nightmare. I had engaged myself (and with pleasure to the acceptants, evident, and to all their relations) to three delightful young ladies in the same day, and could neither decide which to keep, nor how to disengage the other two.' (From John Ruskin's *Diaries*, 29th December 1875)

Night Terrors A sudden **awakening**, occurring maybe an hour into **sleep**, due to an unnamed, and later unremembered, **fear**. It is an affliction that largely strikes **children** of between three and five **years** of age, but one that can, on occasion, continue into adulthood. See **Nightmares**

Nine Nine is traditionally held to be a **magic number**, and to represent the perfect form of the perfected. It also constitutes the threefold elevation of the **Trinity**.

Nine Eleven The number you call (given as nine-one-one) in the US for the **emergency** services, and also the **number** inextricably associated (now, no doubt, also psychically and oneirically) with the terrorist **attack** on New York's **Twin Towers** on 11th September 2001 (the ninth month and the 11th day, in US calendrical terminology).

Nirvana To **dream** of nirvana implies a desire to transcend one's present state and move into another, more advanced state of being – to a state beyond **ego**, and beyond human consciousness. Such an aspiration, needless to say, goes against the **grain** of what it sets out to seek, which is be beyond desire, and beyond volition.
KEY LINE: 'Dissolved is the body, extinct is perception; the sensations have all vanished away. The conformations have found their repose: the consciousness has sunk to its rest.' (The Buddha, speaking in Hermann Oldenberg's *Buddha* 1881)

Nonsense Dreamers are often mystified by the apparently nonsensical structure and content of some of their **dreams**. What appears to be nonsense, however, is frequently the aspect of the dream which conceals its most important element.

Nooses Nooses often represent the threat of being tied down, corresponding to the symbolical **umbilical cord** that still connects many of us to our **mothers**. Nooses may also suggest the **fear** of emotional traps (see **Entrapment**), or the fear of sudden **death**. Paradoxically, perhaps, the Noose of Varuna (in Hindu **mythology**) was a **symbol** of knowledge, and of the **love** of **truth** and **right**-mindedness.

North, The The North, to a Taoist Chinese, was a harbinger of gloom and pessimism. It also symbolized the **Black Tortoise**, with the implication of chaotic **beginnings** to any action about to be undertaken. To a **dream-er**, the north may indicate something that is far away, or marginally out of reach. See **East, South & West**

Noses Noses are obvious appendages – they pre-empt our **faces**, as it were, and give them character. They also expel flux and potentially ingest **disease**. We follow our noses (when we trust **instinct** over rationality), and we are led by the nose (when we **ditch** caution in favour of carnal-ity). 'Nose' carries a semantic link to 'knows', and bleeding at the nose was a traditional sign of **love**. Tycho Brahe (1546–1601), the Danish astronomer, was reputed to have had a **golden** nose made for him after he lost his own nose in a duel (not a lot of people know that). It was alleged-ly attached to his person by a cement of his own invention, which he car-ried with him at all times. Finally, the nose may stand in for the **penis** in certain **dreams**, something **reflected** in the old wives' saw (still current) that large noses in men denote equally outsized appendages.

Nostradamus (1503–66) To dream of Nostradamus might suggest a desire for miraculous (or simplistic) answers to difficult **questions**. This doesn't mean that Nostradamus was simplistic in himself (far from it), but merely that the perception of him relates more to answers than to questions. Nostradamus used a **number** of different prophetic methods to come to his conclusions about the future, one of which consisted of arti-ficially induced **dreams** through a method known as scrying (which involved the use of the reflective capacity of darkened **water** to trigger an altered state of consciousness). Yet another method involved the tak-ing of considerable quantities of **nutmeg** (believed to promote dreaming and **trance**) with a view to triggering the actions of the **unconscious** mind.

Notebooks Notebooks are reminders of the **past**, as well as being emblems of the future (we store them up for future reference). They are generally **self**-reflexive, and may suggest **secrets** that we subliminally wish for others to discover about us – our 'purported' rather than our 'true' selves, in other words.

Nourishment To dream of nourishment is generally to **dream** of the 'desire' for nourishment – this may be either spiritual, corporal, or emo-tional. Nourishment implies necessary sustenance which, in turn, implies the capacity for life. Nourishment may also contain health-giving indices, as well as providing a framework for Christian ideas about the transmu-tation of the **soul** into **Christ** during Holy Communion.

Novels Novels are elucidatory fictions – they are 'true' without, neces-sarily, telling the **truth**. To that extent they resemble **dreams**, in that their sum is (usually) more than their parts. Novels, like dreams, are also

self-referential, in that more is revealed about the **author** than he or she might at first suppose (or even desire). To dream of novels, therefore, is to dream of dreams.

Novelty Novelty implies change, or the desire for change. There may also be the desire to be taken out of oneself, or distracted from real issues that may cause discomfort (see **Changing Personae**). An amusing filmic example occurs in Peter Jackson's *King Kong* (2005), when Naomi Watts' Ann Darrow goes into her burlesque routine in an effort to distract (and, unwittingly, seduce) Kong.

Nuclear Explosions Nuclear **explosions** are manifestations of a **fear** of finality. There is, after all, no comeback from them – if the blast doesn't get you, the fallout will. To that extent they can represent apprehensions about the future, or of unforeseen, and possibly catastrophic, change. There may also be a suggestion of **paranoia**, and of an overarching fear of aggression by others.

Nudity See **Nakedness**

Nuggets On a **Freudian** level, nuggets probably equate with **testicles**, in that both may contain **rich secrets** (in the form of mineral **wealth**, or the ability to manufacture seminal fluid that may, conceivably, fertilize an **egg**). Nuggets are also hard and unyielding, and may embody obstructions, or other stoppages of natural **flows**, when they appear in the context of a **dream** context.

Numbers Numbers, particularly 'one' (the erection) and 'three' (the **penis** and **testicles**) are often viewed as **phallic** in **dream symbolism** – the number 'eight' may have mammary connotations, or refer to obesity. Numbers may also represent important **dates** or other numerologically significant aspects of the dreamer's life, such as **birthdays**, ages, numbers of **relatives**, **secret calendars** of meaningful events, or even disguises. The number 'six' often finds itself replacing **sex**, and 'ten' may relate to moral issues, as in the Ten Commandments. The significance of numbers though, while being to a certain extent communal, cannot be disentangled from the specific associations in the **dreamer**'s **mind**. When numbers appear to refer to amounts of **money** in **dreams**, the specific number is less important than the generalized concept of money, and its significance to the dreamer – money, of course, equates to '**love**' in dream terminology, and may occasionally have **anal** connotations, too.

Numbness Numbness implies the temporary lack of an ability to **feel** – we are numbed by shock, for instance, or by the **cold**. We can be numbed by emotions, too, and the physical sensation of numbness in a **dream** may also relate to an uncomfortable **body** position while **sleeping**, or to a **secret** desire by the **dreamer** to protect themselves (i.e. 'numb' themselves) from an altogether too intrusive emotion.

Numina Spirits or Gods that inhabit places, groves, or living objects, such as **stones**, **rivers** or **trees**. See **Numinosum**

Numinosum A term, coined by theoretician of mysticism Rudolf Otto (1869–1937) in his book *Idea of the Holy*, for anything and everything pertaining to the mystery of Divinity.

Nunneries See **Convents & Nuns**

Nuns Nuns may often represent the **dreamer**'s **sister** in **dreams**, and are subject to just as strict **taboos**. Nuns may also equate with the healing principle, or they may be sombre and threatening and indicative of **repression** and (**archetypally** unnatural) **sexual** abstention. See **Abstinence & Convents**

Nurses Nurses may be a **symbol** of either the **mother** or the **sister** in **dreams**. Nurses, particularly in **male** dreams, can also find themselves transmuted into prostitutes, for the simple reason that they are paid to look after others – they are, if you like, professional 'carers' (it should, perhaps, be reiterated here that **dreams** can be massive simplifications relying on blindingly obvious, and sometimes almost infantile, imagery). See **Harlot Fantasies**

Nurturing Nurturing and the maternal imperative are generally closely linked in **dream** terms. However, nurturing can also be linked to **sexual** servicing, causing potential Oedipal projections and swift **superego** intercessions when things threaten to get out of **hand**. See **Oedipus Complex**

Nutmegs Old English folklore had it that to **dream** of nutmegs portended changes in the **dreamer**'s life. Nutmegs, for obvious reasons, can also represent the **testicles** or the **ovaries**. See **Nostradamus**

Nuts Nuts were considered **symbols** of fertility and life-giving forces in pagan antiquity. More recently they have been linked to **love**, married life and childbirth. See **Birth & Nutmegs**

Nymphs In Greek **mythology**, nymphs tended to portend change – one was privileged to see them, in other words, and never quite the same again afterwards. They were the traditional guardians of feminine qualities, and the personification of the **female** for the **male**. They were purported to dwell in isolated natural areas (near **woods**, **rivers**, gorges, and glades) in which males, as **hunters** – rather than the more socialized and domestically driven females – were wont to lurk. They are an idealized alternative to real life women, therefore, and their appearance in **dreams** may, in consequence, be yet another manifestation of the (so often elusive) **anima**. See **Satyrs**

O

Oak Trees Oak **trees** were worshipped by the **Druids**, and were considered holy by many Indo-European peoples on account of their perceived link to **thunder** and **lightning**. Oaks may also relate to age (hoary as an old oak), or strength. See **Holiness**

Oars Oars drive one forwards, and thus may find themselves the antidote (or signifier) of rootlessness – one doesn't, by definition, need oars if one is **centred**, or on the **right track**, already. Somewhat inevitably, the rowing movement may also find itself linked to the **sexual** (or **masturbatory**) act – the respective **shape** of oar handles and rowlocks surely tell their own story in this regard. See **Paddles**

Oases Oases, like **niches**, suggest places of refuge, and even of **sanctuary**. Their link to **water** predisposes towards an emotional, rather than physical, refuge – somewhere the **dreamer** feels might restore their equanimity. 'Dates' and 'palms' have semantic connotations, too, and curious juxtapositions may occur, **leading** us swiftly away, if we are not careful, from the original motivating source of the dream image.

Oats Oats are a simple (i.e. fundamental) foodstuff, and **sowing**, having, or getting 'one's oats' is a simple (i.e. fundamental) euphemism for the **sexual** act. Both meanings involve fertility.

Obedience Dreaming of being obedient, or of forcing someone else to be obedient, inevitably harks back to **childhood** power struggles, and to a deep-seated (and perfectly natural) antagonism to parental authority – a more or less universal experience, unless one succeeds in neurotically repressing it. See **Neurosis**

Obelisks Obelisks, due to their **shape**, are often **phallic** in connotation, but they may also suggest spiritual or aesthetic striving (the upward movement – see **Above**). There may, too, be a **sacred** aspect to the image, implying some sacrosanct article or idea that may be left un-tampered with only by the expedient of setting it in **stone**.

Obesity See **Fatness**

Obituaries Curiously, to read one's own obituary may be an aspect of **wish-fulfilment**, in that, if one is still able to read, one is, by default, not yet dead. Many **people** (the **author** included) turn instinctively to the obituary column to discover – well, what? That someone of the same name as them is dead, leaving them still alive? Obituaries in **dreams** may perform a similar placatory function, reminding one of one's mortality, while at the same time offering up the comfort that one is not yet quite there.

Obligation Obligations come in many guises in **dreams**, and usually stem from **guilt**, rather than duty. An obligation often emerges only if one tries to **repress** it, and it may, in consequence, hijack inappropriate images in an effort to disguise itself from its progenitor. This aspect of expedient convenience is very common in dreams, and often gives rise to charivari (or seeming bedlam).

Obscenity Obscenity is usually **self**-referential, even though it may seem, at first glance, to be aimed outwards. Very often, too, it is merely the disguise for something else – a **red** herring, even – designed to mislead the **enemy** (for the enemy, read one's own capacity for enlightened self-understanding).

Obsessional Neurosis: See **Obsessions** & **Obsessive Compulsive Disorder**

Obsessions Morbid preoccupations with apparently trivial ideas or artefacts to the exclusion of rational thought. Such obsessions may reoccur in **dreams**, and their source needs to be pinpointed before a correct interpretation of the dream they are contained in may be attempted. See **Compulsions** & **Obsessive Compulsive Disorder**

Obsessive Compulsive Disorder The 'system' behind **obsessions** and **compulsions** (the overriding idea) can find itself reinforced and **locked** in by **anxiety**. The obsessive/compulsive may realize, logically, that if the compulsion is resisted, the anxiety may well be alleviated, while still being unable to achieve this non-anxious state through their own actions. This rationale may find itself reflected in **dreams** manifesting doubt, or even elements of **sado-masochism**. This 'doubting' element may function as an annulment, or alleviation, of **past** experiences – everything is suddenly put to the **question**, or even **blacked** out. The **symbols** which occur in such 'doubting' dreams are of considerable importance, and may help in pointing to the origins of the '**ceremonial**' element often contained within such a disorder.

Obstacles If the **dreamer**, in their **waking** life, customarily **represses** thoughts or actions that threaten them, then this behaviour is likely to be **mirrored** in **dream** terms. Freed from normal constraints, the **unconscious** mind will fabricate appealing situations in which these repressed instincts may potentially be let free – the **superego** will then intervene to put an obstacle in the way of the dreamer's enjoyment of their forbidden **fruit**. See **Moats** & **Repression**

Occult, The Freud wrote an interesting paper about 'The Occult Significance of Dreams' (1925), in which he describes both **prophetic** and **telepathic** dreams as possibly falling under the listing of 'occult' phenomena. He himself was in no doubt that prophetic **dreams** existed, and **questioned** only their subsequent accuracy (a very Freudian quibble, that, wholly negating the original premise!). **Telepathic dreams**, he felt, were a different matter entirely, and did not, of course, solely relate to dreams – on the whole, though, he was minded to accept that certain forms of telepathy do exist, and that they were easiest to access at the exact moment when a thought emerged from the **unconscious**. He believed, in addition, that telepathic messages that arrived during the course of the day could only really be dealt with at **night**, in the form of dreams. If such beliefs seem curious, coming from such a scientifically rigorous person as Freud, it should perhaps be remembered that the scientific basis of any **discipline** only moves forward in the presence of lateral thought.

Oceans Oceans, like **lakes** and **seas** (and all other such **bodies** of **water**), carry hidden emotional depths – the surface is impressive, but the real mystery is contained within. And oceans, like unfettered emotions, are apt to carry the **dreamer** to places they would sometimes rather not go.

Octopi Octopi are notable principally for the number of **legs** they have. For a two-**handed** human, the idea of having eight legs, each with a different function, might suggest an inability to focus on one thing at a time, or a tendency to disperse one's essential energies in unfruitful activities. Octopi may also be threatening, and indicative of emotional minefields – for even a tiny squid, lunging unexpectedly at a human being from the depths of the **ocean**, will cause that human being to **retreat**.

Odours Odours are rare in **dreams**, and are accorded particular significance for that very reason. One has to read the odour, in order to correctly interpret the dream, for it is often a literal replacement for a figurative idea. Unpleasant odours often suggest aggressive or malevolent forces, while pleasant odours are the **unconscious** mind's way of attracting our attention towards something, or giving it a positive slant. Odours coming in from outside the bedroom may also trigger particular dreams (see **Maury**) – a good example might consist of an **escape** of **gas** from a calor **refrigerator**, say, triggering dreams of **mist** or **fog** clogging up the nostrils.

Oedipus Complex The desire, by either **sex**, to possess one or other of their **parents** in an inappropriate manner. The source lies in Greek **mythology**, where Oedipus inadvertently slays his **father**, then **marries**, again inadvertently, his **mother**. When he discovers what he has done he **blinds** himself. The composer and satirist Tom Lehrer wrote a marvellous song spoofing the Complex's near-terminal overuse in certain psychoanalytical and pseudo-psychoanalytical **circles**, which I will forbear to quote here. See **Electra Complex**
KEY LINE: 'When on the following night, much to his dismay, Caesar had a dream of raping his own mother, the soothsayers greatly encouraged him by their interpretation of it: namely, that he was destined to conquer

the earth, our Universal Mother.' (From Suetonius's *The Twelve Caesars* 120 AD)

Offences Committing an offence in a **dream** is a well-known **guilt** trigger, and almost always disguises the **repressed** desire to revolt against one's moral or parental upbringing in the real **world**. To take **offence** in a dream often relates to actions by the **dreamer** themselves, and to give offence may have a similar thrust – the dreamer is conducting a **conversation** with themselves, in other words, and talking up both sides of the debate.

Officers Officers in **dreams** frequently represent aspects of the **dreamer** themselves which have been trained through the hard school of parental, religious, or scholastic authority to control anarchic thoughts and actions that might otherwise tempt them towards an indiscretion. Officers can also act as **teachers**, or as agents of the **superego**.

Offices Offices suggest activities within a formal setting – such a setting provides everyday actions with a spurious significance, according them an importance often out of all proportion to their real substance. Offices may also stand in for a **school**master's study, or a **police** station interview room – mildly threatening, in other words, and indicative of a communally sanctioned status quo.

Officials See **Officers**

Ogres Ogres (in the form of wicked or frightening **monsters**) are generally **archetypes** representing **angry**, aggressive, or overbearing masculine individuals or **symbols**. Their presence in a **dream** usually reflects the **dreamer's** relationship with their **father**, particularly if that relationship was built upon a foundation of rigid **discipline** or an imposed pecking order, with the dreamer very much at the bottom of the pile (both physically, in stature, and psychically, in emotional ramification).

Oil Oil tends to create a slick on which the **dreamer** may very well **slide** – often with no braking capacity, and frequently towards a bottomless **pit**. It is a catalyst, therefore, triggering responses to possibly ill-conceived actions. As well as tripping one up, though, oil may act as a lubricant, simplifying certain actions and releasing blocked up or rusted emotional mechanisms. Oil may **heat**, and it may **pollute**, and each of these actions may be significant in the **dream** context. If a person is covered in oil, for instance, it may imply that they are slippery types, or even, in certain circumstances, in the process of **rebirth**. See **Oil Spills**

Oil Spills For a **child**, an oil spill may represent **parental** disapproval – over **wetting the bed**, for instance, or otherwise filthying oneself up and threatening the sacrosanctity of the household accoutrements. The fact that oil **spillages** usually occur in **water** is also significant, in that water frequently represents emotional depths in **dreams**, or even the process of **birth** itself. The dreamed emergence of a **baby** covered in oil may imply that the baby is unwanted (unclean, **dirty**), or suggest a **fear** that the baby is imperfect in some way, and needs to be disguised. See **Oil**

Ointment The rubbing on of ointment suggests concern about some aspect relating to the rubbed **spot**. This may not be a literal concern, but rather a metaphorical one, as in an **arm** being rubbed, and the concern relating to being 'harmed'. A similar example might see the **dreamer** rubbing the back of a **friend**, or a **lover**, with the implication being that the dreamer feels that there might be some threat to them (from the back, or when they least expect it) from a close acquaintance – the rubbing on of the ointment (**witch** hazel, perhaps?) is thus acting as a **pointing** out, or 'witching'.

Old Man The old man is often a wisdom **archetype**, suggesting thought unconstrained by desire and **ego**. The old man may also represent **death**, occasionally in the form of Old **Father** Time. See **Old Woman**

Old Things Old things are inevitably suggestive of the **past**, and possibly even of outmoded areas of thought and behaviour. If the old thing is cherished, however, an opposite reading might be appropriate – the qualities of the dreamed-of object or person then become important in themselves, representing aspects of the **dreamer** they may particularly value, or wish to conserve. See **Conservation of Energy**

Old Woman A **fairy tale symbol** indicating wisdom and the eternal feminine. **Witches** often disguised themselves as old women to allay the **fears** of those they intended to molest, as happened in the story of **Snow White**. See **Old Man**

Olives Olives represent steady persistence and modest grace. Olives can also relate to peace and achievement – (as in olive **branches** from **sacred trees**, traditionally given as **prizes** at the Panathenaic **Games**), and also fecundity.

Oneirocriticon See **Artemidorus of Daldis**

Oneirology The **scientific name** for the study of **dreams**.

Oneiromancy The purported art of divining the future through the interpretation of **dreams**.

Onions In traditional societies, onions were often said to induce **dreams** of a future **husband** or wife. They also protected against **snakes**, which were considered not to like their smell. See **Odours**

Onyx The **blackness** of onyx is suggestive of mystery, although, curiously, the word comes from the ancient Greek for fingernail (presumably after it has been struck by a hammer). In purely symbolical terms, the onyx is a spiritual **stone**, indicative of the **psyche**, but it can also act as a **symbol** of power and wisdom on the Buddhic plane. See **Gems**

Opals Opals were traditionally considered unlucky, due to their resemblance to the **eye** (their name stems from the Greek word, *ops*, meaning eye) – as a result it was thought that their presence in a **house** would lead to domestic disharmony. This resemblance to the eye may well act on the **unconscious**, too, triggering Medusa **dreams**, in which the simple glance of a malevolent being may turn one into **stone** (see **Mirrors**). The famous opal of Alphonso XII of Spain purportedly **killed** anyone who wore it – the **king** presented it first to his **wife**, then to his **sister**, and then to his sister-in-law, finally trying the wretched thing on himself after everyone else had succumbed to its malignancy. The **Queen** Regent finally prised it from the dead king's **hand** and placed it around the **neck** of the **Virgin** of Almudena, where it has remained ever since. See **Gems**

Openings Parts of the **body** that comprise openings (**ears, eyes, mouths,** etc.) are usually synonymous with the **vagina** in **dreams**, and may, as a result, contain **birth** or **pre-birth** revocations. Openings may also suggest shortcuts, or easy (**wish-fulfilment**) ways out of difficult situations. See **Stockings**

Openness Openness – in the sense of sudden vistas (either physical or spiritual) which may seem to offer enlightenment or elucidation – is a major **dream** trope. The dreaming mind is perpetually **questioning** itself, and the opening up of a **landscape** is inevitably suggestive of potential answers (usually implying a return towards simplicity, or naturalness).

Opera Opera invariably equates with drama, and may imply an excessive dramatization of intrinsically non-dramatic scenarios. The viewing of an opera in a **dream** may indicate a desire for harmony, or it may suggest the feeling that the **dreamer** is always of the **audience**, and never of the players – a sense of outsider-ness, in other words.

Operations Operations, and similar service-related **repairs**, would appear to suggest that we are in need of healing (or that something, somewhere, is wrong). They may act, in this way, as **warnings** by our **unconscious** minds that something is amiss, and needs urgent diagnosis and rectification. **Blood**-letting, in **dreams**, usually implies the loss of vital energy, while the actual loss of an organ has a direct bearing on the physical or symbolical function that **organ** usually provides – **heart/love**, kidney/purification, **hand/friendship**, etc. See **Amputation**

Opiates Opiates are **sleep**-inducing **drugs**, usually containing **opium**, or an opium derivative.

Opium A powerful **opiate** distilled from the dried resin of the opium **poppy**. The **writer** Thomas de Quincey (1785–1859) wrote his notorious *Confessions of an English Opium Eater* in 1821, detailing his hopeless **addiction** to the potent narcotic. **Dreams** experienced under its influence often **reflect** an elongation of normal **time** spans, so that a narrative that habitually takes place within a brief interlude is unnaturally lengthened, often to grotesque proportions (70 years, in the case of de Quincey). See **Artificial Dreams** & **Hayter, Alethea**

KEY LINE: 'All this, and much more than I can say, or have time to say, the reader must enter into before he can comprehend the unimaginable horror which these dreams of Oriental imagery, and mythological tortures, impressed upon me.' (From Thomas de Quincey's *Confessions of an English Opium Eater* 1822)

Oppositions Oppositions, or opposed opinions, may personify (see **Personification**) themselves in **dreams** by such simple expedients as having two **people sitting** opposite one another, or by the bringing together of two **fists**.

Oracles Persistent **questioning** of everything, while it can be enlightening, can also be obfuscating, for there are moments when we simply need to stand still and accept things as they are. Oracles, and other such all-seeing, all-knowing apparitions, are usually **wish-fulfilment** fantasy embodiments, reflecting irritated non-acceptance of a subordinate (or spiritually inchoate) state. The Delphic oracle, of course, was renowned for answers that could be taken two ways, often incorporating equivocal messages that played on the vanities or **naked** ambitions of its interlocutor, frequently to their extreme detriment (*pace* Croesus, Pyrrhus, Maxentius and Philip of Macedon, all of whom were in some way duped by their own vainglory).

Oral Fixations We all go through an oral stage during infancy, in which everything is either ingested or tested in the **mouth**. In some individuals, such oral fixations remain latent (or simply unacknowledged) through adulthood, while in others they rear their ugly **heads** in **dreams** of **cannibalism** and other forms of oral predation. Gluttony and greed (often projected onto others) may feature prominently in such **regressive** dreams, as well as exaggerated emphases on mouths and **lips**. See **Grinding Teeth, Pocketing, Spitting, Teeth, Toothbrushes, Tooth Dreams, Toothpicks** & **Teeth**

Oranges Oranges are suggestive of **breasts** and of fecundity (Saracen **brides** would wear orange **blossoms** at their **weddings** in the hope of fruitfulness) and also of the **sun**. For this reason bitter oranges may suggest the turning of affections, or the inability to procreate.

Orchards Orchards are concatenations of **trees**, all with a similar end in mind (or working towards the same **goal**). Because of the complicated symbolic value of trees, the orchard can represent stultification, multiplication, or fructification, depending on context – even the over-regimentation or collectivization of thought.

Orchestras Orchestras represent more than the sum total of their parts – harmony out of **chaos**, in other words, or the subjugation of the many to the one.

Organs Organs, either amputated or otherwise highlighted in some way, usually represent the **unconscious** mind's desire to draw attention to some aspect of the **dreamer** that is being overlooked, undervalued, or marginalized. A torn-off or discarded organ may also represent **danger**, or a perceived lack of emotional closure. See **Amputation** & **Operations**

Orgasms Orgasms, in **dreams**, are subject to many euphemisms, the most common being the images of 'arrival', of 'coming', and of 'dying' – they may also find themselves depicted in dreams which portray **trips** or **travelling**. See **Avalanches, Flowing** & **Layer Symbolism**

Orgies Orgies can be about sharing, but they may also alienate, or be representative of discarded or wasted energies. We all crave togetherness, but we also **fear** the loss of our essential selves in meaningless or **neurotic** gratification.

Orient, The For many centuries the orient has represented the desired or mystical other. Its **dream** function will tend along similar lines, suggesting, perhaps, aspects of the **self** that are not sufficiently known or understood, and which we sense may be amenable to a spiritual or emotional **awakening**.

Ornaments Ornaments tend to catch the **eye** – and possibly draw the attention away from less salient or salubrious features. However, we also ornament ourselves to raise our **spirits** (and those of others), and this aspect may occur in **dreams** too. Ornaments may also be used for **sacrificial** purposes, or as tokens of respect (as in **grave** goods). It is interesting to note that our society has grown so consumerist that grave goods (and the symbolical placing of spiritual, ahead of material gain) are now more or less unheard of.

Orphans In **dream** terms to be orphaned is to be abandoned, and to view oneself (or an aspect of oneself) as looking after an orphan can often reinforce, rather than rationally oppose, that **reading**. This sense of **abandonment** is usually infantile in origin, and it is fitting that the metaphor it chooses by which to reveal itself should be parentally related.

Orphic Mysteries The **link** between the **worship** of **Dionysus** and Christianity. When Orpheus played the lyre he mastered all natural things, becoming the mediator between man and his primitive **nature**.

The ancient art of **bull**fighting is one of the few remaining **cathartic symbols** of this crucial union.

Ostriches An ostrich traditionally symbolizes stupidity, triggered, perhaps, by the **bird**'s seeming incapacity to **face** up to **reality** (in the form of the **head buried** in the **sand**). Ostriches may also symbolise inappropriate **aggression**, in that one does not expect the average bird to **kick** out backwards with no apparent provocation, as ostriches are wont to do. Could this be their answer to the head-in-the-sand syndrome?

Others We all dream exclusively about ourselves. The presences of others in our **dreams** is simply another aspect of ourselves that is vying for our attention.

Otters Otters are playful, liberated creatures, with few predators, and no qualms whatsoever about using **nature** entirely for their own advantage. Unlike us, however, they blend into the natural environment without despoiling it (save in the opinion, one imagines, of **fish**). This playfulness is almost certainly salutary, in **dream** terms, and is probably meant as an object lesson promulgated by one aspect of the **self** towards its rather more **neurotic twin**.

Ouija Boards Ouija boards were wildly popular around the time of Madame Blavatsky (1831–91), but one suspects less so now (although the **internet** numbers seemingly countless Ouija websites amongst its panoply). However, their meaning remains fundamentally the same, and they will tend to represent our **frustration** at the psychic limitations seemingly imposed on us by the narrowness of our cultural upbringing. We yearn, in other words, to move beyond the rational, but we can often only contrive instant and **artificial** – as opposed to sedulous and unpretentious – methods for so doing.

Outlaws Outlawry suggests a lack of **repression**, almost certainly along **id** lines – the possibility of instant gratification twinned with a status that some (the imagined **audience**, as opposed to the **victims**) may find romantic. To **dream** of being an outlaw is a **wish-fulfilment** fantasy somewhat along the lines of dreaming one was Superman as an adolescent – it is a complaint about powerlessness, in other words.

Out of Body Experiences There has been much debate about out-of-body experiences in recent **years**, with most of it verging on the wishful – there is even a research foundation, the OBERF, which collates information and encourages its members to recount their experiences. The generally accepted theory behind OBEs (as they are euphemistically known) is that the flyer (note the **dream** correlation) is briefly connecting beyond their own **body** to a pre-existing astral whole – a living matrix that unites us all beyond the physical. **God**, in other words. We can therefore assume that the dreaming of an out-of-body experience (as opposed to the experiencing of it while nominally awake, or near **death**), marks a desire for significance beyond the apparently rational – a concealed or non-explicit desire, perhaps, for union with the Godhead.

Ovals Oval shapes tend to suggest the **egg**, which gives us, in turn, the **womb**. In the guise of the *Vesica Piscis* (the Latin for **fish** bladder), it is also the aura that encloses a **sacred** figure, either in medieval art or in more explicit Christian iconography. At the symbolical **centre** of the *Vesica Piscis* lies the *mandorla*, or almond-shaped **heart** (it will hardly have escaped the readers' notice that both, put together, mimic the exact **shape** of the **vagina**). Ovals are therefore likely to suggest both **birth** and potential sanctity, particularly, it must be said, to Christians, in the guise of either the **Christ** figure or the **Virgin Mary**. See **Haloes**

Ovaries One assumes that there are **people** who **dream** of ovaries, just as one assumes that the ovaries will tend to represent the possibilities of **birth**, renewal and regeneration. To that extent they are similar to the **testicles**, and will tend to carry similar revocations.

Ovens In recent **years** (i.e. since the Second World War) ovens have taken on pejorative, alongside the more usual nutritive, overtones. Whatever way one chooses to think of them, however, they remain fundamentally transformative, although whether that **transformation** is a desirable one or an imposed one has inevitably become something of a moot point, depending entirely on the context and framework of the **dream**. In purely **Jungian** terms ovens are **alchemical**, and suggestive of the metamorphosis of base qualities into the higher qualities of what we might reasonably call 'spiritual **gold**'.

Overcompensation A term coined by **Adler** for an over-response to a perceived organic defect or congenital organic **inferiority** – a diminutive but over-aggressive man, for instance, who is obsessed by taller women (see **Tallness**). Such traits, while remaining unacknowledged in real life, are often **unconsciously** revealed in **dreams**.

Owls An owl symbolizes wisdom. It is also looked upon as a **funeral bird**, due to its habit of screeching when bad **weather** is at **hand** – and bad weather often precedes **sickness**. To the Taoists the owl represented **evil**, **death** and unappreciative **children**.

Oxen An ox symbolizes patience and strength. In Christian iconography, it implies pride. According to **Ezekiel** it also represents Luke the Evangelist. **Black** oxen were traditionally sacrificed to Pluto, and other infernal deities, for they implied misfortune. See **Cow**.
KEY LINE: 'To behold oxen in dreams is of evil tendency. Dead oxen signify times of famine.' (From Astrampsychus' *Oneirocriticon* 350 AD)

Oysters Oysters have strong **vaginal** connotations when they appear in **dreams**. Given their alleged aphrodisiacal qualities, they may also form part of a **wish-fulfilment** fantasy scenario, whilst also suggesting hidden **truths** or enlightened qualities that are not immediately obvious to the casual observer (*ergo* the **pearl**).

P

Packages Packages can often represent messages, or even aspects of the **self** that one wishes to dispose of or to **transform** – sending them away (just like sending a **child** away to **school**), may appear, at first glance, to be for their own good, but it is more probably an expedient act, convenient only for the expediter. To receive a package is to have something specific brought to one's attention, with the contents of the package, even if overtly symbolical, thereby becoming significant. See **Packing**

Packing Packing things may mean to 'hide' things, or else to transform them. We also **pack** things that we deem necessary or essential, and without which we would feel **naked**, or in some way incomplete. Packing a thing away for future reference (often a long way down the line) is also a means we contrive to hide unpleasing things from ourselves, shunting them aside until we are prepared to confront them once again from a position of strength.

Packs Packs may hold promise, but they may also threaten. They obfuscate and titillate, causing us to **regress** back to a childish state of unfocused anticipation. Packs are also suggestive of **journeys** and of preparation – the desire, in other words, for change. See **Packages**

Paddles Paddles, like **oars**, are both propulsive and **phallic**, and therefore may be suggestive of either the **sexual** or **masturbatory** act. In E. A. Wallis Budge's famous 1895 translation of the Egyptian *Book of the Dead*, the twin paddles were taken to represent the **love** of goodness and of **truth**, through which the **soul** may find itself propelled forwards on its preordained course – they were, if you like, the two outstretched **fingers** of Horus (the **god** of the **sky**, of **light**, and of goodness).

Padlocks Padlocks denote ownership. To that extent they are suggestive of insecurity, for we have no need of securing that of which we are sure. They are also a means of tying down something that threatens to get away, or of holding it to us without effort. There may also be the added revocation of chastity **belts**, incorporating traditional **male** insecurities about progeny and their potential origin (an insecurity transfigured and even further neuroticized thanks to recent advances in DNA testing).

Pagans The word pagan (originally meaning simply 'belonging to a village') has many pejorative overtones, implying someone 'not like us', or someone ignorant of the **truths** we understand and take for granted. Paganism may also represent uncivilized or ignorant aspects of our **past** lives – aspects we may feel that we have since successfully transcended. There may also be the suggestion (common to all cultures) that urban individuals look down on rural individuals as being in some way heathenish or unregenerate, a view increasingly prevalent in predominantly urbanized cultures like the United Kingdom, in which such nominally 'pagan' country pursuits as **hunting**, **shooting** and **fishing** are increasingly viewed as inappropriately antediluvian, and discriminated against accordingly.

Pages Pages **hide** things, and need to be turned before their buried **secrets** may be unearthed. They may also suggest the story of one's life, or, if they are blank, the potential for change or for new experience – they may even, perhaps, contain a suggestion that one isn't making the most of things. See **Books** & **Burials**

Pagodas Pagodas represent the abode of **God** (just as **churches**, **mosques** and **temples** do). They may also represent the human **body** in its outward manifestation of interior desires or aspirations. Symbolically, pagodas are icons of the divine, with their traditional **dragon** ornamentation denoting wisdom and heavenly **treasure**.

Pain Pain, or the absence of it, may have both symbolical and metaphorical significance in a **dream**, and generally points to a **suppression** of desired outcomes – the ending of a relationship, for instance, or a necessary family schism. It may also point to the existence of **repressed** hostility or repressed aggressive tendencies. Pain in any of the erogenous zones may represent a **warning** that the **dreamer** is giving to themselves against the enjoyment of forbidden **pleasures**. In addition, a **link** can sometimes be found in dreams between **orgasm**, pain, and infantile **sexual** experiences. Pain can also be projected onto others in dreams as a way of alleviation, while real-life pain can be wish-fulfilled away, often by the dreamed-of **amputation** of the offending limb or **organ**, or the shunting of the pain onto different parts of the **body**.

Paint Paint, like whitewash, can conceal **rot** and putrefaction (think of the **biblical** metaphor of the '**whited** sepulchre'). It may also enliven and cheer up what would otherwise be a dull surface (or idea). Paint may also be a means of communication, or of **drawing** attention to something that would otherwise pass unnoticed.

Paintbrushes Paintbrushes are **phallic** objects, and the act of **painting** with them may correlate to the **sexual** act, and to the **emission** of **semen** by the **male**. They may also act as extensions of the **hand**, **mirroring**, or even dynamically enhancing, the creative act.

Painters See **Artists**

Painting The motion of painting may indicate the **sexual** act (see **Paintbrushes**), or it may indicate a desire to **interpret** or 'better' an already existing concept. The act of painting is specific to the interpreter – no two people paint alike – and to that extent it may be indicative of variation within homogeneity (either naturally occurring or artificially

induced). What the painting represents is also important, with a **land-scape**, for instance, suggesting a desire for freedom or to stretch one's **wings**, whereas a miniature or a **portrait** might suggest a concentration on one subject to the **exclusion** of all others. See **Paintings**
KEY LINE: 'I dream my painting, and then I paint my dream.' (Vincent Van Gogh 1853–90)

Paintings The subject of the dreamed-of **painting** is all important here, and will afford clues as to the underlying motivation of the dream. Painting is often about perfecting, or **drawing** attention to something that threatens to elude us. **Hanging** the painting on the **wall** attaches it to one place, and prevents it (or the idea behind it) from dispersing itself in the **ether**. To that extent paintings are similar to **books**, with the particular proviso that paintings are open whereas books are generally closed – or open to only a limited **number** of **pages**, and thus amenable to only a truncated viewing.

Pairs Pairs of things may reflect **mirror** images, or they may reflect contrasting aspects of the same source object or idea. The existence of one thing may imply it's opposite, therefore, as in hate mirroring **love**, or wisdom, ignorance. The **archetypal** (or fundamental) pairing is the **male/female** one, with the one presupposing or pre-suggesting the existence of the other. This concept may be taken considerably further, if one wishes, with any one object or idea intimating the existence of other even as yet unknown reactive or collaborative forces – this apparently anti-rational but nevertheless instinctively sound neologizing tendency is particularly amenable to **dream interpretation**, and probably lies at the basis of the notion of **God's** creation of, for instance, Eve to complement Adam (and of a considerable body of experimental scientific theory to boot). See **Interpretation by Opposites**, **Reaction Formation**, **Rationalization**, **Symbols** & **Transformation**

Palaces Palaces, like **houses**, often represent the physical or causal **body** of the **dreamer** (the abode of the **self**), symbolically elided with aspects of the dreamer's **past** experience. Palaces may also express dynamic potential, and sometimes even the capacity (or the desire) to protect oneself from emotional attack through grandiosity (how, for instance, can one easily **tear** down something which is extremely large?). Palaces may also reflect exalted conditions, and the possibility of bliss.

Palms Palms **nourish** and they protect. They may act as signposts, also, to places of safety or **sanctuary**, whilst suggesting, in addition, the nearness or presence of **water** (representing, in this case, the emotions). In purely symbolical terms, palms carry implications of higher things, and also of intuited **truth**, with **oases** standing in for **sacred** groves, and the foliate or cinquefoil **shape** of the palm corresponding – both semantically and iconically – to **God's hand**.

Pandora's Box Pandora was the Greek personification of Eve, placed on this **earth** to **punish** men by offering them exactly what they seemed to want. When she opened her box of **tricks**, all **evils** flew out of it, leaving only the seeming panacea (or placebo) of hope. In **dream** terms, therefore, we crave her **box** and yet we **fear** it – i.e. we still follow our **compulsions** despite knowing the long-term effects on ourselves and others of our rapaciousness. This is Zeus's **revenge** for Prometheus's encouraging of humanity to take the best part of each **animal** sacrifice for itself, leaving only the offal or the residue for the **Gods**. A similar situation now appears to have arisen concerning our despoliation of the **planet** – we humans want what we want now – this instant! – and to **hell** with the consequences. We are no longer mentally prepared for necessary **sacrifice**, and we have somehow succeeded in unlearning the lessons our ancestors gleaned from the endless storeroom of foreknowledge that is Greek **Myth**. See **Baskets**

Panic Panic, in **dreams**, usually occurs as a result of unwanted changes that are threatening the regular **pattern** of the **dreamer**'s life. Such panic tends to be anticipatory, therefore, and **anxiety** forming, rather than reflective of any immediate **danger** or threat. The **unconscious** mind would appear to be practising on the dreamer, rather as **soldiers** practise their response to ambushes or unforeseen crises in the hope that when they really do occur, the training, and not the **naked fear**, will **cut** in.

Pans Pans are domestic, nurturing and receptive, suggesting constructive social interaction in the form of **eating** and sharing (unless, of course, they are being used as **weapons**). They, too, are extensions of the **hand** (see **Palms**), and may be taken, in **alchemical** terms, as catalysts uniting a number of potentially disparate principles.

Panties Panties (the word is irredeemably **female** in connotation) are a verbal trope for a physical condition, i.e. the desire to see under, or to be titillated by, something that is defined by its apparent absence – (just like the diehard naturists on the **beach** surrounded on every side by **naked** women, who only bother to turn and stare when a woman stands up to put on her underclothes). To that extent panties (and the uttering of the, in itself, inflammatory word, with its **dog**-like 'panting' overtones) constitute something of a mental striptease – an image undoubtedly carried over into **dreams**, where panties will tend to be designed (just as they are in real life) to draw attention to a potentially desired outcome. See **Pants**

Pantomimes Pantomimes are fictional representations of real **truths**, in that the emotions which are conjured up through artifice **reflect** back on real emotions that may have been felt – or are about to be felt – by the **audience**. To that extent pantomimes are suggestive and anticipatory, and are probably designed to draw attention to something that the **dreamer** does not otherwise wish to, or see how they can, deal with. See **Representability**

Pants To an American the word 'pants', with its downward, **mouth-**shutting inflection, applies specifically to trousers, and suggests necessity. The word **panties**, on the other hand, incorporating a mouth **opening**, upwards inflection (almost in the form of a smile), suggests anticipation. This semantic suggestibility can be taken further, with the **ants**/pants liaison only the most obvious – in either case, **dream** images incorporating such items will tend to have a verbal or vocal element.

Paper Blank paper may suggest a desire to communicate (or else a **fear** of being communicated with). Paper covered by squiggles or otherwise illegible script might suggest obfuscation or a desire to hide the true meaning of something. Wrapping paper might suggest the desire to reach out towards others or to be reached out to, whilst brown paper might suggest a wish to be useful or efficient.

Parachutes Parachutes are **saviours** of last resort – they imply that all else has failed, that we are on our way down, but that we may still have one last **egg** left in the **basket**. Parachutes, in their protective capacity, may also equate with **condoms**, or with the desire not to suffer from the consequences of otherwise rash actions (like **flying**). Parachutes may also suggest the freedom to see something from a wider perspective than usual – to take it in globally, as it were, rather than from our normally rather truncated viewpoint. See **Below** & **Failure**

Parades Parades are showcases of pre-arranged, pre-learned, skills. They can suggest role-**playing**, and they can suggest vainglory (as in, 'look at me – see how clever I am'). A parade may also imply shameful actions that have come home to roost, or a desire for conformity and not wishing to stand out in a crowd.

Paradise Paradise can be a real place or an illusion, and the context of the **dream** needs to be carefully investigated before it becomes clear whether we are talking about, for example, something along the lines of Charles Baudelaire's **drug** induced *Les Paradis Artificiels* (1860), or John Milton's spiritually induced *Paradise Regained* (1671). We are all to a certain extent pre-programmed by our **parents** and our **teachers** towards completion through achievement – *ergo* 'if you do *this* well, you will attain *that* desired condition.' So the concept of paradise is omnipresent in us, and entirely amenable to **dream** suggestion, often in the form of a compensation for perceived injustices. See **Compensatory Dreams** & **Heaven**

Paralysis To be paralyzed in a **dream** is normally to be unable to go ahead with some particular action that the **superego** disapproves of. We may also find ourselves 'paralyzed' through **fear**, or through **guilt**, or through **anxiety** at the effects our actions will have on us or on others. **Running** on the spot is a frequent paralysis image, as are **frustration dreams** and any form of **inhibition** getting in the way of what may, at first glance, appear to be a normal everyday action – the underlying symbolism (or symbolic **weight**) of the action, however, is what needs to be addressed, rather than the nominal action itself.

Paranoia A psychiatric disorder characterized by exaggerated feelings of **persecution** or mistrust. Such delusions may find themselves **mirrored** in **dream** images of, for instance, **parasites**, or other such threatening phantasmagoria. If such images occur only in a dream environment, all well and good – the dream is simply fulfilling its protective capacity. Should they begin occurring outside dreams, and in a manner which impinges on the **dreamer**'s everyday life, therapeutic assistance may be in order.

Parasites The appearance of parasites in a **dream** often suggests the existence of energy-sapping carryovers from the **past** which we suspect are still **eating** away at us, creating negative energy cycles. Parasites may also stand for **feelings** of **invasion** and uncleanliness, or for perceived incursions by outside **parties** whom we suspect may mean us no good. See **Fleas, Lice & Paranoia**

Parcels Parcels suggest the **excitement** and mystery of the unknown, and they are, in consequence, the perfect **camouflage** for **birth** desires on the part of a woman. If we send them out to others, however, rather than keeping them for ourselves, they tend to contain particular aspects of our personalities that we may wish to project or offer up to a wider audience in lieu, as it were, of the whole **package**. Parcels may also contain **feelings** or vestiges of the **past** (for we tend to pack things up for safekeeping), and they may even contain things that are defunct – as in the **ashes** of the dead, for instance, in the guise of coffins or **urns**. We human beings also have the tendency to bundle up the things that most irritate us, intending to deal with them at a later date – parcels conveniently **seal things** off from view, and suggest that they have been dealt with in some way, when in fact they haven't.

Parents Parents tend to stand for aspects of the **dreamer** that they either wish – or **fear** – that they have inherited. They may also represent the more mature part of the dreamer, in terms of either experience or **judgement**. See **Fathers & Mothers**

Parking Lots Parking lots are **resting** places associated with **anxiety** – this may seem, at first glance, like a contradiction in terms, but **hotels** perform a roughly similar function. We can stay in them, but only for a certain amount of **time**, and only if we are prepared to **pay**. If we are unsuccessful, of course, in the way in which we live our everyday lives, or in the way in which we are perceived by others (**policemen**, hotel clerks, minor bureaucrats and traffic **wardens**, for instance), these options are no longer open to us.

Parks   Parks are artificial **renditions** of seemingly natural environments –
in that way they resemble **theatres**, and have a roughly similar symbolical value. As well as all the positive revocations of rest, leisure and
recreation, parks may also act as mankind's attempt to **trick** itself into
accepting second best as best – under such a scenario, parks may act as
placebos and compensations for otherwise intolerable impositions, such
as **light pollution**, **smog**, overcrowding, and the 'unnatural' life of cities.
In purely symbolical terms, a particularly well-kept park might suggest a
desire to please or to be well-perceived by others, whilst a shabby, over-
grown park might suggest an ill-concealed disdain for oneself, or for the
effect one is likely to produce on outside parties.

Parliament   Parliament is a forum for debate, and the concept of it will
tend to be called upon in **dreams** for similar reasons. The **dreamer**, for
instance, may wish to debate something privately with themselves, or to
create an environment in which a fundamentally unfair debate might
eventually be perceived as fair (democratic). Parliament also carries with
it the implication of the individual functioning effectively in a communal
or **group** environment, with the inevitable suggestion of power achieved
through compromise.

Parrots   A parrot symbolizes mocking verbosity and the possible inability to think for oneself. There may also be the suggestion of **speaking**
without aforethought, and the parrot may thereby constitute a **warning** to
the **dreamer** to **measure** what they say rather more carefully than usual.

Partial Sleep   A quality or manner of **sleep** in which the **psyche** remains,
at least to some extent, active, i.e. under **hypnosis**, or during **waking
dreams**. Continued **recurrence** of only partial sleep may result in a gradual deterioration of neurobehavioural function, as seen and monitored
during extended **space flight**. See **Microsleep**
KEY LINE: 'Who knows whether the part of life when people think they
are awake is but another kind of sleep, a trifle different from the first, to
which people are aroused when they think they are asleep.' (Blaise
Pascal, whom Nietzsche termed 'the one logical Christian')

Parties   Parties, when they occur in **dreams**, usually have **sexual** connotations, and may represent the sexual act itself. If the party is viewed in
purely **celebratory** terms, it becomes important to note the attitude of the
dreamer to the party – excessive shyness may denote discomfort with
certain aspects of the **self**, whilst an excessive sociability might suggest
the presence of an **Adlerian inferiority complex**, for which the dreamer
is attempting to **compensate** by an exaggerated 'hail fellow, well met'
gregariousness.

Passages   Most of us (the non-Caesareans, at least) emerge into the world
through a passage. The quality of our emergence may have a considerable bearing on our later perception of confined **spaces** (the **author**

admits that he is speculating, here), with breech birth **babies** (of whom the author was one) tending more towards **claustrophobia** in later life. The quality of one's **birth** experience may also be reflected in our **dreams**, with post- and pre-partum images abounding, often in allusive forms. See **Channels & Pre-Birth Dreams**

Passageways See **Channels & Passages**

Passengers Our first experience as a passenger occurs in our **mother's stomach** – we are effectively 'carried' for **nine** months, with all our needs and desires seen to. Could this be why we respond so strongly to air travel, as adults? Certainly, in **dream** terms, **travelling** by **aeroplane** may constitute an extending and broadening out of the **birth** experience, with the added **phallic** revocation of the plane itself. The act of being a passenger is at once passive and dependent – we arrogate all responsibility for our lives and well-being to total **strangers**, which is either high folly, or a tribute to the imaginative, asseverating capacity of the human mind to convince itself of what it feels it needs.

Passports Passports constitute a formal permission to act in a free and liberated way. A passport is also an element of our functional identities, persuading others of our conformity to certain collective characteristics that may – or may not – have any real significance when taken out of context. To be entitled to a passport is the equivalent of being allowed to join a **club**, the membership of which accords no rights beyond the mere impression of simulacrity.

Past, The Someone, I don't remember who, said 'The past is a better place.' **Shakespeare** asserted something similar in Henry IV Part II, Act i, scene 3: 'Past and to come, seems best; things present, worst.' The past does indeed seem a cosy place to many, and this is reflected in the cladding of our **dreams**. The coming of puberty, and with it the **fall** from Eden, can cause untold torment. Some never survive it, and simply revert to the past in a **neurotic** way. This is often reflected in their dreams, which may show **signs** of **regression** or otherwise **reflect** some long ago psychic trauma which has frozen them in time. There may even be an **unconscious** desire to reconstruct or re-experience the past repeatedly, and it is this **wish**, and not the initial **trauma** itself, that is most likely to be the **root** cause of any **neurosis**.

Paths Paths may lead to unanticipated resolutions, but they are also suggestive of hope (see **Pandora's Box**) and possibility. A short path to a certain end (i.e. the path towards a cottage) may imply defined **goals** and a desire for comfort, whereas a meandering path whose end is lost in the far distance might suggest uncertainty and a lack of any particular ambition. A path which splits into two – as well as being suggestive of the **body** and the **legs** – might also indicate the symbolic twofold path of

Love and Action, which together constitute the path to perfection in Islamic philosophy.

Patios A patio is an extension of the **house**, i.e. an extension of the **self**. As its main function is the gathering of **light**, its symbolical value in a **dream** may be a similar one, with the possibility existing that it may represent the **eyes** of the **dreamer**, or their capacity for insight.

Patterns Patterns are **models** or forms of behaviour that consistently reoccur. Dreaming of patterns suggests a similar reiteration of existing prototypical behaviours, with the possibility that these might become **burdensome** if uncorrected. For some **people**, however, existing patterns are not restrictive, but comforting, and the mathematical certainty that underlies, for instance, a **kaleidoscope**, becomes a condition devoutly to be desired. See **Dream Series**

Paupers See **Poverty**

Pavements Pavements are lines of demarcation between two disparate, but nevertheless related, elements. They separate the **house** (the person) from the means (the road) of their eventual removal from the place (the character/personality) that they have established for themselves. The pavement represents slow, locational movement, therefore, whereas **roads** presuppose **speed** and possible disjunction.

Paving To pave something is to replace something natural (the **earth**) with something unnatural (a hard, impervious covering). It is the equivalent of wearing **armour** – the wearer is safe, but they are henceforth defined solely by their outer covering, rather than by what remains hidden inside. Paving also correlates to smoothing, as in preparing the way before one ventures into a new place ('smoothing one's path', 'paving the way'). See **Hiding**

Pawnshops A pawnshop is an **alien** environment that we allow to appropriate articles (or ideas, or resources) that we have not sufficiently cherished, but which we desire, one day, to recolonize. It is the triumph of expedience over hope, in other words, and the **symbol** of thwarted ambitions. The sign of the three **golden balls** which traditionally hangs over a **pawnshop** referred to the Medici coat-of-arms, and to their long association with the Lombards, but in **dream** terms the **empty** balls may as well indicate sterility, and the inability to beget or fructify.

Paying Paying is often synonymous with **atonement** or with the act of **compensation** in dreams. To 'pay the piper' suggests a desire to enjoy things before one can rightly afford them – to have all the fun, and then not to **face** up to the concomitant responsibilities. 'Paying' and '**pain**' are semantically similar, and one may very well find **cross**-relations occurring within a **dream** context.

Peaches   Peaches can be **vaginal symbols** when they occur in **dreams**. A peach is also a thing of **beauty** which spoils quickly – one is therefore constrained to enjoy it swiftly, whilst the going is good. Symbolically speaking, peaches are redolent of the **fruits** of the **spirit**, namely **Love**, **Truth** and Wisdom, first appearing as such in the 8th-century Japanese Shinto text, *The Kojiki*, during which Izanagi (the **God** of **light** and the **primordial sky**) used them to ward off the Ugly **Females** of Yomi.

Peacocks   A peacock traditionally symbolizes pride. Its flesh, too, was at one time considered incorruptible, and it therefore became a **symbol** of the **resurrection**. It was for this reason that **King** George III of England – who lived for the most part in something of a **dream** state, it has to be admitted – insisted on adding 'peacock' to the end of every sentence of the King's Speech, until persuaded by his ministers that the word was considerably more effective when merely whispered, rather than shouted.

Pearls   Pearls are at once **symbols** of the higher **self** and of the gnosis, or **soul** process, which constitutes the unencumbered attainment of the Perfect Way. In purely **sexual** terms they are frequently taken to represent the clitoris, whilst as symbols of chastity and purity they were also seen as **sacrificial** objects, by, amongst others, Cleopatra, Clodius, the **son** of Aesop, and Sir Thomas Gresham, who once **melted** a £15,000 pearl in order to **drink** to the health of **Queen** Elizabeth I (the **Virgin** Queen). See **Gems**

Pears   Pears, when they appear in **dreams**, are often associated with the **penis**, whilst prickly pears might be deemed to represent forbidden **fruits**, such as those growing in the **Garden** of Eden, and vouched for by the **serpent**. Pears may also be taken to represent the benevolent aspect of **nature**.

Pedestals   Pedestals are rickety places, prone to sudden sideways **movements** which may result in the pedestalic equivalent of defenestration. When we place someone or something on a pedestal in a **dream**, we are actually placing chosen aspects of ourselves onto that pedestal, with all the concomitant **dangers** such a choice involves in terms of the possible marginalization of other, less graphic, or less **sexy**, attributes – attributes which may, nonetheless, one day stand us in good stead.

Pelicans   In Christian iconography the pelican symbolizes **Christ**. Pelicans are also lumbering beasts, who nevertheless retain the virtues of **self**-provisionment and self-sufficiency thanks to their capacious beak pouches – to that extent they were often cited in medieval **times** as examples of the worthiness of maternal **love**.

Pencils   Pencils frequently represent the **penis** in **dream** imagery. They may also denote a desire to communicate, with an unworkable pencil suggesting shyness, uncertainty, or some other form of obstruction (a learning disability, for instance) getting in the way of the free dissemination of knowledge. See **Obstacles**

Pendants Pendants often refer to **testicles** or **breasts** when they appear in **dreams**. However irritating this may seem, in terms of meaning, it is nevertheless true that the **unconscious** mind is far more readily sexualized than the **ego**-programmed conscious mind, which consistently **represses** anything it may find threatening. Pendants may also act as signifiers, pointing the way towards, or **drawing** attention to, **questions** (or answers) that the **dreamer** may otherwise ignore. See **Necklaces**

Pendulums Pendulums are traditional **aids** to **hypnosis**, and they may also act (in the **right hands**) as aids to healing, and as **symbols** of the correct balance of life forces. Pendulums also have a tendency to **swing** from one extreme position to another, whilst still remaining attached to a central **point** or focus (namely the **dreamer**). We were all taught the principle of the fulcrum at **school**, and this image will no doubt be present in pendulum **dreams**, frequently suggesting the need to **split** oneself between two often disparate forces (a **husband** and **child**, say, or a **mother** and **father**). This enactive/abreactive element is a powerful one, and gives to the image of the pendulum a potentially very strong curative element.

Penguins Penguins are the most human of all avians, in that they walk upright and tend to **pair** for life, with both **partners** looking after the **children**. To this extent they are convenient ciphers for human behaviour, with their juxtaposed **colour** scheme (**black** against **white**) suggesting the dynamic balance of apparently opposing entities (**male/female**, **love/hate**, **magnetic**/antimagnetic, etc.). Certain particularly well-designed penguins even appear to embody the universal **yin/yang** symbol.

Penis, The The penis is one of the most common of all **dream** images, occurring as a synonym for power, aggression, **creativity** and assertion, in a multitude of barely concealed and often prurient symbolical euphemisms (see **Layer Symbolism**). **Dreams** of the penis are common to both **sexes**, and are very often the result of expedient desires – of the **female** for a mate and a **father** for her **children**, and of the **male** for a female through virtue of providing her with those apparent necessities. The penis, like the **vagina**, then takes on beyond sexual connotations, which occlude any easy or obvious interpretation of the value of the image. There may be **fear** of the penis, too, manifesting itself in dreams of being **stabbed**, say, or pierced through with **shafts** of **light**. See **Lingam**, **Vaginas** & **Wombs**

Penis Envy So-called 'penis envy' may not have specific **sexual** connotations. It may simply represent a **female**'s identification with the masculine in a (quite natural) quest for power – having the 'key' to something, for instance, or the satisfying use of a mortar and pestle, or in terms of her potential for motherhood and for giving **birth** to a **male** child (i.e. dominating the male in herself). This is a case of the **unconscious** mind overriding the conscious one, and insisting, possibly against the **dreamer**'s rational, everyday judgement, that, **archetypally** at least, masculinity equates with power. See **Jealousy**

Pens Pens very often represent the **penis** in **dreams**. Like **pencils**, they are also a means of communication which may, or may not, function effectively, depending on circumstances. A non-functioning pen (particularly in an **examination**) would tend to foment **anxiety** in the user, and might also be used as an excuse to avoid a potentially difficult confrontation – which takes us right back to the potentially non-functioning **penis**, of course, and to the hidden **fear** of **impotence** common to most men at some point in their lives. See **Castration Complex**

Pentacles Pentacles/pentangles imply an esoteric meaning available only to the adept – a sort of exclusive **club** for wannabe **mystics**. The pentacle (or Solomon's **Seal**) was in fact a five-**cornered hat**, representing the five senses, which **magicians** and **alchemists** wore as a defence against **demons** during or after the act of conjuration. Its **dream** meaning is likely to incorporate an element of wishful thinking, therefore, twinned with elemental caution about the **dangers** of **playing** with **fire**.

Pentangles See **Pentacles**

Penthouses Penthouses are privileged areas at the summit of **tall buildings** – they can represent the **brain**, therefore, and also aspirations toward higher things, or a high status. They may also suggest **exclusion** or enforced **solitude** (one thinks of Howard Hughes, **locked** away in his penthouse, going quietly **mad**). See **Above**

People The presence of many **people** around the **dreamer** during a **dream** may, paradoxically, point to **secrecy**, or a desire for privacy, or even to the existence of a traumatic event in the dreamer's **past** which was conducted 'in private' (see **Interpretation by Opposites**). A seething **crowd** of people may also **point** to disparate aspects of the dreamer's own persona, **fighting** for supremacy – or, alternatively, to a collective force achieving more together (by 'belonging') than one person alone can hope to do.

Pepper Pepper spices things up, but it is also abreactive, releasing tensions (through **sneezing**, for instance) that may have been **building** up for some **time**. It is an outside force which works on the inside, in other words, transforming existing situations (and tastes) into something other.

Pepys, Samuel (1633–1703) In his **diary** entry for 29th June 1667, Pepys gives us the following sublime example of an **anxiety** dream: 'I dreamed that I had great pain of the **stone** in making **water**, and that once I looked upon my yard [his **penis**] in making water at the steps before my **door**, and there I took hold of the end of the thing and pulled it out, and it was a turd … I pulled out something and flung it on the **ground** – it looked like slime or snot, and presently it swelled and turned into a **grey** kind of **bird**, and I would have taken it in my hand and it run from me to the corner of the **door**, going into the **garden** in the entry by Sir J Mennes's; and so I **waked**.'

Perfume The main function of perfume is to disguise and **transform** – one could call it 'to **live** a **lie**', or one could call it an 'emphasis on otherwise underemphasized attributes'. The original meaning of perfume came from the Latin, *per fumum*, meaning 'from **smoke**', implying that the word was originally meant to be taken as **incense**, possibly for use within a **sacrificial** environment to counter the **smells** of **rotting** or **burning** flesh. Perfumes, like all **odours**, contain strong revocations of the **past**, and are suggestive of ideas and states of mind as much as of particular **people** or situations.

Peril Peril is a convenient **anxiety** adjunct, providing comfort within a **dream** environment – just as it does in the cinema – by anticipating and preparing the **dreamer** (or spectator) for what may lie just around the **corner**. **Saving** others in **peril** (or being saved) is another regular dream trope, and can usually be interpreted along the lines of the dreamer saving aspects of themselves that they **fear** they are **losing**, or which are underappreciated (or otherwise unfulfilled). A good example might be of a **male** dreamer saving a young **girl** from a bog or **quicksand** – this might imply that he wishes to cherish or salvage aspects of his feminine (**anima**) **nature** that are in **danger** of **suffocation**. A concomitant **female** image might include a submission, of some sort, to the male, possibly in the form of being saved from peril, or otherwise **guided** by a dominant male **archetype** – this, too, suggests that the female wishes to be more 'in tune' with the male elements in her **psyche**, rather than to **fight** them in a possibly misguided or dogmatic attempt to assert her femininity to the **exclusion** of her **animus**. See **Danger**

Periwinkles The periwinkle **flower** has many superstitions attached to it, one of which is that to uproot a periwinkle from a **grave** will bring the perpetrator bad **dreams** for an entire **year**.

Persecution Persecution by dangerous **animals** or hostile men is a regular motif in many **people**'s **dreams**, and is often a **pointer** to an underlying, but normally hidden, **anxiety**. The details of the persecution should then be investigated in order to ascertain whether the anxiety refers to outside or inside forces. A **fear** of alcoholism, for instance, might manifest itself in persecution by a rabid **dog** (the hydrophobic **link**) whilst a fear of **sex** or the **penis** might manifest itself in dreams of being punctured, possibly by people with **knives** or with **spears**. See **Danger, Paranoia & Peril**

Persona The manner or attitude an individual adopts as their way of dealing with the world. A *persona* was the mask worn by a Greek actor, and a *persona grata* is someone whose persona is well-liked.

Personification The substitution, in a **dream**, of a thought by a person. The person dreamed of takes the **place** of the thought, and overrides it, protecting the **dreamer** from its real significance. An example might be a dream of a one-legged man, who takes the place of real thoughts the dreamer might be having about infirmity. **Abstract thoughts**, in other words, need to be concretized in the context of a dream. A **personification**, according to **Jung**, always indicates the autonomous activity of the **unconscious**.

Perspiration See **Secretions**

Petrol Petrol, like **food**, is a **fuel**, without which the human (or mechanical) entity cannot function. It is also inflammable and potentially damaging, and may therefore correlate to **fears** of obesity, or of overwhelming or provocative emotions.

Pets Pets, like **friends**, **reflect** how we want to be perceived by the outside **world**. 'Love me, love my pet' is something of a giveaway in this context, and reflects what, in a **dream**, may **manifest** itself in the unconditional **love** we all wish we were heir to (and that we feel that we deserve). Pets, of course, appear to provide this, without the need, it must be said, for reciprocation in any meaningful or impositional sense of the term.

Peyote The small button-shaped nodules on the stem of the peyote **cactus** contain **mescaline,** and are traditionally used in Mexican **shamanic rituals** to induce **hallucinatory dreams**. See **Dream-Founded Churches** (Number 7)

Phallic Of or pertaining to the **male organ**. Also the stage in psychosexual development where the **child**'s main attention and **sexual** feelings are concentrated on the **genital** area.

Phallic Symbols Phallic **symbols** are representations of the **phallus** which transcend apparent meaning, carrying with them implications that pass beyond the physical into the inferential. Obvious examples might include **towers**, **aeroplanes**, and **knives**. See **Lingam & Penis**

Phallic Woman A woman who appears in a **dream** either using, or in terms of, a **phallic** object. Such a woman is usually a dominant force in the life of the **dreamer**, arrogating to herself what the dreamer may perceive of as an **archetypal** man's role. An alternative, non-oneiric meaning describes a woman who enjoys playing the **male** part.

Phallus The ancient Greek **symbol** of the reproductive or creative force of life. See **Dionysus & Phallus Cult**

Phallus Cult The ancient Greek **cult** of the **phallus** (a cult that appears in many other so-called 'primitive' societies) was synonymous with procreation, which for a long time was viewed as one of the main ways in which mankind could participate in the divine. The cult was also initially related to **star worship** (not the **celebrity** kind, needless to say), but found itself gradually extinguished by the onset of Christianity. See **Dionysus**

Pharaoh's Dream Chapter 41 of Genesis recounts the two great **dreams** of Pharaoh, the first of which narrated the fate of the **seven** fat **oxen**, happily munching away in their **meadow**, who are then unexpectedly **eaten** by seven lean ones, emerging out of the **river**. The second dream describes the similar fate experienced by seven **fat** ears of **corn**, eaten up by seven lean **ears**. Pharaoh called for Joseph (he of the 'coat of many colours', who had been sold into **slavery** in Egypt by his envious **brothers**, **angry** that he was the favourite of **Jacob**, their **father**), and asked him to interpret the dream. Joseph claimed that Pharaoh's dream foretold a period of seven **rich** years, followed by seven years of famine, and that the dream was a warning by **God** to Pharaoh that he must put aside **grain** in the good **years** to counteract the shortages ahead. Pharaoh duly hearkened, put Joseph in charge of the procurement, and Egypt was saved. See **Wrestling**

Philip II of Macedon (382–36 BC) According to the English writer Sir Francis Bacon (1561–1626) – via Plutarch's *The Life of Alexander the Great* (100 AD), one supposes – Philip of Macedon dreamed one **night** that he had **sealed** his wife's **stomach** up with the image of a **lion**. He immediately **jumped** to the conclusion that he was faced with an augury that she, too, was barren, just as his first two **wives** had been, or that she was straying outside the den (as it were). The soothsayer, Aristander, put him right. 'My Lord,' he said, 'your wife is **pregnant**. For men do not customarily seal vessels that are **empty**.' Philip's wife Olympias went on to give **birth** to Alexander the Great. See **Sealing Things**

Philosopher's Stone The **alchemical symbol** of wholeness, or unity, predicated on the purported existence of a substance that would turn base **metals** into **gold**. The search for the **stone** yielded many practical benefits, such as Dresden porcelain, the composition of gunpowder, the properties of various acids, and the **nature** of certain inert **gases**. The Philosopher's Stone also holds considerable symbolic value, and formed part of the basis of **Jung**'s acausal connective principle, which he called 'synchronicity'.

Phobias A phobia is an irrational **fear** of **people**, objects, or ideas. Phobias can be transmuted into **dreams**, with often important subsidiary meanings, and frequently via **ellipsis**. See **Claustrophobic Dreams**

Phones See **Telephones**

Photographs Certain Amerindian tribes still resent or refuse to have their photograph taken because they feel that the photographer is removing something of their essence alongside the image, and that this essential part of the **self** will not be available when the physical totality of the individual is once again required at **death**. The further into the digital age we venture, the more we are likely to define ourselves by images and not by our physical presences. We have already discussed the **masturbatory** elements inherent in the **internet**, and it is inevitable that our symbolic concentration on images as against the written (and therefore 'considered') word will increasingly invest and **fuel** our **dreams**. Digital photographs, in this context, *become* the **reality**, acting as a rectifiable resource around which to contrive the narratives of our would-be lives.

Physicians The so-called 'wise physician' or paraclete (in non-Christian terms, literally 'one called upon to assist'), is an age-old **symbol** of harmony, and is most likely to appear when guidance is called for or **unconsciously** needed. The healing or rectifying aspect of the physician is probably of most importance here, triggered by the need we all have to mend our fractured **souls**.

Pianos There is a strong connection between piano **playing** and **masochism**, and this may be reflected in **dream** imagery. The act of **beating** upon, or striking at, a piano can also find itself symbolically transmuted into spanking or **whipping** fantasies on the part of a masochistically inclined person, or of **sadistic** fantasies in the sadistically inclined. A piano is of course dominated by its player, and the piano itself is feminine (i.e. potentially submissive) in **shape** and concept. There may also be **masturbatory** elements associated with piano-playing (i.e. one often does it **alone**, equating with self-gratification). On a more positive note, the piano can suggest harmony, too, and the unifying of disparate parts into one euphonic whole.

Picking Flowers Picking **flowers** is a frequent **masturbatory symbol**. Doing so may also be equated with **death**, as in the **poppy** symbol in use since 1920 to represent **blood** sacrifice in armed **conflicts**.

Picking Up Picking up things, and in particular **coins**, may relate to **anal-retentive** or **anal-erotic** fantasies associated with a **money** accumulation complex. In addition, given the association of money to **love**, it may indicate a desire to force love out of another person, without the need to earn it.

Picnics Picnics are communal celebrations carrying with them often sur-reptitious echoes of quasi-animalistic mating **rituals**. The fact that they are mostly conducted on the ground (when most people are more comfortable sitting at a **table**), and involve a nomadic search for a perfect temporary environment, merely adds to the **Dionysian** connotations. **Archetypally**, they are places where 'things happen'.

Pictures The pictures one owns are often **reflections** of how one would like to be viewed by others (beau-ideals). This can carry over into **dreams**, where pictures are frequently only reflected aspects of the **dreamer**, held up, as it were, for study or notice. See **Photographs**

Pied Piper, The The concept of being led astray by others is a frequent **dream** motif (the arrogation of **guilt**), whereas its twin concept of leading others astray (the acknowledgement of guilt) is a deal less common. Both encompass wishful thinking, just as the burgers of Hamelin indulged in wishful thinking when they imagined that there would be no revocations after they refused to 'pay the piper' for doing their **dirty** work (**cleansing** the town of **rats**).

Piers Piers are assertive **phallic** excrescences into **fragile** or unruly 'emotional' **waters**. Alternatively, they can act as extensions of a **land**-based and comfort-oriented mindset into **alien** or otherwise uncontrollable areas – the tentative outstretching of a **finger**, say, into the metaphorical **mouth** of a **lion**. They are also **beginnings** and **endings** of **journeys** or undertakings (spiritual or otherwise), susceptible to upset or undermining despite their seeming security.

Pies Pies are **self**-contained entities which suggest **nourishment**. 'Looking for a pie's nest' – meaning to persist in looking for something that you are unlikely to find – is an expression originating in France, where it referred to the **magpie** (or *pie*). We English, in our Falstaffian literality, quite simply transmogrified the idea to a comestible pie, giving the phrase a **surreal** quality that was certainly not its original intention. The fact that human **nature** will always **search** for the best bits in a pie (not uncoincidentally destroying the pie itself in the process) also gives us the likely meaning of a pie within dream imagery – as somewhere in which things that we want are temporarily concealed.

Pigeons A pigeon traditionally symbolizes **cowardice** (pigeon-livered). It may also **represent** the concrete form of an **abstract thought**, such as **love** (turtledoves). A pigeon may seem free, but it **flies** according to strict criteria, and towards strict **goals**, and has many predators.

Pigs A pig symbolizes obstinacy and dirtiness (also **sexual dirt**, *pace* Circe in *The Odyssey*). In Christian iconography, the swine, or **hog**, was also a **symbol** for Satan. See **Devil**

Pilgrimage Making a pilgrimage implies that the pilgrim has a preordained, prefigured purpose. This may suggest that the **dreamer** is discomforted, in some way, with things as they are, and wishes to effect change via a third party (i.e. the pilgrimage itself, or the notional or metaphorical 'wise **teacher**' lurking at the end of the pilgrimage). See **Pilgrims**

Pilgrims A pilgrim is someone who subsumes themselves (their individuality) before a greater, collective purpose. Pilgrims personify the triumph of hope over expectation (think *The Mayflower*), with the implication that the real must be leavened by the spiritual if the **bread** of life is to be maintained. A **dream** pilgrim has a set purpose, therefore, towards a defined, if not necessarily realistic, end. See **Pilgrimage**

Pilings Pilings underpin **piers**, for instance, and are designed to offset the power of **waves** to overthrow them. They are hidden supports that may (or may not) be strong enough to withstand extreme natural catastrophes (*ergo* emotional upsets) – in an everyday context, of course, they are usually perfectly adequate, but the mere presence of them in a **dream** suggests a lurking **fear** of their potential **failure**.

Pillars Pillars – as in the no doubt **unconsciously** allusive quotation below – are very often **phallic**, and suggestive of generation. A pillar stands up against **nature** and challenges it to do its worst (not, in general, a wise thing to do), and to that extent they exemplify mankind, and its 'scream into the **night**'. Pillars are therefore the equivalent of shouting 'Here I am!' into a great and measureless **cave** – they are human comfort tropes, designed to placate us for our inability to have perfect faith (without which, needless to say, we find ourselves, like a pillar, ultimately **alone**).
KEY LINE: 'I was converted into a mighty pillar of stone, which reared its head in the midst of the desert, where it stood for ages, till generation after generation melted away before it.' (From Robert Macnish's *The Philosophy of Sleep* 1830)

Pillows Pillows are comfort inducing (if occasionally stifling), and have strong maternal connotations – it is not unknown, for instance, for young **girls** to stuff pillows inside their blouses to mimic (or satirize) the act of being **pregnant**. Such mimicry can reoccur within the context of a **dream**, often in terms of a 'prior enactment' of conditions that make the **dreamer** anxious or 'expectant'. It is the rough equivalent of venturing an 'Anybody there?' when entering a strange **house**, in the hope of somehow disarming **danger** before it can occur. The ancient Egyptians traditionally placed pillows underneath the **heads** of their **mummies** in order to 'lift them up' and prepare them for the afterlife.

Pills Pills are designed in the expectation that they will cure us, or, at the very least, act as a placebo which will ameliorate an existing unpleasant condition. The very act of taking the pill is therefore in itself significant, for it implies a desire to rectify a situation, rather than merely ignoring it, or remaining on the **fence**.

Pilots The word pilot – possibly stemming from the medieval French word, *pile*, meaning a type of **ship** – implies someone who will **steer** a safe course through potentially dangerous territories. The pilot therefore equates with the **teacher** and the guide in terms of so-called dream **archetypes**.

Pimples Pimples appear to be exterior manifestations of a possible uncleanliness (or disharmony) within. They affect how we appear to others, and therefore have revocations for our **self**-esteem. Should a **dreamer** see themselves as covered in pustules, there must inevitably be an implication of hidden **guilt** or **repressed** troubles emerging unexpectedly, as it were, to give the **game** away. See **Cleansing**

Pin Cushions There simply has to be an element of **masochism** involved in dreaming of pin cushions – the mere act of **driving** yet another pin into an already bristling panoply of pins, twinned with the semantic revocations inherent in the word ('don't pin me down', 'I don't care a pin', 'you're not worth a pin', 'don't pin your faith on him', 'here's your pin money', etc.) must surely **weight** the balance heavily in favour of either a low sense of **self**-esteem, incipient **paranoia**, or some other form of lurking **inferiority complex**. It should also be mentioned that the image of driving many pins into the same cushion may also point to **feelings** of being abused, or of being viewed as promiscuous – the pins, in this context, being **phallic** and intrusive, rather than phallic and generally welcome.

Pine Cones In **Freudian** terms the pine cone may be deemed to have faecal revocations, simply on account of its **shape** and **colour** (at least during the earlier stages of its growth). Its appearance in a **dream** would then contain regressive characteristics (see **Regression**), which might also find themselves twinned with **phallic** connotations, perhaps in terms of sodomy or a carry over from infantile onanism. The pine cone that formed the tip of Dionysus' *thyrsus* (or **staff**) suggests a link to the **goddess** Cybele, and her **castration** cult consisting of **male** Galli (**eunuch priests**), who also frequently doubled as tree-bearers of the pine **tree** cut to represent the goddess and her **son**, Attis, during the great Roman **spring festival** held in their honour each 22nd day of March.

Pines See **Pine Cones** & **Trees**

Pins See **Pin Cushions**

Pioneers Pioneers are generally the first to arrive somewhere, and to that extent, at least, they may equate with **pilgrims**, in that the end is often in

danger of becoming more important than the means. The urge for **newness** (implying a refusal to face back and come to terms with the **past**), whilst not peculiar to the twentieth and 21st centuries, is, nevertheless, something of an adjunct of the so-called 'information age'.

Pipes Pipes are overtly symbolical of the **penis**, in that they carry **liquids** and have a tendency to probe into unexpected places. They have other revocations too, thank goodness, amongst which we might find that of a spiritual **search** (the **water** conduit), or a possible 'last resort' means of **escape** – which may, not entirely uncoincidentally, reconnect us with the **birth passage** (the inverse, or objective correlative, if you like, of the penis).

Pirates Pirates are strong fantasy figures, in that many of us would like to *be* them whilst not **wishing**, in real life, to *meet* them. Pirates are perfect representations of the uncontrolled **id**, therefore, and the tendency that we all have to **repress** the id inside us may find itself exemplified, for instance, in the hamstringing of the pirates' **prisoners** before **walking** the **plank**, or the image of pirates **falling** into the **sea** between two **boats** whilst in the throes of boarding (via Tarzanic **swinging**, of course).

Pistols Pistols almost certainly have **phallic** connotations when they appear in **dreams**, but they may also figure as extensions of the **hand** or **finger**. See **Guns**

Pistons The pistoning process is so obviously **sexual** in connotation (even down to the synchronous mimetic **hip movement**), that it would be extremely surprising if the **unconscious** mind allocated another, more subtle meaning to it.

Pits The image of the pit **represents** a **fear** of the unknown – if we stand on the **lip**, the obvious implication is that although we might conceivably choose to **jump**, we nevertheless can never know for certain what will result from our actions. Perhaps there will be **water** down there, or even (far-fetched this) a means of **escape** from a present situation which is worse, even, than the unknown prospect of the pit. To rescue someone from a pit is to **rescue** an aspect of ourselves that we have temporarily **lost**, or feel the need of resuscitating. See **Resurrection**

Placentae Placentae may represent aspects of the **past** that were once crucial, but are now ripe to be discarded. There may be suggestions of the **twin**, too, in their organic **makeup**, as well as incoherence or lack of communication, in that the placenta is, by definition, inchoate (or otherwise incomplete in and of itself).

Placenta, The See **Placentae**

Plagues **Biblical** plagues were fomented on nations as a **punishment** for **trespassing** on **God**'s prerogatives – it is not too far-fetched to assume, therefore, that **dream** plagues are designed, on a personal level at least, as punishments for perceived infringements on parental **rights** and claims.

Planes See **Aeroplanes**

Planets Each planet, or significant **satellite**, or heavenly **body** in our **galaxy** holds a particular symbolic value, as listed below:

1. **Sun = Apollo = Gold = God** = Adonis = **Horses = Male = Female = Brother = Riches = Yellow** = Dominion
2. **Moon** = Diana = **Silver = Measurer = White = Female = Male = Sister = Growth**
3. **Mercury** = Quicksilver = **Boxwood** = Choice = **Figs = Purple** = Communication = Activity = **Growth** = Expansion = **Education = Science**
4. **Venus = Copper = Love = Green = Daughter** of **Heaven = Egg = Whiteness** = Evolution = Receptivity
5. **Mars = Iron = Warfare** = Divine Fortitude = Upheaval = Creation = Power = Force = **Resistance = Red = Will** = Bravery = Nobility
6. **Saturn = Lead = Tree = Devourer = Evil** = Misrule = **Black** = Venality = Limiting = Defining = **Decay** = Rest
7. **Neptune** = Illusion = **Escape = Water = Rocks** = the **Sea**
8. **Uranus** = Fulfilment = **Spirit** = Matter = Involution
9. **Pluto** = Lord of the Underworld = the **Grave = Transformation**
10. **Jupiter** = Tin = Air = Zeus = Jove = Living Being = **Heaven = Blue** = **Father** = the **Self** = Spiritual **Journey**
11. **Earth** = Strength = **Primordial** = Sustaining = **Mother** = Physical

Planks Planks provide a **shield** or barrier between the **dreamer** and something else which might impinge upon them – they provide security, in other words, or at least the semblance of it. Planking, in purely **symbolical** terms, represents the **shape** of the **boat** which **cradles**, or forms the **seat** of, the **soul**.

Plants Plants suggest natural or simple **instincts, twinned** with a yearning for the **light**. A plant may also **represent** measured and constructive **change**, rather than **primordial** flux – natural **decay**, in other words, rather than variation by force.

Plastic Plastic suggests **artifice** and expedience, while also, to the modern **mind**, carrying within itself revocations of instant gratification. There is a childlike element to plastic, too, reflected in the bright yet often strangely unsubtle **colours** plastic seems to attract to itself. Plastic is therefore a secondary, rather than a primary, substance – an afterthought amongst materia.

Plastic Surgery To **dream** of plastic **surgery** carries within itself implications of dissatisfaction with an existing state of being. It suggests that **self**-esteem may be ameliorated, not by the concerned party, but by outside sources – that beauty is in the **eye** of the possessor, in other words, and not the beholder.

Plates The presence of a plate implies that something exists (outside the frame of the **dream**) which requires, or may require, to be placed upon it. The plate was significant in the case of Salome and the **head** of John the **Baptist**, because it implied a formal presentation (i.e. a closure). Plates may also carry implications of **celebration** or of communality – sharing things from one plate may suggest a relationship beyond **friendship**, for instance.

Plato (428–347 BC) According to the Roman historian and augur (see **Augury**) Marcus Tullius Cicero (106–43 BC), the great philosopher **Plato** advocated a careful **diet** in preparation for dreaming, so that the details of the **dream** (or what he called the 'prophetic **vision**') would not be obfuscated by flatulence. To this extent at least Plato was at one with the Pythagoreans, who forbade indulgence in **beans** for the very same reason, believing that it set the **soul** at **war** with the **body**. The Swedish philosopher and seer **Emanuel Swedenborg** (1688–1772) received a similar **warning**, in the form of a dream, on the eve of his discovery of his seership: 'Don't **eat** so much,' the man in his vision told him. The next morning the man in the dream revealed himself as **God**. See **Abudah** & **Historical Dreams**

Playing Playing suggests a reversion (or a desire to revert) to a childlike status – if we are capable of **playing**, we are also less likely to be a threat to others, or they to us (except insofar as we or they are pretending to play, which is far more sinister). Playing may suggest its opposite (see **Interpretation by Opposites**), too, incorporating a **fear** of **reality** and the implication that one might no longer be able to play (i.e. that one is mortal, and will eventually die) – playing, in this context, becomes symbolical of the **child**'s view of **life** as without obvious consequence, and may suggest a desire to act without taking responsibility for one's actions. See **Gamblers** & **Wagers**

Playing Cards See **Cards**

Plays Watching a play in a **dream** goes **hand** in hand with creating a play, the principle subject of which is oneself. Plays cast **light** on hidden motivations (remember Hamlet?) and may also **reflect** on how we wish to be seen by others (the perfect **audience**, of course, being ourselves).

Pleasure Principle The quest for immediate gratification and the accordant release from **pain** (driven by the **id**). See **Reality Principle**

Ploughing If a man **dreams** of ploughing, it usually symbolizes the **sexual** act. Ploughing may also represent a preparation for the future, in the sense of going over old ground with a view to **finding** a new way forward.

Plumage One could be charitable, and suggest that plumage is a necessary protection from outside elements, but a more likely interpretation involves display, and a desire to be perceived as other than we inwardly are through recourse to outward manifestation. If the plumage is sufficiently abundant, a false first impression can be created, obviating any need for **self-reflection** or fundamental self-improvement.

Plumbing Plumbing traditionally refers to the urinary system when taken in terms of the **body**, and there is a fair to middling chance that this concept is at the back of any **dream** which features it. Being concerned with **water**, plumbing may also refer to the emotions, and to the convolutions (piping) they involve us in. See **Pipes**

Plunging Plunging involves risk taking – in that we seldom know exactly into what we are plummeting – and also a **fear** of the unknown. Many **dreams** will see us teetering on the edge of a **pool** or **pit**, obfuscating. This is merely the natural force of **repression cutting** in to protect us from the possible consequences of our own, often ill-considered, actions. Even if we do take the plunge, the dream will often keep on protecting us via a series of *Perils of Pauline* contrivances (i.e. bringing in a *deus ex machina* or a fall-leavening prop at the very last moment to protect us from oneirically unacceptable **damage**).

Plywood Plywood, being **light**, is also malleable – it is made up of many **layers**, and is therefore flexible, and may be used to the **dreamer**'s advantage. If it is used in the construction of a **house**, say, it may be taken as an unnatural additive to the physical structure, implying, perhaps, the mending of a **broken bone**, or some medical intervention or other (if we take the **house** to **represent** the human **body**).

Pocketing Pocketing something in a **dream** is often a reversion to the period of **oral fixations** that we underwent as **children** – in this context the **pocket** stands for the **mouth**, and we conceal, **test**, or possess things under its aegis. It's a safer form of **cannibalism**, really – if you like or want something, or wish to make it a part of you, ingest it. This may even apply, as in cannibalism, to a hate object.

Pockets Pockets frequently have **oral** or **vaginal** connotations when they appear in **dreams**. Popping something into one's pocket equates with possessing it on some **level**, whereas having something emerge from one's pocket might suggest the process of **birth**, shock, or **creativity**. See **Pocketing**

Poe, Edgar Allan (1809–49) The great American fantasy **writer**, Edgar Allan Poe, wrote his own personal favourite amongst his many stories as the result of a **dream**. *The Lady Ligeia* (1838) seduced him because of her **eyes** and their expression, 'which were even fuller than the fullest of the gazelle eyes of the tribe of the **valley** of Nourjahad … How for long **hours** I have pondered upon it! How have I for the whole of a midsummer **night** struggled to fathom it!' See **Introjection**

Poems Poems in **dreams** tend to contain messages – from the **dreamer** to themselves. Concealing such messages in poems also makes them more palatable, in that it is hard to take exception to a rhyme, or a euphony. Poems, too, act as encapsulations of inferred experiences. See **Poets**
KEY LINE: 'He also told me he dreamed an enormously long poem about fairies, which began with very long lines that gradually got shorter, and ended with 50 or 60 lines of two syllables each!' (From Lewis Carroll's *Journal* of 1859, speaking of Alfred, Lord Tennyson)

Poets Amongst the poets who claim to have been guided by **daemons**, or to have received inspiration whilst still asleep are **Dante**, Tasso, **Byron**, **Coleridge**, Milton, Novalis, **Goethe**, Pope, Tennyson, Heine and Mallarmé. Symbolically, a poet is a superior person who attempts to **lead** others, and themselves, towards the **light** of inferred **truth**. See **Authors & Writers**

Poena Talionis A Roman law which dictated that the perpetrator of a crime should be punished in exact accordance with the **injury** he has promulgated on others. Such 'eye for an **eye**' logic also frequents **dreams**. See **Criminals & Criminal Thoughts**

Pointing Pointing with one's **finger** or with a **staff** tends towards the **phallic** in a **dream**, for the usual reasons. Marking something, or forcing someone to acknowledge you, is a particular **male** characteristic which appears to occur throughout the **animal** kingdom, or at the very least amongst the higher primates. This **archetypal** marking of territory (the formalized possession of something) was originally symbolized by a handprint (think of **cave** iconography) or the laying on of **hands**. Pointing appears to be an extension of this – it acts as a gathering-in of the pointed-to object. A male, if one begins to think about it, is far more likely to point at something than a **female**.

Poisons Poisoning has rather gone out of fashion in recent **years**, but it used to be all the rage, particularly in medieval **times**, when the art of poisoning was often handed down to surviving **family** members as part of their **oral** (or aural, in *Hamlet*) tradition. In symbolical terms poisoning equates with the ingestion or promulgation of negativity – we can even **self**-poison, in the sense that we frequently suffer **guilt** from the consequences of our own actions.

Poker Thanks to the **internet**, poker has once again taken its place in the **unconscious** mind of risk-averse **dreamers** – such a **game**, of course, symbolizes risk-taking without the actual taking of any fundamental risks, for the mere **loss** of **money** within the charitable **shade** of a socially constructed and benevolent welfare state no longer equates with **starvation**. A rigid, fire-stoking type of poker is **phallic**, unbending and 'strait' (in the sense of potentially warding off **danger**), and may also equate with the outstretched **finger**, as in **pointing**.

Poles Poles are natural aspirational **symbols**, because they tend to be set or **buried** facing upwards, as a **foundation** for more ambitious structures. To that extent poles may also suggest fertility (as in the **maypole**) or communality (as in the **flagpole**) or support (as in the **tent**-pole). Somewhat inevitably, poles may also represent the erect **penis**.

Policemen/Policewomen Policemen frequently take the place of the 'father' figure in our **dreams**. They may also represent aspects of the **dreamer** which police other, less positive aspects. A policewoman may conceivably appear threatening to a **male** dreamer in terms of his masculinity, or attractive, in terms of the paradoxical and often **secret** desire many dominant men have to be dominated in their turn – which may go some way towards explaining their appearance as one of the major **pornographic archetypes**, alongside **teachers, doctors, dentists, prison** warders and **nurses**.

Politicians One would like to be able to say that politicians appear in **dreams** in the guise of **guidance** figures, but it would probably not be true. They are more likely to appear as **salesman archetypes**, or as aspects of the **dreamer** trying to convince themselves of something that is, on the surface at least, rather hard to **swallow**. Politicians are the perfect trope for that sort of thing.

Pollen Pollen is an irritant to some, but one to which we nevertheless accord a privileged place because of its aesthetic and regenerative uses. Pollen may also symbolize the dissemination of news, or, as a worse case scenario, a bacterium or a virus.

Pollution To dream of pollution is to **dream** of being polluted, something which is likely to go **hand** in hand with a desire on the part of the **dreamer** to clean up their act, or otherwise transform their behaviour in a positive way. See **Cleansing**

Ponds Circumscribed **bodies** of **water** frequently represent the **uterus** in **dreams**. Ponds may also represent the emotions, with the implication that there exist hidden depths to which we do not readily have access.

Pools Pools of **water** often have **vaginal** connotations. Like **ponds**, they can also represent the emotions, with the surface **reflection** constituting the surface level of what might be termed everyday thoughts. Once the surface is broken, other depths stand revealed.

Popcorn Popcorn is essentially non-nutritious but fun. It may also carry with it implications of 'corn', as in something that is corny, hokey, or populist. The rapid expansion from the original kernel will also have some bearing on the way the image is read, suggesting explosive potential, perhaps, or a desire on the part of the **dreamer** to make a show of themselves.

Popes Popes can often be a symbol of the '**father**' in **dreams**. For certain Catholics, dreaming of the pope may have a **repressive** effect, while for others the very opposite might be the case. One has to be cautious when suggesting readings for religious **symbols**, as the meaning is very much in the **eye** of the beholder – or in this case, the **dreamer**.

Poplar Trees To the ancient Chinese, a poplar represented duality – the **yin** and the **yang**, the **sun** and the **moon**, **light** and **darkness**. Poplars also bend with the **wind**, and are therefore suggestive of compromise and steadfastness.

Poppies Greek legend has it that the poppy was originally created by Somnus, **God** of **Sleep**, and given to Demeter (Ceres), **Goddess** of **corn** and of the **harvest**, to allow her to rest from the **search** for her **daughter** (and, not entirely uncoincidentally, to allow the corn to **grow** once again). The poppy is, in consequence, also the **symbol** of sleep and of oblivion, and it is considered lucky to see one in a corn **field**. Its derivatives, **morphine** and **opium**, encourage **hallucinations** rather than **dreams**. See **Artificial Dreams** & **Picking Flowers**

Porches Porches, being **entrances**, leave themselves open (as it were) to a mass of potentially **sexual** and **birth**-related meanings. A porch can represent the **hood** (or labia majora) that encloses the **vagina**, for instance, or even that which encloses the clitoris. The fact that the porch is usually situated at the front of the **house** reinforces this **reading**, for the house frequently doubles as the **body** in the interpretation of **dreams**. In **biblical** terms the five porches of Bethesda were considered to be the entrances through which the five senses of unredeemed, or unregenerate, passions might obtain ingress.

Pornographic Images Pornographic images, and, even more importantly, the locations used in pornographic **material**, often (and inadvertently, one supposes) reflect dream images. Pornographic images are often hijacked by **dreams**, and transformed into non-pornographic descriptive material (merely because they are so convenient, and, dare one say it, available). See **Bus Stops** & **Subways**

Pornography See **Pornographic Images**

Portraits Portraits are usually commissioned, and they are (generally) designed with a view to pleasing the sitter, rather to alienating them. With this in **mind**, it is likely that a portrait in a **dream** would tend to reflect an aspect of the **dreamer** that they wish held up for view – or, alternately, which they fear *might* be held up to view. There is a long tradition, too, which sees the portrait as containing something of the essence of the sitter (see **Photographs**), even to the extent of being able to influence others in a (usually) malevolent way. This may reflect the fact that portraits are often seen **face** on, with the **eyes** of the sitter apparently boring in (or seeing deep into the **soul** of) the observer.

Ports See **Harbours**

Posses Posses are **anxiety** adjuncts – we all **fear** being pursued by the collective furies, and the implication with a posse is that our transgressions will eventually catch up with us, and stand to be accounted for. The original *Posse Comitatus* consisted of every man over 15, in any particular county, agreeing to bind himself to the general good by turning out, if called on, to maintain civil order.

Postcodes Postcodes being **numbers** that geographically locate us, it seems logical to suppose that their appearance in a **dream** might imply a desire to be grounded or settled in some way. There is also the 'code' element to contend with, and the mixture of **letters** and numbers (at least in the case of UK postcodes) might suggest an equation with **secrecy** or passwords of some sort – a sort of 'open sesame' effect (have postcode, will unravel).

Posters Posters may relate to **portraits** and **photographs** in **dreams**, in the sense that they are external manifestations of inward drives or **goals** (they *want* to be seen, in other words). They are also designed to seduce and advertise, whilst their **shape** (usually, but not always, rectangular), might suggest a **table** or a bill of fare.

Post-Hypnotic Suggestion Plans and suggestions made to or by a person whilst they are in a state of hypnosis, the effects of which are deemed to continue beyond the hypnotic state. To give but one example – the **author** of this **book** unexpectedly cured himself of **stammering** in this fashion, aged 15, through the entirely unenlightened one-time use of a book about **self**-hypnosis.

Postmen Postmen are **messengers**, and through their **medium**, news may be learned or information shared. A postman/woman does the bidding of whoever **pays** them, and there may be hidden revocations of **prostitution** in the dream image, or a **fear** of laying oneself open to outside forces or influences (quite literally, in the case of the postie-hating **dog**).

Post-Operative Dreams Such **dreams** often express themselves in the form of **consolation dreams**. Their **unconscious** motive is to reconcile the patient to whatever **trauma**, either physiological and **psychological**, might have occurred as a result of the **surgeon's** scalpel. To this extent they are extremely important in the maintenance of psychic health. See **Anaesthesia**

Post-Traumatic Stress People with post-traumatic stress disorder (what used to be called 'battle fatigue') usually have **anxiety** dreams, often of a **repetitive nature**. Such **dreams** frequently recreate the source of the original stress as a means of **unconscious**, quasi-infantile, alleviation. Dreams of annihilation are common, as are defence-related dreams (in the sense of the warding off of **danger**). Dreams of this sort are important pointers to the **dreamer's** capacity for adapting to the initial causes of the stress. Such **dreams** may be broken up (see **Breaking**), or interrupted, just as they are in the process of telling or communicating to the **dreamer** some important fact. Such dreams can also act in an abreactive (tension releasing) capacity, protecting the **ego**, and allowing a resumption of its ability to function in relation to the outside **world**.

Postures The taking up of particular postures is an important aspect of the **dream** experience, as each posture has a meaning, and each position reflects a potentially different moral standpoint. If we stand **above** someone, bearing down on them, it might imply that we feel superior to them (or to what they represent), but that we are not confident enough to maintain that position for long or without recourse to threat. Being recumbent or **below** another person may suggest submission, but it may also refer back to **childhood patterns**, during which, despite our innate value to ourselves or others (i.e. regardless of the strength, or not, of our **self**-image), we would invariably be looked down upon by **taller** (or more dominant) beings. As a rule of **thumb**, the spiritual and the moral tends to be set high, while the **sexual** or immoral tends to be set low. Forward or **backward movement** tends to reflect will (or the lack of it), possibly **twinned** with **regressive** (or aggressive) tendencies, dependent on the direction one is **travelling** in. A corkscrew motion might, as with **bathwater**, suggest that one is at the mercy of outside forces, and no longer in directional control.

Pot Holders Pot holders may equate with the **hands**, suggesting caution when reaching out to others (or to unknown or unsuspected aspects of oneself).

Pots Pots are feminine **symbols**, and can have **vaginal** connotations. If the pot is fractured, it might suggest a **feared** loss of **virginity**, or the marring of something that the **dreamer** formerly considered perfect. Symbolically, pots **represent** the causal **body**.

Potters Potters mould and design, taking control of chaotic forms and **guiding** them towards a potentially more useful existence. The downside is that the potter, by taking control, can also curtail, or lose the initial essence of, the medium they happen to be working. See **Clay & Pottery**

Pottery Pottery is **fragile**, nurturing, and confining. In addition, the outside decoration may hide an undecorated, or empty interior. Pottery can also suggest the making of something from nothing, whilst a potsherd can imply fragmentation or disunity concerning something that was once whole (or which had spontaneous integrity, or *barakah*). See **Clay & Potters**

Pouring Pouring **liquids** is often a euphemism for the act of **masturbation** when the image occurs in the course of a **dream**. There may also be the implication of a dispersal of energy or of the emotions – even a pouring away of moral or mental detritus, if the liquid being poured away is putrid or ill-favoured.

Poverty To dream of **poverty** or pauperdom might suggest a lack of **self-worth**, or a **fear** that what one has might eventually be taken away. To be poor in **spirit** is not to acknowledge benefits when they do occur, and to foment negative thoughts when positive ones may be just as easy to contrive. The pauper is a reflection of one aspect of the self, in other words – an aspect which is **crying** out for a patron, a **break**, or someone willing to afford it some charity.

Powder Powder may be **explosive**, and it may be decorative – it can be a sign of decadence, too, in the sense of disintegration, and it can imply a desire (or even the capacity) to be healed. Powder can also symbolize a means of dispersal – the rendition of something into a simplified or fundamental state. The blowing away of powder can have semantic connotations connected with 'taking a powder', or alternately of something disappearing unexpectedly, no longer to be retrieved.

Prayers To **dream** of prayers suggests that there is some request that the **dreamer** may wish to make and which they aren't, perhaps, sufficiently articulating in their everyday lives. Prayer is also an acknowledgment of the spiritual and a downplaying of the material. Symbolically **speaking**, prayer is an emblem of aspiration, designed to secure the **soul** through necessary **sacrifice** (i.e. the voluntary acceptance of a greater power than the merely temporal and expedient).

Praying See **Prayers**

Praying Mantises Praying mantises are the symbolic equivalent of **wolves** in **sheep's clothing** – they are predators disguised as celebrants, in other words, and it is for this admittedly anthropomorphic reason that they have for so long featured in human **superstitions**. Appearing to stand in prayer, they are in fact waiting for other unwitting **insects** to approach and be converted into foodstuff – the purported **eating** of the **male** by the **female** during mating is the stuff of urban and oneiric legends, and has strong revocations of incorporative **cannibalism**.

Pre-Birth Dreams **Regressions** to (or the re-experiencing of) a pre-**birth** state are not uncommon in **dreams**, and may **point** to the existence of instinctive non-visual, non-verbal memory **patterns** whose origins we do not as yet understand. In **Jungian** terms, they are felt to refer to **archetypes** of **rebirth**, **resurrection**, transubstantiation, etc., and to point towards a desire for a higher, more elevated and idealized life pattern – the move from the **mother**-principle (the **womb**) towards the **father**-principle (**creation**). Taken in its more literal sense, the intra-uterine state would seem to be one of unmitigated comfort and security, where all our needs are catered for, and any **dangers** are passed on to us only collaterally by our host. Such regressive dreams, however, usually point up unresolved tensions, or an underlying pessimistic attitude in the **dreamer** which refuses or does not wish to confront an uninviting reality. They are therefore very important dreams in the context of an analysis, and may point to problems or aspirations of which the dreamer is as yet unaware. See **Sleep**

Precognition Foreknowledge or advance information, provided in **dreams**, **visions**, or revelations, about what will happen in the future. Many apparent precognitions are simply the belated acknowledgement of a gradual, **unconscious** move towards some soon-to-be-inevitable end. Dreams may or may not provide **warnings** of such occurrences, but there is no reason to assume that they are the manifestation of some benevolent force – they may, indeed, be **traps**. A nice example of apparent precognition features **Sir Winston Churchill**, the British wartime **leader**, who was often considered to have premonitory abilities – in 1953 he informed Jock Colville (the **Queen**'s Private **Secretary**) that he would **die** on the exact same **day** as his **father**, namely 24th January. 12 **years** later, on 10th January, Churchill lapsed into a coma. Despite all the gloomy prognostications, Colville, remembering Churchill's act of precognition, was adamant that the great man would not die for another two **weeks**. Extraordinarily, he went on to do just that. See **Predestination**

Precognitive Dreams See **Precognition**

Preconscious State The borderland state between the **conscious** and the **unconscious**, as delineated by **Jung**.

Predestination The concept that **God** has foreordained everything, and that nothing that has not be preordained can possibly happen. The atheistical German philosopher Artur Schopenhauer (1788–1860) believed in the significance of **dreams** as heralds of predestined events (without the necessity for God's intervention, needless to say), describing predestination as the working of **unconscious** physiological functions driven by one universal will. Such reasoning brought the philosopher perilously close to a pure metaphysical pessimism – 'everything that happens, happens of necessity'. See **Precognition**

Pregnancy To **dream** of pregnancy has, as its symbolic equivalence, the bringing into **light** of something new – something, however, that has long been mooted. Pregnancy is also about filling, and burgeoning, and possibly even the portage of acceptable **burdens**. To dream of difficult pregnancies might represent a hidden **fear** on the part of the **dreamer** about the true ramifications of becoming pregnant or of venturing in a radically new direction, incorporating, in its wake, an **anxiety**-inducing increase in responsibility.

Premenstrual Dreams Women in a premenstrual state frequently **dream** of wading through **water** or through lapping **waves**. This concept of **flowing** may suggest **wish-fulfilment** triggered by the subliminal recognition that engorgement of the **uterus** is taking place, prior to the beginning of actual **menstruation** – there may, in addition, be an **unconscious** desire to 'just get on with it' behind the architecture of the dream.

Premonitions To dream of premonitions suggests a desired reversion to the instinctual, triggered by a **fear**, perhaps, that materialistic, everyday life, costs more in alienation than it provides in benefits. Real-life premonitions are usually hints from our **unconscious** minds that what we are doing is unwise or flawed in some way. To dream that others are communicating their premonitions to us might suggest an increased need to trust our own **judgement**, via the example of others who already do so.

Prescriptions Prescriptions are actions ahead of the facts – solutions, if you like, to **problems** that have not, as yet, necessarily arisen. A prescriptive posture may be negatively charged, however, and suggest an unbending approach to potential difficulties – the equivalent of **beating** a **child** before it has the opportunity to get into trouble.

Presents See **Gifts**

President, The The US President might equate with **God**, with **leadership**, or with **teaching**, in the **dreams** of an American. Being a settler country, there might also be elements of wishful thinking, in the sense of needing or desiring to belong to a symbolical community represented or personified by the figure of the President. Many Americans dreamed of John F. Kennedy immediately after his assassination – but as if he were still alive. This may be seen in alleviatory terms, or as a manifestation of **dream censorship**. See **Prime Minister**

Pressure Dreaming of pressure is an **anxiety** adjunct – pressure builds and requires alleviation, or else a crisis will occur. **Running** away from pressure in a **dream** (while seeming, on the surface, eminently sensible), probably suggests a **fear** that by not confronting a particular problem, its end result will be unnecessarily exaggerated.

Priests/Priestesses   Priests are **symbols** of the subjective/intuitive spiritual mind, but also of convention and involution. **Archetypally**, a priest corresponds to a **teacher**, a **brother**, or a sorcerer, whilst a priestess would correspond to an acolyte, a **sister**, or a **witch**. This seemingly rather unfair **archetypal** balance, is, nevertheless, prototypically (if not entirely expediently) sound.

Primal Scenes   A **child**'s first encounter (either aurally or visually) with scenes of a **sexual** or intimate **nature** between its **parents**. Such memories can languish for many **years** in the **unconscious**, to emerge only later on in life in the form of **dreams**.

Prime Minister, The   For a British **dreamer**, the Prime Minister would have significantly different revocations than the **President**, for instance, would have for a US dreamer. This reflects the different emphasis laid on the Prime Ministerial function (leavened by the fact that the **Queen**, and not the Prime Minister, is Britain's Head of State). The Prime Minister is first and foremost a **servant** (albeit a superior one), and therefore does not function as **teacher** or moral **guide**, but more as a conduit for decisions in the communal interest.

Primordial Images   An alternative, **Jungian** phrase, which he later discarded in favour of **archetype**.

Princes/Princesses   Princes and princesses are great-**hearted archetypes** representing ideal aspirations **divorced**, as it were, from the intrusion of reality. They are superior beings inside whose **light** we wish, **cannibalistically**, to bask. They personify an unrealistically flawless **world** (see **Wish-Fulfilment**), and their presence in a **dream** throws up more **questions** than answers.

Printing Presses   Printing presses are formalized mechanisms designed to disseminate knowledge, and they would thus relate to **teachers**, **archetypally**, or to institutions of learning. Because they are mechanisms, rules may also be suggested – the **right** way of doing things, perhaps?

Prison   To be held **captive** is to be in thrall to the **past** – there is, by definition, no future in a **prison**, except that which is suggested by the **leaving** of it. It is encapsulated **time**, equivalent, in some ways, to stasis and to the **pre-birth** experience which – in theory at least – is not amenable to fundamental change (but simply to **unconscious** influence). See **Prisoners**

Prisoners Prisoners are **time**-servers – they differ from **criminals**, however, in that they are not necessarily **guilty**. The concept of false imprisonment is quite prevalent in **dreams**, and relates to what the **dreamer** may consider to be unfair perceptions held about them by others. Symbolically **speaking**, prisoners represent the spiritual **ego** held **captive** by the lower passions. See **Prison**

Prizes Prizes are desired commodities that **reflect** aspirations that go beyond the actual commodity itself. They suggest a desire to please and to be well perceived – they also suggest conformity to a communally held ideal. A prize may also suggest an **artificial** reality that the **dreamer** persists in holding as more precious than **reality** itself – the **past** motivating, investing, and **invading** the present, in other words. See **Trophies**

Probation Probation is conditional. One is **waiting** for something to end, but there are **anxieties** attached to the manner in which the waiting must be undergone (or conducted). Probation also incorporates value **judgements** held by others about us. There is an element of helplessness and **frustration**, too, about the image, as if the **dreamer** were in the **hands** of a sometimes fickle fate.

Problems When a **dream** appears to be solving a **problem** that has been troubling the **dreamer** during their everyday life, it should be understood that the dream is merely solving the problem in terms of an irrational wish (see **Wish-Fulfilment**) and not in any permanent or rational manner. Many writers and creative artists might differ with this view of Freud's, however, and with his positing that dreaming is simply a fantasy designed to protect the **sleeper** from **awakening**, with its primary function being one of pacification. But Freud does go on to say that if the dream is correctly interpreted, it will be possible to 'overhear **preconscious** thought taking place in states of internal **reflection** which would not have attracted **consciousness** to themselves during the daytime'. This goes a long way towards explaining how problems that **writers, poets** and **artists** take with them to **sleep** can often find themselves solved when work is once again addressed the next day.

Processions Processions are **ritualistic** invocations of communally held beliefs. Symbolically **speaking**, a procession suggests the possibility of – or the desire for – salvation. One processes to make a **point** – to formalize celebration, in other words, and to ritualize and give significance to conformity.

Prognostication The ability to predict or foretell future events. The Ancients believed that this was one of the **chief** functions of **dreams**. See **Nostradamus**

Projection When people recognize their own **unconscious** tendencies in others and attempt to reject them. Projections, by their very **nature**, obscure clear views of events. **Shadow** projections can cause us to **act**, unknowingly, against ourselves. Only by an acknowledgement (aided by the **interpretation** of our **dreams**) of the substance of the projection, can accommodation and understanding be reached. Very young **children** engage in an early form of projection – while they ingest and explore with the **mouth** all that is pleasurable and satisfying, they also **spit** out or reject all that is unacceptable or unsatisfying. In dreams, such projections are usually shown as **personifications** of the unacceptable in the form of 'other' **people** who act out or do our **dirty** work for us. See **Alcohol & Sacrifice**

Propellers Propellers are both **cutting** and **driving**, and as such they may represent amoral ambition – i.e. it doesn't matter what we **damage** so long as we move ineluctably forward.

Prophetic Dreams Dreams traditionally sent by a deity which appear to forecast the future of others, rather than of the **dreamer**. Such **dreams** can also occur when the dreamer is in a state of ecstasy.

Prophets Prophets act both as **teachers** and as clues to the existence (or **dawning**) of a higher consciousness to which we may, unknowingly as yet, aspire – they are, at their highest levels, **personifications** of the **truth**.

Props Props are adjunctive – we can manage without them, but they give verisimilitude and sustenance to what might otherwise seem like thin gruel. Eventually, when we reach a particular level in our lives, we may feel that we can do without them for good – their appearance in **dreams**, however, suggests that our **unconscious** mind may feel that we still need (or crave) their support.

Prostitutes See **Harlot Fantasies**

Proteus Proteus, the seal-herder **son** of Poseidon, **god** of the **sea**, knew of all things, **past**, present, and future, but hated having to prophesy. To **escape** this fate, he took on numerous horrific incarnations to frighten off supplicants. Only during his midday **sleep** on the island of Pharos could he be, quite literally, pinned down. If the supplicant could hold on to him through all his chameleon-like incarnations, Proteus would eventually turn back into his normal form and deign to tell the **truth**. See **Beethoven**

Proverbs Proverbs act as **message carriers**, stimulating the desire to **learn**, and facilitating its dispersal. Proverbs can suggest **patterns** of thought, too, as well as proactive or benevolent connections to the **past**.

Psyche, The A human being's inner **centre**, roughly equivalent to the *daimon* of the ancient Greeks, the *Ba-soul* of the ancient Egyptians, and the Roman concept of the *genius* of the individual. In **Jung**'s particular case, he called his psyche the **Wise Old Man**, constituting his version of the Wise Man **archetype**. See **Self**

Psychedelic Drugs Psychedelic drugs (**drugs** which contain hallucinogenic qualities) have the power to immobilize the logical **mind** by causing a temporary loss of objective **reality**. **Artificial dreams** experienced in this state usually contain a fair degree of morbidity, reflecting a temporary psychic imbalance. See **Hallucinations** & **Hallucinatory Dreams**

Psychics To **dream** of psychics most probably contains aspects of **wishfulfilment** fantasy, in that, although we may all contain latent psychic powers, few of us have either the capacity or the will to trigger them in a constructive manner.

Psychoanalysis Freud defined psychoanalysis as 'any method of research acknowledging both **transference** and **resistance**, and proceeding from them.' Franz Alexander (1891–1964) called psychoanalysis an 'uncovering procedure' whose aim was the inviting of **unconscious** material into **consciousness** in order to create harmony with the rest of the analysand's personality. Both acknowledged the fundamental importance of **dreams** in this process, with great importance being always attached to the first dream brought by a patient into analysis. **Jung** considered that this first dream had anticipatory value, stemming from the psychic disturbance a decision to attend analysis entails. He further believed that collective images present in the dream would in some sense anticipate the direction the analysis might take, and might, in addition, offer an early and telling perspective on the **dreamer**'s psychic conflicts.

Psychoid A **Jungian** concept that means of, or resembling, the **soul**.

Psychologists To **dream** of psychologists is to wish for answers to often unanswerable **questions** – to questions, in other words, not amenable to formal logic. This outside party (**archetypally**, a *deus ex machina* in all but name) is called in by the **unconscious** mind to rearrange the mind's furniture into a more acceptable (and wished for) symmetry. It is surely invidious to state here that the 'dreamed' psychologist and the 'real life' psychologist have little, if anything, in common, beyond their nomenclature.

Psychoses Freud was amongst the first to point out the clinical and etiological relation between **dreams** and psychoses. Both can contain similar mechanisms and phenomena whilst remaining fundamentally, or causally, unconnected – dreams, in this context, become **secondary** elaborations, amenable to normal interpretation. See **Dali**

Psychotherapy See **Psychologists**

Public Houses Public **houses** are just that – communal meeting places inside which social interactions may take place in a quasi-**ritualistic** form. Their association with **drinking** – and the way we **travel** to and from them on a 'regular' basis – may, at a stretch, allow them to be viewed as maternal stand-ins, particularly, it has to be said, in the case of **males** (who tend to fetishize drinking possibly a degree or so more than most **females** do).

Pudding See **Dessert**

Puddles Puddles suggest spillages and potential disruptions. To a young **child**, this may equate with **wetting the bed**, whilst to an adult it is more likely to relate to the nuisance associated with having to make allowances for something that appears, at first glance, to be **self**-causative. The **water** connection, though, does **point** to something potentially emotional in the puddles' makeup, along the lines of an 'upset', perhaps, or a minor last minute irritation.

Pulling The act of pulling often equates with the act of convincing – we wish to cause a fundamental change in the dynamic or the direction of the chosen article/idea. Being pulled, on the other **hand**, suggests passivity and excessive tolerance, and may indicate low **self**-esteem or an inability to take the **bull** by the **horns**.

Pulque A fermented **cactus** juice invented by the Aztecs and still in common use in present-**day** Mexico. It is made from the agave, or maguey cactus, and can cause **angry dreams**, often leading to real life altercations when **dreamers** wake up under its influence. See **Artificial Dreams & Mescal**

Pulse The pulse relates directly to the **life** force, in that we naturally feel for a pulse if there has been a medical crisis entailing the possibility of **death**. An overall steady pulse presupposes harmony and balance, whilst an unsteady pulse might suggest tension or **anxiety** (possibly about death itself).

Pumping Pumping **water** frequently has **masturbatory** connotations when the image appears in a **dream**. It may also relate to the dredging up of memories or old emotions that were thought to have perished (or drained away).

Punishment Dreams **Freud** believed that this type of dream was the only apparent exception (as opposed to the genuine exception of traumatic **neurosis**) to the fact that all **dreams** are, to some degree or other, **wish-fulfilments**. He believed, in addition, that the critical function of the **ego** was able to interject in such dreams, engaging in an offensive action against the dream and, to that extent at least, controlling it, and avoiding an otherwise near certain interruption of the **sleep** process.

Puppets Puppets are mimicries of their subject, suggestive of manipulation and control by outside forces. If the puppet is the **dreamer** (the most likely scenario) then we may assume that the subject feels themselves helpless or otherwise caught up within the toils of fate.

Puppies Symbolically, a puppy symbolizes empty-headedness and conceit, whereas in traditional **dream** terms puppies are considered masculine and assertive (for the two may, just conceivably, be linked) – this is possibly on account of their exuberance, which surely matches that of young **children** in the playground. There may also be a maternal trigger involved when women dream of puppies, in that they obviously require a deal of **love** and nurturing if they are to make it into **dog**-hood.

Purgatory According to ancient Jewish Rabbinical doctrine, purgatory was a **waiting-room** between two stops – an intermediate state between **death** and corporeal transubstantiation in which the defunct was allowed to revisit its dead **body** and the places and persons who had been closest to it during **life**. Christian theology saw it rather differently, with purgatory as a place of suffering and purgation for mortal sins committed during the deceased's lifetime. Either way, the waiting-room image appears to transcend religious faith, even reappearing in Jean Paul Sartre's 1944 play *Huis Clos* (No Exit), in which the three dead protagonists famously discover that 'Hell is – other people', and that, even though they are offered a potential exit from purgatory, they are not 'free' enough, in themselves, to consider taking it.

Purple The **colour** purple is symbolic of wisdom (the **Buddhic** vesture), and, according to **Swedenborg**, celestial good and celestial **truth**.

Purses Purses are value containers, and to that extent they tend to have feminine ramifications when they occur in **dreams**, possibly relating to the value one places upon oneself, or to the exterior valuation others place upon us, or we upon them. The purse can also equate to the **vagina**, or, in certain circumstances, the **testicles** (particularly as they pertain to procreation).

Pus See **Secretions**

Pushing When a woman **dreams** of pushing, there may be a **pregnancy** implication to the dream, with an extra element added by the **nature** of the **sexual** act, in which both partners tend to push towards each other in the moments running up to the actual fertilization of the **egg**. Pushing may also imply coercion, or achievement through effort rather than by **right**.

Puzzles Puzzles, in **dreams**, often lead to **frustration** and **anxiety**, in that our rational capacities (the puzzle-solving ones) are temporarily suspended during the dream process. Puzzles may suggest opacity, therefore, and possibly even intentional obfuscation, in that we often tend to excuse ourselves from doing necessary things on the expedient pretext that we were prevented from so doing by outside forces.

Pyramids The **shape** of the pyramid is considered to be divinely inspired, and equates to that of the causal **body** (the form taken being that of the spiritual triad) – it exemplifies and facilitates, in consequence, the integration of the **soul** and the **psyche** (or **self**). To this extent it is a healing image, bringing together the lower (northern) and the higher (upper) planes of being. In certain **dreams**, the pyramid may stand in for the progression of the immortal soul as it gradually becomes invested by the divine attributes of **God**.

Pythons See **Snakes**

Q

Quails To the Taoist the **symbol** of the quail, when it appeared in a **dream**, implied military zeal, possibly suggested by the upright stance of the **bird**. More traditionally, the quail evoked great-**heartedness** and fecundity, while its negative connotations included **witchcraft, wizardry**, lust and **soul searching**.

KEY LINE: 'And there went forth a wind from the Lord, and brought quails from the sea and let them fall by the camp. ... And while the flesh was yet between their teeth, ere it was chewed, the wrath of the Lord was kindled against the people, and the Lord smote the people with a very great plague.' (Numbers xi, 31–33)

Quarantine To be quarantined is to be **sealed** off or deprived of the privileges accorded us through membership of ordinary society through no obvious fault of our own. On the surface, then, quarantine might be seen to equate with **exile**, although exile tends to be for a specific causative reason (i.e. there may be **guilt** involved), whereas quarantine suggests bad luck – or being dealt a bad **hand** by fate – more than it suggests blame or culpability.

Quarrels Quarrels may indicate the opposition of two contrasting ideas in the **dreamer**'s **unconscious** – ideas which manifest themselves in literal or symbolical antagonism. Quarrel is also another word for a crossbow bolt, something which throws up interesting semantic possibilities when twinned with the possible schisms and ruptures caused by **argument**.

Quarries Quarries are assets that may be mined when and if necessary. This is suggestive of the **dreamer** digging deep into their resources in order to **find** something precious (possibly originating in **childhood**) that may have lain **buried** for a very long **time**. To **hunt** a quarry in a **dream** probably relates to the **search** for something elusive or indefinable that one suspects will accord more pleasure in the chase than in its fruition.

Quartz Quartz symbolizes the crystallization of **light** and the containment of energy. Quartz is therefore emotionally non-dispersive, but intellectually and rationally permeable. It is the most common of all minerals, and its appearance and significance within a **dream** will tend to **match** that of **crystals**.

Quaternity Quaternity is the principle of **fourness** notionally underlying everything. Even the Christian concept of the **Trinity** carries within it the implication of a fourth, or **evil** aspect, embodied in the **Devil**. It is arguable, too, that the declaration of the Assumption of the **Virgin** Mary by Pope Pius XII was an effort by the Catholic **Church** to incorporate a notion of **femaleness** into what had seemed, hitherto, an exclusively

male fraternity. The Hindu **God** Brahma, creator of the universe, although part of a Triad consisting, in addition to him, of Vishnu and Shiva, is often represented by four **heads** looking to the four different **corners** of the **world**. See **Cosmic Man** & **Great Mother**

Queen Mab The **fairies** employed **Queen** Mab as the midwife, or bringer of **dreams**, when they wanted to favour a human being with a glimpse of the **world** they inhabited. 'Queen', in this context, refers back to the old Saxon word *quén*, meaning a woman, and Mab may well have been a less than queenly figure – more of a Mrs Drudge, if the **truth** be told – fussing and feather-dusting her way through **people**'s **minds**. **Shakespeare** wrote of her as a diminutive person, and 'no bigger than an agate-stone on the fore-finger of an alderman'.

Queen of Heaven Each great civilization has had its **Queen** of Heaven – for the Egyptians she was Isis, for the Phoenicians she was Astarte, while the Greeks had their Hera, the Romans their Juno or their triple Hecate (who incorporated Phoebe, Diana, and Proserpine, depending on whether she chose to dwell in the **Heavens**, on **Earth**, or in **Hell**), and the Catholic **Church** its **Virgin** Mary.

Queens Queens are often **symbols** of the **mother** in **dreams**. **Females** dreaming of queens may be seeking **guidance** via traditional feminine qualities, whereas **males** may **wish**, or seek to serve, some overriding feminine ideal – one thinks of the flourishing of predominantly male endeavour in the courts of Queen Elizabeth I, Queen Victoria and Margaret Thatcher (also something of a queen figure). The male queenly attributes tend to be linked to favouritism, therefore, whereas the female queenly attributes tend towards **exclusion** (of the male, and of non-adherent females).

Questions To **dream** of questions is to suggest the possible existence of answers – we are back to a **wish-fulfilment** mode of thinking, therefore, or a **regression** to **childhood patterns** of thought where it appears that an adult (or some all-knowing being) must have all the answers and, what's more, be prepared to provide them. Mature (or rational, or non-dreaming) **people** know that there are many things that must remain unanswered, and that there are even more things that must be taken on trust. **Ego**-driven beings, on the other **hand**, usually insist, against all logic, that there must be an answer for everything, forgetting that each answer merely points up another question.

Quests Quests are **key** psychological male **rites-of-passage** – they are searches for the **self**, of course, functioning under the guise of duties, **rituals**, and honourable **obligations** (often associated with the **search** for some essential **female** essence the **male** lacks). The prime male quest was that for the **Holy Grail**, which only became visible to the quester when the correct **question** was asked. Dreaming of quests implies that one wishes to be needed or functionally used – that one craves for an overriding purpose that may add extrinsic value to one's intrinsic being. See **Anima & Animus**

Queues Queues are **anxiety** tropes, in that they presuppose a particular desire, whilst also suggesting that that desire must be put on temporary hold rather than immediately gratified (as the **ego** might wish). Societies which know how to queue tend to be mature in terms of civilization but potentially deficient in terms of energy and the *qui vive*. A queue inside a **dream** may have a similar import.

Quicksand For the **dreamer** to be stuck in quicksand may suggest either incipient insecurity, or the need to act fast in a certain pressing situation. Quicksand is **sand** that **acts** 'as if it were alive', and to **dream** of rescuing, or attempting to **rescue** someone from such a subsumation indicates a desire to retrieve something in oneself that may be dying, or to re-enliven an aspect of a situation – a **marriage**, perhaps? the connection of two **people**? – that may be in **danger** of being stifled. See **Sinking**

Quilts Quilts or quilting is a bringing together of disparate articles/ideas/**people** into one homogenous, enhanced, but nevertheless still indi-vidualistically coherent whole (the utilitarian **twinned** with the aestheti-cally pleasing). This 'communion' tends to be security based, in that quilts are reassuring and suggestive of the benevolent incorporation of the **past** into something that may, nonetheless, be of significant use in the future.

Quips Quips are ready ripostes which often disguise hidden insecurities. To be funny is to be accepted, and most of us have constructed daylight fantasies in which we reply wittily and on the **nail**, rather than belatedly and as an afterthought. To quip in a **dream** is often a cheap means of getting out of a difficult situation with one's dignity and reputation, as it were, still intact.

Quivering Quivering is a sign of submission – submission to **cold**, to **fear**, or merely a **sign** that we aren't threatening, and that we may be vul-nerable too.

Quotations The minute something is quoted, the inference is that it has attained a beyond cursory acceptance – that there is some significance to it over and above normal standards. Quotations in **dreams** tend to be reit-erations of already acknowledged **truths**, designed to reinforce already decided on modes of action.

R

Rabbis Rabbis tend to equate with **teachers** and **wise old men** when they appear in **dreams**.

Rabbits A rabbit symbolizes fecundity and threatened freedoms. There are also **sacrificial** aspects contained within the image of the rabbit, and suggestions of **masochism** and **victim**-hood. **White** rabbits have **magical** connotations, too, and may be indicative of **trickery**.

Raccoons Raccoons are distinguished by their banded **eyes**, which may suggest **criminal** connotations in the context of a **dream**, or the **fear** of criminal activity (through the implication of not being able to see behind the **mask** of someone – *ergo* hidden motivations). Raccoons are also **tree**-dwelling mammals, and are 'treed' when **cornered**, giving rise to an image of someone with their **back** against a **wall**, or with few possibilities of **escape**.

Races Races in **dreams** tend to be between the **dreamer** and other, disparate aspects of themselves, leading to suggestions of indecision, perhaps, or of being torn two ways by a particular subject (possibly as a result of aiming too relentlessly at one particular **goal**). **Integration** occurs both at the start of a race, and at its completion (with all the competitors joining in for the finish) – disintegration or partition tends to occur only during the **running** of it. See **Tearing**

Racks Racks differentiate between disparate goods and products (or disparate ideas). Rather like **planks**, they can function as protective or symbolic barriers, keeping incompatible things apart, and acting as way stations for compatible entities. To **dream** of racks is to dream of ordering and streaming, therefore, and of keeping good metaphorical **house**.

Radar Radar is designed to **pick up** possible problems in advance and allow us to forestall them. Radar may also be **linked** to intuition and inference – if such and such is there, then we may infer suchlike. Radar, taken in this sense, almost always refers to **self**-monitoring, rather than relating to a **fear** of outside intervention – it thus becomes an interior mechanism by which we may attempt to predetermine dubious outcomes.

Radiance Radiance tends to reflect goodness, in the sense of hallowed **light**. Radiance marks **spots**, too, and accords them significance, as if something from outside us wished to influence our internal **eye**. See **Haloes**

Radios Radios inevitably find themselves connected to ideas of communication and to the possibilities of authoritative interrelation (think walkie-talkies). There may also be an element of reaching out involved, possibly spiritual in content. On a more mundane level, while appearing to embody intimacy, radios actually reflect its lack – and are thus primarily adjuncts to loneliness.

Raffles Raffles suggest the possibility (but not the probability, alas) of good luck. They may also embody charity without fundamental commitment – **lip** service, rather than service, in other words. Not many **people** read E. W. Hornung's *Raffles – The Amateur Cracksman* (*Gentleman Thief*), anymore, but there is undoubtedly a semantic link between raffles and raffishness, and this may inform the dream reading as well.

Rafts Rafts are salutary vessels, designed for cases of last resort. Symbolically, they represent a somewhat **fragile** protection from stormy emotional **waters**, or a vessel used by the **soul** for the 'difficult crossing from sin to wisdom' (*The Bhagavad-Gita* Chapter iv, 36).

Rags Rags **carry** within their meaning a potentially interesting admixture of poverty and **cleansing**. Rags may also have revocations of **flags**, high jinks and **menstruation**, so the word is something of a symbolical minefield – **whisky** used to be known as rag-**water** by Victorian **thieves** (due to its **colour**, one supposes), and **paper money** was known as rag-money. All this to say that **dreams** will tend to have a **field** day with rags, for their subject may be construed in any number of alliterative and allusive (elusive?) ways.

Railings Railings protect, but at the same time they also obstruct the view. In this way they can represent the civilized barriers we put up between ourselves and our **animal natures** – the thin membrane that separates the **id** from the **superego**. See **Planks** & **Racks**

Railroads Railroads are direct **lines** to specific destinations – in symbolical terms, this would equate with clear-headedness, ambition and, quite possibly, ruthlessness. See **Railroad Tracks**

Railroad Tracks Railroad tracks tend to suggest predetermined destinations, but their parallelism is what really defines them – they are two joined together as one, and they suggest, in consequence, the partnership of two disparate entities, both **pulling** together. There may be an extra edge to this **reading**, however, in that the **tracks** are only amenable to **reverse** or forward gears – sideways meanderings are rare possibilities, and only along pre-existing lines. See **Railroads**

Railways See **Railroads, Railroad Tracks** & **Trains**

Raimondi, Marcantonio (1480–1543) A follower of **Albrecht Dürer**, and the **painter** of *The Dream of Raphael* (a.k.a. *The Nightmare*), in which **monsters** and **demons** beset two **naked**, sleeping women. While they **sleep**, a **castle burns**, and strange **lights** emanate from above them.

The **painting** is, despite its apparent obscurity, one of the most perfect depictions of a **nightmare** ever placed on canvas. See **Fuseli & Incubus**

Rain Rain equates with purification and the resolution of important issues. In **mythological** terms it was considered to be a union of **love** between **heaven** and **earth** – a **sacred marriage** of the Gods. Danaë, the **mother** of Perseus, was impregnated by the god Zeus in a **shower** of **golden** rain. In **Freudian** terms, rain may indicate **urination**, or urine.

Rainbows Only the **gods** are considered to be able to walk a rainbow **bridge** in safety – any normal human being will lose faith and fall to their **death**. Humans should instead pass underneath the rainbow (showing, thereby, humility), and inhabit the lower places set aside for them and their ilk. **Dreams**, curiously enough, **reflect** this image, in that rainbows tend to be aspirational, non-noumenal, and upwardly causative – collective **symbols** of the higher mental plane.

Rams Rams, like **bulls**, are symbolic of sacrificial masculinity, and 'ram feasts' have been held in country districts since time immemorial, with possible connections to Baal **worship** (in the sense of fertility being placed in opposition to **death**), particularly in the extreme west of the United Kingdom, where such influences may well have come to rest thanks to ancient trade links. The strength (and the **weakness**) of the ram is in his **horns**, and one thinks of Abraham happening on a ram caught in a thicket by his horns, and offering him up to **God** instead of his **son**, Isaac – although Muslim authorities believe that it was his illegitimate son, Ishmael, who was spared – as a **burnt** offering (Genesis xxii, 13). See **Banquets**

Ranches Ranches are microcosms of idealized **nature** – they are tamed wildernesses, if you like, suggesting comfort, sustenance, and protection (but not isolation) from the elements – having one's **cake** and **eating** it, **springs** to **mind**.

Rank, Otto (1884–1939) One of the first **students** of Sigmund Freud, Rank differed from **Freud** in that he ascribed the development of **neurotic** tendencies in the individual to the trauma of **birth** rather than to the **Oedipus Complex**. Later in life he moved to the United States, where he was massively influential in the psychotherapy movement. In 1925, he devoted a **book** to the subject of the **double**, or *doppelgänger*.

Rape Rape is notoriously difficult to define in dream terms, because, like **incest** and **sexual abuse**, it contains such apparently immovable **taboos**. It is, nevertheless, an extremely common dream image, and may well find itself used as a **repression** tactic by the **unconscious** mind in its attempt at protecting us from the consequences of our everyday desires. It is worth reminding ourselves here that **Freud** believed that all **dreams** – apart from **punishment dreams** and dreams relating to traumatic

neurosis – are directed towards **wish-fulfilment**, however inconvenient, unconducive, or even downright unpleasant this may sound when perceived from beyond the immediate perspective of the dream environment.

Rationalization The forming of expedient **self**-justifications for **unconscious**, unacceptable, or irrational propositions or behaviours.

Rats Rats often represent the **penis** in **dreams**, for, like metaphorical penises, they **run** up things, and gnaw into things, and are objects of morbid fascination – dreams of rats emerging from **lavatories**, for instance, can imply a **fear** of the **sexual** act (or of the outcome of the sexual act). Rats had a considerably better press in ancient **times**, however, for they were associated with the **souls** of men, and deemed to have foreknowledge and **judgement**, and it is no doubt for this reason that they found themselves deified by the Phrygians and the Egyptians. **People** who dream of **white** rats may be relieved to know that Pliny the Elder considered them presagers of good fortune, while the **god** Apollo was known as 'rat-killer', and the ancient Irish steadfastly maintained that they could rid their **fields** of rats simply by rhyming the beasts to **death** (*pace* Ben Jonson's *Poetaster*). See **Pied Piper**
KEY LINE: 'Just then, by adverse fate impress'd,/A dream disturb'd poor Bully's rest;/In sleep he seem'd to view/A rat fast clinging to the cage,/ And, screaming at the sad presage,/Awoke and found it true.' (From William Cowper's *On the Death of Mrs Throckmorton's Bullfinch* 1782)

Ravens A raven symbolizes ill-luck and **death**. This is due to its alleged habit of sniffing out dying **bodies**, thanks to its acute sense of smell, and of congregating about **sick-rooms** and the **chimney** tops of **mourning houses**. In Norse **mythology**, ravens were **sacred** to the **god** Wotan. In **dreams**, ravens may also represent occluded vision, as in the floaters that some of us have in the vitreous of our **eyes**, the **shadows** of which – like the ravens in Van Gogh's final **corn field paintings** – tend to be cast on the retina in conditions of extreme luminosity.

Razors Razors – particularly in the case of cutthroats – tend to be **phallic** in connotation, suggestive, in the case of **females**, of a **fear** of **sex** and of its consequences (one would not wish to be made **love** to by a razor, for obvious reasons), or, in the case of **males**, **fear** of **castration**. Razors can draw **blood** and they can maim – they are also **symbols** of change, even when used benevolently, as in the controlling of **beards** and **hair** growth, for instance, or in the trimming of forged **passport photographs**. People who dream of **self**-mutilation with a razor may often be symbolically castigating themselves for the quality of their hidden or 'unacceptable' desires. See **Barbers**

Reaction Formation The disavowal of **unconscious** antisocial or unpalatable tendencies by the development of their exact opposites. A good filmic example might include Lewis Milestone's *Rain* (1932), based on the Somerset Maugham short story, in which a zealous **fire**-and-brimstone missionary, played by Walter Huston, lusts after a **prostitute**, Sadie Thompson (played by Joan Crawford), on the tropical **island** of Pago Pago. Instead of acknowledging his real **feelings**, he rationalizes them away by victimizing the **girl**, and turning everybody against her, triggering a tragedy in which he himself is subsumed (symbolically **self**-immolated). See **Rationalization**

Reading Reading presupposes paying particular attention to something, for it is impossible to read in a casual way, without, as it were, losing the plot. Reading may also suggest comprehension (or at least efforts made in that direction), elucidation ('reading between the lines'), and the quest for information and knowledge. This quest for knowledge (*ergo* power) lies at the **heart** of the threat that reading traditionally poses to totalitarian regimes – one thinks of Adolf Hitler, Chairman Mao, and the first great Chinese Emperor, Qin Shi Huangdi, all of whom came to believe in the suppression of written material. The **unconscious** mind is perfectly capable of acting in a similar capacity. See **Books**, **Dream Censorship** & **Libraries**

Reality Principle The reality principle is the exact opposite of the **pleasure principle**, and describes a condition in which adjustments are made to one's desires and urges in acknowledgement of the requirements of society at large.

Realtors See **Estate Agents**

Reaping Reaping implies that we have already put things aside for future provision, and that now we wish to derive the benefit due our forethought. There may also be a suggestion of getting one's just desserts – of 'reaping what we have sown'. The action of the **scythe** (see **Razors**) will inevitably hold revocations of the 'grim reaper', in the sense of the apparently random but seasonally inevitable **reality** of **death**.

Rebirth A primeval concept relating to the solstices and to the hope that **winter** will once again turn into **summer**, or that **illness** will one day transform itself back into health. This **archetypal** notion threads through virtually all **world religions** and dogmas, but it is notable for its absence in almost all secular faiths. Balder, Osiris, Tammuz and Orpheus, for instance, were all **killed**, and subsequently restored to **life**, at the order of the **Gods**. See **Resurrection**

Recollective Dreams The content of **dreams** is inevitably limited by the **dreamer**'s own cognitive and imaginative capacities – they cannot, in other words, contain information that the dreamer has never possessed, even if we accept, for a moment, the possibility of multiple lives. Dreams can, however, contain information that we **repress** or that we didn't know we possessed, as in, for instance, the subliminal memories of our lives before, let's say, the age of three, when we started to be able to filter and digest **conscious** thoughts about the **world** around us. One of the most wonderful aspects of our dreams is that they traduce so-called real **time** – the **past** and the present exist simultaneously and are equally open to the dream's scrutiny, and to its convenience.

KEY LINE: 'Time present and time past/Are both perhaps present in time future,/And time future contained in time past./If all time is eternally present,/All time is unredeemable.' (From T. S. Eliot's *Burnt Norton* – Part 1 of the *Four Quartets* 1943)

Records Records (in the sense of annals, archives, or chronicles) are **past** accounts of our behaviour that can come back to haunt us. They are therefore **anxiety** inducing, even if they may seem, at first glance, to be benevolent – we never quite know, of course, how people are going to interpret them in the future. A good example might be the prevalence of **smoking** in Hollywood **movies** of the 1930s, 40s and 50s – then, it was considered the epitome of glamour, and the fomenter of numerous **fetishes**; now, it's as good as banned.

Recovery Dreams Dreams in which the **dreamer** would appear to be recovering from whatever **neurosis** assails them. **Freud** categorized such dreams as 'convenience' or 'avoidance' **dreams**, designed to obviate further analysis.

Recurring Dreams Recurring dreams are **dreams** that return to the **dreamer** again and again, often continuing through from **childhood** and well into adulthood. Such dreams usually constitute an **unconscious** attempt to rectify defaults or defects in the dreamer's attitude to life. They can also reflect deep-seated prejudices, often triggered by traumatic episodes that have been consciously forgotten. On occasion, recurring dreams have been known to anticipate future events that are, in some sense, waiting to happen because of unconscious decisions and drives on the part of the dreamer. Another side-effect of recurring dreams is that they can artificially immunize us from the real effect of terrible events, by causing us to go over them again and again before they actually happen.

KEY LINE: 'But when a dream night after night is brought/Throughout a week, and such weeks few or many/Recur each year for several years, can any/Discern that dream from real life in aught?' (From James Thomson's *The City of Dreadful Night* 1874)

Red The **colour** red is often symbolic of **feeling** or passion, and is considered a lucky colour. It is also synonymous with **sex**, **excitement** and emotion. Red is also the colour of **blood**, and to that extent it often finds itself juxtaposed with **black**, the colour of **death**. In women's dreams red can apply to the loss of **virginity**, or to the act of defloration, just as it can to **menstruation**.

Red Indians Red Indians – in their filmic 'Cowboys and Indians' incarnation – tend towards the **archetypal** in **dreams**. The 'Red' aspect may represent projected **anger** (at being deprived of what rightfully belongs to the **dreamer**, for instance), whilst the 'Indian' equates with the 'noble savage' **archetype**, towards which many of us pay **lip** service (*ergo* dream service), without wishing to suffer the inconvenience of actually having to make do – as the Indians, in reality, did – in an entirely **self-sufficient** way.

Reduction of Affect The reduction of all the different emotions held within a dream into one overriding emotion.

Redwood Trees Redwood **trees** are the largest living things on **earth**, and they have, in consequence, a particular niche in dream imagery, because they are capable, not only of **representing** human aspirations towards higher values, but also of representing **God**.

Reefs Reefs are hidden **dangers** – we suspect their existence, know roughly where they are likely to be, but never quite know when we are going to **hit** one. They are barriers which contain and dictate both inward and outward movement, and dreaming of them suggests that we are feeling constrained by our perception of **risk**.

Reference Idea The concept that other **people's** actions and words slyly refer to an aspect of oneself that one would rather see hidden – such a person habitually **projects** their own thoughts onto others. Reference ideas frequently occur in **dreams**, in which one's 'real **self**' finds itself unmasked in a public **arena**.

Reflections Reflections of ourselves seen in **mirrors, ponds, puddles** and **water bowls** tend to suggest the parts of ourselves that we wish others to see (and value). The medium in which we are reflected is of the utmost importance here, with a **dirty** looking-**glass**, for instance, suggesting that we may feel tarnished and grubby, whereas the pristine **metal** of a **car** might indicate that we hold a considerably too high opinion of ourselves, or are over-conscious of status. To find ourselves reflected in the iris of another's **eye** might indicate incipient **paranoia**, the belief that we are a **target**, or a desire on our part to subsume, or to be subsumed in, another person or another aspect of ourselves.

Refrigerators A woman dreaming of a refrigerator (which can also be a **symbol** of the **vagina**), may be manifesting a **fear** of **frigidity** in her **sexual** life. Refrigerators are also storage spaces for things that 'have gone **cold**' – this may refer to old relationships, old ambitions, or **friendships** that have been 'put on **ice**'.

Regression The reversion, either in real life or in **dreams**, to an earlier, less mature state. **Psychoanalysts** have long maintained that fantasies have the same patho-dynamic effect as real experiences, and this can be echoed in regressive dreams, which frequently take us back to earlier stages of human development – the infancy of mankind, if you like – manifesting themselves in **cannibalism**, **sadism**, misogyny, man-**hating**, or other such atavistic tendencies. Such regressions, accompanied, as they inevitably are by the defensive postures of the **unconscious**, may **lead** to **neurosis**.

Reich, Wilhelm (1897–1957) Another fallen branch from the **Freudian** tree, Reich developed his orgone theory of radiating energy after his move to New York in 1939. In it, he postulated that organic **illness** stemmed from the blockage of universal vital energies which his 'orgone box' invention would release. He ended up spending two **years** in a Federal Penitentiary, after being indicted for fraudulent claims. He died there.

Reindeer Reindeer, to non-Lapps at least, tend to have cartoonish revocations (Rudolph), with bits of semantic nonsense (rain, dear?) thrown in. In **reality**, reindeer are notable for their antler span, and for their hierarchical **herd** instinct, and this is likely to be reflected in their **dream** significance. The **dreamer** may wish, for instance, to belong to, or to be accepted by, a particular community, or, alternately, to protect themselves or their ideas (the **head**) from outside interference.

Reins Reins imply the capacity or the desire to control or to be controlled, depending on context. To '**hold** the reins' suggests having power over others or over oneself, and the word 'reigning' constitutes an extra semantic layer to what is already somewhat of a **rich** brew. Broken reins may suggest a desire on the part of the **dreamer** to 'get out from under', whereas tight or oppressive reins might suggest the need to '**bridle**' or **repress** one's passions for **fear** of what would happen were they ever to be 'unharnessed'.

Relatives Relatives who appear in **dreams** are generally acting not as themselves but as some aspect of the **dreamer** that they either represent or threaten. A good example might have the dreamer conjuring up a **brother** or a **sister** within the context of a market or a fair. **Markets**, of course, suggest the need to get on with **people** if one is to survive or flourish – to 'come to some accommodation' with them.

Religions Public, rational obstructions between the human being and their private, instinctual relationship to **God**. In their guise as expedient contrivances, religions are mankind's way of projecting **dreams** of **fear** and hope onto **reality**. In psychoanalytical terminology, religions equate to the moral, or **superego** – i.e. they appear to be empowering, but they are usually limiting, in the sense that society needs them to control itself and in order to be able to function as a viable collective force.

Religious Symbols Religious **symbols** are naturally morphological, whereas **signs** tend to be **artificially** contrived. Religious symbols grow organically, as a result of primeval **dreams** and creative fantasies, until they become collective representations of the **nature** of the divine. See **Representability**

REM Rapid Eye Movement. This is the period in **sleep** when **dreams** are most likely to occur. It takes place perhaps four or five times during the course of a normal sleeping night, **beginning** about an hour into sleep, and then reoccurring during the course of the **night**, culminating in a final REM stage just before we awake in the **morning**. It is to this stage that we owe our success in **remembering our dreams**.

Remembering our Dreams The closer we are to awakening when our dream is perceived, the more accurately we are likely to remember its contents. Even the simple act of acknowledging that we dream every **night**, despite the fact that the vast majority of these **dreams** are forgotten upon **waking** – of paying attention to our dreams, in other words – will guarantee that dreams which would otherwise be **lost** will be recalled. The single best means for dream **recollection** lies in **pencil** and **paper** left next to the bedside, for there is something involved in the physical act of **writing** which seems to connect directly with the **unconscious** and to allow the most enlightened possible recall – a **tape** recorder comes in at a distant second place. The most important thing when transcribing dreams is not to interpose oneself (or one's sense of moral rightness) upon them. Simply describe exactly what occurred. The interpretation can come later. A modicum of work done in a state of half **sleep** is also helpful – allow the mind to **zigzag** back through the filigrees of memory that remain, and the dream should return in its near entirety (although one can only ever realistically hope for the 'tail end Charlie' of any normal, extended dream sequence). Only then rise from your **pillow**, snatch at your notepad, and begin writing. If this is not done, it means that a **resistance** to the potential message of the dream is already taking place. See **REM**

Rent Rent is what is required of us for the privilege of benefiting from the foresight or astute forethought of others. It is also what is required of us when we are poor, and to that extent it is a **reflection** of how we feel that we are perceived by a larger society. The value that we place on our **house** is also the value that we place on ourselves, and if we rent ourselves out, there is the inevitable implication attached that we might be **prostituting** ourselves or our talents.

Repairs Repairs to any structure in a **dream** usually refer back to the **dreamer** themselves, in the sense that the **unconscious** mind may be suggesting that 'something is rotten in the state of Denmark', and needs urgently seeing to.

Repetitive Motifs Repetitions in **dreams** are usually caused by **frustration**. If a particular motif in a dream finds itself endlessly repeated, it can, paradoxically, point up the importance and even the possible benefit of the individual ideas concerned. See **Recurring Dreams**

Reporters Reporters are information carriers – convenient **dream symbols** that suggest the need (or the likelihood) that information about the **dreamer** will find itself disseminated to a wider audience. Bearing in mind our 21st century obsession with **celebrity**, the image may find itself taken even further, with the reporter acting as conduit for the ambitions of the dreamer to transcend perceived mediocrity. The need to be persistently recognized or lauded by another, of course, implies (at least in terms of **wish-fulfilment**), a potential lack of confidence and **self**-worth.

Representability In **Freudian** dream analysis, the metaphors, **symbols**, mental ideograms and figures behind the formation of a significant image. Within representability, transfiguration can sometimes occur, as in the **splitting** of one person into two **people** within the context of the **dream** (the reverse of **condensation**, in other words) – examples of such splittings off might include **mother/daughter** and **father/son**. This second stage of **dream work** is also known as symbolization. See **Displacement** & **Secondary Revision**

Repression Repression of anything, in a dream context, creates **fear** and **anxiety** in the **dreamer**. An underlying tension is triggered as a result of the dreamer's fearful anticipation of the repressed action breaking through the **fabric** of the dream, and actually occurring.

Reproaches Reproaches, when they occur in a **dream** context, almost invariably refer to **self**-reproach on the part of the **dreamer**, and usually express **guilt**.

Reptiles Reptiles suggest **coldness** and amorality. Their functional lives appear to be entirely driven by expedience and short-term **goals** (the need to **eat** or to **kill**), and their significance to a **dreamer** will tend to be bound up with the possible **fear** that they engender as a result of this metaphorical inability to get through to what they may represent affectively. Reptiles tend to embody the unknown, therefore, and emotional **failure**.

Rescue The act of rescue is often a euphemism for the **sexual** act in **dream** imagery. Both **Freud** and **Rank** maintained that it reflected the **Oedipus** situation – i.e. the symbolical **killing** of the **father** and the consequent, or desired, rescue of the **mother**. See **Hero**

Reservoirs Reservoirs are backups designed to be used in **emergencies**, or when primary supplies of energy and/or resources are not available. They are primarily **water** repositories, and it is for this reason that they tend to be associated with the emotions, or with underlying, held back **feelings**.

Resignation Resignation, in a **dream**, might incorporate a reluctant acceptance of mortality, or it might suggest a **depressive** acquiescence or an inappropriate susceptibility to **failure**. Acceptance tends to have positive overtones in dream symbology, whereas resignation is predominantly negative.

Resistance Resistance occurs at some point in nearly all analytic and **self**-analytic relationships (*ergo* the relationship between the analyst and the analysand, or the **dreamer** to themselves). It is usually a defensive **measure**, designed to delay the relinquishing of often comforting (because long-standing) **conflicts**. In dream terms, such resistance may be personified by a persecutor, or by the conjuring up of **artificially** threatening situations which it seems eminently reasonable for the dreamer to try to avoid. To that extent, resistance often points to an attempt by the dreamer to reconstruct or rekindle an old **neurosis** – infantile fixations, as **Freud** discovered, are exceedingly hard to **abandon**. Freud described analytic sessions with a resistant client as 'difficult analyses', requiring significantly different measures than those with a more collaborative one.

Restaurants Restaurants are amenable and open to everybody just so long as that person has both the **money** and the nous to dress appropriately. Because restaurants are primarily **public** forums, there is an element of **ritual** about their use, implying that the subject is not necessarily being themselves in the restaurant environment – they are showcasing, in other words, and playing to the gallery, possibly as a result of a craving for **companionship** or for the anonymity of public places. As a result, restaurants have an element of neediness about them, and of latent **fear**. Will we behave correctly? Will we order or do the **right** thing?

Resurrection The age-old concept of something or someone arising from a dead state to a living one again. In **dream** terms, resurrection implies the bringing back into conscious mode of something that has long been **buried** in the **unconscious**. See **Zombies**

Retreating Retreating, both physically and metaphorically, presupposes a **self**-conscious understanding of one's own shortcomings. **Backwards movement** does not necessarily constitute retreat, of course, and the **dreamer** must be clear as to definition. Perhaps the easiest way to define retreat is via the fact that it tends to be involuntary, whereas backward movement may have a more strategic or tactical purpose.

Retreats Retreats represent the **dreamer's** desire to fill a spiritual **vacuum** – to that extent they constitute an outside resource for inner disharmony.

Revenge The anonymous epigram 'revenge is a **dish** best eaten **cold**' about sums up the likely upshot of revenge as gratification, for the ultimate **victim** is invariably the avenging party (i.e. the subject has effectively deprived themselves of the possibility of a hot **meal**). **Dreams** of revenge tend to **reflect** back on the subject of the dream, therefore, and to suggest hidden motivations and **wish-fulfilment** rather than the beneficent outcome of justified sinning. The final revenge taken is usually by the **dreamer** against themselves.
KEY LINE: 'Ah, God! what trances and torments does that man endure who is consumed with one unachieved revengeful desire. He sleeps with clenched hands; and wakes with his own bloody nails in his palms.'
(From Herman Melville's *Moby Dick* 1851)

Reversing Reversing, **retreating**, and **backwards movement** are three very different things. Reversing suggests the presence of an overweening will, ready to make itself uncomfortable if the end result seems worth the **candle** – it is also an acknowledgement of fault or error, and a quite conscious decision to rectify what has already partially come to pass. Reversing is proactive, retreating is reactive, and backwards movement is active, therefore.

Revolutions Revolutions are extreme reactions to perceived shortcomings in the status quo. In oneiric terms, the **dreamer** must be considered to be revolting against aspects of themselves which they find distasteful or not quite up to scratch. The physical act of turning or revolving may also enter the equation, implying, in **wish-fulfilment** terms, that everything that turns around comes around.

Rheumatism The place in which the rheumatism manifests itself is important here – if it is the **arm**, for instance, then certain activities that the arm does (or may potentially do) may be distasteful to the **dreamer** (i.e. **masturbation**, **wife beating**, abuse of some sort). In addition, rheumatism may reflect insensitivity and inflexibility of thought, particularly if the rheumatism manifests itself around the **head** or **neck**. An inability to get into a **bath**, for example, might lead one to suppose that the dreamer was over-cautious about entering into, or effectively analyzing, their emotions.

Ribbons Ribbons are almost invariably **female** accoutrements, designed to set off, or to show up, a particular aspect of the **body**. They may have **wound** revocations, too, and possibly even **menstrual** significance, in that the obvious wearing of a ribbon in a female **dreamer** would tend to draw attention to that part of the **body** which the ribbon emulates, in either **shape**, **size**, or **colour**.

Rice Rice, to the ancient Chinese, represented abundance, divine providence and immortality. This is carried over in the Western tradition of showering a newly **married couple** with rice, in earnest of the **wish** that they never go **hungry**, or in want. In **Buddhistic** terms, rice is a **symbol** of the higher emotions, and may be construed as embodying the **harvesting** of the **soul**.

Richness Extreme richness in a **dream** is usually **wish fulfilling** in meaning or content, implying a desire on the part of the **dreamer** to manifest externally what they would most desire to possess internally. Symbolically, richness is a concentration on a multiplicity of objects, rather than on one single object (i.e. **God**) – it is a distraction, in other words, from the strait **path**.

Riding Riding in a **car** is often synonymous with **masturbation** in a **dream**. Riding on **horseback** can have similar connotations. Riding can also be a dream euphemism for the **sexual** act itself, particularly if dreamt of by a **male**.

Rifles Rifles can often represent the **phallus** in **dreams**. In addition, the **fetishistic** way that many men treat their rifles and shotguns is a direct **reflection** back onto the value they place on their own 'equipment'. The fact that rifles can **kill** as well as project beauty and provide **nourishment** is not entirely uncoincidental. A rifle which is unable to be shot, which shoots blanks, or which backfires against its wielder, is particularly significant (for obvious reasons). See **Castration Complex**, **Guns** & **Shooting**

Right Traditionally the side of the **good** and the **just**. The right was also considered the side of **marriage**, stability and heterosexuality. See **Left**, **Left-Handedness** & **Right-Handedness**

Right-Handedness In ancient times, the **right hand**, because it was usually the stronger, was associated with masculine traits. In **astrology**, the **sun** was associated with the right **eye**. Right-handed auspices were considered good auspices, and the right-hand side of the **body** traditionally represents logic and rational behaviour. See **Left**, **Left-Handedness** & **Right**

Rings Rings often represent the **vagina** or the **anus**. They can also imply binding, or the **sexual** act, particularly when they are seen in terms of the movement of the **finger** towards the ring. The finger on which the ring resides is of particular significance here, as the forefinger traditionally implied a desire to be **married** (although without formal **engagement**), while the little finger suggested quite the opposite. Symbolically, the ring carries with it an endowment of the qualities of one person onto another, and a **gold** ring, in particular, was viewed as a sign of nobility, insofar as, in Roman times, only **magistrates**, senators and nobles were allowed to wear them (pre-Justinian).

Rising If a man **dreams** of rising into the air, it is usually synonymous with images of an erection, or an erect **penis**. In medieval **times**, however, **saints** and **holy** men frequently rose into the air in the symbolical equivalent, one presumes, of spiritual ecstasy. Famous risers include St Dunstan (marginally), St Robert de Palentin (several inches), Ignatius Loyola (two to three feet), Girolamo Savonarola (call it five feet – pre-execution), and the great maestro himself, St Philip of Neri, who allegedly managed an **ascension** of several **yards** on a **number** of separate occasions (although it is only fair to say that many **people** claim the *victor ludorum* for St Joseph of Cupertino). All joking apart, the sense of spiritual rising has a very real part to play in **dreams**, and almost certainly has something to do with wishing to rise up above everyday matters in order to gain a larger, more all-encompassing view of what lies beneath.

Risk Risk is an **anxiety** facilitator – without it, we achieve nothing, but with it, we make ourselves anxious. The **rush** that follows a successfully taken risk, however, more than compensates for any initial trepidation, and this **donkey/carrot** equation most probably carries through into **dreams**, in which risks are taken because our **unconscious** mind instinctively knows that it will be able to secure our safety (or **wake** us up) should things become too **hairy**.

Rites-of-Passage Rites-of-passage (often equated to coming-of-age **rituals**) are nearly always concerned, in symbolical terms at least, with the cutting off of inappropriately **incestuous** ties to **parents** and/or siblings. This is often enacted in a tribal or communal setting, and may represent, at least in cognitive terms, a move from one Kohlbergian (child psychologist Lawrence Kohlberg 1927–87) stage of moral development to another, superior one (at least in the capacity for rational judgement).

Rituals Rituals, in **dreams**, may represent evolutionary desires. There is a part of the brain that persists in believing that if one does a thing enough times – or enacts it with enough vim and **ceremony** – something, surely, must happen. There's more than a smattering of Darwin's 'Theory of Evolution' here, together with a dash of Manifest Destiny thrown in for good **measure**.

Rivers Rivers traditionally contained **spirits**, and were **symbols** of **nature's** force. To the ancient Chinese, the **Yellow** River, or *Huang*, just like the River Styx for the ancient Greeks, represented the natural border between life and **death**. In **Freudian** terms a river may represent urine, or the act of **urination**, whereas to a **Jungian** it might suggest the **passage** of the emotions. See **Secretions**

Roads Roads lead to places (perhaps even to infinity), and their existence in a dream might suggest the necessity for a **journey**. Other **people** travel on roads, too, and so the **dreamer** is guaranteed the possibility of encounters and transitory relationships (with people, things, or life). The condition of the road then becomes important, reflecting perceptions of the ease (or the difficulty) involved in following the waymarked **path**. Finally, the direction of the road – upwards, downwards, **north** or **south**, etc. – will suggest the tendency or gist of the **dream**. **Moving** upwards might suggest a desire for spiritual growth, whereas moving downwards might reflect despair, or **fears** about the future – if one continues with this line of thought, then **beating** eternally across a level plain might imply a fear of change, or, alternatively, a fear of conformity and sameness. A road may also symbolize the inevitability of **death**. See **Above, Below, Crossroads & Pavements**

Roaring A roaring sound in a **dream** – be it from a **river**, a wild **animal**, or a human being – suggests internal flux externalized. The implication here is that the emotion felt is so strong that it cannot find adequate human expression, and needs, as it were, to be animalized.

Robbers See **Burglars, Robbing & Terrorists**

Robbing The act of robbing in a **dream** suggests that the **dreamer** feels that they have, at some crucial point in their lives, been robbed of something that was rightfully theirs. This may refer to **energy**, rights, respect, health, or even material things, depending on the imagery that surrounds the robbery, and on the residual images that remain after the robbery has been perpetrated – paradoxically, this rule will tend to apply even if it is the dreamer themselves who appears to be the **guilty party**. A fundamental case of 'robbery', of course, is that of the **mother** by the **father** (or vice versa), or alternatively of the mother from the father by the **son** – leading to what **Freud** termed the **Oedipus Complex**.

Robes Robes are indicative of status – initiatory, inculcative, transgressional, or honorific. They may also be disguises that the **unconscious** mind annexes to protect the **ego** from the consequences of its own untrammelled thought processes.

Robin Redbreasts A robin traditionally symbolizes confiding trust. The splash of **red** on the robin's **breast**, however, may also carry Christian revocations of the **thorn** the robin was alleged to have plucked from **Christ's crown** on the way to Calvary – an action which caused it to be spattered with **Jesus' blood**. This may then carry over, in **dreams**, to the human **heart**, with all the customary implications associated with that **organ**.

Robots Robots imply sterility of thought and process – repetitive, uncreative acts, without initiative and with little motivation beyond expedience. Such mechanical responses may reflect back on the **dreamer**, or on how they feel they are perceived by outside **parties**.

Rockets See **Fireworks**

Rocking Rocking is often a sign of **mourning**, and to that extent it is a physical indication of an 'enclosure' of the emotions – a closing off from the outside **world**, if you will. Rocking may also be age related (in the sense of infant/venerable), in that a **mother** traditionally rocks her **baby**, while popular convention has a dotard rocking aimlessly – and on the way to nowhere – in a **chair**.

Rocks Rocks may abide, but they can also bushwhack, in the sense that they can appear as if from nowhere (**earthquake, volcanic eruption, underwater hazard**) and undermine the human vessels' progress. To this extent they can symbolize not only obstructions, but also opponents who stand in the way of the **dreamer**'s ambitions. See **Obstacles**

Rods A rod is a euphemism for the **penis**, and it can also indicate any other form of physical extension. It can conduct (i.e. it can transmit, or transmute, energy), and it can also **punish**. In **dream** terms it can become an extension of the **finger**, and to that extent it may also act as a **warning** about the consequences of intended actions. See **Fishing Rods**

Rollercoasters A rollercoaster tends to imply something that may at first glance seem out of control, but which may later prove to have been deliberate or premeditated – a risk taken with a view to grandstanding, perhaps, rather than as an end in itself. See **Dreamland**

Rollo the Norseman The 7th-century **war chief**, Rollo the Norseman (a man of such considerable bulk and girth that no **horse** could carry him), was warned in a **dream** that he was not, under any circumstances, to venture into England, as it was so ably defended by Alfred the Great. Better try France, the dream told him. So he sailed up the Seine towards Rouen and laid siege to Paris. After **marrying** Charles the Simple's **daughter**, Gisela, he became a reformed and humane man (and the not entirely uncoincidental ancestor of William the Conqueror).

Roofs Roofs equate with **hats**, giving rise to the inevitable **phallic** connotations, not least in the sense of providing (or needing) protection. Roofs can also symbolize limitations (particularly of **upwards movement**), and also, quite possibly, of mental capacities.

Rooms Rooms are often **female symbols** in **dreams**, and may, in consequence, represent the **vagina**. They are domestic, also, and can liberate via restriction, *ergo* Virginia Woolf's proto-feminist concept contained in her extended essay of 1929 entitled *A Room of One's Own*, the title of which inevitably contains vaginal connotations, in the sense of suggesting that a woman should have charge of her own **body** (and **mind**), rather than simply being at the mercy of over-dominant men.

Roosters Roosters rise early, they are assertive, and they make a considerable racket in the process. Sound familiar? Yes, roosters are masculine symbols, dedicated to the service of the **sun god** Apollo, to Mercury, and to Aesculapius, for, respectively, waking **people** up, summoning them to their business, and keeping them healthy as a result of prudent habits (early to **rise** and early to **bed**). See **Cocks**

Roots Roots run deep – they provide support and they act as conduits of energy and **nourishment**. They **anchor** things in a **storm**, and allow them to stand firm when racked by vicissitude. In a **dream** they may act in the guise of a **wish-fulfilment**, or as a grounding when the dreamer is **flying** high. They may also contrive to hold us back, in the sense of the **past**, or of our relations. Chopping at roots will tend to indicate a desire to **break** free from all that is attaching us to the **past** – but the image bears a **warning**, too, in that, without those very roots, we may soon lack sustenance.

Rope Rope is frequently a substitute for the **penis** when it appears in dreams. It can also represent the **umbilical**, or **life** force, and to that extent it can be either constraining (in the sense of 'roping something off'), or liberating (in the sense of attaching us to something that will aid and **nourish** us when we would otherwise be at risk of 'detachment').

Rorschach Test An ink blot test, **linked** to free association, invented by Swiss psychologist Herman Rorschach (1884–1922), and designed to elucidate personality traits as an aid to psychiatric diagnosis.

Rosaries To a Catholic, a member of the Orthodox **Church**, a **Buddhist**, a Muslim, a Hindu, or a Jain, a **rosary** (albeit of a differing configuration) will tend to **represent** a focus of **meditation**, in the sense that it aids in the **counting** of **prayers** or of other matters of spiritual significance. The necklet effect will also be important in dream terms, suggesting a circular enclosure, or **mandala**. See **Beads & Necklaces**

Rosemary Rosemary was yet another plant favoured for **dreams** of future **husbands**. It had to be placed underneath the **pillow** on All Hallows' Eve, together with a **silver** sixpence, if the **charm** was to have any chance of working. Traditionally, rosemary is an emblem of **remembrance** (*pace* Ophelia, in *Hamlet*), and may also be used as an aid to love-making or in the pursuit of a desired object or objective.
KEY LINE: 'The sea his mother Venus came on;/And hence some reverend men approve/Of rosemary in making love.' (From Samuel Butler's *Hudibras* 1663)

Roses Roses may be symbolic of the **vagina** when they appear in **dreams**, and also of the eventual **loss** of a woman's **virginity** – particularly if the rose and **blood** find themselves intermingled. For many centuries European folklore had it that to dream of **red** roses was lucky, but to dream of **white** ones was ill-omened. In modern times, red roses have become specifically linked to **love**, purity, and **female** pulchritude, and they are also one of the traditional emblems of England. In the ancient

language of **flowers**, however, each separate rose had a different significance, and one wonders whether aspects of this might not be reflected, **archetypally**, in dreams. The **yellow** rose, for instance, suggested **infidelity**, whereas the faded rose was held to suggest the fleeting aspect of beauty – the **dog** rose implied **pleasure** mixed with **pain**, while the moss rose indicated voluptuous love. Roses are also the emblem of **silence**, as in the expression *sub rosa*.

Rotting Rotting equates with deliquescence and impermanence – with temporality and evanescence. If something is rotten we suspect that there is something wrong with it – a conviction often heightened by our sense of **smell**, or by our sense of what is ineffably right. Rotting in a dream may constitute a signal, therefore, that the **dreamer** is sending themselves about the constitution of certain things, and of their transient **nature**. A good example might be a **pair** of rotting **bananas**, implying problems of fertility triggering relational problems between an otherwise powerfully connected **couple**.

Roulette Roulette is a **game** which requires next to no skill but which relies instead on chance. For this reason it can **represent** a **fear** of choosing, exemplified by the passing over of personal responsibility onto what is the equivalent of a random throw of the **dice** (loaded, in this case, against the **gambler**). It is an **anxiety** trope, in other words, suggesting mixed **feelings** about imminent decisions. See **Gamblers** & **Games**

Roundness Roundness indicates a natural wholeness. A quadrangular **shape** often **reflects** this in normal, as opposed to dream, **consciousness**. Both forms can meet in **dreams**, leading the **dreamer** towards a concept of the **centre**, or **self**. See **Mandala**

Round Tables Round tables bring to mind the Arthurian Legends, and images derived from pictorial representations of the Last Supper. When such **tables** are broken up (the perfidy of Judas Iscariot; the **search** for the Holy Grail), wholeness can, for a time, be **lost**. See **Breaking**, **Mandala** & **Roundness**

Royalty See **Kings, Queens**, etc.

Rubber Rubber can erase the **past**, and we can **drive** on it (in the sense of **tyres**) towards the future. It is flexible, and able to be moulded into whatever **shape** we require of it. It is a natural substance, and capable of protecting us, both **sexually**, and from inclement **weather**. Viewed like this, rubber becomes nigh on a universal panacea, and it is likely that the **unconscious** mind will snatch at it, as a **symbol**, as much for its bouncing characteristics (in the sense of 'bouncing back' from a setback), as for its good natured and eminently convenient amenability.

Rubies Rubies were the original **philosopher's stone** – the Hindu **flowers** of the **sun**, symbolizing all the aspects of the 'higher **mind**' and the **ascent** of the **soul** in search of wisdom (involution) (see **Falling**). This may be because of their resemblance to an **eye**, and to the significance of the **colour red**, which also gave to the ruby its connection to medieval royal fertility. Within **dreams**, the ruby may also signify a **wound**.

Rucksacks See **Knapsacks**

Rudders Rudders suggest a desire for control, or a desire for guided evolution. Because rudders are **hidden**, this **guidance** may come either from the outside, or from unexpectedly close quarters – even from part of the metaphorical **family** '**boat**'. See **Planks**

Rugs See **Carpets**

Ruins One of the greatest of all the early English (Anglo-Saxon) **poems** is called *The Ruin*. Written 300 **years** after the end of the Roman occupation of Britain, it details the scop's (poet's) **journey** through the ruins of what may be Bath (*Aquae Sulis*). Awestruck by the quality of the stonework, the **poet** imagines that '**Giant**'s hands made it'. Ruins can still contain these sorts of revocations, suggesting mystery and **lost** knowledge and the existence of **peoples**, societies, and artefacts the likes of which we can only conjure up in the imagination, or in **dreams**. Ruins, then, suggest the greatness of the **past**, and the transient **nature** of human ambitions.

Running Running without moving forward is a classic symptom of **anxiety**, but must be taken in the context of the particular images and **symbols** that surround the ineffective action. It can also have a physical cause, and be a response, let's say, to a rapid pulse rate caused by **illness**, **heat**, or other sensory input. To that extent it may prevent **injury**, by causing the **dreamer** to awaken from a position that is restricting their circulation. It may also indicate a 'running away' from the control of the **superego**. See **Frustration Dreams & Lateness**
KEY LINE: 'That time I flew,/Both eyes his way/Lest he pursue/Nor ever ceased to run/Till in a distant Town/Towns on from mine/I set me down/This was a dream.' (Emily Dickinson 1870)

Rushing Rushing is a nervous thing, and very often chemically induced. We call a sudden emotion a 'rush', too, with the implication that it has been triggered from the outside in terms of stimulus. For a **dreamer** to rush suggests a **fear** of **time**, and of time's effects, whilst the sound of the **wind** through rushes may indicate a similar transitoriness.

Rust Rust presupposes disuse, or the gradual loss of interest in an object that had hitherto engaged us. Rust also acts on both the interior and the exterior of an article, and for this reason it can suggest spiritual, as well as physical, senescence. Finally, there can be a beauty to rust, and this pictorial aspect may leaven or dilute the pejorative overtones of the image, making of the rusted implement (or aspect, or relationship) a quasi-desirable artefact.

Ruts Ruts slow us down on our way forward – they act as brakes or catalysts, forcing us from our formerly smooth **path** onto a different, and possibly less conducive, orbit. They are difficult to get out of, too, and may suggest a stick-in-the-**mud** or overly reactionary mentality.

S

Sabotage Sabotage is designed to cause outrage and affront. In its **self**-destructive guise – the one most likely to appear in **dreams** – it offends reason, in the sense of seeming to go against **nature** (in the form of the constructive use of our physical and mental resources). When projected onto others, sabotage suggests the **dreamer**'s outrage at their own lack of forward movement, and the expedient blaming of this onto third parties.

Sackcloth Sackcloth is a **symbol** of **mourning**, entropy and pre-reincarnative humiliation, and although few modern **dreamers** would even know what sackcloth looked like, the image itself – due to our familiarity with the **biblical** saying 'sackcloth and **ashes**' (Genesis, Samuel, Esther and Matthew, with only the last two, in the **King** James translation, using that exact wording) – may well pop up in **dreams** in any variety of guises, the majority of which will tend to reflect a sense of loss or of unjustified deprivation.

Sacks Sacks conceal – and, what's more, they tend to store what is concealed for later retrieval. Such an image plays into the **hands** of the **superego**, which may use the image as a warning to the **ego** not to stray too far along the **path** of self-indulgence. The **nightmarish** figure of the sack-man, or *el hombre del saco*, is an **archetypal** children's **myth** figure, common to Spain, Portugal and Germany, and usually consisting of an old man who **kidnaps** unruly or **sleep**-averse **children** in his sack, never to be seen again. This 'man with a sack' image was cunningly used by Beatrix Potter in her *Tale of Mr Tod* (Tod is German for **Death**), in which the vulpine Tod conducts a similar **witch-hunt** on the local bunny population.

Sacred Marriage, The The coming together of the **male** and **female** principles in a positive, rather than a negative, **light**. Age-old **rituals** are still used to **celebrate** the concept of such a union and its mutual interdependence, and include the **carrying** of the **bride** over the **threshold**, and the **exchange**, or **giving**, of **rings**. In **dreams**, such a **marriage** may indicate a desire on the part of the **dreamer** for a complementary union restoring, or providing, some element that is **missing** in their **waking** life. See **Anima, Animus, Dionysus, Marriage, Titans & Wedding**

Sacredness To dream of sacredness is to dream of exceptions. Something which is sacred is, by definition, outside normal parameters, and is, in addition, notable in some particular way. For the **dream** to single out particular objects, **people**, or artefacts, shows that they have a special significance for the **dreamer**, and that they are, to all intents and purposes, beyond criticism.

Sacrifice Sacrifice can be either positive or negative, **masochistic** or altruistic. The sacrificial object is of crucial importance here, as is the fact of whether that object seems amenable to the sacrifice or not. A great deal of **projection** occurs during most sacrificial acts, with the eventual victim often taking the place of the devitalized committer, in what may well become an exercise in aspirational transmutation. See **Shamans**

Saddles The French phrase *à califourchon* (implying a **fork**-like **splitting**) splendidly evokes, by reverse inference, the symbolic meaning of a saddle. It is a joiner-together of two disparate things, whilst also carrying with it an implication of **burdens** borne and duties unwillingly discharged. The actual act of saddling something is a dominant one, and implies a desire for mastery over the chosen object.

Sadism A morbid practice characterized by the ill-treatment of others for **sexual** gratification. Sadism in **dreams** is often the **dreamer**'s response to a perceived 'unfair' domination occurring in real life – of a **boy** or a man by his **mother**, for instance, or a **girl** or a woman by her **father** (to suggest merely two examples). The term derives from the name of the French aristocrat, Donatien Alphonse François, Conte de Sade (1740–1814), a.k.a. the Marquis de Sade, whose **novels**, **plays** and philosophical treatises describe the practice in minute, and frequently gratuitous, detail. See **Killing** & **Masochism**

Sado-Masochism See **Masochism** & **Sadism**

Safaris Safaris are **journeys** made to 'see' things (from the Arabic-rooted Swahili word *safar*, a journey). The obvious semantic **link** here is to 'see far', implying an **opening** out of either the spiritual or the physical dimension.

Sages See **Wise Old Men**

Sailing Boats See **Boats**

Sailing Sailing equates with desired emotional freedom, in the sense of **skating**, in apparent safety, over deep waters. The fact that whatever really lies beneath you may not possibly be construed from the mere shallow perspective of the deck of a **yacht** should more than slightly leaven the **dreamer**'s cruising joy, however – to more fully address the emotional depths concealed beneath the **boat**, it might be thought necessary to at least place a **toe** into the **water**.

Sailors Sailors represent freedom from terrestrial constraints. In symbolical terms, they are the **ego**-conductors of the **soul** (a.k.a. the **pilgrims** of the **night**), driven (at least in terms of the Egyptian *Am-Tuat*, and the **boat** of the **sun** god Ra) by the **sails** of faith.

Sails Sails are often **penile** symbols in **dreams**, but if one delves deeper, it may be shown that they imply enhanced reception, too, in the sense of aiding in the capture of the **soul**'s ambitions. See **Sailing** & **Sailors**

St Denis, Hervey de The **author** of the 1867 *Les Rêves et les Moyens de les Diriger* (*Dreams and the Means of Controlling Them*), this professor of Chinese at the *College de France* had studied so-called **lucid dreaming** for a period of 32 **years** before attempting to set down his thoughts on **paper**. He used the resulting **book** to describe how he was able partially to master his **dreams** from the age of 13 onwards, and to offer **guidance** as to how others might achieve a similar result.

Saint John's Wort As well as being a catch-me-all for **eye** troubles and the **menopause**, Saint John's Wort is also said to induce **dreams** of **spirits** and spectres in the unwary. If the Hypericum was gathered on St John's Eve, before the dew was off it, and placed beneath a **fasting** maiden's **pillow**, she would dream of her future **husband** and **marry** within the **year**. See **Artificial Dreams**

Saints Saints suggest the possibilities of harmony between the individual and the **nature** (or essence) of the Divine. Incorporated into this **reading** is the notion of perfection, and the concomitant attainment of complete liberation from terrestrial ties through assimilation by the godhead. At a more mundane level, saints are **teachers**, and their presence in a **dream** might suggest a desire to be led along an enlightened path, and in an enlightened way. See **Leading**

Salads Salads are mixtures of things, and to that extent they may have **alchemical** revocations, in that the admixture presupposes a collective increase in power once individual articles find themselves conjoined with other, similar articles. If this seems just a little farfetched, then the contents of the salad should be investigated, with the significance of each individual item analyzed – it may then be found that the juxtaposition of any two or three articles produces an increased value equation.

Salaries Salaries are **payments** for services rendered – and services, what's more, that are required from us on a regular basis. In **dreams**, then, salaries often refer to affective or familial relationships, and to the duties and responsibilities involved in maintaining such interactions on a level footing. If a salary is withheld, duties may be being shirked. If the salary finds itself **magically** raised, the **dreamer** may be considering that their value to others is being ignored, and that unilateral action may be called for.

Salesmen/Saleswomen Salesmen **sell** us things they want us to want. In **dreams** salesmen frequently represent the **dreamer** trying to sell themselves a bill of goods which may or may not be judicious, but which the dreamer feels they need. Should the salesman be over-intrusive, there may be a suggestion that the dreamer is trying to convince themselves of something which their **unconscious** mind deems either antagonistic or inappropriate.

Saliva Saliva has healing qualities. A child with a birthmark was traditionally cured by the **mother**, or another woman, licking the afflicted spot every day for between nine and 30 days after **birth** (before having taken breakfast – the **fasting** aspect being of the utmost importance). Saliva in **dreams** may be threatening (as in drooling), restorative (as in healing), or rebarbative (as in regurgitating). It may contain **links** to our **animal natures**, or symbolize a perceived loss of control. See **Healers**

Salmon Salmon are mystical creatures, in the sense that, despite all the scientific brouhaha surrounding their life cycle, their conduct and motivations still remain a mystery to both fisherman and marine biologist – in fact the **author** knows of Scottish gillies who have spent a lifetime studying the salmon's ebb and flow, often on one particular **river**, and who still pronounce themselves mystified by the whims of this capricious and enigmatic **king** of **fish**. The caught salmon certainly provides a connection with the lower **self** (the arbiter of the so-called desire-**nature**), and to this extent the salmon will tend to represent the instinctual, emotionally asseverating part of man in **dreams**. In Nordic **myth** the salmon was the familiar of the **god** Loki (Loke), indulging him in all his stratagems and **tricks** against the Aesir (Odin's chief-horde). In Celtic mythology, Fionn mac Cumhall unwittingly tasted of the 'salmon of knowledge', thereby learning how to outwit his enemies and defend Ireland in its hour of need. This fickle, whimsical element may also be present in the dream, together with the underlying constancy of a propagating fish that will inevitably return to the exact same river, and to the exact same **spot** that it was spawned in, following thousands of miles of **journeying**, and after an interval of **years**. See **Fishing** & **Fishing Rods**

Salt Salt symbolically relates to the permeation of **truth** through the false **levels** of expedient belief. Salt may also carry revocations of youth and passion, which would correlate with the pejorative overtones of the 'spilling of salt', in terms of both **superstition** and incorruption (which salt exemplified). A pinch of salt placed inside a **coffin** was traditionally considered to ward off the attentions of **Satan**. See **Spillages**

Sanctuary Sanctuary is an enlightened aspect of civilization. The idea that one can control desire for long enough to allow another person the benefit of the doubt is only possible in an ordered and literate society (and by this I include so-called barbaric societies that are nevertheless open to the concepts of **totem** and **taboo**). Sanctuary is also about exceptions to the rule and, by process of default, the rule itself.

Sand It is quite possible that sand became connected with **time** way before man thought of placing it in a receptacle and using is as a **measure**

for hours and minutes, for no one, surely, can stand on a **beach** and watch the **tide** ebb and flow over the ever-changing sand without dwelling, even for a little while, on the probabilities of transformation and temporality. In **dream** terms, therefore, sand will tend to indicate insecurity and **fear** of change, with drifting sand obscuring our **vision** of the future, and dis-integrating edifices made of sand suggesting that 'The best-laid schemes o' mice an' men/Gang aft a'gley,/An' lea'e us nought but grief an' pain/ For promised joy.' (From Robert Burns's *To a Mouse* 1785)

Santa Claus The **name** is a corruption of Sankt Nikolaus, the patron **saint** of **children**, and the **night** of his bringing of **gifts** to a sleeping child is sometimes celebrated on the 5th December and also, of course, on Christmas Eve. See **Befana, Bertha & Dame Abonde**.

Sap Sap tends to **represent** the **life** force in **dreams**, but unlike **blood** (which merely thickens or **thins**), sap is infinitely amenable to the **seasons**, and takes its essence from their changes. Sap may also contain revocations of seminal fluid, tears, micturition, sweat, putrefaction and **condensation**, and to that extent may echo the externalization of internal thoughts or attributes. See **Secretions**

Sarcophagi See **Coffins**

Satan See **Devil**

Satellites Satellites frequently represent **children**, in the sense that they appear to be free, but they are in fact forever orbiting (albeit at occasionally great distances) around the **mother** or **father ship** or **planet**. This leaching of essential energy – this amenability to the forces of gravity – infuses the meaning of satellite, and ensures its **chain** reactive role.

Satyrs Satyrs (part **animal**, part human attendants of the **god** Dionysus) are **id** simulacra, in the sense that they personify total freedom of action without any leavening whatsoever of moral responsibility. Symbolically, they objectify the higher aspects of the **mind** (the **horns**, the pointed **ears**) twinned with the lower aspects of the **soul** (the **horse**'s **tail**, the **legs** of a **goat**). In **dreams** they will tend to reflect **wish-fulfilment** fantasies related to the casting off of normal moral constraints and the non-liable pursuit of hedonism. See **Dionysian & Nymphs**

Savings Savings, **money** in the **bank**, **nest eggs** and rainy day money all suggest **constipation**, or the retention of faeces. This 'forcing of issues' is a quasi-constant dream motif associated with **anxiety**, often in the sense of 'are we living our lives well?', or 'how may we ameliorate our lives in some way, without having to change our essential **natures**?' If one retains something (an object, an idea) in the expectation of one day being able to use it, present action is inevitably stultified, leading to iner-tia, **self**-satisfaction, and vainglory. Savings dreams are therefore the '**belt** and braces' **dreams** of the canon, and may ultimately disguise a well-hidden **fear** of **death**.

Saviour A saviour, in a **dream**, can equate with **Jesus Christ**, for in religious terms the 12 **biblical** apostles represent the 12 saviours of the **soul** through which the higher **self** may eventually be raised to bliss. Symbolically, the saviour is often an aspect of the **dreamer** themselves which wishes to protect or redeem a part of the dreamer's essential **nature** that may seem under threat. The saved person or artefact then becomes important, and will suggest clues as to what features of the dreamer's personality are deemed to be most in **danger** – a young **girl** or a **female** rescued by a **male**, for instance, might suggest the **anima**, whereas a woman struggling to draw a **male** out of a **bog** or to prevent a male from destroying himself, might suggest the **animus**. See **Destruction**

Saws In purely **Freudian** terms, the **backwards** and forwards movement of the saw (and its relation to the **hand**) would tend to be linked to **masturbation**, whereas **Jung** might have viewed the saw as a metaphorical **tool** with which to construct new things from old. The **movement** of sawing remains important in both **readings**, however, with, in the Jungian reading, its suggestions of hesitation and setback (when one encounters a **knot**), and the need for energy, skill, and creative determination, if one is to finish accomplishing one's task.

Scaffolds Scaffolds tend to be **warnings** – it is, after all, only the miscreant who actually mounts the scaffold to his **death**, but it is a potentially enormous **audience** which views it, and absorbs its message. Scaffolds, in the sense of scaffolding, are constructive entities, designed to sustain **weight** (or, in the case of a **book's** scaffolding, to carry the weight of an extended storyline), and weight will inevitably be associated with the appearance of a scaffold in a **dream**, too, as will expectation.

Scales For a Muslim **dreamer**, scales will bring to mind the scales of the archangel Gabriel, in which everyone will be weighed on the Day of **Judgement**. Those whose good deeds outweigh their sins will make it across the Al Serát **bridge**, but the remainder will **fall** into the eternal gloom of Jehennam (or Gehenna, the place of eternal torment). The presence of scales in a **dream** inevitably denotes comparisons, in the sense of **measuring** or weighing one thing against another – 'if I do that, then this will happen', or 'how does this compare with that?' If one side of the scales consistently fails to measure up to the other, then it will tend to be the dreamer's **self**-esteem which finds itself on the lower side – in that case the actual description of what is being weighed will come to the fore.

Scalping Scalping implies something valuable being taken from the **head** for the use of another. This may suggest ideas being stolen, or strength (**hair**), or beauty. The symbol of a **belt** full of scalps may also suggest promiscuity, or a failure correctly to value one's fellow human being.

Scanners The presence of a scanner in a **dream** implies a search for knowledge or understanding about something that is threatening the **dreamer**. Scanners 'make sense' of complicated things, and give us insights into the internal mechanisms of externally explicit problems.

Scapegoats The scapegoat is a pre-**biblical**, **archetypal** image, to do with the **transfer** or **projection** of collective **guilt**. The vessel (the **goat**, the **boat**, the person) which carries the guilt is ejected into both a real and a symbolical wasteland, allowing transgression to be replaced by true knowledge. In **dreams** the scapegoat is likely to reflect the **dreamer**'s perception of themselves as the butt for others' guilt projections – there are no easy answers to this, save in the physical condition of the outcast scapegoat, which may betoken the capacity (or not, as the case may be) of the dreamer to carry such a **burden**.

Scarabs In Egyptian **mythology** scarab **beetles** were **sacred** creatures. They **represented** the cause of things, the **soul** of things, their fertility, and their subsequent **resurrection** (via the **god** Khepera – or the 'one who rolls'). Golden scarabs represented the **sun**, whereas **black** scarabs symbolized **darkness**, and the work of **devilish** forces. In **dreams**, if a beetle enters the **body**, life within **death** may be assumed, whereas if a beetle exits the body, the **soul**, or the evolution of the lower into the upper, may be construed.

Scarecrows Scarecrows are **warning** figures – symbolically, they represent **death**, decomposition, and intellectual **emptiness**. If it is the **dreamer** who appears as the scarecrow, the image might tend to suggest vapidity, or the fomenting of a false image with nothing much inside it. If the dreamer finds themselves confronted by a scarecrow (and made **anxious** by it), then a **fear** of being seen by others as less than one feels oneself to be, is probably at the **root** of the scarecrow's appearance.

Scars Scars suggest old **wounds** that have healed but that have not yet been forgotten. Scars are also external manifestations of internal (i.e. emotional) damage – in this case, the location of the scar becomes important. If the scar is near the **heart**, for instance, it might suggest **damage** from an affective relationship, whereas if the scar is near the **head**, the damage may be more intellectual in content. See **Healers**

Scent See **Odours**

Sceptres Sceptres tend to be **phallic**, in the sense that they imply male **pattern** dominance (either in the **male**, or in the **female**). As with wands and **staffs**, sceptres may also imply a more than temporal power, in the sense of a dominance of the physical by the formal, and the capacity to raise those touched by the sceptre (wand, **sword**, what have you) into a lesser (or more humble) simulacrum of the bestower.

Schedules Schedules are **anxiety** indicators, in that they presuppose a **time** limit for the completion of potentially important actions. They are also restrictive, in the sense of negating the exercise of so-called free will in the completion of necessary duties. If a **dreamer** sets themselves a schedule, or finds themselves unwillingly faced by a schedule imposed from outside, any interpreter of the **dream** will be forced into the supposition that either the dreamer does not trust themselves, or alternately that they suspect that others may not trust them to fulfil certain undertakings.

Schizophrenia A morbid loss of contact with, and understanding of, what passes for **reality**. Commonly referred to as a **split** mind or a split personality, sufferers from schizophrenia commonly suffer **hallucinations**, delusions and the **hearing** of **voices**, alongside the catastrophic disintegration of their personalities.

Scholar's Dream, The According to Chinese dream legend, a Taoist **scholar**, elated at passing his Imperial examinations, went walking in the **Temple**. Exhausted, he asked if he might rest in the **room** of a *bonze* (a **Buddhist monk**). While dozing, he dreamed about his future. First, the **dream** told him that he would reach high **office**, and would enrich himself through mendacity – following his **death**, however, he would be forced to **drink** the exact equivalent of his ill-gotten gains in molten **gold**. He would then be reborn into a **family** of beggars, as a **girl**, and be sold off as a scholar's concubine. The scholar awoke shortly after his second death, awash with the horror and the vanity of the world's **honours**, and with the firm resolve to retire to the **mountain** and seek the **Path**. See **Lu Tung-Pin**

Schools Schools are rarely entirely positive images in **dream** terms, largely because, as adults, we usually feel that we have been there and done that, and no longer wish to suffer under such a restrictive regime. Should a **child** dream of school, it is usually in terms of a **resistance** against it, rather than as a welcoming move towards it. Schools are imposed on us by society for our betterment – we are (most of us, at least) convinced of the strength of this **argument**, but not always entirely comfortable about the means with which the argument is carried **home**. See **Students & Universities**

Schwind, Moritz von (1804–71) Von Schwind's 1860–63 **painting** of *The Dream of the Knight* (a.k.a. *The Captured Princess*) is a romantic evocation of the ideals of chivalry. It portrays a **knight** sleeping in a woody dell to whom a **princess** appears, her **hands** bound, her **face** eloquent of wistful **sadness**. Von Schwind painted a number of **dream** paintings, amongst which *The Dream of the Prisoner* and *The Dream of Erwin of Stone Creek* are probably the most notable.

Scientists Scientists **represent** the possibility of rational answers to what may at first seem to be irrational **questions**. In **dreams** scientists tend to appear as **teachers** or **guides**, possessing esoteric knowledge not normally available to uninitiated human beings. Picturing oneself as a scientist in a dream may imply an over-identification with the intellectual at the expense of the instinctive.

Scissors Scissors suggest either that something needs to be cut out of the **dreamer**'s life, or that the dreamer **fears** the **loss** of some aspect of themselves that an outside party may gain access to (**breasts**, **testicles**, or the brain, for instance – *ergo* prefrontal lobotomy). The **cutting** off aspect is important here, implying the necessary truncation of two states of being – an image accentuated by the **twin legs** of the scissors, and by the **eye**-like **finger holes**. The cutting action only occurs when the two sides are brought together, whereas the non-cutting (i.e. protective) action relies on the limbs/**organs** being separated. See **Amputation** & **Shears**

Scopophilia Sexual gratification derived from viewing or imagining images of other **people**, rather than by direct experience. Sexually driven **dreams** tend, by definition, towards the scopophiliac, but should not necessarily be interpreted in a **sexual** way – voyeurism may be as much about **self**-image as it is about sexual **projection**. Scopophilia, according to the Lacanian definition (reforming psychoanalyst Jacques Lacan, 1901–81) represents a fragmentation (or decentring) of a formerly existing unity, occurring in infancy, and in which the child first realizes, thanks to a '**mirror** phase', that a **world** consisting of other **people** and their motivations exists beyond their own personal orbit.

Scorching Scorching can be disguising, modifying and reactive. If an article (or a person) in a **dream** is so hot that one cannot touch it, it suggests that the **dreamer** fears the effect of that article on their physical or mental well-being. Both **fever** and **heat** tend to equate with heightened emotions in a dream context, and invoke potentially life-changing transformations.

Scorpions The sting in the **tail** is the scorpions' most potent dream image – even **astrologically**, this aspect predominates over all others (even the sexual predation). Orson Welles loved telling a so-called 'immortal story', which described the scorpion's essential nature to a T – he even used it in his 1955 film, *Mr Arkadin*. In Welles' version, a scorpion approaches a **frog** at the side of a **river** – 'Take me across on your back,' the scorpion says. The frog laughs. 'I'm not that witless. You'll sting me.' The scorpion shakes his head. 'I'd be mad to do that. I'd drown.' Convinced of the logic of the scorpion's **argument**, the frog agrees to **carry** him. Halfway across, he feels a terrible **pain** in his back. 'You've stung me!' he croaks. 'Why did you do it? Now we'll both die.' With his final breath, the scorpion sighs. 'I know it was a stupid thing to do. But it's my **nature**.'

Scott, Sir Walter (1771–1832) The Scottish **writer** Sir Walter Scott dictated the whole of *The Bride of Lammermoor* (1819) from his sickbed, occasionally getting up and continuing with the dictation in a somnambulistic (**sleepwalking**) state. When he eventually recovered from his **illness**, Scott admitted of the **book** that 'he did not recollect one single incident, character or conversation it contained!'

Screen Memory A *bona fide* memory that is used to disguise, or draw attention away from, another, related memory. The **latent** or repressed memory frequently reoccurs, in altered form, in **dreams**, where it needs careful **teasing** out and unlayering.

Screws Screws may be **sexual** (for the inevitable reasons), but they may also act in an adhesive capacity, anchoring two disparate things together via a physical **chain** or **link**. The **spiral** aspect of the screw is also important, and may contain DNA revocations (the DNA spiral, or double-stranded helix, being akin to the **Golden** Section). This brings us neatly back to the sexual, therefore, and to the link between 'screwing', procreation, and the principles of genetic heredity.

Scripts Scripts contain pre-digested words which negate any need for additional creative input. All that is required is the capacity to act out (and personally infuse) the work of another. This notional dialogue between three **people** (the creator, the enactor, and the **audience**), boils down, in **dreams**, to a monologue with oneself. The equational lynchpin inevitably contains **wish-fulfilment** elements concerned with not taking full responsibility for one's own actions – if another writes the script, you see, they must also take partial responsibility for the outcome of the set-piece.

Scrolls Scrolls traditionally contain **truths** and **secrets** about the **past**. The unrolling of the scroll imitates the gradual unravelling of memory and the belated comprehension which sometimes follows. Scrolls also suggest the passing down of information from one generation to another (again, the physical makeup of the scroll adds to its meaning). In their rolled up form, there may be a **phallic** element to a scroll, too, with the suggestion of a genetic carry-over from one generation to another.

Scythes The scythe is linked to the **cutting** away of ripened or unnecessary items – this aspect is **reflected** in the connection between **time** and scythes, in the sense of **death**, mortality, the Grim Reaper and Kronos/Cronus (Old **Father** Time). In **dreams**, a scythe may also represent a desire on the part of the **dreamer** to clear away the old in favour of the new – if the scythe is threatening, however, the opposite may be true. See **Knives**

Sealing Things Sealing things, in a **dream**, may have **sexual** connotations – if the **vagina** is viewed as an open receptacle, the **penis** then 'seals' it shut – seals, in addition, are signs of ownership (or acknowl-edgements of interest). Sealing the **lips** in a dream might suggest a need to temper the personality, or **rein** in certain aspects of one's behaviour. See **Philip II of Macedon & Sex**

Seams Seams represent the potential **weak** points of a relationship – i.e. things tend to 'come apart at the seams', as well as being joined there. Seams may also work semantically in a **dream**, in the sense of an auspi-cious or '**rich** seam' of some sort – luck in a relationship, say, or success in a joint undertaking – finding itself represented by the **colour gold**.

Séances To dream of séances is to dream of gaining some advantage through outside or unknown forces. This is **wish-fulfilment** taken to its logical conclusion, in the sense that to imagine a séance as providing the answer to any fundamental **questions** is akin to believing in a *deus ex machina* which is benevolently amenable to human will.

Searching See **Finding**

Searchlights Searchlights mark out and isolate issues that would other-wise lose themselves in a collective **fog**. To that extent they can represent the workings of insight, intellectual acuity, spiritual application (the con-centrated focus of **light**), or even caution, in the sense of the **flagging** up of **danger** areas and the **drawing** of the dreamer's attention to them. If the searchlight is focused on the **dreamer**, then it is likely that they feel marked out or unpleasantly earmarked in some way, rather as a **rabbit** might feel when caught in a **car's** headlights, or in the lamper's beam. See **Lighthouses**

Seas The sea, according to **Jung**, is a **symbol** of the **collective uncon-scious**, due to the unfathomable depths it hides. The regenerative aspect of the sea is also important, in that the sea is to a large extent **self-fuelling** and self-fulfilling. In symbolical terms the sea represents the aspect of the astral plane that deals with our desires and, according to Plutarch, our passions (in the guise of Typhon, or Set). Diving into the sea in a **dream** might then suggest giving in to – or allowing ourselves to be subsumed by – our emotions. See **Oceans**

Seasons Seasons usually relate to age when they appear in **dreams** – **spring** equates to infancy (Adam and Eve in Paradise), **summer** to youth (Ruth in the cornfields), **autumn**/fall to maturity (Joshua and Caleb bringing **grapes** from the Land of Promise), **winter** to senescence (the Deluge). Symbolically speaking, the seasons refer to the cycles of the **soul**'s evolution, and this **reading** may also be reflected in dreams, in a sense akin to 'what goes around, comes around'.

Seaweed See **Kelp**

Secondary Revision Freud's term for the semi-rational rearrangement of the details of a **dream** by the **dreamer** in order to give order and a notional semblance of coherence to what, before analysis, or before the full recall of the dream, may seem simply chaotic. See also **Condensation, Displacement** & **Representability**

Second Sight The ability to pick up hidden revocations, to infer things before they happen, or to see things that others are not able to see. The Gaels called this **God**-given capacity **shadow**-sight, or *taischitaraugh*, and it was considered particularly prevalent in the Highland regions of Scotland. Its appearance in a **dream** probably implies a **wish** to see more clearly, *ergo* the desire for a heightened capacity for understanding. There may also be a suggestion of 'shutting the **stable door** after the **horse** has bolted', in the sense of **wishing** one had the capacity to outguess fate.

Secretaries To a **male** (and to some **females**) a secretary may constitute something along the lines of a **wish-fulfilment** fantasy. She (for it is usually a she) is nominally at our beck and call, is dedicated to bringing order into our lives, is a conduit for communication, is employed and not **married** to us (thereby leavening our responsibilities towards her), and, in a dream a least, her submissive presence may suggest the possibility of **sexual** availability. If this all seems a little primitive, not to say infantile – that, after all, is the **nature** of **dreams**.

Secretions In **dream** terms all bodily secretions are interchangeable. Thus urine, pus, **semen**, **milk**, tears, **blood**, **venom**, vomit, **water**, sweat and **excrement** have the same symbolic value, and may substitute for each other in a dream. An example of this might be a man dreaming of urinating in the **garden** of a man whose wife he desires, or a **jealous** woman dreaming of bleeding (in the sense of having her menses) over a rival's **bed** linen. See **Bodily Fluids** & **Menstruation**

Secrets There are open secrets (*un secret de polichinelle* – Mr Punch's secret), and there are closed secrets (secret secrets). The **dream** will tend to **flag** its choice of secret by what it surrounds the secret, or the secret-bearer, with. A sealed room, for instance, might imply a secret referring to the dreamer's **past**, held within the **dreamer**, and that now forms part of the construct of the dreamer's character. A secret held within an imperfectly sealed container, on the other hand, might carry with it suggestions of **Pandora's Box** – the ramifications involved in letting the '**cat** out of the **bag**', in other words.

Sedatives Sedatives imply that we are not entirely in control of our own emotions – that we may need outside help or the emotions will overwhelm us. There are semantic links to both '**death**' and '**relatives**' in the word, too, implying that there might be an element of retained **grief** lurking inside the image, leading to a thought **chain** along the lines of 'if we are grieving we want it to stop and therefore we take sedatives' – that sort of thing. Sedatives are therefore a **dream symbol** indicative of not wishing to confront reality.

Seeds Seeds imply growth, the possibilities of regeneration, and the capacity for looking to the future rather than to the **past** for sustenance. Within Christian symbolism, they equate with the manifesting **God**, or Logos. See **Growing**

Seesaws Seesaws are fundamentally static (in the sense in which the fulcrum does not move, but merely promotes or facilitates the **movement** of other things). The image may therefore give us a **mother** and two **children**, say, or a man and two women who are attached to him. This lack of lateral movement is the **key** to the seesaw's meaning, and implies rigidity and the concretization of relationships – the 'play' element of a seesaw will tend to pall, after time, and foment only **nausea**.

Self, The According to **Jung**, each individual inherits a powerful, holistic sense of self, from which ego-**consciousness** later emerges. This sense of selfhood equates with the totality of the **psyche**. The **separation** between the self and the **ego** causes a severe injury to the psyche, which must be healed if psychic health is to be regained. See **Hero** & **Heroine**

Self-Analysis See Dreams, Self-Analysis of

Selling Selling oneself or selling an object is a **projection** of the individual onto the communal – it implies both a desire to communicate and a desire to dominate (or to be dominated). It also implies that everything has a value outside of its own particular integrity or *barakah*. This mercantile aspect to everything is actually a devaluation rather than a valuation, and the concept of selling may therefore contain **self**-image ramifications within a **dream** (we are valuing ourselves according to others' **lights**, in other words, rather than according to our own).

Semen Semen will have radically different revocations for both men and women. For a **male** it may equate with power, essences and creativity, whereas to a **female** it might be seen as either inclusive, intrusive, or exclusive, depending on the context of the **dream**. Either way, it is a fundamental adjunct of masculinity, and may therefore find itself equated with energy, assertion, control, loss of control, or, when squandered, a **failure** to fulfil one's promise – its appearance in a dream may also reflect a desire for, or a shying away from, necessary **rites-of-passage**. See **Exclusion** & **Secretions**

Sensation The non-perceptual experience, by a sense **organ**, of an immediate stimulus (i.e. without the need for rational thought or filtration through **past** experience).

Sensuality The creative rendering of the sense emotions into something which would seem to pertain to beyond the physical. In its essence, sensuality probably refers back to the earliest stages of the **mother/child** relationship, in which the mother to some extent **depersonalizes** herself, temporarily becoming a mere vehicle for her child's comfort and nurture. This vehicular aspect infuses sensuality in **dreams**, **mirroring** the beyond-rational carriage-mimicking **nature** of our **animal** instincts. See **Depersonalization & Servants**

Separation **Dreams** of separation may indicate a **depersonalized** state in the **dreamer**, in which the dreamer's **ego** may be perceived as **small**, or distant.

Serendipity An 18th-century concept, latched onto by **Jung**, suggesting a happy occurrence or causal relationship that leads to an unexpected but nevertheless synchronous felicity (or sought-after end). Such occurrences often find themselves contrived in **dreams** – a **reflection**, perhaps, of their desirability in **waking** life.

Series of Dreams See **Dream Series**

Serpents Serpents and **dragons** were virtually indistinguishable to the ancient Chinese, but when a dragon took on the guise of a serpent in a **dream**, it suggested malevolent **destruction**. The serpent **cult** (**snake** worshippers) saw the serpent as representing specifically the paternal **penis**, and as such it formed an important part of ancestor **worship**, for the **souls** of Chinese **ancestors** were believed to live on in serpents. See **Mandalas**
KEY LINE: 'Got restless – taste in mouth – and had the most horrible serpent dream I ever had yet in my life. The deadliest came out into the room under a door. It rose up like a Cobra – with horrible round eyes and had woman's, or at least Medusa's, breasts.' (From John Ruskin's *Diaries* 1st November 1869)

Servants The servant is often a **symbol** for the **mother** in **dreams**. Although this may seem a little unfair, it is, nevertheless, **archetypally** true. See **Sensuality**

Seven The seventh stage (in the language of **initiation**) is the highest stage before enlightenment, and is therefore the coveted **goal** of all desire. Its achievement would mean, in theory at least, that the process of the **integration** of the personal **unconscious** was completed, and that the **collective unconscious** would thereafter become illuminated. The appearance of the **number** seven in **dreams**, therefore, is usually considered auspicious.

Sewerage/Sewers Sewerage implies the effective rendition (translation) of outmoded or superfluous artefacts or bodily processes. The appearance of the **dreamer** in a sewer system (*pace* Carol Reed's 1949 film of *The Third Man*) tends to imply a low **self**-esteem, or low expectations.

Sewing Sewing often **represents** the **sexual** act in **dreams**. The result of sewing – just as with the result of the sexual act – is, in theory at least, to bring two disparate things together as one. See **Seams**

Sex Dreams are replete with sexual imagery (for obvious reasons): the insertion of a **key** in a **lock**; the wielding of a heavy stick; the **breaking** down of a **door** by force; the raising of a **tower**; the **entry** of a **train** into a **tunnel**. **Jung**, while acknowledging obvious sexual imagery, advocated a deeper process of **dream work** which took into account the actual images themselves, and why they were the ones specifically chosen by the **unconscious** mind of each separate individual. Such investigations could lead to a quite different psychological outcome than the initial, exclusively sexual connotations that might initially be drawn from them. **Dreams**, in other words, have their own limitations. And sexual desire is beset by protective euphemism. See **Layer Symbolism** & **Urges**
KEY LINE: 'I kissed thee (panting), and I call/Night to the record! that was all./But ah! If empty dreams so please,/Love, give me more such nights as these.' (From Robert Herrick's *The Vision of Electra* 1648)

Sexual Abuse Sexual abuse, like **rape**, is extremely hard to define in dream terms, because the **wish-fulfilment** aspects behind most **dreams**, twinned with the societal and **taboo**-driven **repression** of many of our natural **instincts**, may **mask** its true significance to the **dreamer**. One thing is certain – it cannot, and should not, be taken at **face** value.

Sexual Intercourse The actual act of sexual intercourse in a **dream** frequently refers to the 'making' of the **dreamer** – the blending of a number of qualities which together go towards the creation of the individual dreaming the dream. This union aspect between the **male** and the **female**, the **yin** and the **yang**, the **anima** and the **animus**, can have both creative and metaphysical revocations, and may imply a desire on the part of the dreamer to 'rebalance' something that is out of kilter. See **Layer Symbolism**

Shade Shade can imply being out of favour (out of the **sun**). It may also, depending on context, imply the seeking out of protection, or a desire on the part of the **dreamer** to stay out of the limelight. See **Sanctuary**

Shadows, The The shadow (the **Jungian** version of our *alter ego*) is the unacknowledged part of the human personality. It consists of those qualities and impulses we would rather remained hidden. It has two aspects – one **dangerous**, and one of value. One way of confronting and understanding the shadow is through the interpretation of our **dreams**, leading to **self-education**. The shadow often appears inadvertently, or in the company of same **sex friends**, when we find ourselves acting in ways that are not 'ourselves' but merely the **reflections** of the **wishes** and aspects of ourselves we feel that others may value, to our advantage. See also **Double** & **Dr Jekyll and Mr Hyde**

Shafts Shafts, as in mineshafts, are often **symbols** of the **unconscious**. They can also imply hidden resources, or, if they seem threatening, the unacknowledged, even surreptitious aspects of our essential **natures**.

Shakespeare, William (1564–1616) Even a brief glance through some of William Shakespeare's work will show his **obsession** with **dreams**. *Hamlet*, in particular, gives us, amongst many others: 'A dream itself is but a shadow …'; 'To sleep: perchance to dream: ay, there's the rub': and, 'Oh God! I could be bounded in a nut-shell and count myself a king of infinite space, were it not that I have bad dreams.' *The Tempest* gives us 'We are such stuff as dreams are made on, and our little life is rounded with a sleep …', while the whole of *A Midsummer Night's Dream* is premised on a dream – 'Swift as a shadow, short as any dream, brief as the lightning in the collied night.'

Shamans As part of their initiation into shaman-hood, novice shamans (or 'religious specialists' – the word comes from the Tungus **language** of Siberia) take themselves to a **sacred** place, where they will have a **nightmare** in which they are torn apart, and then put together again (their old **bones** are replaced with new ones). This **rite-of-passage** then gives them the power of healing and of **second sight**. In Greek **mythology**, both Orpheus and Pentheus were torn apart in a similar Dionysiac frenzy – the symbolical '**tearing** apart' allows the mind to **fight** free of its **earthly** shackles, and open itself to the **light** that exists outside the human sphere. See **Flaying** & **Healers**
KEY LINE: '… the shaman's instruction often takes place in dreams. It is in dreams that the pure sacred life is entered and direct relations with the gods, spirits and ancestral souls are re-established.' (From Mircea Eliade's *Shamanism* 1951)

Shampoo Shampoo, like **soap**, usually relates to **cleansing** or purification. The fact that one usually shampoos one's own **hair** is also significant, in the sense that hair is often an indicator of gender and age, and its quality a **symbol** of sexual availability or attraction, particularly in a woman. The act of rubbing is frequently symptomatic of affection (and **masturbation**), and it also mimics an **animal** rite which suggests bonding and the acceptance of the individual into a wider community. Shampooing someone else's hair in a **dream** may then carry ramifications of taking on elements of that person that one either admires or covets.

Shapes Shapes have particular significance in **dreams**, and usually refer directly back to the **dreamer**, and to particular elements that are (or have been) meaningful in the dreamer's life. Shapes are the outward manifestation of inner conditions, in other words, and may offer up symbolical clues which relate directly to the emotional status of the dreamer in their own mind. See **Circles, Mandalas, Squares, Spirals**, etc.

Sharks Sharks are **danger** signals, usually relating to emotional issues (in that they are **water**-borne). The indiscriminate aspect of the shark is also important, in that it tends to **eat** up whatever comes into its **path**. If a shark makes off with a particular limb in its **mouth**, then that limb, and what it represents, is of specific importance (both semantically and metaphorically). A shark coming up from **below** the **dreamer**, for instance, and **tearing** off the dreamer's **leg**, might imply a desire for freedom of **movement**, but the inability to put that desire into practice – the shark then becomes a convenient excuse for not indulging in forward or upwards movement (see **Above**). Sharks may also symbolize mortal **disease**, or threats of mortal disease. See **Amputation, Floating & Swimming**

Shaving The act of shaving often equates with **masturbation** in a dream. In Roman times, the shaving of the **head** was considered a sign of servitude, common to bondsmen and **slaves**. The tonsure of **monks** and Catholic **priests** (which continued until 1972) held a similar meaning, relating to dedication. In **dreams** shaving may therefore suggest a **separation** of the physical from the mental, and may also carry with it revocations of contrition, as in the traditional shaving of the head in **grief** that we hear of, for instance, in the story of Jason and the Argonauts after the accidental killing of Cyzicus, **king** of the Doliones. See **Barbers & Razors**

Shawls Shawls, being **head** and **neck** coverings, may suggest shame or dissatisfaction with one's looks, or even a desire for anonymity based on **past** actions (shawls being suggestive of times past).

Shears Shears may be linked to **castration** or **circumcision complexes** in the **male** (think Struwelpeter/Shock-Headed Peter), or to **fears** of **breast** loss in the **female** (Diodorus wrote in 340 BC that the Amazons traditionally seared (sheared) off one of their breasts to facilitate archery – the word Amazon in Greek actually stems from the *a-* (privative) and *māzos* (breast)). There may also be a semantic link to **height**, as in the word 'sheer', which might suggest an image of a **pair** of shears descending on one from a great height. As with **scissors**, shears also carry revocations of the **opening** and closing of **legs**. See **Amputation & Sieves**

Sheaths Sheaths may represent the **vagina** in **dreams**. The placing of a **knife** into a sheath is therefore synonymous with the **sexual** act.

Sheds Sheds are additional (i.e. as yet un-integrated) storage spaces, usually seen as adjuncts to the main edifice. If one takes the **symbol** of the **house** as representative of the **dreamer**, then the shed becomes a repository for old ideas or discarded **patterns** of behaviour that are nevertheless safeguarded in case they may one day be of use. The shed therefore constitutes an unrealistic, quasi-**fetishistic** fallback position equating to **anal retention**.

Sheep A sheep traditionally symbolizes silliness and timidity, but also, somewhat curiously, the living **truth**. Sheep may also be taken to **represent childhood**, given both their **biblical** and their **fairy tale** associations (the shepherds watching their **herds** by **night**, and Little Bo Peep, for instance). There may also be semantic links to the word 'fleece', as in 'act stupidly, and **people** will take advantage of you'.

Sheets It is the spread-out aspect of a sheet that carries its symbolical value. Being domestic, nurturing, and receptive, sheets tend towards the feminine in **dream** implication, although there can still be revocations of **death** (in the sense of winding sheets) as well as of **birth** (in the sense of swaddling **clothes**).

Shelley, Percy Bysshe (1792–1822) The last stanza (number 23) of Shelley's **poem** *Marianne's Dream* (recounting a **dream** told to him by Marianne Hunt, wife of Leigh Hunt) perfectly describes the English Romantic belief, later annexed by the **Surrealists**, that **waking** and dreaming were intimately connected:

> The dizzy flight of that phantom pale
> Waked the fair lady from her sleep,
> And she arose, while from the veil
> Of her dark eyes the dream did creep.
> And she walked about as one who knew
> That sleep has sights as clear and true
> As any waking eyes can view.

Shells To the Taoist **dream interpreter**, shells might imply famine in this life, followed by good fortune in the afterlife. In more common **dream symbolism** they represent the **vagina** (think of Sandro Botticelli's *The Birth of Venus* 1485–6, in which Venus stands **naked** – save for the holding of her **hair** over her pudendum – in a **floating** scallop shell).

Shelter The appearance of shelter of any sort in a **dream** suggests the **splitting** off of one thing from another. In purely symbolical terms we are dealing with the obscuration of the higher **nature** from the lower, a **reading** further strengthened by the 'sanctuary' aspect of shelter.

Shelves Shelves are storage capacities for ideas, with the strong implication that those ideas should not be intermixed – these are rigid ideas, therefore, and probably hierarchical in inference. They are also likely to be ideas relating to internal (i.e. emotional), rather than external (i.e. physical), subjects.

Shields The **dreamer** will tend to conjure up a shield to protect them from harm or in order to deflect incoming negative energy. One is **blind** behind an upraised shield, however, leading to an instant increase in vulnerability. A shield is therefore a method of last resort, and may well carry with it implications of shutting the **stable door** after the **horse** has bolted.

Ships Ships are the vessels that bear the **dreamer** over the **sea**, and the associated depths of the **unconscious** which suggest the **self**. Semantically, one may also 'ship' extra **weight** or a cargo, and, *in extremis* or when **sinking, water**. See **Boats** & **Yachts**

Shirts Shirts are emblems, in the sense that they carry messages about the wearer (literally so, in the case of **sports** shirts) – a pristine **white** shirt, for instance, might suggest innocence, whereas a bright **red** shirt might imply dominance, or sexual availability (depending on the **sex** of the wearer).

Shivering Shivering, or the convulsive **movement** of the **body** or a **limb**, is an attention gatherer – in real life it implies 'I am **cold, warm** me up', but in the **dream world** it may have other implications, such as 'the part of my body which this limb symbolizes is emotionally cold' or 'I, too, am capable of ecstasy, so please notice me'. Either way, the strongest implication is of a need for affective (rather than effective) **heat**.

Shoes Shoes have many **superstitions** attached to them. One such was that to place them beside the **bed** in the form a T would bring **dreams** of a future mate. In dreams, shoes tend to symbolize the desire to advance spiritually, whilst the discarding of shoes usually implies the shucking off of **lower** things, for shoes *per se* can suggest an excessive attachment to the material **world**. An ill-fitting shoe might **lead** one to suppose that the **dreamer** feels uncomfortable in taking on another person's mantle ('standing in another's shoes') – **black** shoes, in this context, might suggest that there has been a **death**, possibly triggering the identity crisis.

Shooting A woman's rational and conscious **fear** of being **sexually** overpowered by a physically stronger man (whom she nevertheless desires) may mean that, to protect her **unconscious self**, she resorts to euphemism or **symbols** of the sexual act or of sexual aggression when dreaming – shooting, with its revocations of **danger** and of moral improbity, is thus a common and convenient symbol of intrusion for both sexes. When a man **dreams** of shooting, it is usually synonymous with sexual intercourse. See **Guns** & **Symbolic Parallelism**

Shoots A formalized **shooting arena** (in the sense of a syndicated shoot) might suggest either a communal **search** for one precise thing (the quarry), or an indiscriminate, albeit metaphorical slaughter of a specific, pinpointed prey (the victim). If the **dreamer** feels that they are the quarry or murderee (see **Attacks**), then **anxiety** feelings, twinned with **frustra-**

tion, are to the fore – if they are the **hunter**, or murderer, then **self**-complaisance must be suspected. Such shoots/**mobs**, similar to that delineated in H. G. Wells' much-filmed *The Island of Dr Moreau* (1896), are frequent dream contrivances.

Shops Shops suggest barter, or the exchange of ideas for **money**. There may also be a suggestion of **prostitution** about putting things up for sale, strengthened by the fact that one may, of course, **window** shop, but one actually needs to 'enter' a shop physically to get what one really wants. See **Harlot Fantasies & Grocery Stores**

Shorelines Shorelines are specific demarcations, in the sense that they indicate the exact boundary between two opposing forces. Symbolically, they suggest *devachanic* (that is to say **Heaven/World**) **consciousness**, at least in theosophical terms. In **dreams** they can suggest either unity (in the sense of complementarity) or disunity (in the sense of schism), entirely dependent on context – **storm** or calm, for instance; flux or reflux; **chaos** or order.

Shoulders Shoulders may be **burden** carriers, centres of attraction, or **symbols** of directive ability. In a **male**, they are the fulcrum of forward and sideways movement, whereas in the **female**, this capacity is normally invested in the **hips**. For a woman **dreamer**, then, shoulders will tend to have attention-gathering significance, whereas to a male they may reflect the capacity to bear burdens, either wanted or unwanted, an image that frequently sees itself reflected in piggy-back images of the sort immortalized in the Sinbad and the **Old Man** of the **Mountains** story from the *Arabian Nights* (in which Sinbad cannot rid himself of the limpet-like old man until he hits on the idea of making him drunk, whereat the old man loses control of his **limbs**, and **falls** off Sinbad's shoulders).

Shovels Shovels appear intimately associated with the getting rid of unwanted clutter, in that they are usually ejective. In this sense they are probably **anxiety** indicators, in that their use implies urgency and the desire to offload encumbrances (they can also double as **weapons**, of course). More positive indicators might include the shovelling of compost, suggesting fertility, or the shovelling of coal, suggesting energy. Either way, shovelling tends to uncover the **past** rather than referring to the future.

Showers A shower of **rain** is usually a welcome purificatory **symbol**, with a domestic shower featuring as a more contrived **cleansing** process. Showers tend to invoke blessings rather than misfortunes, therefore, and to be uniting rather divisive.

Shrinking A very common motif in **children's dreams**, the **unconscious fear** of shrinking was beautifully expressed in Lewis Carroll's *Alice in*

Wonderland, in which Alice, already a child (i.e. small), became smaller (*ergo* less powerful), and had to **compensate** for this by becoming more assertive than usual (the small yapping **dog** syndrome). Objects that shrink are usually in the process of becoming less important for the **dreamer**, whereas objects that inflate in size are seen to be imposing themselves on the dreamer's attention. See **Growing** & **Smallness**

Shrouds Shrouds suggest the **shadow** of **death**, in that a shroud covers, like a caul, and carries similar **superstitious** revocations (many 14th- and 15th-century English *memento mori* **tombs** show the **corpse** shrouded and skeletal *just as it would be in death*). Shrouds in **dreams** are therefore reminders of death, and their presence may be seen as a **warning** to change the **pattern** of one's behaviour.

Sick, Being See **Vomiting**

Sickles In religious symbolism sickles are used to cut the ties between the lower **nature** (the **ego**) and the higher nature (the **soul**). This **cutting** aspect of the sickle, whilst retaining the sickle's natural revocations of **death**, also implies the death of one particular element of the personality (the severed element). In terms of the communist **flag**, the sickle was the **symbol** of the peasantry, with the **hammer** being the symbol of the industrial proletariat.

Sickness Sickness in a **dream** is generally a **sign** that something is not **right** with the **dreamer**, or with one particular aspect of the dreamer's personality or emotional **makeup** – the sick element is drawing attention to itself, and requires either to be discharged or treated. See **Illness** & **Vomiting**

Sidewalks See **Pavements**

Sieves Sieves suggest **splittings** and desired truncations – the winnowing of the **good** from the bad. They may also suggest sudden **escapes** and porosity. In medieval **times**, those thought **guilty** of **robbery** were often subjected to **trial** by sieve and **shears** (a method of divination also mentioned by Theocritus in his *Idylls*, circa 250 BC). In the medieval version this involved a sieve with a **pair** of shears inside it being shaken by two **virgins** uttering the words, 'By St Peter and St Paul, turn shears to **thief**'.

Signatures Signatures are assertions of **selfhood**. They are proclamations of individuality within the community, and to that extent they equate with the **palm** prints our **ancestors** often placed on the interior walls of **caves**. In a **dream** they will tend to **represent** particularized expression, in the sense that they act as a reinforcement of the **ego**, somewhat akin to looking for one's **name** in the obituary **columns** of a **newspaper**, perhaps – *we* may know that we are alive, but it's always nice to have it confirmed.

Signboards Signboards proclaim things to the outside **world** – they are attention grabbers. If the **dreamer** is tormented by secret **guilt** or **secret** rancour, then the dream's act in notifying the (dream) **world** of these things may function in a leavening capacity, or as a preparation for coming clean in 'real time'. Signboards may also act as a reminder to the dreamer about the importance of certain things that may be being overlooked. See **Signs**

Signs Signs, in **dreams**, always mean less than the concept they **represent**. They are the **reflections** of a **conscious** thought. Signs may be invented or contrived, but **symbols** may not.

Silence Silence is rarely neutral – in fact there is often a sense of expectancy or dread attached to it. What are we about to hear? How will it affect us? When will the utterance come, and what will be its quality? In **female dreamers**, particularly, there is often a tendency to view silence as consent. See **Deafness & Muteness**

Silk Silk generally carries overtones of quality and luxury when it appears in **dreams**. There is also a fatuous aspect to silk, nicely satirized by Jonathan Swift, in *Gulliver's Travels*, who has his Lilliputians leaping over the Emperor's stick – in varying contortions, and every which way but loose – in order to be rewarded with a status-defining **coloured** silken **thread**. This status aspect is important in silk-impregnated **dreams**, and lurks at the very heart of silk as a **symbol**.

Silkiness Silkiness usually equates with **sensuality** in **dreams**, in that something smooth-flowing is generally valued higher than something which contains hitches or obstructions. Silkiness may also contain revocations of **children**'s 'rubbies' – security blankets, comfort objects, or what D. W. Winnicott (1896–1971) called transitional objects – in the sense that the texture of the skin on the **mother**'s **breast** is one of the first sensual objects we encounter, and that echoes of its effect are likely to be used by our **unconscious** mind whenever it confronts the **question** of desire.

Silver Silver was related by the **alchemists** of old to the **goddess** Diana and to the **moon** – to that extent it stands in second place to the **sun**, and **gold**, whilst retaining, perhaps, just a little more subtlety. **Light** reflects off silver, and to that extent it is symbolically seen as more passive than gold – the **female** to the **male** in **archetypal** terms. In **dreams**, silver may also find itself related to age and wisdom.

Silver Cord, The Consultants, **doctors, nurses** and relatives attest to the frequent appearance in the **waking dreams** of dying **people** of a **silver cord** leading to a particular **place** or destination. When the cord breaks, the person dies. Before that happens, the person could go anywhere. A similar cord is spoken of in Ecclesiastes xii, 6; 'Remember him – before the silver cord is severed, or the **golden** bowl is broken … and the **dust** returns to the ground it came from.'

Simplification The reduction of the contents of a **dream** to nothing more than a simple outline, thereby, according to psychotherapist **Wilhelm Stekel**, facilitating a quicker, more instinctual, analysis.

Singing Singing is one of our most immediate and visible expressions of our **feelings**. To interpret its meaning in a **dream**, however, the context in which the singing occurs must be taken into consideration, including the dream furniture that surrounds the singer, and the circumstances in which the song is sung. In addition, the content of the song, who is singing it, and the manner in which it is sung are also relevant, and must be addressed before a full interpretation can take place. Singing inside a **cave**, for example, might suggest that our emotions are being dampened, or turned back on us, whereas singing in a **room** full of other singers might correlate with a desire to assert ourselves and to be heard above the **crowd**.

Sinking Sinking is a frequent **dream** motif – often it is some aspect of the **dreamer** themselves that is sinking into a bog or **quicksand**, an aspect that the dreamer may wish to save before it is too late. In the **male** this may be the **anima**, and in the **female** the **animus**. The downwards movement (see **Below**) of sinking is also significant, in that it implies that the dreamer must act swiftly, before what threatens to become lost becomes irretrievable.

Sirens Men both desire sirens, and **fear** them. It is interesting to note that Ulysses insisted that his men tie him to the mast without earplugs, so that he could enjoy the siren's call without having the physical capacity to follow it and doom himself. In Platonic terms, **earth** sirens (as opposed to celestial/heavenly or cathartic/infernal) were generational, and emblematic of the **sea**, and their motion was deemed to be harmonic. See **Archetypes**

Sisterhood The gathering together of feminine quantities. The '**archetypal**' feminine tends towards nurture, submission and regeneration, whereas the 'imposed' or 'expedient' feminine might tend to value manumission over submission, and inclusiveness over abnegation. The individual character of the **female dreamer** is crucial when it comes to the demarcation of these two disparate aspects of sisterhood.

Sisters Sisters, in **dreams**, are often represented by **symbols** such as **nurses**, **nuns**, and suchlike. There are also strong **incest taboos** associated with them, and this is often reflected in the choice of **symbol** made by the **dreamer's unconscious** mind.

Sitting Sitting suggests peaceful intentions – it is, for obvious reasons, rather hard to be aggressive when seated. Sitting might also suggest **illness** or extreme placidity (think of the **Buddha**). Symbolically, sitting implies acquiescence, which is probably why so many 18th-century **family portraits** show the **female** sitting, with the **male** standing beside her.

Size See **Bigness & Smallness**

Skating 'Skating on **thin** ice' is a rather obvious illustrative euphemism for out-of-control skating when it occurs in a **dream**, the implication being that elements of the skater are unbalanced or disharmonious in some way – 'on the slide', figuratively speaking. See **Skiing**

Skeletons Skeletons are the **scaffolding** by which otherwise ambitious constructions are invisibly supported. If one sees a skeleton in a **dream**, the obvious implication must be that the construction (idea, notion, carapace) has collapsed, and that only the skeleton of it is left. In this way we may see the **death** of a thing while it is still notionally living.

Skiing Skiing has a certain correlation with **skating**, in that **dreamers** often imagine themselves in out-of-control mode when they take to the slopes. Slipperiness is important here, implying a certain elusive quality on the part of the **goal** we are striving to attain. The fact that the goal of skiing is traditionally in a downhill direction (see **Below**) also sets up **resistances**, as we are programmed from **birth** to strive upwards (see **Above**).

Skin, The Skin is the covering on the **scaffolding** of the **skeleton**. It is the outer environment the **dreamer** creates for themselves, and constitutes their **shop window** to the **world**. If the skin is any other than the constituent **colour** of the dreamer, then that, too, becomes important. Skin, unlike character, may be sloughed, however, or at the very least tampered with. This chameleon effect allows skin to be equated to a certain extent with **clothes**, a convenient trope, especially when one is **walking** in one's **birthday** suit through **hotel** lobbies. See **Clay, Nakedness, Tattoos & Tiles**

Skulls Skulls may denote the intellect, and the throwing away, or rejection of a skull, may indicate a desire to rid oneself of inconvenient thoughts. Symbolically, the skull represents **emptiness** and the vacuity of material pursuit (in the absence of spiritual **movement**) – Golgotha, where **Jesus** was **crucified**, was known as the place of the skull, and suggested the as yet unliberated **soul**.

Sky, The The sky represents **elevation**, ennoblement, and possibility. It is also the perfect **symbol** of the Buddhic plane of being, suggesting, as it does, the evolving **life** of the **soul**. To **dream** of a clear **blue** sky is to dream of untroubled progress and **lightness** of being – a symbol of the material made empyrean.

Slang The word '**dream**' has many uses in slang, amongst which we find the following:

1. A beautiful or attractive individual.
2. A brand name, and later a euphemism for, a **hand**-rolled **cigarette**. (US)
3. An expert.
4. A 1920s expression covering a variety of **drugs**, including **opium** and **morphine**.
5. A 1980s word for the effect **cocaine** has on the brain.
6. A word used in 1920s Australia for a six-month **prison** sentence, with the implication that one could serve it in one's **sleep**.

Slavery To be enslaved to something or someone in a **dream** implies the subjection of the will to a more assertive, more dominating, force. This may be an idea, a **compulsion**, or even **guilt** – it is, in other words, a domination by the lower **nature** of the upper. See **Captivity** & **Slaves**

Slaves To have slaves is to desire power – if one is able, even in a **dream**, to force others to obey one's will indiscriminately, it inevitably suggests **feelings** of **inferiority** (see **Adler**) on the part of the **dreamer**, for surely only an inferior being would feel the need to bolster their own vainglory through the enforced truncation of another's span of liberty? See **Captivity** & **Slavery**

Sleep Sleep, alongside **breathing**, **drinking** and **eating**, is arguably our most important function, as without it, we die. It is not a passive state, however, but a necessary withdrawal of contact with the outside **world**. To that extent at least, certain elements of sleep imitate the functions and forgotten habits of the foetal realm. There are two main periods of sleep – D sleep (desynchronized and dreaming), and S sleep (synchronized). These states equate with REM (rapid **eye** movement) and NREM (non-rapid eye movement) sleep. To that extent we are similar to all other mammals, excepting, of course, the spiny anteater, who is apparently something of an anomaly. **Fish** have periods of quiescence rather than of sleep, while **birds** resemble humans in that they have both S and D sleep, although the latter only in small doses. **Dogs**, as we all know, have significant dream **passages**, largely, one supposes, associated with **hunting**, **sex** and **fighting** (what George Steiner calls 'dreams before **language**') – to that extent, of course, they resemble us. As we grow older we reputedly require less sleep, and are more prone to sleeping-related disorders such as **insomnia** (a difficulty in getting to sleep) or **narcolepsy** (sudden and uncontrollable sleep attacks). Certain tribes considered the condition of sleeping **taboo**, and the Malays, for instance, or the Babar islanders of Indonesia, would refuse to consider **waking** a person except in the most extreme circumstances.

KEY LINE: '… But no, like a spark/That needs must die, although its little beam/Reflects upon a diamond, my sweet dream/Fell into nothing – into stupid sleep.' (From John Keats's *Endymion*, I 1817)

Sleep Deprivation Lord Byron, **Edgar Allan Poe**, Margaret Thatcher and Napoleon, all claimed to be able to manage on very little **sleep**, and to suffer no apparent ill effects, whilst the Roman Emperor Caligula was tormented by such terrible **nightmares** that he never managed to sleep for more than two or three **hours** at a time. See **Microsleep**

Sleeping Position Alfred Adler saw the sleeping position as symptomatic of the **dreamer**'s attitude to **life** – disillusioned **people** curl up, isolationists **bury** themselves under their blankets and **sheets**, while optimists snooze on their backs. Such a theory does not take into account, of course, pathological positions caused by **illness** or other morbidities.

Sleepwalking Walking, **talking** and even **driving** whilst still asleep or in a hyponoic (a condition of lowered lucidity) state. Sleepwalking may have a genetic **link**, strikes the young rather than the old, and can often result from unacknowledged stresses or the onset of an **illness**. It is in many ways a **regression** to a primitive state of **consciousness**, and requires a complete absence of the **ego** if it is to function or occur. Emil Gutheil defined somnambulic performance as a dramatization of a **dream** rather than a dream itself. Condillac, tutor to the infant Duke of Parma (the nephew of Louis XV) claimed to have written the greater part of his *Cours Complet d'Instruction* whilst in a somnambulistic state. Other famous somnambulists include the poet **Percy Bysshe Shelley**, and Benjamin Franklin. See also **Amina & Taboos**

Sliding Sliding and slipping have a lot in common with **skiing** and **skating** in **dreams**, and all are, generally speaking, signs of insecurity. '*Multa cadunt inter calicem supremaque labra*' said the **poet** Horace (65–8 BC) – 'there's many a slip 'twixt cup and lip'.

Slippers Slippers are comfort adjuncts, suggesting settled domesticity and continuity (i.e. non-nomadism).

Slipping See **Sliding**

Smallness The **size** of **people** appearing in **dreams** can be significant in terms of their relative importance to the **dreamer** – **tall** indicating important, or adult, and small indicating unimportant, or childlike. Important people were often portrayed as particularly large in medieval **paintings** (**Kings**, the **Virgin Mary**, etc.) whereas unimportant people (human beings, devotees, subjects) were represented as small. Extra small objects in dreams may therefore be less worthy of attention. Jonathan Swift's *Gulliver's Travels* (1726) takes this idea to its logical extremity in his creation of the tiny Lilliputians and the giant Brobdingnagians. See **Growing & Shrinking**

Smells See **Odours**

Smog Smog is roughly equivalent to **fog** and **mist** in **dreams**, for they all constitute a restriction on **vision** and, to a smaller extent, on the receipt of sound. Of the three, smog is the only one to contain dirt revocations, in the sense of the pollution of ideas, relationships, and desired (or **feared**) interactions.

Smoke Smoke, like smog, is a pollutant, and one of its main characteristics is to infuse things with its **odour** (*ergo* to foment ignorance). There are certain positive revocations to smoke though, in the sense of **signalling**, and the residual (or inferential) giving off of **heat**. Smoke's main use in a **dream** appears to be to suggest a lack of clarity with regard to concerted thought and the capacity for enlightened (i.e. smoke-free) decision making. See **Smoking**

Smoking The **dream** revocations of smoking will no doubt be subject to fundamental changes, given the restrictions now placed upon the practice across a significant proportion of the Western **world**. It will tend to become something almost **secretive** – a hidden **vice** or **taboo** that the **unconscious** mind will protect us from, or apologize for, or crave to **break**. Within the context of a dream, it may even take on the mantle of a quasi-infantile (i.e. orally triggered) opposition to authority, the **parents**, or the state, acting in a similar way to a **child** who stuffs something into its **mouth** then looks defiantly across at its parents as if to say, 'Well, Mateys, what are you going to do about that?' See **Records & Smoke**

Snails Snails can suggest **frustration** and small-thinking (the notion of never being free of one's **house**, *ergo* limiting one's ideas). The slowness associated with snails may imply a difficulty in getting on in some way, or of the **dreamer** making few advances in some sphere that is dear to them or for which they have unrealistic ambitions.
KEY LINE: 'Doddiman, doddiman, put out your horn,/Here comes a thief to steal your corn.' (Old Norfolk Nursery Rhyme)

Snakes A snake symbolizes wisdom, fertility, **initiation** and transcendence – he is the mediator between this **world** and the next, chthonic world, for in Christian iconography, the **serpent** was also a **symbol** for Satan. If a woman **dreams** of a snake, it may imply that she **fears maleness**, or the intrusion of a **penis**, but can also indicate a desire for connection. The African Xhosa tribe believe that snakes represent their **ancestors**, and in ancient Greece, both **Gods** and fallen **heroes** were **worshipped** in the guise of **bearded** snakes, whilst the Malays believed that dreaming of a snake portended success in **love**. Australian Aborigines believe that the Great Ancestor (the source of everything), lives at Ayer's

Rock, in a rock **pool** that never dries up, in the guise of a python with scales the **colour** of a **rainbow**. Savinien Cyrano de Bergerac (1619–55) recounts, in his *L'Histoire Comique des États et Empires du Soleil* (*A Comic History of the States and Empires of the Sun*), how God **punished** the snake that had tempted Adam and Eve by placing it inside Adam's **body** to form his entrails, with its **head** sticking out from Adam's groin, always ready to bite woman and **seed** her with its **poison** for nine months. The snake and the staff are the traditional **symbols** for **Aesculapius**, the Greek God of **Medicine**. See **Mandalas**

Sneezing Sneezing equates with release, and to that extent it may have **orgasmic** or **cathartic** revocations when it occurs in a **dream**. It is also expulsive, and may suggest denial or a refusal by the **dreamer** to accept something they are being offered, even if **unconsciously**. Countless cultures consider sneezing an omen to be averted, in the sense that it may imply that 'evil is abroad', as in contagion, **disease**, or in the person of evil **spirits** – this may stem from **plague fears** (of which sneezing was a **death**-symptom), or **myth**-memories relating back to ancient Greece, which told of Athens being 'depopulated by a sneeze'.

Snorkels A snorkel suggests the capacity to do something when, logically speaking, it should be impossible. There may also be **phallic** or **oral** revocations, and the use of a snorkel in **water** may also be significant, in the sense of being able to **breathe** (i.e. surviving) during emotional crises.

Snow Fresh snow will have a radically different meaning than slush or **dirty** snow – fresh snow suggests purity and renewal, whereas slush suggests staleness and pollution. Symbolically, snow, **ice** and frost hold a roughly similar **weight**, implying latency, as in the congealing or solidification of **water** (i.e. the emotions, *ergo* **truth**).

Soap Soap is, somewhat inevitably, a **cleanser** or purifier. It is also **slippery**, and there may be an implication of **laundering** something unwholesome, or of cleaning up one's act, about the image. Finally, given the stinging aspect of soap (if it gets into the **eyes**), it may carry with it implications of not seeing the **wood** for the **trees** (i.e. the subject is so busy working on their image that they don't see what's **right** in front of their **face**).

Sockets Sockets tend to be **female symbols** in **dreams**, just as **plugs** tend towards the **male**. The appearance of the two together may suggest that the male part of the equation draws its energy from the female, and that if they are disconnected, the male part becomes useless whilst the female part remains passive – that only the two together, in other words, foment the charge. When viewed like this, both the **anima** and the **animus** come into **question**.

Socks Socks and feet frequently equate to the prophylactic (in the form of a **condom**), and to the **penis** in a **dream**. British visitors are often amused, when arriving in Mexico City, by large advertising hoardings advertising Durex Socks (Durex being a near ubiquitous trademark in Britain for the contraceptive **sheath**). The generalized covering aspect is also important here, suggesting disguise and the seeking out of comfort.

Sodium Pentothal Trademark name of thiopentone sodium, once commonly used as an aid to **hypnosis** and as a so-called **truth** serum, and now more often as a sedative or general **anaesthetic**.

Soiling Soiling, when dreamt of by a woman, can equate with the loss of her **virginity** or with the act of defloration. It may also have **menstrual** implications, and suggest a loss of energy or of the capacity to procreate. This may carry over into **fears** of **miscarriage** or of **abortion**, both of which may be symbolically akin to soiling. For both **sexes**, soiling may contain revocations of old age, or of the loss of control over one's own **life** – for the soiling of one's own **nest** is often the first sign of long-term physical deterioration and morbidity.

Solar Plexus, The Traditionally, the solar plexus is at the **centre** of balance and harmony in the **body** (remember the games one used to play at **school** in which a person could be unbalanced by a single **finger** to the solar plexus?). To that extent it equates with the fulcrum, in the sense of being a point of symmetry, similar to the centre of a **circle**. This is, of course, reinforced by the famous Leonardo da Vinci drawing of the *Scientific Proportion of the Male Body* in which the upper framing rectangle passes directly through the solar plexus area.

Soldiers One may marshal one's own forces, as in the combating of **disease**, say, or the repelling of unwelcome attentions – one may also be threatened by the forces of others, encroaching, as it were, on one's own sovereign territory. **Soldiers** are expedient **symbols**, then, to be called on when needed, and at the service of the state (i.e. the individual **dreamer**).

Solitude Solitude may betoken individuality, but it can also suggest forlornness and solipsism. We are all **alone** before **God**, and this fact is neither easy to accept nor amenable to creative logic – our **dreams**, therefore, may act as **compensatory** mechanisms.
KEY LINE: 'Others are afraid to be alone, and amuse themselves by a perpetual succession of companions: but the difference is not great; in solitude we have our dreams to ourselves, and in company we agree to dream in concert. The end sought in both is forgetfulness of ourselves.' (Samuel Johnson)

Soma A fermented drink made from the sap of the soma plant (possibly a hybrid of **corn**), and much used by the Incas, the Mexica, the Hindu Vedics and the Zoroastrians, to induce **visions**. The Inca ruling caste banned the common **people** from **drinking** soma on account of 'its peculiar effect and excessive strength'. See **Artificial Dreams**

Somatization When purely mental experiences find themselves converted into actual, physical symptoms, as in 'psychosomatic' **disease**.

Somnambulism From the Latin, *somnus*, meaning **sleep**, and *ambulare*, meaning to **walk**. See **Sleepwalking**

Sons The appearance of a **son** in a **dream** may indicate **Jesus Christ**. For a **female dreamer** the son may represent her **animus**, or the desire for **integration** of the feminine into the masculine. For the **male** dreamer, the son image may act as a desired (i.e. **compensatory**) **reflection** of himself onto another. See **Solitude**

Soul, The The word soul equates to both the Latin word *anima*, and to the Greek word *psyche*, with the joint meaning of 'soul' and '**life**'. The Greeks believed that the soul retained human **shape** after **death**, and it is from this that we derive our concept of **ghosts**. The souls of fallen **heroes** would often reappear in **dreams**, temporarily infusing the **dreamer** with the living **atoms** of the departed. The English Quaker anthropologist Sir Edward Tylor (1832–1917) stressed the importance of dreams in first suggesting to primitive man the possibility of the existence of a soul.
KEY LINE: 'If the human soul is anything, it must be of unimaginable complexity and diversity, so that it cannot possibly be approached through a mere psychology of instinct.' (from C. G. **Jung**'s *Freud and Psychoanalysis*)

Soup Soup suggests the blending of nominally disparate objects into harmonious wholes. In addition, there is the slaking aspect, in the sense that soup is designed to curtail or banish **hunger** (metaphysical, metaphorical, or somatic). The opaque element of soup may also prove important, in that one cannot see 'through it', but one is nevertheless perfectly happy to 'take it on trust', implying that the offering or partaking of soup in a **dream** is generally a friendly or benevolent (nourishing) act.

South, The The south carries with it implications of the **sun**, of leisure, of health, and of easy living. This may reflect the western **world**'s long-standing **love** affair with Attic Greece, but it may also carry solar fulcrum and natural harmony implications. To that extent the appearance of the south in **dreams** is likely to be principally regenerative in meaning. See **East, North & West**
KEY LINE: 'O for a draught of vintage! that hath been/Cooled a long age in the deep-delvéd earth,/Tasting of Flora and the country-green,/Dance, and Provençal song, and sunburnt mirth!/O for a beaker full of the warm South!/Full of the true, the blissful Hippocrene, ...' (From John Keats' *Ode to a Nightingale* 1819)

Sowing Sowing inevitably presupposes consequences, in that 'as you sow y'are like to reap' (From Samuel Butler's *Hudibras*). This cause and effect rule carries through into the actual action of sowing, which may be aggressive, **sexual**, placatory, or **neurotic**. In every case, though, the **fruits** of the action are what most likely concerns the **dreamer** – dry, arid returns imply negative actions, whereas lush **crops** suggest generosity and karmic benefit.

Space To a rationalist space may equate with **death**, with nothingness, and with unknowability, in that it constitutes (at least in abstract terms) inchoate **blackness**. To the superior person – in the Confucian sense, needless to say – it may also equate with a desire for spirituality, for it takes a large **mind** not to be humbled by the concept of infinity and immutable matter. It is probably only through the acceptance of **God** (as the Ineffable, the Absolute, the Supernal) that we are allowed the possibility of a more than temporary, human-sized alleviation of a seemingly logical nihilism. The appearance of such images (**space**, flux, **chaos**) and such **questions** (how is not nothing possible?) in **dreams**, may presuppose, even if **unconsciously**, just such a craving for spirituality.

Spades Spades are functional and, quite literally, 'down to **earth**'. They can act as extensions of the **arm** or as euphemisms for the **penis** in **dreams**. Either way, they generally represent a constructive (albeit sometimes assertive) reaching out. Spades change what they **touch**, too, and they are generally inflexible – in dream terms this inflexibility might tend to refer to the ideas behind the **digging** action, rather than to the digging action itself.

Spanking See **Beating**

Sparks Sparks can be the result of dialogue, or of the coming together of two disparate objects in a brief, transformative unity. 'Briefness' is the **key** here, in that sparks don't tend to shed long-term **light**. In **dreams**, though, sparks may betoken the beginnings of things, or even the triggering of **chain** reactions. A spark may also stand in as a euphemism for chemical/**alchemical** or affective attraction.

Sparrows A sparrow traditionally symbolizes lasciviousness. Why this should be is a moot point, although it may have something to do with **Jesus'** making of the 12 sparrows of **clay** on the Sabbath (from the *Gospel of Pseudo-Matthew*), and the upbraiding that Joseph, in consequence, received, and which he duly passed on to his **son** – Jesus then struck his **hands** together and said to the sparrows, '**Fly!**'. In dream terms, sparrows may be taken to represent the **fragility** of freedom, and its consequent susceptibility to being **starved**.
KEY LINE: 'To hold a sparrow, struggling to escape, forebodes mischief.' (From Astrampsychus' *Oneirocriticon* 350 AD)

Speaking See **Speech**

Spears Spears are likely to be primarily **phallic** when they appear in **dreams**, but they may also represent the **hand**, and be directional. A spear **pointing** in a particular direction may suggest a desire to expand one's **sexual** or terrestrial remit, particularly, of course, in the case of a **male**. In purely symbolical terms, the spear represents the divine ray which, in the ancient Egyptian **religion**, dispelled illusion through the unification of **nature** and **consciousness**, via Horus' decapitation and subsequent infibulation of Set.

Specificity **Dreams** are often disarmingly literal. An example of this literalness might include a man who feels himself to be physically **weak** dreaming that another man **kicks sand** in his **face**; or a woman who feels herself to be unattractive to men dreaming of a specific person, or a specific **number** of **people**, rejecting her.

Spectacles Spectacles are aids to seeing, and this literal aspect is likely to be the first **port** of call in any **interpretation**. Should the **dreamer** define what they are wearing (or what they are observing being worn) specifically as 'spectacles' – and not simply by the more commonly used word 'glasses' – then a semantic link to, for instance, 'making a spectacle of oneself' should be suspected.

Speech Speech presupposes rationality, whereas speaking in **tongues**, or babbling, suggests a more instinctual desire to communicate. Trying to speak and not being able to may take the **dreamer** back to the infant state of being unable to communicate – or it may suggest a **bottled** up **secret** that the dreamer is unable, or unwilling, to confront.
KEY LINE: 'Men use thought only to justify their wrongdoing, and employ speech only to conceal their thoughts.' (Voltaire's *Dialogues*: No. xiv, *Le Chapon et la Poularde* 1766)

Speed Speed, in a **dream**, tends to restrict the power of thought. This may be intentional on the part of the **unconscious** mind, and can function in a protective capacity, rather as a **child** will flap its **head** from side to side (or its **hands** up and down) when it doesn't wish to acknowledge importunate **reality**. Speed is also a recognition of intensity, and it can act, on occasion, as an **anxiety** trigger.

Speedometers Speedometers are **measures** of intensity. To that extent they are **self**-regarding and **narcissistic**, in that they presuppose the need for an **audience** or a **witness** to what should, and perhaps could, be an **integrated** experience – if one is looking at the speedometer, one is, by default, not eying the **road**.

Spending Spending – particularly of **money**, as opposed to, say, **energy** – frequently equates to 'spending **love**', and may refer to the giving away of something valuable. When women dream of spending money, this may indicate an **unconscious** desire for promiscuity (see **Harlot Fantasies**), twinned with the **guilt** such a fantasy can unconsciously engender.

Sperm See **Semen**

Spheres Spheres are consummate wholes – all their contents are, by definition, embraced. To that extent they may imply the possibilities of new beginnings, rather as a person puts on all their **clothes**, and gathers together all their necessary possessions, before venturing forth into the **world**.

Sphinxes Sphinxes are **symbols** of the **spirit** triumphant over matter. They are also **transformative** and unifying. In Egyptian **mythology**, Horus, **god** of the **sky**, of **light**, and of goodness, transformed himself, sphinx-like, into the form of a **lion** with the **head** of a man, surmounted by a triple **crown**.

Spiders A spider traditionally symbolizes wiliness and craft – mystery and independence. **Freud**'s colleague, Karl Abraham (1877–1925), disagreed with this view, however. He believed that the spider represented the fearsome '**phallic mother**', and that a **fear** of spiders was the manifestation of an **unconscious taboo** against mother **incest**. See **Fixed Symbolism** & **Webs**

Spies Spies suggest a desire to know, or to gain access to, hidden information. When the spy seems particularly threatening, then the **dreamer fears** the prying **eye** of others into their internal landscape. Spying may also be a euphemism for **sexual** importunity and the **invasion** of emotional privacy. See **Spying**

Spillages Spillages in **dreams** are usually **linked** to **urination** (micturition), **orgasm**, or **menstrual** processes. As all **secretions** are fundamentally interchangeable in dreams, it is likely that spillages refer primarily to a loss of some sort, in that such secretions and spillages are generally perceived by the suspicious **unconscious** mind as being energy draining, rather than as the natural, regenerative functions they really are. See **Amputation**

Spine, The The spine, taken literally, probably relates most easily to the concept of 'having backbone' when it occurs in **dreams**. It is also both flexible and rigid, and this paradox invests its meaning with a series of **oppositions**. It suggests, for instance, both the power of motion and the possibility of its loss – the capacity to be or to think in an upright and energetic manner, twinned with the capacity to lie supine or to relax into a state of passivity, if that is appropriate.

Spirals See **Labyrinths**

Spires Spires may be either **phallic** or aspirational – wags might descry little difference between the two. Taken purely aspirationally, they might suggest a **movement** upwards towards knowledge or acceptance – a desire to stretch out, in other words, and to make vulnerable. See **Steeples**

Spirits Spirits in **dreams** are often **alchemical** in origin, and originally comprised orpiment, sal-ammoniac, brimstone and quicksilver. Bodily spirits (linked to **alchemy** through **bottle**-imps, *oboth*, or genies) included **animal** spirits which stemmed from the brain, vital spirits which originated in the **heart**, and natural spirits which lurked in the **liver**. The elemental spirits, rulers of the elements, consisted of the salamander (**fire**), the undines (**water**), the sylphs (air) and the gnomes (**earth**). These spirits are often aiders and abetters in dreams, and tend to be brought in by the **unconscious** mind – often via apparently long-forgotten **childhood** memories – in order to facilitate understanding, as well as to act as conduits between the rational and the 'natural' **worlds** (the side which imparts qualities and motions, and the side which receives them).

Spitting The act of spitting, being projectile, is inevitably intrusive. It is not necessarily hostile, however, for it may simply be expulsive, in the sense of ridding oneself of something that one does not want or disapproves of. Here we find ourselves back to **childhood** again, and to **oral fixations** – the placing of something in one's **mouth** in order to test it. Spitting for luck was also common until recent **years** (as in fishwives spitting on the first **coin** they received that day, at the **market**) and originally stemmed from the ancient Greek habit of spitting in order to defuse fascination. See **Spittle**

Spittle Spittle and saliva have always had complex virtues, in that they can be used both to protect and to **curse**. The Zulus believe that a person is made **sick** by the Amatongo (**ancestral spirits**) rather than by the workings of a purely random fate. Should a person be unfortunate enough to **dream** of the Amatongo, the witchdoctor will tell them to gather together the spittle that has collected in their **mouth** during the dream, and hurl it over their **shoulder** – if the **dreamer** is unwise enough to turn their **head**, at this point, in order to see what has happened, the dream is sure to reoccur. See **Spitting**

Splinters Splintering implies fragmentation – it may also imply irritation. If something splinters it is, by definition, fallible and not to be trusted. Splintering may also be seen in terms of rendering (in the sense of a **breaking** down). See **Thorns**

Split Personalities We often conjure up a **number** of characters in our **dreams**, each one manifesting some different aspect of ourselves in their actions – some may even show antagonism, one to the other. Good fictional examples of such activities are to be found in Robert Louis

Stevenson's *Dr Jekyll and Mr Hyde*, **Edgar Allan Poe**'s *William Wilson*, Oscar Wilde's *The Picture of Dorian Gray*, Joseph Conrad's *The Secret Sharer*, and James Hogg's *The Private Memoirs and Confessions of a Justified Sinner*. See **Basements, Depersonalization & Schizophrenia**

Splitting the Body When the **body** is split into its upper and lower parts in a **dream**, it represents a split of the **ego**. The upper part of the body probably **represents** spiritual, idealistic, or platonic desires, while the lower part tends to represent all the baser, more carnal **instincts**. See **Depersonalization**

Sponges Sponges tend to be female **symbols** in **dreams** – this may be associated with perceived passivity (*ergo* the capacity to soak up and expand in order to incorporate outside forces), but it may also be associated with the softness of the sponge, and its undoubted aesthetic value (for it is not only for the benefit of men but also for their own benefit, that women choose to decorate themselves). Sponges may also be **linked** to giving in or being accommodating, as in the expression 'throwing in [or throwing up] the sponge'.

Spoons They used to say that a long spoon was needed to sup with the **devil**, and spoons do, indeed, seem to incorporate fending off or distancing attributes, as well as suggesting carriage and propriety. In addition, spoons in **dreams** may indicate **temptations** given in to and good fortune received (as in the expression 'being born with a **silver** spoon in one's **mouth**').

Sport On the primary level, sport appearing in a **dream** might suggest a simple desire to indulge in it, or point to the existence of an otherwise **repressed feeling** that one ought to be seen to be giving it a go as it is nowadays such a universally approved-of panacea. On the secondary **level** it might denote competition – the acceptance of it, or the **fear** of it, depending on context. On a tertiary level the type of sport becomes important, and needs to be weighed against the **dreamer**s' hidden ambitions for themselves or for their **family**, with **water** sports connecting with the emotions, free-**falling** sports with **anxiety**, and so forth.

Spots Spots are **eruptions** from within that become visible on the outside. They are therefore useful **symbols** for those hidden aspects of the **self** that threaten to reveal themselves to others, and give their progenitor – the **dreamer** – away. They are also blemishes on otherwise pristine surfaces, and may therefore have **anal-retention** connotations.

Spring Spring carries with it inevitable revocations of regeneration, in the sense of what goes around comes around. This **repetitive** aspect is very important, in that it is imbued with an inevitable **feeling** of mortality (and even the possibility of a subliminal **death** wish). In a more positive **light**, spring may also suggest the possibility of a further move up the **chain** of spiritual evolution – the equivalent, if you will, of the **Buddhic nirvana**.

Springing Springing onto something or someone involves taking them, or it, by surprise. People or things springing onto the **dreamer** have the same value, and suggest unpleasant revelations or lurking **dangers** which the dreamer is trying to avoid.

Springs Springs are frequently **symbols** of the **female** breast when they occur in **dreams**. This nutritive aspect also suggests reenergizing, or the emotion of looking forward to something, with **breasts** themselves often taking the role of **eyes** – or ersatz eyes – to the **drinking** infant. Springs may also stand in for the eye, given their natural powers of **reflection**, as well as acting as a repository (just as with **wells**) for human **wishes**. Springs, in the sense of **bed** springs, may suggest the capacity to bounce back – or even the presence of some barrier by which one is consistently frustrated.

Sprinkling Sprinkling and **urination** are inextricably **linked**, with sprinkling **movements** often occurring in **childhood dreams** (which may, or may not, lead to **wetting the bed**). Sprinkling may also be related to the **male orgasm** and to the production of **semen**, as in the 'sprinkling of one's seed on barren (or fertile) ground'.

Spying Spies and spying occupy a naturally voyeuristic **niche** in the **dream** lexicon – sighted **people** inevitably **watch** and compare, **judging**, and subsequently accommodating, their own actions to the actions, or lack of action, of others. Spying is also intrusive, or dependent on the fear of intrusion, and this aspect is likely to be dominant if the **dreamer** feels more than normal **anxiety** or more than normal repressed **guilt**.

Squares See **Quaternity**

Squeezing Squeezing **fruit**, for instance, is often a **symbol** for **masturbation**, and it may also hearken back to our infantile squeezing of the maternal **breast**. Both are **linked**, of course, in that they provide comfort and non-rational (or irrational) security. Squeezing in **dreams** can also be judgemental, in that one can be seen to be making an estimate of something by squeezing it, and when this happens, the identity of the squeezed object should be **weighed** and investigated (squeezed?) by the **dreamer**.

Squirrels Squirrels are somewhat akin to **rats**, if **truth** be told, but **childhood** connotations and **fairy** stories have leavened this view, making squirrels (and particularly the **red** squirrel) something of an **icon**. We are left with the 'storing up of good things for the future' image, and a certain rather unpleasant **phallic** resonance, amplified by the squirrel's habit of nesting in **holes** in **trees**, and of using its **tail** as a fulcrum.

Stabbing Stabbing is almost inevitably **sexual** in connotation. When dreamt of by a **female** it tends to imply, if not an active fear of **sex**, then at least a certain **anxiety** regarding it (or its intrusive aspect) – there may also be a suggestion that one is with the wrong partner (it takes two to tango or to contrive a stabbing incident), or going against one's natural grain in some way (stabbing oneself, or contriving to have oneself stabbed). When dreamt of by a **male** the stabbing motion can indicate excessive assertiveness (or the desire for such), suggesting a fundamental misunderstanding of the notion that assertion is a positive (or innate) masculine characteristic. See **Attacks**, **Murders** & **Murderers**

Stables Stable **doors** are apt to be shut after the **horse** has bolted, and this may be one of the attributes of a stable in a dream – as an empty place, redolent of missed opportunities. Stables will also tend to be **linked** to smells, and **dreams** of stables may find themselves triggered by outside **odours** intruding on – and possibly threatening – the **dreamer**'s **sleep**.

Stadiums Stadiums (or, equally correctly, stadia), suggest demonstrability or demonstration – the conducting in public of something in which the **audience** may have a voyeuristic interest. There may also be a judgemental aspect to the image, suggesting **guilt**, or **anxieties** related to outrages of convention or to the undermining of **taboos**. To that extent stadia can represent one of the functions of the **superego** in **dreams**. See **Spying**

Staff Staff, in the sense of employees, are support adjuncts, as is a staff in the sense of a stick. This curious coincidence (**Jung** might call it a **serendipity**) will tend to carry **weight** equal to more than the sum of its parts inside the **dream** environment. The staff, like the wand, the **sword**, and the **sceptre**, will also tend to have **mystical** characteristics, and may act in the capacity of a *deus ex machina*, allocating to the **dreamer** attributes that they may wish they really possessed. See **Employment**

Stages Stages imply both **beginnings** and ends – **births** and **deaths**, **openings** and closings, **curtains** up and curtains down. Shakespeare's seven stages (ages) of man (from melancholy Jaques's famous speech in *As You Like It*, Act ii scene 7, lines 139–167) are all **endings**, in that, once one stage has been attained and shucked off, it is no longer amenable to a return visit, however much we may wish to do so. Theatrical stages have a similar **weight** to **stadiums** when they appear in **dreams**, except, of course, to **actors** and playwrights, for whom they may have more specific connotations, possibly relating to **anxieties** or ambitions. See **Plays**

Stagnancy Stagnancy may equate to perceived passivity, but with the added worry that there may be something awkward lurking under the apparently torpid and sterile emotional **waters**.

Stags A stag traditionally signifies cuckoldry. Stags are also **symbols** of limited freedoms, in that the stag, within its capacity for **consciousness**, may consider itself free, but we, with our advanced consciousness, know that it is threatened by culling, both natural and, as it were, humanly triggered. The stag is also a **male** simulacrum in **dreams**, and potentially aspirational, as it both mounts its mate, mounts to dominate any competitor, and mounts to greater **heights** in search of safety and privacy. See **Above** & **Climbing**

Stains Stains and **secretions** are often interlinked in a dream context, with stains acting (rather as **spots** do) in a potentially marring capacity. They are giveaways, which imperil the stability of the **dreamer** and threaten to undermine **ego** satisfaction. To that extent they may act as triggers or reminders that activities need to be undertaken to obviate their possible effect.

Stairs Walking up stairs can be a **dream** euphemism for **sexual intercourse**. Spiritually speaking, staircases often act as catalysts between disparate states – betokening moves from a lower to a higher condition of **consciousness**, for instance, or suggesting the possibilities of **upward movement** onto a different plane.

Stakes Stakes and **trees** are often interchangeable in **dreams**, with the stake taking over the active aspect of the otherwise largely static tree. The stake may also be a **sacrificial** one, suggesting **upward movement** or renunciation of **earthly** desires. Stakes may also represent the **phallus** (in the most positive Greek sense of the word) – however, stakes such as those used for the snuffing out of **vampires**, for instance, may have more intrusive revocations, and incorporate **rape** fantasies.

Stallions Stallions carry all the positive revocations of **horses**, with additional revocations relating to the more benevolent and attractive parts of the **male** essence. Stallions, though naturally dominant, are rarely threatening, and to that extent they are probably aspirational, when dreamt of by a **male**, and desiderative, when dreamt of by a **female**. See **Epona**, **Mares** & **Stables**

Stammering Stammering, in everyday life, may occasionally point to the existence of a **secret**, or of a suppressed **question**, which the stammerer wishes to remain hidden – a pathological control of the **speech** process then becomes the stammerer's **unconscious** strategy to prevent any inadvertent blurting out. When stammering occurs in a dream, a similar psychological cause may lie at the **root** of the chosen dream image. In such cases, the identity of the **people** in front of whom the **dreamer** is stammering may provide an important clue to the secret, or to the question, that is being **suppressed**. Particular **dreams** in which stammerers find themselves speaking without a stammer are also significant, in that they may contain within them much-needed insights into the conditions in which the dreamer is stammer-free. Famous historical stammerers include Aristotle, Demosthenes, Virgil, the Emperor Claudius, Louis II, Notker of St Gall, Charles I, Charles Darwin, Isaac Newton, George VI, Somerset Maugham and **Sir Winston Churchill**. Not-so-famous stammerers include the present **author**, who managed to overcome his stammer, aged 15, via **self-hypnosis** (this *à propos* of nothing).

Stamps Stamps are visible authorizations, the implication being that one has paid one's dues and is now entitled to the service offered. There may be an element of immorality about them too, in the sense of **rubber** stamping something with no obvious recourse to ethical considerations – giving oneself permission to do something despite the possible consequences, if you like.

Stars Stars suggest **guidance**, not only in the navigational sense, but also in the form of the ineffable, given that the vast majority of stars exist outside – and will most probably always exist outside – our human remit. Stars also suggest energy and illumination (both mental and physical), and are sometimes taken as representative, both in **number** and significance, of the human **soul**.

Starvation Starvation implies a lack of some essential nutrient without which **life** is impossible. If taken metaphorically, this might suggest a lack of **love** or of familial affection, or even a morbid lack of **self**-esteem.

Stations Stations suggest destinations, and in **dream** terms they are roughly equivalent to **harbours** (in their suggestion of the **anima**) for that very reason. They are not usually final destinations, however, but **transitions** or stages on a **journey**, and this affords them the possibility of a slightly different emphasis, perhaps – one of temporary restoration rather than of final rendition?

Statues Statues, being lifelike but empty renditions of the human form, inevitably suggest the **surreal** rather than the real. In dreams they can represent the false ideal (insofar as they are malleable and incapable of independent thought) or the pornographic (in the sense that they, and the people that they represent, are seemingly at our command). The lifeless and cold aspect of a statue may also be significant, possibly suggesting the **death** of the **spirit** (given that the corporeal aspect would, on the surface at least, still appear to be intact), and one would do well to remember the story of Pygmalion, King of Cyprus, who fell helplessly in love with a statue of his own devising.

Stealing Stealing, in **dreams**, can act as a substitute for **sexual** misbehaviour. It may also represent inappropriate comportment, as in the undermining or ignoring of societal **taboos**. See **Burglars**

Steam Steam would appear to be menacing on the **surface**, but unless one gets very close to it, it is unlikely to cause harm. Thus the expression 'blowing off steam' to describe someone who, while seemingly gruff, is actually unthreatening. Steam may also suggest **cookery** (in the form of nutrition) and **washing** (in the form of purgation). In the case of a steamship with a very obviously steaming smokestack, steam may then equate with **semen**.

Steel Steel is both powerful and inflexible, and these two aspects define it in **dreams**, the presumption being that the **dreamer** is unable to influence or move it from its established position. The shape of the steel, and what it represents, then becomes important, followed by the context in which the steel finds itself – gnarled and rusty and on a **beach**, for instance, might suggest outmoded ideas, bogged down on the periphery of a less important, more transitory place than either the **sea**, or the mainland.

Steeples Steeples, like **spires**, tend towards the **phallic** in **dreams**, and towards the aspirational. They may also act as spiritual markers, reminding the individual of the existence of something other than the material **world**.

Steepness When things get steeper they become more difficult, requiring more of a commitment on the part of the **dreamer**, and considerably more effort. The suggestion of **upward movement**, however, probably hints that the effort is worthwhile, at least in terms of its **goal**.

Steering Steering is about control, or the desire for it. Steering a **boat**, for instance, in a dream, might suggest a desire to rise above or dominate one's emotional condition or the emotional climate surrounding one. The necessity to steer delicately, or by the making of precise movements, is **self**-explanatory, and will garner any significance from its immediate context.

Stekel, Wilhelm (1868–1940) The Polish-born Stekel was originally a **student** and analysand of **Freud**'s, but, together with **Alfred Adler**, he fell foul of his **master** following his advocacy of the so-called 'short analysis', in which the analyst takes a more active participation than in the traditional Freudian **model**. Stekel's influence on succeeding generations was not great, but he had many important things to say about **dream analysis**, and some of his **writings** justly bear re-scrutiny.

Steps See **Stairs**

Stereotypical Dreams Stereotyped **dreams** and recurring stereotypical motifs can point up important **problems** in the dreamer's **psyche**. Their continuous appearance in the **dreamer**'s **unconscious** implies a desire to overcome the problem, twinned with a frustration about its apparent insolubility. Such hidden **conflicts** need to be addressed and resolved if they are not to hamper the dreamer's emotional development. A period of concentrated **dream work** may be the best way forward. See **Recurring Dreams**

Sterilization Dreams of enforced sterilization may hide or reflect an unacknowledged condition of low **self**-esteem, in the sense that we are programmed, as humans, to procreate, and that any **failure** to do so may be seen (falsely, of course) to **reflect** on our humanness. Such **dreams** (particularly if they are **recurrent**) may also disguise a **castration complex**, a **circumcision complex**, or a **hymen complex**, or, more seriously perhaps, an unresolved depressive condition. See **Amputation**, **Depression** & **Manic Depression**

Stevenson, Robert Louis (1850–94) See **Dr Jekyll and Mr Hyde**

Stinging Stinging tends to **point** to small niggles and annoyances, often appearing out of the **blue**, which impair concentration and cause too much emphasis to be placed on trivial things to the detriment of larger issues. Stinging may also be seen as part of a curative process, and this may carry over to truthful, yet nevertheless still hurtful, criticisms, which stinging can also exemplify. See **Critics** & **Nettles**

Stockings Stockings tend to be about **openings** (at least in the somewhat literal **world** of **dreams**), and this may give them **female** connotations over and above their relation to adornment. **Blue** stockings, for instance, taken to indicate a certain degree of pedantry or as a badge of feminine intellectuality, may also, paradoxically, represent openings or byways which the **dreamer** may wish to frequent. Stockings may also represent the desire to receive **gifts** or to be rewarded in a non-judgemental way.

Stocks & Bonds Stocks and bonds represent the desire for material growth and security at the expense (within reason) of control. This gambling aspect is an important one, and is almost akin to **playing** in **archetypal** terms, and may suggest a hidden desire to **cheat death**. See **Gamblers** & **Wagers**

Stomach Ache Stomach ache is what **children** claim to have when they are bewildered by adult actions, or **wish** for some attention outside their normal **times** or **spheres** of influence. This infantile desire for attention is perfectly likely to be carried over into adult **dreams**, and suggests that the stomach ache will inevitably reflect something other than its seeming source – a lack of affection, for instance (one presses a **teddy bear** or a hot **water bottle** to one's stomach for comfort), or a desire to either be a child again, or to have a child.

Stones Voices traditionally spoke from within stones, and ancient man would have seen nothing untoward in **speaking** back to them. The dolmens and menhirs of Stonehenge were likely to have been consulted as oracles, just as we know that certain trees, plants and animals were consulted. Moslems make pilgrimages to the Black Stone of Mecca, contained within the holy sanctuary of the Ka'aba, and Christ, in Christian symbolism, was personified in the rock: 'For they drank from that spiritual Rock that followed them: and that Rock was Christ.' (1 Corinthians x, 4). In dreams, therefore, stones can represent emotional energy, as well as stability, spiritual renewal, and the self. The alchemical stone (the lapis), represents indissolubility. Stones abide. They express the inexpressible. See Tombstones

KEY LINE: 'When Gunnhildr heard the woman saying the same thing so often with a trembling voice, she was curious as to what sort of infant she had been delivered of. It seemed to her that it was a rather large stone, snow-white in colour; it shone so that sparks flew in all directions, as with glowing iron, when the hearth is blown up sharply with the bellows ... After that she woke out of the dream.' (From the *Sverris Saga* 900 AD)

Storing The storing up of things for the future may be neurotic in origin, for in the modern world, and outside times of crisis, we rarely need such fallbacks. In metaphorical terms, the storing up of things reflects fears of energy loss or of losing aspects of ourselves which we view as significant – storing may therefore act as a correlative to the ageing process, and to our fears of dissolution.

Storks Storks are inextricably linked, in most people's imaginations, with the delivery of babies. It is something of a paradox, then, that the Romans had a law called the Storks' Law (*Lex Ciconaria*), which obliged children to look after their parents 'just as storks do'. Given that storks are also renowned for eating snakes, the symbolic resonances of the stork seem virtually unlimited.

Storms Storms tend to reflect emotional upheavals and sudden changes that have either inconvenienced the dreamer in the past (repression), or are about to inconvenience them in the future (anxiety). Storms may also act in a purgative capacity, or imply confusion.

KEY LINE: 'Then Jesus arose, and rebuked the winds and the sea; and there was a great calm.' (From Matthew viii, 26)

Stoves Stoves are female symbols, and frequently represent the vagina in dreams. Heating a stove can also be a reference to the sexual act. Taking the anti-Freudian view, it should also be mentioned that things are cooked up in stoves, and that the stove may therefore act as a euphemism for planning ahead or anticipating things.

Straightness Straightness, directness, ease of access – 'Enter ye in at the strait gate: for wide is the gate, and broad is the way, that leadeth to destruction, and many there be which go in thereat:' (Matthew vii, 13).

The beautiful paradox of Matthew's rendition of **Jesus'** words lies in the fact that one would assume the large gate to afford more ease of access, whereas it is in fact the **narrow** (strait) **gate** that 'leadeth unto life'. So straitness and straightness find themselves interlinked, but nevertheless diametrically opposed. Such juxtapositions are an immensely **rich** seam in **dream symbology**, and throw up the most surprising of bedfellows. Take **straitjackets**, for instance, which occur next in the **book**.

Straitjackets Straitjackets are designed to be constraining, whereas a euphonic **reading** might suggest a jacket designed not so much to constrain as to empower. The disempowering aspect of the straitjacket, however, together with its resolute non-**straightness** (the **arms** are twisted and tied behind the back), hearken back to the **pre-birth** condition, and to the inchoate **nature** of incipient life, which finds itself dream-echoed in revocations of the inchoate (or embryonic) state of **madness**. The wide (straight) **gate**, of course, whereas simple in prospect, affords no control, whereas the straitened gate both **reflects** – and is at the level of – the human condition.

Strangers Strangers, especially those whose **faces** are not easily distinguishable, frequently represent the **unconscious**, or the non-ego. In this case the **dreamer** retains possession merely of the differentiated function, implying that the unconscious is beginning to hold sway, with the dreamer gradually becoming unbound from the **earth** and its hold on the **psyche**.

Strangling Umbilical **neuroses** (the **fear** of, or the conviction that one has been strangled by, the umbilical cord) is often strongly related to **mother** fixations, and to the **feeling** that one is powerless to detach oneself, undamaged, from the maternal presence. On the Indonesian island of Seram, **mothers** traditionally kept the remains of the **umbilical cord** and hung them around the child's **neck** when it was **ill**, and on the islands of Leti, Moa and Lakor grown men would wear their dried umbilicus as an **amulet** – it is at least arguable, therefore, that these practices, by symbolically acknowledging the visceral mother/**child** connection and using it in a positive way, also helped to leaven it.

Straw Straw is viewed by the **Bible** (and by pork-loving **wolves**) as unconducive to permanence, and of little value. Traditionally, if straw (or more particularly chopped straw) was present at a **wedding**, it suggested that the **bride** was no **virgin** (in the sense that the **corn** had already been winnowed). This 'flighty' aspect to straw is probably the most important in any **reading**, but it should also be remembered that straw is often associated with **sleep** (the filling of **mattresses**, the thatching of mangers), and **childbirth** (women were known, until quite recently, as being 'in the straw', in certain country regions). Straw blowing in the **wind** suggests useless effort, while laying straws onto objects might suggest a **fear** that the **dreamer** is close to **breaking** point.

Streams Streams, being only small stretches of **water**, suggest manage-able emotions. They may also be **linked** to micturition (**urination**) in **children**, and to the dispersal of energies. See **Brooks**
KEY LINE: 'Dear Child, I also by pleasant Streams/Have wandered all night in the Land of Dreams;/But tho' calm and warm the waters wide,/ I could not get to the other side.' (William Blake's *The Land of Dreams* 1789)

Streets See **Crossroads & Roads**

String String may find itself related to the **umbilical cord** (see **Strangling**), or to connections between **people**. **Walking** along and hold-ing a piece of string may suggest futility (being strung along), or an inability to move from one particular line of thought ('he only has one string to his bow'). See **Rope**

Struggling Struggling may relate to **birth** traumas, or it may point to **repressed conflicts** that the **conscious mind** is secretly grappling with but still refusing to acknowledge. Somewhat paradoxically, perhaps, struggling may also intimate a desire for peace and harmony, for in **dreams** things are very often marked by their obvious **absence**. See **Symbols & Transformation**

Students Students imply the desire to learn, or the desire to be taught by someone (a **guide**, a mentor) who is learned. This idea of discipleship fre-quently occurs in **dreams**, and is probably related to the **parent/child** relationship we have all experienced (in one guise or another), and the consequent urge to perfect, heal, or recreate it via **dreams**. See **Schools & Universities**

Stumps Stumps are usually related to **amputation**, in the sense that something living has been **cut** off and discarded, and what remains may now be considered truncated or incomplete. The waving of stumps (of **legs** or **hands**, for instance) indicates powerlessness, and a possible inability to differentiate.

Sublimation The overcoming of immoral or antisocial tendencies by their **unconscious** transformation into morally or socially acceptable nor-mative behaviours (an **ascent**). The reformed **criminal** who lectures oth-ers on the perils of a life of crime is a case in point, as is the dreaming of behaviours which in real life we would find unacceptable – in this way our **dreams** protect society, and ourselves, from the **dangers** of an uncon-trolled gratification of desire. For instance, during the **Fall** of Berlin, in 1945, even old women and young **children** were subjected to violation at the **hands** of an incensed (and brutalized) Russian soldiery who, for the space of two appalling weeks, were given free **rein** to behave like beasts for reasons of political expedience. Those **soldiers** who chose not to indulge their baser passions on a defenceless population proved themselves triumphantly capable of sublimation in the most extreme conditions – the others were damaged for life. See **Dream Censorship**

Subliminal Beneath the threshold of **consciousness**.

Submarines Submarines are fairly obvious **penile symbols** (in that they go under and thrust forwards), but they may also relate to **water** and to the emotions, in the sense, perhaps, of 'plumbing the depths'.

Submerging The **symbol** of submerging has a **number** of striking connotations, the most obvious being the act of being swamped by one's emotions (see **Drowning**). There may also be revocations of the **sexual** act, or of losing oneself in a problem of one's own making (in the sense of submerging oneself).

Subways Subways can have strong **sexual** overtones in **dreams**, not only because of the obvious sexual imagery of a **train** entering (or emerging from) a **tunnel**, but also because they present opportunities for inadvertent physical contact which are not customarily available. In nominally **repressed** societies, such as Japan, the United States and the United Kingdom, subways take on even more extreme connotations, and often find themselves used as locations for fantasized sexual encounters.

Succubi The **female** counterpart of **incubi**, the succubus was a female **demon** who appeared to **sleeping** men (at least according to medieval folklore) and constrained them to mate with her. Her progeny were **witches, demons,** or warlocks.
KEY LINE: 'It was he who dressed up for me a hag that nightly sate upon my pillow – a sure bed-fellow, when my aunt or my maid was far from me. All day long, while the book was permitted me, I dreamed waking over his delineation, and at night (if I may use so bold an expression) awoke into sleep, and found the vision true.' (Charles Lamb)

Sucking Sucking (in either **sex**) usually relates back to infantile **oral fixations**, in the sense that sucking was our first semi-conscious act, and constituted our primary means of influencing our immediate environment (i.e. persuading our **mother** to offer her **breast** to us by bawling and making sucking motions). Sucking was therefore early associated with triumph, and therein probably lies its preponderance in sexual display and gratification, and its constituent **weight** in **dreams**.

Suffocation Some see **dreams** of suffocation as relating to the **pre-birth** condition, whilst others relate it to the perceived **trauma** of **birth** itself. Either way, it probably has more emotional than physical resonance, except insofar as it may be caused by an inadvertent clogging of the airwaves whilst asleep. See **Strangling**

Sugar To a present-day **dreamer**, sugar is probably both **sweet** and mild-ly threatening. This paradox may complicate interpretation, in that some-thing that is both desirable and dangerous can lead to **repression**, and, in consequence, to **ellipsis**.

Suicide **Feelings** of suicide may be transient, but their end results are irre-versible. **Dreams** may provide hints as to a suicidally-inclined **dreamer**'s intentions, or, at the very least, point to the mechanisms behind that intent. They may also (more debatably) conspire in easing **people** towards acceptance of **death** as a solution, in the form of **wish-fulfilment** fantasies, which may involve the '**joining**' of those already dead. The protective element of the dream has then, signally, failed – the **ego** has been relegated to object status, and no longer acts as a safeguard. Particularly dangerous, in this context (i.e. for those with pre-existing or even pathological suicidal tendencies), are those dreams which show what we may call an 'absolute pessimism' – in **Freudian** terms this means that the ego has been abandoned by the **superego** and 'left to die'.

Suitcases See **Bags**

Summer Summer may find itself related to the **south** or to the **sun** in **dreams**, and to maturity and gratification. Summer is also about **light**, and the ability to see clearly and without **shadow**, and its presence in a dream may point to **problems** which the **dreamer** feels need eradication by a purgative (i.e. enlightened) source.

Summits Summits (of **hills**, **mountains**, **buildings**, etc.) are generally stand-ins for aspirational **goals**, and equate with anything that involves being **above** something else. Summits are also suggestive of resolution, particularly of affairs of the lower order, or the lower plane of being.

Sun, The The sun is often a **symbol** for **God** and of the Higher **Self**. The **rising** sun controls aspiration, with the motion of the sun acting as a **door** to perception, as well as being a living proof that everything (under the sun) is cyclical. The setting sun reminds us of our mortality, and of the fallibility and fragility of human **wishes** and desires. See **Planets**

Sundays Despite the 24-hour-day, **seven**-day-week **nature** of our modern **world**, Sunday (at least for non-Muslims and non-Jews) still remains a potent **symbol** of rest. The **unconscious** mind is perfectly capable of recycling **childhood** memories to serve its purposes in a gross nominal betrayal of its progenitor's subsequent intellectual and theological devel-opment. Call yourself an atheist? The unconscious mind will dredge up every holy and **religious** symbol it has at its disposal if that is the only way to fulfil its single-minded devotion to the protection of your **sleep**. A trivial aside, here: it's a curious fact, but many well-known **battles** have been fought on a Sunday, including Worcester, Bull Run, Killiecrankie, Lepanto and Waterloo.

Sunglasses Sunglasses both protect and disguise, and this happy juxtaposition makes for a particularly useful **dream symbol** – for wearing sunglasses conceals the emotions, replacing the **eyes** with **mirrors** that can serve to **reflect** our interlocutors back on themselves. We are **projecting** outwards, in other words, without allowing for a reciprocal connection.

Sunrises See **Sun**

Sunsets See **Sun**

Superego, The The superego, according to **Freud**, has the task of upholding the inculcated ideals of **education**, customs, **taboos** and moral rectitude, causing us to **sacrifice** or repress our **primordial** cravings on the **altar** of convention. It represents the observational and critical aspect of our personalities, and takes over, in many ways, the original function of our **parents** as we emerge from our chrysalises into adult life. The superego can also intervene physically, as in a nervous **stomach** getting in the way of a woman's assignation, or impotence besetting a man who is about to commit **adultery**. See also **Dream Censorship**, **Ego**, **Id**, **Paralysis** & **Sublimation**

Supermarkets See **Shops** & **Grocery Stores**

Superstitions We appear to need superstitions and **taboos**. A world **cleansed** of all irrational elements would only have **dreams** to fall back on – and irrational elements, acknowledged in everyday life, act as a correlative to such a state of affairs. Superstitions are our way of **consciously** recognizing our **unconscious** identity with natural objects, and as such they form an important safety valve, or **bridge**, between both states. Bowing three times when one sees a **black cat** or a single **magpie** – saluting kestrels, or **hawks** – **fear** of the number 13 – throwing **spilled salt** over the **left shoulder** to ward off the **devil** – all serve to remind us of the beyond-rational. Lucky charms such as **rabbit**'s **feet**, **coins**, lockets, and **horseshoes** have strong symbolic resonances, too, and humanize a **world** that has, in many ways, become dehumanized by science and a slavish adherence to the judicious. Dreams often choose superstitions as part of their **wallpaper**, and it is important, when interpreting such dreams, to **judge**, first of all, whether the **dreamer falls** into the rational, or into the irrational (or fey) **camp** – because the meaning of the dream will be different in both cases.

Suppression The predominantly **conscious repression** of particular ideas – and the emotions which infibulate them – from the **mind**.

Surgery Surgery suggests that there is an urgent need for change, and that this need takes precedence over even physical integrity. This crisis aspect may have as its source some perceived attack on one's very **fabric** (i.e. getting under one's **skin**), and only resolve itself via radical attention.

Surprise Surprise, wonderment, or befuddlement in a **dream** may **reflect** the presence of a pre-existing **question** – possibly relating to undigested or strange aspects of one's own behaviour or character – already present in the **mind** of the **dreamer**.

Surrealism Founded as an offshoot of Dadaism in 1924, Surrealism strove to incorporate both **dreams** and the **unconscious** into an artistic credo that rebelled against the bourgeois certainties of western culture in the post Great War age. **André Breton** was its guiding force, and it numbered within its ranks, and influenced, many of the greatest **artists** of the twentieth century. See **Dali** & **Magritte**

Suspension Dreams in which the **dreamer** finds themselves suspended between the **earth** and the **sky** (or perhaps ascending a **ladder** or a **staircase** that leads to nowhere) usually indicate a triumph of fantasy over **reality**. They are different in that sense from aspirational **dreams**, in which the dreamer finds themselves **above**, or at the **summit** of something.

Swallowing Swallowing indicates the need for ingestion – this may seem like a blindingly obvious statement, but it is the details of the act (and the objects involved) which are important. Swallowing a **book**, for instance (although not strictly recommended), might imply a desire for knowledge, whereas swallowing something threatening, like a **knife**, might suggest a desire to disarm or **integrate** the hazard harmlessly inside one's personality. Try not to swallow any **flies**, however – just remember what happened to the **old woman**.

Swallows A swallow traditionally signifies a fair-weather **friend** – for they will come and go as they please. Their appearance in a **dream** might suggest transition, therefore, or change of some sort – even the possibilities of mental freedom in a physically un-free **world**.

Swamps See **Marshes** & **Quicksand**

Swans A swan habitually symbolizes grace. The Anglo-Saxons used to call the **sea**, or large expanses of **water**, *swan-rid*, or the place over which swans **ride**. This ancient form of kenning (the metaphorical liaison of two words to create another meaning), is a frequent adjunct of **dreams**, and can work either poetically or literally, as in, for instance, the word swansong, which suggests **death**, beauty and apotheosis. A similar process can occur in dreams, with the **linking** of two disparate objects or concepts equalling considerably more than the sum of the two wholes.

Swastikas The swastika (or *fylfot* sign: also *gammadion*) used to indicate the cycle of life, before it was hijacked by the German National Socialists and temporarily debased from its **mandala**-like eminence. It has still not been entirely redeemed, and any dream which figures it must be scrutinized both ways – via the besmirched and via the noumenal – dependent on context.

Sweat See **Secretions**

Swedenborg, Emanuel (1688–1772) Swedish scientist, philosopher and mystic. See **Bears** & **Plato**

Sweeping Sweeping indicates the need for **cleansing** (*à la* Lady Macbeth), but the to and fro movement might also suggest the **sexual** act or **masturbation**, hinting at **guilt** issues possibly involving the **dreamer**'s sexuality.

Sweets Sweets and candy tend to be viewed, in **dream** terms, as rewards, even when the **dreamer** is no longer remotely sweet-toothed. This is evidence that the image is imbued with **childhood** rather than adult significance, and that our subsequently attained proclivities count for little in fundamentalist dream terms. See **Sugar** & **Syrup**

Swimming Swimming is often synonymous with **masturbation** in **dream** terms. It can also reflect harmony and balance. The forced truncation of the swimming movement (by the attack of a **shark**, say) may imply disharmony, disunity, or the **fear** of **impotence**.

Swine See **Hogs** & **Pigs**

Swinging The word Tarzanic, as in 'Tarzanic swinging' (see **Pirates**), is a **neologism** rather dubiously **coined** by the **author** to represent the free **movement** in **dreams** between apparently unconducive locations via convenient lianas/**ropes/ivy**, streamers/**drapes**, etc., as typically seen in escapist Hollywood **films** of the 1920s, 30s and 40s (plus their modern derivatives), along such lines as Michael Curtiz and Richard Keighley's *The Adventures of Robin Hood* (1938), Sam Wood's *A Night at the Opera* (1935), or Curtiz's *The Sea Hawk* (1940). The swinging, in this case, equates with **flying**, in that it appears to offer an **escape** or freedom perspective where no such escape or freedom perspective normally (or rationally) exists. It is the perfect exemplar of **Freud**'s concept of **wish-fulfilment**, therefore, and almost certainly reminiscent of recollected **childhood** freedoms of movement. See **Trapezes**

Switching The sudden switching from one object (or scene) to another is a frequent **dream** occurrence, and is probably **sleep**-protective in origin. Switching may also equate with the exercise of power, as in the switching on and off **lamps** (i.e. **light/truth**) or the switching on and off of affection.

Swords Swords have strong **phallic** connotations in **dreams**. Even **King** Arthur's sword Excalibur finds itself **plunged** into the **earth** between the sleeping **bodies** of Lancelot and Guinevere, nicely equating priapism with justice (the double-edged blade of **truth**). However, swords may also have protective connotations, as well as substituting for the **hand** in religious or heraldic iconography – in such contexts the sword would appear to betoken outgoing positive energy, implying the desire positively to differentiate between the true and the false. See **Falsification of Memory**

KEY LINE: 'Who tolerates this gadding about of ancient knights in dreams, irresponsibly brandishing their swords, stabbing innocent sleepers who are saved from serious injury only because the weapons in all likelihood glance off living bodies, and also because their faithful friends are knocking at the door, prepared to come to their assistance?' (From Franz Kafka's *Diaries* 19th January 1915, following a dream in which a sword sticks in his back, though causing him no injury)

Symbolic Parallelism An amalgamation of two or more symbolical ideas conjured up by the **dreamer** in order to **suppress** or dilute **unconscious fears** and **anxieties**. At least one aspect of the symbolic parallel usually **represents** a **wish** which is opposed, or frowned upon, by the **ego**. Crimes, for instance, may substitute for each other in a dream context, or even for something else (a **taboo** action, perhaps) that the **dreamer** feels that they may have done wrong. See **Shooting**

Symbolization A general scheme of **symbols** called upon by the individual **dreamer** and used in an individual way. It functions, if you like, in a roughly similar way to a Cartesian or an empiricist view of 'private' **language**, something hotly disputed by philosopher Ludwig Wittgenstein in sections 243–315 of his *Philosophical Investigations*. See **Representability**

Symbols Symbols, in **dreams**, always signify more than their obvious and evident meaning. They are attempts by the **unconscious** to reconcile **opposites** within the **psyche**. They are spontaneous products, not amenable to invention – unlike **signs**. Religious symbols, for instance, though apparently elaborated, are actually collective representations stemming from primeval dreams and creative fantasies. They are therefore artless and uncontrived. **Jung** advised his **students** to learn as much as they could about symbolism, and then to forget it all when they were analyzing a dream. The implications of this advice stem from Jung's belief that, in ancient **times**, men and women did not **reflect** upon their symbols, but simply lived them, their behaviour being unconsciously animated by symbolic meaning. **Freud** viewed symbolism as not a dream problem at all, but merely a topic connected with our archaic forms of thinking – what the paranoiac Dr Daniel Paul Schreber (1842–1911), in *Memoirs of my Nervous Illness*, called our '**root-language**'. See **Fixed Symbolism, Individual Symbols, Representability** & **Symbolization**

Symptoms When symptoms such as **illness**, unwarranted excitation, or **frustration** occur in **dreams**, they are usually accompanied by their own particular set of dynamics or undercurrents – they act as points of **condensation**, in other words, between often disparate ideas and emotional forces. This is of enormous importance in **dream work,** providing potentially precious insights into underlying but still hidden problems, such as infantile **trauma**, or **neuroses**.

Synagogues Synagogues can represent the **superego** in **dreams**, just as **churches**, **cathedrals**, **pagodas** or **mosques** can. They can also, by extension, exemplify **taboos**, particularly to **dreamers** of the Jewish faith.

Synchronicity **Jung**'s concept of 'meaningful coincidence' – the meeting or juxtaposition of outer with inner events that are not, in themselves, causally connected, but which nevertheless point towards underlying **archetypal** messages. When related to **dream symbolism**, synchronistic events can suggest crucial phases in the process towards **individuation**.

Syphilis See **Diseases**

Syringes Syringes often symbolize the **penis** in **dreams**. The contents of the syringe are also important, as is the **colour** of the liquid injected, for the use of a syringe can imply a desire to influence the inner by the outer (**drug**-taking being a case in point), thus highlighting a **weakness** of the inner. Alternatively, syringes can point up a **fear** of being tarnished or unwillingly (for needles hurt) infused by outside influences. See **Vaccinations**

Syrup Syrup sticks, and its main point is that we can't **escape** it once it tarnishes or infuses us. It is both desirable and off-putting for this very reason, and will probably contain **sexual** connotations linked to **guilt** and gratification, virtue and reward. Syrup can also act as a disguise for something that is, by its very nature, bitter (as in **pills**), but which may, nonetheless, (in **superego** terms, at least), act to our advantage.

T

Tabernacles Tabernacles of any sort are most probably related to the **superego** in **dreams**, but they may also relate to **quaternity**, as in the Tabernacle of Moses which consisted of four **onion**-like **layers** referring, in their turn, to the outer physical **body**, the inner intellectual body, and the **heart** and **soul** within the **veil**, which, in its turn, housed the Divine Glory, as typified by the Ark and the Shechinah (a Jewish theological trope describing the presence of **God** throughout the **world**). Such correlations are important in dream terms, and may act **unconsciously** (even unconstitutionally, in the case of an atheist), without the **dreamer** being aware of their source.

Tables Tables suggest community, in the sense that they are gathering places around which **people** share things, such as **eating**, **cooking** or **talking**. A clean table has revocations of a clean slate (a *tabula rasa*), on which anything may be written and on which anything is possible. A cluttered table, on the other hand, might suggest a cluttered **mind**, pointing up the necessity for an urgent mental spring cleaning. See **Cleansing**

Tablets Tablets (the sorts on which things are written) can act as conduits for the **superego**, suggesting laws and diktats, **taboos** and restrictions. Tablets (in the form of **medicines**) are more likely to indicate the implied necessity for a change in condition, denoting a lack of present comfort. See **Pills**

Taboos Instinctive prohibitions against **people**, objects, or types of behaviour. **Dream symbolism**, stemming as it does from the **unconscious**, evades societal taboos, and allows us to experiment with illicitness without suffering the consequences in the form of exile, ridicule, or expulsion from the community. Sometimes these prohibitions do not work, however, and the tabooed desires cause the **dreamer** to enact them through the medium of somnambulism (**sleepwalking**) or epileptic deliriums. See **Dream Censorship**

Tadpoles Tadpoles, given their resemblance to **male sperm** (albeit on a far more grandiose scale), will tend to inhabit **dreams** of **pregnancy**, **pre-birth** and parturition. Their inchoate **nature** is also likely to be of importance, suggesting incompleteness or lack of resolution of some projected task.

Tailors Tailors are the perfect **servants**, in the sense that they do exactly what we want (make us **clothes**) without otherwise inconveniencing us (they are comfort providers, in other words). To that extent they may take an almost maternal role in **dreams**, acting as conduits for the view we have of ourselves, or of how we wish to present ourselves to the outside **world**. In real life our **mothers** often fulfil a similar capacity, reinforcing our **egos** even when they palpably don't need reinforcing (i.e. making us metaphorical **clothes** that we don't need, or which are surplus to actual requirements, but which are nevertheless nice to own).

Tails Tails generally have **phallic** connotations when they appear in **dreams**, but they may also contain revocations of the **devil** or of illicit sexuality, **drawing** attention, as they do, to the rear of the human **body**. They may also suggest aspects of the **past** which we are unable to slough off, and which persist in dogging our steps because they are (or have become) a part of us.

Talismans Talismans are closely related to **amulets**, and suggest a desire for change without the necessity for creative or active input – they're almost akin to **gambling**, in other words, but without the financial **risk**.

Talking See **Speech**

Tallness Very tall **people** appearing in **dreams** can signify a reversion to a **childhood** perspective, when everyone appeared tall. Tallness can also relate to importance, as can **smallness**. In addition, very tall people are often the carriers of stress in dreams, or of threat. Extra large objects may also be forcing attention on themselves.

Talmud, The The Talmud (or Shas) is the book of Jewish law, and a definite stand-in for the **superego**, alongside the **Bible**, the **Koran**, and the Bhagavad-Gita, to name but a few of the myriad **sacred** works that seek to usher us along the **path** to absolution.

Taming Taming things is to impose one's power and dominance upon them – to mark them, in other words, with our metaphorical **scent**. Taming implies a certain superiority, therefore, and even the taming of aspects of ourselves implies the mastery of them by a superior demonstration of willpower. Taming is thus an adjunct of the **superego**, and implies dissatisfaction with (or **fear** of) the existing order or *status quo*.

Tangling Human beings tend to become entangled by their emotions or their interrelationships, somewhat along the lines of a **juggler** trying it on with one too many **plates**. Such confusions often arise when the **dreamer** feels put upon from too many different quarters – the **magical** untangling of surrounding growths is therefore **wish-fulfilment** in origin, and is merely one of the ways in which the **unconscious** mind protects the dreamer from the consequences of an incipient **neurosis**.

Tanks Tanks crash through things willy-nilly, forcing their way over fragile growths, through **houses**, and over **bodies**. Tanks are also defensive, in the sense that they are **armoured** in order to protect themselves from the consequences of their own aggressive acts – in **dream** terms this may seem a little like having one's **cake** and **eating** it too. Tanks are predominantly **male symbols**, therefore (which is not to say that **females** won't dream of them or use them in their **dreams**), and also assertively **phallic**, given the protruding and multidirectional cannon which they display to all comers as a badge of dominance.

Tape Tape tends to be used to mark out boundaries, and boundaries are what the **ego** does best. The use of tape is also imbued with potential **anxiety** (crime scenes, **police** restrictions, the taping of the **mouth** to prevent **speech**), as well as being sticky, and prone to **tangling**. Audio tape may act as a **record**, reminding us of things we would rather forget, or affording us the suggestion of things to which we may no longer have easy access (audio tapes or video tapes being useless without the adjunct of a player).

Tapestries Tapestries are predominantly about symmetry and the steady accrual of significance through patience. They are decorative but also useful, and this may see them incorporate suggestions of diplomacy, in the sense of a painstaking investment in a desired future outcome. Tapestries may also be symbolical of **richness** and of display.

Taps See **Faucets**

Tar Tar has toxic revocations as well as **primordial** ones (in the sense of **primal** ooze). To that extent it may suggest **death** and decomposition, given that, both by substance and virtue, it can prevent **breathing**. The association of tar with sulphur, with **blackness**, and with **burning** may involve thoughts of the **devil** and of **hell**.

Targets Targets very often **reflect** or symbolize the **vagina** when they occur in **dreams**. In certain other contexts they can suggest the **mouth** or the **anus**. See **Arrows**

Tartini, Giuseppe (1692–1770) The Italian violinist and composer Giuseppe Tartini was **slaving** over the composition of a particularly difficult sonata. Dozing off, he found himself in the midst of a **dream** in which the **devil** entered the **room**, snatched up a **violin**, and played the sonata right through. When he woke up, Tartini had the entire sonata clear in his **head** – it was published posthumously, unfortunately, but Tartini did have the grace to call it the *Devil's Trill*.

Tarzanic Swinging See **Pirates, Swinging & Trapezes**

Tattoos A tattoo is the imposition of an **alien** design on a familiar object (i.e. the **skin**). It can **reflect** both identity and ownership, but may also carry revocations of shame and disenfranchisement (as in a **slave** tattoo, or a tattoo imposed upon a **concentration camp** inmate). Given all this, a tattoo may also carry a paradoxical meaning, such as making a virtue of the wearing of a mark of shame.

Taxes Benjamin Franklin wrote to his **friend** and colleague, Jean-Baptiste Leroy, in 1789: 'In this **world** nothing can be said to be certain, except **death** and **taxes**.' Nonsense, of course, but entertaining nonsense – tax, unlike **death**, is a temporary and expedient imposition from the outside in, with death being an inexpedient univocity from the inside out. To that extent taxes (unlike death) are stand-ins for the **superego**, and suggest behavioural (and even moral) limits.

Taxis Taxis imply that desired or convenient activities come at a price – that help may have to be paid for, or contain hidden catches or disadvantages. Taxis are also about restrictions on free **movement** (physical or spiritual), often linked to a desire to surpass or transcend such restrictions.

Tea Tea most probably suggests comfort and conviviality (even to a **drug** addict – tea being early 20s street slang for heroin), twinned with a stretching out or sharing across cultures, in the sense that one is imbibing something exotic in what may be a nominally un-exotic setting. Either way, it constitutes a taking in as well as a reaching out, which is probably what gives rise to some of the spiritual connotations potentially contained within the **symbol**.

Teachers Teachers are often a **symbol** of the **father** in **dreams**, and can also represent the **superego**. They may also, in certain cases, represent **Jesus Christ**.

Teams Teams suggest varying aspects of an otherwise one-dimensional whole (the **dreamer**). This concept of being more than the simple sum of one's parts is an adjunct of **wish-fulfilment**, and most probably refers back to **childhood** when one instinctively considered oneself to be a symbiotic (and even permanent) part of the **mother/child** relationship. The sense of **loss** engendered by the onset of knowledge may partially be offset by the protection and comfort (the correlative, even) afforded by **dreams**.

Tearing If a woman dreams of the act of tearing, it is frequently synonymous with the loss of **virginity**, or even with the specific circumstances of her defloration. Tearing is also an unnatural sundering of otherwise related **parties**, and may reflect a **break** up (or relational breakdown) between formerly harmonious entities. The act of tearing may also relate to **shamanic ritual**.

Tears See **Secretions**

Teasing Teasing can imply affection and it can imply imposition – and the dividing line is sometimes very difficult to judge. Maturity is often encapsulated by the ability to tease oneself, or by the capacity to take teasing without vainglory rearing its ugly head. Teasing can therefore constitute a **rite-of-passage** in a **dream**, but it can also constitute an **anxiety** pointer, relating to old (and possibly now discarded) **patterns** of behaviour.

Teddy Bears In **childhood**, as well as being transitional objects (see **Silkiness** & **Velvet**), teddy bears are also **reflections** of the **self**, in the sense that they can **unconsciously** represent the **child** to itself, and to itself in terms of others. They are therefore likely to represent the **dreamer**, too, when they appear in adult **dreams**, and what happens to the teddy bear thus becomes significant. If the teddy bear is being torn to pieces by a **dog**, for instance, it might suggest that the dreamer feels torn apart by their own desires and impulses.

Teeth In traditional folklore, being born with a tooth already in place foretold that the **baby** would grow up to be a **murderer**. It was also considered unlucky to **dream** of one's own teeth, more especially if they fell out in the course of the dream – this betokened coming sorrow, or the **death** of a close **friend**. See **Tooth Dreams**

Telepathic Dreams No one can say for sure whether **dreams** contain a 'sixth sense' consisting of the capacity either of presentiment or of telepathy. To say that both are extreme examples of **wish-fulfilment** fantasies is simply not enough, however, to explain the various occurrences and prognostications larded throughout this **book**. Both **Freud** and **Stekel** believed firmly that telepathy does exist, but that its foundation was outside dreams themselves. In addition, **Jung**'s concept of the **collective unconscious** would predispose us towards the pro-telepathy argument, with the single proviso that he would not have acknowledged that there was anything remotely irrational, or fey, in the process.

Telephones Telephones can have **phallic** connotations in **dreams**, and telephoning between two **people** may imply the act of coition.

Telescopes Telescopes are naturally **phallic** objects. They may even be called supra-phallic, in that they extend and retract according to the desire of the possessor, unlike the **male penis**, which often seems to have a will of its own.

Televisions Dreaming of televisions may incorporate **mirror** fantasies, for a television would appear, at first glance, to be a mirror. And yet, on switching the television on, it proves to contain within itself the capacity for wishful thinking twinned with what purports to be an approximation of 'real' life, but which is, in fact, a contrived and microcosmic view – dependent on the whim of the producer – whose success is determined by the intelligence (or, even more disturbing, this) the lack of it, of the intended **audience**.

Temples Temples rank alongside **churches, mosques, pagodas** and **synagogues** as representatives of the **superego** in dreams. Temples, like **houses**, may also stand in for the **body** of the **dreamer**.

Temptation Temptation of any sort points up a potential **conflict** between the **self** and the **ego**. For perfect **integration** to occur, the temptation needs to be overcome. Each time the easiest option is taken and the temptation is given into, damage to the **psyche** is likely. See **Discipline**

Tenants Tenants are, by definition, **strangers**, inhabiting a part of the dreamer's very own corporeal **house**. The significance of this will vary, but it may well relate to close relationships, or even, given the correct context, a business relationship or a **friendship**. Should the **dreamer** find themselves a tenant in someone else's house, it may suggest that they are not entirely comfortable with their present situation, or, alternatively, that they are not yet prepared to take full responsibility for the effective **running** of their own lives.

Tennis Tennis is a to and fro **sport**, and this element is likely to be the dominant one in any **reading**. It may refer to the **dreamer** feeling torn (**conflicted**) between two other players (**parents**, say, or two potential **lovers**), but it may also point to routine and unchangeability, in the sense of a competitive game with strict rules to which, nevertheless, one must nominally adhere. See **Tearing**

Tents Tents are temporary housings, and if one accepts the **house** as representative of the **dreamer**, then a tent implies impermanence, or dissatisfaction with the *status quo* or with one's **self**-image. The fact that even the slightest **storm** is likely to undermine the tent reinforces the temporary **nature** of the proceedings, suggesting nomadism and the lack of any permanent **roots**.

Terminals The concept of a terminal or of reaching the end of somewhere in a **dream** (possibly a **journey**), may equate either with **death** or the **orgasm** (the 'small death'). The image of the terminal may also imply a desire for rest, or for something to end.

Terrorists The presence of terrorists, **rapists, burglars**, thieves, and any other assorted miscreants in our **dreams** nearly always points to the **repression** of certain desires that the **dreamer** senses would be too **dangerous** or unsettling to enact in real life. These **id** desires are omnipresent, nevertheless, and the choice of characters who normally suffer on the wrong end of the **sword** of justice only serves to highlight the existence of the hidden **anxieties** which cause such **dreams** in the first place. It is perhaps important to reiterate here that each separate species of thug should not necessarily be taken as a 'literal' representation of the type of crime they specialize in, but rather be taken both literally *and* metaphorically: a rapist, for instance, is someone who imposes something unpleasant on someone else, as well as violating them sexually; a burglar is someone who **invades** someone else's privacy, as well as stealing their goods. See **Robbing**

Tertium Compariationis A concept, extremely useful in **dream analysis**, which acknowledges the **links** between objects which resemble each other simply on a surface **level** – i.e. that have no affective **link** whatsoever beyond the architectural. Examples might include a **light**-bulb and a **pear**, a **guitar** and a woman's **body**, a Frisbee and a **halo**, or a courgette and the erect **penis**. Such apparently whimsical juxtapositions frequently occur in **dreams**, and require effective translation before the full meaning of the dream can be obtained.

Testicles Testicles are a source of interest to both **sexes** (rather in the way of **breasts**), and this may be because they are **spherical**, and therefore not overtly aggressive in **shape**, as is a **penis**. That said, they appear to function both as **symbols** of creativity (just as **eggs** do) and as symbols of vulnerability, thereby incorporating both **male** and **female** characteristics. This is reinforced by the fact that the testicles, like the **ovaries**, **harbour** the capacity to produce both male and female offspring. See **Easter Eggs**

Tests Tests act as communal proving grounds, promoting outrage and venality in roughly equal measure, as **people** go about pretending not to care about their outcomes. Such acts of **repression** will tend to emerge in **dreams** under various guises, one of which we might call the **wish-fulfilment** test result, in which whatever the **dreamer** does, succeeds. The opposite also holds true, and tends to proclaim itself via **frustration dreams** and **inhibitions**. Tests may also reflect an excess of **ego-consciousness**.

Texts Written texts may act as **memorials** to the **past**, and also as **taboo** signifiers (see **Tablets**). If something is written down it tends to remain (there is a sense of permanency about it, in other words), and this is usually a clue to the existence of a **death clause** lurking somewhere in the **dreamer**'s **psyche**. This is further reinforced by the fact that **wills** are texts which, by definition, outlive their progenitors.

Thawing See **Melting**

Theatres Theatres can often symbolize evasion. They are an alternative, or imitation of real life, rather than an answer to it. Theatres are also places in which actions are enacted voyeuristically, in the sense that they purport to come from inside the **dreamer**, but in reality they are manufactured for the edification of an **audience**, and in that sense, though mimetically true, they are not truly 'true'. See **Catharsis** & **Theatrical Performances**

Theatrical Performances Any such performances seen in the context of a dream are usually performances or projections of the **dreamer**'s own life – to this extent they equate with the vast majority of real life theatrical experiences, if one substitutes, for a moment, the word 'dreamer' for the word 'playwright'. See **Catharsis** & **Theatres**

Therapists Dreaming of therapists is an obvious oneiric manifestation of the need for help, or for the capacity to understand oneself and one's own motivations. The therapist figure acts, therefore, as the symbolical antidote to puzzlement, and is, in consequence, just one aspect of a no doubt much larger **wish-fulfilment** scenario. The therapist may also fulfil a roughly similar dream role to that of the **teacher**, and is therefore likely to function as an adjunct of the **superego**.

Thermometers Old-fashioned thermometers measure **fever**, and they are also **phallic** in shape, and intrusive. To that extent they probably represent lust or passion (and its consequences, given their medical ramifications). There may also be **guilt** associations present, in the sense that, if one overdoes something, one usually suffers for it. See **Heat**

Thermoses Thermoses keep things hot when the surroundings are **cold**. In **dreams** they can act as containers for the emotions, suggesting the bottling up of heated passions. One-way **love** may find itself represented by a thermos, as can simmering hatred. See **Heat**

Thieves See **Burglars, Robbing** & **Terrorists**

Thighs Symbolically speaking, thighs represent advance and the power of forward **movement**. In **sacrificial** terms, the thighs of **animals** (and particularly of **bulls** and **goats**) suggested the jettisoning of the lower **nature** in favour of the higher. The thighs may also represent the concept of 'seating' or of 'planting' something, and it must also be remembered in this context that Zeus used the interior of his thigh to quicken the as yet unborn Bacchus (see **Dionysian**), following the **death** of his **mother**, Semele.

Thinness Extreme thinness can suggest **poverty** of emotion and of **nature**, or possibly vulnerability and sensitivity to criticism (as in the expression 'thin-skinned'). Thinness can also indicate a desire to be relieved of **burdens**, with a consequent capacity to move faster, and with less apparent effort. Thinness can also be a correlative to **fatness**, suggesting, in this context, a **fear** of its opposite.

Third Eye, The The third **eye** is that of the **mind**, and its capacities for clairvoyance and the maintenance of balance and unity in the **face** of the gradual evolution of true (i.e. ocular) sight, which it preceded – the implication being that the third eye ceases to function (or goes into abeyance) when normal sight is achieved. Dreaming of a third eye, then, might suggest untapped possibilities, and the importance of the **past** as it relates to the present, and as it may relate to the future.

Thirst Thirst presupposes a desperate requirement for something that may, in itself – and in the last resort – save our lives. This may be exemplified by a cure, or by a spiritual **sea** change of some sort, but it may also **represent sexual** desire, and our **wish** to have our passions slaked rather than denied. Thirst may also correspond to underlying **feelings** of **fear** or of **guilt** in the presence of over-conspicuous spiritual or material consumption.

Thorns Thorns tend to interpose themselves between us and something we want. To that extent they resemble **splinters** in suggesting the potential downside of desire. For a **female dreamer**, thorns may represent a fear of, or trepidation about, the sexual act, and for a **male** dreamer they may relate to a fear of causing pain or discomfort to a partner, or to feeling pain (*ergo* **guilt**) as a result of one's desire-driven actions. **Jesus'** crown of thorns is also likely to imbrue any reading (especially for a Christian), and may add elements of submission and implied humiliation.

Thread See **String, Unravelling & Yarn**

Thresholds Thresholds suggest the possibilities of forward movement and of new experience, whereas hesitating on the threshold might hint at a **fear** of the unknown. Thresholds may also represent desire, in the sense that **husbands** traditionally carry **brides** across the threshold of a **house**. The symbolical severing of a barrier at the threshold of something new can indicate ownership, or the **breaking** (or defusing) of a **taboo**, as in the traditional legality of **sex** as only occurring after a **marriage**, symbolized, in this case, by the legalized fracturing of **virginity**. See **Hymen Complex**

Throat, The The throat is the physical seat of expression and of the powers of communication – it is also the symbolical facilitator of prejudice and of subversion. Microbes (i.e. potential **enemies**) may enter us via the throat and the nasal **passages**, and this aspect of vulnerability makes of the throat a two-way conduit of action and abreaction, particularly given that the throat has a tendency to constrict when we feel ourselves to be under pressure.

Thrones Thrones exemplify the symbolical placing of one person higher than another (see **Above**). Such physical hegemony, be its origin that of natural paramountcy or simple one-upmanship, will tend to find itself reflected in the accoutrements surrounding the throne. If the throne is outside, this may imply a desire to dominate **nature**, or a **fear** that nature is unfairly dominating the sitter – if the throne finds itself dominating a scrapheap, for instance, it might suggest that the power the throne-sitter asserts is valueless.

Thumbs The position of the thumb is inevitably important, with a raised, **phallic** thumb implying positive resources, and a **downward** pointing thumb suggesting negativity. Roman augurs considered a pricking feeling in the left thumb to be a bad augury, something echoed in Act iv scene 1 of Shakespeare's *Macbeth* – 'By the pricking of my thumbs, something wicked this way comes.' The biting of the thumb was long considered a **sign** of contempt.

Thunder Archetypally, thunder was the **voice** of an angry **God**, just as **lightning** was his missile. Thunder may also represent sublimated anger or spiritual unease.

Tickets Tickets carry the symbolical meaning of permissions. They can also act as reminders to oneself of intentions that are as yet unfulfilled. If one requests a ticket in a **dream**, one obviously wishes to obtain something that will otherwise cause **frustration**. A ticket passed to another person in anger may act in a castigatory capacity, or as a **label** of some sort, possibly implying a measure of transferred **guilt**.

Ticking Ticking – as in the ticking of the **eye** – was viewed by the Romans as an augury that a **friend** was about to **visit** you. As nonsensical as this may seem, most **superstitions** are based in physical fact, with eye ticking possibly relating to the crinkling of the eye during the smiling process (something that would inevitably occur at the unexpected sight of the nonetheless instinctively foreseen friend).

Tickling Tickling the septum or the eyelid can often result in a **sneeze**, reinforcing the notion of tickling as a means to an end – as a way of gaining a desired and possibly expurgatory reaction. Tickling may also function as an excuse for otherwise **taboo** physical contact, tickling being, by virtue of its **nature**, manifestly (if not necessarily surreptitiously) harmless. See **Eyes**

Ticks Ticks are strongly related to **leeches** in **dream** terms, except insofar as they do not **heal** but merely irritate. Furthermore, ticks can represent unseen or unrecognized drains on physical vitality, and as such the position at which they fasten themselves upon the **body** becomes potentially important, as this may indicate an area in which the **dreamer** feels vulnerable.

Tics Physical tics often disguise repressed experiences (often sexual or incestuous or otherwise **taboo** in nature). The location and frequency of the tic can find itself reflected in dreams (often elliptically), which may, if effectively analyzed, point to its origins, and afford a means of overcoming the condition. The tic (similar, in this instance, to the **stammer**) acts as a symbolical announcement to the world of the repressed idea behind its activation.

Tides Tides ebb and **flow**, reflecting natural process. Tidal **waves**, on the other **hand**, appear to subvert natural process, but are in fact only another aspect of its function. To that extent tides (being **water**-borne) can often act as **symbols** for the emotional to and fro that constitutes life, with riptides and neap tides constituting merely the constitutional extremes of the sudden clamorous changes that sooner or later assail us all.

Tigers A tiger symbolizes ferocity. It can also encompass mystery, in that, while nominally related to us in terms of our joint mammalian ancestry, the tiger nevertheless appears to function largely **alone**, and without the need for community. Tigers were the traditional drays of Bacchus' coach (see **Dionysian**), and to that extent probably symbolized the potential destroying power of the **god**, in that they are, by definition, largely non-vegetarian, and thus unlikely to enjoy the **grapes** they are so often portrayed as **eating**. The English **poet William Blake** (1757–1827) understood the tiger's **dream**-like mystery, producing a **poem**, *The Tiger*, that itself appears to resemble a dreamscape: 'Tiger, tiger, burning bright/In the forests of the night,/What immortal hand or eye/Could frame thy fearful symmetry?'

Tightropes Tightropes suggest choice and the necessity for quick decisions, in that the tightrope **walker** may go either way (but usually down). Tightropes may also carry revocations of the **umbilicus** and of the ability to communicate between apparently disparate (or unrelated) points of view. See **Below**

Tiles Tiles are both practical and aesthetically pleasing, in the sense that they are surfaces which potentially bear perusal, rather than merely adjuncts of utilitarian design. To that extent they suggest more than the sum of their nominal value, and constitute part of the civilizing process that differentiates man from **animal**. Tiles may also be **symbols** for the separation of the inner from the outer, and in certain circumstances they may even stand in for the **skin** (see **Houses**).

Tills Tills are formal mechanisms for the estimation of value. As such they can symbolize low **self**-esteem or even vainglory, dependent on context (and possibly upon the value depicted on the screen). Tills may also suggest the desire to accumulate, generally in the sense of material things.

Timber See **Wood**

Time Time, in a dream, bears no relation to real time – the **past** and the present (and the anticipation of the future) may exist on a simultaneous plane. Mentions of specific times in **dreams** may relate to the **dreamer**'s age, i.e. 4.30 may apply to a person of 43, or a 'late' time may equate to a person's advanced stage of life. **Repressed** impulses can also be reflected in the act of arriving **late** for something, or of **feeling** that one might be late, and the **anxieties** involved with that **feeling**. See **Clocks, Years & Weeks**

Tire Tracks See **Tyre Tracks**

Tiring Sudden unexpected tiring in a **dream** can equate to a **fear** of the consequences of our actions coming in between those actions and the motivations we have for doing them. This tends to be **id** related, and the tiredness is a function of the **ego** endeavouring to control itself before things have been allowed to go too far. See **Frustration Dreams, Inhibitions & Lateness**

Tissues The main virtue of a tissue is that it is disposable, obviating the need for a more permanent aide to mopping up. Instancy, then, is likely to be its main adjunct in a **dream**, suggesting the presence of an immediate emotional or physical response to an outside stimulus.

Titanic **Disaster** Mrs Archibald Gracie, the wife of one of the surviving **passengers** on the *Titanic*, awoke on the **night** of the **disaster** to a vivid **dream** of the steamship's demise. She threw herself to the ground and began praying, and continued in this manner throughout the night. Her **soldier husband**, Captain Gracie, later affirmed that he had felt himself buoyed up, and his life secured, by the utter conviction that his **wife** was praying for his well-being.

Titans The 12 Titans (six **male** and six **female**) predated the Olympian **gods** of ancient Greece, and stemmed from the **marriage** of **heaven** (Uranus) and the **earth** (Gaia). Their tenure was only ended after a ten-year **battle** with Zeus, after which they were **imprisoned** in Tartarus, giving rise to revocations of both the **anima** and the **animus**, **sacred marriage**, and the **captive** maiden. Both Ovid and Virgil used the word titan as a poetic euphemism for the **sun**.

Toads A toad symbolizes inspiration, as does a **frog**. Toads, to the ancient Chinese, represented long life and the accrual of **wealth**. According to the Taoists, a three-legged toad lived on the **moon**, with each of its three **legs** indicating one of the moon's phases, and in Western Europe it was long believed that elderly or great toads contained a **stone** within their **heads** (the toad-stone) that offered a forewarning against **venom**. All this to say that toads carry strange and often **primal** revocations in **dreams**, linked to both their sound and their appearance, and it is hardly surprising, therefore, that *bufo bufo*, living as he does in **holes**, so frequently finds himself **linked** to the **unconscious**.

Tobacco See **Cigarettes & Cigars**

Toes Toes suggest balance, in that without even one toe, the equilibrium of the **body** is seriously undermined. The individual toe may also be seen as vulnerable, and potentially subject to **injury** or to **amputation**, whilst its **phallic** shape may give rise to indications of a **castration complex**, or to revocations concerning **female** circumcision (in the sense of the elimination of the clitoris, *ergo* the **vaginal** toe). See **Circumcision Complex & Fingers**

Toilets See **Lavatories**

Tombs See **Graves, Inscriptions, Shrouds & Tombstones**

Tombstones The ancient Germans believed that the **spirits** of the dead went on living in their tombstones. A carry-over from this may be seen in a **number** of the **films** of American director John Ford (1895–1973), most notably *She Wore a Yellow Ribbon* (1949), in which John Wayne, as the veteran cavalryman Nathan Brittles, communes with his dead **wife** at her graveside by the simple expedient of placing a stool next to her **grave** and **talking** directly to her tombstone. Tombstones can also represent memories in **dreams**. See **Inscriptions, Memorials & Shrouds**

Tongues Tongues are, generally **speaking**, phallic **symbols** in **dreams**, even when dreamed of by women. The 'sticking out of the tongue' is a euphemism for **phallic** display which carries over from real life into dreams due to its convenience as a unisexual symbol. The extant tongue may objectify a potential desire for communication, whilst a severed tongue may define a **fear** of **muteness** or incommunicability.
KEY LINE: 'It was in my eighth dream that I thought my tongue was so long that I wound it round the back of my neck, and forward into my mouth on the other side.' (From *Thorstein's Saga* 900 AD)

Tools Tools are reminders that there is work that needs to be done, and each individual tool will have its own significance within that **reading**. A large set of disparate tools, however, might indicate puzzlement as to where we ought to address our energies first. See **Hammers, Saws**, etc.

Toothbrushes Toothbrushes can be both **fetishistic** (in the sense of neurotically **cleansing**) or **phallic** (in the sense of foaming and intrusive). The link with the **mouth** is most likely to refer back to infancy, and to infant **oral fixations**. Taken in a literal sense, toothbrushes may indicate the need to take especial care of what one says – to clean up one's verbal act, in other words. See **Neurosis, Obsessions, Teeth & Tooth Dreams**

Tooth Dreams Tooth dreams are amongst the most common of all **dreams**, and were, for a long time, associated with the idea of **death**. The image of a fallen or extracted tooth is deeply symbolical, and can be related to just about any **loss** whatsoever (in **Freudian** terms, this was usually associated with **masturbation**) – this sense of loss being all the more relevant in dream terms because it is a 'personal' loss. Tooth dreams are entirely dependent for their interpretation on the emotion that accompanies them. To that extent the extraction of a tooth may be seen as a good thing, offering comfort and a release from **pain**, or a bad thing, indicating bereavement or a marring of beauty. Teeth **falling** out may also find themselves associated with **castration complexes**, and the **fear** of **impotence** (the inability to **chew**), and the **drilling** of teeth, when dreamt of by a woman, has age-old **sexual** overtones. As if that weren't enough, the losing of teeth can also symbolize the ageing process, the perceived degeneration of the intellect, or a major life change, in the sence of adulthood or approaching senescence. See **Cavities**, **Mouth**, **Teeth** & **Toothbrushes**

KEY LINE: 'Dreamed a quite formidably clear dream of taking a large front tooth out, with part of the jaw, and looking to see how much disfigured I was, in the glass, saying at the same time, "Well, for once *this* is no dream."' (From John Ruskin's Diaries 21st January 1877)

Toothpicks Toothpicks may be taken on one **level** as clearing impediments to effective communication, and on another level as intrusions into the **mouth** space by foreign (**phallic**) objects. See **Oral Fixations**, **Teeth**, **Tooth Dreams** & **Toothbrushes**

Torches Torches are likely to be used by the **unconscious** mind to suggest throwing **light** on an otherwise obscure area. They may also carry **phallic** connotations, not least in the sense of the beam acting as an extension of the bearer or of the bearer's power, just as one's progeny potentially do. The concept of a torch lighting up a **dark** place may also be taken to refer to a desire for either spiritual or mental enlightenment, or, perhaps more correctly, elucidation (from *lux* which means light in Latin, or *lucidus*, which means clear).

Tornadoes See **Hurricanes** & **Storms**

Torpedoes The imaginary firing of torpedoes is one of the most common of all power fantasies, combining **phallic** assertion with control at a distance (i.e. far enough away so that one isn't forced to see the results of one's actions). Add to that the **anal** element, in that the torpedo symbolically correlates to the act of **defecation**, and one is inexorably drawn back to **childhood** and to infantile modes of behaviour, including the desire for fantasy control over one's **parents** and any other large **people** who lord it over us. See **Anal Retention** & **Excrement**

Tortoises A tortoise traditionally symbolises chastity. The **Black** Tortoise symbolised the **North**, to the ancient Chinese, with all that that entails in terms of gloom, foreboding, and the suggestion of false **beginnings** in any venture undertaken.

Torture As dreamers rarely feel **pain** during the course of a **dream**, torture images tend to be purely symbolical, and to relate more to emotional torment than to any real or imagined act of torture. The concentration on one **limb** or **organ** is therefore significant, as is the choice of **victim** (almost certainly an aspect of the **dreamer**) and the choice of implement (almost certainly reflecting specific fears and **anxieties** that have been 'torturing' the dreamer) – a **knife**, for instance, might suggest a **fear** of **sexual** closeness, whereas a cudgel, **club**, or other thrashing implement might suggest **frustration**, *ergo* an inability to make oneself understood or to get one's **message** across.

Totemism A system which predated most formalized **religions** and relied upon the given significance of objects and **animals** as a basis for social organization. See **Totem Poles** & **Totems**

Totem Poles Totem **poles**, while nominally possessing strong **phallic** connotations, may also represent memories when they occur in **dreams**. The implication here is that the totem pole symbolizes the **family tree**, or a **line** of **ancestors** vanishing gradually into the distant **past**. See **Totems** & **Totemism**

Totems In so-called 'primitive' cultures, specific **animals** (or, in certain cases, objects or **plants**) were chosen for each individual as part of their process of **identification** with the tribal unit, to whom that object was thenceforward deemed to have a **blood** relationship. In Mexico, to this day, the first animal that **crosses**, or **flies** over, or burrows under, an imaginary **circle** around a newly-born child's **cradle**, is considered to be that **child**'s totemic animal. This animal will then reappear, in some form or another – **dreams, visions, serendipity** – at a moment close to that individual's **death**. See **Totem Poles** & **Totemism**

Touch Touching the dead was traditionally felt to ward off future **dreams** of the dead person. In Scotland it was considered to forestall a haunting. In conventional **dream interpretation**, reaching out and **touching** someone can have a **number** of revocations, given that one may be touching aspects of oneself (personified in others), or simply attempting to reach out to third parties *per se*. In addition, touching a particular object can suggest a marking out (equating to an attestation of significance), or it may be synonymous with a fundamental **wish** for possession or with the taking on (the allocating to oneself) of some of the object's attributes.

Tourists The appearance of tourists is likely to suggest something that is only of **surface** significance – a dilemma or an irritation or a place that one may **visit** and then immediately forget. There may be an implication of uncertainty, as well, or of the purely tentative **nature** of a nominally earnest quest for knowledge.

Towels Throwing towels around has obvious implications for **wishing** to give up on something ('throwing in the towel'), and this is most probably the first **port** of call in any **interpretation** of what may otherwise seem a rather puzzling act. Towels may also carry suggestions of **menstruation**, or of the metaphorical mopping up of inconvenient emotions (objectified by wetness and **water** imagery).

Towers Whereas in **Freudian** terms a tower is likely to be **phallic-**centred, it is also arguable that it may **represent** a desire to learn, or to have access to otherwise hidden knowledge. The tower, in this instance, may stand for certain specific aspects of the **dreamer** – even the dreamer's **sexuality**, given the tower implications not only of the **penis**, but also of the **captive** maiden. The Parsees traditionally place their dead (whom they consider impure) atop 'towers of **silence**' to be **eaten** by **vultures,** fearing to **bury** or cremate the cadavers and thus subject themselves to possible contamination – a tower, therefore, may also represent a desire to distance oneself from something that one **fears** or despises, as in an '**ivory** tower', or the French philosopher Michel de Montaigne's (1533–92) '**white** tower' to which he **retreated** in 1571, the better to study the **world** through the vehicle of his **mind.**

Towns In **dreams**, the exact placing of a town or a **harbour** can often be significant, and relate to **anima symbols.** Placed at the apex of two outcroppings of **land**, it may represent the birthplace of the **dreamer** (quite literally), whereas if it found itself placed high – on a **mountain**, for instance – it might suggest upward or creative aspiration that is **unconsciously** perceived as difficult or unlikely to be successful without a considerable degree of **struggle.** See **Above**

Toxicity If something is toxic it should be avoided at all costs, and this tends to be the implication of toxicity in **dreams**. If the atmosphere that surrounds the **dreamer** should happen to be poisoned – by **gas**, for instance – then there may be an underlying **anxiety** about a particular familial or relational situation, or a **fear** that one might be being contaminated by a particular **argument** or process of thought stemming from outside one's normal, everyday boundaries. See **Poisons**

Toys Because it is marginally inappropriate for a solitary adult to **play** with **toys**, their appearance in a **dream** would tend to suggest that we are dealing with **infantile** fixations carried through into adulthood. The desire for instant gratification is one such **regressive** characteristic, for an adult ought to understand that immediacy does not necessarily equate with quality, whereas the **child** in the adult (the one who still resolutely pops up whilst the adult is dreaming) might not yet have reached that stage of maturity. That said, the particular toys dreamt of will have an important function to play in defining the adult state of **mind**, and we should be able to infer from them, and from their location, why the **unconscious** mind is calling them 'into play'. In addition, it should be mentioned that toys are, by definition, non-threatening and non-real, and that any reversion to playtime by an adult might suggest a desire not to confront what may seem, at first glance, to be an unacceptable **reality** – the type of toy then, might well **represent** what the adult secretly **fears**

in real life, and which the dream state miniaturizes in order to make unthreatening.

Tracks The **right** side of a track is the **conscious**, or rational side. The **left** side is that of the **unconscious**.

Tractability The tendency among clients or students of a dominant figure in dream **psychology** to dream to order, particularly in terms of **arche-types**. They dream (or at least recall dreaming) the sorts of **dreams** they feel they should be having. Another definition might be 'dreaming to please'. Such dreams are less than useless except in terms of the **light** they shed on the aspirations of the **dreamer**.

Tractors Tractors are work **horses**, except insofar as they are mechanical and no longer made of flesh and **blood**. Their capacity to **plough** and **till**, though, twinned with their sheer power, make of them a convenient **dream** conduit for the preparing of ground for the future, or for the **breaking** down of recalcitrant positions. The tractor is a power tool, then, which the **dreamer** may call into **play** when faced with an otherwise insurmountable (or obstinate) **problem**.

Trailers Trailers can represent emotional **baggage** which we are not quite yet ready to discard. They are attached to us, but by a manipulable (and potentially detachable) connection. To that extent they can equate to modern **marriage**, in which **divorce** is often considered and prepared for before the marriage is even engendered. They may also represent **chil-dren**, or **guilt** associated with **past** actions.

Trains Trains are images of energy and dynamism. The clichéd image of a train going into a **tunnel** does not necessarily indicate a sexual content in a dream, however, but can also imply elements of the **dreamer** being repressed back into the **unconscious**. A train emerging from a tunnel may imply the re-emergence of these traits, and the makeup of the train – **pas-senger** cars, freight **cars**, **coal** tenders, etc. – can indicate a valuable cargo, full of psychic power, capable of being used positively. Should a woman dream of being run over by a train, or of a train passing over her body, then this is usually synonymous with **sexual intercourse**. See **Railroads & Railroad Tracks**

Traitors The appearance of traitors in a **dream** is likely to say more about the **dreamer**'s perceptions of themselves than it is to indicate the pres-ence of any real external threat. A traitor is usually an aspect of the dreamer's own **persona** that they are discontented with, or which hasn't quite lived up to expectations. The cause or object of the betrayal is therefore of extreme importance, as it may shed **light** on the fly in the **ointment**.

Tramps The tramp is an **archetypal** figure, implying **waste** or unexploited opportunities. A tramp may also **represent** the downside to freedom, in the sense that he is generally free to roam as he will, but must, in consequence, remain disconnected from the larger **world** that surrounds him. This should not diminish the positive aspect of the tramp figure, however, which suggests that conformity is not necessarily the only way to go – that free will may also encompass a decision not to be dominated by possessions, **taboos**, and the mores of society.

Trances A trance implies that there is another possible state of **consciousness** to which we may only have access if we let ourselves go – whether this is a spiritual state or merely a condition of vapid morbidity is a moot point, but the **question** still remains. A trance may also suggest an inability to feel or to express emotion – a detachment from the mainstream, in other words, rather in the way a **river** will **branch** off into a succession of largely static (because short-lasting) tributaries.

Transference The **unconscious** endowment onto others (in the everyday) of characteristics pertaining to past individuals or institutions (**childhood patterns**, for instance) significant to the endower. This characteristic may find itself used in a positive, constructive manner within the psychotherapeutic relationship, during which transference and counter-transference may occur (both to and from the analysand, in other words), often in the form of **dreams**. This may lead (if the dreams are correctly interpreted) to the resolution of existing **conflicts** within the **dreamer**'s **psyche**. See **Transference Dreams**

Transference Dreams Dreams which, through **transference**, reveal the **secret**, hidden attitude of the **dreamer** towards their life. If correctly identified, such **dreams** may point to the means by which the dreamer may resolve any long-standing **conflicts** which are holding them back from the fruitful enjoyment of their lives.

Transformation The changing of a thing into its opposite. Such transformations often occur in **dreams**, and should serve to cast more focused attention back onto the original object, in an effort to understand why the **unconscious** elected to conduct the transformation in the first place. See **Interpretation by Opposites** & **Oppositions**

Transitional Objects See **Silkiness** & **Velvet**

Transmigration The moving of the **soul** from one **body** into another, often at the point of **death**. See the 'death of the **father**' section under **Artemidorus of Daldis**

Transparency Transparency suggests a desire on the part of the **dreamer** to see through to the **truth** of something that might otherwise be thought opaque. This may also incorporate the shedding of **light** on something via any transparent medium.

Transvestism Transvestism in a **dream** is likely to be more about the capacity to change than about the actual change itself. It may also incorporate ideas of the **anima** and the **animus**, and the taking on of the characteristics or virtues of the other **sex** – only when such a 'makeover' becomes morbid in content does the dream image turn potentially negative and begin to adhere more to a sexual rather than to a **transformational** stereotype.

Trapezes The **author**'s startling new concept of Tarzanic **swinging** may potentially come into **play** here, implying a fantasy desire for freedom from earthbound cares. All joking aside, the trapeze is a very convenient **dream** trope for getting oneself out of tricky situations, or for negotiating one's way through potentially disastrous breakdowns in communication. Such swinging is often part of a **wish-fulfilment** fantasy engendered in **childhood**, when one's capacity for rational **problem**-solving was as yet unformed – the separated podia of the trapeze, in that context, most probably represent the **parents**, with the child swinging between, and being connected to, both. See **Pirates**

Traps See **Entrapment**

Trash See **Garbage**

Trauma In **psychoanalytical** terms a trauma is what occurs when specific **damage** is done to the **psyche** due to an experience, either positive or negative, and often occurring during **childhood**, when a mature understanding is not yet present.

Travel/Travelling Travelling in company with another person can be synonymous with **sexual intercourse**, whereas travelling solo can equate with **masturbation**. For **Freud**, however, travelling represented the act of **dying**.

Trays Trays, platters and salvers are for presentation – even John the Baptist's **head** was presented to Herodias' **daughter**, Salome, on a tray (Mark vi, 17–29) – the implication being that **affirmation** is being sought for actions that have already occurred. The strength of the tray image may very well refer back to **childhood** actions in which the child would go through the motions of presenting a **painting** or its exercise **book** to a person in authority over it, in the anxious hope of garnering approval or praise.

Treadmills Treadmills suggest **repetition** and pointless labour. They were originally designed to keep **prisoners** occupied and, one supposes, fit, something for which their modern equivalent is still used to this day in health **clubs**. The **circular** shape of the original treadmill could be construed as a **mandala**, although not, by definition, a true one.

Treasure The **finding** of – or the diving down in **search** for – treasure, can indicate the presence, or desire for, a perfect lifetime **companion**. It may also suggest the long-desired **meeting** (or even 'mating') between the **self** and the **ego**.

Trees The **tree** is a motif that often appears in **dreams**, and can be construed in a number of ways: as symbolizing evolution or knowledge; as a **symbol** of physical growth; as a **phallic** symbol; as a non-verbal trope for the process of psychological maturation; as a symbol of **sacrifice**, and even **death**; as a symbol for renewal; as the natural image most conducive to an understanding of Divine **Light**; and as the life principle itself. The ancient Chinese believed that the Tree of Life was a Plum, a Mulberry, or a **Peach**, and that dreaming of the **sun**, alongside such a tree, indicated that a life cycle was coming to an end. Intertwined **branches** represented the **twin** concepts of the **yin** and the **yang**. In certain dreams, trees may also indicate our **parents**. See **Christmas Trees, Cross, Oak Trees, Poplar Trees, Yew Trees,** etc.
KEY LINE: 'I had a sort of dream-trance the other day, in which I saw my favourite trees step out and promenade up, down and around, very curiously …' (From Walt Whitman's *Thoughts Under an Oak* 1875)

Trespassing Trespassing suggests the possible undermining of a **taboo** or some other restriction that the **ego** finds inconvenient or onerous (but nonetheless still threatening and **anxiety** provoking). Trespassing may also represent the simple desire to go beyond the boundaries of expedient behaviour, twinned with a **fear** of the potential consequences.

Trials Trials are what happens when we are caught out in the act of behaving inappropriately (at least insofar as the **superego** is concerned). They are a forum for public contumely, and thereby act as a potential regulating mechanism on the **ego**.

Triangles A simple triangle tends to represent the **penis**, whereas a reversed triangular **shape** tends to be symbolic of the **vagina** when it appears in **dreams** (think of the natural placement of the two **thumbs** and forefingers when both hands are **mirrored** together). Triangles may also suggest the **Trinity**, in the sense of the concatenation of a **number** of forces into one, stronger, all-encompassing force.

Tricking See **Tricks**

Tricks Tricks may be at once playful and intensely irritating. They can hark back to **childhood** and to our then lack of understanding of some of the nuances of what was going on around us, or they can reflect our anger at the present actions of others – even the occurrence of wilful mis-constructions on the part of an apparently mischievous fate. See **Salmon**

Trinity, The Traditionally, the **Father**, the **Son** and the **Holy Ghost** – alternatively the **body**, the **mind** and the **spirit**. Possibly encompassed within the image is the idea of transfiguration, or of the capacity of one particular thing to transform and transmigrate into another. See **Quaternity**

Triplets Three of anything may potentially suggest disunity, whereas two usually suggests unity, the implication being that two will potentially **gang** up against one. This is not true of the **Trinity**, of course, nor necessarily of the **triangle**, although the eternal triangle (in terms of affective relationships) might, at first glance, suggest the **opposite**. The **number** three is particularly significant in terms of its symbolic status, in the sense that it can represent the **penis** and **testicles**, or, in Pythagorean terms, perfection (epitomizing, as it does, the beginning, the middle and the end, in the form of the Deity).

Tripping Tripping on the **threshold** to somewhere (on a **stair**, for instance, or other such impediment) may point to a desire for non-conformity, or even, in some cases, a **resistance** on the part of the **dreamer** to confront some aspect of themselves they may consider reprehensible, inconvenient, or incommensurate with their **self**-image. The cause of such an **unconscious** protest may stem from an unresolved **childhood** situation which needs to be identified before the dreamer can experience undisturbed, or head-on ingress to challenging situations.

Trips Trips may contain within themselves both revocations of **death** and of **orgasms**, depending on context. Examples might include trips to a **cemetery**, or trips into a **tunnel**. See **Travel/Travelling**

Trophies Trophies are **awards** that the **dreamer** might **wish** that they were receiving – for good behaviour, possibly, or for sticking to the rules. Such reversions to **childhood** criteria (*ergo* pleasing one's **parents**) usually denote a **search** for comfort certainties. They are frequently a reflection of the presence (or suspicion) of uncertainties in the dreamer's present day situation – the **dream**, as it were, acts *in loco parentis*, putting things temporarily **right** with the **world** and thus protecting the dreamer's **sleep**.

Trucks See **Lorries**

Trumpets Trumpets tend to be proclamatory, in the sense that they come before, or announce, significant facts or expected occurrences. The trumpet is also one of the closest instruments to the human voice (one has only to think of Louis Armstrong), and may therefore act *in lieu* of the voice, in, say, **warnings** about **danger** ahead. In purely **Jungian** terms, the trumpet may stand in for the voice or **voices**, and be, in consequence, less suggestive in terms of exact meaning.

Trunks See **Baggage & Bags**

Truth The belief in truth is often part of a complicated **wish-fulfilment** fantasy, founded more on expedient truth rather than on any belief that there is some overriding fundamental truth available if only one were to seek it in the correct way (the **myth** of the **Holy Grail**, for instance). Although this may seem unnecessarily cynical, dream truth tends to be the truth that most suits the **dreamer** – for whatever they are, **dreams** are not fundamentally pedagogic.
KEY LINE: 'A dream, the other night, that the world had become dissatisfied with the inaccurate manner in which facts are reported, and had employed me, with a salary of a thousand dollars, to relate things of public importance exactly as they happen.' (From Nathaniel Hawthorne's *The American Notebooks* 1843)

Tsunamis See **Tides & Waves**

Tumbling Any **movement** which lacks control, or which suggests that the **dreamer** no longer has any willpower, may be read in terms of **falling**.

Tumours Tumours, pustules, **spots**, **warts** and excrescences tend to be external manifestations of inner conditions. Where tumours differ from the rest is in their possibility of internalization – they may on occasion reverse the usual significance and **reflect** the outside (resulting from what we imbibe, take in, or are otherwise instilled with) in. They are us attacking us, in other words, and may therefore come to symbolize **self**-hate or self-mutilation under certain specific circumstances. A tumour on another is a visible expression of an internal disharmony that we may suspect within ourselves.

Tunnels Tunnels provide a perfect example of **layer symbolism**, in that they are almost inevitably a euphemism for something else – that something usually consisting of a return to the **womb** via either **sex**, or protective inclination.

Turkey-Cocks A turkey-cock traditionally symbolizes official insolence. See **Turkeys**

Turkeys Turkeys, like **chickens**, carry semantic overtones of **failure**. If you are 'chicken' you are a **coward**, and if you purchase a 'turkey' you have allowed yourself to be **tricked**. To be fair to turkeys, their apparent capacity for stupidity is occasionally leavened by their symbolical significance in terms of **celebration** and **richness**, which is probably the aspect under which most North Americans will tend to view them.

Turning Mattresses It was considered particularly unlucky to turn mattresses on a Friday or a Sunday. If the **mattress** was turned on the Sunday, the **sleeper** in the **bed** would have bad **dreams** all **week** long.

Turquoises Turquoises are traditionally viewed as calmative **stones**, with their **colour** reflecting that of the **sea**. The turquoise also symbolizes the celestial regions (particularly in terms of **Buddhism**).

Turtledoves A turtledove traditionally symbolizes conjugal fidelity.

Turtles Turtles radiate protectiveness, due consideration and steadfastness. Their beaks, however, may on occasion be suggestive of hidden aggression.

Twain, Mark (1835–1910) The celebrated American **author** (real name Samuel Clemens) of *The Adventures of Huckleberry Finn* (1884) wrote of a **dream** he had had foretelling his brother's **death**, in 1858. The dream (which he had recounted to his **sister** that **morning**) showed his beloved **brother**, Henry, lying in a **metal coffin**, **suspended** between two **chairs**, with a bouquet of white **flowers** near him, and a crimson flower on his **breast**. A short while later Twain heard that the steamboat on which Henry had been training for his **river pilot**'s licence had blown up. Twain hurried down to Memphis where he discovered his brother lying exactly as described in his dream, 'lacking only the bouquet of white flowers with its crimson centre.' As he stood there, an elderly lady entered the **room carrying** a large **white** bouquet, with a single **red** rose at its **centre**. See **Flowers**

Twins The twins (Gemini) and the **scales** (Libra) are interrelated, suggesting harmony, unity and balance – for the **number** two is generally counted as symbolic of the duality of **manifestation**, in the sense of **spirit** and matter intertwining. However, two was also the **evil** principle of Pythagoras, and was frequently counted an unlucky number in historical terms, due to its relationship to Pluto (the second **day** of the second month being traditionally allocated to him).

Typewriters Typewriters tend to symbolize the organization of a formal means of emotional (i.e. potentially non-verbal) expression. Now that they have largely been superseded by **computer** keyboards, their significance may well have been arrogated, but they may possibly have gained a historical dimension (relating to the **dreamer**'s **past**) in its lieu.

Typhoons See **Hurricanes & Storms**

Typical Dreams Typical dreams are those which occur with the greatest frequency to the greatest number of people. These include **agoraphobic**, **alcoholic**, **anxiety**, **artificial**, **childhood**, **claustrophobic**, **comical**, **compensatory**, **confirmatory**, **creative**, **daydreams**, **dreams within**

dreams, emission, examination, falling, filmic, flying, frustration, hallucinatory, historical, immoral, invented, lateness, morphine, phallic, post-operative, pre-birth, premenstrual, prophetic, punishment, recollective, recovery, recurring, stereotypical, telepathic, tooth, transference, waking, and wet dreams.

Tyre Tracks Tyre tracks constitute the temporary **history** that we leave behind us – they are an imposition onto the natural **world** by proxy. This proxy element is important because it implies uncertainty about our significance, which is what this symbol is possibly trying to tell us. The fact that tyre tracks manifest themselves as **pairs** is also important, and presupposes an inability or refusal to acknowledge that we may exist **alone** before **God**.

U

UFOs UFOs **represent** the ultimate **wish-fulfilment** fantasy, because they are grounded in logic yet their appearance nevertheless remains unlikely. Their presence in a **dream** may suggest a desire for change, or for that old trusty, the *deus ex machina*, to appear out of the **sky** and relieve us of all our immediate **problems**.

Ulcers Ulcers suggest internal turmoil, possibly resulting from unacknowledged (because **repressed**) **guilt** feelings. Ulcers also evoke dilemmas, in that they are not easy to cure or to access. See **Repression**

Umbilical Cords Umbilical cords suggest symbolical but ultimately discardable **links** between human beings. This disposable aspect, implying a temporary physical union, makes of them convenient tropes for **marriage** and expedient **friendships**.

Umbrellas An umbrella is often a **symbol** for the uncircumcised **penis**. If this seems a little far-fetched, it should be remembered that an umbrella provides protection, can be **opened** and **closed**, and sometimes gets hitched up (think phimosis). An umbrella may also suggest systems of belief (in the sense of encompassing or protective thought). See **Circumcision Complex**

Uncles Uncles are, somewhat inevitably, **male** adjuncts. They may benefit from **taboo** status, and they can suggest dominance of one sort or another (as in 'cry uncle' and 'don't come the uncle over me' – or *ne sis patruus mihi*, as Horace would have it). Come to think of it, the **author** had an Uncle Horace. **Freudian slip?**

Unconscious, The The element of the **mind** which contains **fears, feelings**, desires and memories that are not consciously recognized. **Freud** believed that the unconscious consisted, in large part, of feelings inherited from **childhood** and subsequently modified by the **superego** (the **inhibiting** mind). **Jung** believed, in addition, that the unconscious mind was the doorway to the **collective unconscious**, and that it functioned instinctively.
KEY LINE: 'Everything of which I know, but of which I am not at the moment thinking; everything of which I was once conscious but have now forgotten; everything perceived by my senses, but not noted by my conscious mind; everything which, involuntarily and without paying attention to it, I feel, think, remember, want, and do; all the future things that are taking shape in me and will sometime come to consciousness; all this is the content of the unconscious.' (From C. G. Jung's *The Structure and Dynamics of the Psyche* 1934)

Under Being under something suggests hierarchies, low status, or a disturbance in the natural order of things (in which we generally find ourselves on level ground). This lowering aspect might suggest **repression** of some sort, or merely a feeling of being 'under the **weather**'. Being underground may also suggest that one is having trouble convincing others of the merits of one's point of view.

Underground, The See **Subways**

Underwater With **water** equating to the emotions, being underwater takes on a potentially destructive connotation, in that one's feelings are symbolically **drowning** one. If the **dreamer** is happy being underwater, and seemingly in no immediate **danger**, one might infer that they were enjoying the process of being carried along by events in their affective life, and that this presented no discernable threat to them. See **Submerging**

Underwear Underwear can represent fundamentals, as in 'down to the nitty-gritty' or 'stripped to the barest essentials'. This concept of the 'final vestige' is an important one, because it implies that the **dreamer** is but one **layer** away from a **revelation**. When revelations of this sort are bruited in **dreams**, the surrounding context becomes even more significant than usual, affording the interpreter and the dreamer possible hints as to the source or origin of the disclosure.

Undressing Undressing, when it appears in the **dreams** of an analysand, is often a **symbol** of that analysis, and can indicate **transference** when it occurs, for instance, in front of a **doctor** in the dream. It can also represent a desire to reveal the **truth**. See **Underwear**

Unemployment Unemployment tends to be a **self**-esteem issue even in the **dream world**. To see others going about their useful duties while the **dreamer** remains idle, not by volition, but by default, indicates the possible existence of an **inferiority complex** (particularly if the dream occurs on a regular basis). The image may also act as a pointer towards more desirable behaviour – i.e. the full and creative use of one's talents. See **Adler, Individual Psychology** & **Recurring Dreams**

Unicorns In Christian iconography, the unicorn symbolizes **Jesus Christ**. Guillaume Clerc de Normandie's 13th-century bestiary relates that a unicorn can only be caught by the placing of a young **virgin** in its haunts. The beast will then run up and throw itself at the virgin's **feet**, allowing capture by the hunters. In **dream symbolism** the **phallic** horn of the unicorn accords strangely with the apparently chaste **nature** of the, often **white**, **mythical** beast. In only one eventuality was the **horn** used for piercing – for the unicorn was the one **animal** in the world which dared to confront the **elephant**, ripping out the belly of the pachyderm with one fatal blow. The ancient Chinese, too, thought of the unicorn as a gentle

beast, and considered that it represented wise rule and exalted **children**. When a great **leader** dreamed of the *ky-lin*, it was considered particularly significant, and the **riding** of it even more so. See **Beauty and the Beast, Captivity, Christ & Hunting**
KEY LINE: 'But, like a lion in legend, when I flung the glove/Pulled from my sweating, my cold right hand,/The terrible beast, that no one may understand,/Came to my side, and put down his head in love.' (From Louise Bogan's *The Dream* 1941)

Uniforms Uniforms can act as **masks** behind which the **dreamer**, or aspects of the dreamer, may **hide**. They can also suggest uniformity (even conformity), and they may on occasion act as **witnesses** to the power of the **superego**, rather as a **judge** will remind the court-at-large that small issues of law may have universal applications – that each, regardless of individual will, is responsible to the collective other.

Universities The first universities date from around the 12th century, and were designed to suggest something that was all-encompassing (i.e. in which everything under the **sun** was taught). They may therefore act as symbolical panaceas or **compensations** for perceived lacks in the dreamer's **makeup**, or simply as expedient repositories of knowledge from which the **dreamer** may draw at their convenience. See **Schools**

Unknown Woman, The See **Anima**

Unravelling Unravelling is **linked** to **yarn**, and can incorporate anarchy, **chaos**, and brevity of opportunity in its interpretation. The unravelling of something that was entire may correlate physically (with the bowels, for instance), and metaphorically (with **consciousness**, say).

Upholstery Upholstery can equate with obesity **fears** (see **Fatness**), and it can also suggest renewal and reformation (in the sense that one re-forms a worn out sofa). Upholstery may also point to our perception of ourselves as seen by others, in the sense that a floral, or quintessentially **female pattern**, may suggest a desire to please, whereas a **leather**, or quintessentially **male** pattern, may suggest a desire to be pleased.

Upward Movement See **Above**

Urges All our urges, **sexual** and otherwise (the desire to **urinate**, to **defecate**, to **eat**, and to **drink**) are accorded equal **weight** in our **dreams**. Bodily orifices often substitute for each other, and are symbolically equal.

Urination The desire to urinate is one of the main reasons we have for wanting to **wake** up. As a result, the act of urination may occur, very often metaphorically, in our remembered **dreams**, often in the form of a

burden carried or discharged. The dream therefore both prevents us urinating in **reality**, and acts as a protector of **sleep**. See **Why We Dream**

Urine See **Secretions**

Urns Urns to some extent equate with **vases**, except insofar as they suggest **death**. There is also a possible semantic aspect to the word, in that it euphonically resembles 'earns', hinting that the death of the cremated person may have been well earned.

Used, Being Should a woman **dream** of being used, or of things being used, this may refer back to the **loss** of her **virginity**, or to **fears** of defloration, often contained within a **hymen complex**. Being of use is also of practical value, and can imply a desire for status, common to both **sexes**.

Ushering To usher suggests **guidance**, insofar as direction goes, but it also carries ramifications of service and hierarchy, in the sense that the usher is nominally the **servant** of the one ushered. An usher may also be used to invoke or disseminate knowledge of **secrets** held in the common good.

Using Using, in the sense of deriving utility from, will most probably **reflect** back on the status of the **dreamer**, given that the more use one is, the higher status one should nominally have. In reality, of course, the opposite principle often holds true, and this paradox lies at the **heart** of both using and being **used**. See **Interpretation by Opposites**

Uterus, The An **archetypal**, eternal, life-giving principle, frequently represented, in its most primitive form, as a **circle** with a dark **centre**. See **Vaginas & Wombs**

V

Vacations See **Holidays**

Vaccinations Vaccinations can relate to **sexual intercourse**, and they can also suggest cooperation rather than solipsistic fantasy, in the sense that they are **injections** from the outside (i.e. society-at-large), towards the inside (i.e. the subject), except that they differ from injections in the sense that nothing is potentially taken out (*ergo* they do not constitute a two-way street, or dialogue). With this in mind, vaccinations may be taken as relating – on a purely symbolical basis, of course – to teaching. See **Doctors, Syringes** & **Teachers**

Vacuums Vacuums are static conditions in which the subject is unable to either feed or gather spiritual or physical sustenance. Such moments may be constructive, but they don't tend to be liberating, for obvious reasons. Vacuums and creativity tend to be incompatible, except insofar as the vacuum suggests the need for creativity in order to negate its own static condition.

Vaginas Vaginas suggest receptivity and connection. Being responsive rather than proactive, they tend to exemplify the possibilities of union rather than the dominance of one by the other that the **penis** may occasionally exemplify. See **Hymen Complex, Uterus, Venus** & **Wombs**

Valleys Valleys can often indicate passive states, when **consciousness** and psychic **movement** are at a standstill. They can also suggest the lower emotions surrounded by the higher emotions, in the form of **trees**. In purely **Freudian** terms, they may suggest the **female sex organs**, and possibly even **death**, in the sense of **leading** the **dreamer** to the end of something (*ergo* the Valley of Death).

Valves Valves are controlling **tools** which allow for effect regulation of the needs of disparate functional mechanisms. A valve in a **dream** may indicate a pressure build up in the **dreamer**, and suggest a desire for alleviation, sometimes in the form of a *deus ex machina*.

Vampires Vampires, particularly in the guise of Count Dracula and his mistresses, generally equate to **incubi** and **succubi** in dreams. This **unconscious** desire to be taken against one's will (i.e. not to be held responsible for one's actions), very often finds itself slaked through the medium of **films** and **books**. **Dreams** act in a similar capacity, in the sense that they effectively defang otherwise threatening mental constructs and render them next to harmless, thus protecting the **dreamer's** **sleep**. When this protective capacity breaks down over a lengthy period of **time** (as it does, on occasion), **neurosis** and **paranoia** may begin to occur.

Vans See **Vehicles**

Varnishing Varnishing suggests the covering up or **sealing** of otherwise vulnerable areas. It may also refer to a desire for beautification, or for the glossing over of flaws or errors.

Vases Vases, to the ancient Chinese, indicated a condition of perpetual harmony. The capacity of a vase to hold **water** denoted fertility and compassion. To a **dreamer** with a spiritual bent, a vase may suggest the astral **sheath**, in the sense of a designated **vehicle** for the passage of the **soul**, or higher **self**. See **Urns**

Vaults See **Façades**

Vegetables *Pace* the no doubt **tongue**-in-cheek Dr Johnson, vegetables tend to be inanimate and therefore insentient – this accords them stoloniferous status (see **Roots**), in that their entire relation is to other things rather than themselves, and particularly so when they appear in **dreams**. A **carrot** is therefore not a carrot, but a goad and a **phallic symbol**, for instance. See **Vegetarians**
KEY LINE: 'Sleep is a state in which a great part of every life is passed. No animal has been yet discovered, whose existence is not varied with intervals of insensibility; and some late philosophers have extended the empire of sleep over the vegetable world.' (Samuel Johnson, 1709–84)

Vegetarians Vegetarians choose to go without. This concept of restriction (*ergo* **repression**) constitutes **meat** and potatoes to a **dreamer**, for **discipline** involves **conflict**, which in turn creates **anxiety**. A peculiarly well-balanced vegetarian dreamer (certain Hindus and Buddhists, for instance) might conceivably avoid this maelstrom of emotions, viewing vegetarianism in a positive, unrestrictive, non-**anxiety**-forming **light** – a move towards, rather than a reaction against, in other words.

Vegetation Aspects of **nature**, such as **vines**, **flowers** and **trees**, usually contain symbolical revocations which directly relate to something the **dreamer** feels they lack. This may be something as nominally simple as sturdiness or steadfastness, but anything to do with **roots** will tend to have a more complex identity, very often relating to community, to moral obstacles, to societal restrictions, or to a possible desire to avoid **repressive** or inconvenient (because they cause us to **suppress** our desires) **taboos**.

Vehicles See **Bicycles, Cars, Lorries, Trains**, etc.

Veils Veils, cauls and membranes are all linked in **dream** terms, in the sense that they act as separators between one state and another – for example **birth**, **virginity**, recognition, or the guarding of **secrets**. **Jung** believed that a veiled woman appearing in a man's dreams represented his **anima**. To that extent it functioned as a **projection** of the man's **unconscious** femininity, with the eventual removal of the veil taken as a positive **sign**.

Velvet Velvet may refer to the memory of transitional objects such as children's 'rubbies', or to the texture of the **mother's breast** (a quasi universal collective experience). It tends to be a **female** rather than a **male** image for this reason, and to be comfort-affording – there may, however, be revocations of **death**, too, particularly with **black** velvet. See **Silkiness**

Venereal Diseases See **Disease**

Venom In certain circumstances – a desire not to become **pregnant**, say, or in the aftermath of a **rape** or of **sexual abuse** – venom may equate with **semen** in the dreamed of scheme of things. Venom may also act as a euphemism for **anger** or hostility, either directed outwards or towards the **self**. See **Scorpions** & **Secretions**

Venus Venus suggests both **love**, the pubis (in the sense of the *Mons Veneris*), and, very often, the **hand**, in that to many **people** Venus is associated with the **mound** below the **thumb**, rather than that delineating the **female** pudendum.

Vermin Vermin, strange to say, may sometimes represent **children** in **dreams**. This may have something to do with the invasion of personal space, or with the imposition or commission of irritating behaviours.

Verticality Verticality may suggest both expedient distance from a **problem**, and the power (or the desire) to get **above** it.

Vervain Vervain was considered to be the enchanter's herb, and its **roots**, when hung about a man's **neck**, were felt to have the capacity to ward off **evil dreams** and **nightmares**. Vervain tea allegedly prevents **insomnia**.

Veterinarians Veterinarians might be deemed to be protective of our animal **natures**, just as **priests** or **monks guard** the spiritual. If a **sick** animal, in urgent need of help, appears in a **dream**, both the **animal** and the veterinarian who comes to its aid represent aspects of the **dreamer**, often seen in terms of desire (the **id**/animal), and the governing of desire (the **superego**/veterinarian).

Vicars The Vicar of Bray famously swung with the **wind**, in terms of religious expedience, turning first Protestant, then Catholic, then back to Protestant again, according to royal whim. He lasted through four reigns (Henry VIII, Edward VI, Mary I and Elizabeth I), and died, just as he said he would, as stipendiary Vicar of Bray (lesser tithes only, needless to say). Although Simon Alleyn was hardly an **authority figure**, vicars do tend to denote authority when they appear in **dreams**, and also to carry suggestions of the life spiritual and the life devout. But they also contain a strong dose of Alleyn's comic susceptibility, and frequently stand for **fools** as well as **saints**.

Vice/Vices In medieval morality **plays**, Vice appeared as a buffoon with a **cap** made out of asses' **ears**. To that extent he equates with Bottom the Weaver, then, in William **Shakespeare**'s *A Midsummer Night's Dream* (1596), who also finds himself expediently transformed into an **ass**, in a sublime comment on the somewhat arbitrary **nature** of lust, covetousness and **sexual** desire. Vices in **dreams** may find themselves subject to semantic confusion, with our baser **urges** quite literally indulging in vice-like (clamp-like) behaviour in pursuit of the objects of their affections.

Victim-hood Victim-hood, or the perpetual **failure** to win **battles**, often manifests itself in unrealistic attempts at **compensation**. This can carry over into **dreams**, in which the **unconscious** mind frequently attempts to alleviate the **anxieties** which beset its host, either through euphemism, or creative **projection**. See **Walter Mitty**

Victims See **Victim-hood**

Victorianism Victorianism sometimes represents a **dream** euphemism for asexuality.

Victory To **dream** of victory is to **fear defeat**. This paradox lies at the **heart** of most **wish-fulfilment** fantasies, and leads to some magnificent juxtapositions of nominally antagonistic images. The **truth** probably lies somewhere at the fulcrum of the two images, with the **dreamer** inhabiting aspects of both the **victim** and their vanquisher.

Videos Videos are recording media, and to that extent their meaning in **dreams** will tend to refer to the **past**, with the emphasis on the bearing of **witness** to personal history. They contain an entertainment element, too, probably functioning along **wish-fulfilment** lines (think instant gratification). Now, like audiocassettes, LPs, and shellac 78s, videos have taken on an antediluvian patina, as if the packaging somehow invests the product inside – victims of fashion, then, doomed to be consigned to the **lumber rooms** of **dreamland**.

Vines Vines suggest **burial**, and the dissemination and concatenation of the **self** via one's **roots**. Rabbinical lore had it that the **devil** buried a **lion**, a **lamb** and a **hog** at the foot of Noah's first vine, leading to the three primary end results linked to an overindulgence in **wine**, namely ferocity, mildness and wallowing. Vines may also symbolize the **hand** in **dreams**, and the process of reaching out towards others (*ergo* the desire for community).

Vineyards Biblically speaking, the vineyard is a storehouse of wisdom. In **mythological** terms, vineyards suggest **Dionysian rites**, and the consequent freedom of **self**-expression that pertains to the use (or misuse) of **wine**. **Swedenborg** saw vineyards as the metaphorical equivalents of **churches**, and this view may well be reflected in **dream** imagery, and might possibly refer to the **arching** of **vines** in **unconscious** reverse mimesis of **cathedral** architecture.

Violence The fear of violence and the commission of violence tend to be correlated in **dream** terms. Both are likely to refer specifically to the **dreamer**, in that violence against the individual is generally anticipatory of violence done or violence deserved by the dreamer themselves.

Violets To dream of violets was traditionally considered to bring future good fortune or a change for the better in the **dreamer**'s circumstances. In **colour** symbolism, violet is emblematical of innocence, and suggests, in addition, the **love** of **truth** – it is also the colour of **mourning** and **fasting**.

Violins Violins tend to be **female symbols**, primarily on account of their **shape**, but also because (metaphorically, at least) they are perceived as wearing their **hearts** on their sleeves. Being hollow, the violin also suggests echoes and resonances.

Vipers See **Serpents & Snakes**

Virginity/Virgins Symbolically, the notion of the virgin suggests purity and spirituality, as opposed to impurity and carnality. As the retention of one's virginity is, by and large, a rational decision, virginity also carries with it revocations of the use of the will and of the existence of non-virile desires. Philo Judaeus (20 BC–40 AD), in his *De Cherubi*, maintains that virginity is a state of **mind** and not merely a physical condition, and that the **loss** of virginity may therefore be reversed. This craving for perfection is also symptomatic of virginity in **dreams**, and may, under certain circumstances, contain a **neurotic** edge.

Virgin Mary, The The **Virgin** is often a symbol for the **mother** in **dreams**. She may also form the fourth **corner** of a **quaternity** dream, or quite simply reflect purity or the inchoate (in the sense of her Assumption by the Holy **Spirit**).

Visions Mystics believe that there is a difference between visions and **dreams**. A vision should be truthful, but dreams may deceive, and mean the opposite of what they purport to show. In certain cultures, visions may be brought about by the use of hallucinogenic drugs. In Mexico, for instance, **shamans** and **medicine** men traditionally use the *peyote* **cactus**, the *oloiuqui* creeper, and certain **fungi**, to facilitate this visionary state.

See **Artificial Dreams, Hallucinations, Hallucinatory Dreams** & **Interpretation by Opposites**

Visits Visiting, or being visited, is often a symbolical euphemism for **menstruation**.

Voices When voices are heard in **dreams** they are always significant. **Jung** believed that when a voice interposed itself in a dream, it was a direct intervention of the **self**, and must not be disputed.

Voids Voids are akin to lacunae, in the sense that they are suggestive of **loss**, or of the removal of something that once filled the void the **dreamer** is now seeing. With this in **mind**, voids may be taken to **represent** physical as well as emotional loss, and to imply that the lacuna needs action (i.e. filling), rather than tolerance. See **Abysses, Amputations** & **Emptiness**

Volcanoes Volcanoes suggest latent emotional power, ready to **erupt** when least expected. An active volcano may relate to the **orgasm**, with **lava** acting in lieu of **semen** – however, in this case the destructive element of the volcano would also need to be taken in to account, potentially leading to a **rape reading**, or to suggestions of brutalization. An extinct volcano might indicate a dead or frozen **heart**.

Voltaire (1694–1778) Not **wishing** to fall overly foul of the **Church**, Voltaire frequently couched his criticisms of the established hierarchy in euphemistic **language**. One such is *Plato's Dream* (1756), in which Demiurgos calls his acolytes together and parcels out to them the lumps of matter that are later to be made into the **planets**. Demogorgon is given the **earth**, and fancies that he will be duly congratulated for his handiwork. He is therefore outraged to find himself sarcastically upbraided by his peers for his consummate botching of the **job**. He has, for instance, split the **world** between **ocean** and **land**, thereby complicating communication. He has been cavalier in his choice of **animal**, and slipshod in his tolerance of **disease**. Demogorgon defends himself by attacking the others. Demiurgos steps in, and consigns them all as dilettantes. 'In a few billion years, when you've learned something, you will be able to do better,' he shouts. 'Just as you've done with us?' says Demogorgon.

Vomit See **Secretions** & **Vomiting**

Vomiting We tend to vomit excess articles in **dreams**, and things that we don't really need. The context of the vomiting is important, too, as it may relate to an atmosphere in which the **dreamer** feels particularly uncomfortable – a public **arena**, say, or somewhere **claustrophobic**.

Vortexes/Vortices The concept of the vortex implies the bringing together of a **number** of disparate forces into what constitutes, in essence, an uncontrollable whole. Such a state of flux most probably relates to the emotions when it appears in **dreams**, and may contain threatening aspects, relating to turbidity – the **dreamer** may feel that they require straightforward answers, which the **symbol** of the vortex cannot, by definition, supply.

Votes See **Voting**

Voting Voting equates with choice which in turn equates with a desire for power. If the **dreamer** feels themselves to be powerless, the existence or fomentation of the possibility of suffrage might conceivably provide an element of hope where otherwise there might be only bleakness. Voting is a concept reliant on community, of course, and on a non-expedient morality that protects the **weak**.

Vows Vows are aspirational undertakings (usually of a symbolical **nature**) and in **dreams** they generally relate to the conscience rather than to natural evolution. They are also public demonstrations of private commissions – what Ludwig Wittgenstein might have called public indications of a private **language** (i.e. something that, by definition, cannot be, but which is nevertheless, a necessary concept in terms of the possible construction of a functioning philosophy of the **mind**).

Vultures A vulture symbolizes **rape** and violation. It is consuming and transmutative, and for this reason it was the preferred **bird** of Isis, particularly when it came to protecting the dead on their **journey** to and from the after-**world** (the Kingdom of the Dead). Unlike the Phoenix, the vulture is extraverted and not introverted – it acts as a catalyst to change, in other words, rather than as the repository of change in itself.

W

Wadding Wadding generally acts as a buffer between two disparate, but nevertheless related, entities – it also absorbs energy, and may act in a protective capacity, particularly when it is sound (a **voice**, for example), that is encroaching or threatening the **dreamer**.

Wading Wading through **water** may suggest that we are being held back emotionally in some way, but it may also hearken back to **childhood**, with partial immersion correlating to a gradual move towards detachment from the relational *status quo* (*ergo* the freedom to dip one's **toe** into strange waters).

Wafers The very **thinness** of a wafer carries with it suggestions of an interleaving of some sort (for something is only made thin if a desire exists to fit it between or inside another article). Pictorially, a wafer can equate to **skin**, while symbolically it may represent the **body** of **Christ** – as a sacrament, in the case of the Catholic **Church**, or as an ordinance, in the case of certain Protestant congregations. The wafer may also find itself linked in **dreams** to the **biblical** concept of manna, in the sense of desired (i.e. metaphorically ingested) spiritual sustenance.

Wagers Wagers symbolize our natural human desire to outwit fate (*ergo* **death**). They may also suggest randomness and insecurity, and the **games** that life can play with deserving (for we only accept wagers because we want to win) subjects. The **ritual** of the wager is also important, and suggests a desire to control outcomes, and to define them in **black** and **white**. See **Gamblers & Roulette**

Wages Wages are **compensatory** tokens suggestive of our possible value to others – as such they can act as comfort dispensers in our **dreams**, particularly when we find ourselves in crises of confidence in our everyday lives. They may also suggest the material as opposed to the spiritual, **reflecting** our requirements rather than our aspirations – our apparent qualifications rather than our real attainments.

Wagons Wagons suggest both **forward** motion and the imposition of the will. Wagons may also incorporate the notion of something that is **burdensome** and possibly even intrusive, in the sense that a wagon tends to impose itself on a **landscape**, and, *de facto*, require things of it.

Wailing Wailing is the outward expression of an inner torment. There is a **ritualistic** element to wailing, also, in that it can encompass (or be a part of) a communal expression of a collectively held emotion (*ergo* the west **wall** of the **Temple** Mount, known as the 'wailing wall').

Waiters/Waitresses The principle or tradition of service is less strong than it used to be, but that does not mean that it is not **latent**. It is normal for **dreamers** to extrapolate out either their desires or their **fears**, and service to others can encompass both these emotions. **Anger** at a servitor can therefore reflect anger at one's own passivity, or anger at not receiving what we feel is our due – the anger of others **reflecting** back onto the dreamer as servitor might suggest problems of low **self**-esteem or **projections** onto others of **feelings** about ourselves. See **Servants**

Waiting Waiting implies desire, in the sense that it would not be worth one's while to wait if one did not desire something that might (or conceivably might not) be forthcoming at the end of the waiting period. Waiting also presupposes expectation, in that it allows us **time** to conjure up often unrealistic possibilities. Waiting, of course, is worse when one is young, because **rationalization** is more difficult for the unencumbered, and therefore waiting in a **dream** may signify a temporary reversion to infantile status, in which wanting and **frustrated** waiting are virtually interchangeable.

Waitresses See **Waiters/Waitresses**

Waking **Freud** called every **awakening** from **sleep** 'a new **birth**', twinning the actual process of sleeping with a partial return to the foetal realm from which one is then, in consequence, reborn.
KEY LINE: "'You waked not?'/"Not until my dream became/Like a child's legend on the tideless sand,/Which the first foam erases half, and half/ Leaves legible.'" (From Percy Bysshe Shelley's *Fragments of an Unfinished Drama* 1822)

Waking Dreams The brain activity of an awake person, and that of a sleeping person during the dreaming, or **REM** (Rapid Eye Movement), stage of **sleep**, is roughly commensurable. There is no reason, therefore, why we should not dream whilst awake – assuming, for a moment, that we can allow ourselves a suitable **break** from our pursuit of the trivial. Turn to **Abon Hassan**, for a splendid 'waking dream' story. See **Lucid Dreaming**

Walking Walking in tandem with another person is often **representational** of the **sexual** act. Walking in a solitary fashion frequently represents waywardness, or lack of focus – it is at the same time a **search** for change, and a slow process of change in itself. The actual process of walking may also suggest development or personal progression, in the sense, for instance, of the 'walking off' of our desires.

Wallets A wallet can often be a **reflection** of the **dreamer**'s view of themselves, and it is therefore connected with identity and motivation (think **photographs**, **driving** licences, lucky **coins**, etc.). It is also a containment area, and designed to mould itself to the dreamer's person (or

persona) until it becomes intimately adjunctive – *ergo* a possible additional source of energy or status outside the immediate confines of the **body**, but easily accessible and non-emotionally amenable.

Wallpaper I have often found myself using the expression 'a dream's wallpaper' during the course of this **book**, and it is true that **dreams** do often find themselves coated with modish, immanent, and recently acquired **symbols** or **designs**, hijacked by the **unconscious** mind to furnish the dreamer's **room** in the most up-to-date, if not necessarily the most flattering, of styles. Wallpaper – often **layers** of it – protects the **dreamer** from the full implications of their **unconscious** (and often **repressed**) drives. Strip the wallpaper off layer by layer, and one is faced with a **series** of historical conundrums that need to be **teased** out if one is to discover the underlying motive behind their selection.

Walls Walls are **barriers** (or obstacles) between possible states of being. To **tear** down or demolish a wall suggest a desire to set things **straight** again – to see clearly, without let or hindrance. See **Facelifts**

Walruses Walruses are **male** simulacra, in the sense that their principle characteristics are predominantly what we think of – albeit in a largely pejorative sense – as male (**moustaches**, bulk, dominance, aggression, promiscuity, lack of grace, etc.). For **female dreamers** to **dream** of a walrus might imply a **feeling** of being crushed by the male, or of being unwillingly dominated, not by **right**, but because of sheer willpower or physical bulk.

Walter Mitty Walter Mitty, the eponymous **daydreamer** of James Thurber's novella, *The Secret Life of Walter Mitty* (1939), spends as much of his **life** as possible fantasizing his way towards a more desirable **reality**. During the course of one pallid afternoon spent waiting for his **wife** to emerge from her **hair** appointment, he becomes the intrepid **commander** of an eight-engined Navy hydroplane, a millionaire-saving **surgeon**, a Webley-Vickers 50.80 wielding superstar **gangster** defendant, a single-handed bomber air ace, and Walter Mitty the undefeated, calmly facing the firing squad with a disdainful smile – all conditions, needless to say, with no bearing at all on his present **reality**. See **Daydreams** & **Lucid Dreaming**

Waltzing In Max Ophuls' film, *La Ronde* (1950), a waltz by composer Oskar Straus links ten scenes of men and women (further connected by the carousel of which the waltz forms part) in an erotic charivari, suggesting – according to Artur Schnitzler, **author** of the original play – that we **fall** in **love** not with a person, but with the 'idea' of a person. The waltz is a perfect exemplar of this kind of **projection**, and may, in consequence, act as an **unconscious** trigger in **dreams** for certain desired kinds of behaviour.

Wandering Wandering is primarily a **male** tradition, and its significance will tend to be tellingly different depending on whether it appears in the **dreams** of a man or a woman. To a woman, it may be threatening, carrying revocations of **abandonment** and the **destruction** of settled relationships – to a man it may be stimulating, suggesting change and the arrogation of responsibility for one's actions to the mechanisms of random fate. These **readings** are not set in stone, however, and depend on character and inclination for their relevance.
KEY LINE: 'Though I am old with wandering/Through hollow lands and hilly lands,/I will find out where she has gone,/And kiss her lips and take her hands;/And walk among long dappled grass,/And pluck till time and times are done,/The silver apples of the moon,/The golden apples of the sun.' (From William Butler Yeats' *The Song of Wandering Aengus* 1899)

Wands See **Sceptres**

War War reflects a state of flux when it appears in a **dream** – flux and the **fear** of change. If the war is far away, the changes may be viewed as looming rather than imminent, but if the war is adjacent, or actually involves the **dreamer**, then an internal schism may be taking place, with aspects of the dreamer vying with each other for dominance.

Wardens Wardens are often aspects of the **superego** called in by the **unconscious** mind to circumvent trouble from the **id**. If the id is out to persuade us, for instance, that venality is perfectly acceptable within a **family** environment 'because we deserve it', then the superego might conjure up a warden figure (be it a nanny, a dominant relative, or a **policeman**) to persuade us back onto the **right track**.

Wardrobes A wardrobe, for a **female dreamer**, may refer back to her view of herself, in that it houses **clothes** (i.e. aspects of the **self**-image). A tidy, ordered wardrobe may suggest self-satisfaction, or a desire that things work and function correctly (or appropriately) on an emotional level. An untidy wardrobe may point to problems with self-esteem, or with the way one feels that one is perceived by others – a clean outer disguising a disastrous inner, for example. See **Closets**

Warehouses Warehouses are **sealed** units in which things are protected, and as such they tend towards the feminine when interpreted. They may also represent repositories of ideas, particularly if the **dreamer** is uncertain in which direction to move – a move towards the warehouse might suggest inclusion, away from the warehouse, alienation.

Warlocks See **Witches**

Warmth The desire for warmth may well **reflect** back on the pre-natal condition, and its appearance, and the **dream** furniture surrounding it, should initially be investigated in that light. Failing that, the issue may simply be one of comfort anxiety in an otherwise frigid emotional environment. See **Pre-Birth Dreams**

Warnings Warning dreams can be extremely useful, if the warnings contained within them are translated into everyday life. A **mother fearing** for her **child** (and disguising this by sarcenet chidings); a **pilot** fearing for his **passengers**; a **doctor** fearing for her patients – all these may be and should be readily translated back into how one lives one's conventional, non-dreaming existence. Warnings may also reflect the **dreamer**'s **resistance** to uncovering facts that may be unpalatable – to this extent they point to **weaknesses** in the **walls** of the dreamer's **neuroses**, and are of considerable value in **dream work**.

Warrants Warrants are permissions, and their presence is needed in order to make something demonstratively 'correct'. In a **dream** they may constitute clearances we give ourselves in order to behave in a certain way.

Warts Warts are blemishes on otherwise pristine surfaces, and there is usually a strong element of **guilt** involved in their appearance. They may be charmed away if one is *deserving* of the charm, and this provisional aspect may act as some sort of **compensation** for their sudden emergence. **Dreams** will tend to view them causatively, therefore, and possibly as a result of something that the **dreamer** has done.

Washing Washing often equates with whitewashing, or covering something over to hide or divert attention from it. It may be both illicit, and an elimination (or annulling) of the illicit. It can also be a **symbol** for **masturbation**. Traditionally, sins were considered capable of being washed away (*pace* Lady Macbeth and Pontius Pilate), and the washing of the dead was a necessary **ritual** before the transmigration of the **soul** could be achieved.

Wasps Wasps are frequently seen negatively, in terms of **punishment**, whereas **bees** are generally seen positively, in terms of **construction**. This seems marginally unfair on the wasp.
KEY LINE: 'The sight of wasps marks injuries to one's foes.' (From Astrampsychus' *Oneirocriticon* 350 AD)

Waste Waste presupposes loss and the **sacrifice** of energies. There may also be a **link** with **death**, and therefore sadness. Women who **dream** of waste may be suffering from a **fear** of **miscarriage**, or simply the desolation of what might have been, in terms of lost or **aborted** children, or of **children** unborn or not conceived due to the failure of an affective relationship. See **Abortions** & **Miscarriages**

Watches Watches watch us. This semantic connection is important, and **reflects** back on the significance of **time** in a **dream**, and on its fluidity and non-specificity. A watch may also draw attention to something, as the manipulation of a watch inevitability catches the **eye**. One could even argue that a watch is the most perfect metaphysical accoutrement, and that its presence in a dream is specifically designed to provoke **questions**. See **Clocks**

Water Water implies the possibility of unknown powers or emotions, and deep water represents the **unconscious**, or the **psyche**. Hesitating before entering the water can imply doubt as to one's inner depths, and where the discovery of them may **lead**. Water, particularly when it is circum-scribed, can also **represent** the **uterus**, while uncircumscribed water may represent urine. In **Freudian** terms, water almost always means **birth**, especially when dreamt of by a woman – and when a young **child** is asso-ciated with the **dream**, and perhaps **blood** as well, this becomes even more apparent, and may point towards **fears** of a **miscarriage**. See **Aquarius, Fire, Kelp** & **Secretions**

Waterfalls Waterfalls are release images, and may therefore accompany **wetting the bed** dreams in **children**, or **sexual/orgasmic dreams** in adults. Waterfalls may also suggest the release of pent up emotions, or the smooth outpouring of previously blocked **channels** of communication.

Waves Waves can often have menstrual significance in a **dream**, and may sometimes indicate premenstrual states in women. See **Menstruation** & **Premenstrual Dreams**

Wax Wax is used for literal replication and for providing **light** – it is also malleable (triggering mimicry); it is impressionable (triggering flattery); and it is meltable (triggering domination, i.e. the desire to mould it). To this extent it probably has more **female** than **male** characteristics, and certain **sexual** connotations may obtain in a dream as a result.

Weakness Weakness tends to relate to **self**-perception in **dream** terms, but it may also relate to barriers the **unconscious** mind places in the way of what it considers inappropriate activity – this may be activity that might challenge the status quo, threaten **sleep** continuity, or otherwise undermine the **ego**.

Wealth Wealth is a pejorative word only to the poor. The misuse of wealth (talents, power, influence, potential) is another matter entirely, and probably lies at the core of the image's significance in **dreams**. Wanting everything is a symptom of the **id**; feeling **guilty** about wanting it, but seeing that one gets as much of what remains as is going, is a symptom of the **ego**; being forced to justify one's want by an overween-ing and socially engineering superstate, or by any other sort of self-proclaimed moral arbiter – which will probably end up snatching it all anyway, under the convenient guise of inclusion, positive discrimination, or some other expedient catchword – is a symptom of the **superego**. Superego, ego, and id – the state, the citizen, the **internet**. Don't laugh.

Weapons Weapons are frequently merely extensions of the **hand**, and consequently of the **dreamer**'s desire for power over their immediate environment (both physical and psychological). Weapons may also act as euphemisms for outgoing energy (except, of course, if the weapon is turned against oneself), and may find themselves called on to act in a protective, as well as an aggressive, capacity.

Weather Weather is important in **dreams** because it **reflects** the mood surrounding the **dreamer** (or the perception the dreamer has of the mood surrounding them). A weather front coming in might suggest trouble in store, whereas a sudden precipitation might correlate with loss, a *coup de foudre*, or some other unavoidable influx of emotions. **Rain**, for instance, may equate with **tears**, dispersal, and eventual purification, whereas **snow** might indicate a gathering together of the emotions into one all-encompassing (and possibly comforting) blanket.

Weaving Weaving denotes the natural rhythms of **life**, which ebb and flow like a tidal estuary. To the ancient Chinese it represented the perpetual **movement** between the **yin** and the **yang**. In normal **dream** euphemism, it may **represent** the **sexual** act.

Webs Webs suggest the interconnectedness of all things, with the sticky **nature** of the web acting as a brake to the **celebration**, for it implies that if we want to **escape** this interconnectedness and assert our individuality, we may find it more difficult than we bargained for. In the context of a **dream**, the web is the perfect euphemism for the **family**, with the **taboo mother** figure (at least according to psychoanalyst Karl Abraham) as **spider**.

Wedding Cake In traditional societies, if a young **girl** took her part of the **wedding** cake and placed it beneath her **pillow**, she would **dream** of her future **husband**.

Weddings Weddings are **female** initiatory **rites** at which the **male**, in symbolical terms, acts as auxiliary, rather than as principle. Both parties to the wedding are about to discover convergent, although nominally oppositional aspects, of their own **psyche**. See **Marriage** & **Sacred Marriage**

Wedges Segmentation; wedging; the **cutting** into parts – all relate to aspects of the **self** that we show to others, or that we allow others to hijack. If we are physically **split** (or if something that represents us is physically split) then we suffer from disharmony and dispersion, no longer retaining the strength of the whole. A perfect example might be an **orange**, symbolically representing the **dreamer** (let's call her the mother). The peel (her external carapace – the **face** she shows the **world**) is cut away, and she is segmented (possibly by her **family**), with each loss **swallowing** aspects of her former integrity, until she is simply the memory of an orange (or of the person she once thought she was). She has been pulled in too many directions at once, and no longer retains her individual identity.

Weeds Weeds suggest neglect and misplaced growth – the false seeding of unproductive ideas. They may act as a **reflection** on how we think we are perceived by others, with a rank, natural **garden** implying that our **self**-esteem is at a low ebb, potentially making us vulnerable to outside interference and busy-bodying.

Weeks The passing of **time** tends to denote the passing by of the possibilities of activity rather than the specific of time itself (which is fluid, anyway, in **dreams**). The emphasis on specific periods of time such as **weeks** and **years** is probably not unrelated to **mourning**.

Weeping See **Crying**

Weighing Weighing and **judging** go **hand** in hand in **dream** terms, and the physical weighing of an object is often merely a euphemism for a quality or convenience check.

Weight Things that are of exceptional weight in a **dream** are often **burdens** that we are being forced to **harbour** against our wills. Weight may also indicate reservations, misgivings, or scruples about some desired course of action (e.g. if our **shoes** or **feet** are acting as unwitting drags) or inhibitions that we are attempting to conceal from other parties (weight in a **rucksack**, perhaps).

Wells Wells may sometimes represent the **female breast** in **dreams** – they can also represent the **uterus**. Wells are questioning, too – think **echoes** and **wishing** wells – and may, in addition, represent the **fear** of, or the nostalgia for, trapped or unrecoverable emotions. See **Springs**

Werewolves Werewolves are akin to **demons**, **monsters** and bogeymen, in **dream** terms, acting as correlatives to **unconscious fears**. As with **vampires**, there is a **cannibalistic** aspect to the werewolf persona, given extra acidity by the **child**-snatching, child-**eating string** to the **myth** – paradoxically, this may represent a hidden **fear** or resentment of **children** on the part of the **dreamer**, or a desire to incorporate certain childlike aspects into the dreamer's own personality. See **Incubi** & **Succubi**

West, The The West traditionally suggests journeying and creative endeavour – adventure, and the extension of boundaries. The West may also symbolize the spiritual, holistic state that succeeds death. See **East, North** & **South**

Wet Dreams Nocturnal emissions of **male semen** triggered by **dream passages**. See Ejaculation & Emission Dreams

Wetsuits Wetsuits are designed to keep us dry (*ergo* emotionally unencumbered) when we are in a wet (*ergo* emotionally threatening) environment. This very lack of porosity, though, is their downfall, because wetsuits do not allow for two-way communication. Instead, they are simply that – a protection. It's like expecting a gasmask to intercede in anything more than a prophylactic way between oneself and a chemically-armed **enemy**.

Wetting The Bed Wetting the bed, in **children**, is often accompanied by **dreams**. These can provide a strong **key** to the emotional excitement that is often at the cause of **night**-time micturition. Such dreams frequently involve **armies**, or **enemies**, or fantasized **war** situations, which may **reflect** back or throw **light** on the **family** situations responsible for the bed-wetting in the first place.

Whales Whales are significant **symbols**, and have been so since pre-**biblical times**. The whale may **represent** the emergent **soul** (as in Jonah), or the **lower** passions externalized (as in the **Buddha**'s Nirvanic cutting of his bonds with the **world** and its '**monsters** of desire'). This apparent paradox – this at once concreteness and luminosity – is at the **heart** of the whale's fascination, and stems from its function as one of the few beasts (**vehicles**) that can span the very bounds of the **oceans** (*ergo* the emotions).
KEY LINE: 'When I'm playful, I use the meridians of longitude and parallels of latitude for a seine, and drag the Atlantic ocean for whales. I scratch my head with the lightning and purr myself to sleep with the thunder.' (From Mark Twain's *Life on the Mississippi* 1883)

Wheat Wheat, in the western tradition, has a similar function to **rice** in **Buddhism** – i.e. it embodies a harvesting of the **soul**, and is a **symbol** of the higher emotions. In purely literal terms, wheat may indicate a desire to be fed either figuratively or spiritually.

Wheels Wheels are **circular**, and therefore have undoubted connections to the **mandala** and to transformative unity. They also suggest motion, and the possibility of spiritual or material advancement.

Whips Whips are extensions of the **hand** and of its remit, and therefore suggest the desire for power over others. This reaching out aspect is an important one, except insofar as the whip finds itself wielded by another person, who is threatening the **dreamer**. In this case the second person will tend to be an aspect (possibly **self-punishing**) of the dreamer themselves. A **phallic** aspect to the whip may also figure, particularly in the case of **female** dreamers – either extrapolated, as in an outward projection of a desire for **male** pattern dominance, or apprehended, as in a **fear**

that someone who is dominant physically (possibly a male) will abuse that advantage.

Whirlwinds See **Vortexes/Vortices**

Whiskers Whiskers are, by and large, **male** attributes, but as well as being both **phallic** and pudendal, they also bring **cats** to mind, and are consequently suggestive of **antennae**, and the capacity or the desire to receive communications from the outside **world**. See **Beards**

Whisky Whisky incorporates the concepts of **celebration**, good health (from the Gaelic *ooshk-'a-pai* or the Irish *uisge-'a-bagh*, meaning **water** of health and water of **life** respectively), and companionship (in that it is rarely customary to **drink** alone). With the possible exception of a teeto-taller, a religious zealot, a prohibitionist, or a recovering alcoholic, there-fore, one may safely assume that it stands as an entirely benevolent image, in dream terms, to the informed remainder of the human **race**.

Whistling Whistling occupies **space**, in that it reaffirms our existence when we are **alone** or find ourselves surrounded by **silence**. It also **draws** attention to things, in that when someone whistles we notice them or inadvertently emulate them, often without being **conscious** of so doing. Whistling can also suggest **frustration**, in that we may need to 'whistle for our supper' (or what have you) just as **sailors** used to 'whistle for the **wind**'.

White The **colour** white frequently indicates something that is **sacred** to the **sun**, as **white elephants** were in India, white **horses** were for the ancient Greeks, and white **oxen** were for the British **Druids**. It is also linked to mystical legends, and **represents** purity. The colour white is also linked to **death**, as in white flower dreams, or the bearing of mixed **red** and white **flowers** into a **hospital**, which was considered to foretell a death in the ward. See **Epona**
KEY LINE: 'Perhaps in a recess of the unplumbed future,/again I will find you, white deer from my dream./I too am dream, lasting a few days longer/than that bright dream of whiteness and green fields.' (From Jorge Luis Borges' *The White Deer* 1975)

White Elephants The white **elephant** is a **symbol** of temperance, eterni-ty and sovereignty. In India, the Supreme **God** Indra rides one. Both the Lord **Buddha's** mother, **Queen** Maya, and also Trisala, **mother** of Mahavira, founder of **Jainism**, on the eve of giving **birth**, dreamed that a **white** elephant came to present them with a **lotus**, the symbol of purity and knowledge. *Indian Proverb*: 'Only an elephant can bear an elephant's load.' Thus the tradition that the **King** of Siam (land of the white ele-phant) customarily gave a white elephant to those of his courtiers that he wished to **ruin**.

Whores See **Harlot Fantasies**

Why We Dream There are three main reasons why we **dream**. First for the protection of the **ego** (i.e. the dream prevents emotional shocks). Secondly, for the regulation of the affect mechanism (i.e. the dream acts like a safety valve, discharging excess emotional energy). Thirdly, for the protection of our **sleep** (i.e. the dream protects our sleep by counteracting the effect of internal and external stimuli that may otherwise **wake** us up).

Widowers The image of the widower suggests the **loss** of the **female** element, or **anima**, just as the **widow** suggests the loss of the **male** element, or **animus**. We are definitely talking loss here rather than rejection, given the element of **mourning** inherent in each image.

Widows The image of the widow suggests **female mourning** for the **loss** of the **animus**, and relates directly to the **widower** image, with its correlative **male** loss of the **anima**. In each case the image denotes unwanted disharmony.

Wigs Wigs may suggest a desire to **transform** oneself into something other – something hopefully better, but conceivably worse (for wigs can give away more about the wearer than they sometimes suspect). Wigs can also suggest age and **illness** and the putting on of **masks** or **personas** to address different issues.

Will to Power A term originally coined by the German philosopher Friedrich Nietzsche (1844–1900) in his eponymous 1901 book, and later used by **Alfred Adler** to indicate the fundamental neurotic drive from inferiority towards superiority. See **Inferiority Complexes** & **Neurosis**

Wills Wills are usually **anxiety** indicators, in that they suggest the break-up of the **family** unit (often literally) into **parties** driven by **self**-advantage. Even with the best of intentions, wills usually produce strife of one sort or another, triggering expedient **reflections** on the **past**. More positive aspects might include the desire in the **dreamer** for rationalization and the putting of distance between oneself and one's more selfish or acquisitive drives. The existence of wills in a **dream** also presupposes the existence of a **death clause**.

Wind Wind usually denotes change, in that it tends to **sweep** away or threaten existing structures. Symbolically, it denotes emanation, Divine energy and the energized **self** – i.e. the capacity of the human being to acknowledge otherness. It is also a **symbol** of the quaternary, and the four entrances into **heaven**. See **Quaternity**

Windmills Few people can conjure up a windmill without thinking of Don Quixote (even if they have never bothered to read the **book**). This 'tilting at windmills' aspect **reflects** on the continuous, circular motion of the **mill**, which is suggestive of harmony and continuity, and which is one most human beings aspire towards. The **grinding** aspect is also important, in that it suggests the need for radical **transformation** before betterment or progress can be achieved. See **Mandalas**

Windows   A window is a common **symbol** for the **vagina**, but it may just as well stand in for **consciousness**, and the consequent letting in of **light** – it may also suggest the allowing of one's **urges** free rein. In addition, an open window can indicate the '**world** outlook' of the **dreamer**, and their capacity for receptivity.

Wine   Wine suggests communion in all its many forms. Wine itself is the result of a communion of man and the **soil**, and it requires community for its creation. It is also a **symbol** of wisdom, and was used by **Swedenborg** to signify both 'holy **truth**' and 'truth profaned'. Wine's relation to **blood** is also apposite here, stemming from its traditional **label** as 'the blood of the **grape**'. See **Dionysian**
KEY LINE: 'Me thought I saw (as I did dream in bed)/A crawling vine about Anacreon's head:/Flusht was his face; his hairs with oil did shine;/And as he spake, his mouth ran o'er with wine.' (From Robert Herrick's *The Vision* 1648)

Wings   Wings are aspirational **symbols**, suggestive of desired freedoms and the ability to transcend oneself or one's environment. They may also reflect a desire for peak experiences, or for a **regression** to **childhood**. See **Childhood Dreams** & **Flying**

Winter   Winter is often age-related in **dreams**, implying a gradual coming-to-an-end of ideas, physical attributes, and natural resources. It may also **represent** incipient **death**. In symbolical terms, winter equates with latency, lack of manifestation and unfruitfulness. There are a number of more positive **readings**, however, of which productive stasis (the gathering together of energies) is merely one.

Wire   Wire may be supportive or threatening. Either way, it has the ability to 'cut' through' things if misused. It may also be a means of communication, and may be used to connect or encompass related things – it is at the same **time** both flexible and hard. All these sometimes paradoxical attributes make of wire a complex **dream** image, and one in which the **dreamer**'s personal view of wire becomes paramount. A **farmer**, for instance, might view **wire** benevolently, as a protector of his flocks, whereas a **cowboy** or a **prisoner** might view wire as an impinger of precious freedoms.

Wise Old Man, The   The *Philomen*, or Wise Old Man, was the **dream** entity which, according to **Jung**, personified the balance between his inner and his outer **self**. The Wise Old Man (his Higher Self) allowed

Jung to make decisions that were wiser and more apposite than he could have made without his *Philomen* acting as the **bridge** to his **unconscious**. See **Anima**, **Animus**, **Archetypes**, **Great Mother** & **Wizards**

Wishes Our **unconscious** or subliminal wishes may sometimes appear in **dreams** in the form of super-dramatized enactments or theatrical fulfilments of the wish. See **Wish Fulfilment**

Wish-Fulfilment **Dreams** can fulfil certain of our unexpressed **wishes**, and even, on occasion, provide dreamed precedents for our **unconscious** desires. Such wish-fulfilment dreams **fall** into two main categories: the catagogic, or **downward** fulfilment dream, in which we satisfy our **incestuous**, **criminal**, **sexual**, or other tabooed cravings, such as **suicide**; and the anagogic, or **upward** fulfilment dream, in which we satisfy our **urges** towards the sublime, the ideal, and the benevolent. The great Turkish **poet** and astronomer Nasr-ed-Din recounts how, as a **child**, he once ran up to his **father** and told him of a wonderful dream he had just had in which he was given all the sweetmeats and delicacies he had ever craved. His father, in an effort to **teach** his **son** the value of **money**, replied, 'Well, my boy. If you give me 10 paras, I will interpret this important dream for you.' Outraged, Nasr-ed-Din replied, 'But father, be serious. If I possessed 10 paras, I wouldn't have needed to dream about the **sweets** – I would have bought them instead!' A brilliant literary example of the wish-fulfilment fantasy comes in Isaac Bashevis Singer's story of *Gimpel the Fool*, in which the title character dreams that his dead **wife** returns to him, consoles him, and answers all his **questions** 'with the **eyes** of a **saint**'. The irony, of course, lies in that fact that Gimpel's wife cared nothing whatsoever for him while she lived, and that he is, in consequence, much happier in his dream fantasy world than when confronting the realities of his **past**.

Witchcraft See **Witches**

Witches Witches, warlocks, and warricows are all pursuers of the so-called 'cunning arts'. In Anglo-Saxon, warlock actually means a deceiver, or one who **breaks** his word, and there is a strong **archetypal** connection between witches and **Satan** (he of the cunning **tongue**). Both witches and warlocks tend to be **wish-fulfilment** in origin, and generally relate to the desired empowerment of otherwise helpless or unassertive individuals or classes of individuals through the obtaining of alleged **secret** knowledge. See **Devil**

Witnessing Witnessing is a complex issue. It implies, at one and the same time, connection and disconnection. Connection, because we are interested and **paying** attention to events outside our normal remit – and disconnection, because we are choosing not to involve ourselves in what is happening in front of our **eyes** *despite* our interest in it. We are arrogating responsibility, therefore, and seem content to use only part of our capacities. Witnessing may, in consequence, be acting as a wakeup call when it occurs within a **dream**, or as a spur to **ditch** passivity.

Wives For a **male** to dream uneasily about his wife may suggest **anxieties** about his **anima**, or the quality of his **self**-image *vis à vis* women, as seen through the reflective eyes of his mother (for **mothers** and wives are sometimes interchangeable in men's **dreams**, just as **husbands** and **fathers** may be interchangeable in women's). Comforting **dreams** about a wife may suggest a healthy anima, particularly if the man *becomes* the wife in some form or other – such startling transmogrifications are perfectly normal in the dream world, and reflect different, but often complementary, aspects of the self.

Wizards Wizards are **prayer**-answerers and authority figures, and to that extent they relate to **magicians** in the **archetypal** scheme of things, and to the **superego**. They are called on to resolve insoluble problems, which means that they may also equate to **Jung**'s concept of the **wise old man** or alchemist (see **Alchemy**), in their apparent capacity to translate the lower into the higher. **Black magicians** and **witches**, though, are another case altogether, and relate to the **ego**.

Wolves A wolf symbolizes cruelty and savage ferocity. We all retain a race-memory of the **fear** of wolf **attacks**, and it is probably the collective – and therefore intelligent – coordination of its fomenters that makes the fear of such an attack so all-encompassing. Pursued by wolves! It must seem as though the entire **world** is against one. And this perfectly justifiable **paranoia** translates easily into **dreams** in which unknown elements (*ergo* 'others') would seem to be threatening us.

Woman See **Female** & **Old Woman**

Wombs An actual return to the womb would be a horrifying, **claustrophobic** experience, and not the nurturing, comfortingly dependent event that some commentators would allow. The womb is therefore a symbolical rather than a realistic haven, and any desire to return there is probably **neurotic** in origin. That said, the womb may well represent non-creative creation to a **dreamer** – in that it creates life despite, and not because of, its harbourer. To that extent it equates with its correlative, the **penis**, in suggesting more than it is, in reality, able to offer. It is an inadvertent **tool** rather than a golem, in other words.

Wood Wood is spiritually sustaining and symbolically significant (at least to Christians), in that it is intimately related to **Christ**'s travails on the **cross**. Wood, while nominally equating with growth, may also, perhaps paradoxically, be seen to represent stasis. This is actually the difference between worked wood (in the sense of **furniture**, say) and natural wood (in the sense of **trees**) – the one attests, the other abides. If this difference seems a little meretricious in **dream** terms, it should be remembered that any art is transformative, and capable of relegating the medium to second place behind the message.

Woods See **Forests**

Wool Wool can **represent** an **artificial** carapace or disguise – logically **speaking** we are taking on another creature's outer covering for our own, and then transforming it to suit ourselves (pun intended). Wooliness or wool-gathering may be another aspect of the equation, strengthened by the **sheep**'s reputation as a stupid, or at the very least a susceptible, **animal**.

World, The The world is at once limiting and empowering – it is limiting to the visionary, and empowering to the peasant, and brave indeed would be the person who favoured the one over the other. In **dream** terms the world tends to represent welcome constriction, in the sense that a **child** (the **dreamer** as neophyte) might view the extent of its playground as comforting rather than confining.

Worms A worm traditionally symbolizes cringing – to have 'a worm in one's **tongue**' signified cantankerousness. This negative aspect often carries over into **dreams**, and probably indicates a long-standing resentment against worms, possibly triggered by their role as the happy recipients of human physical decay.
KEY LINE: 'Worms' food is fine end of our living.' (From John Lydgate's *Daunce of Machabree* 1430)

Worries Worries, in dreams, usually reflect **wishes**. They may also **reflect** an existing but unacknowledged condition of alertness that the **dreamer** takes to **bed** with them.

Worship Worship suggests that the concept of 'free will' is a non-starter. Worship also constitutes the symbolical acknowledgment of a higher order by a lower. Its appearance in **dreams** may also carry sardonical intent, and act as a commentary upon perceived enforcements of another person's will.

Wounds Wounds are usually synonymous with the **vagina** when they appear in **dreams**. If a woman dreams of wounds to her **body**, she is possibly dreaming of defloration, or the loss of her **virginity**. A wounded person, on the other hand, may often represent the **Christ** figure. See **Lakes**

Wreaths Wreaths suggest the loss of something precious – something that in life was deserving of **celebration**.

Wrecks Wrecks are **failures** of intent. They suggest that we are not the **masters** of our own destinies, and that random acts may upset our most desired progressions. Continual wrecks in **dreams** may suggest deep-seated insecurities and/or **inferiority complexes** – it is perhaps important, in this context, to discern whether the **dreamer** is sabotaging themselves (**neurosis**) or whether that job is seemingly being done for them by others (**paranoia**).

Wrestling Wrestling, in a **dream**, often points up mental **conflicts. Jacob** wrestled with an **angel** in Genesis xxxii, 24, before becoming the personification of the nation of Israel. French **artist** Paul **Gauguin**'s 1888 **painting** entitled *Jacob Wrestling with the Angel* depicted the event in both pictorial and symbolical terms. Here is what the artist himself has to say about it: 'Art is an abstraction; derive this abstraction from **nature** while dreaming before it, and think more of the creation which will result (than of the model). This is the only way of mounting toward **God** – doing as our Divine Master does, create.' (From a letter to Claude-Emile Schuffeneker)

Writers Amongst the writers who claim to have received daemonic or literary guidance whilst still asleep are **Sir Walter Scott**, Dr Johnson, **René Descartes**, Jean-Jacques Rousseau, Thomas de Quincey, Charles Lamb, William Makepeace Thackeray, Alexandre Dumas, and Charles Dickens.

Writing The very act of writing constitutes a desire to communicate – even spectres often choose writing (or so we are told) in preference to verbal or aural processes. This may reflect on writing's concreteness, for before **computers** and **printing** (recent phenomena both) writing itself was the only means we had of accurately presenting ourselves and our thoughts to a future **world**. Writing in **dreams** is therefore a concretization – or outward manifestation – of inner **urges**.

X

X See **Cross, Crossings, Crossroads & Crucifixion**

X-Rays X-rays allow us, as it were, to see through things – to penetrate mysteries and to plumb unexpected depths. X-rays carry **danger signals** as well, in that we **unconsciously fear** that they may be doing us harm in the very act of illuminating us. This 'can of **worms**' aspect is surprisingly prevalent, and may constitute the major force of the image in a **dream**.

Y

Yachts In **dreams**, yachts, like all **water** vessels (see **Boats** & **Ships**), contain elements of both the feminine principle and the suggestion of **sanctuary** in times of emotional uncertainty – for without them, we **drown**. This sanctuary element stems originally from the **female** as eventual repository of **male** seed – without the females' metaphorical **carrying** capacity, the male **seed** would, as it were, **drown**. Thus, boats as female **symbols** in which males (**sailors**, seamen, **semen**) are carried.

Yang The rational, active, creative side of the Chinese dynamic balance, which, when in tandem with the **yin**, creates dynamic potential. **Key** qualities associated with the Yang include the **sun**, **fire**, hardness, **brightness**, expansion and energy. See **Lingam** & **Yoni**

Yards Yards are outcrops (or add-ons) to existing **houses**. If one then takes a house in a **dream** to **represent** the **dreamer**, yards become either areas of growth (particularly if they are well kept) or **burdens** (if they are a mess). They may also represent **children** or **animals**, if only by inference.

Yardsticks Yardsticks are largely metaphorical **tools** nowadays (except, perhaps, in the **army**), and suggest the need to **measure** oneself against others rather than to survive in a **vacuum**. They may also be **phallic** (it must be said), and prescriptive.

Yarn Yarn is particularly interesting semantically, as it describes both **thread** and story, both of which are interwoven, the one with itself, the other with disparate strands from the outside. Yarn may also have **umbilical** significance in a **dream**, and may act as a unifier of already homogonous principles. See **Unravelling**

Yarrow Stalks To a **dreamer** who uses the I Ching, yarrow stalks are divinatory **tools**. Traditionally, yarrow stalks were a protection against **curses**. In folk **medicine**, yarrow was used to prevent **nosebleeds**, and by maidens to induce **dreams** of a future **husband** – but only if the following song accompanied the placing of the yarrow stalk beneath the **pillow**:

> Yarrow, sweet yarrow, the first that I have found,
> In the name of Jesus Christ, I pluck it from the ground.
> As Jesus loved sweet Mary, and took her for his dear,
> So in a dream this night, I hope my true love will appear.

Yawning Yawning is catching. It is also indicative of weariness and involuntary communication. Yawning in a **dream** may be a **sign** of non-aggression (as with **animals**), or a sign that one wishes to ingest (oxygen, food, **drink**) or somaticize something (emotional **hurt**, an already expelled scream, a **trauma**).

Years There is no such thing as **time**. Years are a fallible human imposition onto infallible non-humanness – an expedient projection of ourselves onto an otherwise inexplicable universe (see **Space**). In **dreams**, years may denote cycles, but they can also denote loss. To some of us they accord the comforting appearance of growth. See **Weeks**

Yeast Yeast is a trigger for growth – it can act as a catalyst, therefore, and as an activator of dormant emotions. The making of **bread** is fundamental to civilized life, and therefore the adjunct of yeast to anything suggests a desire to improve or empower it.

Yelling Yelling often equates with **fear**, in the sense that even aggressive yelling is frequently only a disguise for insecurity. In a **dream** one yells to call attention to something or someone, and one may also yell in demonstration of (or remonstration against) past agonies.

Yellow Yellow is a paradoxical **colour**, as some view it as a **symbol** of peace and harmony (in blazonry it is the colour of **love**, wisdom and constancy), whilst others view it as the colour of **jealousy**, inconstancy, **adultery** and cowardice. Symbolically, the positive **camp** probably wins out in the long **run**, with yellow indicating kingship (it was the Chinese Imperial colour and the colour of St Peter's **robes**). It is also the colour of the **sun**, and thus suggestive of **God**.

Yew Trees The yew is a **symbol** of everlasting life, thus its prevalence in churchyards. In Herefordshire, young **girls** would go to an unfamiliar churchyard and pluck a sprig to place beneath their **pillow** – this would guarantee **dreams** of a future **husband**.

Yin The instinctive, emotional, intuitive side of the Chinese dynamic balance, which, when taken in tandem with the **yang**, creates dynamic potential. **Key** qualities associated with the yin include the **moon**, **darkness**, softness, moistness, response and completion. See **Lingam & Yoni**

Yoga Yoga implies harmony, and the taking up of a yogic posture in a **dream** may suggest a desire to harmonize something that is intrinsically disharmonious. It may also imply the taking up of a passive or meditative position, or the wish to ignore surrounding flux.

Yokes Yoking equates to disgrace and servitude – in Roman times, conquered **soldiers** were traditionally forced to pass under a symbolical yoke made of three **spears**. Yokes may also suggest the harnessing of one idea or object to another more powerful or dominant idea or object.

Yoni The **female sex organ** and **symbol** of receptivity, as construed within Hindu **mythology**. See **Lingam**

Youth Youth tends to be about **loss** in that, by default, one does not need to **dream** of youth if one still enjoys it. In terms of **wish-fulfilment** fantasies, youth suggests **energy** and resilience, whilst 'youth restored' has long been a **gift** of the **gods** (one thinks of Iolaus, Phaon, Aeson and his **son** Jason, and the muses of Bacchus, all of whom enjoyed rejuvenation at the hands of disparate Greek deities). Very soon, youth may prove to be in the **gift** of **doctors**.

Yo-Yos Yo-yos bounce back – that is their function. In **dreams** they probably represent consistent **patterns**, or modes of thought developing across roughly similar **lines**. Yo-yos even **fail** as modes of aggression, in that they are attached to a **string** and therefore have only a limited range.

Z

Zebras Zebras are images in **black** and **white**, suggesting things taken down into their fundamental **natures**, or **split** into disparate emphases – the opposing sides of a **question**, maybe, and the possibilities of unity beyond the question (in the sense that the zebra *carries* both questions and answers). In **animal** terms the zebra is a prey species, and herbivorously passive, and may relate to the feminine principle.

Zen To a **Buddhist** dreaming of Zen, the image might imply completion through process – to a non-Buddhist, the image might suggest the possibilities inherent in other **disciplines alien** to the **dreamer**.

Zero Zero represents the **circle**, the **mandala**, unity and perfection. It may also represent the **female**, and the **enclosure** of inner forces from outside interference.

Zigzagging Zigzagging equates to wishful thinking. The image of a **soldier** zigzagging across a **killing field** is a prime example of optimism and training triumphing over **reality** – common sense would see the soldier refuse the run, of course. Zigzagging in a **dream** is usually an attempt to avoid something bad that we instinctively know is meant for us – something that we feel **guilty** about, perhaps, for the hunched attitude the zigzagger traditionally takes may be interpreted as a **sign** of submission to fate, or even to **justice**.

Zip Codes See Postcodes

Zipping Zipping or closing or **sealing things** are all ways of **joining** two otherwise disparate objects together in a brief union. Zipping shut a **mouth** is a common euphemism for desiring **silence**, whilst zipping on a dress or a **pair** of trousers implies a desire for **self**-protection against outside forces – possibly even against the opposite **sex**.

Zips A zip can relate to **scar** tissue in a **dream**, and it can also represent the **vagina**. It may also act as a **curtain** behind which things may **hide**. See **Zipping**

Zodiac, The The Western Zodiac consists of six ascending northern and six descending southern signs (**north** or **south** of the equator). The six northern signs are Aries (the **ram**), Taurus (the **bull**), Gemini (the **twins**), Cancer (the **crab**), Leo (the **lion**), and Virgo (the **virgin**). The six southern signs are Libra (the balance), Scorpio (the **scorpion**), Sagittarius (the archer), Capricorn (the **goat**), **Aquarius** (the **water** bearer), and Pisces (the **fish**). The Chinese Zodiac is equally split between the **yin** and the **yang**, the wild and the domestic, and consists of the **rat**, the **ox**, the **tiger**, the **hare**, the **dragon**, the **snake**, the **horse**, the **goat**, the **monkey**, the **cock**, the **dog**, and the **boar**. As far as **dream symbolism** goes, the Western Zodiac equates with our place in the universe, and the Eastern Zodiac equates with our dynamic potential. The two are not contra-indicative.

Zombies Zombies, while seemingly alive, are really dead. This paradox lies behind their appearance in a **dream**, and suggests sterility of **feeling** and the inability to connect on an emotional or beyond-automatic **level**. See **Death & Resurrection**

Zoos Zoos are **alien** environments in which primitive passions and emotions are bottled up. This may seem an extreme **reading** at first glance, but however civilized a zoo may seem, there is no getting away from the fact that its main function is to sterilize and sequester, and that this aspect is likely to be paramount in any **dream interpretation**. It is a place where natural urges and natural modes of behaviour are, through expediency, caparisoned.

'... Night's swift dragons cut the clouds full fast,
And yonder shines Aurora's harbinger;
At whose approach, ghosts, wandering here and there,
Troop home to churchyards.'

William Shakespeare
A Midsummer Night's Dream (1595–6) Act iii, scene 2, line 379